Mythimo: Through the Looking Glass of Fairy-tale Archetypes

Janice Walker Jones

Mythimo: Through the Looking Glass of Fairy-tale Archetypes explores how fairy-tale archetypes can help us reclaim our light and guide us on our Hero's Journey to become Whole, healthier and happier ever after.

Jung believed we recognise these characters instantly because they're already 'programmed' into our minds. They're like mental shortcuts that help us understand stories and people - and even understand ourselves better.

Through the looking glass of fairy-tale archetypes, we open a portal to our shadow side, the hidden aspects of our psyche that we often suppress, avoid, deny and don't even really know.

Just as Alice found truth and transformation in Wonderland, we too can solve the mysteries of our being by embracing the reflection in the mirror of archetypal tales. These stories call us to rediscover our concealed desires, traits, emotions and fears, inviting us to integrate our hidden treasures and rise above their silent power that holds us back.

Who in the world am I? Ah, that's the great puzzle!
(Alice, Alice's Adventures in Wonderland)

Published by Synchronicity Press
ISBN 978-1-7645313-0-6 (paperback)

MYTHIMO

www.mythimo.com.au

Mythimo explores the interaction between universal archetypes and the individual psyche, using fairy-tale, mythic narratives, and metaphors to illuminate psychological and emotional processes. It reveals how age-old stories connect people and capture our modern human experience.

The book's title, represents *myths-in-motion*, focusing on how immutable archetypes become dynamically enacted in our inner lives, shaping and reflecting our consciousness and behaviours—showing how the way we think influences our personal stories and the way we act in our outer realities.

The self-help technique, the *Mythimo Method* is a simple seven-step process for integrating our light and shadow sides, making us Whole and happier ever after.

Readers will encounter traditional pronouns and language drawn from the original tellings of stories, narratives, and case studies, preserved to maintain historical authenticity (with no offence intended). The author is committed to fostering belonging and unconditional positive regard, and she means for this ethos to come across in her writing.

Written by Janice Walker Jones
Illustrated and designed by artist Simo
Editing, Media and Marketing assistance by Elle-Louise Burguez

Permit application to use an illustration of Uluru-Kata/Tjuta approved by Uluru-Kata Tjuta National Park/Parks Australia.

It is during our darkest moments that we must focus to see the light.
(Aristotle)

DEDICATION

For my father and mother, Stan and Barbara Walker; my golden children, Simon and Elle; and my animal family in the natural and supernatural realms: you brought me closer to understanding what it means to be authentic and to love unconditionally. Thank you for the goodness of your hearts — from the bottom of mine.

We are not human beings having a spiritual experience.
We are spiritual beings having a human experience.
(Pierre Teilhard de Chardin)

ABOUT TEILHARD (1881-1955)

Pierre Teilhard de Chardin, a French Jesuit priest, philosopher, and palaeontologist, proposed that the universe is constantly evolving toward a state of consciousness and unity he called the Omega Point. He believed humanity's collective goal is to advance this process by developing individual consciousness. According to Chardin, we are spiritual beings having a human experience, not the other way around. His famous quote highlights that enlightened individuals help expand the universe's light by aligning their beliefs, thoughts, and actions with Divine goodness.

Until you make the unconscious conscious, it will direct your life and you will call it fate.
(Carl Jung)

CONTENTS

The innumerable variations within the same fairytale told in different cultures are like a musical theme crisscrossing humanity.

—Marie-Louise von Franz (*Introduction to the Interpretation of Fairytales & Animus and Anima in Fairytales*)

ACKNOWLEDGEMENTS

I am deeply grateful to my children, my mother, and my sisters for their faith in me, and to my son, Simo, for bringing the fairy tales alive through his beautiful art.

My dearest friends encouraged me on the hero's path when I stood at the threshold of refusing the call.

Without the timeless insights of Jung, Campbell, Freud, Maslow, Frankl, de Chardin, and other cartographers of the human psyche, *Mythimo* might still have been hidden in the dusty bottom drawer of my shadow.

I appreciate also all the insight and growth my valued clients and peers have brought into my life. Thank you for your inspiration, healing, and kindness — this round of the Hero's Journey has come to that deeply satisfying fruition, you once all foretold.

The difference between a good life and a bad life is how well you walk through the fire.
(Carl Jung)

INTRODUCTION TO THEMES IN THIS BOOK

THE CRACK IN THE MIRROR—A FAIRY TALE

Every evening before bed, two young girls, identical twins, sat at their dressing table, gazing at their reflections, side by side, in the mirror hanging above on the bedroom wall. Both girls were as fresh and sweet as each other, delighting in how much alike they were and how much they enjoyed life's simplest pleasures. They were inseparable.

But as the years rolled by, neither girl had found their soul mate or made their fortune, and as they aged, the mirror's gleaming gilt edge rusted, and a crack appeared, dimming its once radiant lustre.

One twin lived joyously every day of her life as though it were to be her last, skipping along life's path with ease. The other grew more woebegone, weighed down by her own shadow.

One fateful night, the sad twin found herself alone at the dressing table, contemplating the loss of her freshness and sweetness. Despite the subdued light, she traced the deep lines etched on her face, questioning why she had so many when she had barely laughed in years.

To her astonishment, the cracked mirror began to speak: "Forgive me, ma'am, for disturbing your solitude," spoke the looking glass, "but may I ask you a personal question?"

The lady was tired but nodded and said, "I will answer you truthfully, old friend."

"You and your twin have surely noticed the large crack in my glass," whispered the mirror, "so, why do you still use me?"

"Let's bring in my sister for one last lingering gaze," she replied, "and then I will answer your question."

So, the two ladies sat before the mirror once again, one as fresh, sweet, and cheerful as ever, the other wizened and worn-out in both body and spirit.

"Now", said the weary one to the mirror, "have you noticed the beauty and light that only shines on my sister's side of your glass?" Feeling as exhausted as she looked, she continued, "These days, I must look to her sunny reflection to find the strength to get out of bed. We keep you because you reveal the image of who I used to be and might become again. You are a symbol of hope."

After taking her sister's hand, she smiled a knowing smile that lit up her face and spoke into the mirror with gratitude, "Thanks to you, I have finally been able to see into my soul and am ready to retrieve its brilliant light. I want to become my Whole Self again—just as my twin lives. From now on, there will be no more dwelling on the dark side."

The twins hugged lovingly, and all the weariness lifted from the once sad old lady. Amazed, they glanced fondly at the looking glass once more, speaking in unison: "Look! Your crack lets the light in."

And so, that is the story of the old, cracked mirror still hanging on their bedroom wall today, a testament to their journey of reclaiming their light, Wholeness and joy. **THE END.**

This fairy tale shows us that we all carry both light and dark within. Through the metaphor of twins, it reveals how the behaviours we envy or find irritating in others can shine a light on hidden parts of ourselves.

The cracked, shadowed side of the looking glass symbolises the unconscious — the hidden reservoir where we store the disowned aspects of our psyche. Yet it is so much more: a realm where dreams, symbols, metaphors, archetypes and myths converge, opening a gateway to the collective unconscious: the timeless field of universal truth.

The sad twin, unlike her joyous counterpart, has turned away from her own beauty and light (much like the wicked stepmother did in *Sleeping Beauty*). She only begins to recognise what she has denied when the mirror confronts her. Through this reflection and self-awareness, she begins the journey of integration to oneness — symbolised by the embrace between the twins.

By following the path of these reunited twins, we too can move toward Wholeness, embracing the full spectrum of our emotional life. In doing so, we awaken a renewed vitality and happiness that becomes visible to the world.

N.B. The words Whole, Wholeness and Self are capitalised throughout this text when it is necessary to distinguish them from everyday use and highlight them as the integrated state sought by those undertaking the *Mythimo* quest.

Each fairy tale is a magic mirror which reflects some aspects of our inner world, and the steps required by our evolution from immaturity to maturity.
(Bruno Bettelheim)

FOREWORD

Once upon a time in the human psyche, our ego caught a glimpse of what it would be like if all our psychological parts worked together like a well-oiled machine. But in our mind's eye, we also saw how our self-critical superego's conditional love made us feel below the grade, and our shadowy id fuelled our fears of missing out.

In a flash of insight, through the looking glass of fairy tales, we saw archetypes looking back at us and, perhaps, for the first time, saw who we really were. Some of us saw how we failed to live up to our Higher Self (our soul) by what we had become. Our evasive shadow, briefly emerging, resisted the soul's call for healing. In that instant, we knew, for our full recovery, we must return to loving the Whole of whom we were born to be, reforming dark-side failings and all.

Mythimo is written to help us recognise our mistaken selves (or myth-taken selves) and provide a way for reclaiming our originality. According to clinical psychologist Robertson (1992), if we do not, we are tempted to claim an unreal 'mana-personality' as our own, becoming its pawn and reducing our creative potential. He claims: "As long as we are gripped by an archetype, we are literally inhuman, merely flat figures designed by the centuries to fit all time and all situations. Caught within that grip, there is no development, no change (p.195)."

Through the artful lens of the mythical archetypes of fairy tales, we contact our unconscious patterns of behaviour so that we may reclaim and integrate our disparate elements into a unified conscious Self. To undertake this healing journey, we go through a psycho-somatic process, delving into the personal and collective unconscious to reach our authentic being. Prior, this original Self was over-shadowed by the dark arts of our ego, making misguided attempts to have us fit in with the social mean and think well of ourselves.

Our ego, only too aware (but in denial) of our limits, is at odds with our uniqueness also referred to as our soul essence and its unmatched power. But it seems counter-intuitive that our ego would try to suppress our innate greatness when its role is to talk us up. Our goal is to see through the ego's ambiguity and achieve a feeling of oneness: recalibrating our psychic parts to work in unison. Whether we are in the thrall of living up to some objectified or idealised image of whom we think we should be and are aware of the game we are playing within ourselves or not, sooner or later, our true nature will demand our attention. Until then, our unregulated behaviours will continue to cause our feelings of separation within and without and unintended consequences will follow.

It is one thing to never live up to our superego's idealisations. We will feel inadequate, guilty, embarrassed, or even ashamed of being less than perfect as our shadows regurgitate these negative emotions. But it is another thing to be realistic about ourselves, knowing we were once more open, caring, and creative (and more) than we have become. Our soul, a quantum encapsulated within the human form replete with essence and qualities, compels us to engage in profound introspection, confronting the reality of how we have relinquished our innate beauty—the very essence of our 'poetic basis of mind' (Hillman, 2015). Then, we may rediscover and recover the authentic being, the one-of-a-kind, essential, and destined being who is our better Self.

After experiencing their epiphany, clients ask why they were so blind to their acting in contrary ways to their soul's voice. Their deep beliefs, values, and dreams screamed to be heard in vain. They wonder why they had once chosen to live a life making them angry, frustrated, and sad as they trudged along reluctantly rooted to their unhappy existence.

Now, shadow-healed, they no longer feel conflicted within, incongruent, or separated from others and can confidently forge a healthier and happier path. While not perfect, life has become sweeter, fuller, more honest, grounded, and real. Rewards come more easily.

Our time in this life is finite. Today is the day to ignite our awareness and start the work. A life in accord with its divine potential enriches learning experiences and satisfies the soul's longing. The quality of life that has been our dream is within our manifest power.

Until we bring together our dreams and the behaviours to take us there, our soul aches as we walk in an unconscious stupor. We project a sanitised image, denying those aspects of ourselves we find unacceptable. This discarded energy does not dissipate— it must go somewhere. Projecting and laying judgment on others for our negative traits we are blind to does not rid us of our contradictions. The uncaptured dark side hides in the shadows, stalking us in our dreams and darkening the doorstep of the unlived future before us.

The good news is that reintegrating our shadow elements with the light expands us, strengthening our innate talents and capacities. In a nutshell, the coalescence of all our psychic parts restores our completeness, thrusting our confidence and self-trust into full throttle. We think and act from the Higher Self.

Some of us might aspire to the higher angels of our nature and do the inner work, balancing polarised emotions routinely. In contrast, others resist, denying their duality and lack of tranquillity and over-expose themselves to the dynamic dregs of their dark-side instincts that hold a gloomy power over their existence.

Dark behaviours are products of a wounded ego. When acting from the shadow, folk behave in ways that meet their immediate needs (such as thinking one thing and doing another to avoid any painful feelings). Few people have intentions to hurt us, incognisant of how harmful their behaviour is to others. The harm done to us is consequential, which may explain why the unenlightened find no need to apologise for the pain they have wrought.

Mythimo is not designed to vilify beguiled, game-playing folk who, for reasons manifold, choose not to call a spade a spade or behave ethically or with transparency in their interactions. Sending them love and light energy is alchemical, like turning lead into gold, and will jump-start an awareness of their shadow in them. If we are honest, we are all guilty of unevolved behaviours at some time or another. After all, such demonstrations of animal cunning and raw guts can be hard to regulate and are helpful allies in times necessitating our survival. But there is a time and place.

The mythopoetic *Mythimo* method's overarching purpose is to promote the virtues of keeping our heart, mind, and eyes wide open always, moderating irrational emotions, and harnessing our personal power by forging union within. Some clients describe becoming Whole as feeling freer and lighter and sensing an expansion of their aura. No longer bogged down by shadow density, they feel an out-pouring of their soul's loving energy centre, resonating where their personal boundary meets the universal field, the sacred Source. Such at-oneness is also experienced when one knows they have had an 'aha' moment because they feel connected or in-tune with the Divine.

Being aware, temperate, self-regulated, and open are central to living a kind, whole, fearless, ethical, and fulfilling life. To this end, I am ever-grateful to those conscious beings who have lived by a virtuous personal code for Higher Living, evincing these fine qualities.

They role-model a religion of kindness that makes the world a better place for us all. Without their influence, I doubt I would have developed my deeply felt sense of compassion for all sentient beings on the planet (including the earth as a living entity itself).

Mainly, I thank my beautiful mother, Barbara Walker, a modern-day Vasilisa archetype (and multitudes more). A wonderful storyteller, she drew from her own life the cautionary tales that prepared us for the wiles of the world. She also opened to us the lyrical and magical world of nursery rhymes, songs, and fairy tales (the shortened versions in this book are her retellings as I remember them). This selfless and intuitive wise-woman brought a sense of wonder and safety, sparking our imaginations and soothing our sensitive souls.

But more than any gift she gave, Barb always observed one's right to be themselves, fanning the fires of her offspring's creative originality. A brave, open, objective, and observant matriarch, her anti-hierarchical way of valuing the animal kingdom is now commonplace among Millennials and Alphas. Mum always stayed ahead of the game.

After all, why are different species measured against each other for worth on the planet? Are not all creatures great and small, indeed all sentient life-forms equal in having earned their place and right to be here? Each of us needs to survive the best way we can with what we have without falling prey to the misuse of power by others: those times when animal cunning is necessary for survival in the wild notwithstanding. Still, in a so-called civilised world, clearly, compassion, collaboration and kindness are the more powerful forces for sustainable success, taking all species forward. Why is the majority, the mean, so afraid of giving this paradigm a go when all their systems built on competition, overconsumption, exclusion, and elitism are now in a state of relentless decay?

When benevolence is not returned to me from the external world, I am ever-thankful to feel secure on the inside, which I attribute to being shadow-healed. In the darkness, I know how to find my way back to the light, keeping my faith in the power of empathy alive. Once inner peace is restored, I appreciate my new learning despite its dark delivery.

I also give heartfelt thanks to my life-long mentor, Leila, who taught me what it means to believe in your dreams and have a forgiving heart. And to dad for his awe-inspiring jazz and illuminating guidance from here and the other side—what a pleasure it is to know and love you and be loved in return. Mum, Dad, family, students, clients and friends (human and animal in material and spiritual realities)— you are all my fairy godmothers guiding me towards being a Whole person who shares love, light and a set of helping words and hands in our upside-down world. Thank you for the blessing of YOU.

We must fight against the spirit of unconscious cruelty with which we treat the animals. Animals suffer as much as we do. True humanity does not allow us to impose such sufferings on them. It is our duty to make the whole world recognise it. Until we extend our circle of compassion to all living things, humanity will not find peace.
(Albert Schweitzer)

1 THE INTERLACE OF FAIRY TALES & MYTHS

In mythological literature, fairy tales are the most straightforward and purest manifestations of the collective unconscious, yet they provide profound insights into our psychological realities. In contrast to myths, which link us to the Divine and our original creation, fairy tales focus more on how we relate to the ordinary world and each other. However, both genres contain a catalogue of socially powerful stories confronting the consequences of good or evil on earth, above and below. The psychological motivations of dualistic beings with special strengths but dreadful defects and exaggerated behaviours allow us to see and understand the effects of our limited human understanding and unregulated actions. Both genres explore individual and social issues stemming from our family and intimate relationships (including the relationship between humans and deities) and the effects of disruption and separation, culture, belief systems, traditions, politics, and the power of judgment and choice.

An inside-out or secret-revelation polarity is a common thread tying myths to fairy tales (and to the duplicitous nature of the human condition). We contain the contradictions of the prince inside the frog, or the marginalised duck cum swan, and then Oedipus' wife, Jocasta (his mother) and his slain victim Laius (his father). The revelation arrived too late for the mother-loving and father-killing Oedipus but was the making of the prince and the swan. Oedipus' blindness echoes the fate of Rapunzel's suffering prince (in part), who must overcome immense grief and a long search before recovering his sight and happiness again. The earthbound, supernatural, and quasi-divine figures cut across both genres, spreading the message that we must transcend blind ignorance to achieve self-knowledge.

According to Thompson (1977), characterising fairy tales are their motifs and episodes occurring in unreal times and places. They are populated with miracle-making marvels who kill off anti-heroes to win kingdoms and the hearts of princesses. Nearly always, the hero must undertake a quest before achieving a happy ending. If complexity defines myths, fairy tales generate a simplistic take on human morality. The genre was initially popular with adults with a penchant for satire and the making of psychological correlations between characters and members of their social tribe. Children, too, found fairy tales entertaining, whether told or read, given the host of anthropomorphic animals and supernatural beings interacting with girls and boys just like them. Today, parents still rely on fairy tales to transmit social learning in those precious storytelling moments shared with their young. Acclaimed children's writer Joy Lawn advises that reading our children diverse stories nourishes their imaginations and endows them with a sense of belonging and self-worth. Fairy tales lay the foundations of morality for humankind, tempered by wise-woman wisdom, cynicism and compassion for our common foibles. Fairy tales, like old wives' tales, have an alluring irony, but their ability to inspire hope for a higher humanity holds the most appeal. Like myths, fairy tales guide how we live, outlining in sharpened and heightened form the retribution one may expect for rebelling against the higher order or cultural standards. In the folkloristic perspective of Jorgensen (2019), myths validate social norms, explain why the world works the way it does, and rationalise a society's power dynamics.

The 'Golden Rule' of Christian origin overprints many European fairy tales, but any religiosity is subdued compared with the divine acts portrayed in myths. Myths are also differentiated by the dramatic measures taken by gods to punish the disobedient. Jack might not get his supper for resisting his mother's instructions, but Gilgamesh's rebellion brought deadly reprisals from the gods. Jack was just an ordinary boy capable of extraordinary feats on beanstalks but not unlike the demi-god Gilgamesh, who, in the end, turned his ordinariness into his strength. Regardless, Aesop wrote a fable about clay and tears symbolising our creativity and suffering, which ties in nicely with ancient Sumerian mythology. But did the fabulist suspect we would still be clodhopping about in feet of clay today? In fantasy or mundane settings, mythical and fairy-tale heroes each have a mission to master. Still, paths diverge when one struggles in the grand earthly scheme, and the other engages in violent combat between heaven and earth and hell. Myths, often with fuzzy historical underpinnings, provide a narrative born from a community's traditions, superstitions and beliefs, but so do fairy tales, conveying the values and perspectives that help explain the world and how we might fit in. The former focuses on the pantheon's macrocosmic control over supernatural and natural powers. The latter has its microcosmic lens on the socio-historical structures governing our everyday behaviours. One is fiercely brutal, whereas the other puts an iron fist inside a velvet glove. The universal conflict between light and dark in the soul pervades both genres. But still, the lines blur.

In the fairy tale of Vasilisa, the angry child-devouring Baba Yaga, also renowned for her potent plant potions and aerial chariot, is comparable to the mythical Medea, a scheming sorceress who murdered her children in a raging act of revenge. Parallels with Hecate, goddess of witchcraft and necromancy, are drawn. Vasilisa is like a Greek hero who marches into hell (Baba Yaga's hut) for a heavenly cause. We might compare the super strength of Hercules to Gilgamesh. Both were demi-gods capable of incredible feats, some involving bulls, lions and monsters, but only Hercules (Heracles) rescued Prometheus, overcame mortality and became a God. From the other side of the storybook, Vasilisa completes a series of Herculean labours, earning her freedom and returning as a Promethean pyrotechnician with the gift of fire and light. Darkness was burned to hell by a Faustian fire and reigned no more. Both torch-bearing protagonists strove and suffered, were isolated, benefitted from forethought (hers was due to the tiny doll in her pocket) and experienced unintended consequences. Prometheus, a glorious and tragic archetype, possessed a cosmic-creative power, while Vasilisa's life of hard grind had a magical touch and fairy-tale finish.

The concept of the ingroup and outlier interlacing the mythical and fairy-tale genres has currency in contemporary social debates, confirming both genres still have an essential role to play in what we value and how we behave as a collective and as individuals. We are tested when we come up against those who we consider different to ourselves: the others. Myths give us multi-headed monsters, Sirens, Amazons and hybrids of dogs and reptiles, whereas fairy tales introduce us to frogs (but not so many snakes), fairies, and trolls. Giants are shared between stories along with mothers, fathers, daughters and sons and a raft of relationship issues, ranging from the ridiculous to the sublime. An initiation schema exists across myths and fairy tales, promoting that the pubescent or inexperienced must leave the ordinary world as they know it, venture into the wilderness and only return once they have mastered their mission. This circuitous and heroic path is traceable, either literally or symbolically, across nearly every fairy tale or mythical trope. Consider, for example, the *Mythimo* stable of twenty-two fairy-tale heroes, beginning with Little Red Riding Hood and ending with Vasilisa (and all those in between), to see this archetypal pattern in action.

In common, myths and fairy tales, as acknowledged by Zipes (2012), share a guiding role, drawing upon the ancient wisdom of diverse cultures—it is evident how the profound influence of these myths, originating from Greek, Roman, and various other traditions, paved the way for the development of the modern fairy tale. Together, they offer a compass in a world gone astray, assisting us in rediscovering and reclaiming a path towards self-recognition and rational regulation amidst our insatiable animal appetites for the spoils of the earthly realm. Every story, after all, is a journey, just as every journey is a story.

Themes of transformation and personal growth exist in both myths and fairy tales. In *Vasilisa: The Brave, Beautiful and Wise*, Vasilisa transforms from a hardworking young girl mistreated by her step-kin to a courageous and resourceful young woman who outwits Baba Yaga and ultimately finds her place in the world. Emerging from adversity, she ascends—a beacon of hope for all women. With her fulsome, feminine firepower, she wields a luminous torch, piercing through the shadows, illuminating the path to triumph over darkness and oppression. She becomes the mythologist of her own fate, reframing her trauma and blooming where she is planted to create an exciting and satisfying new reality.

Like myths, fairy tales such as the one about the brave and wise Vasilisa archetype use symbolism and allegory to convey deeper meanings. Her story can be interpreted allegorically, with elements such as the magical doll representing both her inner parent and child, her inner strength and wise counsel. The dark ogress Baba Yaga represents the id and shadow, particularly the fears of rejection, abandonment and non-belonging that we all harbour. Our animal appetites and human ability to be conscious, rational and in control of our primal id come to the fore across the genres. Where the dark Baba Yaga is overwhelmed by gluttony, the enlightened Vasilisa, even when allocated a tiny morsel, remembers to feed her magical doll, as her wise mother told her to do.

Comparatively, in the myth of Gilgamesh, transformation motifs and symbols relate to his personal growth. When his close companion Enkidu dies, he enters the road to humility, learning from one bitter experience after another. His reckless treatment of the Cedar Forest symbolically represents the wild appetites he must tame to mature, whereas his loss of the plant of immortality points to how he must confront and accept the limits of his humanness. He, the once arrogant king, and Vasilisa, the humble servant, must rise from the ashes to reach the apex of their wisdom and contribute as valuable citizens of the world.

The interlace of myths and fairy tales is woven into the fabric of our everyday lives, helping us get to the bottom of them and building a better understanding of who and where we are. The archetypes imprint our souls. Sometimes, we are sage and other times, we are arrogant fools, but we are always presented with a dramatic backdrop.

Myths and fairy tales, through exaggeration, bring attention to the consequences of our good and not-so-good human behaviour. By amplifying reality, they emphasise the profound impacts of our actions and encourage self-reflection on their moral implications.

Orpheus, a divinely endowed melody maker who tamed animals and saved souls, recommended we put our individual passions aside to save our communities. Myths and fairy tales, with their cultural and historical aura and archetypal power, illuminate the duality of existence, the triumph of light over darkness, and the transformative Hero's Journey undertaken by protagonists on their quest for the grail. Like them, as Dr Estes (1992) suggests, "Let's triumph over our travails, living a useful, unbounded and meaningful life worth remembering."

Fairy tales are the purest and simplest expression of collective unconscious processes… They represent the archetypes in their simplest, barest, and most concise form [and] afford us the best clues to the understanding of the processes going on in the collective psyche.
(Marie-Louise von Franz)

2 FAIRY TALE OR REALITY

Once far back in the annals of time in the late 18th century, in the unspoiled woods bordered by the Pyrenees mountains of southern France, where hungry wolves hunted and howled their spine-chilling cries in the lonely night, wandered a lost and lonely child.

The feral boy, who came to be called, Victor of Aveyron, was adopted and cared for by a pack of grey wolves who raised him with their kind of tough love as one of their own. Over a period of about twelve years, the wolves showed the wild boy how to hide, fight, hunt for large prey and share in the kill.

Meanwhile, back in the village, folk, having spotted the strange wolf-boy from afar, gathered their dogs and set out to hunt him down for his own good. Victor's body was battle-scarred from his serial skirmishes with wolves, prey, and predators, and although he could hear, he could not speak to tell his tale.

His captors observed how the pubescent boy behaved and communicated in the natural ways of his wolf clan, using body language, scent marking, barking, and howling. Growling gutturally, he was forcibly led back to the township. Residents provided for Victor's welfare and oversaw his rite of passage as he re-learned human and social behaviours. Eventually, he was taken in by a family devoted to his ongoing upkeep and care.

We will never know if he found the perils of living with humans in a civilised existence more precarious than his early days in the wilderness with the wolf pack. Victor only uttered two words to his French countrymen, lait (milk) and Oh Dieu (Oh God!). Still, he bravely embarked on his second iteration of his Hero's Journey to follow his star.

Victor of Aveyron went from existing as a wolf in the woods to a human life in one of the world's most civilised yet demanding urban jungles. Taken to Paris, he became the subject of intense scientific study and speculation. There, he spent most of his days— in the magnificent 'city of lights', aiming to fulfil his potential (presumably).

We can only imagine the deep wounding in Victor's shadow that he sought to subsume with the light of hope. He made it through, sometimes revisiting the wilderness of his early beginnings, but Victor died alone in Paris at just forty years of age. **THE END.**

Fairy tales are vessels that dive deep into the hidden truths at the heart of every life.
(Italo Calvino)

3 A BRIEF HISTORY OF FAIRY TALES

Oral fairy tales, drawing on folklore, have endured millennia, opening small doors to the natural history and philosophies of real people from times of yore. Some elements of European fairy tales date as far back as the Bronze Age, over five thousand years ago, making the tracing of their various forms of transmissions daunting. But the mythical world of fairy tales, then, now and into the future, evokes memories both mysterious and magical.

Metaphysical mythology arose from our forebears' system of grand beliefs about human creation and destiny and where gods, demons and heroes were both worshipped and feared. At the same time, as everyday folk went about their commonplace tasks, they wove and embellished life events into the social fabric, the story and history of their existence. The folklore, legends and fables they created helped their tribe understand the perils and pleasures of survival in their time, as well as the intensity of emotions aroused between members of the family unit.

Today, these ancient mythic-historical narratives continue to carry profound truths that illuminate our understanding of human nature, the psychology of our intimate relationships and our ways of dealing with reality. As a result of Freud's and Jung's studies of our dreaming minds, archetypal and submerged meanings were revealed below mythological narratives, inspiring further exploration of their transmission, renewal, and influence.

As reported in research from the universities of Durham and Lisbon (2016), the oldest known European folktale, hailing from the Bronze Age, *The Smith and the Devil,* centres on a Faustian bargain struck with a wily blacksmith seeking supernatural powers.

Some scholars consider the second-century Greek story of *Eros and Psyche,* written by Platonicus, the first literary mythic tale of the West. The star-crossed lovers, Eros (Cupido) and Psyche (Anima), conquer all challenges, ending with a marriage made in heaven. The fairy tale *The Frog King* adapts its storyline with its universal animal-to-groom cycle. Reminiscent also of this classic trope is the classic fairy tale of *Beauty and the Beast* (1740) reimagined and made famous by author Villeneuve. But it appears that Perrault's tale of *La Belle et la Bête* served as the original inspiration for Jeanne-Marie Leprince de Beaumont's version of the tale and the Grimm's *Die Schöne und das Biest.* Perrault's *Riquet a la Houppe* (1697) shares a similar trope, posturing that beauty exists in the eye of the beholder.

According to the Brothers Grimm (1785-1859), academics and cultural anthropologists who meticulously collected and preserved archaic stories of the oral tradition, the *Beauty and the Beast* tale may be as old (as is the story of *Rumpelstiltskin*) as the wheel and writing innovations of the ancient Sumerians, existing 5,000 or more years ago. Perrault's *Peau d'Âne* or *Donkeyskin* underpinned the Brothers Grimm's *Rumpelstilzchen,* but the tale's origins go further back. Folkloric stories were unsentimental and not always intended for children. Some of those curated or rewritten by Frenchman Charles Perrault (17 C.E.-18 C.E.), widely credited as the first author of fairy tales, survived generations, conveying cautions concerning the darkness of human nature and dangers of the wild.

His *Cinderella*, for example, has its dark social secrets subverted. It is based on a rosy-cheeked Greek beauty called Rhodopis from 500 B.C.E. who was sold as a slave and taken to Egypt by her master, who gifted her a pair of shiny golden shoes. How generous of him, not! The sight of her in her golden slippers so overtook the sensibilities of Pharaoh Ahmose II, he demanded Rhodopis join his harem. His sole purpose (pun intended) was to fulfil his foot fetish and other sexual proclivities. We may well ask how sexual slavery makes for a happy ever after. Whose happiness?

Perrault's fairy tale, called *Cendrillon* inspired the Brothers Grimm's version originally called *Aschenputtel.*

Perrault braided old tales together to create the macabre fairy tale of *Bluebeard.* The first came from the history of *Conomor the Cursed*, a Breton chieftain from French Brittany linked to Cormoran, the giant of Cornwall from across the channel. Legend from the 6th century has it he was an eighteen-foot giant who built his castle on Saint Michael's mount while being the protector of the English Channel and ruler of Mont Saint Michel on the other side.

About Conomor the Cursed: a prophecy foretold his murder at the hand of his future son. So, as soon as his wife became pregnant, he slew her and the unborn child. A despot, he committed many murders. Like the earlier days of the ancient Mesopotamian mythic king, the gargantuan Gilgamesh, he wielded a ruthless power serving only his ends.

The second theory concerns a 15th century nobleman, Gilles de Rais (a hero of the Hundred Years War). Upon leaving his role as Joan of Arc's protector, he went on to prey upon, rape, torture, and annihilate innocent children by the hundreds.

Perrault's dark tale *La Barbe Bleue* was retold by the Brothers Grimm as *Blaubart.*

We can pretend these horrible, inhumane acts did not happen, are not happening now and will not occur in the future. Or we can break the taboos surrounding truth and the need for transparency and start solving the problems. Many real-life accounts merge into *Bluebeard*—a tale of uxoricide, a sad fact for some women subjected to coercive control and murder by their partners. The dead wives' plight in the story speaks to the depths of depravity in the archetype, which, without a redeemable soul, mercilessly plots and carries out the taking of another's life.

Not to mention the stain blotting the survivors' psyches, trying to put their lives back together again. In toxic relationships with predators, women become tired, dead inside (with no libido) and feel too small, too diminished to fight the battle of getting out alone. It is much more difficult for them when kith and kin are more focused on their assumed shortcomings in managing the situation than on providing hands-on help. But with our understanding and ongoing support, she may have an opportunity as a survivor to find and shine her light once more.

First, there is healing work to do, digging into the shadow, picking up the shards, those destructive fragmented pieces stealing her life force and reconstructing them before she will ever return to Wholeness. Beyond bafflement and with the key to her crisis in hand, she can face and stand up for the truth without equivocation: truths that will set her free.

There is no room for a 'damned if I do, damned if I don't' refrain— look how well it served her predecessors at the hand of the dark captor.

Like brave Vasilisa (and her indwelling doll: her inner child and internalised parent), she saw through her trials without cringing and cowering, seeing light in the dark like a canny cat on the move in the wild. Such intrepid women can bring back the fire and light into their lives. Real-life sufferers of abuse worldwide prove that they can recover, overcoming their fear of and attraction to mentally decayed predators.

According to one survivor of unabating psychological abuse, Françoise Gilot, the famous Spanish modernist artist who founded Cubism, Pablo Picasso (1881-1973), acted as a Bluebeard archetype. Gilot was one of his many muses and live-in lovers. She wrote in her memoir (1964), "I began to have the feeling that if I looked into a closet, I would find half a dozen ex-wives, hanging by their necks." But if we are suspicious of her claims, we do not have to take her word for it. The man himself bragged about his relentless womanising, justifying it as fuel for his genius. Shameless, he gave little thought to the emotional wreckage he left in his wake.

Despite his unconscious Bluebeard complex, Picasso was one of his time's most gifted, revered, and wealthiest living artists. He presents us with an ethical question: Is it not possible to be both great and kind?

Presumably, Bluebeard's surviving wife differed somewhat from the so-called love or sex-struck Picasso women. But perhaps we can typecast her as one of his two kinds of women—a goddess or doormat? In the carnal Picasso's view, she is just like any other woman: a 'machine for suffering'. Today, protests outside art museums are gaining traction worldwide, imploring that we consider the backstory of the tormented women featured in Picasso's art. Like Bluebeard, he believed in men's entitlement to their secret business without trespass from women. It is no surprise that Picasso is the pin-up boy for males of the elite class. But who knows? One day, switched-on new generations of art lovers, may not separate the man from his creations. They will see Picasso's art as reminders of his overt diminishment of women, considering his abstractions of them as profoundly infra dig.

Great art made this macho male famous, rich and self-satisfied, but it did not maketh the man—not coming within a whisker.

Channelling Bluebeard, Picasso upheld male superiority and dominance, remarking that women have no place in male territory. His warning of consequences is barely disguised. He also said, and the symbolism is not lost on us, "To make a dove; you must wring its neck."

Why cannot a great public figure such as Picasso commit to a kinder, more harmonious way of relating, seeking respectful acceptance of differences rather than making them the brunt of his brutality? It seems that Picasso considered greatness and kindness mutually exclusive states. But he might have eliminated his complex had he allowed it to rise to consciousness and afford its expression and regulation. Perhaps if we decode the female figures in his art, we will detect where he found vent and validation but not catharsis.

Alas, matters can be even worse when we are denied the right to choose our marriage partner. These women speak of feeling powerless in coercive and abusive hands. Overnight, a goddess becomes a doormat, from an eagle to a damaged dove. Early into her arranged marriage, the young wife of Bluebeard felt intuitive stirrings, paid attention and acted on her inner sight.

Sadly, our more liberated sisters of the deep past were seen as daughters of the devil, guilty of Eve's sin of tempting the flesh. Ironically, they were held accountable by the same men who derived sexual satisfaction from the use of their bodies. So, it is no wonder that by the 15th century, the German-based treatise on witchcraft penned by men was women-centric. The authorities declared women's use of herbal and magical treatments, ointments, and remedies paganistic, a crime against God. Painful labour was seen as punishment for a woman's sins, and any wise-woman, mid-wife (in other words, not church-endorsed as a physician) who eased a mother's (or her baby's) suffering was deemed the devil's helper. The discrimination went as far as inferring a woman devoid of any self-agency. After all, she needed the devil's authority and help to apply her knowledge and skill.

No matter that, only the rich (predominantly males) were permitted to study and become physicians. No bother that the wealthy and powerful male physicians refused to treat the unwashed poor or that the poor could not afford to avail themselves of their elite services even if they were granted access. This double-bind has continuously kept the 'powers-that-be' on the top, from one generation of physicians to the next, and many of us at the bottom. A rich, male-dominated in-group is a cold, dark and dangerous place for any outsider who tries to get through the door, let alone a fiery woman, daring to trespass into their domain. Any questioning of their modus has been labelled subversive or an act of heresy to the dominant religious doctrine or conspiracy against the State. Heretics refusing to recant were often baked over a slow fire to prolong their suffering.

Things change but don't change. In the 20th century, 150 million people died across the globe because of genocide and war.

We of the West live in a doctors' democracy, potentially reducing human suffering locally, yet how has our reliance on the medical system significantly benefitted us globally? Granted, many caring medical practitioners are working tirelessly in all corners of the world to make a difference. But their good appears to be overwhelmed by inequitable policies, bureaucracy, superbugs, infections, diseases, war, famine, natural disasters, a lack of resources (such as clean drinking water and sanitation in developing countries) and so on.

In other fairy tales, the predatory archetype (i.e., the unregulated one who lurks in the human id as the beastly animal or fearful survivalist of human nature) is always drawn or attracted to its opposite, the loving or the light: if only to feed on or contest it. They come to take the newly born child or to upend the emergent hero on their journey, as is the case in *Little Red Riding Hood, Rumpelstiltskin, Sleeping Beauty, Hansel and Gretel, Rapunzel, Snow White, East of the Sun and West of the Moon, Vasilisa* and many more. The primary archetype (the protagonist) has erred, committing the one forbidden thing. The dark combatant has come for retribution or to hold them to their word, extorting an unfair price, a 'pound of flesh' to mend the mistake and profit from the other's misery.

It is easy for women to swallow the expectations of our culture and society that we must be uncomplaining and compliant to be seen as nice or good. Nice women who have been violated will spend considerable healing time trying to claw back the full fiery power of their insight and voice. They must now recover and restore their ability to act from their once vital animus that has sought refuge in their shadow. Its reclamation will be the larger portion of the holistic remedy that prevents her from being a target for further assault.

The woman's animus archetype equates to their unconscious male energy—in the ways she perceives it to be. A woman I once knew dreamt of a cupid cherub (Eros) holding centre court in a mythical dreamscape of a silvery-grey Italian Renaissance artwork. An elderly wise-woman stooped over Eros on the left side, and a male counterpart stood on his right within the static frame. Before the brief dream ended, a human penis appeared on the cherub and she woke up feeling the presence of Eros, the embodiment of fulsome masculine potency, running through her whole body.

The dreamer knew at once that she was integrating her animus and anima on her approach to Wholeness. She spoke of feeling stronger, alive, braver, and more prepared to stand up for herself 'like a man does' (her out-moded thinking). But she also considered the attributes of the wise-woman (or was she the 'old maid') and the protective, responsible and wise father archetype which she held as a projected ideal for her partners. She began the psychological processing work recognising her psychic components still requiring reclamation and integration while also becoming aware of how the men in her life had projected their internal anima archetype onto her. They railed at and resented her resistance to play the part of the downtrodden service-providing 'Cinderella', which seemed commingled with the nourishing mother archetype harboured in their shadow. Rather than stray too far now away from the history of fairy tales, explanations about the psychological terms and effects introduced here are covered in future chapters and the glossary.

How do couples reconcile such diametric ideals, playing out in the dynamics of their relationships? At least, mythic and fairy-tale archetypes provide a start.

The animal-groom archetype of fairy tales (Aarne-Thompson-Uther Index (1910, 1928, 1961) speaks to the civilised human longing to recover their wild-side. On a darker note, an animal-to-bride groom transition warns women of the many 'wolves in sheep's clothing' out there on the look-out for the unsuspecting. These men use their animal instincts to sniff out what a woman wants to present as her ideal match, pretending to be harmless while masking their malintent to control her.

Beyond *Bluebeard*, Perrault's pen drew further attention to the dangers women face when they put their trust in men. These 'tame wolves' (the sort that engages in the niceties of polite social intercourse) may well have bad intentions with psychically naïve women, as inferred in his tale of *Le Petit Chaperon Rouge* but called *Little Red Riding Hood* for English speakers (also attributed to the Brothers Grimm as *Rotkäppchen).*

Another classic by Perrault, *Puss in Boots, or Le Maître Chat ou Le Chat Botté*, originated in Straparola's *Facetious Nights*, also known as *The Pleasant Nights* (1550-1553). It tells the fable of three poor brothers, with the youngest inheriting a cat, who is actually a disguised fairy. The tale's morality proffers that one must be saved from both the rich who become poor and the beggar who climbs the hierarchy to richness. Perrault's later version echoes the deceitful game-playing of the wealthy and how when emulated by the poor can provide them with a leg up: a matter very much on the minds of the under-class of his time which greatly feared the punishing grip of pauperism. The Brothers Grimm added the booted cat as *Der gestiefelte Kater* to their collection.

Sleeping Beauty, known in versions of the tale as *Briar Rose, Aurora,* or *Rosemund*, is also attributed to Perrault's tale-stable (along with the Brothers Grimm). Perrault's original story titled *La Belle au bois Dormant* was later adapted by the Grimms as *Dornroschen* in their collection. For this tale of dark fairies and sleep-inducing spells, Perrault likely drew from Basile's (1634) Neopolitan tale *Sun, Moon and Talia* and the medieval manuscript (a blend of pagan and Christian elements) of *Perceforest* (1340). In the forerunner, the prince impregnates a sleep-enchanted princess. Her newly born bairn removes some charmed flax from her finger, and as she awakens, only then does the prince return to marry her. Other iterations have the sleeping kingdom set in the ancient Sababurg Castle, county Kassel from whence the Brothers Grimm family came.

With a trope in kind with *Sleeping Beauty*, *Snow White* (attributed to the Brothers Grimm) is based on the life of Margaretha von Waldeck (16 C.E.), daughter of Count of Waldeck-Wildungen, raised in the baroque castle Schloss Friedrichstein. Gaining far too much attention for her beauty, her strict and cruel stepmother wanted rid of her. Margaretha was sent to the Habsburgian Court of Brussels to improve relations between her father and the emperor and enhance her marriage prospects. She and Prince Philip II (the future king of Spain) fell in love.

Reference to the seven dwarfs in the fairy tale concerns the child labour used in the copper mine owned by her brother in her home district at the time. Sadly,

Margaretha died at just twenty-one years of age from suspected poisoning by the father of her prince. Her father's castle can still be seen today, towering over the mythical medieval town of her birth. We can also trace *Snow White* to another version from a Bavarian village and castle at Lohr. It is said the real girl's frightening foray into the forest is often retraced by tourists through the Spessart mountain range.

An early third century Heliopolis Christian story of a maiden was later renamed *Rapunzel* and retold by the Brothers Grimm. In the original telling, a pagan merchant-father was so protective of his beautiful daughter that he locked her in a tower whenever he left the village to peddle his wares. Converting to Christianity, the isolated maiden was devout in her worship and daily prayers. Ardent and loud, her outpourings often intruded into the quiet sanctum of the village folk. When the father returned and learned of her outbursts, he dragged his raucous 'Rapunzel' before the pro-Roman consul. They demanded she renounce her Christianity lest they force him to forfeit his fortunes. Flames could not burn her, and her painful wounds from torture would miraculously heal overnight. And so, her outraged father beheaded her. But on his way back home, he was struck and incinerated by lightning. After her death, the maiden became venerated as Saint Barbara. She protects us from storms and is the patron saint of the military, mine workers and users of explosives. German folklorists claim that the 700-year-old hilltop tower with a single window at its summit known as the Fortress of Trendelberg is the very tower that inspired the Grimm's *Rapunzel*.

During 13 C.E.-14 C.E., Europe experienced many wars, the Great Famine, Black Death (plague), infanticide and cannibalism, wiping out one-third or more of the population. As shocking as it sounds, there is something even more macabre that came earlier.

A trade existed in the London markets for roasted human flesh until at least the 11th century (and probably later). It is horrible to think of where the supply came from, but we can only imagine the most vulnerable becoming victims. While not trying to make too fine a point on this grim subject, before any of us goes into denial about the extent to which humans will go to survive or provide sacrifices to their gods, we know from Roman recorded history that the Celtic Druids were cannibals. A large number of Druids, originally pagans, had assimilated into the Christian way of life by the 9th century. The suppression of many of their beliefs and practices and the gradual phasing out of their ritual of cannibalism no doubt was met with resistance, taking a long time to come to an end. Pliny the Elder said of their cannibalistic tradition: "To murder a man was to do the act of highest devoutness and to eat his flesh was to secure the highest blessings of health." Cannibalism is still taboo and stigmatised by societies, but war, famine and extreme poverty can cause us to do unthinkable things. The point is that humans of all colours and creeds from all points on the globe have had a long history of eating their own; indeed, anything that has a heartbeat and moves. Many more see no harm in consuming anything sentient possessing a face.

Greek myths are rife with acts of cannibalism. Fairy tales portray our brutal animal side, but few of us can get our heads around the gore, accepting that our savagery is real.

Revisiting the times of famine and desperation depicted in *Hansel and Gretel*, parents deserted their homes and children. They butchered their hungry farm animals, keeping them out of the hands and mouths of the enemy, and headed off with a packed lunch to battle or resettle in the unsanitary town centres to find a new means to survive.

These rural, pre-industrial times in history were very different from the religious, socio-political landscape we experience today in developed democratic nations. Still, poverty remains a grim reaper of our modern times. Back then, its cruel bedfellows of malnutrition, filth, disease, beggary, persecution, prostitution, abortion as a means of belated contraception, infanticide and premature demise were left unremedied (in the main) by the patriarchal, hierarchal authority. *Hansel and Gretel* (Brothers Grimm) may have come to the fore and circulated at such soul-wrenching times.

During the 16th century, Katharina Schaderin, a renowned German gingerbread baker accused of being a witch by a fellow baker jealous of her success, was hunted down by a furious posse and burned alive in her oven.

The chances are that Katharina was a wise-woman who not only knew how to cook ginger root but employed a wide range of local plant materials with both culinary and medicinal properties in her recipes. Such women, skilled in cooking, brewing and folkloric, holistic forms of healing, were sought after by the poor in times of injury, illness, birth, and death. But any healing not sanctified by the church resulted in a death warrant. With only a handful of physicians, trained exclusively for the elite classes, available in Britain and less in France and Germany in the 16th century, the common folk relied heavily on the traditional therapies of wise-women handed down through the ages. Ironically, the doctors of the day exploited the same active ingredients derived from plant, animal and mineral sources in their treatments but supplanted the local healers' incantations to the supernatural with religious prayers. Still, well over 80,000 witches (85% female witches and 15% male wizards) were prosecuted for sorcery and heresy. Through the fourteenth to eighteenth centuries, they were hanged or burned alive at the stake, including Joan of Arc (but of different context) for heresy. They tended (charitably or for a pittance) to the needs of the so-called undeserving poor. Many were immolated for crimes they did not commit. The highest number of witch killings recorded (let's call it femicide) was in Germany which conducted the most mass trials and executions ever witnessed in Europe.

Contrastingly, a century or two later, the Russian folktale featuring Vasilisa implies the real witches are closer to home, causing us a far worse injury than the witch doctors practising herbal magic in the woods. The plot reveals a spared wicked witch but a burned step-family of mean girls, aiming to inflict unbearable psychological damage (and worse) on the one they outcast.

According to the Brothers Grimm, in the case of *The Frog Prince*, dating back to the 13th century, this tale is one of the oldest and more beautiful, hailing from the German-speaking traditions. Originally written in Latin, a version of the story harks back to the Roman emperor Nero, often referred to as The Frog. Origins of *The Frog Prince* may also be found in Greek antiquity with the story of *Princess Danaid Amymone.* She carries water upon her head from the river Styx, has a goat-like satyr try to force himself upon her, but is saved by the God Poseidon.

Another tale featured in the Brothers Grimm's collection is *The Fisherman and his Wife.* Links exist with the old Russian tale of *The Old Man, his wife, and a Fish.* The wife is just as dissatisfied and greedy in each of these 19th century renditions, holding the same moral caution for us to be satisfied by any reward received for our good deeds. In any case, goodness is its own reward.

Unfortunately, in the Brothers Grimm tale of *Our Lady's Child,* the adopted child takes for granted her privileged life in heaven and must live a life of purgatory in a giant tree for her sins. Here lies a hint of the folkloric cure for problematic or unwell children (or adults) of placing them in a young ash tree spliced through the middle: as the tree heals, so too does the patient. In the 17th century precedent, there is a tale about a maiden, Ranzolla, who is also ungrateful for her many blessings. Her beauty is reversed by a supernatural, giant lizard who gives her a goat-face. She must beseech a good spirit (a fairy) for her pardon, just as is implied in the latter tale about the Virgin Mary's adopted child retold by the Grimms.

According to the universities of Durham and Lisbon (2016), the tale of *Jack and the Beanstalk* has its origins in a pre-literate time, five thousand years ago. Many different versions of the oral story emerged throughout Europe. The famous English fairy tale *Jack Spriggins and the Enchanted Bean* (1734) became the *Jack and the Beanstalk* tale most of us remember. The Welsh mythic giant Gogmagog features in the Jack Spriggins' story, while Blunderbore is the Cornish giant in one of the versions of the legendry tale of *Jack, the Giant Killer.*

England, like Germany, had a viral word-of-mouth transmission of old-wives' folktales. Many informed the classic fairy tales then and as we have come to know them in our time. An example relating to the modernised, *The Three Little Pigs* came from Dartmoor in 1853, featuring three little pixies, not pigs, who venture from the home hearth to make their fortunes.

Another narrative from England, a revised tale by Robert Southey (1837), has a golden-haired girl entering a house in the woods (like Snow White did). It seems Southey's retelling may have developed nuance from a Nordic tale of a princess seeking refuge in a cave where three princes in bearskins dwelt. But Southey's uncle is said to have told him a story about an intruder, a vixen (female fox) that ate the food she found in the home, inspiring the storyline of *Goldilocks.*

The Danes' major migrations into England through the fifth, sixth and tenth centuries have been well documented. Their shared oral tales have and will continue to travel across the oceans and centuries to find a place in our hearts.

Modern science tells us that humans can pass on memories for several thousands of years with or without the benefit of literacy.

Perhaps, one of the most endearing fairy tales is *The Ugly Duckling* (1843*),* written by the famous Danish writer Hans Christian Andersen, who shared that the tale was an autobiographical one. Hans was an unattractive and awkward child who finally grew into a fine-looking gentleman, possessing ancestral roots in royalty (hence the duck to swan theme). Other Andersen conceived tales are *The Little* Mermaid and *The Emperor's New Clothes,* also published in his extensive collection*: Fairy Tales Told for Children* (1837).

Travelling further north to the kingdom of Norway, we discover the fairy tales and legends collected throughout the Norwegian countryside and northern Europe, recalibrated, and retold by Peter Christen Asbjørnsen and Jørgen Moe in '*Norwegian Folktales'* (1841). *The East of the Sun and West of the Moon* tale has motifs and tropes in common with *Beauty and the Beast* and *The Golden Ass.* Bargains are made with beastly beings as a means to an end, as is also the case in their version of *Three Billy Goats Gruff.*

Our final fairy tale in the *Mythimo* series is *Vasilisa the Brave, Beautiful and Wise,* the quintessential initiation story especially (but not exclusively) for women. It hails from the far north-eastern realms of Russia but is also widely known in Romania and Poland. In some instances, the tale is called, *Wassilissa the Wise.* According to Australian author and scholar Kate Forsyth (2022), this is a hybrid tale emanating from Russia and through the Baltics, predating classic Greek culture, with archetypal roots in the ancient horse-goddess cults. Forsyth (2022) writes about *Vasilisa the Wise* on her website, *Long-Lost Fairy-Tales,* "The tale carries ages-old psychic mapping about induction into the underworld of the wild female."

In keeping with the Slavic folk beliefs which influence the first telling of the *Wassilissa the Martyr* legend (4 C.E.), our psychological interpretations outlined in *Mythimo*, recognise the same oppositional and yet complementary dark and light dualities of the human condition. Light and shadow are two sides of the same coin. Concurring with the dualities of the cosmos through which the one eternal, infinite power expresses itself, we are invited to integrate as one within and without, atoning with the Divine throughout the course of our lifetime. Mind you, the sooner the better— As above, so below. Aldous Huxley (1894-1963), who penned *A Brave New World* believed the only hope for humanity is if a critical mass of us engages in a deep mystical training, learning how to become one with Divinity. Our quest begins by subsuming our personal darkness with our innate love and light. We are divine beings, an expression of Divinity after all, reassures Neale Donald Walsch (2009).

In the case of *Vasilisa, the Brave, Beautiful and Wise* (together with her indwelling doll: both her inner child and internalised parent), when the light faltered, she went into the gloomy woods to face the dark mother-ogress, the fire-hardened Baba Yaga, to bring back the light and flame for her step-tribe.

Back in the days near on the Dark Ages, powerful, wise-women like Baba Yaga were both revered and reviled. The witch hunts and trials through Europe took hold during the centuries preceding the revival of the folk fables and tales powered by the Grimms in the early 19th century. In much earlier, classical, polytheistic times, the distinction between good and evil dwelling within deities or demons was prevalent in the philosophy of Western and Eastern European culture.

Looking back, Baba Yaga, beholden to no religion or authority, would have been seen as a paganistic peasant— a dark witch driven into exile in the densest parts of the forest who sometimes sought refuge in caves. Like other so-called dangerously hysterical women, she was ruled by her womb senses and hence too outspoken with her deficient reasoning powers. Truth be told, she was too busy making fiery weapons and casting spells to protect herself, kith and kin from the raiding Goths (Eastern Germanic, early Christian and barbaric tribes) invading her lands (raping, impregnating, torturing, torching, slaughtering, enslaving, stealing) and subjugating her Slavic people and those of the Baltic Sea region and beyond. Theirs was a polytheistic animism, butting heads mostly with the inhumane arbiters (and arguably, biased interpreters) of the tablets of the Law or Word incarnate.

The simple folk (equally guilty of inhumane acts) were taken by the throat by the oppressive hand of religion raging its holy terror across their lands while they paid tribute habitually to the spirits of the natural world, beseeching them for protection and mercy. The Orthodox Church held power and pomp, but pagan masses saw little reason to curb instincts they regarded as natural, not sinful.

Fairy tales hark back to these pagan times where the animistic worship of supernatural creatures, plants, trees, stones, and celestial bodies was woven into the fabled fabric of their society. Motifs such as enchanted dolls, elves, dwarfs, imps, fairies, trolls, giants, witches, mermaids, and the like feature commonly across the fairy tales because of their magical transformative powers. They take us from trope to truth, turning the ordinary into the extraordinary and back again. Like then, they promise relief from our real-life woes.

Nowadays, humans succeed against different odds than in the past, still relying on the magic of their intuition but believing in a monotheistic Higher Power, the power of science and their own abilities.

The real-life sages of our distant heritage practised their own kind of domestic medicine and homespun teaching for it was at hand and empowered them through some of our darkest days in history, serving them efficaciously. They preserved and handed down their folkloric remedies from the wild and educated each new generation long before a masculine-mechanical-medical-model made its official 11th century debut. Through the decades, doctors' socio-political clout expanded, granting them prestigious status, wealth and access to power and control across communities once dominated by the healing gods of the pantheon and the wise witchy-women helpers of the helpless.

Then, the Age of Enlightenment (17 C.E.- late 18 C.E.) moved in, shifting the thinking and behaviours of the people, promoting a scientific rationale based on logic and intellectual reason over pagan or religious superstition. So, our mythical, irrational thinking was overtaken by religious belief to be superseded again by science and rationalism.

The poor old midwife conjured spirits to charm her potions of belladonna, raspberry leaf and snakewort for birthing babies or she was known to put dried toad skins around one's neck to ward off the plague. Still, methods utilising plants (such as lavender, linden blossom, elder bush berries, chamomile and rose petals etc.), minerals and animals were trusted by the life-hardened peasant and working classes only because they so often worked.

When the Grimms collected their stories, medical physicians, surgeons, and apothecaries became more available in the community for those who could afford their services. Nevertheless, wise-women healers and their ancient tales about the doings and wrongdoings of the common (and not so common) people had not yet been completely driven out. Donkey hair placed around a baby's neck was still being used to ease teething pain when Jacob Grimm was born (and probably even later). Where there is a demand, someone will supply.

Animals are strongly represented in fairy tales and myths. The reader of *Mythimo* will encounter wolves, birds, snakes, pigs, cats, goats, ducks, fish, frogs, bears and a bestiary of European or Australian variety, enhancing one's symbolic interpretations.

Our moderation of our animal instincts and intuition enriches our knowing and doing in real life. Sometimes these natural powers are denied because they have been disowned, mocked or used for fearmongering. It is easy to see how accusing an instinctual, wise-woman using her herbal and plant folk knowledge of being a witch (guilty of heresy and punishable by death) would induce fear and a resistance to employ her charitable services. Creating fear is a Machiavellian strategy of the political class even today.

Another instance of inciting fears in the common folk involves the cunning war tactics of Napoleon. He was referred to as the 'ogre'. Errant children were warned by their parents that the ogre 'Boney' was hiding under their beds (as we might too if we knew an enemy with his ruthless powers was nearby). The reputation of the self-crowned emperor, known as the ogre (in other words, not humane), preceded him wherever he went, stirring up fear and loathing in adult populations, too, but proving to be an effective means for achieving the ends of widespread compliance with local government rules.

After the French Revolution (1789) and as the Napoleonic Wars (1803-1815) raged through Europe, the Brothers Grimm (Jacob and Wilhelm), the studious cultural anthropologists and linguists from Hesse-Kassel, collaborated, collected, and rewrote the old oral folktales. These stories had been handed down for centuries across the small kingdoms of Germany. Educated as lawyers and working as diplomats and librarians, the Brothers Grimm were determined to harness their people's past before it slipped away from the war-torn, famine and disease-ravaged landscape. As two of the most outstanding scholars Germany has ever produced, they reasoned, once the oral tales were set in script form, they would endure.

Even as the natural sciences gradually overtook mythological wisdom across the West from the 17th century, nothing could erode the folkloric imprint in our biological and social unconscious. While protesters were saying that advancements with understanding the workings of the human mind had their roots in myths, scientific inquiry attempted to put the death knell on folkloric philosophy. They ridiculed their impact on our sensibilities and scorned the Celtic faeries popularised by the medieval Druidic bards in the literature of Chaucer and Shakespeare. Catholicism and science became unlikely bedfellows in denouncing pagan mythology, agreeing it had no business trying to convey meaning concerning the great mysteries of life. At the same time, James 1 (King of Scotland) claimed the 'divine right of kings', a throwback to the pagans who glorified monarchs. He appointed himself an ordainee of God, protecting him from criticism or rebellion. But just as religion replaced the freedoms of former types of worship, there arrived other ways for addressing the fundamental questions of the universe, human existence, nature and death. The axiomatic discoveries of astronomer Copernicus superseded any human right to divinity. Following in his footsteps came Kepler, Galileo, Newton and Faraday—all making their mark in the age of science.

Our God-fearing ways may have been overtaken using mathematics to explain our existence, but our sentiments for the mythic tales of yore remained steadfast through the shifting sands of time.

The German Grimms (18 C.E.-19 C.E.) left an enduring legacy with their *Children's and Household Tales*. Italian poet Giambattista Basile (16 C.E.-17 C.E.) collected Neapolitan fairy tales. His *Rapunzel,* and *Cinderella* (with ancient Chinese roots), were published posthumously in *Pentamerone.* Charles Perrault (17 C.E.-18 C.E.), whose published collection, *Tales and Stories of the Past with Morals,* made him a favourite with the aristocracy and courtiers of Louis XIV's Versailles Palace where he resided.

We see each of these authors included our same old favourites in their collections, demonstrating that back in the day, storytelling of folkloric tales travelled with ease between France, England, Germany, Italy, the northern lands and far beyond.

In contemporary times (2005), the Grimm's fairy tales were entered in UNESCO's Memory of the World Register to preserve their folkloric history for posterity. The Brothers Grimm collected over 200 fairy tales and legends over a forty-five-year period. It is heartening to know their life-long commitment to safeguarding the oral traditions of their people's past is so widely appreciated. Not only are the tales safely archived as world history, so too are the original illustrations of their stories.

During and after the Napoleonic Wars, the Grimm's tales (1812) of princesses, witches, talking animals, transformative magic and happily-ever-after endings began to play a small role, influencing the trend towards a warmer cultural sentimentality. The people of the time welcomed the expression of one's feelings and waxed lyrical (after living through the harshest of times) when rendezvousing with nature, composing music and poems, writing fiction and painting pictures. Fairy tales also possessed a magical alchemy, transporting them into the world of their poetic imaginations.

As the Romantic movement took hold across Europe, the Grimm's scholarly and hard-won works were eventually well-received across noble and common households alike. Romanticists placed store in people and things being authentic or unadulterated. They believed we were part of nature and so personified the non-human world with the power of speech. Humans communicated back, recognising the emotions nature evoked in them, and felt deeply their part in the whole scheme of things again. Indeed, even latter-born princes held deep conversations with the plants in the greenhouse.

When emphasis was placed on children's learning needs, the Grimms, proponents of the German Romantic Movement, rewrote tales appealing to the child's perspective. Stories read to them by nurturing caregivers inspired young imaginations to venture out into the world and sow the same sweet memories for generations of children to come.

Visual illustrations of the stories helped the young to grasp meaning and remember the tales, aiding their ongoing learning. Some famous illustrators back in the day were the lithographer Gustav Sus and Danish illustrator Kay Neilsen, Gustaf Tenggren—the Swedish-American artist also later played a role in the animation of Disney's (1937) *Snow White.* English art of note includes the works of Walter Crane and the black and white silhouettes of Arthur Rackham (*Sleeping Beauty and Cinderella*, 1920). And to think, the illustrious and brightly coloured depictions of the fairy tales seen across multi-media since the heyday of the Grimms had their early beginnings in monochrome. In their first published books of the 19th century, the famous Grimms utilised the talented painter Otto Ubbelohde, caricaturist George Cruikshank, and English illustrator Charles Folkard. All in all, there were over 200 illustrations from renowned illustrators chosen for inclusion in the Grimm' works.

Interpretations of the fairy tales have a long history in books, ballet, opera, theatre and movies. The modern film, *Once Upon a Time in Hollywood* (Tarantino, 2019) subverts and reimagines the horrific ending of the real-life actress Sharon Tate (and her unborn child) in 1969 by the murderous Manson hippy-gang with the violence being turned on the wigged-out perpetrators instead. We can wistfully envisage the luminous Sharon Tate as a modern-day Snow White, destined to die at the hand of the malevolent archetype but being saved by a handsome prince to live happily ever after. The diabolical make-believe version of the Manson mob in the movie meets with a horrible end as happened to the wicked witch. Similar vignettes can be drawn from different fairy tales and cross-referenced to Tarantino's movie masterpiece with such a fitting name. In this case, art imitates art, but many who remember the real-life case were relieved that the art took its own path.

We know that many of the folkloric stories retold as fairy tales happened, at least in part, in real-life narratives of history. The case of the feral boy, Victor of Aveyron, who wandered lost in the wild woods of southern France to be raised by a pack of grey wolves, was the basis for the book and movie *Mowgli: Legend of the Jungle* (2018). Wolves raise Mowgli in the dangerous Indian jungle, but he eventually, after many trials must try and fit in with his human tribe.

Other movies sharing similarities to a famous fairy-tale trope include *Kate and Leopold* (2001), which brings two time-crossed lovers together when Kate is awakened from her deep sleep by noisy Duke Leopold in the apartment above. Another nod to *Beauty and the Beast* is from the film *The Knight Before Christmas* (2019). The fifties' classic starring Audrey Hepburn, *Sabrina,* is Cinderella reimagined. Still more examples of art imitating art and life exist.

Then, there are the fairy-tale inspired posters and artworks. Visual arts of the Grimm's era included the cutting-edge works of Lotte Reiniger, who launched her successful career on the back of her silhouette styled films interpreting the Grimm's fairy tales.

In summarising twenty-two fairy tales in *Mythimo,* efforts have been made to stay close to the versions that many of us recall from our childhood. However, as there are so many different sources and retellings, some may find that their recollections differ slightly from those included. My versions are those memorised from my early beginnings with my story-telling mother and other caregivers.

For example, there are 60 or more translations ascribed to the story of *Little Red Riding Hood* who walks across the woods in a red hoodie to visit her grandmother, including an Italian version from the 10th century called *The False Grandmother.* In Europe, the tale is also known as *Little Red Cap.* Some say that the image of the pre-teen girl known as 'Red Cap' was inspired by the 'Schwabische Jungfrauen' of the Swabian region of Germany who wore distinct red headscarves, exhibited virtuous qualities and a strong work ethic and were regarded as positive role-models for young girls.

Another tale titled *The Wolf and the Kids* shares motifs with *Little Red Riding Hood* and has origins pinpointed to Greece around 400 A.D. It travelled the trade routes to Africa and China in oral and written form before enjoying a revival in Europe.

There are hundreds of sources of readily accessible information that will corroborate or contradict the author's research of fairy-tale origins. However, there exists a scientific model for classifying, dating and appropriating them called phylogenetic analysis. The process looks at the common motifs utilised in stories across cultures (such as supernatural entities, magic objects, moral coding etc.) and attributes their origin, according to the region where the archetypal tale is most predominant. The inspirational Joseph Campbell (1949) tells us that fairy tales, like myths, offer a timeless narrative structure that not only captivates our imagination but also illuminates the historical tapestry of our shared human experience, enabling us to comprehend our place in the world. Borrowing from Symonds (1873), myths (and fairy tales) are the 'everlasting elastic tissue of human consciousness'.

Examining the provenance and nature of fairy tales and their archetypes reveals that when masks fall away and truth comes to light, the human journey toward self-understanding begins.

The persona is that which in reality one is not, but which oneself and others think one is.
(Carl Jung)

4 THE MYTHIMO QUEST

At this juncture, you may be wondering what fairy tales have to do with the notion of healing our psyches and making us Whole and happier ever after.

To be effective, any psychological process utilising fairy-tale archetypes requires the client to either retell and summarise their favourite version of the story or work with a counsellor to make meaningful connections between their personal life story and a relevant fairy tale of their choosing. My story summaries are designed to serve as prompts in later pages. From the outset, one must accept that no person or archetype is all evil or all good, black or white, but corresponds to gradients in between, individuating one person from another. One thing is sure: almost all of us can utilise fairy-tale archetypes and their positive or negative emotional attributes and energy to highlight and heal our psychic shadow. But our efforts with the inner work must be sincere and ongoing.

Analytical psychologist Carl Jung (1875-1961) and mythologist Joseph Campbell (1904-1987) spoke of the rediscovery of myths as a set of immutable psychological types (archetypes) that evoke universal emotions. Archetypes are inborn, invariant models or patterns of human knowledge, character, personality, and behaviour (etc.) transmitted intergenerationally from ancestors. In the same way, a young child inherits and knows instinctively what behaviours to do at a particular stage of their development (Wadsworth, 1989), the unconscious archetypes, comingling with our subjectivity, influence what we think, say, and do. In light of Jung's (1959) theory, we can explore myths and fairy tales for meaning relevant to us and how we live our lives today.

Take the Goldilocks archetype's sense of self-entitlement and compare her to how corporate entities behave in modern times, exercising their 'right' to take whatever they want from nature without conscience. We soon come to realise that there is nothing new under the sun about human behaviour.

Many honest souls will relate to the motifs of the *Goldilocks* tale (for example) when examining their own behaviour. Soon they will even agree with Jung (1959) and Campbell (1949) that resonant archetypes, metaphors and symbols embedded in stories, artefacts and artworks are grist for the mill of a reflective mind, revealing more about themselves than first expected.

Reflective experiential learning (Kolb, 1984) is the central tenet of the *Mythimo* quest, whether it is your journey to Wholeness or mine. If imagination is the queen of truth, then active self-reflection is its king.

To enhance the reflective process, artist Simo modernises and reassembles timeless fairy tales under the sunlit Australian skies in a sparkling gallery of twenty-two mythopoetic mythograms. A sensitivity is apparent in his depiction of the ancient rock formation, Uluru. The ancestral creator spirits and sacred stories, revered by the Anangu, offer these traditional custodians moral remedies for past, present, and future ills. Our curated collection of Western tales, interpreted through Simo's iconographic paintings, captures their archetypal power and illuminates the profound psychological imprints on our collective psyche, shaping our modern reality. Within the universal, inside those deeper symbolic layers, our true colours of Self lay waiting to be found.

Like many Australians, Simo's ancestral origins are in Europe. Still, in his mind's eye, he has always imagined the sunburnt Australian bush, with the sun on his back, birdsong and soft twinkle of the running creek, as the backdrop to the Continental fairy tales he enjoyed through childhood. Just as the stories brought by white settlers from the old countries were introduced to Indigenous peoples' lands, so too were their rabbits, foxes, and carp. The artist's rendition of that woodland wonderland of wise and wilful archetypes such as *Hansel and Gretel* speak to these early foundations of our great southern land. Our native marsupials and botanica feature in *Our Lady's Child; Rumpelstiltskin; Three Billy Goats Gruff; Puss in Boots; Little Red Riding Hood; Bluebeard; Rapunzel; Sleeping Beauty; Cinderella; Snow White; Vasilisa; The Ugly Duckling; Emperor's New Clothes and The Little Mermaid.*

The Australian dingo supersedes the grey wolf in *The Three Little Pigs,* a Tasmanian Tiger (Thylacine) becomes the beast in *Beauty and the Beast,* and a Diprotodon takes on the role of the white bear in *East of the Sun and West of the Moon.*

The reimagining of these classic tales in our modern piece of Oceania proves their transcendence of time and space and enkindles potentially another fairy-tale revival. This will be true, at least, for those of us undertaking the *Mythimo* quest that takes us to the summit of the Self.

Join us in willing bewitchment on a journey through the vibrant colours of the Australian wilderness brushed in the same hues as a Heysen, Streeton, Russell or Roberts' palette: the burnt golds, blue violets, rich russet browns, sage greens and ghostly whites of the whispering gums stood between sunshine and shadow of the bush. In this new light, the psychic fragments of *Red Cap, Jack, Vasilisa* and their mythical peers can be discovered, demystified and contextualised to our personal realities. Sympathetic to these traditional archetypes, we will find parts of us— loving and light, and others potentially shadowy, shouting 'cooee!' as we embark on our very own journey into the deeper leagues of our psyches. Both our positive and negative attributes retrieved will resource the integration process of our emotional life required to make us Whole and revivified.

Our nobilities, flaws, foibles, and falsities as old as time are explored in a present-day mythos through a philosophical and psychological gaze on some of the most fascinating fables of human reality and make-believe ever told.

Mythimo, while not the last word on fairy-tale and archetypal analysis provides an honest account of how humans operate on any given day to survive, cope, gain a competitive advantage, and think better about themselves. Much of what the author shares about archetypes has come from the raw material of her and her clients' dreams, reflecting her personal commitment to the belief that dreams are the 'royal road to the unconscious' (Freud, 1900). Our dreams, operating on the edge of consciousness, serve as a bridge, interacting between our unconscious (the personal and collective underpinnings) and our consciousness at the top of mind. According to Jungian psychologist Robertson (1992), they are a natural source, providing the bulk of our unconscious material, giving direct access to our indwelling archetypes (also termed 'cognitive invariants'). Archetypes are the building blocks of our unconscious, lying in the deep substratum of our psyche that would otherwise remain unconscious if not for our delving. Robertson (1992) contends that the more rapid access we establish between the two psychic states, the more we grow and accelerate change in our lives.

Suppose we do not recognise, process and steer the instinctual behaviours of our latent archetypes in the right direction. In that case, we too often experience more pain than the pleasure our instincts promise and ego desires and needs. In uncertain times, we may find ourselves in a dark cave of despair. But when we increase our consciousness to create a fuller and whole-some life, we restore a crisper sense of clarity for finding our way out. What better way of living than one that moves us onwards and upwards to where we love and are loved in return? And although, to a jaded, cynical mind, this may sound like a myth, our hearts know this loving, and light state of being (referred to as having empathy) feels more natural. Besides, [it] optimises our body's homeostatic physical functions.

Studies indicate our capacity for emotional empathy is inborn. How much caring concern we feel and demonstrate for other sentient life has its roots in our nature and how this loving quality has been or not been nurtured. We are the product of our genetic inheritance, familial and cultural influences, social conditioning, inherent beliefs and values, and much more. Therefore, why some people are sensitive (e.g., vicarious empaths whose caring receptors rarely shut down) and others indifferent to the hardships of their fellow beings (e.g., sociopaths) can be complex. Most of us accept that it is a combination of 'nature and nurture'. Perhaps the person lacking empathy in one situation will show it in another. Or could their insensitivity be due to their poor treatment at the hands of others through the developmental years? Maybe, being hardnosed helps them cope with their own challenges. Still, their inborn empathy has had to have gone somewhere. Jung (1959) assures our biological make-up cannot be cast off or vanish into the ethers.

Repressed empathy can be found in our shadow, waiting to be reclaimed. Our sense of wellbeing will not be fully felt until we constellate and reintegrate the emotional energy of our disowned psychic fragments. As with any healing journey, we must first acknowledge that something feels wrong in our organism and then find out what we must do to make things right.

Can our in-wired empathy also be a virtue or even a moral or ethical obligation? Before we can be good citizens doing good things in the world for others, many great philosophers (such as Schopenhauer, 1840) said that we first need a developed sense of compassion and empathy to fuel our good intentions and deeds. Our take on this depends on our essence, beliefs, and value systems operating quietly within us. One thing hanging over the direction we take, being empathetic or not, is the power of choice in situations within our control. It can come down to whether we choose to put our self-interest above the needs of others, asserting aggressively our agenda. This is an ethical dilemma most of us face regularly. Still, suppose we decide to become the better version of ourselves. In that case, we will switch on our cognitive awareness, be sensitive to the impacts of our thoughts, words and behaviours on other living beings and act the same way a caring person would— making a choice within our control.

Being the best of who we were born to be, does not have to be a chore or a killjoy to life's pleasure. Innately, we know when we let others down, we are only letting ourselves down. We feel it in our souls. Depending on our standards, we may feel guilty or ashamed and marinate in self-recrimination or deny it. In any case, we shove these awful feelings into our shadow, out of sight, but never entirely out of mind.

When caring about others, we feel good about ourselves, and our developed sense of self-esteem and wellbeing attracts more happy and healthy energy into our lives. It is this simple and accessible. We change for our betterment while improving the quality of our relationships and how we live— everyone in our orbit can be a winner. Potent alchemy for turning the lead of our lives into gold exists— it is as old as Methuselah and perennial as the grass.

Was *Mythimo* written to vent a moral, and ethical doctrine with vain ambitions of influencing a fallen society? No. Long ago, fairy tales were written to fill those shoes by employing the honey of enchantment over the bitter salt of judgment and attempts to oppress.

Today, fairy-tale analysis can go one step further. Each of us is naturally good, and once we recover our shadow, revealed to us by the fairy-tale archetypes, we will find it natural to live with maturity and integrity. The author's motive is to share how becoming a Whole person is within reach and provides a return on investment that keeps on giving. Our integration of dark with light reconciles us with the inner child who is ready to live without vanity in the mind and corresponding suffering in the body. Essentially, we dissolve the rigid shell encasing our consciousness, releasing our child-like curiosity and openness to return our harmonic resonance with nature.

I undertook this protracted project because if I had had access to this information when I started out on my own on the hero's path around five decades ago, I would have taken the world in my stride rather than carried its weight on my shoulders. My solemn aim is to spare those with the same naïve and vulnerable hearts any unnecessary *over-learning.*

Herein are the fruits of my life-long labours invested in studying our human motivations and behaviours. My grail is to be lovingly helpful, making complex concepts accessible to anyone who wants to learn more about how and why humans behave as they do, guiding especially the 'emotional and sensitive' souls of our world. Sensitive people care profoundly, and most need a map of the human psyche to reach their breakthrough.

Have you ever experienced a time when you needed to talk to someone, connect with them, and feel safe in your skin, only to find that the contact felt superficial or incomplete? The other person seemed detached from you, distracted, and was not listening to your story. Their tone was dismissive, and you felt like a pawn in the game. Perhaps it was a case of one-up-man-ship with the other wresting control, holding all the power over the direction of the conversation. In any case, the interaction felt lacking and wrong. You left with a head full of questions, feeling robbed of an opportunity to engage fully with a fellow human being.

In the fairy story of *The Little Mermaid,* who suffered a fate like this with a prince, we learn when our energy is not a good fit with people or places, we seldom end up feeling satisfied, let alone loved in return. In these environments, we rarely land on our feet. Instead, we find ourselves being the wild one in a tribe of unwild ones, and the things that matter to us will make no sense with what matters to them. When we are ready for change, the unwild ones often pray for continuity with how things are, which suits them. Like The Little Mermaid, we will feel an odd misfit: different, possessing negative connotations, not different-good. No wonder the infatuated mermaid, who desperately ached to belong, cut off her tail, replacing it with legs, mimicking the unwild tribe.

We are our wild selves (and best tempered by healthy rationality) when we are our authentic, inimitable selves.

We each possess a uniqueness, providing a fully potentiated power. Why must we spend a lifetime covering up our specialness by homogenising ourselves to fit in and belong to a mainstream majority? In other words, we unplug ourselves so that we may merge with a group of others who have also denied their authentic selves and created an illusionary ingroup. We fear to be an original identity, lest we become outcasts.

After Meghan Markle married Prince Harry, she likened herself to the archetypal mermaid, saying she had no fear of depth and a great fear of shallow living. She saw the world as her oyster and refused to become trapped inside the hard shell of a royal reality. But her feelings of otherness began to mute her voice, as was the fate of The Little Mermaid. She made sacrifices until she could no longer bear sinking into the cold, rank and file of royal life where she wondered if she could survive. Meghan strove to find a more nurturing place for herself, Harry, and the children where they would share a loving family life and thrive. Later, she spoke of regaining her voice. Sadly, for Prince Harry's mother, Diana, fondly known as the fairy-tale princess, her mismatched spouse quizzed the very meaning of love, bringing her no such health and happiness ever after. Neither woman of considerable status chose to be identified as victims. Although enduring challenging childhoods, both women's inner child was even more determined to vote for love above royal privilege. As courageous questers for truth, love, and contentment, their stories share a humble philosophy of honouring value over cost.

But for many of us everyday folk (or everyperson archetypes), we feel like an identity waiting to happen, a void waiting to be filled. Sometimes, we sense that we are having the time of someone else's life, not our own. But mostly, we are not even consciously aware of our subordination, spending our day in a routine, going to school or work, following procedures, coming home, eating dinner, using our computer, or playing with the kids. Even meaningful activities can land us in a rut. Routine feels safe to the dumbed-down and comfortably numb version of ourselves. We can try to cocoon ourselves like this, but threats from within and without will still come our way. For now, constant pressure exists for us to be and do the same as everyone else in our peer group.

When we feel emotional distress, pain, and hurt, whether its source is baseless or actual, we grow fearful.

Some of us reflect on what is going on, make meaning from what has happened, and consider the lessons learned. Others, unwilling to remember or contemplate the circumstances, succumb to the pull of their egoic defences, slipping straight into avoidance or denial. When we try to rid ourselves of the pain, such as dumping it on someone else, the agendas and games of human interaction begin.

Humans engage in tactical manoeuvres. Most of us can accept a place for life and death strategies when protecting kin and kith from a ruthless enemy and when our love, peace, and survival are at risk. Politicians across the globe even engage in dummy runs for the advent of warfare systematically. But then, everyday game-playing, which sounds harm-free, when done routinely, can bring any of us down.

There is no denying that if we are not self-aware and sufficiently brave to be our authentic, Whole selves and behave with love, truth, and compassion (i.e., our light qualities), we will stumble on the rubble of life's road sooner or later. Even having become self-actualised and individuated, we will still inevitably come up against stiff opposition, only we will cope far more effectively, taking the knocks in our stride.

Time-honoured philosophies have outlined the four human cardinal virtues: justice, wisdom, courage and temperance (requiring self-regulation of our competing desires). Let us not lose sight of them as we come up against our ignorance, fear, hate and greed.

This book and related colour-plated mythograms and healing process ask us to go within ourselves and uncover the Original Self we have buried beneath the social camouflage. Like emperors in new clothes, the age-old question of 'Who am I?' comes to the fore once more. It dawned eventually on the emperor to act when he exposed himself, a prisoner of the dense psychological wilderness called his dark side—an unsettling condition felt but yet not seen, acknowledged or recovered. His archetypal lesson keeps on giving— better to take charge of events before events take charge of us.

We must explore the same evergreen question when we step into the experiential journey of *Mythimo* (my quest has taken ten years and continues), remaining receptive to life's great mystery. Only when we accept our aloneness, our nakedness, can we find the at-oneness, peace and joy we seek.

At heart, are we kind and caring, seeking a good and satisfying life for ourselves and wishing and acting on it for others? Or are we competitive adversaries with cold, entitled, self-interested hearts in the thrall of our dark traits always playing to win? Do we vacillate between our two sides (unintegrated), depending on our audience and whatever favours our ends? Do we even know?

Is it possible and worthwhile developing a personal code for Higher Living to become our authentic, Whole Selves who commit as conscious, compassionate collaborators, collectively striving to leave the world a better place than when we entered it?

According to an article, Rules for Living in *Womankind* (22), having a code of conduct and enshrining it in a spot to view it is useful when you haven't the willpower to act in the ways that make you most proud. But even thinking about your values and behaviours is a worthwhile exercise in itself.

How many repressed fears, self-fashioned myth-scripts, archetypes, and agendas are we running in our unconscious heads? Why are we hiding behind masks and playing games, disguising our true, fully fuelled, unadulterated selves? Where did our creativity go: our energetic expression of life, sense of humour and thirst for fun? Has our protective ego buried our guilt, embarrassment, and shame far down in our depths, the id? Why? Is it because we are fearful of rejection, abandonment, and scarcity? Then, we dig down our discarded fragments ever-deeper like entombing bones.

The trouble is that many potentially healthy, dynamic self-qualities are interred with painful ones. Still, they cannot lay dormant. As it happens in fairy tales, a bone starts to sing one day, revealing what was once concealed, and things begin to surface and unravel before ever getting better.

Life feels real, right? So, why are we pretending? While society's rules for refinement help tame the wild in us all, they send the message that play-acting and games are good. Some seem necessary for political diplomacy and maintaining the status quo during global security, health, and economic crises. But games don't always serve us. Have you ever rubbed shoulders with a 'smiling assassin' who seduced you with charm while stealing your lover? Then you know the pain and suffering that a scheme or agenda delivers. Such contrivances are deeply entrenched behaviours of people who cope using dominance, power, and control. The more territorial they are, the more they fear and feel threatened. Still, as with most power plays, someone must lose for someone to win. Winners think well of themselves. But our topsy-turvy world shaped by super-capitalism could use more self-aware, compassionate achievers who embrace the win-win paradigm.

Underscoring the philosophy that we all can do well—or that someone else's success is also our own—is an emerging belief that takes us beyond survival and security on Maslow's Hierarchy of Needs (1943). Thinking well of others' success can elevate us into the sensory realms of belonging and self-esteem. Acts of altruism and kindness feed our conscious intelligence and positive self-regard. Survival of the fittest is now superseded by survival of the most adaptable—a perspective meaning different things to different people across contexts. Mostly, it means someone need not have a killer instinct or view others as subordinate to their success. If a critical mass of humanity believes scarcity prevails and there's little room for others to thrive, we will focus on and manifest that. Such selfishness is problematic—it goes against who God intended us to be and will catch up with us sooner or later. *The Fisherman and His Wife* tale delivers this truth bomb.

Talented artist Simo has joined me to develop *Mythimo* in a quest to connect deeply with our divine potential, share with others and make a difference. As an Australian artist, Simo feels deeply about capturing the magic of the Australian landscapes being eroded away by development, mining and deforestation, raising awareness about the destructive impacts of human activity on our natural environment, and inspiring change. We hope his unique depictions of sacred Uluru and array of bush flora and fauna found nowhere else on earth help preserve the memory of an unspoiled outback broken only by the haunting call of native birds and rousing rustle of leaves in the wind.

We feel like winners because we have stayed the course together on a shared Hero's Journey through the conception and completion of our mutual project. Woven into the art and storytelling is a new modality, imagery and set of metaphors with a fresh analytical inflexion for understanding the classic cautionary tales from the Brothers Grimm and friends.

Through the fullness of time, as novices facing new and difficult challenges, we pressed on through personal trauma—learning to view our problem-stories through the lens of timeless fairy tales, reframing those shadows into strengths-based narratives. Now, as a mother and son team, we share that hard-won wisdom with you. Our work consists of a spiritual code, compassionate ethos, and applied mythos for psychological development based on human-like archetypes that enchant, enlighten, and move. Especially in these uncertain, disconnected times, there is every reason to place hope and faith in their gentle guidance and healing powers.

Mythimo's quest to lead us out of the woods to the shining summit, where we perceive and feel at-one with the life force in all that is, calls out to all heroes.

Shall we go through the looking glass?

To myself be true. But if I am only here for me, What shall I become?
(The Enlightened Emperor)

5 INTEGRATION AND INDIVIDUATION

Fairy-tale archetypes, mirroring our lives, unveil a tapestry of human existence encompassing drama, pathos, lust, crime, good and evil, love, light and darkness, devotion, and every conceivable aspect. Within their tales lie rebuke, remorse, repentance, consolation, practical wisdom, philosophical reflection, redemption, and truth. These characters, often based on real people but exaggerated for effect, reflect reality itself. Though their settings differ from ours, their struggles, aspirations, and rewards resonate deeply. Their narratives embody rags-to-riches transformations, guiding them from peasant to philosopher to prince.

Understanding fairy tales demands no exceptional intellect or spiritual gifts. Their symbols are easily recognised and apprehended through contemplation and self-reflection. They speak to us in meaningful patterns, illuminating our path and missteps. Swiss theologian Karl Barth wrote that human error is rooted in pride, dishonesty, and laziness—burdens of the ego and cardinal sins we battle throughout our ever-changing journey.

Through the looking glass of fairy-tale archetypes, we face ourselves, our fallibilities, and our capacity for growth. They inspire us to embark on the inner work of reclaiming and integrating our shadow aspects, transforming our emotional lives. By doing so, we move towards holism, experiencing a healthier happily-ever-after.

The *Mythimo* mythopoetic process and archetype cards are embedded with rich symbolism to foster understanding and overcome self-defeating myths that blind, bind, and limit us. They help us bring our powerful light and loving qualities to the fore. Such cognitive awareness comes through devoted practice: self-reflection, contemplation, meditation, guided breathing (which calms heightened sympathetic nervous system arousal), visualisation, affirmation, and dream journalling. Once enlightened to our shadow traits, we take systematic steps, and our dedicated inner work brings healing, emotional freedom, personal power, and soul growth.

Freud (1913) contended that symbols are the first building blocks of concept formation. Hence, ancient archetypes, springing unbidden from the deep unconscious (during dreams or reflections) and bypassing the ego, are received as instructions by the 'knower' within to take form in our reality.

Mythimo's premise is that when we reflect on, identify, and transform the mythical beliefs and behaviours exemplified by archetypes, we develop higher cognisance that overcomes confusion and aimlessness, resulting in emotional freedom and personal power, leading to self-actualisation (Maslow, 1943). Jung (1959) offered that we could only achieve full efficacy by integrating unconscious and conscious elements. He termed the integrated, emergent self the individuated Self.

Archetypes are vaults in unconscious memory that surface when we dream or contemplate deeply. Their reflection of our traits, active or archived, provides insight into reclaiming our full potential.

Mythical elements of self, both positive and negative, once denied, are called from their shadowy snare to be reclaimed and recalibrated into an integrated whole. It is not complicated—just seven relatively simple steps to reconstitute us into the fullness of our light. Focus shifts from the negative pull of the past to being and doing our best in the here and now.

When we choose authenticity and transform self-defeating patterns of thought, emotion, and behaviour—what I call the *Mythimo* quest, process, method, or healing journey—a reborn, 'de-mythified' self emerges. The authentic self feels confident in its own skin. This act of truth distinguishes our innate qualities while new horizons open as we organically transform and grow.

Take Little Red Riding Hood and her near-death-by-wolf. She was ill-prepared for this first encounter without a memory to revisit. Though she ignored universal wisdom to be careful, she miraculously lived to tell the tale. Embracing *Mythimo*, she would look back on her experience and undertake the seven steps (R.N.R.R.R.R.I.):

First, she **Reflects** on what occurred (utilising *Mythimo* cards as prompts); second, she **Names** her errant thought, emotion, or behaviour (e.g. foolishness) —without discernment; third, she owns and **Reclaims** this behaviour. Then she **Reframes** it with a positive, strengths-based perspective, making it acceptable in fitting circumstances (e.g. one can be foolish only in safe, playful contexts). The fifth step is to **Recalibrate** her light and shadow settings by tempering inappropriate behaviour with a counter-behaviour that balances it. For example, foolishness can be moderated by wariness. Applying an approximate/opposite action helps regulate and change negative emotions and behaviours. If someone feels fear, they can incrementally approach what they fear, breathing deeply, adjusting their posture, and standing tall. To regulate her tendency towards the errant trait, the sixth step requires consistent, mindful practice applying the counter-balancing behaviour. By doing so regularly, she **Regenerates** herself and the story she tells. Finally, when she has applied herself routinely to these six steps, the seventh follows organically: she **Integrates** her shadow and light behaviours (foolishness with wariness) until a positive behaviour (e.g. appropriate playfulness) is demonstrated adaptively across her life. The challenging part is doing the steps that enable psychic and emotional integration, but they soon become a healthy habit when reinforced.

Once the psyche has been integrated, our shadow still lives on. We narrow our attention to another unconscious trait, and the cycle continues—such is the ongoing integration process.

By step seven, Red Cap would have regenerated an integrated, balanced self, edging ever closer to holism. If she were four-dimensional like us, becoming whole would be perpetual practice. We have many fragmented psychic pieces, developing since we were barely five, waiting impatiently to be reclaimed and integrated.

Red Cap can continue adventuring, finding things out, being curious and careful with each novel experience. But she could take a negative stance on processing her traumatic event. She could blame her mother and grandmother for releasing her before she was mature enough. Having faced near death, she might internalise shock, fear, and anger, becoming phobic, too afraid and withdrawn to be spontaneous again. From another perspective, she might carry self-recrimination as punishment for her 'foolish' self. These responses are hardly the tenets of a self-actualised, emotionally free person living a fully realised life.

Self-actualisation is an innate drive propelling us along our grail quest to fulfil our potential. Have you experienced that feeling when the going gets tough where part of you wants to give up, but something deep inside won't let you?

Under pressure, the tough get going until they reach their self-actualised state. But there is no rest when we reach our best. When we've achieved one goal, this drive demands we set the next challenge and start moving towards its conquest. This is why psychic integration is so important. We're more likely to reach our potential peak when we've channelled our duality into one fully charged power source.

Before we get ahead of ourselves, let's explore how human beings operate and why we say and do what we do. Simply put, we can behave adaptively, demonstrating respect, openness, objectivity, positivity, compassion, and cooperation (our starlit traits). Conversely, we can interact from self-interested positions with closed minds and hearts, convoluted intentions, ruthless competitiveness, exclusion, and revenge (our maladaptive behaviours and universal dark traits).

Competing fiercely instead of exercising healthy competition means aiming to win at any cost—the ends justify the means. Adopters of ruthless behaviours seek to destroy competitors rather than beat personal records that deliver longer-lasting benefits without causing unnecessary harm. The unhealthy competitor carries a manipulative tendency with no tolerance for others' perspectives. If the pathological opponent assesses differing solutions as inconsistent with or more knowledgeable than their own, they dramatise the situation as a fight to the death. Life is a battlefield to these maladapted folk: only if an idea can be reappropriated as theirs might they accept it. Depending on what's at stake, the resilient self-actualised person may chuckle, seeing a hidden compliment in the other's attempt at competitive, toxic transaction. Their emotional intelligence might even steer the transaction towards win-win.

The fairy-tale villains and heroes of Cinderella and Snow White epitomise our dualities: the dichotomy of enlightened and dimmed-down human nature. These archetypes have attracted allegorical analysis, seeing protagonists as symbols of spiritual truths and Christian virtues whilst antagonists convey what it means to sin.

We have power to choose how we facilitate our motivations across life's myriad milieu. It may be fitting for an individual to be cold and competitive to survive a war. But we'd expect a more compassionate philosophy from parents raising children and in how siblings relate within the family setting.

However, during the many wars and Great Famine that brought central Europe to its knees in the early 14th century, harsh survival tactics trumped sensitive, kind child-rearing.

When we look deeper into Hansel and Gretel, we're reminded of these dark, dangerous times. Many accounts exist of starving parents abandoning and even cannibalising children so they and remaining offspring (the more useful ones) could survive. Yes, it feels impossible for humans to own such atrocity, but it's the truth. Desperate times necessitate desperate measures.

Harking back to the wild boy of Aveyron left in the French forest to fend for himself in the 18th century, we wonder how he might have developed differently with human love and nurturing from birth. Children need to be held close to their carers' beating hearts to feel in rhythm with them and the world. This is how they develop trust and security. Studies show that language patterns strengthen in the brain if infants receive tender focus, are spoken and sung to frequently (e.g. lullabies), and are read nursery rhymes. Fairy tales help their young minds grasp (even partially) the fundamentals of the reality awaiting their debut. If we're too busy, stressed, or desperate (as the wild boy's unknown parents presumably were) to connect with our child's developmental needs, they cannot develop skills that enable them to read, write, or learn other abilities as well as those receiving loving care and attention.

How many of our world's adults have missed necessary developmental milestones and are trying their best to catch up and exercise frustrated, untapped potential? In the extreme, some disenfranchised join militia groups or rogue armies to feel the drive for belonging raging in us all but which, earlier on, was not satisfied. When we live in a private world without war, we're fortunate not to be tested to its extreme. Our day-to-day life in a first-world country is comparatively comfortable most of the time (though we cannot assume this for everyone). Still, our social fabric becomes frayed by threats from competitors who believe we must be taking something from them whenever we appear to have an edge. Their win-lose thinking and related behaviours attempt to intimidate, infiltrate, humiliate, violate, isolate, and even eradicate our sense of worth in a grey or cold war. The dark fairies, trolls, and witches are apt examples. And regardless of where we stand, we're equally capable of doing the same.

Psychiatrist Dreikurs (1897–1977) asserted that inappropriate human behaviours are underpinned by four mistaken goals driven by our biological need to belong and be loved. When we behave in misguided ways to gain Attention, Power, Revenge, or for reasons that (unconsciously) confirm our Inadequacy (helplessness and avoidance), we're *mistaken* because we ultimately fail in our quest. How does behaving dysfunctionally endear us to anyone?

Accordingly, if a lover experiences unrequited love and then, in an unconscious act of passionate rage, destroys their love interest's property, they show signs of being hurt from rejection and wanting to hurt back. But how will 'getting even' achieve belonging or love from the person whose property was destroyed?

The logical consequence of revenge is that one becomes angry and isolated, triggering a vicious cycle of consequential events. Cross-thematically, when individuals self-sabotage this way, they're living down to feelings of inadequacy tucked crookedly inside their shadow. We can also argue they misused their power, seeking any form of attention to feel less invisible and validated. They were sorely mistaken if they thought making someone else feel pain would relieve theirs. The wicked fairy-tale step-kin archetypes come to mind.

When someone doesn't express anger respectfully, they've likely repressed it in the shadow. In the absence of effective regulation, our five natural emotions—Fear, Anger, Grief, Love, and Envy—can become toxic. Imagine that the aggrieved has stirred negative emotions into a poisonous brew of jealousy, possessiveness, and depression until mounting pressure erupts into raging, destructive panic. Panic leads to erratic behaviour that fails to win admiration.

If this is patently self-evident, why are there ever-increasing cases globally of domestic violence? Why do so many fall prey to mistaken goals? And why would someone have a plan to be 'inadequate' and dependent to feel loved and belong? It might be easier to understand someone craving attention, power, or revenge than acting as an inadequate victim who evinces pity. Whom is someone likely to attract with learned helplessness?

There's no doubt that every one of us, back in childhood or more recently, manipulated someone to give us what we needed by acting needy, getting attention, and making them feel sorry and provide for us. Someone behaving this way will always find another who relies on the company of someone from a place of inadequacy. Indeed, the underbelly of what drives the world's health and social systems depends on this co-dependent mindset.

Why do we repress, give away, or misuse our power, act vengefully, and think we're empowering ourselves when we're enabling our enfeeblement? It sounds like our wounded, duplicitous ego has something to do with it.

Consistent with Dreikurs' (1968) theory of chasing mistaken goals with unfitting actions is Villeneuve's (1695–1755) original story of *Beauty and the Beast.* A malevolent fairy feels scorned after the prince refuses to marry her, so she vengefully turns him into a beast. Her only reward is becoming more embittered and resentful: hardly improving her chances of acceptance and love. Conversely, Beast is later transformed into a handsome prince, finding his true love, Beauty (Belle).

Are we to be led along by a ring in our nose (like, presumably, the storybook's Piggy-wiggy was) because of unconscious beliefs? Our psyche's wounded imprints (e.g. our fallen myth-scripts and archetypes) were adopted by our inner child long ago. Myth-scripts, commonly called schemas—patterns of beliefs—

are powerful drivers for thoughts, memories, and behaviours. When fragmented and left unchecked, they lead to negative manifestations. Do we blindly let this wounded psychic force compete with our positive drives and needs? If so, we're likely enthralled by the mana-personality, says Robertson (1992), causing us to believe deep down we're, of sorts, an archetypal magician, wise-one, princess, sorceress, ruler, or emperor (to name a few) or otherwise rejecting and projecting the image onto someone else. In this case, there's no leaping from the falsified self to true selfhood where one feels oneness with the Godhead: one must engage in recognising, reclaiming, and integrating the denied and projected alien traits; otherwise, we remain trapped, acting against our self.

When conflicted this way, we feel in conflict with an enemy running roughshod over our deepest beliefs and values that are in-wired as our personal code for living. Some consciously develop a spiritual system, whilst others have one hidden inside the psyche, not yet consciously aware of its scope or workings. This formless personified archetype, representing our innateness, can be heard crying out for attention in soul-searching moments and seen symbolically in dreams. Whilst Freud might have seen the archetype as a singular mythological reference, Jung made ties between our archetypal dream images and multiple mythologies or folktales from various times, places, and cultures. Decoding the metaphors elucidates meaning and gives reasons why we feel psychic and physical discomfort. The body feels dis-stress when any psychological conflict occurs, to let us know we need to attend to our wounds and pain—pain is nature's warning signal.

In the case of the emperor in The Emperor's New Clothes, he doesn't heed his nervous apprehension. Whilst appraising his so-called finely tailored apparel for his forthcoming procession, he has an inner conflict raging, causing great angst. When standing on the podium imagining himself a picture of sartorial elegance, his naked body exposed, he suffers public humiliation, refusing to acknowledge the painful truth. His Higher Self spoke in vain, trying to win the battle against his pride and ignorance.

Despite ensuing unsettled, anxious feelings, we often ignore nature's messages. Our mind doesn't want or have patience to acknowledge uncomfortable feelings or competing rationale, so it tells us to deny what's happening inside our heads. Denial is a critical ego defence in our psychic circuitry, helping us survive. But denial poses a corollary: the more we deny facts, the more we delude ourselves, making choices that don't serve us as time goes on.

We remain in denial as long as our mind and body can hold reality at bay, but inevitably our ego starts showing signs of cracking. Mentally exhausted from ongoing wrestle, our depleted body succumbs to accidents, ailments, and illness.

A mind worn out from inner conflict lends itself to stress, anxiety, and depression. With unsatisfactory results from chemical treatments to mask or treat depression, it's time to heed nature's signal, search for the root cause in our unconscious, and plan a resolution. My clients often experience sleep deprivation due to emotionally tainted memories, over-thinking, negative thoughts, and fear, creating a vicious cycle. Their self-confidence dwindles, and they become indecisive when faced with life's ambiguities. One client put it this way: I am always in two minds about everything, with one side of me picking the eyes out of the other. I feel so uneasy and exhausted all the time. You'd be surprised how many people overlook the logical consequences of their negative thoughts and emotions on their physical bodies.

Consider how the true self (remember, the one we were born with) wants us to behave one way, but our myth-script drives us to act in another. It's as though our left foot doesn't know what the right foot is doing. This behaviour is hardly a recipe for a well-directed life. Imagine being on track towards your career destination. You see yourself capably striding along with your end-goal in sight. You come to the fork in the road and must decide where to place your next step. Such a fork in the hero's road always represents a choice.

Do you take the new job offering at 'A' or stay in the outworn job at 'B' (assigned such as it's not your 'calling in the moment')? Let's say you step out on the left foot and decide to stay in the known job at 'B'.

However, before you put your foot down on the place marked 'B', a voice inside calls the hero in you to take a risk and change direction towards 'A'.

But another voice, sounding fearful, niggles at you. Likely, this one is from your survivalist id or self-critical superego in the unconscious recesses. You've taken risks and made mistakes in the past, and your ego doesn't like to admit your lack of confidence. The fear felt has triggered your shadow, placing you in a quandary.

You stand there, pontificating, hopping nervously from one foot to the other. You feel extremely uncomfortable. In which place and when should you put your foot to the ground? All this toing and froing, and with such uncertainty, you grow increasingly anxious.

At the crossroad, you try to apply mental reasoning. Perhaps, you wonder, the voice urging you to take 'A' was your intuition speaking? Trust your instincts, you hear your loved ones saying, but you cannot feel any certainty in your gut.

Animals (real and fairy-tale varieties) don't appear to experience such equivocation. But humans must balance instincts, shadow, intuition, and rational thought when discerning what to do and which way to go. Many surrender to trusting that whatever decision they make, things will work out fine. Still, we have a complex web of psychic parts to access, harness, and use.

How can our rational mind alone, when under duress, have the necessary clarity and unity of our mental modules for making the right choice? How can our intuition function at its best when we're distressed and not feeling grounded? And after all, humans tend to assign meaning and intention to random occurrences, sometimes superstitiously or irrationally.

Here we are—a dweller between thresholds, procrastinating whilst possibly missing opportunities, not knowing which way is up. We're betwixt and between in what can be called a liminal state.

We're here but going there, transitioning to an imperceptible, unknown place in our future. We feel threatened about what we don't know and cannot control, becoming fearful of erring and falling through the cracks. Again, some decide to surrender to trust.

To gain understanding, imagine that we're spiritual beings, white-light energy, and have expired our physical embodiment, and in energetic form, loiter, awaiting our fate. Are we going to heaven, hell, or another parallel dimension? We're threshold dwelling, unsure of our transition in time and space.

The fairy-tale heroine, The Little Mermaid, felt unsettled when faced with a Sophie's Choice: kill the prince and return to her mermaid-life or let him live and love another whilst she departs the material plane for good. For the record, her moral sentiments cause her to act wisely. In the end, she transcends as a Seraphim to the highest angelic realms. Still, she shows that random occurrences, threatening our peace and composure, impede our ability to think with the crystal clarity necessary for survival, but also for flourishing. Besides, it's not always possible for us, emotional and sensitive types, to remain calm and centred in a crisis. But this is the very reason to engage in a healing journey that reconstitutes our dark and light sides into one functioning unit. From wholeness, we behave with temperance and fully potentiated personal power. And our rediscovered trust and faith start to switch off our worry gene.

Our genuine, original self has innate competency for managing existential angst. We're born with the id, a primal, instinctual, enshadowed part of the psyche. At first, the id is innocent (like the allegorical figures of Adam and Eve were in the beginning) yet to be filled with disapproved, furloughed fragments of ourselves. Our ego, our interface with reality, begins developing around age three, as we start taking risks to do what we want. Our superego (our internalised parent, moraliser, and inner critic) emerges at five. We may recognise its interference as part of the so-called 'monkey-mind', scolding or telling us we're inadequate or should be doing better to be worthy. Therefore, our shadow starts small, expanding from early school days and, depending on how often we feed it, continues to grow. Think of Pinocchio's ever-growing proboscis.

We're equipped to cope with these major components of the psyche. But the rub is getting the tricky triad of the conscious ego, id (repressed urges, impulses, and instinctual drives), shadow, and superego to work in unison like a well-oiled machine. Put another way—as our soul would like it.

It's theorised that we can access unconscious elements of the psyche through dreams, deep reflection, and triggered or 'aha' moments. When we judge others' traits or behaviours or face disapproval for our own, we can use arising emotional reactions as insights into shadow material.

Suffice it to say, when we talk of subconscious or mental content under our conscious awareness, we assume the unconscious is within reach of consciousness.

Dreams provide the primary raw material for exploring the unconscious, Robertson (1992) asserts. Their inherent mythological referents led to Jung's conceptualisation of the collective unconscious.

We can imagine it as the broad base of an iceberg beneath a deep sea containing ancient images and behaviours recurring since time immemorial. Our personal unconscious layer, filled with overlooked, forgotten, fragmented, and repressed memories, contaminated emotions and behaviours, sits on top. Consciousness is at the tip of the iceberg.

Some refer to the unconscious (not conscious) as the subconscious (below conscious awareness), calling them a bridge to the conscious state, offering symbolic or metaphorical information to decipher. To simplify, these writings consider the unconscious and subconscious as one and the same, as processes sitting outside our conscious awareness.

Many people claim access to unconscious (personal and collective) material when meditating, reflecting, visualising, dreaming, daydreaming, astral-travelling, in out-of-body or near-death experiences, and through hypnosis. If one is receptive, there must be several ways to access psychic archives.

Jung believed that studying fairy tales and mythology and establishing a gateway to archetypes offers a proven method for gaining insight into the workings of our personal and humanity's collective unconscious.

In *Mythimo*, we rely on Freud's (1966) foundational personality theory and concept of the tripartite psyche, comprising the id, ego, and superego.

Jung (1959) built on Freud's concept of the unconscious id, which holds repressed instinctual urges and primal impulses, by defining the personal shadow to encompass both our disowned traits and material inherited from our ancestors, as well as the universal archetypal patterns of the collective unconscious. In these writings, the terms shadow and id are generally used interchangeably, acknowledging both our animal and personal repressions.

When we have a healthy sense of ego, we function as a positive, energetic, and harmonious entity within the social construct. The ego is an in-wired part of our survival and coping mechanism. But we're conscious of only some of our ego-workings, whilst other parts are repressed or just hidden from our consciousness or mindsight. This notion, and how it plays out in our reality, is the crux of our active learning through *Mythimo*.

The ego is twofold: it manages our identity by organising thoughts and making sense of our reality, and it controls instincts—especially the socially unacceptable ones. Aligned with the superego, it rejects what it perceives as psychic dregs to the shadow. A healthy superego keeps us on track, disciplining us to live by our moral ideals and reach goals. But it can become overcritical, setting unrealistic standards that harm self-esteem. It may also be tainted by emotional memories from wounded childhoods and later experiences. Ego functions shape rational thought and emotionally charged memories, which together trigger our psychic defences automatically. Only some are maladaptive.

We may bury our traumatic memories deep in the unconscious, but they, like mutant zombies, rise unbidden from the shadows from whence we once drove them.

Remember when we were unsure about which direction to take at the fork in the road. Our intellect reasoned that staying at 'B' was the safe, sure way. But our intuition called 'A' our hero's path. Our emotionally charged memory from the shadow contradicted. Our uncertainty and lack of confidence were triggered. Sure enough, as night followed day, we were left in a quandary, anxious and not knowing which way to turn. In this moment, we fulfilled our own prophecy of failing—and failed to act. Conflicted mental energy and nervous decision-making don't augur well for making the right choices, let alone moving forwards.

The ego's defences rush in to protect us, necessarily or not, from perceived threats to our existence or identity. It aims to avoid experiencing anxiety and pain in the real world. As we know, it's not always successful in achieving its aims. Its defence mechanisms are often imperceptible to us as they only surface fleetingly in our mind's eye when our emotionally laden memories are triggered or come to light in our dream-state. Those same complex memories enshroud our clear thinking. However, to the world, judging by the egoic mask we wear, our persona, we appear calm, composed, and totally in charge. If only they knew.

Personas are egoic interfaces that smooth the edges between our reality and the outside world. We can liken their function to the 'mana-personality' (Jung, 1959), a projection of an archetypal image into the world (the guru, sage, ruler, etc.) that hides the true self—sometimes referred to as our God within us. Paradoxically, the persona acts to present our best version to society.

Then, there are times when we lock horns with someone and get told to quit being so defensive. Sometimes we recognise that our protests are too impassioned and disproportionate to the level of contention experienced. Other times, we remain oblivious, denying the truth. We're unconscious of our contradictions arising from having beliefs about ourselves or something else that doesn't align with what we're saying or doing. Perhaps Our Lady's Child, a fairy-tale archetype notorious for her lying, didn't see her lies, which is why she didn't own up to them until facing a slow burn on a fiery stake. Perhaps she suffered from cognitive dissonance (we all do from time to time). She didn't believe she could betray the Virgin Mother, so she chose to pretend and got herself into all sorts of bother whilst living in exile in an enormous ash tree in the woods.

However, when our ego behaves in healthy and mature ways, integrating well with our Higher Self, we're empowered to take the high road, living a compassionate, cooperative, and creative life. We see an example of this kind and courageous functioning in the acts of pardon and forgiveness in the same fairy tale featuring the Virgin Mary. Our Holy Mother gives tough love for a spiritual purpose in Our Lady's Child. As the narrative unfolds, we find that the central character, the other mother figure, has had her children taken away because of her ongoing deceptions. In the end, the desperate mother confesses and is redeemed by the merciful Mary, who exemplifies what it is to be congruent, integrated, and united with the sacred Divine. It's a harsh tale.

Defences can be unhealthy and, left unchecked, lead us down the wrong path of self-interest, competing with callous disregard for others, causing rifts and separations. The ambiguity is striking—acting in self-interested ways only leads to no-one else being interested in being with you.

Defence mechanisms can make us overreact, like wanting to kill a fly with a sledgehammer. Other times, we close off or shut down, resisting information coming into view to which we take umbrage. Even competing within ourselves, the conflict between what we believe and what we say and do, leads to a distressing existence. In extreme cases, psychologists talk about severe psychological pain becoming a psychosis that eventually causes schisms in the psyche. Such a divorce from reality puts us at odds with most others and the divine within us until we can return to good mental health under qualified medical guidance. Here, an inference is made to the deeply conflicted, ego-centric, non-cognisant fairy-tale archetype of Bluebeard. He engaged in a murder spree when his victims, a series of nosy, uncontrollable wives, wouldn't follow his strict instructions.

We're beginning to see why the ego might encourage us to cover up our authentic self with the mask of our persona, an archetype born from myths and the idealisations of who we'd prefer to be. For example, the ego might aspire to be of a higher social class than we were born into, as it feels very uncomfortable living with the truth of our roots. It tells us that to belong, we must reach beyond our lowly born tags, driving our subsequent lofty behaviours and making the mythical ideal appear a reality. The characterisations from the television show *Keeping Up Appearances* are classic examples.

Remember the poor miller's son in the fairy tale of *Puss in Boots*? All might be well and good for the boy were there not an unconscious self-loathing because of low social status. Whilst some people are down to earth and satisfied with their station (such as Daisy and Onslow in the TV show mentioned), others experience conflict within themselves if they believe belonging to the underclass makes them unworthy (take Hyacinth Bucket from the same TV show). They believe deep down they're inadequate or deeply flawed. Embarrassment and its darker cousin shame, lurking in the shadows, have a way of coming out with a howl or hiss when we least expect. When we say someone acts shamelessly, we can appreciate how our social sense of shame is a corrective strategy for keeping our behaviours in check. However, shame can be a dangerously intense, negative, and contagious emotion, often passed on to our nearest and dearest (by means of nature and nurture) intergenerationally.

When left unhealed, shame depletes self-esteem, worth, and the life force itself. Depression, anger, rage, resentment, acting-out (living down to the internal schemata), powerlessness, and loneliness are some by-products of shame. It's no wonder that the ego disowns the shamed parts of the self and buries them in the shadow, so it's not constantly reminded of its shortcomings. The ego's persona showcased to the world is a mythical disguise, projecting (i.e. a typical defence response) its flaws onto others and away from itself whenever shame and pain get triggered. But not everyone puts a sanitised self on show; some people do the opposite, letting their rough side rip, indicating they're oblivious to how others see them, have psychological pain, or just don't care either way. Still, the persona (or similarly the mana-personality) can become so dominant that it takes over the individual's identity, leading to a loss of authenticity and individuality.

As the well-known fairy story goes, when the humble fisherman returns to his sea shanty, his greedy wife's sense of entitlement (born from shadowy shame) is set off when she learns that he hasn't taken full advantage of the fish-genie's bestowments. Full of vengeful resentments, she makes his life a living hell by projecting her pain of inadequacy upon him. She does this by misusing her personal power, emasculating him with her dictatorship and treating him as if he were merely her servant, demanding he and the genie give more and still more again. But nothing will fill the ever-growing wound in her ego and hole in her soul, even the attention she attracts when she achieves kingly status.

Jesus' words to the ambitious wife of the fisherman Zebedee might just as easily apply to her when he said that favours aren't granted in return for sacrifices. Remember how the fairy-tale wife's husband spared the fish-genie for goodness' sake, not for any reward. Therefore, for the wife to heal, she must start by changing her 'tit for tat' way of thinking.

Besides the ambitious-on-steroids, there are people who've become pathological liars. Habitual and compulsive lying indicates the mechanics of unconscious ego defence are in play. By putting up a fortification, the ego protects the person from the hard facts of a reality they cannot face. Perhaps they're masking feelings of inadequacy (e.g. not having equal status, power, and the money their peers have acquired or failing their idealised self-image) by exaggerating the truth. Liars of this ilk lie so often and to such an extent their lying becomes compulsive. As their audience sees straight through the lies, pathological liars only lie to themselves. And as Dreikurs (1968) would say, they're mistaken if they think their behaviour will achieve their goal of love and belonging.

We can reference a compulsive liar to the fairy tale of Pinocchio and gain insight into what might drive a person to act this way and what likely consequences they might expect.

Would a real-life inveterate liar see the actions of the well-known puppet boy as acceptable? Being at first naïve and curious, Pinocchio does tell the truth, only to be cheated, so he reacts by telling lies to protect himself in the future. But the fact remains, he lied to the one he loved most, causing only disillusionment and disappointment.

The harsh and false accusations of a significant other can transform a sensitive child into a seasoned liar. In this scenario, the child introjects the negative characteristic (i.e. by swallowing up the indictment and turning it into a faulty belief). Ultimately, a potentially honest person grows into the liar the parent assumed they'd become: a self-fulfilling prophecy. Once again, psychiatrist Dreikurs (1968) contends that being deceitful isn't the way for any of us to become accepted and loved. Separating the person from the errant trait allows us to believe in the innate goodness of the individual whilst working on their faulty beliefs and behaviours.

Together, in *Mythimo*, we explore our ego-defences through the process of unpacking a compendium of 22 fairy-tale archetypes and their dualistic behaviours relevant to our inner life. Each trope helps us understand how our ego makes mythical masks to shield our way through life and how these shadowy self-protections prevent us from risking to act from the totality of our power source. We're so desperate to belong within the tribe and terrified that our point of difference will alienate us that we self-impose inadequacy to stop us from going after our goals. Most of us are also likely hiding the everyday varieties of dark side fragments such as our anger, fears, frustration, resentment, guilt, and repressed sexuality. But are these suppressed emotions as harmless as our ego likes to pretend? No, is the enlightened response.

Along with these negative (but rarely heinous) attributes, we've buried our shining qualities such as forgiveness, hope, trust, creativity, confidence, clarity, courage, empathy, unconditional love, and compassion. You name it, and you'll find it in someone's shadow, but once reclaimed and integrated, it adds another lightning bolt of power to their light source. Life gets better when we shine an affirming light for good.

By now, we may be ready to accept that we humans are two-sided beings of dark and light energy, spiritual and physical substance, doing our best with what we have in our dualistic reality. We're materially dense but filled with the light of the Divine, even if it's not always clear to us. We might be sometimes self-contradictory, but not necessarily a two-faced or even split personality, as is inferred by the term alter-ego. Whilst most of us are unaware of what's hidden in our shadow, when we shift from a calm, restful state to an uneasy, emotionally triggered one, we cannot help but notice. This said, few of us behave as the stereotypical, good or evil Dr Jekyll and Mr Hyde.

One wonders whether the monstrous acts of fairy-tale archetypes like Bluebeard might reflect disordered personalities shaped by trauma or underlying mental illness, including traits of narcissism or sociopathy. Could extreme early experiences foster dissociative coping mechanisms or maladaptive patterns that manifest in destructive behaviour? Whilst no single diagnosis explains such cruelty, these figures illustrate how trauma and personality disturbances can converge to produce profoundly harmful actions.

Can we then feel mercy and show them compassion?

Atrocities committed by others have us condemning them for their inhumanity or forgiving them for their mental illness or unfortunate circumstances. Some are born that way or become that way through trauma. Some act benignly until they're under the influence of drugs, drink, and or hate incitement. They're in our midst, threatening peace, even survival.

These folk require professional medical care to become healthy and rehabilitated as positive contributors to our society: not seeking pardons as only a last resort to save them prolonged jail time. How on earth do we untangle these perennial perplexities justly, competently, ethically, and morally?

Most of us aren't malignly maladapted. Still, we'll do better by ourselves and others once we've decoded and reclaimed our dark sides, fusing them with conscious light.

Coping and surviving is one thing, but aren't we meant to thrive?

When bound to the repressed mythical self, we may still plough ahead in the egoistic power stakes to enable our domination of others and achieve material superiority. We might even appear to live the perfect life to others peaking over the fence to see what goes on in our family home. But something (the bliss felt from oneness and kindness) will always be missing. The profoundly loving and nurturing relationships (including those we have with ourselves), emotional freedom, sense of wellbeing and self-esteem, and enduring forms of material success will elude us.

The fairy tale *The Fisherman's Wife* makes a compelling case for self-mastery over greed and other flawed human behaviours. We might even reach old age unscathed only to find that our lack of tolerance, patience, and resilience to life's hardships suddenly gets tested. We haven't had sufficient hardships to strengthen the psychic muscles necessary to cope.

We begin to understand ourselves as modern-day beings at a new level through the lens of so-called anachronistic folklore. Conscious myth reimagining can help steer us through life's various rites of passage, leading us back to the right path where our original, healthy, and sacred Higher Self yearns to tread.

If you've ever overseen a bunch of people tasking in teams and experienced growth in your status and wealth, you might look back and see how easy it was to buy into your own success, switching into the guise of someone you weren't, acting superior and feeling entitled. Those close to you may have bravely pointed out that you'd changed. You'd have initially ridiculed, denied, and vehemently opposed their assertions but slowly would have come to feel and know on the inside that what they were saying was true. Gradually, the tell-tale signs materialised in the external world, becoming self-evident to you. Knowing you needed to get back to base, you commenced your self-reclamation quietly but surely. You know, the time when you were centred, open-minded, optimistic, curious, trusting, humble, and grateful. You were content with the simple pleasures of life with loved ones—they were enough, you were enough.

Mythimo enables our return to authenticity by recognising our feelings and fears and, ultimately, facilitating our integration. We understand how we act in ways incongruent with the overshadowed original self buried inside by mobilising a self-reflective practice (utilising the 22 fairy-tale mythograms). The archetypes, in both their light and shadow forms, influence our thoughts, emotions, and actions, shaping our behaviours and steering our destiny. The *Mythimo* self-directed seven-step healing journey is strengthened through meditations, guided breathing, visualisations, journaling, and reflecting on our behaviours and dreamscapes. *Mythimo* helps us square our beliefs with the actions we take.

To reiterate, we Reflect on our thoughts, emotions, or behaviours (utilising *Mythimo* cards as prompts), Name and Reclaim our current feelings and fears shoved down into the ego's shadow; Reframe our perspective such as seeing the positives and strengths that have come from our ordeals. This often entails rewriting our personal narrative, highlighting the new learning gleaned from the experience; Recalibrate our out-of-whack behaviours by tempering them with a counter-behaviour that balances it out; regulate ourselves so we adopt as a habit our new healthier behaviour. Through osmosis, the culmination of our sustained efforts and the natural progression of the steps already taken, we emerge Regenerated and Integrated.

In a nutshell, our shadow's negative ego defence mechanisms and by-products must give way to and be absorbed by our healing light. By utilising the *Mythimo* method, subsumption of the shadow occurs—it diffuses gradually, becoming smaller until it reaches equilibrium with our inner light. As long as we're human beings existing, the shadow will exist in some form. And that's why we must continue to feed ourselves light—to maintain its lead over the dark side. *Mythimo* shows us how fairy-tale archetypes help us reclaim our light and become fulfilled and satisfied. It provides a method for rebirth, self-transformation, and sustainable success for one committed to being an enlightened and self-actualised person.

To explain, here's a shortened version of the process described by my client, Laura, who relates to the fairy tale of Cinderella. Laura took these steps to regenerate her original, fully empowered self:

Case-study—Laura and Cinderella

1. Reflecting and contacting a mythical archetype with whom I resonated (i.e. Cinderella).
2. Exploring the fairy-tale trope and motifs; experiencing an 'epiphany'.
3. Recognising I shared conflicting behavioural traits that were both negative and positive (e.g. by opposing my potential as well as being self-affirming).
4. Realising, through self-reflection, that my actions clashed with my beliefs and values (I was doing what others expected of me, and I felt put upon but did what they demanded to keep the peace. I drank to forget stuff).
5. Developing my personal code for Higher Living to align my actions with my beliefs and values.
6. Reimagining what my life looked like (I imagined waving a magic wand); using visualisation, guided breathing, and meditation (I also chose to customise my healing by incorporating emotional freedom technique [EFT]—tapping). To let go of the painful memories feeding the negative patterns in my life, I sat with my fears, allowing them to be, and gradually

reframed them into a positive orientation in how and when they did serve me. I gave permission to my pain to leave.

7. Having a 'cathartic' experience on a bodily level: I sat with my anxiety, doing my controlled breathing exercises and gradually felt the distress leave my mind and body.
8. Dreaming and analysing my dreams' symbolic messages from the unconscious; realising my shadow was attempting to make contact with me.
9. Continuing the inner work, journaling, reframing my story, and using self-affirmations to communicate with my shadow until we could let go of the darkness together; self-regulating.
10. Visualising the regeneration of my coalesced self encircled by light.

Laura said, "I appreciate that I reach the ascent to self-actualisation for a time, but then life changes again, and I fall back and must start climbing again." She continued, "And at least now I'm better equipped to relax, feel more present, and feel energised doing what I have to do."

In her feedback, Laura wrote: "This was a compelling healing experience after I'd had enough with my life. Even though it made me feel exposed and vulnerable, I knew this was to be expected. I just had to keep taking one step at a time to get to the other side, releasing the old scripts running (if not ruining) my life. I also sought support from my therapist, but I was no longer dependent on alcohol and other drugs. My friends were my sounding boards. As I peeled away the layers of shadow and reconnected with my inner child through the fairy-tale work, I became refreshed. It took a year, but I finally knew how to feel happiness again."

Laura's story (like any client's narrative) is the critical resource for stripping away the mask or myth-script, according to Robbins (2006), when contextualised to the archetypal Hero's Journey paradigm. Framing the client's narrative as heroic provides a potential pathway to their character maturation, a more creatively vital existence, and the faith in their ability to progress onwards to the next iteration of their Hero's Journey. Because our psychic processing is all about our memories, dreams, and reflections, we must arrive at a relevant point: our moment of truth. We experience a sense of enlightenment which is key to our personal growth, becoming confident in our ability to transform and develop. Once we become conscious of the dynamics playing out in our psyche, the unconscious has given way. Feeling emotionally freed and buoyant isn't just an empty promise.

You might be asking, but what does transformation look and feel like? We can gather clues by looking at the Greek word for our experience of transformation: Anakainos—ana meaning back or again and kainos meaning new but different. In the New Testament, we're encouraged to renew and transform ourselves through the "renovation of the mind (anakainos)" (Romans 12:2).

Everyone experiences transformation in their unique way, but universally speaking, a person feels renewed and centred with a plentiful supply of vital energy. Clients describe it as feeling freer, lighter, and more optimistic. The mind begins generating bright ideas again, and they feel trust and peace within themselves. They're motivated and determined to keep moving ahead despite obstacles crossing their path. Many refer to how they can think more positively in regulating errant emotions and thoughts and have faith in things working out well for them. Others describe themselves as unshakeable and empowered. To this end, the Russian fairy-tale heroine archetype, Vasilisa, is again evoked.

Before Vasilisa made it home, she first had to get to know her own level of competency. Like the modernist poet T.S. Eliot said, "Only those who risk going too far can possibly know how far one can go."

Testing our limits is a common theme, recognisable through the stories retold over the coming pages or when casting the colour-plated *Mythimo* cards to chart a hero's course. The inner self is necessarily tapped into and explored. *Mythimo* is a depth experience.

Such self-discovery spurs a reboot of our settings, putting us on course and heading in the right direction. The act of journaling records our inner workings and catalyses our creativity and inspiration. When the self comes to know its strengths and limitations, it's ripe for making appropriate choices and solving problems more effectively.

A wounded ego encourages us to escape the hard facts of reality with the mistaken goal of avoiding pain, as was the case in the tale about the pilloried naked emperor. Comparatively, a relatively healthy ego, as seen in *The Ugly Duckling*, urges us (warts and all) to return to the real world and try again. Because only in facing the truth can the self optimally operate and feel satisfied, and only then can the incomparable rewards for living an authentic life be found.

Analogously, we can compare our states of getting us through our life journey by choosing which plane to take when we travel. Should we decide to fly in an aircraft where the mechanic denies there's a flaw in one of the engines? Truth be told, it malfunctioned on a previous trip and is likely to bring the plane down on the next. A mechanic in such denial lives on blind faith and hope alone. Or will we decide to fly belatedly to our destination in a machine that was grounded for three hours whilst a team of forthright mechanics repaired the faulty engine? Now, and only now, there's more certainty to our hopes for landing in one piece and the right place. The other choice seems downright delusional.

When we know fully what we're dealing with, the crux of the matter is explicated. We can confidently make choices and problem-solve to create what we want and need from life as we move forward. We feel a sense of empowerment in the randomness we call living. Although there are no guarantees, as the great Greek philosopher Socrates reminds us from two thousand years ago, "A life unexamined is a life unlived." Put in its literal context: if we don't dig below the surface (such as checking on the maintenance safety record of an airline before we fly with them), we may not get to live out our lives. Yet, Socrates meant something far deeper.

Few of us know ourselves, let alone whom we get into bed with along life's road. *Mythimo* aims to guide us to the nub of our real nature, positive and negative, and the ways that regenerate our Whole Self.

Let's remember that we're a soulful light who embodied human form when coming to life in the material realm. But how easy it is to be overcome by the egoic illusion that tells us to forget who we really are and why we're here?

In a nutshell, we're light beings who engage in conflict in the dense earthly arena with dark energy within and without, to which we either overcome or succumb. Ours is an experiential journey of learning and growth.

A choice exists for us to reconstitute ourselves as fully potentised, awake beings of love and light. We either remain unaware and separated or conscious and united with the sacred Divine. But there's difficulty accepting we're indeed spiritual beings, learning and being tested to evolve into our highest vibrational form.

When we reach this understanding, the rest makes sense and naturally falls into place. It provides a defensible rationale for living an ethical, spiritual, and kinder existence with other sentient beings. Even the non-believers who don't share this moral sentiment won't have to suffer when we take this stance. We wonder why they call anyone with a benevolent temperament 'weak' when no harm is caused to them. What stirs their overreaction?

On the other hand, the dark side of life manifest on earth can be threatening. It harms, kills, and maims thousands of living beings every minute of our existence.

Taking a fresh look through the lens of fairy tales engenders a light-handed approach to dealing with the darkness casting its long shadow upon us. Fairy tales have always delivered sensitively a cautionary if not sombre message about life's spiritual truths. Ironically, there are no illusions about human nature in the world of make-believe. Still, we must be open to receiving the everyday truths that fairy tales and myths share with us.

Those with an ethical disposition, demonstrating open-mindedness, impartiality, responsibility, accountability, a sense of fairness, and a dedication to a cause are more inclined to want to do the inner work to better themselves than someone satisfied with how they are. But this isn't to say that a self-satisfied person is always unethical—perhaps there's little incentive.

When we're open to receiving new and engaging information, our spontaneous and intuitive creativity flows, and we enter the zone, the field of the collective unconscious, where time doesn't exist. And in that deep, dark space, we may locate our bliss.

Coming back to earth, humans, as animal beings from the biological standpoint, possess instinctual bodily sensibilities, requiring self-regulation to stop us straying from moral codes and causing chaos.

Our reasoning mind and egoic interface must make sense of these competing energies within so we can interact in the reality without. If we cannot differentiate and know which of these psychic parts is in charge at any given time, then we'll be confused at the very moment we need to be discerning, making good choices and decisions.

Keen insight requires our id (animal instincts), ego-consciousness, ego-unconsciousness (shadow), and superego (inner-parent, conscience, or critic) to hum. The deepest part of ourselves, commonly known as the Higher Self or soul, beckons us to integrate all our psychic fragments in harmony, empowering us to achieve our utmost potential in both the physical and spiritual realms.

Our natural, authentic self we were at birth aligns with our Higher Self, called such, as it has an open line of contact with the Divine. The Higher Self is in-tune with all nature of the cosmos, encapsulating the Godhead or universal energy source.

Because our essence feels altered, we must now cut through the guise and guile we cloak and shield ourselves in and return to our origins. Our soul, from which flows our wholesome intent, is the source of our personal power.

Whenever we take on new experiences and do so self-efficaciously, we reach the peak of human actualisation. Yet, too often, our own maladapted fragments hold us back. Our Higher Self recognises the need to reclaim our full potential in order to gather the strength to reach the ultimate goal—the Holy Grail of our journey. In this physical realm, our (soul) and authentic self (original embodiment) are two expressions of the same being.

To reiterate, our holism begins with the healthy integration of our ego, superego, and id-shadow (in accord with our soul). But as we grow and life presents more contests for the ego, we drift from centre. We need to find our way back to our origins so that our behaviours follow suit when we hear the Higher Self think and speak. In this context, this is what's meant by congruency, integrity, and being Whole. All psychic parts of the self are in sync and symbiotic with the soul and the Sacred. We'll drift in and out of this state of being described by Robertson (1992) as engaging 'the god within' because ongoing work is necessary and must be undertaken with an attitude of humility. Humility, as many of our mythic and fairy-tale archetypes instruct, doesn't come easily to the ego. Furthermore, the personal unconscious is always just ahead of our grasp; it acts as a portal to the collective unconscious, where many of our inexplicable supernatural experiences occur. As human beings, we tend to be imperfect, using our shadow traits as a necessary tool to learn from life. Lastly, beyond our rational mind and physical senses, we're intuitive beings seeking our total reality and communion with all its surface meanings and unconscious depths that comprise the reality we live in. We cannot get rid of unconscious energy entirely (and wouldn't want to), but we can see and subsume parts of it into consciousness incrementally as we go along.

Intuition evolves in us from a young age as a dynamic force, individuating us in the most potent ways and transforming us from an ordinary existence to ordinary people achieving extraordinary feats. Like Jack who felt a hunch to climb the beanstalk to success, we, too, can have life-enriching peak experiences. Intuition is a source of super-natural power, enabling life-forms to feel at one and in-tune with nature and the Divine, the Godhead.

How does a dog or cat know the time when its owner is about to walk through the gate? They sense patterns and possess a powerful instinctual sense of smell, but some accounts go beyond biological explanations. Just as animals (e.g. migrating birds) use their senses to perceive events before seeing them unfold in their environment, we human animals have the same capabilities. But in all the white noise, we forget to tap our powerful, super-natural sixth sense.

According to the author and professional intuitive, Belinda Davidson (2020), in her book *Find Your Light*, we might confuse our feelings of fear with our intuition. We need to distinguish between them. If we're urged by our fears to follow or resist a specific trail, we may end up off track. Davidson recommends meditative practice for calming our central nervous system, taking us beyond fear and into a clear state of mind. Only when we're settled can we trust and follow our feelings in the gut linked to our intuition. This is helpful guidance when we're at the fork on the hero's road and cannot decide between route 'A' or 'B'.

Once regulated and distilled, our instincts (purposive fears included), intuition, and rational mind serve as a powerhouse of mental energy. This nerve centre sharpens our perceptions for discerning the truth and our problem-solving competency. So, we're reminded once again to get the best out of ourselves and the life we experience; our psyche must be balanced and integrated.

It's time to re-explore the cautionary tale about an unintegrated psyche (of the essential three components of ego, superego, and id-shadow), conspicuously demonstrated in the traditional Goldilocks archetype.

Pre-pubescent yet out in the woods on her own, Goldilocks presents as an independent, bold, and self-serving young girl with a predilection for perfection (I can hear some of you thinking—welcome to the Millennial world). Her curiosity and instinctual id (i.e. urges to survive: feed, flee, fight, fawn, and sleep among other things) take her out to explore the wider world, leading her into the bears' abode (does she have an early desire to start nesting and reproduce or is she a rebel or self-saboteur?)

Her under-developed ego ignores the small rational voice trying vainly to control her wild instinctual impulses. And as for her superego (i.e. her mother's moral code imprinted within)—it didn't stop her from trespassing and trashing her neighbours' home, but it did spark her inner critic.

Usually, by just five years of age, a child has a fair understanding of right and wrong. Goldilocks is a rule-breaker who flees the scene when confronted by the bears. Some clients say that as a child, they always admired Goldilocks' image and her derring-do, even her fastidious behaviour, and in reflection, concede they emulated her at times. Others claim they found her brash, self-interested, and indifferent to the needs of others. She's a narcissist, lucky to get away with her audacious law-breaking.

But the pre-teen was oblivious to her negative traits already relegated to her shadow. Most kids reckon that folk behaving like the enigmatic and spoilt Goldilocks archetype in the real world suffer consequences or should. And it appears that most of us do until we get the message to change.

But are there incorrigible folk with no desire or intent to change and become better people? You bet. Most receive a wake-up call.

Our client, Sussane, shared she thought it was fun to drop in on acquaintances unannounced. She always felt anxious but thought it was just her excitement about the pleasant sense of surprise she brought to the households she visited. But when she arrived, she felt that her visit made her new friends uncomfortable. She put their apprehension down to their embarrassment for having a messy kitchen or their social ineptitude in failing to offer her a cup of coffee. She found she nearly always had to remind them their home needed a swift broom taken to it. And as for a biscuit, she always had to ask for one. How rude, she secretly thought: their lack of social skills explains their inhospitality, and her sophistication unnerved them. However, she never stayed long as she didn't wish to wear out her welcome.

Then one day, as she arrived, one of her acquaintances wouldn't open their front door, telling her she couldn't come in as her visit was unexpected. It turns out she was having coffee and cake with close friends inside, and they'd all brought a plate to share. But not Sussane. She was refused entry. A shocked Sussane got the message and left in a huff. It was a lesson that hurt to the core.

Like Goldilocks, she was a taker, childish in her outlook, and an uninvited intruder of others' boundaries.

Today, after completing the *Mythimo* method, Sussane has reconnected with her ability to filter and heed social signals. She's mindful of showing respect and consideration, treating other people as she expects to be treated.

It turns out that Sussane had buried her empathy in her shadow along with her feelings of rejection at a very young age. When her mother abandoned her, moved across the ditch with a new partner and was never heard of again, Sussane suffered.

Transformed today, Sussane now thinks before acting and considers her impacts on others before zealously seeking attention and going after what she wants. Where prior, she had unrealistic expectations people should drop everything to make her feel wanted and special, she got into reflecting on the responses she received from other people.

Eventually, after recording her dreams and reflections in her journal, she realised that she also possessed a proud streak of white superiority. She must have at one time also hidden her pride in a dark corner of herself.

After her *Mythimo* experience, Sussane now feels genuinely more comfortable and confident. These days, she feels happier because she's stopped criticising others and immaturely projecting her rude behaviours onto them. But Sussane is aware of the possibility of a relapse of her latent tendencies if she fails to do the ongoing conscious inner work and reframe her story.

She recognises that if she feeds the 'dragon' within, the dragon will re-emerge and breathe its toxic fire again. Sussane regulates her impulsivity and reflects after she acts these days. In short, she's reconnected with her original self. In refining and following her personal code for Higher Living (which includes thinking before she acts), the quality of her relationships has improved.

Perfectionists, like the Goldilocks archetype, are inflicted with the misery of never being able to feel happy unless ever-elusive perfect conditions are achieved. Sadly, perfection is always out of reach, as the human condition is, by definition, flawed.

A conflicted superego reacts as an inner critic when we feel our emotions kick into over-drive, making us hypersensitive to getting things 'just right'. We can end up being lonely and unhappy when we see everything (including ourselves) as not being enough or good enough. This refers to our biological need to be loved and belong and how we resort to mistaken goals and dysfunctional behaviours to meet these needs. As Dreikurs (1968) so wisely taught, feelings of inadequacy (and avoidance) are deeply tied to behaving as a critical perfectionist and comparing ourselves with what an idealised self 'should' be and do. Interestingly, without the benefit of a caringly attentive mother in childhood, Sussane's superegoic mother within, being wounded and over-compensating for feelings of inferiority and guilt could never be pleased. No wonder Sussane wasn't considered pleasing company by those she visited.

Proud perfectionists harbour a repressed, inadequate self in their shadow which comes out in ways other people may sense as an inferiority complex. Therefore, many perfectionists deny ever being one. Having an inferiority complex but identifying and acting as a perfectionist seems counter-intuitive. Contrastingly, sometimes a person with a superiority complex equally presents as a perfectionist. The act of judgement or having a 'sense of entitlement' comes to mind. When we delve deeper, we find there's a yearning to feel completed by another. They feel entitled and demand (unconsciously) to have the hole (i.e. something missing in their life) inside of them filled. Folk subscribing to the Goldilocks archetype have feelings of inadequacy, silently howling out in pain to be seen, heard, and supported under their vain and varnished veneer.

Because the ideal cannot be guaranteed and is out of reach, many of us fall for the allure of its exclusivity, thinking achieving it will lift us into the social stratosphere.

It's better to embrace and heal our fundamental human imperfections, accepting we'll never be the ideal work of art we might once have dreamt we were. Better we concern ourselves with making continual progress than seeking perfection.

The beautifully groomed Goldilocks seems very much alone. Where is her mother, we may well ask? Does the tale infer one ends up alone when they act selfishly?

As a young girl, we wouldn't expect her to be ready to step out on her own and begin exploring life without the safety net of a loving family. But unlike

Hansel and Gretel, she always behaves independently in self-assured ways, suggesting no emotional suffering or abandonment. This rite of passage to self-agency naturally steps up during adolescence.

There comes the point when we're out there on our own, running our own race and fighting our own battles, untied to Mother's apron strings. And then, one day, after a cycle of trial-and-error, we ascend beyond surviving, now belonging and feeling good about ourselves. We confidently reach our destination, entirely on our own steam, achieving self-actualisation. At this vantage point, we start to thrive.

As the Red Riding Hood archetype learned the hard way, our early iterations of venturing forth are where we leave our naivety behind. We build our ego-defences to protect us from perceived threats of harm. We erect a compromised 'false or mythical self', fuelled by hormones and hot air to contact the outside world, exuding a persona of self-reliance. We fake it until we make it. At maturation, we'd like to believe we've grown genuinely confident and have the self-efficacy to quest successfully for the goals we hold dear. But only testing ourselves in the wider reality can we find out.

If, as children, we feel like undervalued nothings in our parents' eyes, our little egos might find the power to defend us by insisting we're 'something'—so that our spirit for life isn't squelched. If the mother rejects us, we might try soothing and reassuring ourselves that we're 'really, really something', and over time core wounding presents as an inflated sense of self-importance. Goldilocks does come across as being oblivious to customary boundaries, entering a house in the woods, and others' personal space. A runaway? Goodness only knows what's happened to her in the past.

When people are unaware of the 'real' motivations behind their thoughts and actions, it's difficult for them to make appropriate choices consistently. They may also be baffled as to why their love relationships never seem to work.

If Goldilocks (as an adult) did the inner work, she might find the real Goldilocks buried beneath her persona or mana-personality and the emotional scarring from which it feeds. After all, something motivated her to ignore the risks and dangers ahead, desperately searching for a place where she might belong: to be accepted and loved for herself.

With mistaken goals, Dreikurs (1968) would posit that she gained attention by misbehaving only to be shooed away instead of being asked to stay and share supper with the family of bears. Whilst it appears the mother cared well for her daughter (gauging by her well-kept appearance), she may have been lax in catering to her emotional needs. Not all mothers develop secure bonds with their offspring, fomenting ambivalent or disorganised (or inconsistent), and anxious and insecure attachment styles inside of them which cause the child's ongoing psychological disturbance. Over time, all the chipping away at our original self (the inner child) fragments our wholeness, caused also by our later independent experiences, and we start to act out. Perhaps Goldilocks' covetous behaviour fills a hole that unconditional love was meant to seal through the crucial emotional stages of her development. As psychiatrist and educator Dreikurs (1968) told us time and time again, all humans have a basic need for unconditional positive regard and acceptance.

The wee Ugly Duckling orphan archetype also suffered the cruel fate of abandonment and exclusion for different reasons. He was taunted and rejected because of his difference until he finally caught up with his innate nature. His true and beautiful self was reflected to him in the shimmery waters of a lake, and he eventually found his rightful and glorious place within his tribe.

Imagining that the mythical figures are human, Goldilocks' future adult challenge is to overcome her infantile strivings and mistaken goals, developing a mature orientation within herself. Only then will she stake her claim in the world as a grown-up person. Like the Pinocchio archetype, if she continuously lets her wounding, infantile instincts, desires, and fantasies rule her, she'll only fortify her defensive demeanour as she grows older. A continuance of her maladaptive ways won't serve her in the end. Feelings of superiority, masking the feelings of inadequacy at her core, gush out in unexpected, over-reactive ways. Goldilocks clumsily broke nearly every item she handled.

Unless she addresses her shadow behaviours, they'll inhibit her from becoming the natural, whole person she must become. Goldilocks needs to reset her goals in a reframed story that aligns with her beliefs, values, and strength-behaviours if she's ever to be accepted and loved and have the self-esteem and confidence to live a life well-lived.

To reiterate, becoming our original, Whole Self again takes work and a willingness to experience the pain of letting go of ingrained mistaken thinking and negative patterns. Even though we reach a point where we know the shadow shards of us must be processed for change to occur for the better in our lives, sometimes it feels more comfortable (to our ego) to forget our quest and resort to our habitual ways. The truth is we're not taking on the challenge to become whole again for anyone other than ourselves and the quality of life we aim to live.

Even if given an ultimatum from the love of our life that they want rid of our problematic behaviours, once and for all, the only motivation to suffice must come from our inner drive.

Analogously, we can compare our quest to a climber striving to reach the summit of Everest. Any climber with an external motivation of becoming the new record holder will barely have the endurance, stamina, or success of the climber who wants to get to the top because they possess an insatiable, unrelenting force within, compelling them to keep going until the peak is reached. With intrinsic motivation, they act in concordance with the divine within, instructing them to complete their mission. This kind of self-actualised hero also often has a charitable service for someone else resonating with their intrinsic purpose at heart. Research teaches us that we're likely to achieve success if we first align our goals with our personal code: our beliefs, values, and moral philosophy for Higher Living. So, if ever we're given an ultimatum by the one we love and know they're right deep down, we need to reflect on and check our beliefs and align them with rightful actions. Only then will we find the energy to reset and act accordingly. Otherwise, other people's threats or punishments are powerless to change us.

Psychologist Lawrence Kohlberg (1958) contended that moral behaviour can be taught, modelled, learned, and developed through the cognitive processes of moral reasoning. He coined the Six Stages of Moral Development to explain the underpinning reasons driving human beings towards their goals. His rationale is espoused in a renewed context by educationalist Rafe Esquith (2007), contending we have a drive for reaching our goals because of our intrinsic motives—we:

- Do not want to get into trouble.
- Want a reward.
- Want to please somebody (even ourselves).
- Want to follow the rules.
- Are considerate of other people.
- Have a personal code of behaviour and aim to follow it.

The sixth driver, our personal code of behaviour, is inextricable from the aims of our authentic self: that integrated state we're gradually reconstituting.

According to John White (1982), our education in moral intelligence develops virtues such as prudence, courage, temperance, benevolence, clarity, independence of mind, wisdom, humour, and vitality—the hallmarks of an educated person.

Our quest is to untangle and integrate the mess of disparate parts of the psyche that spearhead our survival and regenerate them into a whole. This means becoming aware of and integrating the psyche's key aspects: the conscious ego, our present awareness; the unconscious ego, linked to the subconscious and preconscious, including the voice of our soul, dreams, spiritual insights, latent potentials, and visualisations; the id or shadow, holding instincts, repressed impulses, genetic patterns, and darker elements hidden from awareness; and the superego, the inner critic or moraliser, which can operate consciously or unconsciously.

Is it any wonder that most of us struggle to feel unified and centred with all these complex psychic working parts to recognise, manage, and regulate, let alone when they're working at loggerheads? However, it looks harder in words than it is in reality.

To reiterate, the authentic self emerges through integration and healing; it's not fully realised whilst inner aspects remain divided. When parts of the psyche oppose one another, authenticity cannot be embodied. Through deep inner work, these conflicting elements must be reconciled and brought into a coherent centre. The *Mythimo* method offers an effective pathway for restoring inner unity. Extraordinary things in life await the ordinary person who acts from unity and a sense of personal responsibility, accepting their life unfolds according to the choices they make. No-one is to blame, and there's no victim, but we're accountable for every living, learning moment. This true self has firepower, igniting its creative spark where unlimited possibilities abound. We can feel fully alive, stepping to the beat of our drum as we climb the metaphorical pinnacle of existence.

To be clear, people may be victimised without choosing to remain victims. Whilst the climb is steep, it's possible. This doesn't excuse their persecution and the perpetrator of the unacceptable act against them. Regardless of whether offenders take responsibility, those harmed can refuse to keep paying the price.

A Japanese proverb reminds us: An evil deed remains with the evil-doer.

The need to be 'real' comes up for consideration repeatedly and in many contexts. Evolved folk seem to find out this truth early and act on it unequivocally: 'Be yourself, everyone else is taken', goes their mantra. But how do we know if we're being authentic or just being a mythical version if a large part of our information is buried in our shadow? If it's repressed down there, why on earth do we want to dredge it up and face our fears? Change is painful.

Changing a mind that's already made up is extremely difficult. We reject the truth about life, society, and ourselves because it doesn't fit or favour our static picture within. We need to become aware of any confirmation bias we hold, manipulating information to fit the rationale we hold most dear. If we're not mindful of what's driving us, motivating us to think and act, we're not in charge of our life force and have no hope of ever channelling it for our forward motion.

Our world comes as much from within as it does from without. Again, being real, or in other words, acting from an integrated whole of self, where reclamation has occurred of our hidden treasures of both dark and light, leads to loving relationships and genuine and enduring success. Lives lived this way bring satisfaction and rewards that make our reality meaningful and pleasurable. These natural consequences will occur if we follow the standards of our personal code for Higher Living and come to terms with the fact that we have a responsibility to live this one life to its fullest by doing and giving our best.

There are times in our life when we've already experienced a feeling, perhaps only a fleeting one, of being whole at the core—that deep sense of wellbeing, centredness, certainty, and connection. Many of us have also felt the strange body alerts when acting from our wounded ego, shadow, or incomplete self. With these kinds of issues, our souls feel out of whack, and as the Greek philosopher Epicurus (300 B.C.E.) shared, we must look after the health of our souls, no matter our age. He contended that pleasure is the absence of pain in the body and trouble in the soul. In other words, a simple life brings us simple but arguably the most important of pleasures.

Can we, the more fortunate, ever get back to base and count our blessings of having a pain-free body and an untroubled soul? When we've healed our souls, we possess the power to be unified, grounded, confident, calm, and happy. Happiness is a proven preventative of pain.

Before reaching this contented, pain-free, and untroubled state of being, we must first learn how to read the pain signals sent from our body-mind organism day in and day out. And to intuit at this level, we must stay open to new ways of being.

Mythimo offers a collection of 22 archetype cards that represent both our favourable and unfavourable traits (and much more). These archetypes, often featuring animals, are given human characteristics in the analysis, much like how they're portrayed in fairy tales, in order to connect with our own humanness. Even the supernatural entities not tethered to the reality we know have transferrable qualities to ordinary folk like us. These colourful and symbolic cards help us identify important elements of our human condition and ecology with ease.

As we go about our daily lives, we see the connection between our body-mind health and the external environment and how well or not we're navigating our way.

The card paintings present the psychological pathways along the invisible mythic road we take, showing us the forks in the road where logical but unforeseen consequences will play out because of our decision-making. We owe it to ourselves to be as pain and trouble-free as possible in preparation for the personal journeys before us.

Through the looking glass of the fairy-tale archetypes, we come to understand how the shadow elements, denied by the ego, lurk in our unconscious and have an inextricable relationship with how we function and how our life events potentially unfold.

Our ego and superego link directly with the shadowy id, which corresponds to our somatic being. Here in the shadow, the energy is dense and heavy, finding its natural place in our body. The same applies to our instincts (e.g. life-force for survival, fear, sustenance, sex and procreation, sleep, greed, denial, revenge, tribal loyalty, fighting, fleeing, rooting ourselves to the spot, fawning or hiding, etc.). These elements are all part of our psychic make-up, contributing to our emotional reactions and how we make sense and meaning from our earth-realm reality as a light-being, a soul.

Our ego is both conscious and unconscious energy, influencing our psychic output during our wakefulness or sleep. When we become mindfully aware, the light and luminous sensation is felt in our third-eye chakra as an 'aha'—that moment of truth, confirming we've made contact with the Divine. But unconscious energy runs deeper, communicating with flashes of light emanating from the deeper regions of the psyche and felt mostly in the solar plexus.

Our Higher Self operates on the highest vibrational light frequency, flowing to and from the Divine, experienced as a golden glow radiating in a continuous loop from the crown to the heart chakra, and radiating outwards with great warmth to where our boundary meets the world.

Although our minds may be in an unintegrated tangle, we may still experience moments of enlightenment. However, when fully integrated, we experience readily the state of illumination, and our heightened intuition becomes second nature. Our body, mind, and spirit function as a unified entity, with energies that interweave seamlessly. To reiterate, once positive and negative energies have been transformed into a singular unit of light, we're able to operate optimally.

The message for whole living espoused in *Mythimo* is drawn from a miscellany of myths, fairy tales, human experience, spiritual teachings, education and psychology, and Western and Eastern philosophies. As always, the dynamic whole is greater than the sum of parts. Some of you may have already recognised how the symbolic meaning of the Chinese Yin and Yang, with its Tao and metaphysical origins, influences the personal code and writings of the author. Like the opposite or contrary forces embedded in Yin and Yang, our conflicted parts of self are meant to be complementary. An analogous explanation of this principle is to think of the opposing positive and negative charges in a battery necessary for creating a spark and delivering momentum. Likewise, our dark side (shadow and id attributes) and our light-self (the consciously aware ego) are inferred in the male and female Yin and Yang symbol. It conveys how valuable and essential it is for each of us to operate with integrated power. There can be no positive without the negative and vice versa.

Take a closer look at the symbol and see how black is inside the white and white is inside its black counterpart. Our interconnected and interdependent parts spark each other, as the Yin and Yang symbol connotates. We feel the electrical force running through our circuits when our dualities collide and generate friction. Still, the power is even more remarkable when we unify and channel it in one direction. We're not separate but share in the oneness with the polar effects of our cosmos. We experience night and day, dark and light, black and white, fire and water, ego and soul or fear and love. What we see in nature, we can search for inside of ourselves. Once we're on our way, we can steel ourselves to the journey, and as in client Laura's case—our life begins anew.

Mythimo may sound like a complicated process to do, but the systematic steps are quickly mastered once one makes a start. By the time we're in the groove of doing the inner work, we wonder why we didn't start doing it sooner. We can see how much better we feel emotionally, mentally, spiritually, and physically. Besides, we look so much fairer (and fresher) when we gaze again in the looking glass. When shadow aspects are brought into awareness, they lose their unconscious power. Living with greater presence and love prevents them from overwhelming us. In this way, emotional maturity emerges alongside a return to childlike emotional freedom—innocence regained through awareness, not naivety.

Now we've learned how to self-govern our dark side, there's no reason to allow it to bloat again. *Mythimo* is a process we can self-facilitate, but we must be patient with ourselves as we take our first small steps on our healing journey of self-discovery and actualisation. But if impatience is in the shadow, here lies an opportunity to reclaim and regenerate it as patience. Just as it takes time to instil our negative behaviours and habits, it may take as much time (or it feels that way) to transform them.

Good and unhealthy behaviours have their roots in the deepest parts of human nature, requiring a dedicated effort to integrate and keep them intact. A physical fitness regimen requires an ongoing commitment and so does maintaining our integrity. Still, *Mythimo* is an accessible activity that can potentially diminish errant traits within three weeks and reveal the first signs of our sustainable expansion within three months. Everyone is different.

Let's call a spade a spade. Having to face fears can send many of us packing or into the flight, fight, freeze, fawn, or hide mode. Our egos can put up a powerful defence against soul-enriching endeavours. So, whilst we probe for the truth about ourselves, we'll do so gently. Following the renowned writer Oscar Wilde's (1854–1900) clue that we humans only accept the truth if it makes us laugh, we must foster light-heartedness and optimism when doing our deeply sincere inner work. Not taking ourselves too seriously will take the edge off our fears that emerge from our bidden dark side.

Both the writer and artist have quested to deliver an enlightening, entertaining, and educational set of self-help techniques to engage enquirants of all ages. In the colourful and inspiring universe of myth-making and remaking, we're destined to find an avenue for our own stories, no matter how personal they seem to us. Even better, being deeply mythopoeic, we human beings can rewrite our pasts, crafting beautiful, loving, and fulfilling endings and new beginnings to our stories as we heal and advance in the days to come.

Our earnest wish is for our readers to immerse themselves in the *Mythimo* tools, setting them to the task in a mindful way. Our aim alike is to become our better angels. Socrates' teachings from over two millennia ago remain true: if ethics can be taught, they can be learned. Many of us know what our empathic side would do when we choose our thoughts, words, and actions. Now, we have the opportunity to embrace our Higher Selves by stepping out of a personal darkness that contributes to the collective's fragmented moral rationale, permeating our potentially wonderful world. This need not be a distant ideal, chore, or punishment. Our comeback to Wholeness is our return to Eden.

Working through this book (which later unpacks the richer meaning of the 22 archetypes), utilising the mythopoetic *Mythimo* cards, and journaling our reflections, reframed stories, dreams (and more), the seeker studies and comes to understand themselves and others better in this vast mysterium we share.

Channelling Dr Estes (1992): Let us turn to archetypal stories for psychic shelter when we need a good teacher and healer to lighten our hearts and the darkness, to guide us on the better path of hope and renewal.

Such an inspirational mentor is Vasilisa. The Russian fairy-tale archetype, brave, beautiful, and wise, shows us how to handle life's tests even when we land in a landscape of doom. She shines the light to overcome the dark. That which nearly killed her made her stronger, and she, who grasped the thorn to hold the rose, reached the summit of human potential. None of us will live forever, but her story and ours will.

We all are men, in our own natures frail, and capable of our flesh; few are angels. (Shakespeare)

6 ENCHANTED BY STORIES

Telling our story from the heart to someone holding the space for us creates intimacy, reduces stress, potentially shifts perspective, and is where our self-discovery and healing journey begins. Here are the bones of mine:

As young children playing in the great outdoors, we held a deep reverence for the natural world, engaging with it in ways that gave the trees, flowers, and creatures a life equal to our own. We felt the divinity in all living things around us, just as the myth-making Greeks and Romans did, finding our place amid the bush, rivers, hills, sea, and sky as we foraged for wild gooseberries and played our games of make-believe.

Instinctually, we sensed the spirit in all sentient beings and the inanimate. If something existed, it must have a right to be here.

The Celts of the Western world also sensed sacred energy in all life forms, and this animistic and mythical legacy lives on inside many of us today. With origins across Ireland, Wales, Scotland, and Britain (and the Romani gypsies of Eastern Europe and beyond), there was still something innately Cornish—stoic and forbearing—distinguishable in my kin. But for a moment, setting aside my European ancestry, it was my early interactions with First Nations children in my Australian community that most profoundly shaped my perspective on values such as equality, equity, inclusivity, and privilege.

Together, we considered the idea of some humans claiming dominion over other humans, as well as over the natural world, and inflicting unnecessary harm on other species—a win-lose scenario, and therefore invalid. Instead, we, as individuals, developed an understanding that we conscious-rich humans were only one part of nature's matrix. We believed then (and I still do) that all living entities are deserving of respect and compassion as we exercise our God-given leadership competencies in the earthly realm.

I harken back to yesteryear when our dear mother would read us enchanted tales at night, and we would act them out by day. We played games imagining the sky was sea and we, like mermaids, swam in the air and saw the grass as seaweed. Like alchemists turning base metals into gold, we transformed at whim the natural elements into magical props for our vibrant storytelling.

Away in our mythical lands, our whimsical fantasies nourished us more deeply than the milk, eggs and bread waiting on the family table. Then, as nightfall crept in, the familiar and anxious motherly cries could be heard in the distance, beckoning us back indoors for a bath, tea, bed and stories. After a full day away from the hearth, we finally came when called.

My sister and I were convinced we were witches. Our whiter than white straw hair and bold, lively, inquisitive dispositions raised suspicions that we were different and wildly so. We reinvented our dogs as wizards or wolves; birds as mind readers; and cats as siblings. To us, the poor chickens were cooped up for some strange adults-only reason in the neighbour's backyard.

We were discouraged from visiting the concrete and wire structure housing the roosters, hens and hatchlings. Most times, the keep-out rule suited us. If we had befriended the chooks, we would never have eaten their eggs, let alone ever eaten them. After all, you do not eat your friends, asserted the sagacious George Bernard Shaw (1856-1950). Not that we had ever heard of him or his philosophies back then.

Then, one day, our curiosity got the better of us, and we decided to go down to the forbidden territory. We had naughty intentions. Big sister shared a thrilling new game of doctors and nurses, assuring that this den of doom was the place to play it. Typically, after the fun and games, I left behind a tell-tale trace (my red plastic sunglasses), and we all got flogged harshly with the razor strop, bringing all the magic and delight of our fantastic adventures almost to an end. Things were never quite the same again. Our never-ending story of carefree days paled as shame crept in to blight our bliss.

Such jarring reprimands from the dishpan hands of over-wrought mothers threw us off those glorious, fluent feelings of freedom and fantasy conjured together as a pair of white witches in the wild. Still, ours was a happy childhood.

Some years, hence, following our fantastic flights of fancy in the unspoiled great outdoors, the old musty outhouse seemed an odd place for anyone to find quiet retreat. In the old days, most of us lived in areas devoid of sewage. Still, at seven, I remember an unforgettable time in that old rustic shack that proved to be forever life-altering.

Upon entry, greeted by the familiar faint smell of sawdust, masking the foul effluent in the old tin can, a wave of strange stirrings swept over me from head to foot. I felt 'other-worldly'. What occurred next blew my mind.

As I leaned against the wall for support, I traced myself rising beyond my body. For a brief while, while hovering above the scene, came a voice, speaking directly to me from on high as clearly as the peeling of a bell.

"This world is a dream, not real. You live somewhere else a long way away and are watching yourself living your life down here. You are only visiting this place, so don't take things so much to heart. One day you will return here and know that what you hear today is the truth. Remember, this life is but a dream." *The words are paraphrased but are still very close to what I heard.*

Awestruck, the truth of these words resonated within every part of me and from that day on, moved by the strange and inexplicable experience, I changed.

Looking back as though it were yesterday, I see the whole drama unfolding in my mind's eye and experience again those mysterious, transcendental feelings—those woozy sensations consuming me as I peered down at the dusty bowl of the outback toilet. But I can appreciate what psychologists might say about my memories, such as us having no way of keeping the memories intact from such a time so long ago, and how they become fragmented distortions in our minds as the years march on or that I suffered a dissociative state, disconnecting from reality due to trauma. However, whatever the cause, because I could not produce the information alone, it must have originated elsewhere. I entered another realm, the astral or deep unconscious, as happens the same when we experience what Jung (1959) called a Big dream.

Specific memories and dreams operate out of the same limbic brain region. I remember my significant memories as vividly as my big dreams that occurred through the various stages of my life and from a very young age.

Most of the memories I write about in this book are corroborated by my older sister, whereas siblings often have differing recollections of the same shared childhood. Sometimes, it comes down to only the Self and God knowing the truth about these matters, and that knowledge is indeed enough.

As young and inexperienced as I was, I knew my experience was weird and numinous but honest. There had been flashes of a similar nature in the backyard on previous days that I chose to ignore so as not to miss any play-time. But by the third time, I went under its spell, entering an elevated state and receiving the message. There, I felt a connection between my brain, an invisible wire and someone else (my grown-up self?), residing in some unfathomable place above.

After coming down from the heights of other-worldliness to ordinary reality, I ran back to my mother, who was nearby, incinerating rubbish in a forty-gallon drum. I cried to her as I ran, "Mum, Mum, this life is but a dream…this life is but a dream!"

To which she dismissively replied, "Go on. Go, get in the bath."

Running past, I reached the bathroom and, seeing my sisters lined up already in the tub, said breathlessly, "this world is but a dream."

"Who told you that?" quizzed my older sister.

"I heard it in the toilet," I responded elatedly. "It was a grown-up voice. It's the truth, I tell you."

"Yeah, yeah," Susie said with an exasperated tone. "Get in!"

I did not bring it up again for a while (continuing to recount the phenomenal experience through the decades of my life), but it was indelibly inscribed in my mind. I was resolute in my belief and account of my encounter with the metaphysical on that mysterious day and still am.

After that moment, saying I was transformed is an understatement. Everything about me felt different. My eyes perceived things in a new way, as though I had emerged from a cocoon into the light. Like the fairy-tale princess with narcolepsy, having slept a hundred years, I awoke suddenly. Since then, the belief endures that we are born asleep into the world and spend our lives gradually waking up to what is real, what truly matters—only becoming fully awake when we die: a reversal of our conditioning in this upside-down world. The next day, when I returned to my ordinary world, I remember being at school—where I stood, what I wore, what I was thinking. I realised I was no longer a young child, and I had to start growing up to look after the little kids and steel myself to the task. There's no mistaking how my mind felt connected to that faraway voice—an invisible, unbroken cord between me in the present and the other source of consciousness in that timeless, unforgettable place. Today, I can put into words the ineffable experience that happened to me at seven: my soul was ignited. Now, more than body, mind and emotions, I had reclaimed an awareness of my SOUL. With a bird's eye view, the invisible became visible. I could see into people's hearts and glimpse the bigger picture of what was happening in my life and all around me (if only I would switch on this heightened awareness more often). On a lighter note, I would have been born in a toilet seven years earlier if it weren't for my mother's urgent cries to the nuns to get her into a hospital bed. And then, my rebirth in an outhouse at seven? Do bathrooms hold some special significance for me?

This supernatural experience has deepened me in ways that have stayed with me throughout life's journey. Science might attribute my out-of-body experience to elevated carbon dioxide levels inhaled from composting materials in the outhouse. Ours, however, was kept sanitary and was never overly pungent. Still, a different kind of alchemy took place inside me that day. I had a similar experience when I fainted during a Girl Guides' parade and remained unconscious for around ten minutes. During that time, I had vivid dreams that closely mirrored what was happening in reality (I found out later). This was another significant journey into the realm of higher altitudes which had a lasting impact on my worldview.

As I write this, I know others have also had a transformative peak experience such as astral travel, out-of-body, near-death experience (NDE) and other altered states of consciousness with similar effects to mine. They tell of how they have been consciously expanded with a new attitude. As a result of their elevated perspective, most people have a deeper understanding of their inner world and its impact on the outer world. They stand, like the brave fairy-tale archetype Vasilisa did, at the nexus of where their inner world establishes contact with their soul, and the outer reality, and look to marry them in wholesome union. From this higher vantage point, this mysterious power brings a sublime sense of peace to their inner life.

Due to my studies in teaching, human behaviour, and psychology, I have deepened my understanding of these experiences that lead one to self-actualisation and satisfaction. Maslow (1943) might have described my toilet epiphany as a peak experience, marked by spontaneous feelings of intense joy and wellbeing, sparked by an early awakening to truth and a sense of the interconnectedness of all things.

Neale Donald Walsch (2009) asserts that once we establish contact with our Soul, the consciousness of Pure Being, everything in our life changes, including how we perceive our human existence. He explains that we cannot retrieve this higher level of awareness from our minds because it just isn't there. The wisdom of our soul, our indwelling Knower, far surpasses the power of our body and mind—it is our gateway to God.

Isn't it marvellous that we can tap into the power of our integrated, non-dual self, at one with the Soul and the Divine? More than just a thought experiment, it's a body 'felt' experience. However, how can we attain this state, and once we do, maintain it? Being in oneness or Whole brings immense joy, peace and a feeling of security but it is a 'moving feast', requiring our ongoing inner work. As I matured, I realised enlightenment was only the first chapter of the story.

The myth-making of my ever becoming a teacher was that of my jazz musician father, not my own: I longed to become a performer. I remember sitting in a car with him when I was six when he said, "You will go to university to become a teacher."

The kids in the neighbourhood and my younger sisters turned to me from time to time for learning support. Aside from the wonders of telling and singing stories with learners, I could never overcome my true ambitions or squelch the critical voice of my superego (my internalised well-meaning parents). I heard I did not have the gifts or grit to make it as a performer but the *gypsy* in me never lost sight of the dream.

Early on, as a young adult, I saw myself as the rejected *Ugly Duckling* seeking their place. So, with some trepidation, off into the wondrous world, I strode again to test my newly hewn reality, finding and communing with whatever and whoever crossed my path. Influenced by psychology, dreamwork, art, and the philosophies of metaphysical science, my mantra became 'as above, so below'. I believed the macro-cosmos mirrored itself in the earthly-micro, discoverable in all places from the sublime to mundane: a single cell indicating the whole of the body; DNA, the individual's blueprint, and the soul, a miraculous hologram (of sorts) of the original Self.

I was 24 before consciously choosing to unite and regulate my inner and outer worlds into one congruent me who operated consistently and universally. Integrity begins when you self-regulate, applying filters to say what you mean and mean what you say. Still, in an environment where one must keep up appearances, conforming with the majority's way of seeing and being, you can quickly become an outlier—the Ugly Duckling archetype.

Studying the astral through transcendental meditation lit the way through what felt like a trip into the *umbra nihili*, a state described as the shadow of nothingness. As finite beings, we stand on the low way, surrounded by an infinite cosmos ever-expanding above. This liminal state leaves us exposed and vulnerable due to incomplete knowledge and understanding, rendering us nearly null and void. Yet the emptiness reflected in the vast outer macro-realm connects effortlessly with our inner world, evoking a sense of serenity—as though we've come home to a loving place where we belong. This inner calm from feeling insignificant but safe in the *umbra nihili* contrasts with the mainstream impulse to fill the inner chasm. We cling to possessions—sentient or inanimate—to ease the ache within. Still, relief is fleeting. We keep accumulating, and yet the void expands to accommodate. A vicious cycle of greed, over-consumption, discontent, and fear takes hold, just as it did for the fisherman's wife in the fairy tale. To overcome our flawed thinking and fears, healers promote the universal idea of returning to love as the solution.

Learning to love ourselves, the greatest love of all, is the capstone of our heroic journey to evolve our souls and reconnect with the Divine. Yet, it is also a touchpoint that must be reached before we are ready to receive true and lasting love from someone else. Such are the derivatives of my spiritual learnings borne from my various leaps into the void.

Self-love can be the most enduring love of all: the only sure salve for the painful nothingness. It is the highway to completeness. Love can be many things, but in this context, it differs from the commercial notion of love peddled in the 21st century. The nature of love in its various forms, including romantic love, was explored by the ancient Greek philosophers such as Plato and Aristotle and their ideas have had a lasting influence on Western culture.

The media attempts to convey an uncensored view concerning the diversity of human preferences in love, gender and sex. Still, heated romance remains a temporary state of affairs for many of us, with its euphoria fading away or upcycling to a more stable state of the heart. Romance is as ephemeral as life itself: it takes us on a journey, a mystery tour with its destination unknown.

When we feel deep affection for another, there is a stirring in the heart, warming and opening in our creative minds, bringing us closer to our Divine origins. Our views become kinder and more tolerant, no longer clinical and closed.

Meaningful love is a mover and shaker, stirring our senses intensely. But it isn't sentimental, an abstraction or artefact, or a crashing crush of hormones. Its sacred bones go much, much deeper than the novel.

Alone, from the window threshold of our inner and outer views, our gaze is drawn to those in the exuberant throes of romance, making us feel invisible—like the wicked sisters felt when seeing Cinderella with the prince. The projected illusion is one of eternal intimacy and bliss, as they entwine and appear larger than life in contrast to our singularity and feelings of smallness and anonymity. Staring, our craving and desire redouble in joy and despair. We have only seen the scintillating silhouette, yet our imagination fills in the contours with a richness of life from which we feel barred. Minds play tricks. An outer world reflects that we are incomplete in a world without love. However, love is nourishing and enduring to the soul with transformative powers for turning the ordinary into the extraordinary. True love has its source in Divine truth. Love is a sacred fire, leaping in luminous circles, recognising and claiming its own beyond the visible.

When the light fades, shallow love ends in a fast burn or shady show. Like you, I have loved for keeps and for a fleeting time. Many of us know what it feels like to have loved and lost, and they say it is better than never having loved at all.

Now is the time to ward off our bitterness. Rather than becoming hardened through a lack of tenderness in our lives, we may love ourselves with an accepting heart— my story began, sustains and ends on this note, as does yours. Then, we are no longer burdened with a constant yearning to find another to do the kind work of filling our gaps. We have no drive to project our needs onto another while expecting them to overthrow themselves accommodatingly, customising a response for us. When we love ourselves, we go beyond the vanities of intense attraction, self-interests or narcissistic needs. We are comfortable spending time alone, quietly biding our time as the universe unfolds as it should. We will never be lonely when we give our inner love room and time to blossom. Our self-love reveals itself in an abundance of nourishing riches.

French Enlightenment writer, Voltaire (1694-1778), described self-love as an instrument of our preservation, necessary for the perpetuity of humankind and enabling our pleasure. Interestingly, he warned that we must conceal it. Self-love differs from self-centredness: self-love (self-compassion) is the wellspring from which we share our love and light with others. Our challenge is to reclaim it, refill it to the brim, and let it shine.

That remarkable day, I hovered above my seven-year-old self, gaining access to a place within and beyond my soul and its overflowing cup. This spiritual fount has calmed me in times of great tumult, torment and trauma, sheltered me in times of loss, loneliness, and despair, and amplified the beauty of all forms of love.

With this healthy mindset, there is no chasm, longing to be filled with another's resources. One is not as dependent on recognition, praise, rewards, power, and possessions to affirm their place in the world. Sticks and stones may break our bones, but the cruel words of others are empty vessels on broken harbours. Mean acts rest with the doers. Their behaviour only betrays their lack of self-love and emotional intelligence. According to the social activist Parker Palmer (1939 -), we must all embrace our brokenness as an integral part of our life. He sees our Wholeness not as us becoming perfect but as the result of the healing and integration of our broken hearts and parts. When Whole, slights and assaults are powerless against our self-belief as we sail headlong into the hot winds of the unknown. We stand mended and ready, our sensitive hides thickened by healthy scar tissue as we go forth to stake our claim on love without conditions. Instead of feeling hurt and angry, we begin to feel empathy for the wrong-doers, sending them our light and love, little by little. And then one day we feel forgiveness for them and forgive and enrich ourselves.

Not every material domain is welcoming, but we feel an emerging sense of belonging. We have knowing minds and radiantly loving hearts, ready to magnetise like-spirited folk into our sphere. When we are fortunate to share our love, a burning ring of fire melds our souls as we enter Eden.

In this state, we believe in the infinite possibilities of our universe and are open and brave. Our curiosity is ablaze, lighting the path before us as we head home together. To that place where the blue sky is the sea, we are ready to live in the rhythm of each new-born day.

Now, entering my winter years, I back myself with faith—facing down my overactive conscience, the cynics, and applying the same self-belief and tenacity I encourage in my students. With a deeper understanding of archetypal power, I channel Jack's adventurous spirit to climb my own beanstalk and boldly share my reauthored stories. This is the soul's daily task—to love itself. Isn't that how we carve a lasting place in this creative world we all long to belong to?

The German philosopher, Nietzsche (1844-1900), reminds us of the importance of balancing fitting in with our tribe and being true to ourselves. He said: "The individual has always had to struggle to keep from being overwhelmed by the tribe. If you try it, you will be lonely often, and sometimes frightened. But no price is too high to pay for the privilege of owning yourself."

Marianne Williamson (2013) agrees, telling us that the sage always lives on the outskirts of town and rather than fear exile, must be proud of their courage in being who they are.

My story is really our story. What comes to mind is the Grimm's fairy tale, *The Wolf and the Seven Young Kids.* Granted, there were not seven of us, but the mother protecting her children and keeping the wolf from the door rings true. Our beautiful mother was widowed at just thirty-eight and raised four daughters bravely and wisely on her own.

Then, after only a few all-too-short years, along came my magical boy. Together, at a tender young age, we ventured into the wilderness—wending our way through a mythical maze of mayhem, worldly wonder, and struggle. The enchanted tales of my childhood sprang to life once more, this time in his beautiful heart and mind, as we shared our story-telling times. We finally came out of the woods, landing on our feet: wiser, braver, and kinder.

Our story is also the narrative of thousands of others on this planet making the most of the plot where they are planted. But some are still lost, fearing the power in their hands to do what their heart truly desires.

The truth of my story shows how connected children are with our sacred Source, having not long left the spiritual realm to exist here on earth.

Like Little Red Riding Hood, we start our journey with minds wide open to every moment, loving to learn and learning to love. If we can see through the eyes of our inner child again—discerning which way to go without the burden of judgment—we grow strong legs for our Hero's Journey. Otherwise, emotional wounding dims our light, and we grow weak and weary, allowing fear to take root. Having done the inner work to reclaim and integrate my dark side (and the work continues), my inner child is free to come out to play. These days, living in a positively reframed story-line, she follows her bliss, creating a reality aligned with her authenticity. It feels good because it's the right thing to do. Vasilisa, the brave warrior archetype with her magical inner doll, shows us the way. I hope that, like us—enchanted by the spell of childhood fairy tales—you'll feel inspired to take steps toward reconnecting with your indwelling child, key in hand, ready to open those mysterious doors to new beginnings.

What lies behind us and what lies before us are tiny matters compared to what lies within us. (Oliver Wendell Holmes).

7 NOWHERE TO SOMEWHERE

When truly in love with someone, we'd rather be nowhere with them than somewhere without them. But being nowhere has its scary moments. Fear is what we learn, suggests Marianne Williamson (2013). She assures us that love is what we are born with, so we must return to our natural loving state, stare down our fears and get cracking on our way to somewhere with someone to love—starting with ourselves.

As adults seasoned with experience, coping with life's disruptions and vagaries, we fare better than teenagers do when experiencing feelings of helplessness and hopelessness. Adolescents who feel they lack control and direction—especially when compounded by trauma or isolation—may become vulnerable to painful thoughts and, at times, suicidal ideation.

As one of the lucky ones, having a kind mentor long ago, I rose above my own grim ideation and continued on my Hero's Journey to my 'somewhere'.

Just three years after dad passed away prematurely, I was expecting my first child. At barely 15 years old, I felt lost, a 'nowhere girl', standing on a perilous precipice. Looking back, I realise I lived in a daze of depression but also knew the struggle that came with bringing a vulnerable little life into an uncertain world. My fears had me by the throat. Through no fault on my mother's part, I felt totally outcast.

Back in 1972, although everyone seemed to be falling pregnant out of wedlock, mum was understandably concerned and embarrassed by my predicament, putting strain on our bonds. So, despite her love, there was no real sense of belonging for me.

I had become a fringe dweller, ashamed and cut off for behaving in socially unacceptable ways. Lucky for me, my boyfriend and his mother were caring people. Still, I felt very much alone as I looked out into the unknown before me, wondering how the future would unfold. Channelling the goddess Amphitrite who tamed the tempestuous waves to bring calmness to the seas, I held on tightly through the turbulence.

There are choices that only we—blessed with free will as the final arbiter of our destiny—can make. For those of us who are fortunate, love, family, health, wealth, and education become the most significant domains of life; only we can decide how to shape them beyond childhood. So, through the challenges, we must stand alone with our faith, facing the harsh headwinds of reality.

Bracing for the future as a pregnant teenager, I took the first steps into the void with no clue about where I was heading, depending on love and faith alone and surrendering myself to the wild flow of the current.

I wondered if the fairy-tale novices, Little Red Riding Hood and the Little Mermaid felt some of the same fear when crossing from their known ordinary world with their family to the other, deep unknown side of the woods or reef where their fates awaited.

My unborn child was registered for adoption to appease my anxious mother (and the next-door neighbours whose voices had taken up residence in her head), assuming it was the best option for our family and the baby. Despite feeling vulnerable, fearing a severing of ties, and initially going along with the plan, I struggled with the idea of giving up my child. But hundreds of other girls the world over were taking this route at the time.

Still, the more my autonomy grew as a young woman (granted, a woolly-headed one), running her own race away from home and on her own path, my mother's influence lost sway.

Then, out of the blue, my prayers were answered. My mother-in-law-to-be spoke to me—woman to woman. I recall her looking me straight in the eye and saying, "Why not keep your little baby? You will be glad you did in the long run—you will have to live with the decision you make now for a lifetime." She continued, "So, take your time. I know you can do this, and what is more, do it well."

In that Kairos moment, her well-chosen words resonated deeply; they chimed. A bell rang in my soul; I heard the call of the wild and knew what I must do.

While so many young women in the seventies were anguished and alone going across state borders for forced abortions or having their babies and then having to give them up for adoption, I had a wise and compassionate mentor. Even the terminology used back then had blaming and damning connotations. Despite talk of shot-gun weddings, it seemed acceptable for the young men to 'sow their wild oats' without being held to account for impregnating the girls. Media espoused the seventies' shame-free sexual free-for-all for men and women alike, but things were very different on the ground. The double standards caused a great deal of confusion. Our generation still valued chaste women, intimating that unmarried females refrain from sex or otherwise burden themselves with a bad reputation. Girls like me were damned if they did and damned if they didn't. Take the pill, engage in pre-marital sex and ruin your name, or don't, and get pregnant only to abort or adopt your baby out. No wonder, with such an ambiguous social discourse, many of us were uninformed and ended up in the family way (well, also with the helping hand of nature). Back then, no one could accuse us of only wanting a baby, so we could claim welfare payments instead of going to work—there were no handouts for the younger and most vulnerable of girls. Things had not changed much from Shakespeare's day when he wrote plays questioning the social norms that limited women's opportunities, including forcing them into lives of seclusion (or the nunnery) or arranged marriages but never allowing them the sexual freedom enjoyed by their male peers. The issues he explored in the late 16th century remain relevant today due to ongoing gender-based discrimination and inequality.

So, betwixt and between, I ventured forth, in a total state of unknowingness, living each day at a time. I had a few fearful outbursts, running back to my mother for an overnight stay, only to wake up the next day knowing I was more invested in moving forward on my own steam with my baby kept close. Sometimes I would see myself being a single parent living at home with my mum and sisters and frighten myself into staying my course.

Worse, if I took the adoption papers seriously, I would soon be without the little baby for whom my affection grew daily. Standing on this fretful threshold also fostered fear of developing too strong an attachment to the baby. What if circumstances changed and I had to go through with the adoption? Where oh where was my hero's way, I wondered?

Faith was my only antidote to feelings of insecurity: fear not, for God strengthens me (Isaiah 41:10). My dear mother always put it another way: "Don't worry—things have a way of working out in the end." And what if they don't? Then, we haven't reached the end yet.

When I had grown uncomfortably numb, my mentor stepped up and took me in.

Leila had been through many ordeals along life's road but never lost faith in the prevalence of goodness in the world. Her heart of gold, sunny disposition and unwavering optimism soothed my nerves, helping me find the inner strength to face the realities of keeping and raising her son's child. As the birth approached, I crossed the divide, making a firm decision to be a mother. His father, innately kind, stood by us. With the help of family and friends along the way, I stepped up to my responsibilities, doing what I had to do.

Nobody said it would be easy, but nobody said it would be as hard. Reflecting now, I wonder how two young lovers, too young to be married, ever dreamt they could meet their baby's needs and become plugged-in parents. But with desperate times demanding desperate measures, we grasped the thorn, pledging to do our legitimate best.

In 1973, few had a strategy to get through the physical and emotional demands of birthing new life. Although I routinely attended the ante-natal clinic for physical check-ups, there was no information (oral or written) openly available to prepare a woman for childbirth. Wanting to believe what I heard—giving birth is painful but the pain is quickly forgotten— I was unprepared for what lay in wait. A Big dream experienced just weeks before going into labour kept me going. I will never forget the powerful maternal promise I received from the archetype.

My baby son and I endured our birthing experience mostly unassisted. A disapproving, crosspatch maternity matron made sure of this, turning on her heels, leaving me alone for hours on end in a sterile room and snapping at me, "Stop your groans! You were woman enough to get pregnant— be woman enough to deliver your baby quietly."

Turning just 16 years old, four days before his birth, I was overwhelmed with fear and sadness in that moment. How could a birthing room where beautiful little babies made their entry into the world be so harsh? And here I was, bringing, little by little, a tiny new life into it. Confronting.

But as cold and cruel as the world can be on the one hand, on the other, it gave me the most precious of glorious gifts: a baby son to have and to hold.

Indeed, all the physical pain was quickly forgotten. Now, there was someone else to live and strive for, and he, our higher cause, would be loved, adored, and cared for, no matter what befell us.

Together but alone, my baby and I began to muddle our way through the days ahead. My love and genuine effort as merely a child-mother always seemed barely enough. Guilt weighed on me. It turns out that many first-time mothers of all ages experience feeling out of their depth and lacking competency. In trying to live up to an idealised image of mothering, I was very hard on myself. I still wish I could live the experience all over again, doing it so much better with my beautiful love-child. But I had walked that hero's path already and there would be no second time around, in that moment in time, in any case. Consequently, much of my shadow healing work centred on the unresolved issues of this peak experience—an experience that brought both birth trauma and a profound sense of strength and joy yet also led to later self-recrimination for feeling less than a perfect mother in my youth All in all, my son continues to be a golden gift. Fortunate, indeed.

Clarissa Pinkola Estes (1992) contends that child-mothers may not have experienced enough to benefit their offspring or be sufficiently engaged in giving them the attention they need for their development. Years later, when the child-mother matures, she may live her life vicariously through her son or daughter in superficial yet meaningful ways, helping her to realise her identity unrealised so long ago.

My children, both golden miracles in their own right, have devoted their lives to their artistic creations just as I would have liked to have had the courage to do so long ago. Rather than continuing to live through them, I am now venturing out on my own creative journey. We walk side-by-side, encouraging each other along, knowing how fortunate we are to have each other.

After my baby son's birth and through the coming three years, there came the dawning that the bonds of our teenage family were becoming increasingly tenuous. Ultimately, his father and I separated, but our mutual love for our son provided a caring and respectful way to raise him over the years while keeping our genuine fondness for each other alive. Now, fifty years later, our son is a man, a great man, and his father and I are still friends, life-long friends. If we have any wisdom to share with others that might make their world a better place, this is it: If your marriage ends and you have children, act with your children's needs at the centre of your negotiations. Forgive the past together, focusing your attention instead on forging a satisfying future as individuals. Treat each other with empathy, dignity, and common decency; think and behave reasonably and do not overly involve lawyers. If you feel you must win, and the other party must lose—seek psychological support.

The elixir I bring home to you is to tell yourself to grow up and become a better version of yourself. Well-adjusted and healthy children are what really matter in the end. Nothing said here has not been said before. But who is listening? If adolescents can leave a marriage with a toddler and survive and thrive while remaining on good terms, then surely anyone of sound mind and emotional integrity can do as we have done. Well, if they really want to, that is.

Many of us recall that dull, dream-like haze of our teenage mind, trying to figure out how we arrived in this place and time on earth. Feeling powerless at the fork in the road, we pause. Will our actions now be the determinants of our future quality of life?

Nowadays, teenagers have an even greater need for caring mentors and role-models to assist them through the perplexing maze of despair, hopelessness and helplessness. They need sages to compassionately lead them from a place of uncertainty to a path of purpose.

They may not think they need the elder's caring guidance to take them from nowhere to somewhere, but indeed, if research and statistics and personal accounts are accurate, they do. Vasilisa had her inner maternal-doll for support.

If in times of uncertainty, our confidence, clarity, and rationality elude, as my narrative shows, we can always turn to love, hope and faith. The archetype Snow White did. After wandering alone and sleeping in the woods, she was mystified waking up and seeing the mysterious little cottage. I can relate. When my son was still small, we lived outdoors in a tent, enduring all types of weather and relying solely on ourselves without much to our name. Despite the challenges, that year of living rough taught us valuable lessons in love, resilience, freedom, and above all, faith that we were being watched over, and still are. Although we appeared to have lost everything, we gained so much. Years later, I took a path 'A' and everything changed. Like Snow White, we stumbled upon a cosy little cottage in new parts, which turned out to be the beginning of a wonderful new chapter in our lives. It felt like a miracle.

If only we had had a picture of what the finished jigsaw puzzle looks like before attempting to put each interlocking piece of our life down. But this type of wishful and 'magical thinking' never did solve a conundrum. Indeed, life is a series of journeys where we, and we alone, must weigh up our choices, to take risks and venture out into uncertain terrain from the moment we are born right up until that unknown date with destiny. Even the dying, in their last moments, speak of the new journey they are going on, rather than intimating that a final curtain is closing on them. What supernatural secret do they come to understand at the pointy end?

Recalling those indelible, fear-filled formative years, the future resembled an empty thought bubble—like those drawn in comic books—shaded only in dull greys by the traumatic memories of Dad's protracted illness and loss. I was too afraid to fill the emptiness with ideas for manifesting what I wanted in case my dreams were dashed again with those dark images of trauma, abandonment and despair.

Focusing on 'surviving' adolescence, before the brain has fully grown, in an eco-system where you are safely protected by elders (if you are lucky), you are capable of putting one foot in front of the other and shuffling along. You carry out the motions and sleep-walk through each day, hoping you will somehow make it somewhere on the skyline.

Make it where? You do not really know despite what words you mumble to your loved ones to calm their fear. There is no end picture to strive toward, you don't even know in which direction you are headed, but you just keep going along for the ride anyway.

Our generation would say that going steady with a love interest was 'going with them'. Elders would laugh and say, "Going where? Where are you going with them?" But I, a nowhere girl, shrugged.

For many teenagers, fifteen is not the landmark year it was for me. But from conversations today with young people, they often feel like they are walking around in a mental fog. They are on auto-pilot or ready to be led by a ring in the nose (presumably, like Piggy-wig from the *Owl and the Pussycat* poem was). Like me, suggestible, they follow any fad or charismatic individual who seems to be in control of whatever is going on. Cool exteriors mask their tumultuous inner worlds. The truth is, many of today's teenagers are as adrift as I was.

Expectedly, research shows that traumatic events such as divorce and parents' death add another layer to the depression our young experience. Our father was taken too soon from our family unit, dying before we were launched. Life went from being a comfortable middle-class existence with a mum and dad, fitting into a suburban norm, to becoming the only family on the block with a single parent at the helm. Too often, tongues were wagging more than hands were helping. I still recall the naysayers' body language and suppressed words conveying: How is she going to raise four girls on her own, and with two of them at tween-age? She'll never do it. She can't even drive a car, let alone steer them through their future careers. This is a train wreck waiting to happen.

And just as our identities were labelled, the wheels started to fall off the wagon——for me, in any case. Our selfless mum dedicated herself to our care. We were very fortunate, indeed. But how were we faring psychologically? Poor mental health was a taboo subject rarely spoken about unless impacting someone else in a faraway place.

Before my baby, I was living in my head, envisioning a way out of living with four other women. Truth is, we were always a bickering bunch, as often tribes of insecure women left to their own devices are wont to be.

Visions of escape began to dominate my dreams. I hitch-hiked my way up and down the coastline. I didn't yet hold a driver's licence, and there was barely enough cash for train fare. What else could a teenager do? How does one get instant gratification?

My sister was introduced to this dubious and dangerous form of getting around by a friend, which seemed a fun idea at the time. Wanting to appear cool and impress, more than wanting to protect my life, I even thumbed it solo. The thrill of the risk and feeling autonomous overtook any consideration of consequences. I was a vessel of emptiness, waiting to be taken anywhere by anyone exciting to a new experience. After all, the downtrodden Cinderella got whisked away in a coach, and her life was transformed for the better there after. Perhaps, there was hope for me yet.

The fear of being caught out by my mother was more of a concern than travelling in a car with a stranger. Though, I doubted ever being sprung—as even serious delinquents do.

Sometimes, kindly Christian folk would pick me up and explain how I was placing myself in situations that could cost me my life. Deep down, I knew they were right. But as actions speak louder than words, it took a sexual assault and a potentially fatal encounter to cure me of ever hitch-hiking alone again.

To be fair to myself, I was experiencing the challenges of puberty and grappling with complex grief and acute stress, which left me feeling different from other kids my age. Our family's difficult circumstances demanded I act older than my years. But not in the ways I assumed.

Parents in survival mode may place too high an expectation for maturity and responsibility upon the older siblings in the family, requiring they share the caregiving and even providing roles to compensate for the loss of a parent.

Indeed, this was an intergenerational pattern from both sides of my family. Arguably, expecting responsible behaviour is the making of what we call self-agency in young people, proving to be the making of them in adulthood.

My father, at 16, sacrificed all of his modest pay to help his mother and six siblings, living in a non-welfare state of England through the Second World War (WW2) years. Earlier on, my Australian grandmother, at just nine years old as the family's oldest child, had to play 'chief cook and bottle washer' when her mother left all of her children behind in the post-First World War (WW1) years.

In keeping with the theme of the survival stress of our forebears, our widowed, caring mum, doing her personal best, had little time beyond providing for our survival and security, and the rest was up to us. Isn't that enough?

Dizzy me had long dreamt about getting out and having a go at designing my own life, whatever that space might look like. I sometimes brooded about certain inequalities and imagined myself in an outside world, getting what I wanted on my own terms. I recognise now how mum, with limited resources, was more interested in being equitable, sharing what she had where she felt it was most needed. As one does. None of us would trade our incredible mother for anyone or anything and would give everything to get her back into the land of the living. We take comfort in knowing she is in a higher place. Good mothers are the greatest blessing of them all. How fortunate are those whose mother is golden?

But back then, I only wanted to feel heard and valued, be loved affectionately, and experience a sense of true belonging. In hindsight, I see that grieving for our father (while mum grieved for her husband) were complex feelings none of us was ever encouraged to openly express and process. We are all in agreement that our unprocessed pain led us to become chronically depressed human beings.

Few spoke of anxiety and depression back then, so none of us had our downheartedness named or treated. Depression can lead to fuzzy-headedness, fatigue and immobilisation. Your mind is so preoccupied with its ruminations you cannot see the forest for the trees.

Kids haven't had enough todays to understand about tomorrow. Like so many other teenagers who experience negative feelings about themselves and how others react to them, I could not focus and see the pathway in front of me.

Vital learned information to keep you safe or propel you forward seems way back, lost in your brain, and not readily retrievable. You are totally ensconced in your own susceptibility, like a sponge ready to soak up everything, especially somebody else's attention— an identity still waiting to be identified.

Can you see the correlation with Little Red Riding Hood who sets out on her inaugural solo trek across the woods, cloaked in invisibility, until her bright red hoodie draws the wrong kind of attention from the hungry wolf?

What occurs psychologically plays out in the brain's anatomy: The *frontal lobe* (forward-most region of the cerebral cortex) encompasses the regions responsible for our judgment, reasoning and problem-solving that are still under development until age 25. The brain's function is based on the 'use it or lose it' principle, and as the child moves into the teenage years, redundant grey matter in the back of the brain is pruned away to make way for emerging synaptic connections. In short, a lot is happening inside our heads. In effect, the *prefrontal cortex*, the 'smart brain' (situated at the very front of the frontal lobe behind our forehead) where we process decisions in a rational way to control our wild impulses, is developed last. It is part of the *neocortex,* which is humanity's newest evolved brain part. Its later maturity just happens to coincide with our emergent autonomy, when as young adults, we start to separate from parental control to test our critical thinking skills and working memory and develop our social behaviours. Therefore, teens are prone to poor judgment.

As teenagers enter the anxious 'tweens', experiencing challenges, their psyche rests on a threshold, torn between the instinctive responses of the flight, fight, freeze, fawn and hide of the *amygdala* and the still developing 'smart brain' (*prefrontal cortex).* When threatened, teenagers are more susceptible to impulsive (even dumb) choices driven by emotions, aggression, and instinctive behaviour because the *amygdala* floods the smart brain with fear chemicals slowing it down and triggering flight or fight. Tweenagers feel forever on the cusp.

I was an emotional mishmash, driven by impulse, seeking sensational pleasures outside the house, trying to catch glimpses of the future through a mind-fog. It is no wonder my concerned mother so often told me I was crazy. But sadly, in an emotional whirlwind, I chose to take her words literally, introjecting the belief I was insane-crazy. Only decades later did I realise what a detrimental decision it was for someone to swallow up derogatory and self-limiting labels.

Suppose you believe in metaphysical causes of illness and can accept the supposition of therapist and author Annette Noontal (1996) that our body is a 'barometer of the soul'. In that case, you will not be surprised by my take on my own 'tweenage' health issues.

I was plagued by sequential bouts of tonsillitis. What emotional distress, I was not resolving internally, manifested in my body as a physical symptom. The more I ranted, raved, risk-took, and felt unheard, the more my throat health (and ability to communicate) suffered. My tonsils were a pus pocket, the reservoir of my emotional wounding, fuelled by social anxiety, fear of separation, and feelings of gross inadequacy.

The lungs are also associated with feelings of grief, so I experienced recurrent chest infections. Even my amygdala was out of whack —continually torn between fight and flight, while the prefrontal cortex, still under construction, was gaining attitude: negative attitude. The more my forebrain grew, the louder loomed the inner judge, and the more pain concerning being not good enough got shoved into my psychic shadow.

Famed author Clarissa Pinkola Estes, PhD (1992) shares that women raised by kin who are different to them, not acknowledging or appreciating their uniqueness, set out on epic Hero's Journeys. Time and time again, they quest to prove their worth without even knowing why.

On the one hand, I had this overwhelming drive to get out there and have a go (the innate drive and need for self-actualisation at work); on the other, this inner voice kept telling me, "Who do you think you are? You can't do that. You are not good enough, in fact, you are nowhere near enough—are you crazy?"

Without plugged-in role-modelling, mentoring, and encouraging, positive strokes to prop me up, this problem-story fuelled by my inner critic had me carte blanche, rendering me useless. Sadly, many other teenagers feel just the same.

I hung in limbo, an ensemble of separate parts waiting for something or someone else to make me feel Whole. I knew not what. And waiting like a lamb to the slaughter, or more aptly, liaising as Little Red Riding Hood did so dangerously with the wolf, I was prime for the pickings.

The exiled Ugly Duckling archetype, whose urge to rove persisted until he found his belonging place (there exists a so-named syndrome), demonstrates how one should keep questing. So, I did; never giving up and doing what needed to be done.

Estes (1992) lists the indicators of the Ugly Duckling Syndrome as repetitive, compulsive behaviour; looking for love in all the wrong places and knocking on all the wrong doors (hard to know the right door when you have never hit one). The wrong doors are easier to recognise as they reinforce our well-honed sense of non-belonging and therefore feel natural. The trouble is that the orphan archetype or ugly ducklings have a long-entrenched habit of ending up in the very places that reject them all over again. Thus, etching the neural grooves deeper in their brains and reinforcing the negative recurring patterns of their life. Not only lovers reject them but also friends, siblings, parents, workmates, interviewers, and worse, they reject themselves. I know because it has happened to me.

Later on, my three years of marriage came and went in a blur but then came the opportunity to begin anew. Depressed and lonely and desperately wanting to give myself away, I emerged, looking for a signpost. There had been no deep healing of wounds. With all that experience behind me, I came stumbling in, toddler in tow, into a grown-up reality. Rather than seeing myself as a strong, young woman who had come so far on her own with her young child, I could only see an inadequate self, separated and full of wild ideas. Why feel so inferior when I had made genuine progress, and where did this self-defeating script come from?

Living in a family of five women: one brave widowed mum and four rivalling sister-siblings, with 'the rug pulled out from under your feet', tests anyone's mettle.

The absence of fathers is a common thread in old tales of the oral tradition and is equally as meaningful in contemporary times. I always felt like an odd one out but was not alone in my self-diminishment. We might have been the only single-parent family on the block in the sixties, but more and more single families appeared as divorces became more accessible in the following decades. Couples severed their ties on the grounds of irreconcilable differences, shifting away from the blame games congesting the law courts in the past.

All four of us, from the same gene pool but with DNA (and collective archetypes) reacting uniquely to the lived experience, felt a resonance due to our shared mitochondria. Sometimes we felt the intimacy of closeness through our like-spiritedness, and other times we were as 'chalk is to cheese'. We all took turns at cheesy concern and chalky carping.

As a young girl of about five, I remember saying to my mum, "Dad's the softie, and you're the hardy." Mum laughed it off, but I often heard her comment on my remark, betraying her sensitivity. Still, I thought after I had said it, they sometimes swapped orientations.

Dad always told us he did not want us to end up like his three sisters, who were constantly squabbling. He would say, "There you go at it again, just like my bickering sisters." His displeasure with our negative carry-ons stuck in my awareness, remaining after he died. I wanted to uphold his values and keep his tradition of thought alive. Why? Because he was a kind and generous man of moral principle, an intelligent, talented man and one worth living up to. Dad was like the sun in our family: a shining light who took the high road with humility and compassion. Mum, was the moon, sharing her secret stories and lighting the dark corners with her caring, and intuitive wisdom.

Back then, a myth-script played over and over in our family and in my mind (fed by the sceptical superego). It read we would never be good enough, and when anybody else did well, they robbed us of our opportunities. In any case, we did not deserve the same level of success because they were better and luckier than us.

False and limiting beliefs such as these are fuelled by fear and mistrust. One of the effects of our suspicion made my family behave in hurtful, untrusting ways—we all did.

Deep down, all I ever wanted for us was to collaborate as a family and to share our resources, lifting ourselves up together, just as the Mediterranean and Eastern families have done successfully for centuries. Given their sustainable familial achievements, I could never understand the opposing view. Today, I look to fairy tales and the cases of the collaborating brothers in *Three Billy Goats Gruff* or *The Three Little Pigs* to see how much more beneficial cooperation can be over competitiveness. Still, more experience has also shown me that, depending on context, both perspectives can have their merits.

It took me a long time and a lot of hard-won lessons from negative experiences to become conscious of the schema running in a loop over and over in my head. The self-talk said: "We do not trust you because your ideas are crazy."

Such an unregulated inner voice perpetuates hurt and negative expectations.

Referred to as having a 'chip on your shoulder' because others see too clearly the burden you carry around. In other words, your psyche has a faulty internal drive controlling you. If only I had paid as much heed to my mother's retelling, time and time again, of the adage, 'Sticks and stones may break my bones, but words will never hurt me' to help me get through. When our inner speech is positive, regulating our emotions becomes easier. However, if our inner speech is negative, it feeds our negative emotions and behaviours, making them expand and more difficult to control.

Emotional intelligence (EI) may be equated to how well we understand and interact with others. Do we respond in self-aware, composed, and empathic ways? In contrast, our behaviours can be irrational when we carry the weight of accumulated emotional pain, clouding our rational thoughts and subsequent good judgment.

Self-regulation of emotions requires a personal discipline equal to self-mastery for emotional and sensitive types especially. One must also have the *motivation* to do the reflective practice to control outbursts of emotions such as anger. Temperance is one of the great virtues, according to Aristotle. But first and foremost, before governing our dark wildness, we must be consciously *aware* of the underlying memories freighted with emotions triggering it from the shadows.

The fears of being rejected and outcast lay in the recesses of the psyche. Deeper yet is the universal fear of death. Thanatophobia is naturally wired in all of us to improve our chances of survival. But it is commonly triggered by feelings of insecurity. It is also activated when we have an ambivalent (i.e., neither here nor there) and insecure attachment to the people and places dominating our lives. As counter-intuitively as it sounds, our fear of death does not originate from our ego's reluctance to close the curtains on our ephemeral show here on earth. If we are lucky, we have a lifetime of gradual decay in the physical body to prepare for our big exits (by the way, 'exits' and 'exist' are a fascinating word play, illustrating how life and death are inextricably entwined).

Our fear is more about the loss caused by severing ties with those we love and departing for a different and unchartered destination from which there is no return. The notion that we will never be with loved ones in this place and time again fills us with dread. Fear of the cause of death is another matter again.

Caring about others, understanding, and relating directly to their emotional pain and how they feel, having *empathy*, is another pillar of emotional intelligence. We have all come to know people who lack empathy for reasons, medical or personal, and we can empathise with them, imagining what it must be like to live in what seems to us a wasteland of the heart. Not until we have learned how to self-manage, fostering states of *awareness*, *regulation* and *empathy*, can we aspire to have the *social skills* and *motivation* that bring us closer to those with whom we interact. People turn to us as role-models and mentors when they observe and know we are centred, self-efficacious, and emotionally intelligent leaders on the hero's way.

Contrastingly, to those people who come from a place of love and acceptance, some come from suspicion (fear) and judgment. Others' judgment of me and what I am doing in the world can be a trigger. Deeming me crazy, eccentric, airy-fairy, too sensitive, too enthusiastic, too defensive, unworthy, shoddy—a 'space cadet', has stirred my ego defences.

If I had a dollar for every time someone threw a derisive remark my way, I would be a wealthy woman by now (not saying I am alone on this one).

The offenders lacked empathy in attacking me without provocation, and my Higher Self urged in vain for me not to dignify them with a response. But alas, too often, I chose to be wounded. Before reclaiming and integrating these disowned parts of me in my shadow, I felt hurt every time someone insulted me, unaware of how else to handle their sneers.

Should we assume the stance: 'what they really think of me is none of my business?' Can we put the emotional pain away, forgiving and forgetting, when the person taunting us is someone with whom we have an emotional attachment? Do we expect better from them and engage in relationship repair work? Do we fight fire with fire and lash back with equal malignancy or move on?

What if saying cruel comments to others is not part of who you are or want to be? What if a vicious cycle is catalysed that harms both parties?

After trying all the above, the only way forward for me was to take responsibility for my emotional wounding, triggering my shadow and doing the inner work to turn it around.

My personal code says being sensitive is an attribute, not a fault, so rather than take offence when being accused of being sensitive, I now take it as a compliment, no matter the intention behind the remark. Reframing it, I remind myself that I would not be as intuitive, perceptive, caring or creative if I denied my sensitivity. This helps keep this touchy trait from retreating into the shadow and over-reacting when it cops a poke.

Moving forward, I now empathise more with those not sensitive by nature. They fill the roles that take a mind-over-heart approach, such as bankers, health administrators, business leaders, and politicians, to name a few. Dealing with our critical health and wealth matters takes a cool head.

There is no escaping the fact that we all hold responsibility for how we respond to others' words and actions. In this context, the 'Choice' theorist Glasser (1998) comes to mind, and I remind myself regularly of his famous words, "The only person whose behaviour we can control is our own."

There are intrinsic differences in the lenses through which we all see the world. For example, whether we choose to operate compassionately or indifferently regarding the plight of others. Granted, there is a time and place when survival and security are at risk, where being a fragile flower becomes a self-indulgent redundancy. To my way of thinking, and so, infected with some bias, acting sensitively is akin to getting down to raw emotional authenticity, where one can make intimate connections.

Now that my sensitivities (and perspective) have been reframed in this positive orientation, balanced and integrated, I am accepting of them and no longer triggered. This said— it is challenging for emotional and sensitive souls to get past feeling hurt when their innate traits are trampled on by others they care about. This is their Achilles' heel. The tougher types have different brands of hurt in the id, such as being dismissive, too detached, uncaring, and lacking emotional intensity, such as romantic passion. They may be aggressive with their passions but lack sensuality and tenderness.

The stern stoic may think all the warm and fuzzy behaviours are silly, but they, the stalwart in the storm, will sometimes feel empty, disconnected from their loving wellspring.

We all sit on the continuum somewhere between empathy and emotional detachment. Still, we will do well to remember that many an interaction without love and compassion at its centre is merely a transaction or game.

Ironically, the person who rejects the emotional and sensitive traits most likely has bundled these attributes off into their shadow so long ago that they barely remember having them. They are triggered and over-react when these traits are seen in someone else. Therefore, they have their own inner workload to manage. The emotionally stunted have just as long a row to hoe.

Adults who attended boarding school may be sufferers of the so-named syndrome. Boarding School Syndrome results from very young children fending for themselves before being emotionally developed to cope with such a mechanistic environment. These cold institutions do not always provide for their needs of privacy, safety, security, justice, love, belonging and wellbeing. Many syndrome sufferers find intimate attachments challenging when they mature, putting walls up that defy and avoid sensitivity and loving feelings. The 'Cinderella Law' has now been put in place to protect such children from the emotional neglect and abuse that create deeply seated scars, mental health problems, and even suicidal ideation.

To be overly sensitive or insensitive? Neither position is better than the other, only thinking makes it so. Both imbalanced orientations of being too emotional and not at all emotional indicate that some shadow reclamations are in order.

Author Debbie Ford (2010) espouses in her ground-breaking shadow work the benefits of chasing down the dark side. She writes that reclaimed negative traits such as 'laziness' for workaholics and 'selfishness' for those who become exhausted from over-giving bring them back into a balanced state. Being a little lazy and selfish cannot be wrong when these out-of-balance dispositions are moderated.

I learned through self-reflection that I would feel more balanced consistently and universally once I undertook the necessary shadow work. As part of my discovery, I recognised I would be less battle-scarred and would have gone further ahead with achieving my dreams if long ago I had developed an internalised 'locus of control'. According to Rotter (1954), an individual can bring their unsettled feelings back to their locus or centre rather than deflecting them away from themselves, projecting them onto others. To operate from our centre, we can start by asking why we feel a particular way in situ and consider what learning can come from the experience.

My early conditioning in a family who collectively felt like 'victims' after the death of the much-loved man-of-the-house had me believing that I had little power to shape my own life. For many years, I had an external 'locus of control' and thought it was the 'done thing' to blame others, fate and outside events for whatever occurred. Figuratively speaking, I was like the middle brother pig who built his house from sticks, expecting unrealistically it would weather any storm. But after experiencing enough pain, there came the point where I began to see my part in influencing how my destiny played out. There was a direct relationship between my choices and the consequences I was experiencing. Even when I chose to do nothing in some situations, I was still making a choice. Cause and effect or karma are not new concepts, but I had to call a spade a spade before I could connect the dots and start seeing the bigger picture, the completed jigsaw puzzle. Once I assimilated this awareness, a greater sense of personal power and responsibility became mine. Now, acting as Big-Pig would do, I had the benefit of my prior experiences guiding me from the centre of my being. It felt like a positive way to go. In that moment of clarity, life changed for the better.

To come to clarity, we must develop the ability to momentarily stand outside of our emotions and see through the illusions before us. Our darker elements, hitherto unconscious to our ego, trigger our emotions by hooking into our painful memories and hurling them into the midst of our current interactions. Emotionally charged memories and shadow elements (like our denied anger, frustration, guilt, shame, vulnerability, sensitivity, and more) act symbiotically.

There are still testing times. I must work very hard to keep these recycled emotions out of my thinking and behaviours, having the self-control to 'not give myself away' when opposed by another person. My elastic face, full of animation, always betrays the different thoughts running through my head in face-to-face circumstances before I even open my mouth. But in the case of phone conversations, where you do not require a 'poker face', I have exercised greater emotional control during contentious business negotiations. This might be a helpful strategy for you, too. I can stay grounded, live in the moment, and achieve a win-win outcome for all concerned. Goleman (1995) might say I demonstrate 'emotional intelligence' in these interactions. When we maintain emotional control, we circumvent any waste of energy spent dwelling and sharpen self-awareness of our own behaviours. This kind of inner work, over time, leads us back to our Whole, fully functioning Self, who is not susceptible to emotional triggering.

The five women in my primary family, whom I love dearly, all experienced the same reactions from their interactions, one way or another. Can we shake things off and start anew? Indeed, we can. If we want to change the plot or our schema, we can. But we must want to do it and be totally committed to the change. We must be prepared to go back a step each time before we can take two steps forward and persist until we break the chains of the debilitating narrative overlain on our original, unadulterated selves.

In my family's case, we run on a myth-script about the matriarchal archetype. A wounded feminine shadow encoded into our DNA from the annals of our family ancestry, haunting our dreams. She rises unbidden to randomly threaten, disrupt and disempower us with her hostilities and resentment for bearing alone the heavy yoke of family responsibility. Paradoxically, our mitochondria come from centuries of strong Vasilisa-type women who birth strong Vasilisa-type daughters. All of us respond to the deep-seated collective earth mother archetype within our psyches who knows instinctually what must be done and does it to save her young and the life-blood of her tribe. Like the many other warrior women among us, the keepers of the flame, we have been born with the light to undo the dark. But first, we must become conscious of our gifts of strength and leadership and heal.

All of us can draw inspiration from the story of the fairy-tale archetype, Vasilisa, who is put down, almost to the point of sure death, by her vexatious step-family. Not yet aware of her innate power, she does not know how to revolt against their aversive mind games holding her back, and only her initiation into the vast unknown will give her the light she needs. She is expected to do the heavy lifting for her step-family's survival. All the while, her radiant qualities of kindness, beauty and wisdom embodied in her fearless inner child are denigrated. As the Russian oral tale goes, Vasilisa goes into the dark woods, facing her fears of its primordial depths and primaeval dark mother, and returns with light and fire. Its mysterious force extinguishes her darkest enemies. She is finally free. At the height of her powers, she lives a loving life full of creativity, vitality, Wholeness and happiness ever after.

Transforming our life starts with the Self, tells Vasilisa the Brave. When one of us in the relationship changes, the invested other will follow. By the time Vasilisa returned to a home of matriarchal malevolence, she had grown into her own identity, and her gift of light and flame overwhelmed the blackness of her past. In real life, our light and loving nature subtly influences the inappropriate behaviours of those around us. For any relationship to thrive, our 'plus one' must also process and integrate their shadow elements and grow towards the light. Otherwise, they will be left behind. How many people do you know who have said their relationship ended because one of them had outgrown the other? While a fairy-tale transformative process may sound 'airy-fairy' it occurs dynamically, chemically and organically when one commits and applies themselves to acting from their light, not shadow. Degrees of enduring change result, transforming the Self and one's life for the better, little by little.

As actor Brad Pitt once said, "People don't change; we just grow by degrees."

Many fairy-tale tropes reflect how an individual evolves in character and spiritual depth from when they start their journey to when the story ends. Take the Little Mermaid archetype, for instance. Her life lessons took her from the self-denying maiden, cutting off her tail to spite her essence, to becoming a woman standing tall on the moral high ground. By degrees, she evolves into a sky seraph on her way to the highest heavenly realms. Her end inspires us to hang our shining star from the highest bough from the very beginning.

We can see parallels between the Little Mermaid and our own psychological and spiritual growth. In early childhood, our mind and body develop rapidly. Around ages three to five, our ego begins to form, and we start to sense the unconscious through dreams, imaginary friends, and other psychic experiences. These early experiences introduce us to a sense of soul, a feeling that there is something beyond the material world—a higher goodness or spiritual dimension.

As we grow up, we begin to understand that there is more to life than just the thinking mind. We learn from mistakes, develop empathy, and strive to become the best version of ourselves. Like the Little Mermaid, who undertakes an act of selflessness to achieve this, we gradually discover that true growth often involves sacrifice and a deeper connection to something beyond ourselves.

The Divine has coded and loaded us with a unique soul-essence tuned for a sympathetic relationship with it. Our Soul Self is the knower within, programmed with a virtuous value system to help us enact the dispositions of compassion, empathy, open-mindedness and joy. If only we would open ourselves up to our divine DNA by listening and self-regulating before we act. We need not work alone. The Divine is at our back as we quest, seeking our return to love and Wholeness, operating in full vigour to realise, to manifest our seeded intentions in a golden harvest. But before we venture out on our own from the home hearth to the broader reality, several transitions must be made.

As a teacher with many years of experience, I have seen how school life is a microcosm of society and why teachers must masterfully foster students' agency and social competence to ensure their future contributions as good citizens of the world. Educators and caregivers alike have the balance of power with equal responsibility in their hands to lovingly support and shape our innocent young, who have so much to learn about the wiles of this wild, dense realm. Content knowledge is one thing, but feeling secure and confident, thinking critically, knowing how to reason and make sound, ethical judgments, and participating in society autonomously is another. Their wellbeing matters most of all.

Harking back to the earlier days of my journey, I was a fortunate toddler growing up in post-war Australia in a semi-rural environment bordered by woodland thickets at either end of the dirt road on which we lived. Deep wells of rainwater dotted our acreage, roaming horses and bulls paid visits and myriad bush creatures like lizards, birdlife and poisonous snakes shared our glorious home. There was much to mystify a young imagination, kindle curiosity and propel leaps into first-time adventures.

We lived in a mythical world of white witches, wizards, cowboys and Indians and magical mermaids who swam under the blue banner of a sea-sky. Sometimes we were fire fairies (where the hair on other kids' heads—and ours—took some serious singeing from the blaze on the end of a burning stick). Just a mob of 'hairy oubits', according to our Scottish dad. We played in bushlands full of illusory hungry wolves all day long while agitated bulls, tired of our piercing squeals, gave withering looks. I recall that in our young minds, all the fantasy creatures were just as real. If we could imagine them, their detailed features would soon be discovered in the shadowy silhouettes of the scrub. From the treelined hilltop, we even saw that the Indians gathered, preparing for their assault on us cowgirls waiting below. They were indeed unforgettable thrilling times of wonder as we wandered through the uncut bush.

Days filled with wonder were capped at night by the re-telling of fairy-tale favourites shared with us by our familial storytellers. Such memories! Oh, the joy then, and the nostalgia now, knowing our wise, brave and beautiful maternal princess has ascended to the heavenly astral, rather like our own version of the sensitive, intuitive and caring little mermaid.

So impressed were we by the messages channelled from the nightly tales that we played out the parts of heroes, higher angels, and villains all day. As the youngest then, I often assumed the dodgiest roles of the younger pigs, the hapless little girl in the red hoodie who got eaten by the wolf, or worse, Cinderella's ugliest stepsister with the horrible, tortured feet. Well, at least until the older children got bored with the central roles or wanted to dabble on the dark side for a while after seeing me play the lesser part with so must gusto.

The most telling memory is when I kept trying to draw my mother's attention away from her newborn baby girl by solemnly telling her I had just dodged a bite from a giant snake. We kids had worked out mum's instinctual fear and I aimed to use it against her. Each day, we took off to play in the bush without supervision, only returning home for quick top-ups of food and water or when the night began to close in, and our figurative wolves came stalking in the now dark scrub. The catch-cry of all mothers in the sixties appeared to be, "Come on, kids, outside! I have got housework to do." So off we would go, without a second thought or care in the world, ready to paint a bright new day on the backdrop of our scorched backyards.

Alas, there arrived the time when the snake story no longer hit the sweet spot. Savvy mum checked with the scotty schoolmarm next door and discovered that my snake scare was a mere fabrication. All my mum had to say was, "You will turn out like the boy who cried wolf, you know. One day a real snake will bite you, nobody will believe you, and nobody will run to help you, not even me." Sprung! I recall the guilts. I never played that game again, ever!

However, I did not miss the opportunity to compare mum's life to *The Old Woman Who Lived in the Shoe* when I felt my newborn sister received far too much of her attention. As mum was telling me the rhyming folktale, I interrupted her. I asked her why any woman would have so many children if she did not know what to do with them, implying mum had better stop reproducing before things caught up with her. Dear mum only smiled wryly.

Tales of times past in the oral tradition hold potent messages for all folk of all ages. Their transmissive power around the globe supersedes that of the written word tenfold. For personal, social, cultural, historical, and political reasons, the classic archetypes still speak to us and our human condition as much now as they did back in their heyday.

Most of us can remember how fairy tales directly appealed to our young imaginations, arousing our budding sense of morality, desire for thrilling adventures, and aspirations for happy endings. As adults today, we may still sense their subtle elixir of social truth, heard but never stridently dictated. According to psychologist and writer Bettelheim oral tales from childhood inspire us to be brave and embrace life's struggles so that we may come to know our Original Self, our inner child. Bettelheim (1976, p.1) wrote:

Fairy tales intimate that a rewarding, good life is within one's reach despite adversity—but only if one does not shy away from the hazardous struggle without which one can never achieve true identity. The stories also warn that those who are too timorous and narrow-minded to risk themselves must settle down to a humdrum existence—if an even worse fate does not befall them.

So, starting out as a blank page upon which, our life will be writ, a Tabula Rosa, we begin our journey as the archetypal Little Red Riding Hood, the novice, and over the years and through many iterations, evolve into the brave sage, Vasilisa.

I, like you, can trace the milestones of my personal journey, the ongoing Hero's Journey, through each of these twenty-two fairy-tale tropes whether I choose to reflect on the past or seek direction for the future. Our personal narratives, contexts and purposes may be solely our own but the archetypes, the cognitive invariants, remain the same and belong to us all for eternity. As I pen these words and hear the refrain of the famous jazz song, 'That's Life' playing in my head, I rewrite the lyrics thusly:

I've been Jack, a cat, Little Mermaid, a pig and played the goat.
I have been up, down, over and out in a Red Cap and coat.
Sometimes, I was Cinderella, an ugly duck, even kind-hearted Belle,
Then Goldilocks, a frog, a witch and a princess under her spell.

Every archetype is within us all—just add soul. Most of all, I am inspired to be just me—as I hope you are being you. We aspire to fill the shoes left behind by the brave and wise women from whence we came—mothers, grandmothers, Godmothers, and mentors who did not try to be anyone other than themselves. Each of them stood up in times of great adversity, walking to their heart's beat and paying homage to their originality. No matter that society told them they were not pretty or smart enough, talented or anywhere near good enough to make it. In the face of darkness spreading across the world, these modern-day Vasilisas, anchored in truth and wisdom, refused to let others dim their light or put out their sacred fire. And, in their own way: make it they did.

Now, more than ever, our communion with each other, sharing a large vision for the evolution of our human consciousness and creating a compassionate and caring world for all, is vital for overcoming the dark forces. As the Indian mystic Osho (1931-1990) shared, the darkness is always there—only by increasing the light can it have dominion over the darkness fed by our collective failure to adopt virtuous dispositions in our wonderful world.

In the face of dark moral aridity creeping over our blue planet, impacting its dependent life, our collective contribution to unconditional love, fire for right, and faith-fuelled light must blaze to reach an indomitable Divinity. As beings of love and light, we understand that our struggles reflect the invisible battleground of the macrocosm in which we are encapsulated. As we overcome our individual dark elements, transmuting them into light, we add luminous energy to the universal field, conquering the dark cosmic corners by degrees.

As a fellow human being having a spiritual experience, with love as my driving force, I have travelled from nowhere to somewhere: just an ordinary woman still grasping at the nettle. Like Jack and the Beanstalk, I take on demands that ask the best of me. As our fairy-tale hero Vasilisa forged on to brave the harsh elements bearing the torch, I am inspired to rediscover the fire of all that is good and shine on, living my strengths-based story.

Our quest is to light up the human spirit and this is the elixir I aim to bring home. But as Jung (1959) suggested, before anyone can make the world a better place, we must each put in the moral effort to recognise and reclaim the dark aspects of our personality—an essential condition for self-knowledge and our light to prevail.

Like Vasilisa, we are trailblazers on the pilgrimage to our psychic realisation. No matter what battles arise, the joys are sure to follow. Will you reframe your life-story where pain exists and join us on our faithful trip to that fairy-tale finish?

The aim of life is self-development to realise one's nature perfectly —that is what each of us is here for.
(Oscar Wilde)

8 FIRST, KNOW THYSELF

Who am I?

The act of projecting our loving light into the world sounds simple enough. But first, we must come to know ourselves, understand our strengths and talents, and own those dispositions we have delegated to the controls of our shadow and mana-personality (or myth-taken self).

We may think we know ourselves, but unless we have experienced many different challenges, achieved or overcome peak experiences, worked through the consequences effectively, had a change of heart, and seen ourselves in a different light, chances are we only have come to know a small part of ourselves. This view is supported by clinical psychologist Robertson (1992) who writes, "We can't be one with our total reality unless we first face who we are and what we desire" (p.199).

Even when we have dug down into the accessible recesses of our subterranean unconscious, exploring the deeper meanings of our meditations and dream-state messages, and dissected our narrative, there are parts of us still hiding in our labyrinthine psyche.

It is one thing to believe we know ourselves but another to do the inner work with the shadow that returns us to love and a sense of wellbeing. Knowing ourselves is not about finding ourselves but about regenerating our original essence both the light and dark of it. But when someone asked the iconic folk musician and poet Bob Dylan (1941-) how one goes about finding themselves, he replied, "Life isn't about finding yourself, man. Life is about creating yourself."

Drawing from Dylan's perspective, we can imagine recrafting ourselves as sculptors sculpting marble, bringing the inborn figure out of the rock by following its natural grain. Michelangelo was known to say that the statue was already complete within the marble block before starting his work. He just had to chisel away at the superfluous material to unearth it. As we travel life's road, we are the diamond in the rough, drawing out our higher human consciousness and qualities. The rough is our hungry animal side, ensuring our survival needs are met first.

According to the evergreen philosophies running like social threads through time like those of Socrates, Plato, Aristotle, Jesus, Fromm, Spinoza, Teilhard, Schopenhauer, Marx, Maslow, Freud, and Jung (and so many other greats), we are primarily driven by our instinctual passions. But when acting primarily as animal beings (the evolved ones at the top of the Hominidae tree), we are not holding onto the reins, and unless we do some inner work to expand our awareness, we control too little of our behaviours than we care to admit. In other words, we may falsely believe we know who we are and how and where we are going next. But nearly always, we only find our blind spots when we get to that fork in the road, wondering why we are lost, alone and spent. Some find themselves in a whole world of trouble.

Paradoxically, the illusions and the stories we create about ourselves help us to cope with living in the society to which we must belong.

Considering that we are informed by history, philosophy, our mentors and lived experiences, and abide by age-old traditions and values, it is challenging to find valid reasons to change how we believe, think and act. But why not when these systems start to fail us on a personal level?

We must overcome our fear of reality and truth, and confront the illusions we fabricate, if we are to put our unique purpose and talents to good use. Our full potential for love and success can only be realised when we accurately assess who we are, where we belong, and when we fully engage our innate strengths. Social psychologists have developed various typologies to help us understand where our strengths and limitations lie. Drawing on Triandis's *individualism-collectivism* dimension and Maslow's concept of *self* and *transcendence*, we can identify four fundamental orientations.

Are we viewing life as a *Self-preoccupied* journey, focusing solely on an agenda of achieving more power, possessions and pleasure for ourselves? The overly ambitious fairy-tale archetype, The Fisherman and his Wife comes to mind.

Or are we a *Collectivist?* People of this orientation enjoy being of service to others. They commit to a cause, in religion, politics or public life. Here, we can compare The Three Billy Goats Gruff who worked together against a common enemy. Perhaps we are the type of person who spends time developing knowledge, skills, and qualities to improve our lot. Then, we subscribe to *Individualism.* Here, Jack and the Beanstalk corresponds. He feared not his giant challenge, utilising his full skill set to succeed.

But suppose we centre on an ultimate purpose or mission, having altruistic values to provide philanthropic care in the world as if we are one-humanity. Then, we assume the stance of *Self-transcendence.* Vasilisa the Brave, Beautiful and Wise archetype acted from such a stance, proving her compassion for others once establishing her happy-ever-after place.

Still, there are many different typologies to guide (but not define) us.

How we orientate ourselves has a lot to do with our motivation for doing the necessary reflection and psychological processing work that evolves us into a better, more empathic version of ourselves: the Whole, powerful, self-determined and faithful Self.

If we are not moved to go in this direction, then chances are we might type ourselves as *Self-preoccupied.* Like the Fisher's wife or Goldilocks, there may be no perceived purpose in self-development. Their dominant need for pleasure is already satisfied by self-indulgent lifestyles. They argue that the less they feel and show concern, the less the pain. Less pain, more pleasure. In fairness, they may live a contented life, feeling no drive to invest time and energy into an esoteric experiment for evolving the Self. And a perfectly good one at that, they argue. Only the fullness of time will tell. And we say: each to their own.

Collectivists might do the personal work, but only if it fits into the picture of the cause in which they are currently engaged. An example would be when The

Three Billy Goats Gruff shrugged off sibling rivalry and collaborated in tricking and overcoming the troll because each of them wanted to survive.

The exponents of *Individualism and Self-Transcendentalism* have a personal code for Higher Living, driving them onwards and upwards, evolving their consciousness, and expanding their light. Those most likely to take on the inner work for increasing their emotional intelligence fall into these two typologies. Like Jack or Vasilisa, these folk can weather the pain of getting to the crux of the matter, leading them to self-governance and growth and appreciating the satisfaction that invariably follows. Some traits or people fit into multiple classifications, highlighting both the limits of typology systems and the undeniable uniqueness of each individual.

People attracted to self-growth have universal or personal role-models who have inspired their quest to do the depth work, such as Jesus, Buddha, Gandhi, Mandela etc. Otherwise, they may look to emulate the strengths seen in sporting heroes or the ordinary folk in their lives who have achieved extraordinary feats in their own way. Many of them strive simultaneously for a cause and might climb Everest, raising money to build a school in Nepal. They reach the summit for the school but graduate from the peak experience with a spirit of self-efficacy not experienced by them before—a win-win.

Excellent outcomes await the enlightened individual, such as achieving self-actualisation, emotional freedom, an increased sense of social justice and the ability to activate change in the various fields that ignite their passion.

Individualists and *Self-Transcendentalists* develop a meaningful rationale concerning their place in the world and have a wholesome capacity to love and be loved in return. Individuals who act with these capacities will also be resourceful and resilient and have meaningful social interactions, enabling them to belong, contribute to and do well in the material world.

Our most vigorous drive is to belong. We need to be in the company of others and be accepted by them. Our need for inclusion is stronger than the will to live and is more powerful than our desire for sex. This may explain why many teenagers impulsively seek intimacy with strangers, trustworthy or not. It's rarely just about momentary pleasure or pain—it's a longing for connection, belonging, and testing their identity beyond the safety of their upbringing.

If you are a *Collectivist*, your preference for being in the company of others will be highly activated. In the scientific study of human behaviour, we know that humans must relate with other humans and find unity. The absence of links affects us profoundly. Our mental health problems may develop into psychosis if this hard-wired genetic code is routinely disputed or denied. Social connections keep us well and young.

Abraham Maslow's Hierarchy of Needs (1943) acknowledges our first need to survive (i.e., food and water) and, once preserved, we need to feel secure (i.e., having shelter and tribal attachments). When humans feel safe, they begin to forge intimate bonds which enable belonging: love and belonging within the family, tribe, or social structure. After these significant human motivations are met in a hierarchical sequence, humans begin to feel good about themselves (self-esteem/ego health). Once they have achieved the rewards and satisfaction that a healthy ego has quested for, they have the agency to achieve the goal of individuating themselves. In other words, they go after peak experiences that could make or break them but reach the peak of self-actualisation by sustained effort. The *Self-transcendentalist* chooses to ascend Everest for the satisfaction of their peak experience while supporting a cause close to their heart.

After trial and error, they reclaim their original self-strength, innate talent and newly forged competencies, gaining spiritual altitude and emerging ready to care for and share with others.

It has been said while we are alive, even after a climb to the apex of Everest, the quest for self-actualisation never rests. So, the ranked positions on Maslow's Hierarchy (1943) never stand still for us. We face too many changing conditions. No sooner might we think we have reached the summit than we are confronted by yet another mountain, a novel experience, arising with each twist and turn on our path. Still, our soul ascends upwardly to new heights on the invisible spiral staircase each time we master increasingly complex challenges.

If belonging is our greatest need, then our greatest fear is ostracism. When we belong to a tribe (i.e., family or work or social group), we form, norm, storm and perform together with a uniform set of beliefs, values, traditions, customs, and procedures. There is a tacit understanding: conform or be prepared to be sidelined. Groupthink comes to mind. Sometimes we storm with kith and kin but return to a homeostatic state that keeps us interacting in the familiar patterns that feel like home to us. Some conditions are inevitable, others acceptable and affirming, some are tonic, others— toxic. Still, we sense that we belong there just the same.

We adjourn or mourn when someone dies or leaves the group. We induct newcomers into our way of doing things that have always been done a certain way and must continue in that vein. We conform to produce and reproduce, and our conventions almost have a life of their own. It feels safe to do things together and to know what to expect. But, sometimes, we rebel. We disagree. We see things in a different light. We try to reason with our people, but they disagree, not understanding our perspective. They differ as we ask for a modification to the norm. We fear we will be hated, banished from our clan, and alienated for speaking up against wrong-doing. The outliers who seek to innovate and stray from the old pattern, groupthink, stir up a storm.

Our fears run deep. We feel a sense of isolation come over us even before any confrontation has occurred. In response, we back down, reassuring ourselves that we belong here and ask: How can I risk losing my identity by being cast adrift? Out there, I have no connections, no network, only a big empty me on my own alone facing a perilous precipice looking into the yawning void.

The paradox of life persists: When we are ostracised by an ingroup, we have the opportunity to take care of ourselves in solitude. Inside this cave of despair, we can choose to become a better version of who we are today. We can take the time out to work our way back to balance, recognising our dark aspects and returning to our authentic state. But at this point, it is crucial that we reach out to the hero within. We need them to go forward.

In our mind's eye, we may see our indwelling hero reaching that fork in the road where alone they must decide which direction to take. In any case, they must meet and overcome their nemesis. Can we see them battling it out and winning victoriously? Or do they succumb to the shadow? Done right, the Self gets a power reboot and the strength to press on.

Take the lost and alienated Ugly Duckling, clumsily acting out of place. He stumbled into the cave (of despair) not to find himself but to retreat from the incessant attacks he received for being different. Paradoxically, he found himself anyway. He emerged regenerated with the energy to keep moving without any particular destination in mind—but a plan had been writ for him and the world outside began to make sense. His place in the tribe was settled once he rediscovered his essence.

If we risk standing up and being counted as individuals with the courage of our convictions, we gain traction and support the more we persist. There will come a time when our differing ideals, ethics, and passions become accepted as having a right to exist by the people with whom we relate or make bonds, but we must keep going regardless. The Ugly Duckling reminds me of what it must feel like to be a step or foster child or a discarded animal trying to fit in with a new tribe. My rescue cat, Apollo, young, gifted, and black, lets me know how grateful he feels for the genuine outpourings of my besotted heart. Animal and human orphans (indeed, all sentient life) deserve our support, unconditional love and light because we care and need them more.

We see the shortage of empathy around us and the impact on living beings. We dream of making a real contribution to the goodness of our globe before our brief time here ends. Suppose we are to become true citizens of the world, members of humankind who have mastered prejudice and channelled our compassion into a single system of open-minded understanding. In that case, we must first know ourselves and express our unique essence in our capabilities.

Oft time, for many of us who engage in self-awareness and self-reflection, we come to realise that we can only truly understand ourselves—our place and purpose—by testing our originality within the social collective. We might shy away. We might feel lost. Yet it is precisely in these humbling moments that we make contact with our souls. But how can we be sure our innate substance will harmonise with someone, somewhere, within the reality of the wider world as we leave the cave of self-containment, our familiar comfort zone?

First, we must know who we truly are—and have the courage to be that person.

Knowing others is wisdom, knowing yourself is enlightenment. (Lao Tzu)

9 THE SOCIETY 'I' MUST FIT INTO

What is society, really? How deeply do we grasp the inner workings of the vast, human-made system in which we are each expected to find our unique purpose and rightful place? Without formal training in the humanities, we draw upon our reservoir of experience, filtered through interpretation and coloured by perception.

Much of our early understanding is inherited: passed down through the values, narratives, and behavioural models of those who shaped us. Their worldviews inform our beliefs and social attitudes. Yet, endowed with a rational mind, we must learn to think independently, engage in critical inquiry, challenge inherited norms, and remain curious about perspectives beyond our own. Through this dialogue between received wisdom and self-discovery, a more conscious understanding of society can emerge.

Society is as we find it. To some, it is a melting pot of cultures, customs, languages, and values where we strive for personal goals in a reliable, friendly, and fair system. Others may see it less favourably if they have not felt accepted for who they are and cannot access the resources they or their children need to survive, let alone thrive.

Innumerable books unpack the inequity meted out on humanity to help us grasp what is happening in the world. Dexter Dias' book (2017), *The Ten Types of Human: A New Understanding of Who We Are, and Who We Can Be*, opens eyes, minds, and hearts, and prompts debate on poverty, inequality, and the unevenness inherent in globalisation.

As the first unit of society, the family shapes us and prepares us to participate in the larger human collective. Schooling is similarly influential, and when families are unloving, the effects can ripple outward, creating dysfunctional school and community life.

When we venture into society from the home's haven (or hell) and find sympathetic ideologies and structures aligned with our own, we will fit in comfortably as new contributors to the groups we join. We may slot into the dominant group, predisposed to conform to conventions, maintaining the status quo. We have been trained at home to 'not bite the hand that feeds us'. We like to believe our government and society in Australia nearly always provide for our survival, reassuring our sense of security and affirming our place of belonging.

Humans want to establish good standing within their social framework to feel good about themselves; our egos tell us so. As designers of hundreds of thousands of different dialects spoken around the planet, we demand the power of free speech. If we have adequate words to express our feelings, we can use them in Australia (within the limits of human decency). However, when we want to communicate abstract notions such as our feelings, matching them with the right words may prove challenging.

Knowledge cannot enter our awareness if we cannot manipulate it into some form our mind recognises. Fortunately, we can turn to symbols and metaphors for creative expression. Art, poetry, storytelling, myths, dance, and music help communicate what lies within where there are no adequate words.

But symbolic, sublime language in social constructs must be decoded through our personal filter, intimating that a divergent assortment of interpretations exists. We must remind ourselves of the diversity of strong opinions about pet subjects and know that our unique analysis arises from the limits of our 'positionality'—our thinking and feeling experiences. Hence, we must check and transcend our underlying biases and assumptions to become objective and verify whether our view is well-reasoned and supported by reliable evidence.

Sometimes we find elements of society so abhorrent we drive the truth underground into our mind's secret hiding place.

It takes guts to get to the truth about society, let alone about ourselves. Too much is expected from a limited subjective self without a flawless record for all-knowing. We begin by acknowledging that we cannot accept everything we see and hear verbatim. To get the whole story, we need to diversify our sources and look for crucial information from valid, alternative media. The information glut does not make this easy. Facts are also embedded in symbolic forms such as spiritual artefacts, art, dreamscapes, folklore, and myriad creative works.

We must check that our news has a bona fide source, mainstream or underground. So much of it is gratuitous gossip when all we want is the unadulterated truth. We owe much to the doubters, rebels, and freedom fighters throughout the centuries. They did not swallow whole what was fed to them as sacrosanct. When they saw people suffering, they thought critically and investigated all sources of information available to them. They acted with the heroism it takes to make improvements. These warrior archetypes still fight for their rights in democracies or even under fascist regimes.

On the micro-level, when we do not stand up for our truth and 'fight for right' in matters impacting our personal reality, we risk experiencing internal conflict. Symptoms manifest as a troubled psyche with shadow elements erupting volcanically when we least expect, and the body following suit by succumbing to distress and illness. Remember how The Little Mermaid archetype denied her truth and became mute?

The social tribe has its collective shadow, too. Information that runs counter to social-political agendas will make its way underground before it makes the light of day. With a bit of digging, it can be uncovered. Despite the ideology of 'free speech' promoted as part of the constitution, there are areas of information that cannot be openly available to us; otherwise, the whole socio-economic-political system would become threatened. As social members living a comfortable existence, we turn a blind eye rather than challenge the norm. It behoves us to wonder why some information is considered taboo, questions get suppressed, and dissenting views are met with intolerance. These characteristics are tenets of a subtle form of indoctrination. If we accept foregone conclusions without being encouraged to evaluate information and form our own position, we risk our hard-won freedoms. We may not recognise their loss until it has gone. Complacency, history has shown us, may ultimately attract unbridled aggression.

The much-peddled prediction from Australian trend-setters of the eighties claiming that the 'have nots would be challenging the haves' in our lifetime is undoubtedly borne out every day. People are marching in the streets the world over for personal freedoms and against the quality of life compromised because of heavy-handed governance, corporate greed, global terrorism, and pandemic management. They confront the injustices leading them to become the working poor, struggling with the increasing cost of living.

If our country were a wasteland and our children were starving, what would we do if we still had any fight left? Most of us are fortunate and may never face such a soul-shattering situation requiring a Sophie's choice of sorts. Can we find the empathy within us to care about our fellow humans who become alienated through no fault of their own?

All that is light, such as truth, can be driven underground. Anyone with a stake in keeping things in the dark demonstrates selective memory, denial, and strong resistance if their fabrications are scrutinised. Put another way: if someone is driving information out of sight, they do not feel secure in defending it. There must be holes in their argument.

Let us take a brief look at history. Society at large has repressed truth so that it can continue to commit the same lies, unchallenged, as we stand back in our zone of complacency, fearing our exile if we speak out. Only when a lie impacts us personally may we allow truth to enter our awareness. Our leaders may not always realise when they have caused harm, as they often lack the habit of self-reflection.

Before World War II, British Prime Ministers Stanley Baldwin and later Neville Chamberlain pursued a policy of appeasement which emboldened Hitler to pursue territorial expansion for Germany. This approach inadvertently enabled the Nazi regime to gain momentum. At the time, public justifications for appeasement masked deeper fears and political motivations. Groupthink—the uncritical conformity to a perceived consensus—played a role then and may still influence those who feel pressure to uphold dominant historical narratives.

We widely accept that the assassination of Archduke Franz Ferdinand triggered World War I. Yet deep-rooted tensions among the major European powers had been building for years. Germany rallied its population by claiming Russia threatened its territory and freedoms. Behind the scenes, however, economic motives loomed large. Influential bankers and industrialists had long pushed for war as a means to rival the colonial empires of Britain and France. Resources such as French and Belgian coal, along with Luxembourg's iron ore, made conquest all the more appealing.

Several peace attempts during World War I were made under a cloud of futility, even as millions died on both sides—the Central Powers versus the Allied Powers. Though peace was publicly discussed, both sides chose to entrench rather than concede, prolonging trench warfare and pointless slaughter until the

Armistice in 1918, after four brutal years. The formal terms—penalties and reparations—were finalised with the Treaty of Versailles in 1919. Peace is never easily won. Wars are sustained by a fierce sense of duty and honour, deep mistrust of the enemy, and the hollow promise of glory and patriotism, making it painfully difficult for either side to lay down arms. Still, there is more to this story.

Before the war ended in 1918, word of the grand deception spread, and thousands of soldiers—feeling misled and betrayed—began to rebel: deserting in Russia and Germany, mutinying in France. Though brutally suppressed, these uprisings revealed growing disillusionment. Yet this resistance is largely absent from dominant historical narratives. Omission, after all, is a convenient form of untruth.

Had peace come sooner, the harsh penalties imposed on Germany—territorial losses, disarmament, and heavy reparations—might have been tempered. Instead, a humiliated and impoverished Germany became fertile ground for nationalism and extremism, paving the way for World War II. Governments rarely admit that, for a powerful few, war has often served ambition and wealth at the expense of millions of lives.

The truth compels us to question authority and stop accepting everything we're told at face value. Governments often portray the enemy as evil and their information as propaganda—while excusing similar actions on their own side. But when one narrative is presented as education and the other as deception, isn't that hypocrisy? Does spelling out the truth make me ungrateful to those who laid down their lives for freedom? Am I unpatriotic, a traitor? Hardly. But you are entitled to your opinion. Otherwise, I would be an indoctrinator who does not believe in fairness or equal opportunity.

Is acting with a sense of superiority and exclusivity, an 'us and them' mindset, a sustainable orientation in a world rife with divisive thinking? In the 21st century, we choose a 'have and have-not' paradigm, more recently referred to as a 'winners and losers' hierarchy. With this type of wounded thinking, will warfare not continue to rise from the shadows? Only now, with advanced technological nuclear capabilities, humanity's murderous ways will redouble from intolerance, hate, and prejudice mounting across the globe.

Parasitic mega-corporations pursue global profits, exploit natural habitats, and spread toxic tentacles into poorer countries. They sweep up cheap labour whilst failing to contribute to the growth of their workers and communities. There are two sides to every story, however. I am on the side of the debate that argues the means can never be justified by the ends, and people cannot be used as a means to an end. No longer can we engage in the jealous rejection and exclusivity of others or deficit ideologies that demean humanity. Robbing Peter to pay Paul is not a sustainable and ethical way of living: it is a soul-less approach infused with banal administrative indifference, especially unconscionable in an era when we know better.

The fairy-tale existences of the elite often come at a steep price to common folk. In the case of war, everyday citizens must sacrifice their lives for the greater good, trusting in the wisdom and goodness of their leader. Is it selfish to question giving up our lives for our country when we are not convinced that our leaders have the moral compass to protect our best interests? The English WW1 platoon commander and poet, Wilfred Owen (1893-1918), who died in action a week before the Armistice was signed, writes about the glorification of war and the exploitation of the common people:

> If you could hear, at every jolt, the blood
> Come gargling from the froth-corrupted lungs,
> Obscene as cancer, bitter as the cud
> Of vile, incurable sores on innocent tongues—
> My friend, you would not tell with such high zest
> To children ardent for some desperate glory,
> The old Lie: *Dulce et decorum est Pro patria mori.
> (*It is sweet and fitting to die for one's country).

War is death's feast. Machiavellian political and corporate chiefs, motivated by economic reasons, live by the outmoded patriarchal, hierarchal paradigm that awakened light-beings rail against. Their approach takes a human toll, taking away from the value of the profits that maintain their winner's advantage.

While we are talking negative archetypes, the best-known are the pusillanimous politicians of the West and East. They promise when elected to return us to a golden age where we will have equal access to a thriving free-market economy in a peaceful world. They tell us not to fear for the future of our children. Let there be good leaders who practise what they preach.

I have lived through times in our Australian democracy where cultural, scientific, and intellectual capital and quality of life were genuinely on the ascent. However, our complacency and fear of being an isolated island nation have fostered elite deceit, greed, and exploitation. The more we deny that some of the so-called greats who orchestrate our systems are betraying the most vulnerable, the more complicit we become. Our quality of life might be comfortable, even very satisfying, but why, with so many resources and riches in the world, are so many humans and animals still struggling to survive? Something's up. Saying it has always been this way does not mean it's the right way.

We must be true to ourselves while contributing as citizens of the world. It is time to open our eyes and be wary of groupthink mentality. When we read the news, we must question what is said and why it has been said or skewed in a particular way. As someone who spent many years writing for different magazine titles, editing and publishing niche newspapers, I have some idea of the spin journalists can put on a story to promote the ideologies and products that pay for their print-run and wages.

One of the most potent human ego defences is our propensity to 'deny' what we do not wish to see and believe. Not only do we try to ignore the blind alleys of our personal psyche, but many of us refuse to believe our social construct has a dark side. Few folks can accept that they cherry-pick information to confirm their biases.

To awaken, we must practise looking for elements that might have been left out of the story. We must become more self-aware, rigorously checking our opinions for unconscious biases, and practise critical thinking whilst questioning so-called experts. While it is challenging to know what has been omitted, scanning several sources will help us reach our own conclusions. As ethical citizens, we must maintain a curious and open-minded approach to alternative perspectives.

Where are the equity, equality, and fairness for the work-a-day folk (the new class of poor), being told to sacrifice their personal code—and sometimes their health—whilst those in privileged positions reap super-profits? Isn't there something dark about the top tier of society having dominion over the governance of our globe, maintaining the status quo so that the rich get richer and the poor get poorer?

Many businesses today invest in technology such as robotics and artificial intelligence to replace workers. These executives face an ethical dilemma: Does one trim the fat on the payroll to maximise bonuses? Or bolster human resources to improve efficiencies for customers and safety for teams? Our automated systems mean fewer vacancies to fill, resulting in lower unemployment figures to report. A neat and socially acceptable way to reduce payroll burden.

Alfred Adler (1870-1937), the Austrian psychologist, was one of the first to point out how human beings cover up their internalised sense of inferiority by pursuing the external rewards of superior status, wealth, and power. So, taking liberties with Adler's philosophies, many of the elite are rich on the outside but poor on the inside. Poor on ethics. Despite this, if anyone relies on wealth to feel secure and better about who they are, they are mistaken. None of us, whether rich or poor, can escape life's universal equalisers of sorrow, pain, illness, loss, loneliness, and death.

Whoever we are, we can choose to take control over our inner reality. Why don't we decide now to heal and enrich it?

Most of us are feeling a form of cultural bewilderment in these times of great uncertainty. Call it cognitive dissonance. Far from being subversive or cynical, we can check the plain truths about the society we must fit into that few of us care to see. We know something is up when we see our wealthiest entrepreneurs donating millions to political campaigns. Do we honestly believe their donation is purely goodwill? Few people are quick to give away bucket loads of money for the benefit of someone else without getting anything material in return.

The tension can be unbearable when our private beliefs conflict with our public behaviours. Imagine being a leader who does not believe in going to war at the expense of innocent lives but then concedes to the party's will, declaring war and sending national troops in. A horrible scar is carved into one's conscience. For me, I recognise my cognitive dissonance when I see a manipulative tactic at play but go along with the ruse for no other reason than it suits my need for peace and contentment at the time.

Let's look to the tale of *The Emperor's New Clothes*, where the noble leader's vanities cause him to be duped into appearing naked before the plebiscite. We soon see that we are just as easily deceived when we overlook the naked truth. Wearing the camouflage of rich and exotic apparel to hide a soul poor in honesty and integrity is no success—so the moral goes.

We are prone to self-deception when the truth might reveal something unacceptable, and our ego makes it so. According to the fairy tale, at first, everyone ignores reality. And it is only a young child (not yet concerned about being different and breaking with conventions) who calls out the truth about the sky-clad emperor. If we break away and state the facts, others might call us paranoid, negative, unhelpful. In times of war, we could be called a coward or tried for treason. Often, we are mocked, and that might be all it takes to make us feel sufficiently alienated, so we shut up and crawl back, conflicted, into the cave.

Once the child points the first finger, the other onlookers join in to pillory the emperor, who continues with his charade. Later, we can presume his catalysed consciousness will reflect on his actions more honestly. But deep within him, a little dark voice of denial tries to save him from reality—that he has made an absolute fool of himself and lost his dignity. The dark voice from his id, where his ego drives shame, will unite with his ego, telling him it is not his fault and masterminding his mental escape route. Being proud, he will justify what he did, denying responsibility. Deep down, he knows he is a self-interested weak character, but he will dismiss these messages to avoid pain.

In moments of conscious awareness, he has an opportunity to grasp, name, and process his exposure-shame in his shadow and begin healing. But if he blocks it out again, those who also need to cling to denial and self-justification will stand with him as he manipulates a new reality. The ego always wins—in the short term.

A worse consequence of our pride and denial is that they trigger the patterned lesson of humiliation, recurring until we notice. Ego strategies, driven by fear of the unknown, make us cling to limiting beliefs and behaviours which backfire, preventing us from reaching our full potential and leading to stagnation and frustration.

Our shadow behaviours, like any lie, catch up with us in the end. So, we must do the inner work to develop our cognitive consonance and emotional regulation.

While some stories we hear from the mainstream or underground may not be entirely accurate, there are equally as many authentic accounts worthy of further investigation. It is important we seek out objective evidence and consider multiple perspectives to determine what is right. The big question remains: who is the arbiter of truth?

In some countries, seekers of truth and dissident doubters still have their freedom and lives threatened or taken by ruthless indoctrinators. Often, when these same social orders are overturned, the quality of human existence improves, relieving the suffering of ordinary people worldwide. Currently, over 40 million people are enslaved, not to mention the millions more captured and trafficked as sex slaves. Adults and children. This is an irrefutable truth, and a great tragedy allowed to transpire as the powers-that-be sit on their hands counting their profits. Where are the ethics, empathy, legality, or human kindness in that?

While we contemplate the terrible plight of the world's enslaved, and not to diminish their ordeal, we must remember we are slaves of a different kind. We now live inside an economic bubble engineered by the purveyors of Artificial Intelligence, who press for partisan and personal advantage and grow more affluent as our spending costs inflate for daily staples, making us poorer. AI must be used for the power of good, not just for a privileged few, but for all.

Imagine how the loyal subjects felt when the filthy rich but naked emperor paraded before them: not a pretty sight, but a funny one. This is a serious matter, despite our mirth. Oscar Wilde suggested humour helps lessen the ugliness of the reality we face, making it more bearable without diluting our motivation to change it.

Imagine if the *Self-preoccupied* emperor became aware of his human frailties impacting the society he led. Indeed, he would become a better leader by knowing himself. Only in understanding the Self can we know others and lead them effectively. An awareness of our illusions is the first condition for creating personal and social freedoms. Words alone are not enough. Only leaders whose deeds are congruent with their words can become dynamic agents effecting change that makes our world better.

Our society, past and present, demonstrates that inconvenient information not serving the top one percentile's agenda is driven into the shadows. Is it any wonder that as participating members of the 'collective' that the elite created, we can behave similarly? If we can't beat it, we resign ourselves to joining it.

If trying to catalyse change in the world is too much for us, we can work on ourselves. Freud (1856-1939) reminds us that we can overcome our personal oppressions without society having to change. We can be the change we want to see within the spheres where we feel connected and have influence.

But first, we must know and heal ourselves to radiate truth and light. We must decide on our ethical stance. Some aspire to become blazing beacons shining their torch on companies and directors using unethical means. Others throw their hands in the air, wondering where to start. The soldier and poet, Wilfred Owen, killed by gunfire at the young age of 25, authored his anti-war poems that vividly depicted the sad plight of the doomed youth and horrors of the killing fields to stem the military madness of modern history and plead peace among nations.

Soldiers, on the threshold of death's door, rarely get a moment to sleep, let alone experience the luxury of remembering a dream. Our dreams reveal reality with their universal and personalised symbols, metaphors, and literal expositions.

They can help us prepare, as a form of psychological rehearsal, for what we are about to face. Many of us laugh them off, ignoring their latent messages. But our dreams illuminate our dark corners and point us in the right direction for moving forward. They also convey helpful information to our tribe and beyond. The truth prevails and comes to light somehow, whether we like it or not.

As the light-bringer, Jesus, said, "Recognise what is in your sight, and that which is hidden will become plain to you. For there is nothing hidden which will not become manifest." In plain language: everything hidden will ultimately be seen. We will do well to remember the radiant Christ when trying to discern and heal our hidden shadow patterns.

Modern Psychoanalyst Carl Jung (1875-1961) frames it similarly. He describes how the disowned traits and emotions we try to ignore and push down into our shadow develop a life of their own. According to Jung (1959), these personifications eventually become so enlarged that they create a situation outside of ourselves that we cannot avoid.

Does the shadow only contain negative energy? No, but dark-side energy often causes a negative emotional response from us. Otherwise, we would not have cut it off and driven it down there in the first place. Better to do the inner work now and impede the onward march of our shadow elements before they expand to continuously disrupt our peace and wellbeing.

Jung's mentor, Freud (1966), taught him that our unconscious or hidden mental material, such as denied facts or symbolic information from dreams, can affect our thoughts and behaviours in a self-negating way when not faced. Jung stressed how the efforts of our unconscious to break through to our conscious awareness re-doubles in recurring dreams, and our unconscious will always find a route of entry to our awareness.

Some of us are more receptive to the literal and metaphorical information in our dreams. We look for meaning inside the subjective and objective symbols imprinted in our psyches. Likewise, we search for personal relevance in the narratives and stories of the social collective, such as in the motifs embedded in myths and fairy tales. They draw us in, so they must offer clues for how to live in our reality.

The puss in the thigh-high boots might say: Why look a gift horse in the mouth and turn away from the opportunity?

Symbolism often points us toward a higher state of selfhood and guides the realisation of our dreams in the waking world. Freud (1913) said that symbols from our inner psyche help us perceive and form concepts. According to Jung (1959), what lies inside will lead us to what is waiting for us in the outside reality. Life is forever paradoxical.

When we probe through the layers of self, we find our repressed dark narrative: its dynamic force can break us, but it also holds the transformative power to complete us.

Are we game to reclaim it? Can we even be bothered? If the emperor had recovered his denied good leadership traits, his people would have eagerly followed his lead.

First, we must push past the social groupthink telling us that our original thinking is self-centric or ignoble. Others assert the age of narcissism must end, and ordinary individuals have no right to believe they can make an extraordinary contribution to the world. Some shake their heads, whispering under their breath: Dulce et decorum est Pro patria mori.

Subtle, surreptitious messages of this kind abound in media.

When Reddit and GameStop subscribers coordinated an assault to rifle through the stock exchange and unhinge the Wall Street titans who engineer stock market outcomes, the big boys got the picture. They turned the tables on the little guys soon after, but they realised a united front from a large band of ordinary people could usurp their power. So, united, we must stand.

We will continue to find ways of sticking it to the one-percenters controlling our world in their very uneven way. It seems obscene that a child on one side of the planet dies of thirst while a magnate quaffs a magnum of Foch champagne on the other. They say that the dying child is not their problem. If the rich and powerful have made their money from the little people and won't own the issues they help manifest, who owns the problem?

Who wants to be like them anyway? All the luxury in the world is no match for a soul in rapturous rapport with the Divine, tapping into its full creativity and experiencing the joys of compassion and emotional freedom. Let us never forget that the best things in life are still free.

But we must be rigorous with our self-inventory before we can step into the authentic Self's shoes made for walking along the hero's path. Can we become conscious of the cultural imprints and archetypal patterns that quietly shape our psyche, often in ways unconducive to empathy, equality, equity, and access?

Many of us in the West carry what American scholar Peggy McIntosh (1989) calls 'an invisible knapsack of white privilege'—a bundle of unearned advantages embedded in the structures and systems of our society. Because these benefits are so normalised, we often remain unaware of them; yet they leave unconscious imprints that shape our perceptions and responses to others. Recognising this privilege is the first step toward dismantling inequities and standing in solidarity with those who have been systemically disadvantaged, including Indigenous peoples. As Gloria Steinem once said, "The first problem for all of us, men and women, is not to learn, but to unlearn."

Many Western cultures also grapple with ingrained male privilege and the sense of entitlement it carries. When women respond to this dynamic by expecting financial reward for intimacy, it can reinforce outdated transactional patterns: men may interpret provision as a form of ownership, and the cycle of entitlement and inequality continues. True equality calls for both men and women to step outside these inherited scripts and resist the transactional behaviours that feed patriarchal norms. If we adapt the perspectives of privilege and its hungry bedfellow, entitlement, we inadvertently feed into the patriarchal paradigm and limit our potential as world leaders. We—first, those of us in a position of advantage—must reject the notion of entitlement and strive for equality, independence, and self-sufficiency. By doing so, we can break free from the constraints of 'us and them' or 'us and the exotic other' mindsets and pave the way for a fairer future.

Can most of us ordinary folk accept that we are manipulated to fit the mould of a bit-part player in the social play orchestrated by governments answerable to the elite? We may be content with one of the consequences: being unimportant and free from the heavy burden of responsible leadership. We have anonymity, can fly under the radar, and feel comfortable and satisfied with our freedoms. But history urges us to remember what can happen to complacent folk in a rapidly changing world with self-interested leaders at the helm. Is it really that sweet, dying for one's country, when that country cares little about our welfare and suffering?

Rather than resent the unethical practices tolerated in our liberal democracy that we find so unjust, we can be satisfied in having the freedom of speech to impugn and cast a light on ruthless behaviours.

Everyone's day of reckoning arrives, and we will all pay the price when failing to come from the heart—that place of empathy, love, light, and fairness that seems to transcend all personal, national, cultural, and ethnic boundaries. Can we embrace an extravagant fairness that blesses both giver and receiver?

The wheels of the immutable universal law of cause and effect never stop. Suppose I let go and let God, sending energy or demonstrating empathy toward the unempathetic and trusting that the power of good compensates for all the inequities through time.

There is hope for us if we feel invisible, trapped, stuck, or on the treadmill to nowhere, even when we have lost heart. If we need to know where to start, we can start by working on ourselves as the good sages recommended. By narrowing down on bettering ourselves and improving the areas in which we have influence, we will inevitably contribute as caring world citizens.

But remember this: When we commence our inner work for healing, our defensive ego, spying on our soulful endeavour, will powerfully arise to dispute our passage. We must learn to doubt our doubts. As Saint-Exupéry famously wrote in *The Little Prince* (1943), "We can only see clearly with the heart. What is essential is invisible to our eyes."

Despite the uncomfortable visceral response, we must bravely stay the course until we sense the light shimmering on the skyline. And so, we go with Goethe's (1790) insightful words in mind, "…man who thinks without prejudice can rise above his time and is nowhere and everywhere."

The truth is that man's real life consists of a complex of inexorable opposites—day and night, birth and death, happiness and misery, good and evil. We are not sure that one will prevail against the other, that good will overcome evil, or joy defeat pain. Life is a battleground. It always has been and always will be — and if it were not so, existence would come to an end.

(Carl Jung)

10 SPECTRE OF THE SHADOW

Behind every act of cruelty or coldness, every trauma and suffering, there lingers a shadow in need of compassion. The philosopher and theologian Albert Schweitzer (1875-1965) emphasised the importance of living a life of kindness when he said, "Constant kindness can accomplish much. As the sun makes ice melt, kindness causes misunderstanding, mistrust, and hostility to evaporate."

Our small acts of kindness are a way of us taking responsibility for creating heaven (compassion, peace and harmony) on earth in our daily lives. Our loving and light perspective creates a ripple effect that extends far beyond our individual actions. Schweitzer would tell us to pray for the hard-hearted among us, sending them our empathy and, if the opportunity ever presents itself, encouraging them to take the hero's road to enlightenment with us. Even though they have caused us harm, when we send them compassionate energy, we also release our pain before it locks itself down in our shadow.

Can we reframe our stance by understanding, despite appearances, a hard-hearted person is in psychological trouble? They would not say and do the hurtful things they do if they weren't—loving people don't interact and react with meanness, do they? To borrow from the 19th-century author Robert Louis Stevenson, everyone will, sooner or later, have to sit down to a banquet of consequences. So, there is no need to wish for bad outcomes for others; they are already working (unconsciously) on that for themselves.

The reality remains that it will be more the ones who have suffered at their hands who will take responsibility for changing and strengthening themselves for the betterment of their lives and society. Can we view those driven by hidden agendas as teachers who enter our lives to reveal our shadow elements, inviting us to engage in reframing and inner healing?

The aim is not to label people in ways that reduce them by ignoring the many layers of their multi-dimensional selves. It is a delicate balancing act calling a spade a spade while demonstrating dignity and respect for people whose behaviours cause harm. To judge people seems equivalent to condemning them, which is antithetical to caring about their welfare and wellbeing. Still, as has been said before, we cannot lift our behaviour without recognising where it betrays the better angels of our nature.

Beware scepticism and denial of the truth for they annul the reality and its remedy. But first, we must overcome the spectre of the shadow. As individuals and members of the collective we experience fear and anxiety when we acknowledge the dark aspects of our personalities. It can be difficult to face the shadow, as it challenges our self-image and our understanding of who we are. However, according to Jungian psychology, it is important to integrate the shadow into our conscious awareness in order to become Whole and balanced.

While we may struggle to own the deeply ingrained guilt, jealousy or shame in our make-up, some shortcomings are quicker to access and identify and less complex to regulate. For example, after recognising that our meanness is due to being envious and threatened by the strengths of another, we can work on transmuting this negative emotion back to the light of tolerance and kindness without arduous effort. Americans, potentially the most competitive nationality globally, mitigate their jealousy by seeing the more successful as inspiring role-models or 'expanders' saying, "Good for you!" when someone else wins. Soon, this reaction to others' success becomes second nature and envy is transmuted into charitable feelings. After all, if they can be successful in a fierce environment, so can we. At first, some may barely get the goodness out from between clenched teeth but will eventually get into the swing of things. Try it. It works.

Start by identifying those less complicated behaviours to regulate and then move on to the more complex shadow fragments. Exponents have told me that once they got a grip on their negative thoughts that fed into their negative behaviours, they took the reins and regulated their shadow impulses. By acting temperately, consistently, and universally, soon, you will become a more temperate person—much like the premise of Plato's promise.

Some of the more potent inner shadow dispositions require persistent discipline to capture, regulate and recalibrate. To operate optimally, we need to know both the outer edge of our competence and the upper limit of our personal power. Importantly, we all need to develop a spirit of patience and tolerance in all we do and with whom we interact. If we do not, we will give up before progress is made.

The 'Serenity Prayer' and 'Desiderata' have always been effective sources for helping us develop a philosophical understanding for living life. Desiderata speaks to our graceful surrendering of the things of youth, and the other refers to our need to know the difference between what we can and cannot change (and control). Both guide us to accept the things over which we have no control. These examples reveal the limits of our human efficacy. Still, we must stretch ourselves to the broadest boundaries to touch our peak potential within the world's mysterious and unlimited field. At the same time, we need to balance this drive with realistic expectations—and, paradoxically, learn to doubt our doubts. Many psychologists have observed that inflated expectations of ourselves and the world, especially within the time frames we set, are a common source of unhappiness. So, by releasing super-expectations (without compromising our values or potential), our sense of happiness—or at least satisfaction—can grow.

Myriad sources of guidance remind us to LET GO of our desire to change others so they may fit our mould. Our time is better spent developing our light power, locus of control and sphere of influence. We can transform our shadow behaviour and breathe fire into a new way of life. You know, the one that was always intended for us by the Divine.

As we travel on our experiential journey out of the woods and into the clearing, we build understanding to reframe, recalibrate and regenerate our behaviours and story. Our goals are to develop a personal code for Higher Living, serving our emotional health and leading our soul on its upward spiral progression. In a nutshell, we learn how to:

- Develop a non-judging, guilt-free awareness of our dark side.
- Undertake a rigorous self-inventory, identifying our unique strengths.
- Reflect, explore and learn from past trauma (or lessons) to reframe and reimagine our future and strengths-based story.
- Train and tame our ego-body-mind, eliminating triggers so we react rationally and calmly to challenges.
- Process the messages from our dreams and archetypes, undertaking the inner work to stay connected to the language of our unconscious domain.
- Allow empathy feelings to flow and be felt by forgiving (not justifying) our unconscious transgressions and those of others (to let go in a paced way).

We learn how to own and regulate the underpinning beliefs and subsequent behaviours, triggering our inappropriate emotional reactions. From a calm and composed state of being, we appreciate every moment, moving along the hero's path, ever-ready with an open heart and lit mind. Our refreshed personality develops a new personal reality full of luminosity, vitality, gratitude, love, peace and hope. The inner child, freed from shadow wounding (such as trauma), becomes Whole again, carefree and game to take on and achieve, acting on its own steam to surmount life's peak experiences.

Before we get ahead of ourselves, because the healing journey, taking us to a new personal reality) is not an instant transformation, let us consider whether we have the legs for it.

The steps involve reflecting, naming, reclaiming, reframing, recalibrating, and regenerating an integrated Self—the one you were born to be, before all of life's tests wore you down and you lost heart.

Helping us get to the bottom of our human behaviour are the fairy-tale archetypes. As we hold up their magic mirror, we catch a glimpse of who we really are. Apart from several syndromes of the human condition that are based on behaviours and named according to archetypes (e.g., Cinderella Complex or Peter Pan Syndrome), most of us will find meaningful correspondences with many of the positive and negative aspects revealed across the tropes of *Cinderella, The Little Mermaid,* or *The Ugly Duckling* (and more).

The Vasilisa archetype epitomises our striving for a heroic victory over the worst of odds. No doubt, Vasilisa, the expander, will inspire us to follow her fulsome feminine firepower. She reframes her dark reality while recasting a new and brighter one, and so might we.

Psychoanalyst Bruno Bettelheim (1976), who wrote his seminal work on fairy tales' enchanting powers, cautioned that to achieve self-agency, we must first have the firm and persistent resolve to leave our comfort zones. Which need will be the stronger in us? Will it be our need to be our authentic Self with its fully potentiated power? Or are we too timid to take these steps, avoiding the growing pains and the positive changes that we irrationally fear threaten our survival?

No one is questioning our need and drive to survive. To live long enough to journey through our striving years and into the silvery distance—where the pressure eases and leisurely pastimes take guilt-free precedence—is a hope we hold dear. Yet, we also wish to have the mental and physical health to fully enjoy these newfound freedoms.

Such indulgence was impossible for our harrowed forebears with whom we share our gene pool. They had few idle moments between hunting, gathering, feeding, fighting, fleeing, and reproducing. Almost at the brink of extinction 75,000 years ago, our ancestors evolved behaviours, helping us respond today to the challenges of our survival. But in the main, our brain struggles to discern between life-threatening situations and perceived threats, doubling the trouble in an overly anxious mind. Today, the more fearful (or genuinely threatened) of us might possess inborn wiring with survival as the dominant setting. Scientists speak of our brains having a 'negative bias', keeping us safe and secure but caution how we will come up against a negative inner voice when we want to take a risk to expand ourselves. Then there are those among us predisposed to taking risks, leaping out of comfort zones without looking twice.

Sleeping Beauty and Snow White spent a good while sleeping, subsequently getting out of harm's way. Symbolically speaking, their lives had become stagnant, and as day follows night, something had to end for something new to begin. But if we are out there tackling the things terrorising us, as did the traumatised heroine Vasilisa, our acts of survival leave little room for the luxury of sleeping deep. She was proactive, courageously tackling all that stood in the way of her dreams until she achieved them.

In common, as we journey along life's road, humans are programmed to strive for elevation from any inferior starting block to the next progressive platform and so on to a position of superiority. Remember: Dominion over all life forms with which we share planet earth? Wrongly or rightly (and depending on how one interprets the biblical reference), this is who we humans are and why our species has survived thus far.

As we advance, the altruistic centres in our plastic brain may expand and thus alter our purely survivalist orientation (think less *Self-preoccupied* and more *Transcendentalist*). If those leaders most in need of a strong dose of empathy were to experience such an expansion at a soul level, this might mean less dictatorship, war, genocide and oppression around the globe. We live in the hope that Plato's wise and humane promise of 'Philosophical Kings' will one day rule our world. First, we must start seeing kindness as a strength.

Humans are concerned with commonplace survival wherever they are unless they have already succumbed to commonplace death. On one side of the world, someone is still struggling like once were our predecessors due to violence and war, and the lack of shelter, disease prevention, water, food and nurturance. On the other side, another human is in a similar contest but primarily for their sound mental continuity and physical connectivity with a comfortable existence that has taken ancestral lifetimes to forge. At the centre of a private world, we find the unique identity of the Self who must live precariously between life and death every day: a survival dependent on inherited circumstances, chance, and the consequences of choice.

In a broad-brush sense, we choose to live in love, creativity, and unity or self-imposed fear, restriction, and separation. Why are these opposites, and not love versus hate? Because fear is the basis of hate, as it is for other negative emotions such as anger, blame, shame, guilt, resentment, obsession, frustration, envy, etc. We fear our fear, and so, from our conscious gaze, it hides while our body (tangible and tactile) speaks silently in anxious, shaky tones. Our mind archives our abstract notions of knowledge, while our bodies store and express kinaesthetically our emotional experience. We cannot deny our felt bodily responses: they are visceral and real.

The amygdala is part of our brain hardware, where emotions, memories, dreams, and instinctual responses interact. This nerve tissue elegantly processes the uncertainties of our existence, sending us signals. When facing threats, folk with an overactive or enlarged amygdala (often the same emotional and sensitive souls alluded to earlier) are easily triggered into the nerve-wracking flight or fight (or freeze, fawn and hide) mode when no real and present danger exists.

Then there are others blessed genetically with a well-functioning amygdala (or who have done the inner work to regulate their emotions) who sense the signals and respond proportionately. Perhaps this was the case for another fairy-tale queen who remained calm during a high-risk negotiation with a whacky Wesen (an imp or Fuchs Teufel that's as wild as a fox-devil) named Rumpelstiltskin. Had she not regulated her emotions under pressure, she would not have foiled his claim on her beautiful baby girl. We are beginning to understand that there is a connection between our brain wiring and the need for us to regulate our wild emotions with the reins of reasoning to reach optimal outcomes in our human interactions.

Consider that each of us, mere mortals, must live with the knowledge and primal fear that we will expire at anytime, anywhere. On the positive side, fear will keep us alert to the vagaries of chance, keeping us and ours safe from threat.

Through myriad, malevolent causes, many of our fairy-tale archetypes face the threat of imminent death. Yet. the gentle sharing of these tales by our caregivers helps to prepare us from an early age for our human reality. They show us, at the same time, that most trials can be overcome, and life will go on. Sometimes, life even gets happier and much better.

The archetype, Sleeping Beauty, best proves that despite the dark pall of portended death from her infancy, we can overcome the curse by living a whole and rewarding life. The fairy tale implies an immortal existence with a happy-ever-after ending for princesses but not so for ordinary little girls and boys. Tucked up in our warm beds with our beloved mothers (if we are truly fortunate) softly sharing the tales, we happily believe in the illusion of eternity for long enough to feel safe and secure before drifting off to sleep.

However, as we grow older, we do know now that a happier ever after is within our reach, providing we are prepared to reclaim and regulate our dark aspects of self. We must bring ourselves back to the oneness we need before we can experience a sustained level of happiness.

Existential angst in the form of anxiety strikes at random. An anxious mind and body do not naturally make for a carefree, creative spirit. According to Susan Jeffers, PhD (2005), "Fear creates anger, blame, self-protection, judgment and closed hearts." Jeffers goes on to say that in the case of love, "We relax, take charge, act compassionately, and open our hearts to a state of feeling harmony and warmth." She also implies that we become more resilient when we are open and loving, dealing stoically with whatever 'curveball' comes our way.

And there will be curveballs. Where there is life, there will be strife. Put another way: there is no life without fluctuations oscillating around a mean equilibrium. We long for the peace and harmony of a balanced life, but the only fixity of which we are sure is death. Our constant instability is characteristic of any living organism. Our ability to direct awareness and thought to control or regulate the inherent chaos is our humanness. It is this same consciousness that imagines and creates. For all our great intellectual ponderings, the origin of our consciousness lies inside an infinite supernatural field far beyond the contemporary explanations of science. Therefore, as fanciful as fairy godmothers may seem to a purely rational mind, on an intuitive level, many of us have reason to believe in a universal, omnipotent, miracle-making, supernatural Divine force.

You may have had an experience where you were at your lowest point, and something appeared out of nowhere to give you strength, but just as quickly, it disappeared into the ethers once it succoured you. You marvel and wonder what on earth it was. A miracle-maker will often appear spiritually, symbolically or in material form to remind the exiled one of their inner strengths. In that glorious moment of truth, we know a transcendental potency in life exists, (that the rigidly practical and sceptical amongst us in the natural realm might deny).

It is a creative vigour at work in the person. Something once unseen becomes a fleeting flash of consciousness in mind. Like a dream floating in and out of the light of reason, it often escapes before being understood. But once grabbed by the tail, its hidden messages elucidate the mystifications of our reality as nothing else can.

As anyone who has tried to grasp an unconscious gem that has shone briefly in the corner of the mind will tell you: its urge to become hidden again is as powerful as our drive to catch and fix our mindsight upon it. Both dreams and shadow stories, emanating from the unconscious, share this elusive quality.

We are an original tapestry: a tangle of beliefs, values, philosophies, attitudes, impressions, perceptions, biases, prejudices, assumptions, appearances, real experiences, and unreal myths. Some are hewn from nature and the essence of nurture inside the 'I' self; others are borrowed and introjected from kin, kith, or assimilated from the universal field.

We can only fully capture and understand the 'I' self in those unpredictable moments of lucid discovery when we make deep personal contact with the matrix. As a unique being in and of ourselves, we can seem different from our 'I' who meets and intermingles with another being. Nobel laureate G.G. Marquez puts it down to us having three lives: the public, private, and secret. Psychologists add the blind self (that others see but remains unknown to us).

French philosopher Sartre (1905-1980) says we cannot know who we are except through the intermediary of another person. Martin Buber (1878-1965) with his 'I-Thou' proposition sees two ways of relating to the world: 'I-It' and 'I-Thou'. The former stance objectifies others, seeing them as a means to ends while the latter acknowledges the inherent value of other beings, leading to empathy, dialogue, and mutual respect. Here lies the potential to transform our understanding of ourselves and the world. Naturally, we place ourselves in the centre of our spheres of influence as the 'I' but not for the purpose of exploiting and manipulating others to serve us. The 'I', continues to reside inside the relationship, family, community, nation, and universe, acting like a ripple-ring flowing out. But we approach other beings with respect and empathy, acknowledging their inherent worth as manifestations of the Divine—hence, putting us all on equal footing which potentially leads to equal partnership, collaboration and co-creation. However, as we soul-grow and expand, we are still intact but see ourselves becoming increasingly insignificant in the grand scheme of things. The irony is not lost on the sage who contends the more we know, the less we think we know.

The classical Greek Hippocrates, father of the 'physician, heal thyself' ethos, considered man's condition inseparable from his relationship with the environment. This juxta-positioning of the 'person with place' will be a source of contemplation for most of us. We may even wonder how we have survived, given some of our early environments, and come this far. Unconsciously, we feel insecure in any climate where our vulnerabilities are exposed. We want to feel expanded (not reduced) by our experiences, so we fear the revelation of any shortcomings already sent to hiding. We deny, disguise, or bury our primal fears of being exposed, damaged, or exterminated. Fears concerning love, unforgiveness, loss, trauma, immobilisation, separation, rejection, abandonment, suspicion, guilt, shame, and so on leave a bitter taste in our organism.

If we push out of view the psychic elements that make us feel uncomfortable, we do not have to face up to them, let alone show them to others (but others DO see us). We all know how awful our minds and bodies feel when we experience fear and self-doubt.

No wonder we try to avoid or run away from what feels wrong.

Others' judgments can leave us feeling rejected and separated from the acceptable. When judging that we are not enough, we invariably seek to bolt onto ourselves someone or something else that makes us feel worthy of membership in the tribe and feel safe again. Addictions are toxic add-ons to our original Self that often start when our sense of belonging, and self-esteem have done a runner and allowed insecurity to fester. Addicts are often blind to the harm they are causing themselves and others. They act in angry, selfish, indulgent, obsessive and detached ways that make them check-out from the responsibilities and relationships of their reality. According to therapists in the field, addiction invariably indicates that the person suffers from unresolved past trauma and abuse. However, when asked directly, the client might initially fly into a rage of denial.

We quickly judge drug addicts as weaklings or criminals who cannot face the real world by taking substances to escape. But before being hasty judging self-medicators, many of us must face that we also avoid the harsh reality of truth. Our infinitude is an irrefutable truth we fear the most.

The truth is that when we judge others, we have already judged ourselves unworthy. We may not know it because the judgment is lurking in our shadow. By projecting judgment onto others, we take a breather from carrying its psychic weight. However, relying on this approach to address our inner struggles isn't sustainable for achieving lasting emotional relief and freedom. Any sense of peace gained is merely fleeting.

When we feel genuinely better about ourselves, we have higher doses of self-esteem, empowering us with derring-do to create, innovate and make loving contact with others. Yet, given a double dose, this self-tonic can soon turn toxic, manifesting as arrogance, envy and selfishness, as seen in Snow White's wicked stepmother. Aristotle tells us that self-compassion is vital and a product of us perceiving we are good because of our good works in the world.

Remember to be virtuous, one must act virtuously. Many of us can only really love ourselves unconditionally once we have addressed the shadow parts of self that make us seem too flawed to love. We can tell ourselves that we are good and lovable, but there will always come a time when we are triggered and fall back into feeling inadequate and unlovable. These are the reasons that make our shadow reclamation work so important.

Narcissists may display too much self-love but many of them cannot fill the void of not feeling loved sufficiently by their caregivers in childhood. Everything is about them *(Self-preoccupied)* because not enough was about them when they were developing. Narcissists (and borderline personalities), sociopaths, and psychopaths are somewhat alike. Some behave in ways that tell others they are the centre of the universe, the stars of the show, and if you want to be in their orbit, you better serve their needs and sacrifice your own: be the satellite to their planet. Their brand, the 'I-It' kind, is not the type of self-love alluded to by the great philosophers through the ages. Loving oneself is a natural by-product of becoming integrated, melding shadow with light into oneness. One is congruent when interacting with others. The Self is no longer conflicted between being envious or kind, angry or tolerant, shameful or forgiving. Hence, it feels possible to love the Wholesome Self unconditionally.

Therefore, we need to question any feelings of elevated self-worth derived from the putting down of someone else. This behaviour is poison to the integrity of the authentic Self and its relationships. Still, we cannot shy away from making observations of human behaviour and well-measured assessments, thinking critically, and discerning who and which of their behaviours have implications on the quality of our life. But if we are honest, we will see that what most inflames us about another's actions, we are capable of or at least have been capable of doing ourselves. We may not have committed the heinous crime they have, but there will be some acts we have done that we still consider atrocious, a skeleton in our closet, as it were, that we have not yet made peace with within our psyche. To heal our shadow, we must connect the dots and put a name to our problem-story.

We can use another person's peccadillos as indicators of what potentially lies beneath in our shadow. As the wise Confucius said, "When we see men of a contrary character, we should turn inwards and examine ourselves."

We can always decide whether we will be vain or humble human beings. Why is humility good for us and society?

Humble folk are grateful folk who want to pay their blessings forward by serving and helping others. Their helping makes them feel genuinely good about themselves, and healthy self-esteem endows resilience, reducing anxiety and stress. The humble among us know much more than they think they know, motivating them to keep learning and sharing what they know. So, these so-called 'no ones' from nowhere are really something. Jane Goodall (1934-2025), the renowned British primatologist and anthropologist, comes to mind. Goodall lived up to her name as the humble hero whose influential voice for good still inspires millions globally to conserve, care for and protect animals in their habitats.

All of the virtues stem from a place of humility. A humble 'no one from nowhere' rises above limitations to be everywhere and ready for everything. Goethe (1791) might deem them the universal person with nothing left to prove.

Still, too many people, neither humble nor narcissistic, feel inadequate and struggle with accepting themselves and standing in their power. They have furloughed aspects of their strengths. Upon reclamation, psychic fragments (like fear and self-loathing) can be transformed into their luminous counterparts of courage and self-acceptance. After the inner work is complete, the person will begin to feel and live positively. They return to a state of self-compassion experienced before the wounded ego wrought pain and suffering upon them. Put another way: their over-shadowed inner child will be healed to live a revivified life again. Everything they need waits on the other side of fear.

We always have a choice, even by not making one. Do we own up to the fears and insecurities (that have us in their thrall), or do we project them, recasting them onto others? Do we respect someone self-righteous who hides like a cowering child from their imperfections, or instead a humble grown-up who is secure in admitting their foibles, saying their self-improvements are under construction? Better to be a diamond with a flaw than a pebble without one, according to Confucius.

Kierkegaard, the Danish philosopher and existentialist (1813-1855), warned of the pain that comes from abandoning our authentic, flawed selves in favour of a sanitised persona. According to him, the deepest form of despair is choosing to be someone other than ourselves. This may explain the dull ache in our hearts as we wonder if there is more to life than what we are currently experiencing. We might have chosen to remain stuck in our comfort zone, which, as Bettelheim (1976) warned, is not the way to go as it makes our ordinary world increasingly more uncomfortable over time.

Either way, we can pretend to be someone we are not or be who we are. The power of choice is empowering, and we need no one to grant permission for us to make this choice. As Glasser (1998) reminds us, we only control one person's thoughts and behaviours: our own.

We are free to choose to act in a certain way, and we take full responsibility for so doing (unless we are not free with limited access to human rights). As stated before, we all act according to five hierarchical, genetically encoded categories of needs (Maslow, 1908-1970) – 1. survival; 2. security and safety; 3. belonging, (love and acceptance); 4. self-esteem (personal power, competency, and achievement); and sitting right at the apex is—5. self-actualisation (freedom, independence, autonomy, and a sense of fun even when we are learning new things). Incidentally, according to Jungian analyst R.A. Johnson (1989), the archetype of the number five signifies our root essence, our quintessential (or soul) Self.

All our behaviour, positive or negative, is an attempt to satisfy any of these needs at any given time. But before we can feel safe, we have had to survive and so forth, moving up the hierarchical ranks of Maslow's (1943) model. Sometimes we are conscious of the behaviour we are choosing. Other times, we unconsciously act to try and meet a need. For example, sometimes, we will wear a mask to disguise parts of us we perceive as liabilities when trying to belong to a group. In this case, we may wear expensive clothing, speak with affectation, and talk up our achievements to imply we have the higher status required for membership. All the while, our authentic Self stays out of mindsight. Still, our right to choose prevails. Groucho Marx's famous quip, "I don't want to belong to any club that wants me as a member" implies that the most alluring if not illusory sense of achievement is always slightly above our station. We have all heard of people loving only the one they cannot have or who gets away including The Little Mermaid archetype.

Have you ever felt a sense of nervous anticipation while standing in line outside a trendy club waiting to see if the manager deems you worthy to enter? A lack of supply creates demand.

Exclusion creates an illusion of superiority, and most marketing managers milk the concept when creating their campaigns. But such behaviour was a lesson in the making for the archetype The Fisherman's Wife, whose greedy grasping to make it to the Godhead only took her full circle, right back to the bottom rung. If someone excludes you, they must need to feel superior. Ask what is driving that need and empathise with the poor mistaken soul. Aronson (2012) expounds on the virtues of social inclusion, describing it as a way to create an atmosphere of compassion and respect, enhancing our motivation and achievement.

Suppose we see the more successful living the dream we aspire to live as the image of our imminent expansion? When we see the symbiotic relationship, there is no need for an 'us and them' mindset. They provide the necessary benchmark that motivates us to action. An archetype devoid of humility, the Fisherman's Wife had seen and resented the riches belonging to her neighbours and demanded she received the same and then some.

Being aspirational is good, but ambition on steroids and exploiting others as the means to meet your ends are not.

There are times when our need to feel significant overwhelms our conscience. We may deprive someone else of satisfying their needs, such as in the case of putting others down to feel elevated, or denying them equity and access, as the shadow riven stepsisters of Cinderella did. But wherever someone is brimming with eagerness, another will be ready with their demands to take advantage. Being sacrificially good or mean all the time are not choices that will ultimately make us feel happy, healthy, and in control of our own life — they squeeze the libido, the life-force, out of the psyche. We burn out, suffering from emotional exhaustion. When we choose effective, responsible behaviours, we will, in practice, learn to balance things out and self-regulate. As tricky as it might seem, our thoughts and actions become congruent, leading to outcomes that satisfy our needs and evolve us.

But why bother tuning our psyches towards emotional freedom and joy when so many face real threats to their survival?

Many of the world's populations struggle to achieve adequate shelter, warmth, food, water, oxygen, safety, and security and face an increased risk of violation and poor health. Some face terrorism, slavery, and death. In these conditions, many will still reproduce, but their offspring will invariably suffer or die. Their levels of choice in meeting their needs are indeed limited. Our existence sits in striking contrast to people born in countries like South Sudan, Somalia, Yemen or Western Mozambique, for example. We often hear the phrase 'first world problems' to describe how our daily stresses are insignificant in light of the plight of our war-torn or impoverished neighbours. Interestingly, our psychological stresses can trigger the hyperarousal response to the same unhealthy levels as those living under real physical threats to their survival. We cannot underestimate how emotional pain triggers survivalist modes that throw out our equilibrium. We have an innate drive to return to our resting or homeostatic state no matter what goes on around us externally. We can choose to hasten this natural process with a positive effect rather than feed into the fear and anxiety keeping us skirting around and delaying the fulfilment of ourselves and our altruistic duty to humanity.

One of our states of being that promotes feelings of balance and fulfilment is loving and receiving love in return. As human beings, we need to belong. First, we must be accepted unconditionally—just as we are. The trouble is: When someone does not feel good in our company because of our behaviours or their different beliefs and values, they tend to snub us. This highlights why we need to be reassured from conception by parents and significant others and throughout our lifetime, time and time again, that we are loved—not because of our gifts, what we achieve, and the value we bring to them, but just for being who we are. Free of the effects of judgment, criticism, labels, and punishment for being 'unique', we can rise to our next stage of evolution and shine with self-esteem, personal power and competency. But we need to feel secure in who we are, quirks (our works-in-progress) and all.

Parents, teachers and indeed all caregivers and influencers of children can take a leaf out of apostle Paul's book (1 Corinthians 14:3). The Corinthians learned how prophecy is hearing God speak and that the words heard intend to edify, exhort and comfort someone. Parents' words and actions with their children are self-fulfilling prophecies. Showing delight in having them near and kind words of encouragement edify the strengths of their young and everyone else with whom they interact. We of spirit occupying human roles are wired for goodness, and as Socrates said, "All souls are immortal, but the souls of the righteous are both immortal and divine."

Conversely, cruel words and actions lack goodness. Still, some of our most traumatised are also awakened and courageous, going on to do good deeds because of—not despite—the pain and suffering they have endured. Fairy tales such as *Beauty and the Beast* inspire a positive turnaround, leading to emotional freedom and the happiness that follows.

Freedom means experiencing a carefree joyousness, but its flipside implies we are solely responsible for ourselves. Accountable for our decision-making, choices, and consequences. A self-efficacious person does not look around for someone else's support; their first response is to try and conquer the challenges they face on their own steam. A person who has become Whole and free does not falter before the summit, worrying about what someone else is saying or doing or looking for a leg up. Such external matters are trivial compared to the goals they have set for themselves to reach a new personal best.

We cannot stop someone from cruelly criticising how we look, think, sound, or behave. They see our different position as a threat to their existence. Aristotle contended that a clever mind could entertain a different point of view without accepting it. Still, we can only control how we respond to our opponents' put-downs. Do I let their judgment affect me, or can I recognise that they want to feel elevated in themselves by putting me down? How poorly must they feel inside? One with healthy self-esteem can be satisfied with this thought philosophy, knowing the other person has a right to their choice of behaviour, misguided as it might seem. Institutions have laws and regulations to protect us from others' machinations. When they fail, we can seek recourse. In the meantime, we must take solace in knowing that the person bullying us is hiding their overwhelming feelings of fear and weakness. Why else would their behaviours be so exaggerated and out of whack? A balanced person does not have to act hurtfully to be seen and heard. The more bravado and strong-armed power they exert on the surface, the weaker they must believe themselves to be on the inside.

We need to feel accepted and have a sense of belonging, but we must appreciate that we cannot 'belong' to every tribe we encounter, nor would we want to. We will forge a sense of strength and personal power by being compassionate to the other person in testing circumstances, achieving what we set out to achieve, acting with integrity and being respectful and positive in our outlook.

Often when confronted by others' rejection, we experience hurt or angry emotions. These emotions cloud our ability to find and show empathy towards those who set out to harm us or are ignorant of the harm they cause. Once again, we can choose compassion — granted, a place at high reach when we are reeling from insult, discrimination, ostracisation, or emotional or physical abuse. We can assume that the archetype The Ugly Duckling (aka the young Hans Christian Andersen) took this high road. Despite feeling excluded, he never stopped focusing on finding a place to be himself and fit in rather than plotting a retaliation. He did not stop until he got there.

When we are confronted with feelings of powerlessness and our need for autonomy is not met, we may well be experiencing the force of our ego. Our ego tells us in its roundabout way that the power and recognition we need are ours when we control our environment. This also implies having a sense of superiority over others sharing the same space. But when we are in the grips of our ego, we are easily fooled. Instead, we can choose to be humble and sage. Taking a deep breath, we initiate a rethink, reframing our way of seeing the situation and appreciating we do have the choice of staying grounded and humble in our personal power. Then, we demonstrate integrity and composure in the face of challenges. According to McFadden (1998), we fulfil our need for control by taking charge of ourselves (our emotional wildness) rather than having power over others. We are self-regulating beings, achieving our optimal power by choosing to believe, think, and act in ways that we know are good and feel to be the right thing to do. Beyond just considering the consequences of our actions, we are inclined to do the right thing. Kant said that we know it to be the good and right thing to do because, put in the same circumstances again, we would choose to repeat it consistently and universally. Utilitarian principles of moral philosophy encourage us to make choices and act in the way that promotes the greatest amount of happiness for the greatest number of people—in other words, acting in ways that afford the greatest utility.

The rub for spiritual beings having a physical existence in the illusory earth realm is that we need to have cognitive consonance—a state of being where our awareness and feelings are aligned and in harmony with the actions we deploy. Otherwise, we soon become conflicted and confused. We already struggle with how society prioritises the things that don't matter over those meaningful things that do. Next, we are confronted by how humans are not being their authentic selves and say and do things at odds with their souls' intent. While it sounds simple enough to follow through on what our heart of hearts is telling us to do, every day, everywhere, millions of people act in ways that betray their better judgment and soul-knowing. Discordant behaviour leads to psychological distress and shadow expansion. On the other hand, a Whole Self functions with all the components of the psyche working in unison and alignment with behaviours—with cognitive consonance. When including the perspective of our soul, according to Neale Donald Walsch (2009), we find the pathway to eternal peace.

When faced with change, we can become highly anxious in fearing the threat of making wrong choices that bring negative consequences. It can be agonising to make a choice when it requires a change of mind and the grief of giving up deeply be-friended beliefs. Pain is felt in our physical body as it reacts to our psychic purge. When we contact our shadow fragments and begin their reclamation, we will experience tangible effects, psychosomatic symptoms, in our 'pain or shadow body'. Some clients experience a temporary pounding in their heads, stomach upsets, a rise in temperature, shivers or night sweats. As the psyche lets go, so the body follows. The tightly coiled elements of our anatomy begin to move, make space, and release chemicals. Mentally, for a time, we may feel as if we are in a state of suspended animation, uncertain about what lies in wait, evoking fears —the not knowing, the not acting. The fairy tale *The Frog Prince* leaps to mind: the princess had to sublimate her supercilious airs by submitting to the will of the frog. How else could a royal humble herself and kneel to a bottom feeder? Her state of cognitive dissonance, her beliefs in direct conflict with her behaviours, would have caused no end of mental anguish and physical stress. In the moment, she chose to go against her inclinations and kissed the slimy frog.

No matter what we choose, there will always be consequences: naturally or socially enforced. Even with great power, we will not become immune to life's random effects, fluctuations, or natural ups and downs. No matter how far we evolve, at some point in time, a test will arise where we could easily mishandle ourselves and land back on our heels. The brave semi-mythic king archetype Gilgamesh suffered a humiliating loss. Still, it took a second defeat on his Hero's Journey before he was ready to return to the ancient Mesopotamian city of Uruk as a reformed man and better leader: Gilgamesh 2.0.

Ignoring consequences when weighing up alternative actions will result in a likely deprivation of freedoms in some way if the worst happens. Fun is often the first pleasure sacrificed. According to Glasser (1925-2013), people of all ages desire fun in their lives. There is a connection between learning and this biological need (so, we learn from pain and pleasure). As we have already discussed, and as contended by Glasser, our functional requirements, similar to Maslow's, are survival, love, belonging, power, freedom, and fun. A sense of enjoyment and satisfaction best describe Glasser's (1998) application of the word 'fun'.

Humans learn from the satisfying, if not enjoyable, consequences of their actions as much as they do from any adverse outcomes. Interestingly, we tend to remember the impact of unpleasant effects twice as much as the positive ones because of our brain's negativity bias, keeping us vigilant to harmful threats. Therefore, when dealing with the negative results of poor choices, we experience more powerful feelings. The good news is that these powerful feelings can be reframed and channelled into new strengths-based stories with positive ways of thinking and acting.

Satisfying experiences grow our confidence. Confidence leads to self-empowerment, which operates in a feedback loop with our sense of worthiness, value, and self-esteem. Activated self-esteem is like poetry in motion. In this contented state of being, we tap into our creative wellspring, a major fuel source for achieving self-actualisation. It figures. In this state, we are confident that our authentic Self is enough. In fact, it is fine and good. When feelings of enhanced self-esteem kick in, we may believe that our creativity is 'on fire'. Our fire is our spirit. Our human spirit is our creative force, and our creations are dynamic when coming from within a place of belonging in our tribe. We have a choice: follow our wild passion, fire, or plod along, denying our very essence.

Our fairy-tale heroine Vasilisa, with her little-big doll nestled against her breast, faced daunting challenges in her environment. Like many fairy-tale heroines before her, she was the quintessential fall guy, bearing the brunt for others. But after surviving her life-threatening ordeal, she emerged as a tour de force, carrying the torch to a better future. Traumatised by the dark figures in her life, she literally worked her way out of the pain. Dr Estes (1992) explains how she did it: *The doors to the world of the wild Self are few but precious. If you have a deep scar, that is a door.*

In contrast, due to her constant deception, the hapless mother in *Our Lady's Child* faced a baptism by fire. Both oral tales convey that when we have the will to do the right thing, our life force is aflame with the Spirit of the universe. The alternative position warns that we may extinguish our mojo and weaken the bonds with those we love through our unenlightened acts of repudiation. When faced with opportunities to accept the truth and grow, what will we choose?

We soon learn through lived experience that we need each other to grow. When we live a *Self-preoccupied* life in the 'ivory tower' we are not allowing ourselves to interact with others who might grow us through feelings of pleasure and pain. We become impervious, separated, shut off but often, at the same time, content or complacent—safe but becoming stagnant. Rapunzel, the fairy-tale archetype, the princess in the tower, only began to 'live' when cast adrift in the woods, pregnant and alone. Then, having become free, she created a new song-filled life to become discoverable a second time by her prince.

As the bitter witch in the *Rapunzel* tale reveals, emotional freedom eludes us when we seek perfection in a flawed world. Along the way, as we progress, we may begin to see that we exist only because of our imperfections. Voltaire (1694-1778), the French author-philosopher, wisely quipped that perfection is the enemy of the good. Perfection is an end in itself with no room for improvement. It is clear to us all that each of us is not perfect. None of us on earth is ideal physically, psychically, or spiritually. When we refer to another folktale of yore with the artful miller's cat archetype Puss, we see that he is wise to this principle. The crafty cat (an *Individualist*) encourages an imperfect young man of poor status to raise his expectations for himself. Despite his lowly born tags, Puss urges him to act as if he is successful already, and he, duly motivated, makes it to the top.

In other words, expect the best (not perfection). Others may tip us off but be aware that the responsibility and effort for making the necessary improvements to our flaws and progress on the hero's road rests with us and us alone. We must take charge, bringing light, order and calm to our messy individual and collective realities.

No matter the headwinds we face, there is little dispute that we will fare better with a well-developed emotional intelligence. With self-awareness, self-regulation, internal motivation, empathy, and social skills, we become well-resourced to confidently venture forth, going beyond ourselves to live our best lives, and doing good in the world with the Divine force at our backs.

In *Star Wars* movies, mythical characters exchange the goodwill phrase, 'May the FORCE be with you' when they are about to confront a colossal challenge. Staring down the spectre of the shadow is no mean feat. So, may the force be with you, and every hero on their brave new journey of discovery and storytelling.

Looking down from the highest of high vantage points in the heavens is heard a whisper: Get cracking, heal thy shadow with thy light: this is your Hero's Journey.

No one can become conscious of the shadow without considerable moral effort.
(Carl Jung)

11 FREE ME FROM MY DARK SIDE

Have you ever known someone defined by a single personality trait? Family and friends often assign fitting nicknames. My explosively volatile client, Tony, earned the moniker 'Stormy'—and as the proverb goes: 'names and nature often agree'.

Who wants to be known primarily for one part of themselves, especially a negative trait? It reduces the person. Think of Snow White's dwarfs: Dopey, Sleepy, Grumpy. Such names—supposed terms of endearment—are pejorative, reductive, and reinforce negative behaviours.

Consider someone hot-headed who flies off the handle when challenged. We either tiptoe around them or get wound up ourselves, letting fiery words rip, wishing later we'd responded calmly instead of reacting. Stormy let his emotions seize him rather than regulating his explosive emotional energy. His story offers insight into the need for psychic integration.

Case-study—Stormy (aka the Mad Max archetype)

Stormy's spontaneous emotional eruptions resulted from repressing parts of himself he couldn't accept, reacting to the slightest provocation. He harboured unpleasant emotional memories from different life episodes that felt as overpowering as his angry outbursts.

This shadow part—negative and disowned—overshadowed his positive, light qualities. Someone once told Stormy that his anger dominated and controlled him, making him even angrier. His anger ruled him; he could no longer rule himself. To understand him better, let's review his story of the past:

Stormy was a grown man who hadn't learned to regulate his emotional impulses and possessed no motivation to change. His only outlet was hooning down the highway in his hotted-up Holden or getting into biffs when road rage got the better of him around the local shopping precinct.

His ex-wife once told him he'd become mentally unwell. Stormy rejected the notion of being angry and bitter, taking offence whenever others affected by his mood swings pointed out his frailties. Rather than accept he'd instigated many fights with his wife and that his aggressive rants caused her to leave, he chose to live in an uncomfortable state of cognitive dissonance.

Stormy suffered from denial of his dark behaviours, contributing to the expansion of his negativity and emotional volatility. He wore the label like a badge, reinforcing his wild disposition. But being called 'Stormy' signalled he was expected to behave that way, so he fulfilled his promise. Poet Ralph Waldo Emerson's observation applies: *What you do speaks so loudly that I cannot hear what you say.* In plain sight of everyone else, his shadow remained hidden from him.

Life becomes nuanced with typical interactions: work, falling in love, raising children, losing loved ones, serious illnesses, accidents, reverses of fortune. These are likely events in anybody's existence.

Everyday events turn unnecessarily detrimental when a person fails to resolve the underlying causes of their explosive emotional reactions. How can such a person be taken seriously in domestic situations requiring a calm, composed response, let alone during an emergency?

Psychoanalyst Dreikurs (1968) contended that the biological need to be loved and belong could lead to acting out. Emotional situations give rise to mistaken ideas about which behaviours might satisfy our needs and goals. A bully exerting power or taking revenge harbours faulty beliefs—perhaps that victims will show them respect. But fear is not respect. We may act out inappropriately, as Stormy does, to bring a group's attention back to us. His actions are self-serving and fit the *Self-preoccupied* typology.

Stormy might even attempt to prove his inadequacy by evoking sympathy from onlookers who see him as the poor, misunderstood bad boy who knows not what he does. But none of these misguided attempts to receive love and feel we belong succeed. We may even become outcasts—our greatest collective fear—for behaving in ways that don't respect social rules and personal boundaries.

Here, my client Sussane, whose behaviours were reflected in Goldilocks, also comes to mind.

We need to recognise the drivers of our dysfunctions before transforming them into functional behaviours. It requires inner work to locate what's at the source of our faulty functioning. Once identified, we can begin making choices: reauthoring our problem-story by focusing on our strengths, developing emotional intelligence, and self-regulating to act in ways that serve our best interests and the common good.

Stormy didn't regulate his emotions, behaving like a young child with an undeveloped ego. His wife told him he had to choose: Would he admit that his rage ruined their quality of life and start his healing journey? Or would he ignore all the signals and remain in arrested development? She warned they might need to separate.

The mythical character Peter Pan is conjured when we think of an adult who never wants to grow up. However, Peter Pan also exemplifies an inordinate state of freedom that doesn't come naturally to real people like Stormy. He moved back in with mum.

The clan may be fond of him, even enabling some of his unrestrained outbursts. But are they only repressing their own frustration, stress, anxiety, hurt, and mounting anger when he has a meltdown? Sooner or later, the truth will out. Most of them quietly think Stormy had best mature soon, or they'll have to ask him to leave. Tension builds between family members. The frustrations will only grow, and then one day, the proverbial will hit the fan. Stormy will stomp out with threats of never returning. A rift occurs that may take years—a lifetime—to mend.

His is undoubtedly a clear case illustrating how we must become aware of ourselves, our errant behaviours, and our impacts on others. There is no time to waste. We must work on freeing ourselves from the bondage of our repressed and denied traits—our dark side.

Stormy had become a legend in his family for being hot-headed. Part of him enjoyed standing out, having a cheeky identity all his own. He drove his doubts downward, distorting the truth. His self-talk reassured him that he was another Mad Max, the heroic 'bogan' archetype whose fury was justified.

Stormy saw himself as the family's central hero who livens up the joint; besides, he might be invisible if he didn't stand out. As he thought, he acted and so played out his destiny—some destiny: one of ranting, raving, and throwing temper tantrums.

Tony is 29 years old, still living at home, in and out of courier work, drinking alcohol every night trying to get over the fact that his latest girlfriend ran off with his baby and best mate. He mostly misses his best mate. He lives from week to week, splurging his earnings on his beloved Holden, grog, and his mum (in that order). He bought her a smart TV and laptop last year. She needs a new washing machine next. Damn the money. He feels better about himself when he's doing deals. He feels better still when he sees how his mother softens when he gifts her. And then there's the fact that he feels a tad guilty about her still doing his washing. Damn it. His mum loves keeping busy. He brushes his guilt aside.

Stormy can rationalise just about anything. For instance, his road rage isn't his fault. 'Those dickheads are out to get me.' Even when his ex-wife cried out of desperation, 'Why can't you see that you create these dramas?'— Stormy saw her as just another pain. Since she'd left, there was nobody to get in his way. He could do as he pleased, right? But wait. There are other people living at home. A brother, a sister, mum and stepdad, and his grandma living in the granny flat. He thinks (and he's sick of thinking) that at least they know when to shut up most of the time. He doesn't know he's exhausting. Still, they leave him to his own devices, and that's the way he likes it.

Stormy found the tribe's enabling of his wild outbursts comforting. He never thought he'd have to leave. That is until mum and stepdad recently warned him not to take them for granted or he might end up in real trouble. Real trouble meant living alone. How could they do this to him? One night, when they were all at a family dinner, he went off. That was it. They had had a gutful. How does the saying go? You can lead a horse to water, but you can't make it drink. Or you can talk until you are blue in the face, but if the other person isn't willing to listen, what can you do?

Not long after the dinner, at a cousin's wedding, Stormy completely lost it. The family was mortified. Enough was enough. They'd had it with Stormy. He had to go. The police were called. They took him down to the station and held him overnight to calm down. The following day, he had to front the magistrate. Maybe if Stormy hit rock bottom, he might experience his version of an awakening.

He'd seen something similar happen to another mate, Ross, a few years back. Tony thought Ross had looked pathetic when he cried, asking everyone for their forgiveness. Ross told Tony recently that he'd kept it together for over a year now and was feeling better than he had in years.

Eventually, circumstances forced Stormy to live with his grandmother, the only person who would have him. The family knew his manipulative nature but hoped that getting arrested, held in a cell overnight, and losing the comforts of the family home might be enough to shake him into submission. His granny did her best to manage his outbursts by making it clear he could not treat her the way he'd treated everyone else, or she'd call the police herself.

Stormy smartened himself up. He knew that his nan wasn't to be toyed with. Slowly, he started to listen to her. She told him about how her husband (his grandfather) came back from the war and was never the same again. She said it wasn't easy living with a man who'd lost his sense of purpose and battled demons only he could see or hear. But she loved him. She said Tony's mum had had it tough growing up. And so, they all did their best to survive and get by. Granny told Stormy she understood that sometimes rage was the only way to express feelings too painful to name.

Tony started to soften. He gradually stopped drinking. He got more stable work. And he got into Men's Shed. There he met a bunch of good blokes who didn't judge him. For the first time in his life, he felt he'd found his tribe. The men at the shed were his mates. They talked about things that really mattered. They built things together, practical things.

One day, one of the men told him there was this '*Mythimo* quest' that had helped him sort out his emotional baggage. Intrigued, Tony said he'd give it a go. After all, he'd started to notice that when he was calmer, life seemed more manageable. Perhaps it was time to work on the parts of himself he'd been denying all along.

The Mythimo Quest: Stormy's Transformation

Through the *Mythimo* quest, Tony began to see his patterns clearly. He recognised the Mad Max archetype in himself—the justified fury, the isolation, the need to be the hero of his own story. But he also saw how this archetype had trapped him in a cycle of destruction rather than genuine heroism.

He learned to name his emotions rather than letting them explode. He practised self-regulation. He began to understand that his anger was often masking deeper fears: fear of inadequacy, fear of abandonment, fear of not mattering. Through the quest's reflective exercises, he started to reframe his problem-story.

Tony began to integrate his shadow. He acknowledged the aggressive, reactive parts of himself without letting them rule him. He found healthier outlets for his energy. He learned that true strength wasn't about dominating others or proving his toughness—it was about mastering himself.

The transformation wasn't instant. There were setbacks. But each time he slipped, he had tools to help him recover. He learned to pause and breathe and ground himself before reacting. He developed empathy by considering how his actions affected others. He started to rebuild bridges with his family, one cautious conversation at a time.

This client is now relying on their ethos, rationale, and strengths to forge a future. With self-agency, they become a functioning member of society who is potentially sexually and economically potent, responsible, and poised to reproduce and take care of their offspring—engaging in the circle of life.

Only the fully developed individual who has swept out the dark and dusty corners of shadow and integrated it with their original light-Self can be fully autonomous in the world. As we've seen, our unhealthy ego-defences keep us bonded with immature, self-defeating behaviours. Through the *Mythimo* steps and his conscious effort, Tony reframed his problem-story into one of strength and resilience, transforming old wounds into sources of power. Therefore, we must free ourselves from our dark sides before returning to a balanced and resilient state—ever-ready to face any blessing or blight rising to meet us on life's road.

Paradoxically, what doesn't kill Tony will make him stronger. When one is alone in the cave of despair, according to some of the greatest thinkers in history, we're more highly receptive to the wise inner voice. As Campbell's mythical Hero's Journey (1949) for real life promises, when we take on a severe ordeal or peak experience and survive, we receive an injection of personal power. A stronger, self-actualised Self emerges not ever seen before. Anyone who has hit rock bottom and had to climb back to function knows what this means.

At this juncture, Tony, as the genuine article—a grown and mature man—can be reunited with his clan. Because he has changed, a change occurs in the chemistry and dynamics of how others relate to him. It's not always comfortable for the other parties to adjust to the reformed person. Therefore, our tribe often enables our negative behaviours because they fear adapting themselves to our changes. When the right moment arrives, Tony may even ask them to address him as Tony and not Stormy anymore. He has now named his new narrative and swears to live by it.

Tony has learned his lessons and is blessed with renewed strength to function effectively, dynamically, and in an ever-evolving way. He has come so far, he's unlikely to turn back as he progresses in the direction of his dreams. Sure, there will still be stumbles along the stony way, but now freed from his dark side, he'll know the difference between what serves him and what doesn't.

Men cannot remain children forever; they must, in the end, go out into hostile life.
We may call this education to reality.
(Freud)

Case-study—Sussane (aka the Goldilocks archetype)

Sussane is another client who decided to change for the better. Like many of us, Sussane had an unintegrated psyche but overcame her limitations. She had the strength and motivation to eventually steer herself back onto the hero's path to achieve her goal of self-actualisation. While her emotional corrections differed from Tony's, she sought the same sense of connection, vitality, and empowerment.

Not all people have repressed aggression and anger in the shadow, but we all have unpalatable human behaviours deposited there. Because anger can precipitate violence, it evokes fear. Our species has a long memory of its dangers. So, our ego denies having ugly, angry feelings or, because it knows they exist, justifies their expression.

Passive-aggression creates confusion and can be dangerous, hissing out in unpredictable and disguised ways. It can come across as a mind game, confusing others about our intent. If better regulated and channelled, anger can be an effective motivator in times of duress. In essence, we need to accept that every emotion has its function but can become contaminated when not processed effectively.

Sussane presented as a (self-described) hurt, frustrated, and passive person at her wit's end. She realised she would have her work cut out processing her uncomfortable feelings when she chose to deal with them. The journey is worth it in every case, but like any hero, one must be fully prepared for the challenges lying in wait.

For instance, if we start to get real with ourselves, as client Sussane did (who initially saw herself in Goldilocks), we'll feel a voice of opposition from within telling us to leave things be, that our efforts will be a waste of time. As already stated, social conditioning and our proud egos make us excel at avoiding the unpleasant and burying the unacceptable, forbidden, and improper behaviours contrary to the tribe's norms.

Our normative traditions, laws, rules, and guidelines urge us to go along to get along. While our conformance is necessary for us as a collective aspiring to live in peaceful and prosperous environments, it stands in the way of conducting necessary post-mortems of our dark sides.

Sussane spoke of how she became an observer of her thoughts and actions, recognising that her pride (and how-dare-you brand of anger) had prevented her from seeing how her social behaviours were inappropriate. Coming from a well-to-do, socially connected family that extended warm hospitality to all, she struggled with how her ego had defended behaviours that offended others.

Through the *Mythimo* process, and by viewing her story through the lens of Goldilocks, the penny dropped. She realised she'd been ruffling feathers by dropping in uninvited, assuming a warm welcome was her entitlement. Feeling unsettled, she reflected, "If people are unanimously reacting this way, perhaps I need to reconsider my approach. What might their reasonable expectations be?"

Rather than simply capitulating, Sussane chose to engage with her friends in ways that respected both her needs and theirs. This shift was not a compromise of self but a conscious step toward mutual understanding. As a result, she eventually began receiving more invitations and found a genuine sense of belonging.

Her alternative had been to do nothing and accept feelings of loneliness. Previously, her sense of entitlement to 'warm hospitality' fed a negative inner voice and unregulated behaviours that breached her friends' boundaries and pushed them away. Had she not acted when she did, ongoing denial and painful rejection might have led to an emotional breakdown.

As another Self-*preoccupied* type, Sussane recognised she needed to cultivate empathy for others' needs to foster lasting social connections. When she faced the childish, self-centred traits within her shadow through the *Mythimo* process, she became the well-rounded person she was born to be. By reframing her problem-story through Goldilocks, she felt empowered to move forward into her next adventure.

Sussane continues with her daily practice of self-reflection. She has become a keen advocate for developing emotional intelligence to support our biological need for belonging, fitting in, and finding our unique place in the world. Sussane supports the notion that we cannot rely solely on our IQ when making decisions. Many of our dilemmas require us to make difficult choices. We can apply moral reasoning and ask whether what we're doing feels right and whether we would do the same thing again consistently and universally.

The great philosopher Kant (1724-1804) asks us to consider the needs of others, acting humanely and with dignity because of our moral duty. This requires we work within the social norms that yield what is best for all concerned, filling the gaps and our imperfect interactions with love, light, and compassion.

Interacting ethically with others requires the conscious cultivation of emotional intelligence. Sussane embraced this inner work, and through her reframe and reinvention, she transformed her life and relationships. Freed from her dark side, feeling 'free to be me' (while reading the room simultaneously), she forged new bonds of belonging—genuine, mutual, and in some instances, enduring.

Be yourself; everyone else is already taken.
(Oscar Wilde)

12 THE HEART'S COMPASS

Our emotions serve as an inner compass—what we might call the heart's compass—guiding us through the landscape of human connection. Emotional Intelligence (EI), as defined by Salovey and Mayer (1990), refers to the ability to observe and recognise our own emotions (and other people's) and to regulate our behaviour effectively when relating with others. The theory, more recently popularised by psychologist Daniel Goleman (1995), is undergirded by five pillars: self-awareness, self-regulation, intrinsic motivation, empathy, and social skills.

Each component is compatible with the aims of the *Mythimo* process, leading us to identify, reclaim, and integrate our disowned dark elements in the shadow, returning us to Wholeness. When we care about others and tend to their needs, our sense of belonging, wellbeing, and self-esteem are enhanced. Everyone and everything benefit from our renewed state of totality.

Self-Awareness: The Foundation

As we have already discussed, reclaiming our Whole Self starts by sharpening self-awareness in the psyche. When the ego asks the Self to look away, the aware one chooses to look anyway. Self-awareness is the cornerstone to unifying our multiple parts, dwelling within and without. Our interdependent ego, superego, and shadow must make peace with each other to atone with our Higher Self or Soul.

The self always has a choice. We can remain unconscious to a large part of who we are—the part which clashes with the world in ways leaving us fearful, angry, frustrated, envious, isolated, depressed, guilty, and, at worst, ashamed. Otherwise, we can choose to get to know ourselves deeply by observing, actively listening, and taking on board the truthful reflections of Self.

Self-awareness must be switched on in our prefrontal cortex. The switching-on part does not come naturally to us. Its state feels different from when we are on autopilot or when we have those spontaneous, from-the-gut stirrings. The moment we switch on our self-awareness, we begin running our thoughts, words, and anticipated actions through a filter, which can feel odd to the newly initiated, like an extra burden to carry. When a person routinely engages in metacognition—thinking about their thinking—they develop more insight, recognising the thoughts that led to their behaviours and helping them make better choices for themselves in the future.

We have biases in our thinking, conditioned through familial, social, historical, cultural, ethical, and political contexts. We can take so much for granted and not know it. However, any bias can prevent us from being objective, truthful, and fair. Still, we must press on and unpick the significance and meaning of the negative patterns of our thinking and behaviour.

As Goleman (1995) sagely suggests, "When we make a conscious decision to know ourselves by becoming a 'spectator' evaluating our own words and behaviours as objectively and honestly as we can, we are on the path to becoming an emotionally intelligent and authentic adult." His words point to the art of self-reflection, which is the first key to our personal growth.

Self-awareness is prepared to say we are not perfect and have room for personal growth. There is personal power in this brand of humility. Our awareness probes down into our shadow to retrieve and recalibrate our arrogance, regret, and resentment dwelling among other negative fragments of self. The best news of all is that our awareness finds not only our hidden toxicity and limitations but rediscovers our latent positive traits. Can we recall when we behaved with compassion, creativity, enthusiasm, trust, spontaneity, joy, or a hearty sense of humour?

The benefits of becoming more self-aware outweigh the short-lived negatives and range from gaining greater control over our emotional reactions, irrational thoughts, and impulses, feeling more centred with heightened mental clarity, and becoming calmer and more composed around others. The more we live in this reframed story, naming, expressing, and sharing it, the more we evolve over time into a well-rounded human being.

Self-Regulation: Mastering Our Responses

Self-regulation, the second pillar of EI, frees us from enslavement to the highs and lows of emotions. It will take a good measure of learned self-regulation to keep up the good fight for our self-awareness to win out over our ego defences. The coherent Self can better regulate irrational emotions emanating from the id—that shadowy place where our raw instincts and disowned parts coalesce to form our dark side.

Without self-regulation, those with unresolved emotional baggage in their shadows will react to challenges in disproportionate and inappropriate ways. Rather than acting in the present moment, past fragmented emotional memories cause us to misconceive and misread what is happening outside of the time-space context. They also lead us to project our shortcomings onto others in acts of judgment and blame.

To have emotional intelligence, a strong emphasis is placed on our need to engage in a rigorous practice of routinely monitoring and modifying our beliefs, thinking, and behaviours as we navigate the ever-changing landscape of our existence. We must take personal responsibility and become more truthful with ourselves. Are we sustaining our self-awareness concerning our positive characteristics and shadow attributes? Can we be bothered taming our wild emotions with well-developed reasoning, patience, and composure? Or are we slipping back into negative patterns the craggier and steeper our pathway becomes?

Emotional regulation begins with observing our thoughts and reframing our negative thinking with positive, self-affirming statements and stories that bolster our drive to participate in living our lives to the fullest. Remember, our thoughts lead to our behaviours, which lead us onto the path of our fate. As we sum up ourselves and others, let us not jump straight to criticism and judgment, but train ourselves to start by thinking, saying, and writing something positive about what we see, identifying the strengths.

Self-regulation is not a destination but an ongoing practice. Our quest to be authentic is one thing, but maintaining our integration is another. Life is ever-moving, so we must accept that the fitness of the psyche is like the fitness of the body. We must continue training to maintain our peak levels. When we regulate our thinking and behaviours effectively, we tend to exude wellbeing and become more accomplished in our interactions with the world.

Intrinsic Motivation: The Inner Drive

The balanced Whole Self has clarity, connecting readily with its internal drivers for living by its personal code. Intrinsic motivation, the third pillar of EI, springs from that independent ever-striving essence urging us on, keeping us going with dogged determination until benchmarks are superseded by our personal best. Proponents are motivated to do something because it feels like it is the right thing to do, not because of the lure of an external reward or fear of consequences.

Comparatively, an incomplete person may be inspired to act by the allure of competition and the prize for beating another engaged in the same game, feeding on the win. But emotionally intelligent individuals find their motivation from within. They ask themselves: Are we motivated towards self-efficacy where we experience a personal transformation so enlivening we can never go back to how we were before?

Our genuine emboldened feelings sustain our internal drivers and vice versa. When we connect with intrinsic motivation, we become active and informed citizens, moving through the world with purpose and authenticity. This inner compass guides us to pursue goals that align with our values and serve our growth, rather than chasing external validation or meeting societal expectations.

Self-mastery means we are now a new and better version of who we were at the start of our Hero's Journey. Here, our reality expands, setting us on course for living life abundantly rich with manifold blessings. When a person fails in relationships, loses heart, and is more often cynical than inspired, they will significantly benefit from reconnecting with their intrinsic motivation through the *Mythimo* healing method.

Intrinsic motivation flourishes when we have done the inner work to know ourselves deeply. It is the natural consequence of self-awareness and self-regulation working in harmony. Once we own our hidden strengths and the limitations that drag us down, we can become our better, complete, and illuminated selves. We are worth the undertaking of psychological healing to reach this state of emotional freedom.

Empathy: Connecting with Others

Empathy, the fourth pillar of EI, transforms our relationship with the world around us. When we have done the work of self-awareness, self-regulation, and connected with our intrinsic motivation, we naturally extend this understanding outward. Empathy is our ability to recognise, understand, and share the feelings of another. It is the bridge between our inner work and our outer relationships.

A high emotional intelligence quotient (EQ) indicates that our ego is regulated, coming from empathy rather than fear that we might be outdone or loathing when we feel outdone. In people with high EQ, shadow elements have likely been befriended, nurtured, and reintegrated. This inner integration allows us to see others with clarity and compassion, free from the distortions of our own unresolved pain.

EI theory espouses a paradigm shift, encouraging us to embrace a new social perspective by seeing everyone competing in the same pond to meet their needs, not as an enemy to beat. Emotionally intelligent folk facilitate compassionate, empathetic, and authentic social interactions. When we practice empathy, we resist the impulse to project our flaws onto others or to judge them harshly for the very shortcomings we harbour within ourselves. When we are overtaken by contempt, anger, and hatred, empathy slips away. Allowing ourselves time and care to regulate these emotions helps restore our capacity for empathy.

Self-compassion and empathy engender hope and trust, which in turn fuel creativity and motivation to participate in society. Our proactivity leads us to be with others in pro-social ways, tending to their needs as we have learned to tend to our own. The rewards are profound: when we care about others authentically, our sense of belonging, wellbeing, and self-esteem are enhanced.

Social Skills: Bringing It All Together

Social skills, the fifth and final pillar of EI, represent the culmination of all that has come before. When we are self-aware, self-regulated, intrinsically motivated, and empathetic, we naturally develop sophisticated social abilities. These skills allow us to navigate complex interpersonal dynamics, build meaningful relationships, and contribute positively to our communities.

Feeling comfortable in our skin is the most important social skill leading to personal success. When we are self-aware and regulate our thinking and behaviours, we exude wellbeing and extend empathy to others. The more we engage in positive ways in social settings, the more accomplished we become in our interactions. We are attracted to achieving goals that serve both our best interests and the common good.

Integrity is central to emotional intelligence and to social skills specifically. Aristotle, Plato, and Kant alike have taught us that we must act in virtuous ways to become virtuous. If we feel we lack the moral fibre to be the best version of ourselves, we will establish the best we can be by acting in the ways we know to be good. We enter the path to Wholeness by acting with integrity.

Social skills enable us to communicate effectively, resolve conflicts with grace, inspire and influence others positively, and collaborate towards shared goals. These abilities emerge naturally when we have done the inner work of the previous four pillars. We learn to listen actively, to speak truthfully yet compassionately, to navigate disagreements without defensiveness, and to build relationships based on authenticity rather than performance.

Many clients presenting for support with the *Mythimo* experience do so because they have recognised limitations in their ability to connect with others meaningfully. They have found their lapses sometimes even caused a separation from those they love, leaving them feeling lost. They essentially became separated within (not integrated) as much as they became separated without. Through developing all five pillars of EI, they find their way back to authentic connection—with themselves and with others.

The Journey Forward

Such a knowing mind and heart are not made in a day. It takes time and effort to shine a light on who we really are and where our unique place and purpose is in the world. But as day follows night, we will grow the five pillars of our emotional intelligence and rejoice in our newfound personal freedom: a far greater freedom than we ever supposed we had when we were half-hidden in our shadow.

When living an unhappy life due to errors in our thinking, behaviours, and goals, it is high time to implement our strategy to engage in more introspection and do the inner work to develop our EI. The premise is that we have owned up to who we are, know that we can do better, and are prepared to go through the process to become our optimal Self. Fairy-tale archetypes can help with this endeavour. Each archetype corresponds to a pillar of emotional intelligence, highlighting where we can focus our efforts.

We weren't made to run on mere psychic fragments—it is time to bring the sum of our parts fully online and shine our light. Our best version must venture out and sing from the rooftops, "I am free to be me." Now, that's what the culmination of the five pillars of Emotional Intelligence is talking about—a heart's compass pointing towards the light, time and again and again.

We can easily forgive a child who is afraid of the dark; the real tragedy of life is when men are afraid of the light.
(Plato)

13 CHOOSING THE LIGHT

From on High, we are promised that the light will shine in the darkness and darkness will succumb. Our hearts have been filled with light since the moment we were created, providing us with a constant source of truth, hope, love, joy, peace and guidance. When we gaze into the face of a new-born baby, we remember this to be so. It is up to us whether we let our light shine out of the darkness that encroaches upon our every day in some way. Why have some allowed their pain and suffering to alter their original makeup, acting and appearing like dull, shifting shadows as they carry out the motions of their lives? The choice is ours—it always is.

Our personal code constructed from our inner system of beliefs and values drives our outer life's direction or put this way by Neale Donald Walsch (2009): "Our state of mind creates our reality, and our present reality creates our next state of being." Our ethics and values help us to narrow our focus and choices. It is up to us whether we embrace the light over the shadow, value people over profit, or prioritise wisdom over wealth. Others may diametrically oppose our values, and we shouldn't mind unless we are expecting a close and harmonious connection with them. There are many examples of knowledgeable folk who have valued people over profit, becoming powerfully wealthy and thriving within the social groups they genuinely hold dear and support. These philanthropic people must have well-lit hearts with what Buddhists call, Mudita. Mudita is a mind state that only the truly enlightened can reach. Having overcome the emotion of envy, they appreciate another's beauty, success, wellbeing, and joy as if it were their own. They see a winner as an expander who broadens our perspective by showing us that we can be brilliant and that the wildest of dreams do come true. The love and delight proud parents feel for their children's accomplishments, which go beyond what they have ever achieved themselves, is another form of Mudita.

At the foundation of *Mythimo* are the personal success stories of my clients, integrating themselves into Whole, healthier, and better functioning human beings. They followed their heart compass and chose the light. As discussed earlier, the premise behind EI holds that self-awareness, self-regulation, empathy, intrinsic motivation, and social collaboration are human traits leading to our success: success for both the individual and society. For some, these qualities will also bring wealth and civil power. Still, for many of us, living in a first-world country in peace and relative material comfort where we are free to individuate and live a healthy, happy, loving, peaceful and sharing life, life is the dream already realised. But when our behaviours and outcomes run counter to our beliefs and values and we find our dreams slipping away, we need to accept that our decisions and the subsequent events, the unintended consequences are interrelated. What we have experienced in the past can become a pattern that may directly influence future events. Unless we are prepared to change the thinking and behaviours that serve us poorly, we can expect the same result (and sometimes with redoubled magnitude) moving forward. Suppose we hope for a more satisfying existence without taking the responsibility of undergoing the psychological processes that turn our lives around. Expecting everything to turn out well without putting in the appropriate effort is a reliance on magical thinking which ultimately diminishes and devalues our personal power, striking another blow to our self-esteem and causing an uptick in poor outcomes.

Our self-talk must narrow down on the positive, telling us to be in the here and now because we have no control over changing the past, and the future is unknown. Perhaps even more constructively, we can take charge of our lives and say: Up until now, I have made some poor choices. However, I did the best with what I knew about myself and the world at the time. From now on, I am going to think before I act. I will switch on my knowing Self who has learnt from the lessons past and make choices that support my values and goals going forward. This is a lesson in reframing. Because we cannot go back, it is reasonable to suggest a different, positive perspective to ourselves for living in the present. By reframing our past experiences as opportunities to learn what we did not know before entering the challenges we faced, we are supporting our sense of self and strengthening our resiliency. Reframing is an exercise in rational thinking that affords regulatory powers over our emotional reactivity. But we must reinforce our positive thinking with positive words and actions.

People who are considered overly emotional act during times of anxiety and threat from their emotional impulses overriding the rationale centres of the brain. When they learn to regulate their emotions and stay calm during calamities, their reasoning powers kick in, helping them make better choices. The better choices they make, the more confident they become. They take more calculated risks, surpassing their perceived capabilities in ways associated with conquering peak experiences and being their brilliant best. They become ever-more determined to keep going until they make it and will not give up despite the roadblocks or the pain. When they reach their goals on their own steam, the individual has proven their self-efficacy to themselves. This state of self-actualisation sits on the zenith of human experience. But human nature being what it is, once these heights are reached, a person looks confidently around, seeking the next summit to attempt. Aristotle may have nodded, telling us that this was evidence of the human soul's essential longing for something beyond itself. Self-actualised people are evergreen, continuing to throw themselves wholly into their lives, reaping an increase in health, wellbeing, and success. Ever-ready to shine their light, they also develop a sense of generativity, meaning they become morally inclined to pay their success forward to others. This is good for both the individual and society.

Paradoxically, we can only learn the lessons of life for achieving our objectives in new contexts by surviving the experiences related to going after those goals. Remember how Little Red Cap only learned about the danger of wolves by being tricked, gobbled up and regurgitated by one. Her adventure would have been a different story had she known the truth about the wolf before she took her first steps.

It is like a café owner saying I only want to hire someone with experience, and the applicant counters with the point that they will never have the necessary experience unless someone hires and trains them.

The point is we must get a start. If it is not provided by someone else, all the more reason for us to find Path A on our Hero's Journey as a meaningful way for ourselves, even if it involves taking a left turn. However, life must be a learning or relearning journey for the Soul, or we would already know what we need to know, before attempting anything new.

If life is just for empty-headed pursuits, why is it so full of life lessons we must endure? Once again, Maslow's Hierarchy (1943) says that first, we must survive, then have our safety taken care of; next, we need acceptance from the tribe to feed our need of belonging. A boost to our self-esteem will follow, fostering our agency necessary for becoming actualised individuals. When we are autonomous and free to be ourselves, going after our purposive goals, we experience confidence and satisfaction. Life becomes pleasurable. Becoming self-sufficient takes effort for most of us, as was the case for the Big-Pig archetype of *The Three Little Pigs*, who built his safe brick house. His younger brothers were far too self-indulgent (think *Collectivist* vs *Self-preoccupied*).

It is essential for our emotional health to understand that most people are good, but some behave badly when stressed and facing a perceived threat. We choose the light over the dark but can slip and make mistakes. Most people want to be good, according to the ancient philosopher Socrates. He contended that it is in our nature to pursue good for its own sake, and we do not consciously go toward what we believe to be bad: a moral stance remaining unchallenged today.

In the main, no one with sound mental health sets out with the intention to harm another person. Their harmful behaviours are linked to how they are wired to cope and self-preserve and are often the result of their shadow. People with agendas or ulterior motives to get what they want no matter the expense to others have a mindset of ego ethics. They have functioned quite well, coping from a position of self-preoccupation since childhood. Many have roles in governments and large business enterprises and fare well in the context of wealth, status and power. But we do not know the truth hidden behind the closed doors of their private or secret lives. Research consistently points to high self-esteem, self-worth and satisfaction being associated with open-minded, inclusive, altruistic, and empathetic behaviours, not self-interested ones.

The path to a well-adjusted life is understanding and accepting that we cannot change others and how they behave. We can only take control in changing how we interact and react to the external world around us. The fairy-tale archetype, Vasilisa, the light bearer, demonstrates that we must bloom wherever we are planted. When faced with exogenous causes of suffering, she focused her energy on what she could control, enabling her to press on step by step, moment by moment. Using the central part of her frontal brain, she remained calm, steadfast, and determined to tackle each test before her without looking beyond and yearning for a way out. Vasilisa was methodical and, eventually, was free to go her own glorious way. Vasilisa's example sounds simple enough to follow but regulating our fight, flee, freeze, fawn and hide instinctual brain responses when in the middle of a crisis is an ongoing battle for many of us as we go about our daily lives. Anxiety is one of the more predominant health issues of our modern age.

Some of us come into the world never knowing that there are people out there or in our inner sphere who see us as a competitor, a 'frenemy' (like the fallen star, Kevin Spacey's character said in the television series, *House of Cards*, "Friends make the worst enemies").

If we are brutally honest, our primary thinking is always about 'me and mine': after all, we are born alone (as a unique entity) and will die alone and must make critical choices in between on our own to survive. We are the arbiters, deciding how we must live our existence. Socrates cautions that this is no small matter. No wonder we pretend the responsibility lies somewhere else in a bid to feel secure. Our God has our back, but we are responsible for choosing the actions that take us forward.

Many started out by believing we possess unique selves, talents, strengths, limitations, and advantages and must run our own race to open doors. Once inside, we should prove ourselves to our leaders for validation and our place in the system.

We assumed everyone else was concentrating on achieving their personal best and endgame and had no idea they were running an agenda that might implicate or impact us. Soon we saw that these agenda-driven folk were observing us, gathering intel to use against us to make themselves 1. look better, 2. feel superior, 3. win the race. Fourth, in cases of malicious intent: they seek to dim your light.

When a supervising psychologist told me over thirty years ago that many ordinary folks among us are extremely calculating and have 'agendas', a feather could have knocked me over. Despite considerable experience in teaching, and owning businesses and leading several employees, I was shocked by what he said. I had never fully appreciated how false some everyday people arc, and the lengths they will go to win, and all in the name of a day at the office. Highly competitive corporate types were necessarily tactical as if they were at war. Still, despite my best efforts, I could hardly fathom the schemes of a person motivated to undermine others who have caused them no harm except for merely existing and pursuing their own goals. It seemed unbelievable to me that anyone would interact with someone else in ways that were not transparent and from a place of goodwill. It was easy to understand how people act out when unhappy and under duress—but this? —That there are people with hidden, ulterior motives that suck you in to further their cause did not align with my beliefs or values. Fancy someone treating every interaction with someone else as a transaction that must deliver some reward to them— is there no empathy in their hearts? It all sounds very naïve now. Once I woke from my sleep, I soon recognised the win-lose strategy at play. There must be a whole lot of fear underpinning their behaviours.

Are they the Lady Macbeth archetype, desperately trying to rub the blood stains from their hands? They haven't yet reached the understanding that one can achieve their dearly held goals without necessarily anyone else having to lose. Not every interaction is like a game of chess or a round of sports. Perhaps, they held a faulty belief that if someone else succeeded, it prevented them from reaching their goals. If someone else received something, they would get less: a scarcity mentality. Mostly everyone raised in a family of competing siblings catches a glimpse of the picture. The dark step-sisters may have been pretty too, but they were too obsessed with Cinderella's beauty to see that all the girls could be as lovely if they chose living in their own light.

It is wonderful to liaise with other people within the same system and know they are not motivated to outdo you with their toxic intent. Such awakened beings often create the change we wish to see in the world. Imagine a team that is focused not on the other members' talents, quirks, and outputs. All members concentrate on doing their personal best, directing and centralising their gaze, strengths and energy on the common values and goals of the organisation and the clients they are employed to serve. They find ways to collaborate to get essential requirements met (and beyond) and progress the business. While not a new idea, and despite its logic and benefits, it still needs to gain sufficient traction. Why? Because we are in the thrall of our shadows— our fears and perceived threats have us acting out as if every dire imagining will manifest. We act like tribal warriors engaged in territorial warfare. We are without the loincloths and lethal weapons but still employ primitive tactics. The signs are hidden from view because they are not socially acceptable behaviours. When a smiling assassin or one with an iron fist in a velvet glove tries to victimise us with their callous disregard, we are often baffled by their cunning. They see us as a means to their ends. As Plato and Kant contended, everyone has a right to be a means unto themselves, and no one should be manipulated and utilised to serve selfish aims. All life, sentient beings with the breath of life (the nephesh), has a right to be treated humanely and with respect and dignity. And we, with dominion over the world, have the responsibility, the duty, to uphold that right.

Can we not focus on our own performance and our personal best and contribute to the light of collaborative harmony, not the darkness of discord?

I remember my grandmother telling me when I was a little kid running my first footrace at school. She said, "You ran fast, and you nearly won. But you looked around to see what the other runners were doing and took your eye off the finish line."

I argued, "But I needed to see where they were so that I would run faster to beat them."

The elder smiled and replied, "Sometimes people fall over if they fail to concentrate on looking straight ahead. You would not want that, so fix your eyes on the finish-line and run your fastest."

My mum chimed in, "You will win the next race if you do not waste time looking around at the other runners. Just look straight ahead and run, run, run."

I remember being shocked when I still ran second despite taking their encouraging advice, proving my kin had overrated my natural abilities. Still, I wasn't one of those competitors who got their kicks from tying a better runner's shoelaces together before the race.

I have loyally followed my mentors' wise counsel to this day. I know that focusing on running my own race and doing my personal best is a good clean way to achieve satisfying outcomes. It feels right and light in my heart, head, and Soul, and what is more, philosophers Aristotle, Plato and Kant would approve.

A black-and-white view of the world (win or perish) may have sufficed in survivalist times when life was barbaric. Fifty thousand years ago, our choices centred more on whose turn it was to keep watch, which of the men (and women) were in the current hunting group, and who of the tribe was heading off to confront the hostile neighbours. The women would likely fight over whose turn it was to sleep with the father of their children and whose contribution to the tribe warranted access and the larger share of the meat, grain, and grasses. Polygamy was common for dominant males with dibs on the group's gene pool. With much of the same brain wiring today as in the past, is it any wonder some people are in fierce competition with others perceived as a threat, stopping at nothing to sabotage them, fearing they will be done over themselves? Such a dog-eat-dog world. Leaping to mind is the wicked stepmother of the story, *Snow White,* whose comparisons and envy of the beautiful princess turned malignant as she schemed to extinguish the naïve maiden's light. Why did she have to be the MOST beautiful, couldn't both women be beautiful?

Our ancient brain-wiring aside, there is a more rational way for managing our envy of rivals' competence. The former espouses the benefits of a winner-loser world even when the alternative for win-win is achievable. A negative, unconscious (and natural) trait of envy buried in the shadow-self can be far less difficult to unplug than burning jealousy or ruminating resentment. A combination of these elements boiling away in the organism, as applies to the vile stepmother, spews out its poison on the owner, receiver, and all in its wake. Psychologists tell us that envy is a worthless emotion as it does little to benefit the owner (reframed, it can motivate our pursuit of goals though) and has the power to flatter its recipient (who gets a boost to their self-esteem, knowing they are enviable). Does the perpetrator, under an illusion, believe their dysfunctional behaviour will somehow influence the curtailment of competence or spoil the beauty of their nemesis, making them superior and more admirable? Another mistaken goal, if ever there were one. Had the vile stepmother, and from what I understand, there are still a few among us, taken a closer look in her mirror and saw that her comparisons with a young, beautiful girl were like comparing 'apples to dragonfruit', she might have calmed down. If only she knew how to regulate her animus with more aplomb. It was irrational to conceive that Snow White's beauty was the cause of the queen's bitter and withered demeanour. Could she not take responsibility for caring better for her ageing face and body, asking the younger for beauty tips rather than victimising her? The toxic and quixotic queen needed a reality check and a stiff dose of Mudita. Natural beauty radiates from our light inside, after all.

Sadly, shadow-selves are operating out there in our natural world in every corner. Their extreme actions reported in the daily news are often just as malignant as those showcased by the dark fairy-tale matriarchs and patriarchs. Most of us come from a wellspring of wanting to do our best with what we have, relying on the foundations of our reasonable disposition (our genetic nature) and relatively functional upbringing (nurture). We are fortunate if our nature and nurture have coalesced to bring us a well-adjusted life. If our bedrock feels anchored when our lives are disrupted and facing emotional upheaval, we reach within to calm down, take a deep breath and operate from a rational and grounded place of being. We discern and can make better decisions when our mental faculties are at ease. Functional human beings also experience challenges and crises that throw them out of kilter, and stress and dysfunction take over. We all have emotional wounds requiring attention, processing, and healing to restore us to our full light. As you have come to know, I recommend the efficient *Mythimo* method to those willing to do the necessary inner work.

Had the wicked queen engaged in the *Mythimo* healing process, she would have learned to regulate her behaviours, and (utilising the mythopoetic *Mythimo Cards* as prompts):

- Reflected, and identified (named and reclaimed) what was harmful in her thinking;
- Acted mindfully in stressful and negative moments; and chose to regulate and tone down her harmful behaviours;
- Realised that Snow White's beauty had no bearing on her own beauty;
- Focused on being the best version of herself (reframed her lens and story positively); counted the positives of her physical appearance and inner strengths, and shined;
- Undertaken the inner work to (recalibrate) the dark elements of self (including the buried belief of being beautiful); balanced dark aspects with her light and hope (e.g., reconnecting with feeling beautiful and tempering her envy and bitterness with the light of self-compassion);
- Opened her heart and developed a new personal code, a code for Higher Living with empathy and collaboration at its core;
- Opened her mind, practising self-awareness to maintain her positivity;
- Chosen appropriate behaviour for the future; continuing with her inner work, living and sharing her strengths-based story until she had (regenerated her version 2.0)— organically integrating parts of herself back into a cohesive Whole Self.

As said before, people can shy away when faced with an outline of the inner work they must undertake to effect positive change. They deny an effective system of healing that requires them to step out of their comfort zone and call a spade a spade. They find the *idea* of doing the exercise too confronting. The ego is lazy and tells us to refrain.

Is it appropriate to call out our negative human behaviour? After all, aren't most of us good? Doesn't it go against the principles of unconditional positive regard to recognise flaws in someone's shadow? It takes all kinds of people to make the world go round, right? And why emphasise our negative aspects when we have so much good inside?

First, we must separate the person from the behaviours. We call out our negative behaviour, not cast aspersions on the person. That's where archetypes help — they let us externalise the problem-story, gain distance, and reflect without re-entering the wounds. Good people have a dark side that, once recovered, expands their light-fuelled firepower. We are much more than our behaviours but can be reduced by them. The point of *Mythimo* is for us to see our light and dark traits reflected in the fairy-tale archetypes, own and work through them and our negative schema to return to a clean slate of authenticity—revived and brilliant. It is not about becoming someone you are not. It is about being who you were born to be and loving yourself for being you.

To love ourselves as the Divine loves us feels more natural as we progress on our *Mythimo* journey. We must act 'as if' when we begin. Great philosophers assure us that by acting as our better selves, we become what we aspire to be. Our virtuous acts change our chemistry one degree at a time, gradually transforming us until we achieve our desired edification. Perception is key. Naming and describing someone's behaviours truthfully in a healing context is not derogatory but essential for positive resolution. Most people have good intentions, but few are yet to become integrated beings. The ancient concept of holism still feels new, and we struggle with reclaiming our discarded parts in shadow or we don't yet appreciate the full extent of the benefits that will come from the endeavour. But not a day passes when most of us wish we could recapture our old buzz again

Our unbidden memories, shadows of the past, urge our inner work. We see the shadow but must choose the light. Memories locked inside our inner child are ready to be rediscovered, reframed, lived and shared. Suppose we embrace our total reality and the world around us with a curious and open mind, and heart filled to the brim with empathy and light, radiant in a luminescent glow of energy as Abraham Lincoln (1809-1865) inspires with:

The mystic chords of memory will swell when again touched, as surely, they will be, by the better angels of our nature.

14 THE MYTHIMO HERO'S JOURNEY

All societies are evil, sorrowful, inequitable; and so, they will always be. So, if you really want to help this world, what you will have to teach is how to live in it. And that no one can do who has not himself learned how to live in it— in the joyful sorrow and sorrowful joy of the knowledge of life as it is. (Joseph Campbell)

The Hero's Journey represents our independent venturing that provides opportunities for us to grow and make good in the world. The eminent American mythologist and scholarly writer Joseph Campbell (1904-1987) popularised the mythical pathway model. As a literature professor, Campbell recognised the pattern of the hero archetype, central to storytelling in folklore, fairy tales, myths, religious and spiritual stories and rituals, books, drama and more. His seminal work, *The Hero with a Thousand Faces* (1949), unfolds the metaphorical, mythic path of the hero in seventeen steps. But for ease of use, many find the condensed twelve steps, as revised by film-maker Vogler (1996), more manageable and just as valid *(refer to the end of this chapter for the diagram).*

Starting as a beginner, our steps follow a regular pattern no matter who we are, where we are, and whatever we are about to do for the first time. Once we have reached and overcome the challenges arising with each milestone on the circular path, we finally return to our tribe, revealing the worldly-wise person into whom we have grown. For example, the semi-mythic king Gilgamesh mastered his lessons, completing his first revolution and returning as Gilgamesh 2.0, and we follow suit in our personal context.

As first-time questers, such as a child on their first day of school, a teenager starting a new career, parents bringing a child into the world, or an elder moving into a nursing home, in each case, we are going beyond our ordinary world and our self as we know it. There are countless 'first-time' situations in the earthly arena where we explore and test ourselves; in each case, we are always the hero archetype on their Hero's Journey.

The Hero's Journey is a symbolic map of human psychological development through our lived experience. We all ask: Where are we going, how are we going, and where do we go next?

We can trace every hero's undertaking whether we follow the storyline of a real-life person's narrative or a fictitious one such as a mythical or fairy-tale archetype. The underlying premise of the *Mythimo* method is that we can see ourselves and the real world in the fairy-tale archetypes no matter how fanciful the story appears with its supernatural twists. After all, the three-dimensional types relate directly to the human condition and, although make-believe, seem very real, reflecting the psychological fabric of our everyday lives and historical leanings, spiritual truths and timeless relevance. Australian author Joy Lawn tells us that children develop empathy by standing in the shoes of story characters, but it is just as important we all see ourselves in the stories we read.

More of us is revealed in a single narration of the tale than hours spent in lonely rumination might bring to light. There are elements of folklore, magic, and mythology that coalesce into a moral question of eternal value that all people of all ages can approach on different levels (cultural, social, historical, philosophical, psychological etc.) and interpret differently according to their age, lifestyles, struggles, and aspirations. Furthermore, the fairy-tale archetypes, both entertaining and instructive (i.e., edutainment), keeping us at a safe distance, will not affront our senses or turn us away from the deeper digging we must do to understand the unlit foundations of our dark side. Many of us are scared of our own shadows.

Mythimo presents a gallery of twenty-two fairy-tale archetypes synthesising a broad range of their strengths and limitations akin to our human nature, serving as keys to our reality and the diversity of lessons we encounter. In these times where we feel humanity may have lost the plot, its moral compass and direction, the age-old archetypes serve as reliable reference points as we venture towards new horizons.

From the confines of our ordinary world, the journey begins when the universe whispers a call to action in our ear. We must address our fears of embracing change, or we may refuse our calling. If we advance, inspired by a mentor, we find ways of going for it, such as devising a new approach. Opposition arises as we step up. We must overcome our threats, pushing through our battles to stay on the move. At the crossroads, paths diverge. We stand on the threshold, where we must make tough decisions to gain impetus. Crossing the intersection, we encounter tests, allies and foe. Some drive us into the cave to reflect and reframe our modus operandi. When we emerge and are ready for the ascent, even more ordeals confront us. Strategies are chosen so we may straddle the schism and get to the other side of overcoming.

Rewarded for our efforts, we suddenly feel aligned with our soul's purpose and rally to press on, leaving our ordinary past well behind. As we round the bend of our homecoming, a force majeure (it feels that way) confronts us. It has the power to take away our newly won resources, and we wonder if we have the will to break through. Haven't we come too far to give up now? After mastering our challenges, we emerge wiser, resurrected, and transformed into the self-efficacious one who has seen and done it all. Our kin and kith's arms stretch wide as they step towards us, open to receiving the fruits of our grail quest. And the twelfth and final step is done.

We take this circuitous route whenever we engage in any novel experience or enter unchartered territory, and the twelve steps can be overlaid on any event, past, present or future. Our journey requires us to employ a process of enquiry, deciding at step five whether we continue on the calling at 'Path A' or return to the known world of 'B'. Consequently, we surface with the knowledge we did not possess at commencement. But there are no guarantees, and there never are. It would not be a learning journey if there were. Necessarily, we must take that first step into the wild unknown to start figuring things out for ourselves as we go.

The Hero's Journey implies we become heroes because we stayed the course, completed the novel quest and have learned from the experience. In Australian speak: We gave it a go! Whether successful or not, we showed courage, gained wisdom and are willing to share our hard-won secrets with the uninitiated before they set out on a similar path towards the other side of today.

We must walk consciously only part way toward our goal,
And then leap in the dark to our success.
(Henry David Thoreau)

There are twelve (12) stages of Campbell's monomyth (i.e., the lone hero's path). The Hero's Journey and the term 'monomyth' are used interchangeably to describe the universal, archetypal pattern discoverable in the narrative of historical events, mythical, personal and fictitious stories, fairy tales and real-life accounts shared in oral or written form across cultures and from all corners of the globe.

Ordinary World (Step 1): Every person takes the Hero's Journey. Their ordinary world is their everyday life complete with socio-cultural-economic influences, norms, traditions, values and beliefs etc. (e.g., their *positionality*). It is here where they contemplate making a change to their normal routine.

Call to Adventure (Step 2): The universe stirs the hero, confronting them with a choice to stay in their ordinary world, the comfort zone, or to heed their psychological stirrings, calling them to adventure.

Refusal of the Call (Step 3): The hero is uncertain. It feels safer in their comfort zone than out there, where they must confront something new and inevitable changes. They fear the unknown, and at first, the hero might be inclined to refuse the call.

Meeting with the Mentor (Step 4): Standing on the cusp of the comfort zone— the past—and the new experience (and the unknown future), the hero, stands on the threshold. It takes the meeting of a mentor (could be God or their inner hero or anyone who provides a lesson: helpful or challenging) to crystallise the right message that catalyses momentum.

Crossing the Threshold (Step 5): The hero decides to cross the threshold to enter the beckoning pathway. There is trepidation as the new world offers unknown choices, constraints and temptations and life lessons to be learned.

Tests, Allies and Enemies (Step 6): The hero feels like they are being tested on every level by the unforeseen. While some tests are simple, others challenge their capabilities and resilience. What does not kill the hero can only make them stronger. But they must sort out their allies from their adversaries, for far greater tests await and they must be prepared.

Approach to the Inmost Cave (Step 7): Inside the cave, while the hero reflects, a new understanding emerges with a new approach to living taking shape. So, they must reframe the old story, enlist their strengths, and make personal adjustments to enter the reality of the new world ahead.

Ordeal (Step 8): Tests can feel life-threatening when we are confronted by a nemesis or even the dark parts of our shadow-self. An ordeal strikes at the hero's core which will make or break them (it feels that way at the time, in any case). The test will impact the hero's body, mind, emotions, and spirit to such an extent that they may ultimately hit rock bottom. Still, the hero must forge on regardless.

Rewards: Seizing the Sword (Step 9): Rewards await the hero who has the resolve to rise and fight another battle, 'seizing the sword'. But there still remains a risk that all hard-won prizes may be temporary and lost.

The Road Back (Step 10): Pushing on, the hero strives to return with their gains, the 'elixir of life' to share with their tribe. They hold the fruits of something new, a life lesson, a skill or resource, a fresh source of wisdom. Still, adversaries lay in wait to usurp the hero as he approaches the home base, but the hero puts up a stronger resistance.

Resurrection (Step 11): The hero's competitors have failed to halt their journey—but nothing will ever be the same. Returning home, everything looks altered. They realise the past must be surrendered for the sake of what lies ahead: power, old vendettas, outdated beliefs—even the illusion of control—must be relinquished, as the humbled Gilgamesh once did.

An epiphany dawns: they glimpse the universe's ineffable truth (Oneness) and feel both amazed and transformed. Having walked alone, severed from kin and split within, they now stand exposed. In this raw state, they begin to integrate their fragmented self and align with the Divine. A synchrony sparks—their awareness ignites, and transformation unfolds.

Whether it is the ancient Sumerian king standing atop the ziggurat beating his chest, Moses on the mountain channelling God's code, or Jesus agonising in the Garden of Gethsemane, all heroes once seeing darkness for what it is and embracing the light will become one again with the Source. But life does not stop there. If only we could bottle the revelation and never lose mindsight of its essence.

Return with Elixir (Step 12): The transcendental hero returns and shares their elixir, the fruits of their labours: hard-won wisdom and other resources for the common good. Now, more aware and potent than they have ever been, they gaze about them to find a new, even higher peak to climb and begin the search for the path that will get them there.

And so, their next Hero's Journey begins.

The Hero's Journey framework adds depth to our interpretations of reality. We can better understand how fundamental and universal the outlined steps are when we overlay them consistently on our own life stories (both the problem and reframed ones), milestones, and landmark experiences. We can use the model to time-travel back to our past, stay in the present or use it to see where our choices will take us into the future.

There are commonalities between us when we step through the twelve stages from being in our comfort zone at step one, motivated to action mid-way and experiencing a change in our material world and within ourselves by steps eleven and twelve. Looking back over the journey, the sequential, cyclical steps, we see how we grew along the way, accepting the bad with the good (between steps seven and ten), regardless of the outcome. All the in-between steps are integral to the whole undertaking.

Besides the twelve-step framework, there are further layers to incorporate to deepen our understanding of our experience. These insightful resources help us find our true identity (who) and what, when, where, how, and why we think, behave and experience what we do in the world. I refer to the host of mythic and fairy-tale archetypes (archaic symbols of our humanness) that relate to us, especially when overlaid on the twelve-step arena representing our life in motion.

The *Mythimo Cards* enable an exploration of the dynamic interplay between a person, their purpose and place, and the light and shadow dimensions of the relevant twelve archetypes. An individual's story comes to light when correlated to a specific archetypal pattern and where it lands on the 12-step path. Casting the archetypal cards in this manner, prompts one to reflect on the past or present or projects them into the future where the natural, logical or unintended consequences of their beliefs, thoughts and behaviours play out.

The result is a seamless narrative, summing up who we are, where we currently sit in our reality, how we are going, and where our decisions will likely direct us, according to 'the pattern'. We are the mythologists of our own fate.

For example, suppose we select Little Red Cap for Step 1. We recognise at once from the archetype that we are about to leave our ordinary world to go into the unknown. We are initiates and seekers with a sense of openness and curiosity. If we have travelled a *similar* way before, we will know to add carefulness to our approach, heeding the wisdom of those who know well this path. But no two experiences are identical, and Red Cap faces the novel.

However, as novices, we may have to overcome our flawed thinking preventing us from taking the first step, and we might not feel very heroic (our deliberations will transpire between steps two and eight). Suppose we slip into the cave to reclaim and integrate the shadowy naïve and careless fool within, accepting that we will become braver with each tentative step, facing the fear and deciding to do it anyway. Suddenly, some courage is fuelled but tempered with down-to-earth common sense. Are you beginning to see one's correlation with both sides of Red Cap's nature? But are we not all heroes?

We are the protagonists of our life stories, personal realities, and psychological journeys. It takes great courage just to be ourselves as we face the trials and tribulations along life's rugged road for most of us. When we step into the void of unknowing, we must suspend our doubts, assumptions, biases, judgments, and fear of *what we do not know* (especially as adults). We must trust that the new field of unfolding will offer us clues and answers. We relearn the skill of being free, relaxed and open, and accepting, like when we were young children, putting off the intellectual critic-judge and stresses of worldly adult conditioning and constraints.

Despite our sense of adventure to go exploring, we cannot escape our inner doubts; they are healthy signs that our ego is just looking after us. So, we tread carefully into the new arena. Isn't it usually at night when we make these dangerous forays beyond our confines into the wild unknown? That is when our unconscious mind bubbles up in our dreams and reveals what exists in the world of make-believe and, therefore, in our unconscious psyche. Archetypes populate the wilderness, but we don't see them until we look more closely, or they appear to us as dream visitors.

Notably, in making dream journals, journaling in general, drawing and doodling, meditating, and art appreciation, we learn to read nature's signs too and decipher our inner codes that unlock truths about our fears and desires and illuminate the passages written on the walls of our inner caves.

This work undertaken alone will be a highly personal experience with a tailor-made outcome. When we seek help from a trained counsellor, coach or therapist (another mentor) or work on our integration in a group workshop, their expert guidance can illuminate the path and keep us honest and faithful to the process. We do the necessary work while being supported. Workshops provide synergies with fellow seekers who serve as sounding boards and motivators along the journey. They show us how working collectively on the self serves humanity's best interests.

Our enlightenment is potentially everybody's enlightenment because we are all ONE, intimately connected as a species inhabiting our extraordinary sentient planet.

When we each stand in the shadows of the mountain, we wonder how long the climb will take. I cannot stress enough that *Mythimo* work needs grit and stamina to see it through to the end, and even then, once transcended, there will always be a higher mountain to climb, given we are all incomplete, imperfect beings in motion. We are always in process. (See the *Mythimo Method Handbook* for further elaboration on the *Mythimo* method.)

If only every person on earth had a personal code of ethics by which to live, imagine how that might improve our lives as individuals, families, communities and as the human race. I know mine has done me proud for a long time. I fall short of my principles now and then and must reconcile going left when I should have gone right. That is the nature of the beast.

My father's personal code included seventeen principles for Higher Living—among them: practice your talents to educate others, be kind to all sentient life, run your own race, take the bad with the good, and never give up when things get tough. These principles, along with the Golden Rule, shaped my foundation and continue to guide my work.

What similarities or differences do you see between my code and yours? People begin writing theirs down, often starting with the Golden Rule or recognising the quiet influence of mentors—fairy-tale archetypes included.

We look up to our heroes, often immortalising them. My father's code for Higher Living is woven into me, fused through my own experience. At times, I stray but return to it—reflecting in the cave until I find my way again. In doing so, I keep his light alive. However independent we become, we are shaped—deeply and often unconsciously—by those we're bonded to. We may revise the code for our time and context, but its resonance endures.

Call them role-models or mentors; they are our heroes who have gone before us to learn and share what they have learned, teaching us how to survive and reach our potential more efficiently.

Still, there may be no greater teacher for any of us than the lessons derived from our deeply moving experiences, such as suffering the loss of our most beloved heroes. When they leave for the spiritual realm, our eyes are opened a little more widely with every heart-breaking goodbye. We see things we have never seen before—the fundamental principle—a profound knowing about being spiritual energy living in a physical reality and understanding the difference between illusion and reality and what really matters.

I refer to and am guided by my personal code habitually. Have I ever strayed from my habit, its ethos, or path? Certainly. My body's shadow signals have gently alerted me each time. Yet the *Mythimo* process—alongside my own effort—has helped guide me out of the cave and back on the hero's path toward step nine. At times, I lingered there longer than I liked.

Ruminating on past missteps clouds our energy field and draws more of the same. As energetic beings, our actions ripple outward—nothing is lost. Energy cannot be destroyed, only transformed.

Pessimism leads to a loss of personal power—optimism to proactive power. Our call on the hero's path is to take charge, recognise and process our energy, transforming the negative into a positive state of mind, and our actions will follow. As the American philosopher William James (1842–1910) said, "The greatest discovery is that a human being can alter their life by altering their attitude."

Tempering and turning a negative situation around with a positive attitude is what everyday heroes do. They start out doing their very best but if they fail at first, with lessons learned, they go harder to reach their destination. When adversity strikes and we resist its lessons, our energy falters and our connection to the Divine can feel strained. Yet, as sages and prophets remind us, even in suffering, we're called to be grateful for the lesson we didn't yet know we needed. This truth echoes through folklore and fairy tales—*The Little Mermaid*, for instance, ultimately accepts her choices and their cost with grace

I found a connection between my personal journey and the story of *The Little Mermaid*, as so many other women have done who sacrifice their authenticity in the name of love. The sea becomes the sky for our self-effacing heroine transforming from a mermaid to a seraph of the supernal. At the crux, we shared the same affliction: The giving up of the self to get the elusive man because of feeling different, out of place and never enough when being who we were born to be. Women like this are attracted to emotionally unavailable men because their authentic Self is denied or unknown to them.

Making the connection between feeling flawed, inadequate and not worth the fight led me to counselling. Then, working later as a counsellor for years and learning from my intimate sessions with clients that poor self-worth afflicts many across society influenced my development of the *Mythimo* method.

Through our reflections, we begin to see what we fear. It wears one down over time to fight for what is right, just and fair. Accepting the consequences of being treated poorly comes easy when we feel deeply flawed for whatever reason. In repressing her animus, the woman has starved the very part she needs to feed. The more she begs to belong, the more nervous and uncertain she seems.

Still, to come to this realisation, she could not have let the flame burn out in her, not entirely, in any case. Her remnants of hope will cast light upon the path before her as she navigates her way to a new life. But she will need to do the psychological work and find dependable support.

On another note, we see again that our universe has an intelligence of its own when it arbitrarily intervenes to give the mermaid a break along her Hero's Journey. After her ill-fated moon-shot for the prince, she is tested again (at step ten) and rises to her higher angelic level (by step twelve).

The Divine rewards her wholesome choice, granting her a better outcome than her becoming 'sea-foam' but not the deliriously happy ending she sought. In contrast with Cinderella, Snow White, and Sleeping Beauty, The Little Mermaid does not win her prince; she is incapable of rejoining her sea-kin, living instead as a spirit among the vast ethers. The subtle and reassuring tone of the narrative appeals to us to step outside our assumptions and think beyond the known. We can then see The Little Mermaid's fate through a positive lens: she has transcended the ordinary world of struggle and survival and is now a free and evolved spirit exploring and functioning in the higher realms in blissful ascension.

The mermaid now moves with greater freedom and wonder. Perhaps her commitment to doing no harm guided her evolution to a higher state of being. Ultimately, she reminds us to stay true to ourselves while upholding a strong moral compass, whatever our fate.

Her pearls of wisdom are the elixir she brings home to us: Even when we make sacrifices for love, there is no guarantee it will be requited. We only sometimes get what we want, but we get what we need. One thing is clear—our physical death is inevitable.

The Little Mermaid nods from heaven at the Sufi proverb:

"When the heart weeps for what it has lost, the spirit laughs for what it has found."

For those of us still earthbound and seeking love, the Hero's Journey repeats. Each time, we draw on past strengths to face the unknown—wiser, braver, and more resourceful. Through reframing our stories, we begin to live them with purpose and power.

Many clients in counselling learn to appreciate the adversities that once threatened to break them. One shared how loving herself for surviving her struggles gave her a renewed outlook—she saw herself as a work of art shaped by resilience. Hope and gratitude became her antidotes to depression. By keeping her expectations broad and open rather than fixed, she found greater ease in facing the day (but, for some, medication remains an essential part of the path).

This strengths-based narrative approach works consistently for most people, especially those who have decided to have a show-down with their shadow through the *Mythimo* experience. They do the heavy lifting, coming to terms with their disowned elements, and taking steps to re-orientate these as positive qualities. Clients remain hopeful even when there are setbacks in important areas of their lives where before, they were quick to give up on their goals and lose their motivation.

Before the Hero's Journey process begins for a client, we discuss the benefits of becoming Whole again and the imperatives of an optimal mindset, knowing the goals they are working to achieve, and establishing the most effective practice routine to adopt.

Note: For detailed practical applications, step-by-step processes, and workshop materials for implementing the Mythimo method with clients, please refer to the companion volume: The Mythimo Method Handbook.

There is no sugar-coating the level of effort that must go into the practice if the client expects to change themselves and their lives and emerge from the final stage as integrated. The approach is like working out in a gym daily, where you must exert yourself and feel the strain of the exercises on your muscles if you expect a buff body in a few months. Some clients quietly toil away on their visualisations and affirmations while working out at the gym and simultaneously get body and mind into shape. It is incredible how their body speaks to them in different ways during this kind of shadow work. But there are also headaches and gut bloats, and according to clinical psychologist Robertson (1992), some people experience extreme physical reactions such as flu, intense muscle aches, pains, and nausea. It is not unusual for clients to experience mood swings between depression and elation, alternating between tears, angry outbursts and feelings of liberation as the old way of being breaks apart. The body purges toxins accumulated from years of suppressed emotions and limiting beliefs.

Reframing one's negative story from the past into a positive version means we must not feel sorry for ourselves, dwell on our struggles or see ourselves stuck as the victim, even when we have come from terrible situations. We must honour our suffering, but we need to get over it by accepting what was and get on with what will be.

Neurologically speaking, we have to form new neural pathways to replace the old. Our habit is to ruminate negatively because that is how we have been thinking for years, and it has become our default setting. With some effort, we forge new connections in our brains. Only by repetition and believing wholeheartedly in our new story can we effect a relatively permanent paradigm shift.

Case in point: Viktor Frankl wrote about his reframing of the *Man's Search for Meaning*, in 1946, after surviving the Holocaust's horrors. His iconic story recounts his time in Nazi concentration camps between 1942 and 1945. The eminent psychiatrist survived by finding meaning in his intolerable suffering, keeping his hope and spirit alive by maintaining his faith. When facing his darkest nights of the soul, he visualised a future when he would be free to walk and talk and stand upon a stage telling his story. Frankl could hold up his head, knowing he had never lost sight of his higher goals even in hell. Spiritually, he was never captured.

Despite the war's atrocities, he maintained his sense of humour and was grateful for having his shirt on his back, being alive in his wrecked body, and in good company with fellow victims. He also had compassion for his captors, knowing they struggled to survive, too, albeit their circumstances were much better, but he recognised their torment of being human, none-the-less.

There was a time when Frankl, seeing how fragile his body had become, genuinely did not think he would make it out alive. But he had internalised a strong belief passed down by his father before the war: "Do not lose faith because, ultimately, it does not matter what we expect from life but what life expects from us."

Frankl went on after the war, despite the devastation of losing his pregnant wife and many relatives and friends to the tyrannical regime, to set up a practice in Vienna as a psychiatrist and to teach and have a family. The author received accolades worldwide for his humanitarian work and was lauded as a hero, helping thousands upon thousands of people.

Perhaps this is why people like Viktor Frankl succeed where others fail: They go past the default setting of 'poor me' thinking to the positive: 'I am here to make something good of what just happened to me' thinking. There is little bitterness in the genuinely enlightened. Their acceptance that 'what is, is' helps them get over the hump of hate and despondency more quickly. They may have suffered enormous losses, but they see a purpose in surviving and a good reason for it. Being the only one out of ten who survives becomes the impetus to honour those who did not and let their voices be heard again through oneself as the messenger. We serve a higher purpose.

When we start our Hero's Journey again (and again and again), there's a transformation in which we evolve from victim to victor (or victim to survivor to thriver) as we start on our next first-time experience. When we self-regulate our inner voice, having it tell us we can, we will. The great German writer and scientist Goethe may have whispered in Viktor's ear (as he whispers in ours now) that magic happens when you believe in yourself.

Our Hero's Journey, *undertaking the Mythimo* process, is a healing journey with a heroic ethos at heart, peeling away layers of pain and hidden information, fortifying our core, and reframing our reality positively in our strengths-based story to make us stronger.

As we embark on our next Hero's Journey into the deep terrain of our psyches, wandering and wondering, we will heal more effectively the more we spend quiet time reflecting in the natural world. Recent studies show our self-esteem, concentration levels and creativity, and abilities to take risks and make discoveries are enhanced when we immerse ourselves in the natural wilderness. The fairy-tale archetypes vouch for it. The Ugly Duckling found his cave in which to soul search and emerged bigger, brighter and better.

Like us, our mythical heroes are in and of nature. Our being in the natural world is akin to being at one with the elements of earth, air, fire, and water. The Indigenous peoples, Celts, Pagans, and thousands of other tribes (and poets) of the earth knew well the glorious feeling of communing with the wild. Every day of our existence, we must remind ourselves that there is a fundamental principle, a magnificent interplay of unseen forces at work, underpinning our existence.

When we commune with nature's raw qualities, we enter an instinctual world. Here, we can find words that speak from the heart. Feelings arise freshly in the moment, at our spiritual centre, while emotions are recycled feelings held in the body and recorded by the mind. Only by reconnecting with raw feelings in the present can we release those stuck, looping emotions—those myth-scripts that keep us circling.

Ironically, life's truths are often most visible through myth. What is creative and destructive, nurturing and predatory, becomes tangible in the world of make-believe. Myth is not separate from us; it mirrors who we are. When we compare ourselves to mythic figures, we access deep emotions and recognise the universal presence of heroes, villains, victims, and shadowy archetypes within our own unconscious.

Psychoanalyst Jung (1959) coined the four significant archetypes (among others) of the persona (our egoic mask), the shadow (our id and then some more), our Self, and the anima/animus. Modern Jungian therapists might cite twelve: The innocent; every-man-woman-person; hero; outlaw; explorer; creator; ruler; magician; lover; caregiver; jester; and sage. When we think of the sage Vasilisa, we can also add warrior to the list, whereas the outcast duckling relates more to the orphan archetype. Astrologers have their twelve. It is no coincidence that the hero's path comprises twelve steps.

Twelve is a powerful number embedded across many contexts in our earth and heavenly arenas and as we know from Jung (1959), numbers are the most powerful and primitive archetypes for bridging our inner and outer realities. When we dream of specific numbers, it pays to pay attention. Twelve symbolises the gates of Heaven, Divine order, authority, and also represents the membership of a jury. It is a combination of the numbers one and two (totalling 3): our individual identity and the duality of our existence but ultimate atonement with the Divine.

For *Mythimo,* we utilise twenty-two fairy-tale archetypes, selecting the twelve 'main types' echoing our relevant personal conditions. Then, overlaying them on the Hero's 12-step path for context, is a relatively simple exercise for the enquirer.

On a personal level, each of us resonates with the light and shadow aspects of certain archetypes, shaped by our own unique experiences. We can connect with these mythological figures through fantasy, reflection, dreams, hypnosis, immersion in nature or art, and moments of insight or revelation. The mythopoetic *Mythimo Cards* also offer a proven path to this inner contact.

Like a bombshell going off in our hearts and minds, we can struggle with being shown our dark side replete with its poisonous thoughts. Hate can fill the heart as much as love does, but we all know which feels better to hold.

The Hero's Journey demands we face our hidden shadows and integrate them with our light. Archetypes open our eyes. Only through this inner work can we become the hero within. I remember admitting my feelings of inadequacy—a crucial step on my healing path.

Some might say perfectionists always feel something is missing or broken and needs fixing. Nothing is ever enough. But as the eminent educator, Parker Palmer (1939-) said, "Wholeness does not mean perfection: it means embracing brokenness as an integral part of life." A perfectionist must accept the imperfect parts of themselves to feel Whole; otherwise, feelings of lack and longing persist. This gap, symbolised by an emptiness within, often leads us to seek fulfilment through others, possessions, addictions, even idealised archetypes—but true completeness comes from within.

A sense of lack begins when, as young children, we are dependent on our mothers (or other caregivers) during the earliest months of life. We sense her loss when she steps away to attend to other priorities. Our ego-centric world is momentarily shattered in her absence, and we fret that she may never return. This evokes a primal fear—separation anxiety—and over time, the brain's neural pathways become shaped by the recurring stress of perceived abandonment. Yet, when caregivers return predictably and offer comfort, we begin to build secure attachment, which helps to mitigate the long-term effects of our separation anxiety. The infant gradually internalises the sense of being held, loved, and remembered, even in absence.

Still, our desperate aloneness can overwhelm and confront us. We are solitary beings, in the sense that on some level, we came into and will leave the material world alone—just like every living thing. We forget (though not in our souls) that the spiritual realm keeps us close. With biological drives urging us toward clans, tribes, and communities, is it any wonder that isolated selves yearn for belonging and communion?

We feel such emotional intensity when rejected by somebody we love. I recall my deep distress many years ago, having just broken up from a relationship with a man who did not reciprocate my feelings. I sobbed as my heart broke, hearing the lyrics of Roy Orbison's *The Only One* playing on the radio. The song spoke to my loneliness—feeling like the only one with a broken heart, the only one in a crowded room who felt utterly alone.

I felt deep consolation connecting with the song's story, as if sharing a heart-to-heart with a close friend. I later learned Roy Orbison, a visceral empath, lived with immense pain, which made his music resonate so deeply. His words and melody touched my soul, reminding me I wasn't alone in my loss. That song became a healing balm, helping me piece myself back together during my early *Mythimo* journey. As author Knost (2014) notes, music holds profound healing power.

By making 'connections' with others sharing the same plight as myself through the powerful language of Orbison's song, I felt a 'sense of belonging'. My eyes opened to why I had felt a sense of lack and inadequacy in a nonreciprocal union. I discovered how my shadow feelings were triggered when I felt abandoned and gradually began to regain my belief that I was enough. In time, I felt strong enough to start my Hero's Journey anew.

Back then, like now, songs and stories (and my dream messages) were the key to unlocking my secret self. In times since, I have worked with clients who achieve the same result from plugging into their dreamscapes and songs and all manner of other symbolism and signs, including the reading of nature's formations, literature (and the Bible), automatic writing and doodling, spiritual visions and messages and works of art (such as the *Mythimo Cards*).

Words and art give us meaning, but each of us interprets them through a personal lens shaped by culture, beliefs, and experience. True freedom to create meaning comes from the Original Self's consciousness. Our evolving view of the world may sometimes clash with societal norms, but as long as we respect law and ethics, this is our right. When personal views conflict deeply with conservative society, mental distress can arise. But, as one wise soul said, "You don't worry about fitting in when you are custom-made."

We need to find the balance between being comfortable in our own skin and finding our place in the wider world, and this is where the development of our emotional intelligence comes into its own as we embark on our next Hero's Journey. And then, we have much to learn from our animal friends.

There is something very doggy about a dog. Animals are comfortable in their skin (at least until humans cruelly steal it from them). They are reliable and honest in being themselves and are REAL. So very sage.

Along the Hero's path, we will meet many who wear masks—hiding their true selves out of fear or ambition. Some deceive to gain advantage; others conceal imperfections even from themselves. These façades often stem from the fear of not being enough or facing rejection. Recognising this helps us navigate the journey with greater wisdom and compassion.

Then, we will feel safe again when we make friends with others with whom we feel at one. Not all of us have the privilege of being in the company of like-spirited souls with whom we can drop the mask and say and do as we feel at any given time. Opportunities such as these are intermittent or random. Those rare and deliciously spontaneous moments when we encounter a 'soul mate' cause us to believe our spiritual communion will last forever. This meeting of minds occurs when we are on a new calling and have arrived at Step 6 (or reached the reward at Step 9) of the hero's way: Tests, Allies and Enemies. If the delicious chemistry with our new ally sustains, and we are wise, we'll do what is practicably possible to share our lives with them.

Looking back over ALL significant life events embedded in our personal stories, re-stepped out over the hero's path, we will readily recall the synergistic sparks felt when making real connections or experiencing our beautiful BIG dreams and memories. They can be traced along the circuitous route and mostly found at Steps four, six, seven, eight, eleven and twelve.

As a physical entity, we are indeed custom-made and, in our singularity, utterly alone. But to feel we are alone in this world like it is a pathological state of being is an illusion sponsored by our ego.

Our ego seeks control to help us survive, often driving fear to keep us alert. The amygdala triggers anxiety, but many hide their vulnerability behind a mask of bravado. Consider the harsh reality of war—where people are pressured to act against their deepest instincts under groupthink.

Fallen soldier Wilfred Owen's poems about the reality of war shed light on the hostile and heroic world of the 'masculine ideal' promoted throughout history. Women can subscribe to the false ideal as much as men. Cowardice is a reviled human trait. Just thinking about it makes us feel weak and awkward. We push these feelings down into our organism out of our sight because we cannot bear looking at them. They hide in our id. The more we push stuff down into the shadow, the more it bubbles over. The ego sensing the id's displeasure increases its camouflage. All the while, we feel an uneasiness within, our body reacts. Our superego instructs us to keep things together and not be stupid and weak.

The fallen war heroes, like brave Wilfred Owen, whisper lowly to us from heaven to stop the fighting, fleeing, freezing and hiding and start living authentically, and now.

In the eager chase of ego's gain, a soul lesson follows, laced with pain.

Here's the rub: the ego gives the soul a vehicle for growth, which is good. But when ego-driven pursuits bring suffering beyond what we can bear, it feels anything but.

The soul's wisdom doesn't always need to be learned in the bitterest of ways.

There is a choice. We can access a gentler path—one that reaches into the dark fragments within, not to destroy them, but to transform them. And in doing so, we stand tall in the light once more.

Fairy tales, taking us on a virtual walk into the wilderness, have restorative effects on the mind-body as we escape into the natural world of animals, tall trees, and hopeful, happy endings under sunlit skies and moonlit nights.

First, we must sum ourselves up to know our totality. We can start with the fairy-tale archetypes agitating alchemically deep within our unconscious, holding up a looking glass in which to see clearly our foibles and nobilities.

When we choose empathy over anger, we connect with our Higher Self's compassion. Practising *Mythimo* helps you stay calm during attacks, understanding that others' pain drives their behaviour. It doesn't justify or excuse it. This awareness grows into empathy and compassion—for they know not what they do. We take the lead, setting and promoting a good example.

We feel the sublime state of empathy nourishing every cell in our body. This visceral experience is the same when our self-integration occurs. Consistent positive feelings over time will mend the void created by our sadness, gradually leading us to heal and reconnect.

For each kindness, there is unbearable cruelty. War rivals peace. Justice lies only in the narrow lens of a victorious arbiter or is the advantage of the stronger, according to Socrates. Joy and grief, love and hate, are separated only by a fine line. As Shakespeare reminds us, "There is nothing good or bad, but thinking makes it so."

We individually apply judgment and values to our lived experiences. It can be a harrowing realisation when we see the harsh elements of reality without any whitewash. We can choose not to see the hellish side of life, but it will still exist in the world, unchallenged and unchanged, if we continue to bury our heads in the sand and ignore it.

Taoists believe in opposites complementing each other. Yin and Yang symbolism reminds us that we cannot experience the fullness of white without black as its contrast and vice versa.

Animals such as wolves, foxes, cats, owls, and rabbits are truthful embodiments of what they are within. They have evolved to operate in the real world for the purpose of survival and procreation, playing their part as prey or predator.

Humans have upset the balance, prioritising too often their built environment over the natural one. Is this human quest for superiority over all species driven more by a collective fear of our lack? The more we separate from each other, from our natural world (other humans, fauna and flora), we separate ourselves from the Divine. Now, that does not feel good.

Isn't our spiritual purpose more than meeting the 'four fs' of survival (feeding, fighting, fleeing, and mating)? May a fifth f of 'flourishing' be added so that we become conscious of all sentient beings whose existence is nothing short of miraculous?

While the outer world is accessed through our five senses, our inner world—of thoughts, imaginings, reflections and dreams—often feels intangible until our fleeting thoughts stir deeper emotions. These feelings, good or bad, carry energy, and the body becomes the barometer, translating our conscious and unconscious mind into physical experience.

Many illnesses, whether somatic or psychosomatic, have metaphysical roots. For example, someone holding on to sorrow and resentment may suffer constipation—stagnant emotions building physical toxins that block release. We are holistic beings; body and mind are intimately connected. So, mental health and wellbeing are just as vital as physical fitness.

When clients begin to let go and express themselves authentically, their bodies eliminate the waste.

Psychoanalyst Jung (1959) contends in his theory of the 'collective unconscious' that our unconscious thinking has links with a communal archive of the oral tradition. Our subjective psyche communicates with this objective psyche (and the universal unconscious repository containing archetypes, myths, tribal rituals, social mores, language and symbolism (and numbers) and it communicates back to us through our dreams, reflections and revelations. According to Jung, our primordial instincts began when we were preconscious in egg form. Every time we take the Hero's Journey we engage that archetype.

We each carry a personal myth from childhood—formed by our early wounds or sense of belonging—that shapes how we see ourselves. Mine told me I was flawed, inadequate and unworthy, a belief rooted in early pain and triggered when my father died prematurely. I believe it is intergenerational.

Through *Mythimo*, I learned that beneath our struggles often lies one defining emotional moment. Healing begins when we bring that hidden story into the light, name it and reframe it to start anew, living to our strengths.

We long to feel complete again. But instead of embracing our true selves, we wear a mask to fit in, hiding the parts we think are unlovable. The ego helps us get by, but our deeper Self wants more.

True transformation begins when we welcome our shadow and integrate it with our light. The illusion of lack dissolves, and we reconnect with the Divine—fully ourselves. Like the Hero's Journey, fulfilment comes from leaping into the unknown, falling, rising, and sharing what we've learned.

Without faith, we regress to survival mode. With it, we move toward the Godhead. Life offers the tests we need. When we temper our perception with a personalised spiritual code, we act with purpose rather than reacting from fear.

Survivors of torture shine the torch to show us the way. The returned hero, surviving on a sincere belief that the truth must be shared so no one else suffers such darkness again, walks beside us as we tread the hero's path.

Frankl became highly successful in his family life and profession, healthier and happier ever after. Our emotional freedom and self-efficacy lead us too to these same rewards.

Fortunately, not all of us must go to war to get to the harsh realities of truth. Millions perish before they can return to tell us what hell they have seen and how we must change for the better. Imagine what these doomed heroes would share about awareness, empathy, and forgiveness. They would urge us to know our ego and how it shifts our focus away from the things of life that really matter to create illusions, separating us from love and light.

Let us not be afraid of our reflection. Our transformation and transcendence beckon. Today is the first day of tomorrow, so let us begin our Hero's Journey, weaving our personal stories anew along the mythic *Mythimo* way.

Every man carries within him the eternal image of a woman, not the image of this or that particular woman, but a definite feminine image…The same is true of the woman: she too has her inborn image of a man. (Carl Jung—the anima and animus archetypes)

AUTHOR'S PERSONAL CODE FOR HIGHER LIVING

1 Always give others their fair share.

2 Life is a teacher, so enjoy learning and teaching.

3 God-given talents are to be practised so one can entertain and educate others.

4 Recognise the existence of the spiritual dimension.

5 Be kind to all sentient life, considering their suffering before acting.

6 When you are loving and kind, it will come back to you in unexpected, good ways.

7 Other people sense more about you than you realise. Be yourself.

8 Run your own race, concentrate on beating your personal best.

9 Look after your animals because they look after you.

10 Work before play.

11 Finish what you have started before starting something new.

12 Always have a thankful heart.

13 Forgive and become friends again quickly.

14 Take the bad with the good. Pain is a teacher that makes us stronger.

15 Exercise some self-constraint.

16 Respect life but know that death can be better than torture.

17 Never ever give up, even when the going gets tough.

Saint Francis of Assisi once wisely taught: "Start by doing what's necessary; then do what's possible; and suddenly you are doing the impossible."

ARCHETYPE: THE HERO'S JOURNEY—12-STEP PATH

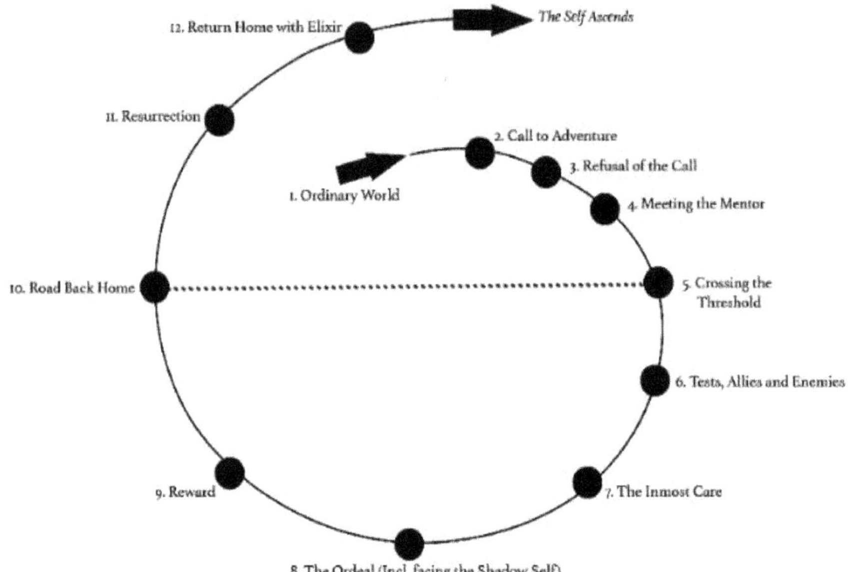

The cave you fear to enter holds the treasure you seek. (Joseph Campbell)

15 ARCHETYPAL REFLECTIONS

Spanning global historical narratives and tales of mythology, fiction and fantasy, a vast cast of colourful archai provides insight into how humans operate in the real world. Women commonly identify with Joan of Arc, Aphrodite and Wonder Woman, while men are likelier to draw parallels with Nelson Mandela, Eros or James Bond. The truth is that we can be more than just a gender-specific self because we all possess both male and female or yin and yang energies and are multitudinous.

By no means do the clients I interview believe, for one minute, they are as fanciful or wield the same superpowers as the comparable characters but see something real inside them that resonates. The essence of age-old fairy tales and myths are germane to us.

Depth psychologist Jung wrote extensively on how the study of fairy tales contributes to our understanding of the structures of the deep unconscious. He told us (1959), "Fairy tales are instrumental symbols with whose help unconscious contents can be canalised into consciousness, interpreted and integrated." We are irresistibly drawn into their enchanted world not because they are fiction but because they reflect our humanness in ways both dark and light. While the ego is lapping up the fantasy, kidding itself and living in illusion, the fairy-tale archetypes own up to their imperfections. Our deepest survival instincts, including our in-wired negativity bias, are in-tune with their veracity.

Egos enjoy optimistic endings, and we feel encouraged that we, too, can overcome our trials. After all, our egos are that part of the psychic structure where the 'rubber hits the road' as we navigate our way on our Hero's Journey. To survive its physical and psychic demands, our ego must put its best foot forward—yet in doing so, it inevitably interacts with archetypes, accepting or denying their guidance while being confronted by their reflection of the hidden self.

Myths and scripture feel primeval, transporting us to the moment our ancestors first experienced wonder and embarked on the endless search for meaning. Exploring related oral traditions—folklore, and fairy tales—offers lasting insights into how we thought and behaved then and now. Alongside this understanding, we come to recognise the magical, supernatural powers of our mythical human and animal archetypes—figures who journey to make the impossible possible. Much like the Taoist insight that white exists only in relation to black, we can use fanciful fairy-tale archetypes to see reality more richly. Subtly nuanced unconscious information, otherwise overlooked, comes into sharp relief.

Deep within our genes, archetypes remain imprinted—passed down from ancient forebears—pointing to a shared reservoir of unconscious patterns within the human psyche. According to Robertson (1987), this substratum is vast and ancient, filled with inherited images and behaviours—what Jung called archetypes—that continuously repeat not only throughout human history but throughout the very fabric of life itself.

An archetypal influence can ripple through the mind—like a hero's bravery, a goddess' goodness, a dark mother's dangerous detachment, or a villain's evil—as either light or dark energy, depending on whether it is acknowledged or not and how it is primed and mediated within the individual.

Our identity—built from the structures of Self (ego, id-shadow, and superego)—begins forming between ages three and five (Jung, 1959). We store emotional memories from early experiences and rely on the ego to protect us from vulnerability, shaping coping behaviours that help us survive. Through the ego's persona, we project a mask to appear as favourable as possible, driven by a deep need for acceptance and survival.

Beneath our conscious ego and persona, the personal unconscious quietly works with the id-shadow and superego (and connects us to the collective unconscious). It expresses itself through dreams and archetypes, symbols, stories, deep reflections and creativity—a rich source for self-understanding. Otherwise, when unconscious feelings don't emerge naturally, it takes mindful persistence to access this hidden material.

Jung and Freud theorised that the unconscious is an archive of subdued impulses, desires, emotional memories and traits tied to threatening or traumatic experiences (and more). Its purpose is to protect the ego, but the ego quickly raises its own shields, defending against the emergence of any dark or unsettling material. Our shadow is always poised to be triggered when old emotional patterns and memories stir, so it's no wonder the ego is quick to guard itself. Fond of favourable outcomes and self-affirming experiences, the ego will do anything—to avoid, deny, project, or camouflage parts of the self it cannot bear to face. Our ego strives to preserve our pride and dignity. We all recognise this behaviour because others often chide us for being 'defensive.' Still, how else can our ego help us appear worthy within the reality we navigate?

Digging deeper beyond the layers of our subjective psyche, we discover the objective psyche of the collective, where many of our universal mythical archetypes and familial and socio-cultural heroes of the past have dwelt since time immemorial. Why they must be preserved at such a deep level within us is an extensive subject for another time. But I can personally attest to the existence of the collective archive of archetypes and our ability to access them.

In one of my Big dreams experienced when I was 15 and pregnant, I dreamt of an African tribeswoman who gracefully gave birth to a large snake. My unconscious had contacted a universal archetype connotating fertility and representing the umbilical cord connecting humanity with Mother Earth. When I awoke, I felt deeply affected by my dream and was suddenly sure that I would birth a son (and told everybody so), and I did within a few short weeks. The dream images were unmistakable and memorable.

The naked woman possessed glossy black skin and a commanding presence, and the enormous snake wrapped around her torso had the patterns of a python with prominent black markings. Still, she seemed strangely related to me. When I finally researched the symbols later, looking to see if the meaning went beyond the personal, I recognised that the woman I contacted was from African folklore known as the goddess Mami Wata or La Sirene. She is a mythic priestess closely related to Mamba, the water spirit worshipped across many different religions of West, Central, and Southern Africa and the African diaspora of the United States. However, being universal (and formless until activated in a personal dream), the archetypal mother from the collective unconscious travels on a universal passport, transcending the boundaries of time and place to appear in the receptive psyche of a conscious recipient from any culture, language or time zone.

It was astonishing to discover that the universal archetype is a mermaid-like figure, a water spirit associated with themes of fertility, grains, creativity, birthing, rebirthing, fortune and fame. She holds a snake and a mirror, representing her ability to see into the future, helping her devotees recreate their image and reality. Mami Wata makes conceptions known, but in my case, she came to let me know about my son's pending birth. She spoke to me silently, soothing my birthing fears while inspiring my further study of the spiritual realms. Never before had I read or seen any information or images related to Mami Wata, who can appear as male or female (or as animus or anima archetypes) in visions. I could not have produced the information on my own (and personal computers were not yet invented). Another peak experience that I will never forget in my lifetime. I have never stopped feeling remarkably close to La Sirene.

Robertson (1992) researched race and dreaming and describes how a white person dreams of an African American person more as a shadow figure, and vice versa for African American dreamers. Not all material or metaphors from the dark recesses of the mind have negative connotations. Big dreams like mine have us wondering if we have lived lifetimes in cultures where these mythical figures were worshipped. Could it be we astral-travelled and met them in the etheric realms? Still, according to Jung (1959), our collective unconscious is other worldly, allowing us access to the universal compendium of symbols known as the Akashic record. Suppose you dreamed of being in the Hundred Year War between England and France, or any war in history for that matter, and it felt real. Your unconscious may have accessed the Akashic library, or perhaps parts of you (i.e., the inherited cells from your forebears within you) that were embodied there once upon a time made the connection. According to Jung's model of the unconscious, our personal unconscious, full of memories, emotions impulses, desires and symbols of our lived experience, is a mere tip on the unconscious strata. Lower, resides the tribal and cultural elements of the collective, and deeper again are the remnants of our racial and primordial origins.

Roughly speaking, modules within the brain project images from the top of the brainstem to where they are visible as we dream. The spontaneous bursts of cellular activity within the spinal stem during the dream-state light up a memory borne spontaneously from certain cell clusters. In the case of historical settings, we may have accessed a cell carrying the coding of an ancient forebear or an archetype of collective humanity (such as my experience with La Sirene). Robertson (1992) points to neurophysiologic research, supporting the notion that dreams release genetic programs.

Male dreamers often dream of soldiers thrashing it out in blood and suffering on the battlefield with images projected vividly within their minds (i.e., the visual processing centres).

While our nonconscious distils information isolated in our shadow, it must also filter elements of our psychic inheritance that interplay with our thoughts, behaviours and schema in our waking reality. Whether we make sense of what is going on deep within psyche (or not), we respond in myriad ways to its energetic activity.

It is a marvel to consider that our outward behaviours originate from and are signifiers of the deep-seated beliefs, values and thoughts within us, instinctually relatable to archetypes. Know thy archetypes; Know thy Self.

My unconscious conjuring in the dream-state of the primaeval, maternal tribeswoman archetype served as a visualisation to mentally rehearse my son's birthing. An otherwise nervous young woman became prepared for what was in front of her on the hero's path. Our moments of great trepidation are assuaged when we make contact with significant and mysterious forces in our universe that are otherwise unavailable to us. Something about our chemistry in these moments opens us to those supernatural dimensions, the fundamental principle, beyond the mundane. In that state of awe, we feel at one, at ease.

Between the sense of knowing and the rhythmic feelings I experienced in that Big dream (which are unforgettable five decades later), there is no doubt in my mind that I had breached the boundary of time and space, making contact with the universe as old as the dawn of time. Dreams allow our minds to time travel to the past and the future. Many of my clients have discussed their precognitive dreams, foretelling events before they occurred.

Only through a revelation, an 'aha', dreaming (including day-dreaming), contemplation and reflection, immersion in nature, creativity, meditation and visualisation can our indwelling mythical material canalise into consciousness. The concept of the archetype being an original model, a one-of-a-kind, sits comfortably with our understanding of the Whole Self as an original article, uniquely representing the unification of the individual's conscious and unconscious shadow elements. To reiterate, archetypal patterns reside deep within us as a universal reality that goes beyond what can be read by our five senses. If we consider that each main type, by definition, can only exist if it is unique (like each of us), then we come to understand how specific patterns of developed human behaviour (i.e., schema) can correspond. (Another thought: So, if you and I are the same, only one of us needs be here).

Let's say that one of our behaviours is nurturing a life (like when we conceive, nourish and birth it). Then, we attribute traditionally the behaviour to the mother, not the father archetype.

Jung (1959) coined more than twelve archetypes, but the most popular applied in contemporary contexts include the four main archetypes of Self, persona, shadow, animus/anima (which we have already touched upon). To remind: he also identified the mother; earth mother; primordial mother; dark mother; hero and child-hero; victim; villain; sage or wise-one; maiden; artist; innocent-child; caregiver; ruler; lover; jester; magician and trickster; rebel; explorer and the 'everyman/everyperson' archetypes that are on call (among myriad others) to come to life inside of us at any time, any place, but mostly only contactable in our dreams and active reflections.

Some fairy-tale archetypes equating to Jung's assemblage are Our Lady's Child as mother or dark mother, Vasilisa as hero or sage, Jack and the Beanstalk as magician or trickster, and Bluebeard as villain—to correlate but a few.

Let us remember the cultural archetypes of our generations of Western society from the 1920s until now. They range from and are classified as the *Greatest Generation* (born before 1920 to 1924): a survival era impacted by The Great Depression, WW1 and WW2; *The Silent Generation* (born 1925-1945), otherwise referred to as *The Builders* who cautiously rebuilt the world after the wars to experience a golden age of relative creative expression, consumerism, peace and security (sans the Cold War); next came the *Baby Boomers* (born 1946-1964), so-called because of the uptick in birth rates post WW2; they were impacted by the Vietnam War (1955-1976).

Baby Boomers worked hard with 'greed is good' influencing many. They often later regretted prioritising wealth over time with children, yet valued independence and home ownership for belonging.

Generation X (born 1965-1980) are better educated but often debt-burdened yet demonstrate deeper parental involvement than their time-strapped parents.

Generation Y or Millennials (1981-1996) are better educated than generations before. Still, in becoming disillusioned by the 'work before play' belief systems of their parents and grandparents, they focus more on meaningful pursuits and fulfilling them than building wealth. Consequently, Millennials without sufficient means to become independent live at home with their parents for far longer than any generation before. This conscious generation emphasises creating wellbeing, healthy self-esteem and resilience for living on an increasingly uncertain planet.

Generation Z, Zoomers (1997-2009) focus on technology and how it can transform our world. As the reach of artificial intelligence widens, Zoomers value individuals' authenticity and being real when interacting (possible because they spend a lot of time inside unreal computer games). As they mature, they collectively appreciate diversity and altruism and focus on meaningful interactions, establishing global collaborative connections to make the world a better place.

Generation Alpha (2010-2025-) enters a turbulent world aligned with the Age of Aquarius. They will become agents of technological invention and systemic transformation, highly adaptable and globally-minded.

No matter which generational archetypes are domiciled within us, overlapping at their boundaries and commingling, none is better than the other. Each has pros and cons relative to progressing our species and its collective consciousness through time.

Jung's archetypes (1959) possess two sides, positive and negative attributes (like humans), influenced by personal experiences in diverse cultural and social contexts when expressed in human behaviour. While the archetype's integrity never alters, its pattern manifests according to the individual's unique reality. Thus, the universal hero archetype, for instance, retains its innateness but is shaped by the individual influences of its human host. The hero inside of us is built by our beliefs, values, thoughts, feelings, personality, motivations, behaviours and schema. Hero archetypes come in as many different shapes and sizes and types of journeys as there are humans in existence.

Whether we are birthing, loving, venturing, warring, creating, destroying, or dying, natural contact with the power of the archetypes, universal and local is possible (but not probable).

When I gave birth to my son all those years ago, I made contact with the primordial mother archetype (and the in-dwelling maiden, lover, victim, and rebel were also sparked). With my cast of archetypes' schemas in conflict, no wonder I had felt prior that I was standing on shaky ground. However, I felt more confident about bringing my baby into the world after the reassuring maternal dream messenger stepped up and showed me that I was up to the task. Interestingly, Mama Wati appeared to me in the same image she appears to others in her own culture (according to the images I researched). In line with how archetypes play out according to our personal context, my psyche chose to focus only on her intuitive powers, and birthing and nurturing competencies rather than other aspects of her character or mythology.

Not all of us will enter the dream-state and be shown in vivid detail the workings of our unconscious that I, fortunately, experienced before going into labour—a lucky coincidence of REM sleep, my openness, faith or something unknown perhaps. As this dream taught me, positive archetypes make contact to enable us to explore the inexpressible, unknowable powers that lie beyond the material, visible life. Many are the supernatural mentors and teachers that arrive when we are ready for the lesson. Carolyn Myss, the best-selling author of *Sacred Contracts* (2001), refers to archetypes as the 'architects of our lives'.

If only I could bottle the transformative essence of the experience to share, though I do carefully mind my words to impart my elixir.

Contacting our primitive underpinnings through archetypes helps us reconcile the discrepancies between what we see, what we're told, and what we feel. These inconsistencies unsettle the knowing spirit, which seeks harmony while the ego struggles to make sense of a dualistic reality. Is it any wonder that spiritual beings feel lost when disconnected from the Sacred and Divine?

As physical beings, we inhabit an ego-driven, unnatural world, objectifying the built environment and sensing something vital is missing. To fill the void, we often reach for inorganic or external substitutes—yet this only deepens the schism within. Our mental health suffers as the separation from our organic, soulful nature grows. Paradoxically, myths—though often dismissed as unreal offer a path to reawaken our connection to what is innately real.

Long before human life appeared, the natural world had its trials but could exist without us. On the other hand, humans living in the natural world in crowded proximity, without introducing the structure and systems of civilisation (such as clean running water, sanitisation and medicine), would succumb to the spread of disease. Mother Nature (an archetype we all recognise) has super-powers for giving and taking. She nearly wiped all of us out 75,000 years ago.

Humans, while instinctual, also have the consciousness and free will to decide between behaving violently or benevolently. Despite not being wired for violence, we still routinely commit senseless acts of savagery. We may become so threatened by the instinctual forces of nature within that we over-compensate and unleash an embodied dark archetype. The archetype could be the animalistic id or other shadowy entities, monsters, villains or villainesses. The Bluebeard archetype is a prime example.

For millions of humans, violence has increasingly become (again) a natural part of the reality on the planet. When we are fearful and strike out, we disconnect from the empathic energy of the Divine. Feeling separate makes us painfully aware of our lack of connection.

With the human collective so often operating from a default sense of 'lack' many awakened voices are calling for a new system of thought—a new paradigm or complete reset. Can we strive to become better versions of ourselves and live our best lives? Can we take responsibility for our actions without shifting the cost onto others? Will we share what we have when we have more than we need? Perhaps we can begin to see ourselves as micro-parts of the macrocosm, naturally inclined to sustain balance through ethics, compassion, sustainability, and care. This reflects the state of individuation—our true selves in motion. Yet when these ideals remain unpractised, they risk becoming little more than noble sentiments. Still, there is hope that the Alpha generation may carry this proposed paradigm—Plato's promise—into lived reality.

Through our global trials, the hero, everyperson, caregiver and collectivist and self-transcendentalist archetypes must emerge anew in us. Consciousness has given us the responsibility of stewardship, with the threat of far-reaching consequences for our ill-directed creation or destruction. Currently, we blinker our eyes, not seeing the weight of our dangerous actions until they come back to hurt us directly. Can these be the behaviours of self-actualised humans with dominion over the earth?

The truth will always out. Truth becomes self-evident, and our denial will not make reality go away. It is time we summoned the sage hero within to take charge and be a voice for truth. We must go beyond the mundane to bring an enduring spirituality into our lives. In doing so, we may then heal ourselves in a cycle of regeneration, living harmoniously in balance with nature instead of playing God with it.

Implementing myth-work like the *Mythimo* process in our reality provides gentle but firm opportunities to put into action Plato's 'know thyself' (to heal). When large numbers of individuals engage in their personal healing quest and a critical mass is reached, we are on the way to healing the collective, one person at a time. Granted, it seems an impossible fantasy that millions of us would begin to see that we are behaving as three-dimensional mythicised archetypes doing our best to conform to a socio-cultural norm. And that might be okay if it were not for the fact that wounded emotions in our shadow contaminate the way we enact our archetypes, mobilising the negative traits over the positive, and separating us from our authentic centre. But we can work backwards from the archetypes to do the inner work, reclaiming and integrating our conflicted parts and becoming authentic—just add Soul.

And what of the notion that no man is an island (John Donne, 1624)? Are we so afraid that being our original, individual Self will somehow destroy the fabric of the family, tribe, society, and the world? If we are all in this together, a part of the main, as Donne implies with his, "never send to know for whom the bell tolls; it tolls for thee," there is no denying our interconnection and the overarching conditions we share. However, must we all share the same perspective? As discussed before, groupthink dumbs us down and dilutes our personal power. We know when groupthink has gone to the extreme when we witness the behaviours of individuals belonging to a cult or a mobocracy. The mob may be pushing for social justice but end up in a frenzied state where anything goes (including violations to individual dissenters) to meet their mobocratic ends.

There may be no 'I' in 'team', but there is a 'me'. We, without forgetting to love ourselves, can adopt a pluralistic ethical stance, digressing from the egoic ethics of modern times and embracing the compatible tenets of relativism, Kantianism and utilitarianism (culturally permitting).

It is time to strike a balance; it is always time. Indeed, self-actualised individuals are more often the courageous, caring and sharing human archetype, a coalescence of the hero, sage and caregiver. By taking good care of themselves, they are more likely to possess the Mudita mindset and commit themselves to lifting others up with them.

Psychoanalyst Erikson (1950) referred to this giving behaviour as generativity. We act to promote wellbeing not only for the common good but to promote our new generations' survival and that of the whole species. We are the generators of giving; we pay it forward.

Some say wanting to improve the world goes against the optimistic belief that the 'world is perfect as is'. If we interpret the poetry, '*the universe is unfolding as it should*', as a nod to sitting on the side-lines, doing nothing and letting things be, we are wasting an opportunity to create a kinder, more sharing world. The famous line comes from the inspiring poem of *Desiderata* (meaning 'things wanted or needed'), espousing the idea that whatever happens only happens because there is still learning to be had. Things would not occur if we knew how to manage the experience efficaciously in the first place This educative philosophy gives us a starting point, a code of behaviour for Higher Living. But it does not speak to what we humans can do once we go 'next level'. When we have become conscious of the problems and how we might solve them, the sky is the limit. We move on to bigger and better things. Besides, we have an ethical duty to help others wherever possible. The good Lord tells us that, and we listen being altruistic by design.

Today, we have reached a tipping point by laying too heavy a human hand upon the natural world in which we operate. Meanwhile, the intense suffering, exploitation, and torture of those hidden from our private view will continue. We are the bystanders, the unwitting voyeurs aware the bullies viciously control the victim, and unconsciously thinking, while it is them, it cannot be us, saying all is well in our world so far away.

A solution-focused paradigm may well seem like a 'doomsday prophecy' to those with a peachy view of the world as it stands. We are all entitled to our perspectives and opinions. But if we do not see the problem, its solution soon becomes superseded by a domino set of larger issues. Foremost, we know the Divine did not intend this to be an '*us and them' or 'have plenty and have-not'* world. We are in the world and of it, and our geographical borders grow closer with every passing year.

Some of us who seek the truth concerning our species' history of poor stewardship may resonate with the lyrics from *When all the laughter dies in sorrow* by the band Chicago (1972). The words of the anthem—our call to action— go like this:

When all the laughter dies in sorrow
And the tears have risen to a flood
When all the wars have found a cause
in human wisdom and in blood
Do you think they'll cry in sadness
Do you think the eye will blink
Do you think they'll curse the madness
Do you even think they'll think
When all the great galactic systems
sigh to a frozen halt in space
Do you think there will be some remnant
of beauty of the human race
Do you think there will be a vestige
or sniffle or cosmic tear
Do you think a greater thinking thing
Will give a damn that man was here.

Are we modern humans behaving like the mythical character of Icarus, who used wings fashioned from feathers and wax to fly but despite his father's warnings flew too far aloft and too close to the sun? Will our life story be, as his was, a chronicle of a disaster foretold?

We have many lessons across mythology already inherent, learned and shared to help us forge new ways of thinking and behaving in these uncertain times of existence on the planet. They await our rediscovery.

While we are polarised by strong passions, diverse beliefs, egoic ethics, internal motives, abuse and violations we will remain distracted from the worthy contributions we can make in this world. It is time we reflect and undertake a powerful self-inventory of our biases, assumptions, and perceptions, allowing room for our greater understanding to emerge. That is if we are truth-seekers motivated to become the full bloom of our authentic selves.

No matter what, we nearly always have the power of choice. Do we want to have the time of someone else's (mythical or real) life or our own? We can hide our vulnerabilities behind the structural order of our culture and groupthink to make our way safely through our existence. Our compliance with traditional systems and social orders brings rewards and nearly always provides us with a protected and predictable lifestyle (until it does not). Suppose we pour ourselves into the conventional, hierarchical frameworks of religion, law, and politics along with their social and cultural systems, rites, routines, ceremonies and popular trends. In that case, civilian life has proven benefits such as security in numbers. But we might only achieve a generic life of sorts if we fail to distinguish ourselves.

According to Socrates and his charge, Plato, an unexamined life is not worth living. Both posited that we were born with consciousness and, as such, have a responsibility to use it. If we do not think critically and question authority, we are no more than the animals in their natural habitats ranked beneath us as we operate in our manufactured strata of human power. Science shows how we outcompete the other species—nature says we win. But we see our sentient underlings as born only to eat, sleep, work, die, and procreate, or if truth be known, be artificially inseminated and grown like fungi and then butchered in factories—cruel, unconscionable and unnecessary behaviours of the human species, motivated by ego ethics and greed.

The magnificent natural environment in Australia has suffered significant damage from mining in The Hunter Valley, Great Barrier Reef, Pilbara, Juukan Gorge, and Tarkine, compromising natural ecosystems.

Deforestation hotspots like the Amazon, Congo, and Borneo have suffered significantly. Queensland, my home state, is a shameful leader in mammal extinction worldwide, with nine unique bird species recently added to the endangered list, along with dunnarts, potoroos and frogs. Heavy-handed mining and deforestation destroy millions of vulnerable lives. In my hometown alone, more than 200,000 wildlife are wiped out yearly.

Talk about our sense of human privilege!

As Australian philosopher Peter Singer (1946) states, "The question is not, can they (animals) reason? Nor, can they talk? But, can they suffer?" He goes on to say, "The capacity to suffer is the foundation of all rights."

Where there are rights, someone has a duty to uphold them. We need an ANIMAL AFFAIRS minister in the senate NOW! Otherwise, that someone is US. Would we wish this miserable, unnatural world inflicted on animals upon ourselves?

Millions of human beings live, suffer and die this way as we enjoy cheap goods they produce and resources they mine. The Central African Republic, rich in minerals, has become an open orphanage.

Starvation, disease, and suffering are rampant while vested interests exploit resources. Dark forces—both human greed and shadow entities—perpetuate these crimes. Only the ego would deny this evil that the Soul sees clearly.

Who is allowing the inhumane crime of using sentient beings to serve exploitative ends to go on? Sadly, we all are. Where is the showing of respect and dignity to all conscious life as Socrates entreated? Our going along to get along is but one by-product of groupthink we are all in together. Suppose there is nothing more that we can do. In that case, we can at least switch on our thinking brain, become conscious of what is going on, share the truth, and make ethical choices not to participate (e.g., by not buying the cruelty-related products; not voting for parties that promote the ill-source etc.) in the depravity.

We become monsters when letting things be is our excuse to turn a blind eye to inhumane acts. Doing nothing still constitutes a decision not to act in defence of the harmed voiceless. Kant urged that when we face ethical dilemmas, our decisions must be based on a sense of universality, rights, duty and respect. Would we consistently and universally act the same way again if placed in the same position? If it is the right thing to do, we *feel* deeply that we are doing right. This leads us to an archetype that typifies our collective apathy.

The *Rumpelstiltskin* trope typifies the bystander archetype. The Wesen is a law unto himself, an opportunist jumping into a situation where a father has thrown his daughter into an unjust dilemma and denying her any paternal duty. She suffers terribly while he sits on the fence somewhere unseen out there.

As bystanders witnessing something heinous but not intervening, we might think we are innocent, but deep down, we know differently. In our shadow, there will be torment and perhaps guilt. We can heal ourselves, but we must be sufficiently stoic to call a spade a spade first: no equivocation.

Only with our consciousness becoming Whole may we recognise and truly understand our part and place. Ours is an ancient, sacred, and divine universe with an eternal intent for love and compassion. Science tells us that the emergence of our species came as a result of extraordinary coincidences, making the earthly realm compatible with our existence. An invisible force orchestrates our birth, death, rebirth, growth, and decay cycles in a circadian rhythm according to the fundamental principle and natural laws. We naturally abide, syncing with it our heartbeat and breathing, and all our waking, sleeping and bodily functions. When we feel at-one with the rhythms, we are in-tune and in a symbiotic relationship with the natural world. We feel the wonder, breathe easy. We feel good.

Some of us are so far out of whack due to our stress and emotional pain that we may not be able to explain what it feels like to merge with the circadian rhythms and the Divine or tap into our highest potential. We cannot expect consonance with the universe if we are cognitively dissonant. One part of us believes that the world is perfect just the way it is, yet we have seen and understood with our own eyes the atrocities belying this belief. When our psychic systems conflict, we have a problem.

Our history tells us that we are only ready to face our problems when they become full-blown and undeniable. On the other hand, the sage archetype can pinpoint the causal effects earlier, so issues are remedied by quick and effective action. A good scout, they know what it is to be prepared. Less waste is attached to their solutions. Remember what Jung (1959) said about our avoidance of troubles within us: Denying a problem is at the root of an even more significant problem about to manifest.

But US psychologist, John Dewey (1859-1952), said it just as neatly in a different way: "A problem well put, is half solved." The fairy-tale protagonists alike confront their problems, surmounting them in unique ways that often leave them better off than before their arduous journeys began. Take Jack who took matters into his own hands, confronting a cannibalistic giant but still managing to bring home the golden goose.

We know that if the truth is unpalatable to the ego, it will be shoved aside in the shadow unless we find ways to bypass the ego defence. Rather than bombard and confront the ego with the raw truth, introducing it to relative mythical archetypes enables us to accept the existence of the shadow twin inside before the ego rises in defence to reject it and hide it again.

Myths stimulate and renew our thinking systems and how we see reality, recasting our world views, especially when we have reached a fork in the road or lost our way. Our sensitive storytellers, minstrels, mystics, and artists also whisper truths about us in their creative offspring, convincing us of the consequences of our actions, igniting our imaginations and inspiring us to make a difference.

Mythical and symbolic images and metaphorical language, corresponding with us and our indwelling archetypes, de-shroud mixed messages, helping us grasp what really matters. Take post-war poems such as *Wasteland* by T.S. Eliot (1922), alerting us to the human ineptitude leading us down a blind alley into a future where our ecology and spirituality lay to waste. Many scientists alike ask us to reject our egoic notion of omniscience and face the facts. The poetry of Samuel Beckett (1906-1989) speaks to the human hubris and overreach that have enslaved our natural world, exploiting it to the brink. In each case, artists of pen, song or brush hold up a mirror to an unconscious society that sometimes seems hell-bent on making a barren, fiery hellhole of our beautiful blue planet giving its best to sustain all life.

A crack forms in humanity's mirror; not so pretty, so many turn away.

But post-modernist poet Leonard Cohen (1934-2016) recites in *Anthem*, "There's a crack in everything; that's how the light gets in." He implies that cracks are necessary. Do the cracks serve to direct our focus and responsibility towards rectifying the broken situation? Would we not appreciate the light unless we could see the ill-effects of the dark and want to do something about it?

While perfection may be the enemy of good according to Voltaire, if the cracks are causing harm, we should prioritise improvement over perfection. Cohen does not suggest disregarding the flaws either but tells us to shine our light into them, mending them through our goodness and improving reality by being our loving selves.

Poets such as Cohen have an uncanny sense of recounting the chinks in our collective armour. They delve deeply into their own, facing their brokenness and creatively expressing it in poems, their projected light. Being blessed with consciousness, we can embrace our healing in the same vein. Some things can be let be, but never the self-defeating schema that brings us down individually or collectively. There is no sense to it.

We turn a blind eye to our sense of entitlement and insatiable demands, impacting the ecological balance on which all sentient life depends. Our planet, just right for inhabitation, is coined the 'Goldilocks Zone' of our Solar System. Ironically, we mimic the fairy-tale archetype of Goldilocks' intrusive, entitled, and disrespectful behaviours taking whatever we please from nature, pursuing all things 'just right' for us – the chosen ones of the Goldilocks' Zone. God's spoilt brats. The collective suffers from a sense of exclusive privilege, a superiority complex. But every life form has value and deserves to be valued. God asked for our good leadership when granting us dominion over nature, but we assumed supremacy, exploiting sentient beings as means to our ends. Apostle Paul might consider the state of our stewardship untrustworthy. Aristotle turns in his grave.

But we can shine a light into the cracks, taking inspiration from the poets and the humble earth mother archetype. She uses all her senses to plug into the Divine, and its goodness and grace inform her choices for ordering the chaos, restoring balance and rhythm. And then she lets things be until the wheeling cosmos turns to usher in the next season.

Once we live each day balanced and down-to-earth, we enter the enlightened path and finally put our hoe on the right road. We may occasionally venture off but strive to stay connected to our part and place, contributing to the natural world around us. We take what we need and gladly give back our spare. We know our strengths but recognise and accept imperfections, yet we feel the drive to improve ourselves. We take risks, are honest with ourselves and learn the hard lessons that evolve wisdom taking us to the mountaintop of our best life.

We come not from the anthropocentric position but rise to the mantle of good stewardship, self-responsibility, and compassion for all living nature (the earth itself is a living organism). Within reason, then, no living form on the planet is seen as being in our way and subject to our merciless cruelty or exploitation.

As responsible stewards, we are mindful and merciful when measuring and monitoring the impact of our actions and continuously make amends. Utilising our superior powers of observation and reflection, we rigorously check our interference with nature's careful balancing act: this is what having dominion and exercising generativity means to many of us today.

We may wonder at this juncture, whether the redeemed mythic king Gilgamesh or the fairy-tale emperor, shamed by his exposure, eventually came to their senses during the resurrection phase of their Hero's Journeys and experienced such an epiphany.

Social archetypes: the Millennials, Zoomers and Alphas (and now the babies born as generation Beta) face upward battles and inner conflict as technological advances such as artificial intelligence pose the risk of engineering vast material gains for some and poverty for others not witnessed in the past. We must get a handle on the brave new world. How do the elite reconcile their slogans for a fairer, more inclusive world with their rapacious grasp on our politico-economic systems? Where is the generativity in their actions?

How will our youth ring the change, benefitting the ''haves' and the 'have-nots' in fair and measured ways? Poverty is just as cruel a grim reaper, as war, terrorism, resource depletion, health-system failure, climate change and pandemics. The great migration of desperate populations is underway, and the time has come to reset our belief systems: within and without, at both the micro and macro levels. We still live in an era where the economy rules, but whose economy?

Economist Thomas Piketty warns inequality may reach frightening levels. The disenfranchised will naturally seek support from those with stability. As Donne reminds us: if a clod be washed away, the mainland is the less. Let's prepare rather than live in fear.

When we see and accept the broken bits of our ignorant or dark collective behaviours, we are halfway toward transforming them and taking the better-lit way. To make a difference: Think global, act local. And we need inspiring governments to lead the charge.

Which heroic and stoic archetypal role-models can we consciously draw from and develop within us to prepare for the coming changes, good and bad, as well as the technological advancements and disruptions?

Our individual behaviour is shaped by socio-cultural archetypes interplaying with our egoic needs.

Once we place our foot down on that map to the future, we must step up and become the *Collectivist-Transcendentalist* hero archetype whose quest is to heed the universe's call, do what it must do, overcome, and return with an elixir to share. Otherwise, if we *are too timorous and narrow-minded to risk ourselves, according once again to Bettelheim, we must settle down to a humdrum existence—if an even worse fate does not befall us.*

Eminent psychoanalyst Jung (1959) speaks of the hero motif as one that must overcome the darkness and all obstacles to achieve goals. The challenge is to receive enlightenment, facilitating consciousness to triumph over the unconscious. We have the natural powers to hear, think, feel, sense and see; let us value them by putting them to the good use our creator intended. Resonating with the higher chords of our nature provides greater opportunities for our spiritual growth. As we sally forth on our heroic path towards our mature selfhood, we begin to nurture the supra-mind of our Higher Self, which grants us exceptional rewards such as heightened intuition and profound insight, enabling us to transcend the time-bound earthly arena and reconnect with the eternal infinite. Some everyday heroes will be blessed with revelations from the Divine and visitations from ancient archetypes in dreams.

Alongside the hero stand other useful archetypes for improving ourselves and how we interact in society and with nature. They include the lover, ruler, seeker, creator, caregiver, sage, and so many more. They are commingled and reflected in the fairy tales of *Cinderella* and *Snow White, Beauty and the Beast, Rapunzel, East of the Sun, West of the Moon and Vasilisa* of the *Mythimo* series. Still, they are universally found, in diverse forms, deep in all creative expressions and artefacts, primordial to present day.

The central ideas discussed here have been widely debated in psychological circles since the early seventies and were popularised by the Jungian and archetypal psychologist James Hillman (1926-2011). From their research and applications, we know that archai imprint our psychic and emotional patterns and their inherent stories shape who we are and what we do. While Jung (1959) posited that the higher-order archetypes of the collective were difficult to observe through our experience, modern archetypal psychologists are more encouraging, saying both collective and local archetypal contact is within our purview. Speaking from my experience: if our imaginations rediscover who we are in their images, then the dynamic archai can help reimagine us.

Hillman (2015) speaks of our psychic struggle with our indwelling daemons (positive and negative aspects), leaving us conflicted and exhausted. If a client has unmet needs, undealt with emotions and has lost hope, inspiration, and motivation, contact with archetypes helps to revitalise their imaginations and cultivate their creative expression—those activities of the poetic mind, the blessed Soul.

Many clients present wanting to deal with the passive handicaps of their childhoods, where their emotional patterning originated in their shadows. Recognising their archetypes and utilising them as sounding boards, they seize the reins of their psychic reality, not the other way around. Hillman also contends that when we understand the symbolic 'speech of the suffering soul' through reflection and acting to regulate and moderate our behaviours and outcomes, we are on our way to soul healing. And it is the archetypes in us, and us in them that help us along our journey.

Our biggest challenges to conquer are our fear of change and the mistaken thinking allowing things to remain unchallenged and unchanged in the interest of perpetuity.

Remember the Boomers who regretted not spending more time with their kids as they worked long and hard pursuing their material quests? Still, according to Australian author Bronnie Ware (2011), some also wish to have had the courage to live a life true to themselves and not the life others expected of them.

An indwelling socio-cultural archetype (the one that heroically rises to every challenge with a will to survive) is encoded in the Survivor (1982) song, *Eye of the Tiger.*

Almost every fairy-tale archetype must battle for survival with a brave heart to overcome adversity before reaching the treasure trove of selfhood, emotional freedom and happiness ever after. Life calls for us too to be our strongest selves, but only some will get their Holy Grail. Will we?

As regular people cum heroes of the ordinary world, we must decide to set out on a new revolution of our Hero's Journey. Our many first-time experiences and the stories created are retraceable over the inner hero's twelve steps it took to complete them. Some experiences were petty; others peak, and some in between. We have survived to tell the tales, and there must be thousands of them. Now we are ready to set out again to achieve the extraordinary: to be real, to love, be loved in return, and truly belong. Poet Waldo Emerson (1803-1882) concurs, saying, "You must try to do something beyond what you have already mastered in order to continue to grow."

Our reach must be higher than our grasp. How else can we find out what we are made of and look back satisfied and say to ourselves that we lived a life well-lived?

What are our mythic archetypes, and when will we harness them to guide us home?

Fairy tales since the beginning of recorded time, and perhaps earlier, have been a means to conquer the terrors of mankind through metaphor.
(Jack Zipes)

16 CONTACTING ARCHETYPES ON THE PATH

On the path, we make contact with archetypes — timeless patterns that stir something deep within. *Mythimo* utilises twenty-two classic fairy-tale tropes and archetypes that play out in familiar (and magical) settings, reflecting the intricate interplay between the positive and negative traits that define the human condition. These stories explore family and personal relationships in ways that still resonate with contemporary audiences. By drawing upon their archetypal energy, we can confront and engage with the complex web of unclaimed shadow emotions that shape our lives — be it anger, fear, self-doubt, or even forgotten courage, compassion and empathy. Contact with these archetypes helps us regulate emotion, reduce the grip of the shadow, and guide us toward deeper self-awareness and personal growth.

As we now understand, myths and fairy tales are deeply rooted in our unconscious, speaking directly and tacitly to us about the challenges of our reality and how we must maintain the good fight for what is loving and right. What better way to feed our 'poetic basis of mind' and expand the light in the world-soul? But first, we must establish conscious contact with them.

The hero archetype seen in all fairy tales resonates most with us because it reflects our innate desire to prove ourselves and grow, and because it's a resonant symbol in daily life and culture. Driven by inner conflict, pain, and longing for fulfilment, we're called to action: to begin our own transformative Hero's Journey toward a healthier, happier life. But first all good heroes must face what they hide. As therapist John Bradshaw (1933) so famously quipped, "We are only as sick as our secrets."

John Keats (1795-1821), the marvellous Metaphysical poet, described the world as the 'vale of soul-making'. After experiencing overwhelming odds, setbacks, and ongoing suffering, he saw, by the end of his short life, how pain was necessary for schooling our mind and making our souls.

The universal Hero's Journey reflects our innate desire for discovery and growth. Beginning as novices separated from the Divine Source, we persevere through tribulations to achieve heightened consciousness and merge with the Sacred, emerging as enlightened sages. We can only imagine the actions of the novice archetype Little Red Cap as her adventure concluded at Step twelve. On bended knee before our maker, she was ever-thankful for having her life spared, atoning, and vowing to act obediently going forth.

The thematic steps are traceable beyond the archaic fairy-tale stable from which the girl in the red hoodie hails, spanning beyond the 200,000 years of ritual, ceremony and myth-making of the anatomically modern human (Homo sapiens): it is what we do.

Our parallel pathways of the spiritual and material realms are cyclic (like the monomythic journey) from our conception to completion (the endpoint where we cast off our mortal coil, returning to spiritual form).

On a macro level, the twelve-staged Hero's Journey enables us to learn from every lesson, aligning with the cyclic pattern of our experiences and the universe's natural laws.

Poet and novelist Proust (1871-1922) who also knew illness and suffering wrote, "We do not receive wisdom; we must discover it for ourselves after a journey that no one can take for us."

So, our Hero's Journeys are our soul's unfolding: through birth, death, and every life experience encountered *en route*. Although invisible to us, the symbolic cycle sits within a spiral infrastructure, emulating the human quests designed to evolve us ever-higher and nearer to what we perceive as our Holy Grail or the Godhead. The Hero's Journey serves as a guide for us to embark on a rich exploration of the transpersonal fairy-tale archetypes, but within the context of our personal experience. As we complete the cyclical journey from the Ordinary World (Steps 1-5) to the Special World of the unknown (Steps 6-9), our transformation is activated. Returning to the Ordinary World (Steps 10-12), we emerge as the master of both worlds, an evolved Mark II version of ourselves. Some, for different reasons, do not complete the twelve steps the first time around but might take another tilt at it later. The process of personal growth and transformation can be challenging and complex requiring multiple attempts.

Implementing the *Mythimo Cards* designed for this purpose gives a deep understanding of how the metaphorical and archetypal twelve-step path relates to us. For our subjective journey at the micro-level, we overlay our specific selection of twelve archetype cards upon the macro framework comprising the hero's twelve steps.

In this way, more nuance or context is gleaned, helping us clarify who we are, where we are going, how we are going, and where we will go next. Compare the process to playing a board game: only hands-on practice makes clear the instructions and explanations.

By using the selected archetypal cards, we can recreate the key touchpoints in the cycle of soul evolution and test the lone hero's choices and how they will play out in the future. To move with the cosmic flow, we must pay non-judgmental attention to the symbolic meanings and trust that our choices on the path will evolve in ways that grow us. Although we may feel like we're at a crossroads and can't see what we're searching for, we must recognise the imaginary cord that runs through us from the start to the end, connecting us to our ultimate goal. The moment our inner 'everyman' archetype steps onto the path, the Hero within is already awakened—and each ordeal, struggle, and reward along the way deepens our becoming. This is the true impetus for the soul-making journey.

Natural laws, such as cause and effect (karma), attraction, or synchronicity and more are brought to light through the relationship of the selected archetypal cards and their corresponding steps on the hero's way. Having discovered layers of meaning, the querant formulates specific questions to guide their real-world decisions and find alternative perspectives and a range of different solutions to problems that might otherwise evade.

Because we each have a customised curriculum for our soul learning, the number of individual lessons is inexhaustible. *Mythimo Cards*, myth-mantic by design, provide multiple insights but serve as a *guide on the side* by inspiring the seeker to elucidate their own contextualised meanings.

The *Mythimo* archetypes have been grouped together as a typology for understanding human behaviour. As a psychological typing tool, they are mere indicators and not the first or last interpretation of how fairy-tale archetypes play out in our individual realties. They are designed to guide, and inspire curiosity and deeper exploration of the self, rather than be the definitive word.

Freedom of association is central to the *Mythimo* method, placing clients at the centre of the collaborative process. Just as dreamers often grasp their personal dream symbolism better than analysts by focusing on how imagery makes them *feel*, the same applies to fairy-tale metaphors. The most effective way to elucidate mysteries is relating them to our individual needs rather than relying solely on packaged descriptions. Consider the packaged analyses presented in *Mythimo* as starting points. When emotionally stumped, the answer might be staring us in the face—The same lessons seem to be stuck on repeat but remain strangely opaque until we are ready for a breakthrough. In this case, we must follow our feelings rather than our intellect to explicate the deeper significance of the archetypal analogies or metaphors to find our way. Jung (1959) suggested we close our eyes and step back into the dream or archetype that confuses us, activating our imaginations to complete the picture. Robertson (1992) recommends comparing myths and fairy tales to our personal narratives (journalling these) to get a feeling for the general problem-story we are dealing with but looking more closely at the variations to get a specific handle on our issues. We can delve into where our strengths, issues or limitations correspond, and focusing on our strengths and lessons-learned, reframe and 'live' the stories we tell ourselves and others.

To this end, the *Mythimo* method urges us to take a familiar fairy tale rich with metaphors we can relate to and bend (but not break) sections of its meaning around our situation. We are not Red Cap going across the woods to grandma's house but an individual starting on something new where we must face fears and adversaries, make smart decisions and emerge in one piece, all the wiser for our experience. Therapists engaging clients in this process report how the metaphors enlightened solutions (where other approaches fell short) and helped people come to terms with their struggles. In some cases, they positioned two chairs to face each other to get a dialogue underway between the client and the archetype(s). In keeping with Perls' (1969) Gestalt psychotherapy, the client spoke to the empty chair, imagining the archetype sitting there before starting a conversation. They alternated between the two chairs, shifting from being themselves in one to the archetype in the other, responding to their own statements and questions from the latter's perspective (as they imagined it to be).

Meanwhile, the therapist recorded the to and fro, explicated the symbols and synchrony, and acted as an objective mediator to maintain the flow.

The signs and symbols we receive along the way help us to connect with our karmic (or if one prefers, sow and reap) lessons. Still, the most obvious clue is that the testing circumstance (upsetting our emotional equilibrium) in which we currently find ourselves is the lesson our soul must learn. Just as solutions contain the problems, so applies the soul lesson.

As philosopher Eckhart Toll (2001) asserts, "Life will provide you with the experiences that are most helpful to the evolution of your consciousness" and he goes on to say, "how do you know this is the experience you need? Because this is the experience, you are having now."

As part of the *Mythimo* process, we select twelve cards from the set of twenty-two and keep them aside in a specific order. As already discussed, a straightforward method for overcoming blind spots is to read the cards in correspondence with the twelve stages of the Hero's Journey. Whether we decide on accepting our current call to action or refusing it at step three (staying as we are) or evaluating a potential consequence ahead at step eight, the dynamic tool evokes a deeper understanding of what we are doing, how we are going and where we are likely to land next because of our choices.

Despite our ability to highlight what others do wrong, we may be self-blind due to our ego defences. But help is at hand. When we select our relatable archetypes, they provide the keys to unlock the mysterious door. Let us not forget that there will always be others we know who will point out our flaws at every opportunity and regardless of their intentions, we can choose to use their tips to self-improve. In the case of the naked emperor, an honest child was the first to recognise his disgraceful public exposure. The emperor's 'pride cometh before his fall', but once he reclaims his unconscious vanity and arrogance, assimilating it with his sense of humility, his self-respect and respect for others will return. We all know someone just like him who could do with a dose of the same medicine. Perhaps it is us.

Our selected fairy-tale archetypes, analogous to our condition, steer us straight to the crux, conveying messages and meanings, helpful in discerning the very lesson we need and clues for how to master them. These so-called *fictional* stories might be embellished, taking flights of fancy into the supernatural, but not only do their exaggerations cause us to feel at a safe distance to take notice. They fulfil our biological and spiritual need to move beyond the limits of our reality, inspiring us to 'have a go' at achieving our dearest-held dreams.

Our nocturnal dreams and fantasies are sparked by archetypal power, motivating us intrinsically to get out there and try. By now, we are recognising how contact and engagement with the fairy-tale archetypes can increase our self-awareness, regulation, empathy, creative expression and mobilisation to go after our goals. Once we have strengthened these four pillars of emotional intelligence, the fifth, social skills, falls into place. As we know by now, being a good social fit while expressing originality is key to an extraordinary human life. Once, someone this daring might have been called an eccentric — but today, our authenticity is revered.

Our soul's mission is to move through life lessons with grace, ascending the invisible spiral stairway. Neale Donald Walsch asserts our earth quest is to grow soul consciousness. Buddha urges us to make the most of physical form: "To discover our world and give ourselves to it." We're dually challenged to achieve both physical wellness (health, wellbeing, happiness, love, belonging) *and* soul growth—no mean feat for any hero.

Each fairy tale embeds archetypal themes, mythical, metaphorical imagery, psychological plots, and 'humanesque' behaviours from which we can personally draw parallels, helping us make moral, ethical and spiritual sense of how we act and interact daily. As Goethe told us, the secret is to act and not react. Because when we do, our dark unconscious bursts through, causing mayhem and regret. A confident, composed, congruent and caring person, on the other hand, becomes well-sought after in social settings. Often, the individual has mastered emotional intelligence and is at-the-ready for leading the collective into a better world.

Again, along the path, we encounter archetypes both within and without — dynamic, three-dimensional psychic patterns shaped by physiological, psychological, socio-cultural, and historical influences. Jung's canon offers one such typology, encompassing human orientations, motives, and behaviours through figures like the Hero, Innocent Child, Sage, and Jester. *Mythimo* presents another overlapping typology with its 22 fairy-tale archetypes. Yet, we are never defined by just one; these archetypes' boundaries blur and interact as they merge with our personal experiences. While one archetype might serve as a primary indicator for us, the full picture is always richer and more complex.

As we learned with the Four Quadrant (e.g. the *Collectivist*) typing tool, typology systems classify our personalities into different groupings, such as the four basic types of optimistic, pessimistic, trusting and envious. Another typology that most of us are familiar with, even if some do not approve, is Astrology (Western or Eastern) which categorises us into twelve types. But there are hundreds of typal systems available, serving as indicators, to help us know ourselves and others better. Psychologists worldwide have clients who, in rejecting the notion of growing up, identify as the *Peter Pan* type but several more fairy-tale archetypes are linked to treatable complexes and syndromes.

Mythimo is comprehensive, but as a largely Western typology, it reflects only a portion of the vast global human experience. Yet once tapped into, these essentially universal (invariants) archetypes begin to shape-shift—becoming fluid and dynamic as they intermingle with our personal realities, and filter through our individual perspectives. Couched in counselling terminology: As we encounter different archetypes along our path, our responses to them are never neutral or universal—they are shaped by the complex interplay of our individual chemistry, unique essence, and lived experience. Concepts such as *positionality*—the social and cultural positions we each occupy—and *intersectionality*—the way aspects of identity like race, gender, sexuality, class, and ability intersect—help us understand how we resonate with certain archetypes while feeling distant from others. These frameworks remind us that our engagement with archetypes is deeply personal and socially influenced, offering us a customised, evolving map of meaning that unconsciously steers us or, if we choose to work with them, serve as a tool for conscious self-inquiry and transformation.

Archetypes exist within three dimensions — appearance, personality, and story. Humans share these same three dimensions, yet we carry a much richer fourth: the soul. It is this soul dimension that elevates us beyond the archetypal pattern we embody. While archetypes serve as valuable tools for self-understanding, they cannot repair a distorted perception of reality or replace professional medical or psychological care when needed. They're especially helpful for generally healthy individuals who occasionally need compassionate counselling to navigate life's challenges. As the Buddha taught, our unique essence is key to healing. We must commit—body, mind, and soul—to the *Mythimo* journey. True transformation happens when we fully engage and apply its wisdom in all areas of life.

Harking back to the case studies already observed, these clients contextualised the fairy-tale tropes to their personal stories, not the other way around. In this way, the integrity of the querant remains central to the *Mythimo* healing process. Mythic and fairy tales have a plasticity allowing their metaphors to be moulded around the client's narrative in a meaningful way to them. For example, Stormy Tony did not say when comparing himself to the Bluebeard archetype that he killed his wife, as Bluebeard did in the self-titled fairy tale. Instead, Tony drew imaginatively from the trope to connect the applicable components to his real world where he had dreamt of killing his father, bending it to fit his problems, and hence, elucidated solutions to progress him on his path. Tony took a look through the fairy-tale looking glass and ultimately rediscovered his authentic Self.

When holding up a mythic mirror, we need to look for the mundane, moral and spiritual elements in the archetypes to find relevance and clarity in who we are, what we do and how and where we are going. But how can we face and come to understand our many indwelling parts that make or take away from who we truly are?

When we marry, we get into bed not only with our partners but with their parents and our own. Add the archetypes—cultural, social, historical and personal—in the marital bed with us. Is it any wonder we need help staying out of divorce courts? Plato's wise words from over 2,400 years ago, entreating we know ourselves, are more apt than ever.

As previously discussed, the non-invasive, non-threatening *Mythimo* method is an accessible and self-directed way to directly know our subjective psyche on a deeper level.

By hand-picking or randomly selecting twelve cards from the *Mythimo* gallery and placing each one in order on the twelve stepping-stones of the Hero's Map, profound insights soon come to light. Clients often marvel at how accessible—and accurate—the reflection of their deeply personal inner world can be. Through this reflective exercise, we can develop a more objective view, identifying obstacles, self-defeating patterns, problem-stories, and potential solutions. The fairy-tale analogies reveal the unintended but probable consequences of our actions and choices as we respond to mentors, friends, foes, tests, ordeals, and rewards encountered at the various stages along the way. Clients who are at the crossroads speak of the relief they feel in having the alternative paths presented on their customised Hero's Journey. They feel a greater sense of self-acceptance (in seeing they are a part of the mean, the collective), better equipped and more at ease for making important decisions and taking the next step.

Underpinning the order of the *numbered* (numbers are archetypes) *Mythimo* archetype cards is a symbolic, *macro-level* Hero's Journey. It begins with the novice — the girl with a beginner's mind at ground zero — Little Red Riding Hood (or Red Cap) and moves systematically through the tropes of the remaining twenty-one fairy-tale archetypes, ending with the victorious, hermaphroditic warrior Vasilisa, the Sage (card twenty-one). This numinous heroine ventures into the wild world and, surrendering to it with all her heart, returns transformed—having mastered both worldly and underworldly domains.

Thus, beginning with the innocent, novice, 'everyperson' or fool archetype, we come full circle to the heroic Sage. It's a case of art imitating life, and life imitating art—especially when viewed through Keats' lens of the world as a vale for schooling the mind and making the soul. The final card being numbered twenty-one is no accident; it reflects a deliberate synchrony. The age of 21 is a socio-cultural milestone, an archetype in its own right, marking the legal age and access to adult rites and rights, and reflecting the important biological, developmental and spiritual changes that specifically occur during this period of life. From this example, we see again just how multi-layered the archetypes are in our psyche and outer reality.

Mythimo's 22 archetypal cards (ordered from 0—21), imply that the soul begins its cyclic journey at Ground Zero. Little Red Cap (0) takes her first step at step one in childlike innocence and self-orientation. But over time, evolves through a series of reality checks to become an authentic expression of worldly and soul wisdom (i.e., Vasilisa who is represented by the number 21) by the time her step twelve is met. These two universal archetypes are the alpha and the omega on the *macro level* of the Hero's Journey, and all other fairy-tale archetypes that sit in between (ordered numerically from 1-20) assume their default position somewhere from step two to step eleven (this means some will sit on the same numbered step together), depending on their distinguishing characteristics of light and shadow. It is always important to take note of the numbers assigned to the archetypes. Jung argued that numbers, as primordial archetypes, carry a great significance in the cosmos.

So, there are archetypes within archetypes rather like how a nested Matryoshka doll works. If seen as a Russian doll, the Russian heroine Vasilisa nests every other fairy-tale archetype within her, each of which contains strands of other collective archetypes, ancient myths, and metaphors, not singular but commingled as multitudes. Interesting, given the maternal energy in the trope.

A rich comprehension of how the *macro-system* of the Hero's Journey the *Mythimo* way is beneficial as it adds another nuanced layer to the client's reading (this optional, advanced layer is discoverable in the *Mythimo* advanced course), but it is not crucial to elucidating pertinent information for the client's benefit. Everything one needs to know about the *Mythimo* method, at this stage, is within the pages of this book and complementary tools.

Let's return to the core of the *Mythimo* method: the personal level where clients begin contacting archetypes on their healing path. They select twelve cards from a set of twenty-two, which reflect who they are and their current state—creating a remarkable synchrony. These cards are placed on a twelve-step journey map in the order chosen by the client. Each selection and its meaning is unique, with the client's input shaping the interpretation within their own context, which the counsellor supports and reflects. For instance, if, through the process of sortilege, a client picks Rapunzel at step one, we know at once (analogously gleaned from Rapunzel's tempestuous ousting from the tower), that they are experiencing a disruption to their ordinary world that provides the impetus for setting forth in a new direction. When read in conjunction with the default *macro-card* of Little Red Cap at that position, further nuance is gleaned about it (but let us not over-concern ourselves with that *advanced* learning stage, for now). Still, we know at once that she is being tested in ways never experienced before, and so on. Does their journeying begin and end there? No: every circle's end is its beginning, and vice versa.

As deep and long as one's shadow goes, so too is the process of reclaiming and integrating it back into our light. And woven into that shadow are often the intricacies of trauma—the tangled threads of a problem-story shaped by trauma, pain, fear, or silence—all of which must be carefully witnessed and worked through on the journey home.

So far, we have learned we are all on a mission to free ourselves from the emotional pain stuck in our shadow, holding us back from living our love and light-filled best life. To heal, we must undertake the *conscious* Hero's Journey, no doubt, over and over, mastering one lesson after another, particularly when we embark on a new phase in our lives.

The twelve steps, indelibly written in the stars, apply to everyone, everywhere and at every time. Yet, only in being conscious do we absorb our learning and evolve, promising our passage will be all the more rewarding the more aware we become.

Rapunzel's ordinary world was suddenly disrupted when she was banished to the woods alone and pregnant. However, she faced her ordeal head-on at Step 8, and her resilience was rewarded with songful contentment by Step 9. By the time she reached Step 12, Rapunzel, self-aware, responsible and evergreen, was able to finally reunite with the love of her life. The archetype spells eventual recovery restored stability and a refreshed existence for the client who chooses her.

Some may refuse the call, clinging to the mythicised self, not appreciating that it has become contaminated from unprocessed painful emotions and trauma, and remain in their (uncomfortable) comfort zone. But change happens in our lives sooner or later, whether we are in the driving seat or not.

As Jung (1959) cautioned, whatever lies unresolved within (our psyches) will eventually erupt in magnified proportions in the light of day. Taking charge, acting rather than reacting, is always the better option.

Unconscious were the fish-wife and her hapless husband. They received many cautionary signs from nature during their rags-to-riches journey. The fisherman felt uneasy, knowing their greedy demands on the fish-genie couldn't end well. Still, the unconscious archetype ignored the conflict, carrying on, only to see their lives unravel from riches back to rags, where their journey began.

Nature signals what's coming if we are conscious and heed her signs. Before we dive into fairy-tale archetypes, let's see how these old stories teach us more about reality and ourselves than we realise. Better yet, they reveal and heal our dark side by restoring our shadow to the light—a transformative process for the poetic soul.

Fairy tales are more than true: not because they tell us that dragons exist, but because they tell us dragons can be beaten. (Neil Gaiman)

17 A FAIRY-TALE TRANSFORMATION

Against the edge of hard, dark, brooding wood,
Between the poor, the plenty, and all that's good,
I stood, as silence rang her charming chime —
Calling deep from the wild, to mark my time.

Once upon a time, in a faraway place where the woods gave glory to God, lived two young men who spent a lifetime searching for the commonplace history of their people's past—the legendary oral archive preserved by the elders' storytelling around the fire.

Here in Australia, our First Nations peoples have long recorded their creation stories and mythic traditions through rock and bark paintings, body art, ritual, story, song, dance, and ceremony—deeply connected to the land and passed down through generations. The mythic sources explored in *Mythimo*, however, draw not from these rich oral Indigenous traditions, which belong solely to them, but from the Western canon—specifically, the European folktales collected by the Brothers Grimm.

Together, in the early 19th century, the scholastic Grimms, devotees of fairy-tale conservation, travelled through the small kingdoms of the German landscape to retrieve hundreds of age-old folkloric stories. They actively listened to tales at the kitchen hearth of handmaidens, in courtiers' parlours, and the sumptuous surroundings of an educated middle-class. Day and night, the brothers chronicled the oral heritage of different ancient dialects and had their works published for posterity. In their lifetime, almost a rags-to-riches story in itself, they finally received recognition for their unique contribution to German history and culture.

Their famous first edition (1812), now succinctly edited and referred to as *Grimm's Fairy Tales*, is still amongst the most widely read books ever published. From early beginnings two centuries ago, these tales have entertained, stimulated, and soothed to sleep both children and adults alike. Although centuries old, the themes and archetypes still ring true to our personal experiences, encompassing both simple pleasures and those that are disturbingly dark and dangerous. Fairy tales are perennial, speaking to the human condition and our inner lives in the same way today as they did so long ago.

For this reason, the timeless tales provide clues, helping us cope with our existential conundrums and to understand ourselves, our modes of behaviour and motives. Willans (2012) asserts that fairy tales and myths, in their replication of our real-world trials, elucidate mysteries and give meaning to our lives. By seeing ourselves inside the fairy-tale tropes and observing the positive ways mythic archetypes strive to overcome their challenges, we become ever-hopeful of slaying the dragons in our personal realities. They teach us that we can develop the same levels of unwavering belief, resilience, and even heroism to get through to the other side where our treasure awaits—if only we can press on until the end, as they do.

Psychoanalyst Jung (1959) said when writing about the power of the hero archetype that "Only one who has risked the fight with the dragon and is not overcome by it wins the hoard, the treasure hard to attain."

Since time immemorial, parents, grandparents, and caregivers have opened us to the world of folklore and fairy tales, reassuring us that we are not alone in our struggles. We are comforted knowing that we will recover and start again, reauthoring our personal stories positively, on our circuitous paths with the benefit of our newly forged wisdom. It is the destiny of all heroes that every start ends on a new beginning.

Yet, the paradox remains: we only learn the very thing we need to know before taking on something new—after we have experienced it. Life, lived forwards, learned backwards, is indeed a journey for schooling the intellect and making the soul.

When we first venture from the home hearth, it is as though we need an old head on our very young shoulders. This only happens in myths such as when Athena (Greek) was born fully formed from Zeus's bisected forehead, wearing a full suit of armour, rearing to take on her leadership role as the resourceful goddess of wisdom, warfare, courage, intelligence, wisdom, handicraft, and freedom. Her traits seem imprinted in the psyche of Vasilisa — both were torchbearers.

According to the eminent psychoanalyst Bruno Bettelheim (1903-1990), we mere mortals must reflect on our experiences to learn coping skills, build resilience, and fortify strategies enabling us to navigate our way through the days of our lives. When we do, we establish a greater sense of their meaning. Fairy-tale wisdom cannot come too late or early.

To help our children develop and prepare for reality's vagaries, we can read them fairy tales, sparking their conscious awareness about different archetypal behaviours and their consequences. Nurturing a child through shared fairy tales or nursery rhymes at bedtime helps the child feel less alone, developing a sense of trust in their carers and the world, according to Dr Maria Montessori (1870-1952). Montessori contends these activities foster the development of children's language and reasoning centres of the brain. Dr Montessori is not unique in her belief, as Einstein (1879-1955) also asserted children become more intelligent if their parents read them fairy tales. As we age, becoming conscious of fairy-tale archetypes also helps us increase our emotional intelligence quotient.

Without regular tender sharing moments between carer and child, we may grow up with an inner voice telling us we are insignificant or unworthy. Adults with low self-worth will imagine that others are living ideal lives, and only they are the imperfect ones living a flawed existence. Fairy tales help us see we are not the only one who feels rejected, angry, sad, humiliated, scared, and alone. However, these mythic archetypes also demonstrate that no matter the challenges we face, we can find a way to overcome them, returning to peace and contentment once more. Fairy tales engender and restore hope.

As Bettelheim (1976) states, "For a story to hold the child's attention, it must entertain him and arouse his curiosity. But to enrich his life, it must stimulate his imagination: help him to develop his intellect and clarify his emotions; be attuned to his anxieties and aspirations; give full recognition to his difficulties, while at the same time suggesting solutions to the problems which perturb him" (p.5).

To this end, the German poet Schiller (1759-1805) wrote, "Deeper meaning resides in the fairy tales told to me in my childhood than in the truth that is taught by life."

Many of us will concur with Schiller's appreciation of the dynamic learning instilled by fairy tales. Parents often choose books containing the same stories they cherished when young, experiencing the creative joy they once felt all over again. How could we ever forget the message to obey our mothers after learning of Red Riding Hood's tricky tangle with the wolf? Can you recall feeling sorry for Cinderella when bullied by jealous siblings? And who could forget the lesson about three pig brothers sharing the same struggle with the wolf at the door? Each had a different work ethic, with the less diligent attracting a potentially fatal date with the starving wolf.

For many of us, fairy tales, myths, and scriptural fables were our first introduction to a moral, ethical, and spiritual system of thinking and doing. One of our most challenging lessons to learn as a tenderfoot is knowing when our emotions are running wild and recognising when we must rein them in, regulating them with our rational thinking. Through our formative years, if we have not sufficiently exercised self-control, we may struggle later with temperance or taking decisive action. Unfortunately, many of us dwell more in a state of ambivalence than in being proactive, and a certain pall of futility creeps into our lives. Roosevelt observed that folk like these neither enjoy nor suffer much, because they live in a grey twilight.

Goethe's guidance to act courageously and not react still rings true. Can we unlearn the thinking that has led us to the impasse, taking a faithful leap into the abyss—as did Little Red Cap? Fairy tales imply a rewarding future lies ahead for the initiate heading out into the unknown, who faces fear, regulates their emotions, and learns from the consequences of their actions. We understand that a personal journey starts with the first step (the hardest one to take). If we keep going, we will complete the quest, satisfied, matured, and individuated for our efforts.

Our identity struggles to surface as we take our first steps from the family nest into the broader reality. Still, with forbearance and perseverance, we eventually resolve the conflict in our psyche. Through all our trials and tribulations, if we keep going, we reach self-actualisation. Andersen's *Ugly Duckling* trope taught us it is not always easy to find where our people and place are, but if we remain true to ourselves, a sense of belonging will ultimately be ours.

Bettelheim (1976) further contends that children's survival depends on being self-centred to compensate for their vulnerabilities. But as we grow and develop, we must foster a deeper inner resourcefulness to rely more upon ourselves. A sense of self-sufficiency does not mean isolation from our social group. On the contrary, being autonomous requires reasonable expectations about what we can do for ourselves and not what others can do on our behalf when they are busy coping with their own existences. Still, at the heart of every venture lies a need for safety, trust, and hope.

Being a survivor of the Nazi prison camps, Bettelheim, like Frankl, learned first-hand how valuable a sense of hope is in the face of potentially crippling adversity. A host of fairy-tale archetypes such as Jack, Hansel and Gretel, Cinderella, Snow White, and Rapunzel undoubtedly concur. Aristotle tells us our self-love derives from our love of the good. Humans want to be good and do good in the world, and when we achieve both, self-love comes easily. The hopeful, faithful, and forgiving archetypes, Hansel and Gretel, show this to be true.

The fairy-tale heroine Vasilisa stayed grounded, remaining true to her faithful convictions, carrying the light of burning hope and goodness through her dark trials to victory. This kind of person is a beacon of wall-breaking womanhood, a lightning rod showing us the way, a new goddess for the pantheon.

Fairy tales reassure us when we have lost faith that good begets good as a natural consequence. Author Marianne Williamson (2013) contends: "Miracles are our right."

Fairy tales explore the complex problems of family and social life, making causal connections and offering a code of ethics that we, child or adult, can live by. Good people can behave badly, and bad things can happen to good people. While the tales do not explicitly moralise self-righteously, readers understand which actions lead to specific outcomes. The faerlorical inspires our optimism and faith: powerful resources when facing the unseen, unknown, and uncertain future.

Many a young boy born on the wrong side of the tracks in 17th-century France could take heart from Perrault's *Puss in Boots* (1697), implying that even a 'cat may look at a king.' The subversive tale is a call for equalising and harmonising the different social classes. If it were good enough for a noble to find a commoner worth marrying, then a commoner was worthy enough to access a noble.

These concise, cohesive, life-like stories communicate the hidden psychological meaning underlying our experiences that can be so easily overlooked in the helter-skelter of today's lifestyles. Positive archetypes demonstrate a strong moral code without always assuring a socially just outcome. 'Doing right because it is the right thing to do' and the Golden Rule are the moral mainstays, serving as learning scaffolds for character construction. Perhaps then, fairy tales shared between caregivers and our young form the cornerstone of the child's developing personhood and emerging citizenship. As adults, we know mythic tales sharpen our lens on reality, reminding us of the illusion of appearances and that we all have flaws. They give us hope that right will prevail in the end, telling us anything is possible and, most of all, through our pain and sorrow, we will be made a better person.

Overlaying a map of the human psyche on any fairy-tale archetype provides essential keys to our conscious ego, superego, unconscious id, and shadow. Fairy tales, embedded with archetypes, symbols, metaphors, and relatively simple plots representing good and evil, help us identify parts of us otherwise hidden from our awareness. Suppose we have lived a broad spectrum of life experiences by the time we reach adulthood; then, there will be even greater psychological value waiting for discovery in the tales.

The conscious ego might see our success but fail to acknowledge that we always want more or are much too greedy (in shadow) to feel calm and contented. We answer the nagging voice from our superego, insisting we should be doing much better than we are. Going after more and still more may have been The Fisherman and his Wife's remedy, but fairy-tale tropes such as the *Little Mermaid*, *Emperor's New Clothes*, *Beauty and the Beast*, *Goldilocks*, and the mythical *Gilgamesh* indicate our varied human responses.

In almost every fairy tale and myth, there exists 'one forbidden thing' to which the protagonist submits. The mermaid's father told her not to swim beyond the reef; Beauty should not have overstayed her family visit; the fisher's wife was warned about her greed, and Gilgamesh went into the Forbidden Forest. The forbidden doors of the *Our Lady's Child* and *Bluebeard* tales came with potentially fatal consequences.

Fairy tales broach the complex concepts of death and loss, helping children learn in a non-threatening way about life's harsh realities. Through their lens, much of our childhood wounding, emotional trauma, and broken dreams are laid bare. Still, as a gift that keeps on giving, when we become adults, they have an innate ability to plumb our depths, revealing our dark side so we may reclaim and regenerate it into light.

We are better off not denying or escaping the existence of our shadow; otherwise, we enable it to defeat us by stealth. The shadow is better out than in, as many a now-awakened denialist who has suffered from a psycho-somatically induced illness will have to concede. We are only as sick as our shadow, our secrets.

In the tale of *Rumpelstiltskin*, the miller's daughter finds herself in an impossible situation, making desperate bargains that will come back to haunt her. But the story's true wisdom lies in what happens when she finally speaks the strange little man's name aloud. The moment she names him, he loses all power over her, combusting in fury. This is the work of shadow integration: when we name our hidden shame, our secret fears, our disowned rage—when we speak them into the light—they lose their tyrannical hold over us. The shadow has power only whilst it remains unnamed and unknown.

As we learned before, naming and taming our shadow parts, requires we become more emotionally intelligent—self-aware and regulated, empathetic, motivated, and socially adept. Getting the balance right between being who we are and regulating our behaviours to fit in with social norms sounds easier than it is for some of us. While I have on occasion been cautioned to curb my enthusiasm by more inhibited types, I have not driven this personal characteristic completely into shadow as I age. There is a difference between taming the tiger before letting it out of the cage (allowing sufficient time to read the environment) and suppressing our natural inclinations because we feel afraid, guilty, or ashamed of them. As I have learned first-hand, a conflicted psyche leads to depression, anxiety, lack of motivation, and even immobilisation. The poor little Ugly Duckling archetype, when experiencing criticism and contempt, never became super-defensive or gave up on himself. It is all a matter of emotional intelligence, discernment, and maintaining one's balance.

To reiterate, before we know where to begin with our inner work, we need to discern and own up to our habitual behaviours impacting our lives negatively. In shadow, these flaws are inflamed with shame. Later, when subsumed into light, the aspects of self still exist, but we use them to act rather than behave reactively.

Nowadays, there is no emotional pull on my equilibrium when someone with mean intent says I'm bonkers. I know I'm not, and I have come to accept and love my points of difference. As the brilliant but hyper-sensitive Hans Christian Andersen wrote in *The Teapot*, "Imperfections we all have, but we also have compensations."

Herein lies the rub. Sensitivity, being seen as a weakness, crawls into a hidey-hole in shadow. Only through owning and reclaiming the sensitivity and doing the inner work to transform and integrate it back into the self will the individual feel the fulsome firepower of innate creativity again. We cannot be complete if we have disowned and sent psychic fragments to the shadow. Nor can we be Whole if our overreaching superego convinces us we should have done better.

Psychoanalyst Jung (1959) proposed we are latently still Whole even after separating from our disowned parts in shadow. We await restoration. If we reflect, listen to, and elucidate meaning from our dream and archetypal messages, we can contact, reclaim, and integrate our outcast aspects. Then, we can regenerate into a single functioning unit, harmonising our tripartite psyche of ego (conscious), shadow (unconscious), and superego (unconscious and conscious). We become consciously aware of what we are believing, thinking, saying, and doing. There is no psychic conflict between these states of being. Jung wrote (1970):

The reason why consciousness exists, and why there is an urge to widen and deepen it, is very simple: without consciousness things go less well. This is obviously the reason why Mother Nature deigned to produce consciousness, the most remarkable of all nature's curiosities.

As spiritual beings hailing from the immense wave of the unified energy field of the universe, incarnated with consciousness here on earth, we can choose to live in light and love or shadow and fear. The more we embrace enlightenment by healing our shadow scars, we vibrate with higher frequencies, emitting light into our lives and back into the cosmic field. Quantum physicist William J. Bray

(2012) proposes that our consciousness paints the universe into being. What colours, light or grey, are we choosing from the world's rainbow palette to evolve the world-soul and our own?

Fairy tales open our eyes to where our behaviours are harmful and adding to the darkness in reality. Archetypes such as the greedy wife, vain leader, violent husband, and untruthful mother or father expose what goes on behind the forbidden doors of not only ours but our neighbours' homes.

If we are honest, knowing our family is not the only dysfunctional one on the block is liberating and comforting. Humans hate to feel out on a limb on their own. But being one of many does not let us off the hook. As a first step, though, we are permitted to accept flaws in our human condition because this position provides a non-threatening impetus to mending our broken bits integral to our Wholeness.

Jack Zipes (2012), a professor emeritus of German, comparative literature, and cultural studies, shines a light through his writings on the insightful quality of fairy tales and how they help us distinguish between falsehoods and truths. Peeking into the fairy tales of *Puss in Boots* and *The Emperor's New Clothes*, we see how foolishly impressionable some of us can be concerning wealth, power, and status. Becoming aware, we might now concede that our material achievements do not always correlate with the eternal properties of wisdom, truth, joy, meritocracy, and ethics.

In the case of the canny cat with human swagger, his wiles led to the elevation of his master's station at the expense of the established nobles (although they did not know or mind). Suppose ordinary people could lift themselves from the 'four fs' (our animal drives of fleeing, fighting, feeding and fornicating/mating) and demonstrate the same levels of critical thinking and abstract reasoning. In that case, they, too, could look at a king.

Zipes (2012) provides a rationale for how fairy tales have influenced, shaped, and, at times, destabilised the cultural paradigm. As the archetype profoundly changes, according to Zipes (2012), so do we on an individual level: "If there is one 'constant' in the structure and theme of the wonder tale, it is transformation."

Beyond awakening us to our positive or negative attitudes embedded in our problem-stories—fairy tales illume our mental and emotional processes in the same way our creative juices flow when we make art and dream. We hear a hungry wolf is on the attack in the woods or a giant is chasing a young boy as he frantically descends a ginormous beanstalk, and our anxious hearts leap into our throats. Our thinking voice barracks loudly for the protagonist to make a speedy and safe getaway. We are right there with them through every emotionally charged minute.

Bettelheim (1976) advances his theories of how fairy tales impact children's development in his ground-breaking book, *The Uses of Enchantment*, and writes, "The form and structure of fairy tales suggest images to the child by which he can structure his daydreams and with them give better direction to his life" (p.7).

By the time the child is three years old, they are already conscious of fitting in with kin and kith and will repress thoughts and behaviours receiving disapproving feedback. Our desperate need to belong and feel accepted causes us to conform to our familial, social, and cultural norms lest we become outcasts. The more of the authentic Self we drive into shadow, the more emotional baggage and psychic scars we accumulate. This is where sharing fairy-tale readings with our children can reassure a young mind about what consequences are likely from their specific actions and how they can survive them.

Bettelheim (1976) asserts that fairy-tale tropes and make-believe characters with relatable emotions help the child make sense of the conflicts and conquests in their reality. The child's imagination ignites as they enter the mythical world. For example, a real boy may not feel as shamed for defying his mother once he hears that Jack's misadventure with the magic beans turns out very well in the end for the matriarch who punished him for his disobedience.

Already reprimanded and having learned the error of their ways, the young's psyche does not also need the burden of lingering shame. Shame is a toxic second-hand emotion that keeps one trapped in patterns. Learning that the fairy-tale archetype has made amends with the mother resonates with the child, who seeks parental approval for their abilities.

Bettelheim (1976) puts it this way: "As the stories unfold, they give conscious credence and body to id pressures and show ways to satisfy these that are in line with ego and superego requirements." (p.6).

Many girls growing up have a wild girl hiding in their id that writer Naomi Wolf describes as the little girl's good dark side. Wolf (1993) states, "We do better to reclaim that little girl's secret darkness and potency than to create belief systems based on denial. If we face up to our dark, potent past, the implications may be profound" (p.287).

Wolf's wisdom resonates in the philosopher George Santayana's words (1863-1952), "Those who cannot remember the past are condemned to repeat it."

It is easy to see how we drive disapproved traits that are constituents of our authentic Self underground whilst growing up. By puberty, anyone who dares to shine too brightly with individual exuberance may become ostracised by the old-line establishment.

The Russian fairy-tale archetype, Vasilisa, was an outlier. Many of us can relate who have stood up for our beliefs despite external pressures urging us to comply with the dominant narrative. Australian author Kate Forsyth (2022) says of Vasilisa the Wise:

"The tale carries ages-old psychic mapping about induction into the underworld of the wild female."

Fairy tales reassure little girls and boys that they can be caring and courageous at the same time without being left out. Taoist Lao Tzu (500 B.C.E.) wants us to let the world know who we are—not as we think we should be or, more aptly, how our superego tells us to be.

Psychic mapping overlaid with familial, societal, cultural, and historical material is made conscious in the mirror held up by the fairy-tale archetypes. We gaze in and see ourselves, and unconscious behaviour patterns are soon made clear. Sometimes we may see a pattern of persecuting others with our meanness. Other times, we find a fear of rejection hiding in our id. Providing the narrative does not go above the child's head, they too can see and reclaim their repressed psychical elements such as their fear of abandonment, anger, guilt, and shame before psychological disturbances take root.

The tale of *Hansel and Gretel* serves as a metaphor for our quest to survive and thrive as we set out to explore the world. Most of us will venture out from home at some point. For some, like Red Cap, leaving the nest may be a thrilling adventure without enough thought given to dangers waiting. But others will weigh the pros and cons. Different approaches with similar results. We experience a series of toing and froing until we finally find a stable foundation to build our lives upon, one brick at a time. The unassailable and industrious Big-Pig comes to mind.

Nature prepares and prompts her adolescents to enter the vast unknown to initiate their independent life. If well-prepared, we set out with hope, a positive outlook, and an in-wired resilience for coping with our challenges. Our unique and complex interplay of genes and biology (our nature) and how we have been raised and influenced (our nurturing) form our rudimentary inner systems. If we expect the best of ourselves and the best to happen, we will look for it. In the guiding spirit of prophet Kahlil Gibran (1883-1931), reframing means our quality of life is determined not by what happens but by how our mind looks at what happens.

Fairy tales share with us what it feels like as a sole agent entering the unknown beckoning world. Many of us will concur that events can leave us with a sense of being lost in the deep, dark, and impenetrable woods. We set out with our kitbag just half full, containing mentors' wisdom, love, beliefs, and values to back up our nascent self-esteem, confidence, and resilience. By the end of our journeying, our hard-won outcomes will fill the bag.

Running under the surface of our youthful bravado lurks a less confident self, untried and with an identity not yet proved true. We must deal with fear, resistance, put-downs, idealisations, procrastination and our own pervasive list of expectations.

Departing from the house on the edge of the wild woods extends our boundaries, and through our new experiences, we broaden our mental and spiritual horizons. Suddenly, we become smaller and feel insignificant in an expanded environment. These are great expectations for those of us sufficiently content with the personal efficacy and freedom such an adventure engenders.

Like the biblical Joseph's grail quest to become a free man after being sold as a slave by his jealous brothers, our freedom seems king. Locked up in Egypt, his dreams prophesied events, and not only was Joseph freed, but he became the Pharaoh's chief adviser. Still, freedom remained Joseph's richest reward.

Often though, we feel overwhelmed by the unlimited freedoms before us. We might sit tight in our complacency, knowing that our potential lies dormant. During this time in our life, we could be referred to as sleepers and likened to the comatose Snow White or Sleeping Beauty. Meantime, meaningful learning opportunities are lost. Were we indulging blindly in magical thinking, waiting for someone else, like a supernatural helper or charming and influential leader (metaphorically known as a white-knight rescuer or fairy godmother), to give us a hand and a leg up? This is avoidance.

How can we know the world when we do not know ourselves? Snow White's stepmother sneered at her mirror, and seeing only her rival's resplendent, natural beauty reflected, she missed the revelation. Arguably, had the stepmother poured over her own flaws cast back to her from the looking glass, she could have done the inner work to constructively reform herself into a beautiful and wise alpha woman. We contract ourselves with our cynicism, envy, and pretentious behaviours and end up in a small and static state.

It is better to engage in rigorous self-assessment and develop the full potential of who we were intended to be. We can turn to the practical and optimistic archetype Beauty or Belle of Beauty and the Beast to find a model of behaviour based on inner strength. Beauty was made of stronger stuff than we might first assume. She was not overly sentimental and did not hold overly high expectations for the future. She knew her shortcomings and recognised those of her father and the Beast with open eyes, heart, and mind.

Belle rationally appraised the situation and acted with emotional intelligence to do what had to be done to save her family from ruin. She said yes to her Hero's Journey. But is the archetype Beauty also playing out the role of the martyr or saviour? Has she divested herself from any tangible prize, her only incentive being goodness as its own reward? We know the warm and nourishing biological glow we experience when realising we have done the right thing.

Beauty did not see her immediate journey as one leading to lasting love, happiness, status, and material success but she followed her heart's compass regardless. She saw a time of need in the family and served this need with a loving heart, maturing to meet the day's challenges. The fact that the beast transformed into the handsome prince was the bonus, the unintended consequence she never saw coming.

Teenagers cannot see around corners, behaving as though they have only tunnel vision. Still, only the lived experience can give us far-reaching vision and profound insight over time. And we must all work at sharpening it, schooling the mind and making the soul.

Undoubtedly, his everyday struggle for survival led the bigger and elder of *The Three Little Pigs* to take the more arduous but enduring option. The choice to build a brick home meant it would take him longer, cost more, and involve more work. Yet, the more he put in, the more he got out. The archetype, Big-Pig, did not falter with the scope of his ambitious project; he just ran his own race. Deep down, in his heart of hearts, he knew he had to complete his housing project his way: the sum of his heritage and life experience told him so.

Nowadays, Big-Pig is content with the rewards of his achievements. He enjoys being a role-model and team leader, sharing his safe home with two younger roustabout brothers. As they mature, they gradually learn life lessons, developing personal responsibility and the ability to discern the best choices. If they stay on this path, each will have a brick home of their own before too long.

Big-Pig demonstrates the choice we make at the crossroads between our immaturity and emerging grown-up self. A transformation from living by the 'pleasure principle' to the 'reality principle' occurs when we develop competency to function when facing the force of threat, human or otherwise.

In the Norwegian mythic tale of the brothers, *Three Billy Goats Gruff*, all their home fields of green grass were consumed. They had to make a choice. Stay where they had outgrown the resources and perish or go forwards across the bridge and pass by the gatekeeper—a starving troll.

Not only do they decide to venture forth, but they also collaborate and devise a strategy to outwit the troll. In unity, their power, greater than the sum of each of them, overcomes the odds—an improbable feat, which alone they could not have achieved. Together, they have found a way to enjoy the grass on both sides now. No wonder they live happily ever after. Well, until they don't.

Most of us set out wishing the best for ourselves; only we do not always make appropriate choices or take the steps needed for the best to happen. Using our intuitive mind as part of all our decision-making is appropriate. But being impulsive and not weighing up potentially life-altering options will not do. Big decisions require more of our mental apparatus. When we need an on-the-spot response to a significant threat, our rational mind—slow, deliberate, logical, and thorough—often proves the better way.

Interestingly, when we are integrated, we will find that our judgement and decision-making skills improve because we can regulate our impatience, over-excitement, and random anxiety.

The Tortoise and the Hare archetypes remind us about the times when we weigh up the speed or steady-wins-the-race approaches to our problem-solving. According to the Chinese, crises are opportunities waiting to happen.

The Chinese were the first to tell their version of Cinderella's rags-to-riches story back in 9 C.E.—the girl with superior beauty and virtue because of her unrivalled smallness of foot. Up until 19th-century Europe, the inferior sibling was often made to live and work amongst the ashes. But, having been degraded by their siblings, the cinder-dweller often had more than sufficient motivation to get out into the world and outdo all of them.

This is a universal tale about an oppressed but beautiful young woman who is also kind and hardworking. Despite being cruelly treated by those meant to love and support her, she is prepared to put her best foot forward (literally). Hers is a story about the power of forgiveness, thankfulness, and hope: hope for acceptance, love, a life worth living, and how our belief can make us decide we are worth the effort of going after and achieving our dreams.

When Cinderella comes of age, she steps out into a world validating her as worthy. If not for her fairy godmother turning up at this juncture, she may have become increasingly anxious and insular. Our current social norms encourage young women to look beyond the prince-rescuer, realising their own potential in overcoming burdens at the hearth. Today, through applying herself to study, creative pursuits, and work, the downtrodden girl goes beyond needing to fit the mould of the glass slipper to succeed.

On the other hand, Goldilocks does not cast shadows of self-doubt upon her sunny, enthusiastic personality. She is pre-pubescent and filled with curiosity as she steps out to explore. Right now, she has a sense of complete satisfaction with herself. Like us, when we are approaching puberty, we begin to identify with peers for role-modelling, turning away from the learning our wise elders try to provide.

Goldilocks appears a motherless child, a curious outsider, breaking into the well-run home of an integrated family unit of bears. "How do the others live?" she asks. This exploration is how we begin to see beyond the insulated walls of our home-life and realise there are multitudinous modes of living out there. Our identity is in-the-making. Our newly evolving, broader sense of understanding may help fill the gaps gouged by the harsh dysfunctions of our primary family. We are searching for something which feels 'just right'. It can be a lonely quest.

Through Goldilocks' lens, she ventured alone on that rite of passage to make contact with her original self-identity. She tested life and found out who she was not.

There is perhaps no better story to highlight our vision-quest for the true Self than *The Ugly Duckling*. It is one thing as a fledgling to reject our hovering parents' advice. It is another, altogether, when the mother rejects or neglects a helpless child. Sibling rivalry prepares us for our integration into the wider world where comparisons and competition are rife. But if our parents tell us time and time again that they are OK (and the rest of the family unit, including our siblings, are OK), and we are not OK, we might internalise the rejection, believing they must be right.

When we believe we are terribly flawed on a deep level, we might expect only the worst from ourselves and begin to fulfil the prophecy of misbehaving. Goethe said centuries ago, "If we treat people as they are, we make them worse. If we treat people as they ought to be, we help them become what they are capable of becoming."

At a time when a young child needs to feel secure in a safe haven, there is a vulnerable child somewhere at risk. When a child's safety is compromised, it is a tragedy. Unfortunately, we have a poor track record when it comes to harming our own, something that is rare in the animal kingdom. We must strive to do better.

Even when we share the same DNA as our kin, it does not guarantee the compatibility of temperaments and perspectives. We can empathise with the unease felt by the ugly duck archetype, knowing he lacked the skills to escape the hostile environment in which he was born. Over time, he could not stay and survive; something had to give.

Other fairy-tale archetypes acting in ways indicating they do not feel OK about themselves include the Little Mermaid and Our Lady's Child. But other fairy tales' dark kin—witches, trolls, Wesen, evil fairies, vain emperors, greedy fishers, and wife killers—engaging in self-defeating behaviours will benefit all the more from taking a stiff dose of self-compassion.

According to the author of *I'm OK, You're OK*, Thomas Harris (1969), the most common proposition for a child put in a precarious position is to take on the 'I'm not OK; You're OK' stance. What we tell ourselves carries a powerful potency and is where our reframing must begin. We see our caregivers as large, strong, and worldly-wise compared to our small, weak, inexperienced self.

However, children who suffer significant abuse may develop the most harmful 'I'm not OK, You're Not OK' orientation, which can have potentially debilitating psychological effects that can last a lifetime without early therapeutic intervention. The pain of being rejected and denied by the only unit of security in the world can lead to a loveless hell of the psyche.

In the seventies, development psychologist Mary Ainsworth (1913-1999) dug deeper into the existing parental-child attachment theories. Her research led to a better understanding of how a child develops their sense of belonging and security. Psychologists have categorised four different attachment styles: 1. Secure—when the child feels consistently secure and protected; 2. Ambivalent-insecure—when the child senses that their mother's level of care is inconsistent; 3. Avoidant-insecure—when the mother routinely dismisses the child's needs; 4. Disorganised-insecure—when the child's needs are mismanaged harshly, with the parent putting fear into the child and then, on the other hand, reassuring them.

Knowing that our need to belong is the strongest of all human needs, we begin to understand how important it is to behave in empathetic and inclusive ways, especially in taking care of our children. According to Aristotle's moral principles, if we want to become virtuous, we must act virtuously. And soon, our positive behaviours become our habit.

Even though the attachments we have with our primary caregivers from infancy play a part in how we manage our emotional attachments as adults, we do have the power to heal and change. Take the mother archetype from the *Our Lady's Child* fairy tale, who is banished to live in a tree for telling lies to the Virgin Mary. Ultimately, when faced with a fiery punishment, she repented. The redeemed mother was freed, her children were returned, and she became most thankful and virtuous.

If we were not so fortunate to be raised with a secure attachment, we might not demonstrate the levels of empathy, confidence, and calm of those who were.

Suppose we are aggressive, disruptive, dismissive, unempathetic, or insecure. In that case, we know there is pain in our psyche requiring our attention and care.

Fortunately for the Ugly Duckling archetype, the damage from step-sibling rivalry and rejection from the stepmother was not permanent. His hopeful predisposition and the will to keep going until he found his place in the world indicate the resilience of his swan-progenitor's genes. The famous tale's author modelled the archetype on his own life, which is very telling about the emotional suffering the irrepressible Hans Christian Andersen endured. We are never alone in our suffering. Andersen shares his elixir that will help us break through too.

Like Cinderella and so many others of our fairy-tale friends, the duckling landed in a step-family. But as we know from the news bulletins, cruelty occurs in both blood-tied and blended families.

Nothing whatsoever makes bullying acceptable: the victim is worn down into believing they are not OK. Knowing with a dedicated counsellor's support that bullying is commonly a symptom in step-family systems provides a small measure of mental and emotional relief to a young, lonely victim.

Knowing that the perpetrators' behaviours are unacceptable, even unlawful, is helpful for the victim's recovery. They develop greater resilience when they innately believe that they themselves are OK.

When children are dealing with irrational caregiver behaviours, inequities, and abuse, they can slip into their insular world, ruminating in unhelpful ways on the injustice. It took the miraculous arrival of a supernatural godmother to turn Cinderella's life in a dusty twilight around. Fortunately, she never gave up hope, grasping at every opportunity to start anew.

Our little ones do not ask to be conceived and born and only hope to be accepted and loved by those bringing them into the world. Science tells us that our brains are not wired to prioritise abuse and violence. Studies show that humans have evolved, preferring cooperation and social bonding over aggression. Whichever the case, we human beings still have a long way to go.

Dysfunctional behaviours of kin and step-kin indicate they are not in a place where self-compassion thrives, let alone being ready to love anyone outside themselves. The annals of history are filled with inspiring humans (and mythic archetypes) who overcame dark and dreadful odds, restoring them to goodness and light. Bettelheim and Frankl, each balanced true grit and their poetic basis of mind to fuel their transformations.

Still, our need to belong is even stronger than the will to live. Well, nearly always, according to my client Lindy.

Case-study—Lindy (Session One)

Not long ago, a client, Lindy (33 years), presented for *Mythimo* counselling. As we launched into our 90-minute session, Lindy, visibly shaken, opened up about how her unconscious had spoken to her in a dream the previous night. She had dreamt of standing alone on the edge of a deserted train station on a cold, dark night (indicating how deep her fears of rejection and separation went). Grieving for her mother, who had taken her own life twelve months earlier,

Lindy's schema carried themes of abandonment and loss, which became central to our ongoing dialogue.

Lindy discussed for the first time how her mother was in and out of foster homes as a young child before finding her forever home. She carried an emotional scar her whole life. Her mum was a kind mother but did not show affection or act as unreservedly plugged into her kids as other mothers seemed to do. Still, it appeared that her mum's unprocessed painful memories left Lindy feeling insecure and inadequate and hence, lacking in confidence. Her single mother was brave, resilient, and self-sufficient in raising kids independently. However, she did worry and ruminate excessively and suffered bouts of anxiety and depression.

During these times of low wellbeing and by spreading herself thin caring for the needs of the tribe, a mother's lapses of attention to the ego-centric child may evoke feelings of insecurity in them.

Lindy understood that her mum felt harried by the enormity of the demands of single motherhood when she heard her say from time to time that she would prefer to die than keep up the struggle. Words like these did nothing to calm the developing child longing for a reassuring hug.

There is an air of ambivalence in many mothers. We are battling and juggling competing demands for our children's sake, but our individual Self requires the oxygen to exist. The truth is, we can love our children more than life itself and still long for space and time alone.

While fairy-tale parents who abandon, barter, or betray their children may be exaggerated archetypes, their echoes ring true—people often feel cornered by circumstance. No mother or father is perfect. We are, after all, children of the universe, some not yet emotionally mature with still so much to learn to school the mind and make the soul.

Through our ongoing sessions and her inner work, Lindy recognised that she had an ambivalent-insecure attachment style, impacting the quality of her intimate relationships in adulthood. Together, we created an initial *Mythimo* healing plan focused on Lindy's depression, loneliness, and desire to move beyond her mother's death. We set exercises for Lindy to undertake and for preparation for the next session.

Many of us can relate with Lindy's journey of needing to heal the past with the mother she now mourned—a mother with whom she felt very close, sharing immense feelings of understanding, love, and compassion. However, because of Lindy being born where and when she was, she struggled with missing out on the depth of affection, encouragement, and emotional security that are the products of a secure attachment. Lindy vowed to reframe her problem-story, focusing on how far she had come despite her traumatic beginnings.

Ambivalence is an airy-fairy, 'maybe-maybe-not', 'loves me-loves me not' state of being, the opposite of being centred, confident, decisive, grounded, and secure—hallmarks of the self-efficacious individual.

Clients who present for counselling have shown me so much of what it is to be still influenced by the attachment pattern made in childhood with their caregivers. Until healed, they go on to reinforce the pattern.

Case-study—Lindy (Session Two)

Lindy shared how she felt the men of her romantic relationships would love-bomb her initially but then, once having conquered her, became detached and distant. The rhythm, moving from emotional intensity to aloofness, can be traced to receiving and not receiving loving attention from her spread-thin parent. Concerning staying the course with her gentlemen friends, it was a 'damned if you do, damned if you don't' scenario for Lindy, explaining why she identified readily with the sense of futility inherent to *The Little Mermaid* fairy tale.

Together, we cast the *Mythimo* Cards upon the twelve steps of the Hero's Journey, with the mermaid at step one, and began a deep analysis into the archetype's bearing on where and how she was going.

My experience has shown me that a man with an ambivalent-insecure attachment style will think he is looking to form an authentic connection but is more inclined to push anxiously for early sexual intimacy with a new love interest. Once the sex is over, it feels more natural to maintain a casual, no-strings relationship. He thinks his conquering of the woman is proof of his charm, machismo, and worthiness. He likely attracts a woman with the same ambivalent-insecure attachment style who mistakenly reads his signals for sex as genuine gestures of appreciation. Naturally, these gender-specific roles are not carved in stone and are often reversed. A problem occurs when she grows accustomed to receiving his intense attention and develops real feelings, but he is already looking over the fence. He doesn't trust her feelings because he can neither trust himself nor his caregivers. He feels safer when love-bombing someone new. But once he feels secure, an unnatural state for him, he feels uncomfortably numb, loses faith, and moves on to the next thrill.

Both are stuck trying to satisfy the low-bar demand for security when engaging in casual sexual encounters, leaving a sustainable sense of belonging and self-esteem out of reach. The 'four fs' become pronounced in their anxious lives: fleeing, fighting, feeding, and fornicating.

How do folk with the ambivalent-insecure attachment setting transmute the energy, developing instead a secure attachment style within? Once again, as we begin being self-compassionate and doing the necessary shadow work, we turn things around for the better.

Case-study—Lindy (Further Sessions)

Lindy put in the inner work, reclaiming her shadow fragments and fusing them with her light. Incidentally, her original *Mythimo* card layout on the Hero's Journey map had Beauty and the Beast at Step 12. Like Belle, Lindy underwent a transformation of the heart, learning to look for lasting beauty within, not out. She now relates to others without fear and mistrust, establishing more feelings of security with family and friends.

Lindy made the decision to live consciously, reading the signs, and making informed decisions aligned with her values. She reports how she is standing in her full voice and power these days. Lindy finds that she expects and receives more respect, and communications have improved across all of her relationships. There is no going in hot pursuit after elusive, ambivalent, and mismatched romantic partners because they *look hot* anymore. She knows her worth, stands tall, and follows her bliss. The Little Mermaid archetype still dwells within her; only now, she functions from her strengths as a free-spirited, sensitive, and intuitive empath, helping other women heal as she has done. With her spirits uplifted, Lindy enjoys going it alone with new levels of emotional freedom. Lindy reports that she has not had a one-night stand in months. Today, she says, "I am free to be me."

The *Mythimo* process is accessible, comprehensible, and self-managed for many clients. The bravest are those who have had tough childhoods but reframe their experiences as the making of them, and undoubtedly, they are the most soulful of us all.

These clients often have something in common. They grew up with an ambivalent or avoidant-insecure attachment or the more toxic disorganised attachment. They speak of how their caregivers consistently treated them as if they were nothing more than a nuisance. The little duckling experienced the same, as did Jung, Dickens, Andersen and Beethoven.

As adults, clients may need support to reconnect with their feelings as they have become experts at avoiding them. They might re-enact the treatment their caregivers gave them. Attachment patterns are contagious, perpetuating from one generation to the next.

While more than half of us say that ours was a secure attachment style, more than 25% of us fall into the category of avoidant-insecure. Imagine being barely seen and not heard and treated as nothing but a thorn in a mother's side from the time you were born? If this is the vale of soul-making, then many of the enlightened amongst these folk have received advanced schooling to possess the most poetic of minds in our human collective. While their young egos wept, their souls rejoiced.

Therefore, ALL of us must play a part in helping our young who are at risk. We can make a great start by showing higher levels of understanding and compassion and lending our helping hands.

Often in a state of fight or flight, the fledgling is ever-ready to take the bolt from the nest when the right (or what can turn out to be wrong) moment arises. Inside an incomplete mind, they have difficulty discerning which is which. From a positive perspective, there is a chance to remake themselves by finding suitable role-models and becoming part of a new niche. Unfortunately, some, through overwhelming fear, stay put, not taking off to assume a fulfilling adulthood. Still, remaining in a hostile environment is not really a safe place and can create scars lasting a lifetime.

When they do flee, they may go from the 'frying pan into the fire', not having the foreknowledge or outside support necessary. Indeed, most people who live on the street have fled from physical and emotional abuse.

I have consulted with many clients who left a toxic relationship, assuming love and light awaited them in their subsequent union. Some clients went from one unhealthy relationship to another until they had done the inner work necessary for knowing and loving themselves. Only when we have learned the life lesson of loving ourselves can we understand the world and the people living in it with us. Aristotle tells us so from the heavenly realms.

According to the Gospels, disciple Matthew is attributed with "Love thy neighbour as thyself" (22.39). Matthew implies we love ourselves and entreats we love our fellow humans in the same way.

When the time arrives, we see our reflection with opened eyes; we begin to understand what characteristics we value in ourselves and others. We also better recognise the human aspects that cause harm. Invariably, most of us struggle in relationships with people who lack empathy, manage us by fear, are cold, indifferent, play mind-games, or are cruel.

Fairy-tale archetypes embodying these negative traits show us that we are deluding ourselves if we think carrying on regardless, denying reality, works. The truth always outs.

It always works out better when we direct our focus back to ourselves instead of being pernickety with the peccadillos of others. We have the choice to continue avoiding our dark patterns of the past, but they will continue darkening our doorstep until we embrace the goodness and light-making of our souls.

Suppose a person at risk leaves the dysfunctional home, entering the heart of a brighter, more compatible tribe. Here, feeling supported and loved, they can turn a negative into a positive. We are the arbiter, choosing to make good or stay rooted in the grudge of grim memories. A continued focus on the new way forward and living with a reframed story will help us leave the pain of the past behind. The swan soared, and so might we.

Healed clients talk of how they took flight and rose like a 'phoenix from the ashes'. Others left but carried the heavy emotional baggage of their wounded inner child around for much too long. Now, from the benefits of therapy and distance, they look back to say, "I'm OK, and I can now say that you were OK, doing the best you could with what you knew and had back then." They say this stance makes them feel good.

Harris (1969) discussed how adjusting our perspective to the 'we're each OK' mindset helps us find the levels of peace and personal satisfaction necessary for good relationships.

Reframing our stories in a positive light influences our self-talk, strengthens our self-regulatory powers, and manifests in positive actions and behaviours. Shifts also occur on a cellular level in our body-mind.

Quantum physicists like William J. Bray (2012) posit that change happens on a subatomic level within us. When we change the way we look at something, whatever we are looking at changes in response.

Nelson Mandela (1918-2013) puts these findings into lay terms when he encourages us to look at someone or something through a positive lens because they tend to grow, living up to our high expectations (just as Goethe promised centuries ago). It starts with the alchemy of a can-do attitude, feeling good inside, and the reassurance of caring mentors to initiate change and turn lives around.

Our Whole selves stand poised to support others going through what we have endured, delivering the fruits of our life lessons and victories as healing agents in society. Success feels much sweeter when shared.

The more we explore and look for solutions to the big questions driving our everyday existence, such as "Who am I? What meaningful thing am I meant to be doing? Where am I heading, and how am I going?"—we begin to grow into true adulthood, ready to take on the world with all its complexities, creativity, challenges, and rewards.

The *Mythimo* method utilising the Hero's Journey and archetypes is purpose-built to tap into rich insights, helping clients draw their own conclusions and make the best decisions to propel their lives positively into the future.

However, some clients present with more complexities. They, like the Ugly Duckling did, phrase the question more urgently, asking, "What is to become of me?"

Theirs is the archetypal root story about the dispossessed outsider struggling to find where they fit in, shares Clarissa Pinkola Estes. Estes (1992) says, "It contains a truth so fundamental to human development that further progression is shaky without integrating this fact: one cannot entirely prosper psychologically until this point is realised" (p.167). Estes points to how humans must evolve beyond the territorial behaviour of excluding perfectly good individuals if humanity expects to evolve.

Other fairy and mythic tale archetypes showing us the inner pain of exile are Vasilisa, Sleeping Beauty, Snow White, Our Lady's Child, Hansel and Gretel, Rapunzel, The Little Mermaid, and Gilgamesh. But there are many more, the world over.

In the Norwegian tale, *East of the Sun and West of the Moon*, a young maiden (given up by her father to a giant bear) who violates the forbidden does not wait to be rescued. Instead, she undertakes an arduous journey, making sacrifices to win the prince back. The tale reminds us that after a transgression, choosing the long path of redemption can be transformative and restore what was lost.

Yet beyond the fairy-tale promise of restoration lies a harder question about those whose losses were never of their own making.

Take the real children of the world, through no fault of their own, who are treated differently, seen as wrong, a nuisance, and not considered part of the well-resourced in-groups? When our young feel inadequate, less vital energy is spent on developing their strengths of Self. Labels are introjected (internalised), telling them they are not good enough to amount to anything or belong. Sadly, with insufficient experience to make conscious comparisons, they believe the negativity and then must spend a good part of their lives suffering or trying to undo the hurt.

Though difficult and undeserved, these early wounds often mark the beginning of an inner journey much later in mid-life—the healing Hero's Journey. Choices made in earlier years, often shaped by survival, external expectations, or inherited beliefs, begin to feel hollow or misaligned. As the unconscious pain rises into awareness, it disrupts the status quo, reshaping how individuals see themselves, others, and the life they've built. They want out. It's not uncommon for people to leave long-standing careers, marriages, or even their hometowns in search of something more authentic—something that reflects who they are becoming, not who they had to be.

At this juncture, we can take note of Joseph Campbell's (1949) words, "We must be willing to get rid of the life we've planned so as to have the life that is waiting for us."

The Little Mermaid chose to leave behind her ordinary world when she went beyond the forbidden reef. However, her story reminds us that we must be careful about what we wish for. So often, with the promise of a joyful future in our hearts, we make foolish or irrational choices and lose our sea-legs, bringing challenging outcomes. Client Lindy resonates and shares, "We can't change those negative experiences, but we can reframe how we see and express them. Even when we feel lost, we might wind up finding a more beautiful path."

In *The Frog Prince*, the spoiled princess is forced to honour a promise, guided by her father's insistence. Though unimpressed by the frog, she learns that surrendering control to the unknown future leads to transformation—for both of them. Her pride softens into acceptance, paving the way for lasting love.

Much like the red-capped archetype—hopeful, naïve, and ready to jump into the unknown—our own journey involves facing fears and overcoming trials. Through this experiential schooling, we are reborn and ready for a reset.

Relating to Cinderella as a child, I found her rags-to-riches story a comfort. As Zipes (2012) assures, fairy tales provide both compensation and revelation.

Many of us are interested in cleaning the slate and raising our vibrations to live a higher quality of existence, without a shadow dragging us down with its hang-ups.

Take the Russian fairy-tale archetype, Vasilisa: she teaches the torches to burn bright and fills the cosmos with her light.

When the wild called, Vasilisa came of age, regenerating herself as a warrior, wise and fearless. Her elixir motivates us to integrate because then we are capable and ready to ignite dreams and transform our lives.

If we forward to the end of her journey, we find a beautiful and joyful young woman who overcame tests of murderous proportions with her step-kin and the arcane Baba Yaga. Vasilisa emerges as a self-actualised heroine fit for modern times who might well marry a tsar but, on her terms, her own steam. She is the firebrand who accomplishes complex tasks, challenges the status quo, and spurs change, helping to make the world a better place.

The numinous hero-archetype of Vasilisa lives inside us all, both male and female. She is present when we hold up the looking glass to find our brilliance and clarity, inspiring us to spark our fire and shine. Vasilisa guides us away from the subordination, indoctrination, and dependency that dim our soul. Her pocket doll is both her curious inner child and wise indwelling mother, leading her out of the darkness into the light. Clever Hansel might have left his breadcrumbs behind, but brave Vasilisa blazes the trail for us to follow.

By embracing the Vasilisa archetype, we enter the forbidden forest, face our demons, and recover our better angels. She did not go gently into that dark night but raged against it, and her burning spirit fuelled a firestorm. When our job is done, and we come out of the woods, brandishing our lamp, illuminating a path in the darkness for all to see—We have embodied her. Cometh the challenge, cometh our fulsome feminine firepower.

While not possible to cast out our human murk entirely, as there will always be an entity somewhere feeding it (let it not be ourselves), by the goodness of our loving hearts we will complete our mission here of cultivating our minds and souls and making a meaningful contribution to the evolution and flourishing of the world-soul.

Shakespeare (1564-1616), waxing Taoism, or so it seems, says in *All's Well that Ends Well*, "Good without evil is like light without darkness....is like righteousness without hope." One cannot exist without the other. We need the propellant tension between positive and negative energies for our momentum. But let there be more LIGHT.

The time has now arrived for our journey of self-discovery through the wild woodland world of fairy-tale archetypes. The universal hero begins with the novice Little Red Riding Hood and, after a complete (duodecimal) revolution of the circuitous path, reaches their transformation with Vasilisa, the brave Sage.

Later, you will read about a fallen mythical hero, Gilgamesh, who wends his way along the same twelve steps of his journey. He illustrates how none of us is but one archetype, a notion apprised by poet Walt Whitman (1819-1892), who said, "You and I contradict ourselves; we are large, we are multitudes." At the very least, we are universally all twenty-two archetypes, each commingling between themselves, our individual chemistry, and those deeper collective and tribal archetypes within as we take the twelve-step round with our every new odyssey.

Individual heroes venturing forth from the known zone to a new horizon start a new chapter in which their personal journeys will be writ in body, soul, and psyche. In the twelve-step process of the novel experience, the hero 1.0 encounters a variety of fairy-tale archetypes, both light and dark. Their embodied, corresponding, and consequential life-learnings rise to meet the hero at the right time and place, urging them to follow that star, no matter how far.

Through the combination of art and psychology, the *Mythimo* ensemble of fairy tales enlighten the universal and personal assignment of the hero, demystifying the significance of the archetypes showing up on our particular path.

And when we come to its end, making our return with new levels of nerve and verve and ready to serve, we are the masters of two worlds, the 'ordinary' and the 'special'.

Just as Cinderella ascended from the cellar as the belle of the ball, our fairy-tale transformation feels just as revivifying. The returned hero 2.0 makes their debut, standing tall at the nexus of the next peak experience and where life's real magic begins. Lean in a little closer, they have such an incredible story to tell.

The universe is made of stories, not atoms.
(Muriel Rukeyser)

18 FROM NOVICE TO SAGE

0 LITTLE RED RIDING HOOD

Little Red Riding Hood (PERRAULT/GRIMM) – (also Little Red Cap or Red Cap)— The *following is a personal retelling of the tale:*

SYNOPSIS OF FAIRY TALE

Once upon a time, there lived a fair, young maiden adored by all and especially her grandmother, who lived far across the woods. The elder always indulged the child with affection and gifts. The latest, a new red-velvet bonnet, became such a favourite of the little girl that she became known as 'Little Red Riding Hood'.

Then one day, her mother asked her to take a basket of fruit, cake and mulled wine to her ailing grandmother. Before she set off, the mother urged her daughter to hurry along, tread carefully and keep to the path. She reminded her to mind her manners and refrain from talking to strangers. Little Red Riding Hood reassured her faithfully as she hurriedly headed for the deep, dark woods.

No sooner had the girl entered the thicket than she was approached by a big, rangy wolf. Being inexperienced, she had no idea of the extent of the animal's treachery. Still, she cordially told him she was going to the cottage sheltered under the three giant oaks on the other side of the forest. Little did she know the wolf was salivating in anticipation of the delectable meal he would make of her.

He padded politely alongside Little Red Riding Hood as she walked briskly along the track. His words were soft and encouraging as he urged her to stop and smell the fragrant flowers, hear the musical birdsong and take in the enchanting magic of the wild woods. Soon the charmed child became overwhelmed by the natural wonders, mis-stepping off the beaten path. She did not see the wily wolf steal away to the grandmother's cottage.

Once there, the crafty carnivore tricked his way inside, gobbling the startled granny up. Quick as a flash, he disguised himself in her long nightdress and cap and climbed into bed, lying in wait to devour the little girl.

Meantime, back in the fragrant forest, Little Red Riding Hood had lost all sense of time and place while flower picking and singing with the birds. When she finally realised how many hours had passed, she hastened onwards to her grandmother's.

Red Cap felt strangely anxious as she opened the unlocked door and called out, "Good morning, Grandmama!" Oddly, there came no reply. She made her way to bed, instinctually feeling something was not right. It was then she spied the large dark figure lying under the bedclothes.

Beastly features confronted her on the supposed grandma she found in repose and so she began to question the oversized eyes, ears, nose, hands, and jaw. Suddenly she recognised the peckish predator's furry features coming into view. But alas, it was much too late, as he had already begun to wolf her down.

The over-gorged wolf soon fell into a deep sleep, snoring so loudly that a passing huntsman overheard the rattling and gurgling sounds coming from the cabin and rushed in to aid the elder. He could not believe his eyes. There, lying in her place on the bed, was the big grey wolf instead. For such a long time, the woodsman had searched for this dangerous menace to the village in vain. But not this day. Unhesitatingly, he grabbed his shears and cut open the unconscious creature's belly, releasing the little girl and then the grandmother. Miraculously, they were both still alive and in one piece. Together, they quickly filled the wolf's gaping stomach with large stones so that he would drop dead on the spot when he woke up.

The triumphant survivors were so relieved in how events turned out that they held a small celebration, devouring every skerrick of cake and wine found in the wicker hamper. Taking the advice of her wise mother, Little Red Riding Hood vowed she would never go off the beaten path and talk to strangers in the woods ever again. **THE END.**

PSYCHOLOGICAL PROMPTS

0: Key soul learning: To develop being curious but careful (Self-Awareness)

Little Red Riding Hood, a naïve, pubescent girl filled with spontaneous, imaginative wonder, embarks on a rite of passage, the maiden's initial quest into selfhood. The red cap symbolises her first foray into fertile womanhood, and the full basket of cake, fruit and wine, her reproductive potential. She must prove her readiness to the grand matriarch for the Oedipal detachment. Throughout history, girls at seven years or younger were seen as having reached the age of consent long before their unripe bodies and unworldly minds were ready. Little Red Riding Hood must prepare for the world of female traditions as a homemaker, child-bearer, and nurturer. Her mother oversees her initiation test to check whether her daughter can remain faithful to the proven path.

Fate is about to turn on the light for Little Red Riding Hood's impending transformation towards fecund femininity. Still, it will be a folly-laden journey for any maiden oblivious to the temptations and traps about to surface.

She feels inadequate inside her shadow side and fears failing on her first venture. To compensate for her lack of social competence, she seeks attention and power by wearing the symbolic red bonnet. She suffers from social anxiety, as so many of us do, but she is keen to make social connections, taking her out of her ordinary world and into new settings. Here she is saying, "Look at me!" The problem is that she attracts the wrong kind of attention. To the conquistador type, she is a blank page upon which they will want to write their name, leaving their dark, indelible mark.

The wolf symbolises the wiliness hardwired into testosterone-fuelled males, always ready to make coital conquests, proving their dominance and ensuring the continuance of the species. Meanwhile, Little Red Riding Hood is open-hearted, curious, playful, careless, joyful, gullible and vulnerable. Infatuated by the wolf's attention, she risks giving away too much of her privacy and endangering herself and her grandmother.

Nature helps buffer the risks of lust-incited danger with an increase, when one reaches adolescence, in mental deductive or reasoning powers. Little Red Riding Hood spots the red flag, but even though she picks that the picture isn't quite right, it is too late. Still, our protagonist recognises that we must employ our conscious thinking to figure out whether what we see is as it appears. Teenagers may be preoccupied with identification and critique of physical appearance but often lack sensitivity to the feelings of others. Little Red Riding Hood takes time to ponder and comment on the fascinating features of the male wolf, but her facility for processing novel information is not failproof against the predator.

Red Cap foolishly chooses to ignore the warnings of her mother as she steps out on her Hero's Journey and commits the one forbidden thing by talking to a stranger. Like any other novice, she possesses a propensity for impulsivity (id) and is impatient with advice (ego). If an alarm had gone off sooner and struck a chord with her moral conscience (superego), she might have erred on the side of caution. However, her yet-to-be-fully-developed brain leaves her woolly-headed, oblivious to the logical consequences of her behaviours. Besides, she wants to do things her way and is disinclined to cloud her optimistic vision or slow her progress with mistrust. She stops to pick the flowers (another emblem of her potential loss of virginity and flowering fertility) and escapes into a tweenage mind-fog. This takes her off the safety of the well-trod path. Little Red Cap, unconscious of her predicament, puts herself in a helpless position. But when life took her to the verge, she had no choice but to rely on her decision-making and leap into the void to face her primal fears. Luckily for her, a rescuer was at hand, a skilled older male, a woodcutter, who knew the lay of the land. Unlike the wolf, he is the epitome of self-restraint in the company of females.

Cut from the wolf's stomach, the young woman was reborn via a caesarean section, still with her purity intact and renewed with sharpened survival skills, ready to take on the world in her own right. Fortune favoured her that day, expressed in the symbol of the 'three' giant oaks sheltering the cottage. The number '3' represents protection from the Holy Trinity in Christianity and is considered a sacred, fateful, dynamic and lucky number across many different belief systems and mythologies. Jung correlated the number three with the stages of human life (e.g., child, mother, grandmother).

Recognising her close escape, Red Cap will regulate her dangerously impulsive behaviours with her hard-won rationale. She has become one of the female 'tribe': a proven product of her upbringing, striving to live up to her promise in the eyes of her female elders. Now, in her second iteration, she crafts her personal code for Higher Living in a brave new world through the culmination of her forebears' stories and her own pivotal experience.

Little Red Riding Hood journeyed from her mindless folly, **Fool** to **Novice.** She emerged with self-awareness and adequacy to meet life's tasks. Through sharing her elixir of joy, self-acceptance, and a healthy balance of curiosity and caution, she has earned her seat at the matriarchal table. With her open heart and eyes and a receptive mind to learning, she embodies the novice archetype—ready and eager for the next exciting peak experience on life's path.

SELF-REFLECTIONS

Step forward with curiosity and care, like the girl in the red cap learned to do. Life calls you to leave comfort behind, explore new paths—whether physical, creative, or spiritual—and trust that experience is your truest teacher. The wild invites change, challenges, and risk; yet freedom never comes with guarantees. Begin with your inner work.

Pause at every fork in the road. Reflect on your choices, notice your blind spots, and seek guidance from those who have walked similar paths. Release the past and let the horizon guide you.

As you open yourself to new experiences, remember the lessons of your own story.

In the past, you may have been gullible and taken impulsive risks, ignoring subtle warnings. Rather than judging yourself, see it as a chapter that gave you insight and resilience. Reframe that story: from now on, you move forward with self-assurance, weighing courage with discernment, and trusting the wisdom you've gained.

Stay open, playful, and curious, but also aware. Let uneasy feelings be your compass. When fear or resistance arises, pause. When your intuition nudges you forward after careful reflection, take the leap.

Courage and spontaneity serve your growth best when tempered by experience. Observe your emotional patterns and relationships. Avoid idealising others or giving away your power. See challenges and people clearly and venture into the deepest caves to reflect—of circumstance, of self, of relationship—before acting.

Peak experiences transform you. By integrating your shadow into the light, you rise from difficulty renewed, empowered, and ready for the next adventure.

Love every part of yourself, light and shadow alike, and work on the limitations that can hold you back.

Your journey will not only bring personal growth, wisdom, and joy, but also inspire others to embrace their shadows and step into their strengths.

You are more than capable of living a fulfilling and satisfying life, and the journey you take will be nothing short of amazing.

So, embrace the hero within and take that first step towards a brighter tomorrow.

There are two wolves inside us all. One is evil, the other is good. The one you feed is the one that wins. (Cherokee wisdom)

LIGHT QUALITIES (NOVICE)	**SHADOW ATTRIBUTES (FOOL)**
Curious	Careless
Playful	Foolish
Joyful	Gullible
Vulnerable	Infatuated
Open-hearted	Inadequate
Naïve	Oblivious
Spontaneous	Impulsive
Receptive	Helpless

PROVERB: There is no teacher like experience.

AFFIRMATION: I take a leap of faith into unchartered territory, open to learning as I go.

GAME OF LIFE: Attention-seeking to feel valid (Consequence: Attracting negative attention and judgment).

REFLECTION QUESTION: Is there more to this story I am not paying attention to?

ANIMAL SYMBOLISM: Wolf/Feral dog; Galah

Wolf/Feral dog:

Canines, viewed as guardians of hidden knowledge in many cultures, teach that we must have sufficient rest, trust our abilities, tame our wild appetites (including tendencies toward promiscuity), and foster loyalty, respect, and unconditional love.

Galah

'Galah' is Aussie slang for one who plays the clown or fool. Her pink feathers mean fun; her grey undercoat—our unseen shadow elements. Her white head represents our innocent, carefree inner child.

ONE SMALL STEP TO TAKE TODAY:

I will practise reflecting on my life experiences and listening to elders' feedback to develop my self-awareness.

MEDITATION PREPARATION (to practise at dawn)

Welcoming a new day, I inhale positivity and release negativity. Envisioning the joy of learning ahead, I feel empowered by the universe, facing challenges with faith. Bathed in warm daylight, I step out with a skip, embracing life's offerings.

It's never too late to be what you might have been. But each of us must be sure to bring our beginner's mind. (George Eliot)

1 JACK AND THE BEANSTALK

Jack and the Beanstalk (GRIMM)—*The following is a personal retelling of the tale:*

SYNOPSIS OF FAIRY TALE

A young lad had come of age and was expected to assume some of the household responsibilities. One morning, his mother instructed him to set forth for the market, sell the dairy cow for a decent sum and return home promptly with the money. So, Jack left with the cow, but on the way to the market, he stopped to talk to a stranger. The stranger offered a deal on the spot for the cow, which meant Jack did not have to continue the long route to the marketplace. Without a second thought, he agreed to swap her for a bag of magic beans. When Jack returned home and showed his tired and hungry mother the small bag of beans, she cursed his madcap youth, beat him, sent him to bed without supper and threw the so-called useless seeds straight out of the window.

The following day, a strange magic had done its work, and a towering beanstalk sprouted its way towards the heavens. Jack did not hesitate. He hurriedly clambered out the window and fervently climbed the ginormous stalk.

Before long, he found himself in a spectacular land high in the clouds: a lush and spectacular world of plenty. In the near distance stood a great hulk of a man afore a magnificent castle. Jack could hardly believe his eyes. Behind the giant stood his wife, who held a large goose in her arms, which began to lay eggs made of pure gold. Jack was gob smacked, contrasting this world of great plenitude with the scarcity and simplicity of his own.

The longer Jack gazed in amazement at the surreal scene; he began to recognise the goose as the very same bird that had once belonged to his family before it mysteriously disappeared long ago. His journey to this wondrous world on high had now taken on a new meaning with an urgent purpose. Now, the mission was to retrieve the golden goose and return it to his mother.

In an almighty rush of adrenaline, ingenious Jack grabbed the goose and darted away with the lumbering giant in hot pursuit, calling out, “Fee, fi, fo, fum! I smell the blood of an English man.” Never mind, thought the lad as he fled for his life, leaving opulent treasures behind and scrambling to get a foothold on the beanstalk; a bird in the hand is worth two in the bush.

Although almost out of breath and his heart beating loudly, Jack descended with speed and agility. Swiftly down the long and winding stem, he confidently went with the goose safely tucked under his arm, until he felt the earth rising to meet his feet. He reached for his axe, felling the preposterous plant in one skilful blow. As for the enraged giant, he was never seen or heard of again.

Jack’s mother, who could bear no more loss, delighted in his safe return. But when she saw he had brought home the golden goose, she could not contain her tears of relief and joy. In her eyes, Jack had finally come of age, proving himself to be a dexterous and dynamic fellow ready to take on the world and make good of his opportunities. **THE END.**

PSYCHOLOGICAL PROMPTS

1: Key soul learning: To develop skills for creating your own rewards (Intrinsic Motivation)

The story of *Jack and the Beanstalk* highlights that life's transactions can be random and unfair, portraying the tension that can arise between authority and one's nascent aspirations.

Jack, a son in a single-parent family, takes charge as the 'man of the house' to compensate, trading their long-serving cow for an intangible commodity: the magical beans. Such harshness reminds us of our sense of human privilege and how nature dictates victory for the most adaptable species.

Jack is a maverick, cavalierly making an inequitable, dodgy trade with a stranger, given that he holds all the family's worth in his two hands. He takes the easiest route, using his smarts, rather than the harder, proven path to the top. He seeks a higher life with only a shallow understanding of what is at stake, acting confidently, speculating to elevate, and predicting his risks are proportionate to potential gains.

Although Jack's primitive and instinctive id fuels his mischievous, mercurial actions, he seems to know what he is doing, rationalising that the cow, past her use-by-date, must make way for the promise of something better. He grasps the nettle with both hands, but he is skilful and resourceful in manipulating circumstances to his liking.

On the other hand, his hard-bitten and conservative mother is initially in disbelief and scorns his irrational choices. She sees Jack's devil-may-care attitude and indulgence in magical thinking, assuming that a heavenly hand will lift him out of the doldrums in one serendipitous sweep. Ironically, the apple does not fall far from the tree, for she is wilful, acting on her impulses and throwing away the magic beans.

As he watches his dreams fly out the window, Jack's inner voice reminds him of how good things can and do happen out of the blue: there is a seed of unknown potential in everybody's life.

Poor Jack harbours several fears in his shadow, mainly that he is incapable of progress. But despite his worries, Jack is capable, adventurous and proactive. He hears the call of his awaiting manhood and sees a vision of a wider world than the one his mother ever knew. However, Jack suppresses his argumentative side as a poor match for his tough-love mother. Her angry beating fails to immobilise him, though, and he steps into his agency, making choices to create a new life beyond the limitations of their past. When he held those beans, he felt their pulsating portent in his hands, figuring there was nothing to lose and everything to gain. He saw a window and took his leg up.

Jack does the one forbidden thing, going after the impossible, risking his life to seize the golden goose from the giant. He had refused to repeat his father's fate: dying young from illness and leaving behind unfulfilled promise and sorrow. Instead, he rose quickly to become the mature and responsible provider, with the power shifting from the elder matriarch to the younger, bold enough to jump at any opportunity. Adolescents become increasingly more in tune with current trends, assuming the lead and possessing a daring spirit that, when the stars align, allows them to manifest their goals and fondest dreams.

The great giant living above us in isolation is a metaphor for abstract concepts beyond our human understanding and five senses. It represents the vast, unfathomable world that confronts an adolescent used to living within the confines of family and school life. Carl Jung (1875-1961) reminds us that something 'beyond the grasp of reason' exists, and it seems Jack was onto it. The young male's actions, fuelled by rational human thought sprinkled with intuitive and instinctual prowess, humbled the supernatural giant. Jack reminds us, in that moment, that the impossible is possible.

But moving forwards, our 'can-do' Jack must balance his over-confidence according to his moral compass and take a 'bird (goose) in the hand' approach. One major win going to his head could distract him from the bigger (the giant) picture of his future. He has the power to create his own rewards by calculating risks, being resourceful, aligning his talents with his endeavours, and staying true to his potential.

The next time demonstrative Jack answers his call to adventure, he will rely more on his natural skills than on the lucky stroke of magic and ducking and diving his way through.

Jack's elixir to share as a **Trickster** turned **Maverick** is to act from one's innate skill-set and employ high levels of determination and motivation to overcome life's giant challenges (such as feeling underestimated or experiencing illness, sorrow or loss)—we must push harder and higher to achieve our greatness and fulfil our wildest dreams.

SELF-REFLECTIONS

'You' become the idea whose time has come, ready to put your capabilities to the test and attract the breakthrough to success, just like Jack. Opportunity knocks, and as you step outside your comfort zone and leave the safety of the well-worn path behind, you lean into your dearly held goals with impeccable timing and a universe conspiring at your back. With each new challenge, important people come into your orbit, and you use your adaptability, creativity, and resourcefulness to turn abstract ideas into tangible achievements.

Ignore the naysayers and be willing to speculate to accumulate. Bargain for what you're worth and remain proactive in seeking opportunities that align with your skills and energy. As you progress on your journey, reflect on whether your current path fits your natural gifts, strengths, and learned skills best. Be discerning about the company you keep and avoid magical thinking or shortcuts that compromise your integrity. Remember that every Hero's Journey comes with challenges and consequences. Any misuse of power can attract opponents who make judgments that one is a user, shallow social climber, or confidence trickster. Arguments with partners and accusations of manipulation may occur over one or the other's relentless angling to get what they want. But many a maverick will tell you that following your rising star will always come at a price.

You press on with your quest, inspired by Robert Browning's poetry that 'a man's reach should exceed his grasp'. However, in life, there will always be limits to observe. Going too far out can result in a tumble, so stay grounded in truth and fair play without losing sight of your dreams.

Serendipitous signs illuminate the way to your integral Self and the making of intimate relationships. However, caution against choices based on superficial appearances. As Shakespeare warned, 'All that glitters is not gold'. In pursuing fair and equitable partnerships, there may be power struggles and adjustments to make, but never compromise who you are. Your self-belief and unique abilities are the cornerstones of achieving your full potential. Trust that the universe supports you in wanting to see how far you can go on your own steam, transforming the ordinary into the extraordinary.

When you feel the fresh green shoots pushing within, you are ready, capable of turning dreams into a new narrative. From your modelling, your peers will understand that to manifest rewards, you need to act not out of fear but by going out on a limb, utilising your full capacities with belief in what you do and knowing that the Great Power will never forsake you.

The only way to do great work is to love what you do.
(Steve Jobs)

LIGHT QUALITIES (MAVERICK)	**SHADOW ATTRIBUTES (TRICKSTER)**
Adventurous	Dodgy
Creative	Shallow
Confident	Over-confident
Proactive	Argumentative
Skilful	Mischievous
Demonstrative	Wilful
Resourceful	Magical-thinking
Manifestative	Manipulative

PROVERB: Grasp the nettle with both hands.

AFFIRMATION: I am capable of doing all that I must do.

GAME OF LIFE: Misusing power to get what you want (Consequence: Expecting instant gratification but attracting trouble).

REFLECTION QUESTION: Does this endeavour align with my natural born gifts and talents?

ANIMAL SYMBOLISM: Goose

Geese symbolise protection and have a friendly, sensitive, and guardian-like nature. As 'watchdogs', they warn of disruption and urge us to listen to our instincts. They also represent social grace, luck, and balanced Yin and Yang, bringing fairness to all aspects of our lives.

ONE SMALL STEP TO TAKE TODAY: I will practise sensing when it is the right place and time to put my unique skill set to use.

MEDITATION PREPARATION (to practise within two hours of rising)

Inhaling golden light, I embrace positivity and release negativity. Envisioning a joyful day, I see myself, standing in my power, confidently facing challenges. Seeds of effort sprout into the blossoms of my dreams.

There are far better things ahead than the ones we leave behind.
(C. S. Lewis)

2 THE LITTLE MERMAID

The Little Mermaid (HANS CHRISTIAN ANDERSEN)—*The following is a personal retelling of the tale:*

SYNOPSIS OF FAIRY TALE

The king of Mer ruled all the lands under the sea. He fathered six beautiful mermaid daughters who swam freely in the azure waters of the deep, but he forbade them to float and linger on the surface or go beyond the reef. Still, they dreamed that one day they would enjoy the warm sunlight, bathe in the magical moonlight and see the earthen lands that beckoned beyond. The king told the shy little mermaids his strange tales from the past about human beings who had entered into their watery realm. He aimed to quell the girls' curiosity and warn them of human unpredictability.

However, the princesses could not stay meek little mermaids forever. When they reached tween-age, they ventured beyond the boundary of their sea-home.

Once upon the jagged reef, the big waves broke wildly upon the colourful coral of the shallow waters, and the sky was not the sunlit reflection of the aqua paradise they envisaged. As they shyly peered above the surf, the heavens took on a dull, dark and menacing glow. Right at that moment, as the oldest sister foretold of a great storm brewing, a violent wind drove a small but fancy ship straight into a snare of rocks along the shore.

The youngest mermaid was the most derring-do. She took off against her distressed sisters' pleas. Finding a young man drowning in the deep, she towed him swiftly to safety on the water's edge, singing him awake with her siren's serenade. But just as quickly, she fled, knowing better than to linger too long with the young man. From a safe distance, she saw human girls fast approaching the poor sea-drenched fellow. They rallied around him, crying out excitedly, "It's the prince! It's the prince!" The mermaid watched as the young man looked upon all the pretty faces before him, quietly asking in vain, "But where's the lovely young maiden who saved me?" The girls went schtum and glum. Nobody knew.

Meanwhile, the mermaid fixed her sights on the cave of the sea witch, swimming hastily to find clarity and comfort in her nebulous hidden world. Oh, dear. The Little Mermaid had fallen hopelessly in love at first sight. But how could she ever be with a human prince?

The witch warned that the only way the union would be possible was to transform from a mermaid to a human being. The spell would entail a swap of her sea-tail for two legs, and she would pay a painful and heavy price for the exchange. She would be rendered mute. The witch cautioned that the prince must genuinely love her, or all efforts would be in vain.

If perchance in the future, the prince betrothed another at dawn, the mermaid would dissolve into sea-foam. Nonetheless, the besotted mermaid willingly partook of the magic potion that would change her forever.

Now appearing human, the caring and beautiful mermaid plucked up the courage to visit the palace to become better known to the prince. Still, without her voice, she could never speak of her love for him, leaving little chance for there ever developing a mutual bond between them.

Then one day, out of the blue, the prince set sail for faraway lands to meet a beautiful princess whose parents and his had arranged their marriage. Secretly, he imagined that she was the mysterious maiden who saved him that fateful day from death on the rocks.

Upon learning the truth, the mermaid wept deep, salty tears, finding little comfort in her sisters' advice: "If you kill the prince, you will save yourself!" The Little Mermaid's loving heart rejected the lowly act. She bravely prepared for the consequences of her ill-conceived choices and despaired at the futile sacrifices she had made.

As dawn broke, the sentimental mermaid threw herself into the swirling sea, where her body began to dissolve slowly into sea-foam. Surprisingly, she suddenly felt the warmth of the sun beams upon her and sensed a great upliftment within.

She was redeemed. Existing now in pure white light, she took on the angelic form of a seraph.

Soon after, the selfless spirit ascended the earthly realm as an eternal daughter of the air. Once she had spent three hundred years in God's kingdom, The Little Mermaid, serene and beautiful, was transformed into a free spirit of love and light, possessing a human soul in Heaven. **THE END.**

PSYCHOLOGICAL PROMPTS

2: Key soul learning: To develop loving yourself (Self-Regulation)

We expect a happy ending for the sweet, impressionable mermaid where 'love conquers all' as portrayed in the Disney (1990) retelling of this tale, but in the original story, it is not meant to be. It is love at first sight that blinds the mermaid, who fails to act in her best interests or achieve a happy ever after marriage.

Suffering in silence, the maiden hopes her actions will speak louder, conveying her untold story. Her empathic nature allows her to feel others' pain and her own unrequited love. The prince is not aware that the one he truly loves is right under his nose, not the one farthest away. Like Odysseus, he is immune to hearing the tempting mermaid's siren call. Her highly-strung infatuation clouds her judgment, making it difficult to see things clearly, leading her to commit the one forbidden thing of venturing beyond the reef and trying to be intimate with a human. As she enters the cave into the deep still waters of rumination, the sensitive mermaid emphasises the importance of being meditative and reflective to find clarity. Information beyond our comprehension that has not yet come to light hides there.

Our torment can throw us off balance when we love someone or something too much. Our choice of words and actions can go awry, and we must ask ourselves, "Am I obsessed with wanting only what is out of my reach?" The Little Mermaid's co-dependent behaviour, driven by her passion for being with the prince, leads her down a path of self-sabotage and sacrifice. When falling for him, the conflicted mermaid makes a deal with the devil to get what she desires above all else. She is prepared to give up her family, home, and self-identity to become what she perceives the unattainable man wants. A victim of mistaken goals, who has she become without her voice, phosphorescent tail, life-force and innate ability to swim through life's tumultuous tides?

The mermaid's fears and uncertainties stem from her belief that only perfect people are loveable, excluding herself from loving contact. Becoming mute, she loses her intuitive yin, leaving her feeling confused and out of her depth in an unsupportive environment.

However, through her healing journey, she, the Jungian archetype of the explorer (partly), will discover that authenticity, sensitivity and vulnerability are greater strengths than physical appearances. Opposites attract in life's duality, and we are initially drawn to one another by a giddy mating magnetism, yet our differences can ultimately lead to feelings of separation, loneliness, and maladaptive behaviours. Love and hate are flip sides of the same coin: light and shadow, pleasure and pain. The pipe-dreaming mermaid puts faith in her plan but does not have the resources or the voice to make her dream a reality. The elusive prince symbolises her animus, and the sea witch, her shadow side.

In the beginning, hers is a sentimental fantasy, distracting her from fathoming karma's enigmatic truths beneath the surface. She knows to keep her potentially dangerous secret confidential, seeking counsel from only those she trusts. Still, she is none the wiser until forced to ask the 'Hamlet' question.

At the end of her Hero's Journey, she models what can happen when we refuse our calling and, in her case, decide *not to be*. However, her mistake in not acting very 'mermaidy' shows us that we must dive deeply into our unconscious to the gestating DNA of our destiny to know if we are flowing with or against our tide. With matters of the heart, the answer is as unchanging as her archetypal power. It is the first tenet of human love: Only when you love yourself can anyone else love you in return.

To open ourselves to the calling of our fate, where our essential potential can be realised, we start by communing with our Higher Self. Everyone and everything have a purpose and place in time. Here, we tune into the positive and negative energies in our lives and recognise when something is discordant with our divine channel. Denying adverse conditions does not make them go away, and our minds and bodies send us anxiety, aches and pains to signal the dissonance. But, with our finger on the cosmic pulse, we feel serene and enlivened, acting in self-supporting ways that achieve our aims.

Despite the mermaid's tenacity, her love's labours were lost, and reaching rock bottom, she finds, guided by her moral compass, a small reef of refuge in a cruel sea. Her shimmery aura of contemplation reflects the Delphic depths of the liminal realm of the unknowable where the right answers reside. Plato (and Kant) whisper victory if she follows her personal code: and she does the right thing because it is the right thing to do.

The receptive mermaid, finally loving herself and acting in sync with her spiritual side, transforms, becoming a **Free-spirit** in the sky, elevating her from the co-dependent **Pipe-dreamer** who once sought someone else to complete her and make her whole.

We learn that what goes around comes around. If we try to force the mysterious hand of fate with our tenacious grip, our efforts may amount to naught. However, if we concentrate on regulating our wild emotions and causing good, we progress spiritually, feeling good enough to be seen and heard and worthy of love at long last.

The human soul is essentially a longing for something beyond itself. (Aristotle)

SELF-REFLECTIONS

Taking inspiration from the archetype of The Little Mermaid, you delve deep, turning inwards, seeking to elevate your intuitive understanding of life's mysteries. But as you confront your disillusionment, you find yourself sinking into over-thinking and mistrusting others. Despite this, you still find solace in believing that your past pains have sharpened your ability to heal.

You find yourself conflicted, caught between the impulses of your free-spirited self and the sentimental dreamer, leaving you feeling all at sea. You long to answer the call of the wild concerning matters of the heart, home, health, work, and beyond but are hesitant to take the plunge and make a change. Nevertheless, you accept that what hasn't yet killed you has made you stronger and resolve to take another step forward, even if the reeds on the river's far bank seem out of reach.

Perhaps you leave behind predictable people and places because you dare to dream of something beyond the ordinary, something exciting or 'perfect'. Relationships with opposites are alluring, but they can also lead to heartache and lovelorn longings. It's important to remember that when we feel alone, we can find comfort in meditation, reflection, and prayer and that the answers we seek are often only accessible from our unconscious and dreaming mind.

The mermaid archetype reminds us that we have repressed parts that need to be acknowledged and addressed to achieve Wholeness. Reclaiming these psychic fragments, we break free from the emotional patterns holding us back. It's not always easy to confront these shadow aspects of ourselves, such as the trauma of past abuses and wounds, but doing so can lead to a profound shift in our reality. Look for your hidden strengths and reframe this outworn story.

It's essential to recognise the difference between our egoistic wants and the spiritual needs of our authentic selves. We can attract lasting love and intimacy by forgiving ourselves and learning to love ourselves unconditionally. In relationships, we must identify when we are in a state of lust, not love and avoid trying to change the hearts and minds of others. The only behaviour we can control is our own, so, we must focus on empathy, emotional freedom, and clarity when making decisions about the future we want to live and with whom we choose to share it.

By confronting our fears and completing the inner work to resonate with our soul and the cosmos harmoniously, we, male or female, can overcome our shadow attributes and begin to heal our animus or anima blockages.

For women, the yin or feminine energy of The Little Mermaid is often associated with relationship problems, menopause, pregnancy, hormonal imbalances, and sexual dysfunction. Reclaiming her animus grants her the 'oomph' to sort underlying weaknesses out. For men, the repressed anima feminine energy, showing signs of contamination, manifests as bitterness, withdrawal, passivity, secrecy, and sexual dysfunction alike.

By utilising our sixth sense to connect with and integrate the discarded aspects of our psyche, we achieve heightened consciousness and a sense of self-love, agency, and wise decision-making to emerge stronger than before.

The Little Mermaid archetype is a powerful tool for exploring your unconscious mind and discovering your true Self and the nature of the mystery you find yourself in. When you heroically rise after meeting your dark side, you are ready to share your learned wisdom and truth and heal others in their darkest hour.

A quote attributed to poet Walt Whitman is a salve for the heart-weary mermaid inside us all: "Keep your face always toward the sunshine, and shadows will fall behind you."

LIGHT QUALITIES (FREE-SPIRIT)	**SHADOW ATTRIBUTES (PIPE-DREAMER)**
Free-Spirited	Pipe-dreaming
Intuitive	Highly-strung
Sensitive	Co-dependent
Meditative	Secretive
Empathic	Perfectionistic
Confidential	Conflicted
Healing	Enigmatic
Serene	Sentimental

PROVERB: An untold story makes for a heavy heart (M.G. Leonard).

AFFIRMATION: I am good enough to be seen and heard.

GAME OF LIFE: Assuming inadequacy (Consequence: Refusing one's natural gifts and life-calling).

REFLECTION QUESTION: Is my heart open to receiving the call of the universe?

ANIMAL SYMBOLISM: Dugong; platypus; fish; starfish; and green turtle

Dugong:

The Dugong awakens our consciousness to unconditionally loving ourselves and finding peace and harmony. If we break free from the traumas of our childhood, we expand our power to nurture ourselves and our loved ones in the best possible ways.

Platypus

The platypus, earth and sea dweller, is a yin symbol. It signifies the duality of our material and spiritual worlds. It reminds us to dive deep to discover our true selves. We should move towards kindness and unconditional love while avoiding envy and jealousy.

Fish

The fish is a symbol of spirituality, emotions, and grace, representing the importance of making soulful connections. They remind us to regulate our emotions and avoid being trapped in past patterns when making decisions.

Starfish

The starfish symbolises a call to action from the universe that tests one's sense of justice, presenting a conflict between ego and spiritual values. One is prompted to act from the truth found only in the heart.

Green Turtle

Turtles represent the conflict between personal protection and pleasing others. One should be careful taking risks and avoid sticking their neck out. The shell indicates safety but also symbolises our ego defences hiding undesirable traits to keep up appearances.

ONE SMALL STEP TO TAKE TODAY: I will practise regulating my negative emotions by telling myself I am good enough to be seen and heard.

MEDITATION PREPARATION (to practise at dusk)

Inhaling golden light, I embrace positivity and release negativity. Fear fades with dusk's transcendent touch, connecting me with the Divine and bathing my soul in the truth and light of who I am.

Jesus said not to lay up for ourselves treasures on earth but to lay up treasures in heaven instead. (Matthew 6:19-21)

3 OUR LADY'S CHILD (MARY'S CHILD)

Our Lady's Child (GRIMM)—*The following is a personal retelling of the tale:*

SYNOPSIS OF FAIRY TALE

One cold autumn day, with no cloud in the sky, a poor woodcutter living in the dark forest with his young child witnessed a miraculous visitation from the Blessed Virgin Mary.

The Holy Mother of Jesus asked him if she could take his beautiful daughter to the divine kingdom of Heaven, promising her a golden and abundant life ever after. The weary woodcutter nodded slowly, watching in awe as his little girl was lifted on high by the Virgin and her glorious host of angels to live in their luminous paradise.

Several years passed, and when the girl turned fourteen, the Virgin Mary explained she was going on a long, faraway journey, meaning the girl would be alone but still protected in Heaven. In preparation for her departure, Saint Mary entrusted the young and beautiful maiden with the keys to the twelve doors of the heavenly realm. However, she warned that while a key existed for a thirteenth door, to touch it would be a mortal sin.

But once the Virgin had left, temptation overcame the curious child, so she unlocked the door with the mysterious key. An astonishing sight greeted her, for standing before her was the Holy Trinity in solemn conference. Rushing away from the remarkable scene, she looked down, filling with horror and dread. Molten gold from the forbidden key coated her index finger, set fast.

When the Holy Virgin returned, she promptly questioned whether her blessed child had opened the thirteenth door. Despite the Virgin Mary's persistent prompts for a truthful response, the timid and tormented girl hid her hands behind her back, stubbornly denying what she had done.

But the pure-hearted Virgin possessed divine powers for seeing through all fanciful human schemes, past and present. Consequently, the maiden who had sinned was banished by the Great Mother to live out her life in the woodland wilderness where the giant trees whispered ancient secrets to each other. A hollow Ash tree became her only shelter. If this was not enough, she was made mute.

Despite her handicap, she eked out a lonely and wretched existence in the wild until one day, a kindly king, catching a glimpse of her, swept her up on his fine horse and headed for his castle. Before long, his regency fell in love with the shy but charming lady of the tree. Although she could not converse with the monarch, she faithfully fulfilled her duties day after day and eventually bore him three beautiful children.

Meantime, over the years, the Virgin Mary would visit upon the fruitful queen at the birth of each new baby, encouraging her to tell the truth about once opening the forbidden door. Alas: her ongoing denials would have dire consequences.

When given an ultimatum to finally own up to her lies or hand over her baby to the Virgin, the queen withheld, choosing to sacrifice her kin rather than tell the truth and repent her sins. As a result, there grew much negative talk about her and unrest crept across the land, threatening the stability of the monarchy.

After the Virgin Mary seized the third child, the kingdoms' people spread rumours about the queen, who, becoming empty and bitter, began detaching from her royal duties. Where on earth were the king's children? Everyone assumed she must have ended the life of the royal offspring with her own hands, eating their bodies to remove the evidence.

By and by, the outraged common folk staged an uprising, demanding their king sentence his sinful wife to death. She was a witch, no less, and must die by burning. The reluctant king relented.

As the flames rose higher and higher around her on the stake, the intense heat began to melt the ice of her hardened anger, gold on her finger, bitterness and foolish pride. The stricken queen's broken heart opened, laying bare her soul for all to see.

Ever-compassionate, the Virgin granted the desperate royal mother one last chance to confess her sins and redeem herself.

Finally, as she was about to be enveloped by flames and choked by smoke, the remorseful queen yielded, miraculously crying out the truth in full voice. Folk turned to the heavens wailing, and just like that, the merciful Virgin Mary brought to fall torrential rains, extinguishing the fire. The king, feeling immense relief, rushed to his spared queen's side hearing the famous words of philosopher Plato ringing in his ears: The truth will set you free.

A flash of white light revealed the Virgin, with three noble children wrapped lovingly in her arms, descending gracefully from heaven to reunite them with their humbled mother and beloved father.

Repentance, opening the door to forgiveness, slowly untied the queen's tongue, enabling her to speak her truth bravely and use it for good forevermore.

Still today, she fills with unbound joy when recounting her great blessings: The Great Mother's forgiveness of her sins, the love of her children, her king and kingdom's support and the amazing grace of the Holy Trinity who made it all possible. **THE END.**

PSYCHOLOGICAL PROMPTS

3: Key soul learning: To develop being your truth (Self-Regulation)

Whether we believe in karma or not, most accept that our choices and actions have consequences. Many of us believe 'we reap from what we sow'. Our Lady's Child archetype teaches us that lying has painful consequences and that forgiving our mistakes is only possible if we confess and repent. However, Bloch (1980) argues that lying does not always come from an unkind intent and citing Hanlon's Razor: "We should never attribute to malice that which is adequately explained by stupidity." Suppose we avoid assuming the worst of others, regardless of the reason for their actions.

While little lies seem to lubricate social interactions, larger lies cause harm. Blaming drugs or alcohol for our lies only shows that we are unwilling to take responsibility for our actions. Our Lady's Child archetype acts from a place of denial, driven by fears of not living up to her ideal self or the feminine forte set by super-achieving women and mothers. So, she does the forbidden thing (and is untruthful) and must live with her shame. Poet Browning (1855) warned that letting the truth slip would count as a crime in our souls.

No matter our beliefs, owning up to our mistakes is the first step towards self-efficacy. We can ask for forgiveness and self-forgive, and forgiveness from others will often follow. However, first, we must apologise with genuine regret. Forgiveness provides emotional release, reducing the likelihood of recurrent harmful actions.

The Holy Mother tests if her child is obedient and truthful similar to how the serpent tempted Eve with the apple. Most teenagers, susceptible to the taboo, make mistakes while exploring with their agency, but upon showing remorse, generally receive a second chance. However, the caught maiden denies her errors and, squandering her golden opportunity, becomes voiceless, empty, withdrawn, and marginalized— a lethal recipe for females in any era of history. The numbers twelve (permitted doors) and three (children), common archetypes in fairy tales, tell us that she has disobeyed Divine authority and that her fate is invoked, respectively.

With cold detachment, she mocks the privilege of the mutualistic bond between Mother Nature and child-bearing women, collaborating in the natural mystery of birthing life. Earth mothers have a miracle in their hands, co-creating when they nest, conceive, bear, and nourish their children through the warp and weft of their daily lives.

Our creative calling is not limited to motherhood but cuts across all our creative pursuits (the arts, business, home-making, socio-politico, self-growth, etc.) When we ignore this calling, we go into a holding pattern, much like Mary's child, requiring a long thaw before our bitterness melts and soul-fire returns.

When feeling lonely, we should check if we're following the program set by our Higher Power or if fear and pride have hindered our heart's centre from keeping time with the Sacred.

Fuelled by the fire of the Holy Spirit, Saint Joan of Arc followed the path of her truth. At just nineteen, heeding God's calling, she bravely led the French army against the English during the Hundred Years' War. They burned her alive in 1431, but the pope declared her a saint in 1920. In her journals, Joan mentions the Ladies' Tree, a towering beech known as the Fairy's Tree, where French folk seeking healing powers placed flower wreaths of faith for the Blessed Virgin. Similarly, in that era, Christians perceived elm trees and their bark as purifiers, symbolising the martyr's blood, truth and Divine justice.

The tree motif conveys that if we stand tall in our truth, we are freed, becoming who we are meant to be in our unique earthly role. A fertile and fruitful future awaits those comfortable in their own skin. However, for Joan, it meant martyring herself as Mary's heroic son had done centuries before. Fortunately, many of us will not face such a monumental test of faith. Still, we must pay attention to our forebears' wisdom, who have travelled the terrain before us or risk consequences. The best teachers don't coddle but cultivate our growth. They show how denials root us to the rot of deceit, as demonstrated by the proud lady of the tree who withholds the necessary sacrifice of pride— feeling threatened, her ego takes precedence over the greater good. A baptism by fire follows, where the smouldering negativity of unkindness eventually burns one out.

On the other hand, self-acceptance leads to self-love and prepares us for a reciprocal, loving, supportive and symbiotic union.

Compassionate Mary urges us to surrender both our light and dark, for no matter our human scheming, we are protected from severing ties with God. Suppose we risk admitting a mistake to a loved one or colleague, facing our consequences with respect and grace, or standing up for what we believe in a hostile environment. Her elixir teaches us to come down to earth and be honest with ourselves, facing our fears, hubris and innate strengths fearlessly. The young queen feels at one when reconciled with the king (her animus) and children (her inner child).

Living our truth is not just a matter of personal integrity or moral responsibility but also a path to meaning, emotional freedom, creativity, abundance and joy. In the end, it is only by being true to ourselves that we can be true to others and truly be alive. We become part of something greater than ourselves to find our place in the grand scheme of the earthly arena.

So, along with their cautions, all the remarkable and inspirational women of grace, grit and gumption who have gone before us hold a favourable augury, promising that when we transmute the slow burn of our shadow pain, we will spark the inner light of our soul and start creating our best lives.

Like them, let us embrace both our shadow and our light, vices and virtues, starting by saying what we mean and meaning what we say with awareness, courage and love. This is how we make peace with ourselves.

Our Lady's Child journeyed from a **Schemer** to **Earth Mother**, emerging with heightened self-regulatory powers and a rekindled instinct to protect and support kin and kith. She no longer saw any purpose in fearing and withholding the truth, for the truth had set her free.

A gentle tongue is a tree of life, but perverseness in it breaks the spirit.
(Proverbs 15:4)

SELF-REFLECTIONS

The mythic Mary's Child's narrative collides with your own in reality, as the opening of a new door brings unintended consequences and delays. It takes time for the seeds of creativity to germinate and flower in the world. As we wait in the wings, the sun continues to rise, seasons change, and we face a new day of joy or struggle.

We have internalised the Earth mother archetype and live according to her sacred truth and light. But Mother Nature gives, takes, creates, and destroys, and we make daily compensations for her dualities. She urges us to call a spade a spade, digging for the truth and taking responsibility for our part in all we do, in contrast to the latter-day fairy-tale queen's dysfunction.

Another lesson from the lying lady of the tree is to accept compromise and make good, blooming where we are planted. Our endeavours can always be better directed if we want to advance to the next level of our Hero's Journey. Otherwise, our aspirations, when manipulated by our hungry, dark depths, cause wrong turns. Careless mistakes may morph into maladaptive behaviours. The exiled, untruthful and voiceless maiden represents the loss of power we suffer when we don't accept who we are and the reality of what is. Being honest with ourselves leads us to be frank with others, and others reciprocate. Our over-reactions to life events are indicators of any unresolved psychic elements and painful emotional memories stagnating in the deep pond of the unconscious, requiring our attention. Journalling our story helps us understand.

Mothering and mentoring our inner child who fears being alone, unwanted, and inevitably claimed by death will stimulate a catharsis. We can take charge of the healing process by reconnecting with the World Creatrix (Mary) archetype, as she nourishes the born and detaches the dying from the earth-bound matrix. Grasping the reality that all things must pass helps us address the fears feeding our shadow and brings us one step closer to reclaiming the deep-seated power of our anima/animus archetypes.

At the right moment, a sign from the Great Mother appears, indicating alignment with the cosmic flow, and blessings abound. Birth is a miracle! Each of us is chosen from a vigintillion pool of candidates for earthly lessons and soul growth. Her message for womankind is though we are at-one with the mystical wonder of nature, women require the different other to seed new life. This realisation inspires gratitude, humility and a grounding in reality, directing us away from the sway of ego's desires and delusions and towards the Higher Power. And, as for you, acting in harmony with the heavenly orchestration, you will soon feel driven in the direction of your dreams, your intentions fuelling the fruition of your creative offspring.

Relationships forged or reformed now have the potential for stability, and your choices will decide their long-term fate. So, act mindfully, balancing yin and yang energies for a deeply rewarding hero's quest, from concept to completion. Reframe your problem-story of yore to reflect your strengths.

As you round the home-bend, sharing your epiphany in strong voice: 'the truth will always out', may compassion be your compass.

The truth will set you free (Plato).

LIGHT QUALITIES (EARTH MOTHER)	SHADOW ATTRIBUTES (SCHEMER)
Feminine	Scheming
Nourishing	Untruthful
Fruitful	Detached
Down-to-earth	With-holding
Truthful	Empty
Co-creative	Bitter
Responsible	Threatened
Compassionate	Unkind

PROVERB: As you sow, so shall you reap (Galatians 6:7).

AFFIRMATION: I fearlessly embrace my feminine creative powers.

GAME OF LIFE: Scheming to get what you want (Consequence: Feeling empty).

REFLECTION QUESTION: Am I being honest with myself?

ANIMAL SYMBOLISM: Kangaroo; Crow

Kangaroo

The kangaroo totem focuses on motherhood and nurturing others, promoting kindness, friendliness and cooperation over competition.

Crow

The crow, symbolising wise guardianship, is the 'Great Black/Spiritual One' in Buddhism. It utilises tools dexterously to advance but represents the potential for craftiness in one's shadow.

ONE SMALL STEP TO TAKE TODAY: I will practise regulating the way I express my truth.

MEDITATION PREPARATION (to practise upon waking)

Inhaling golden light, I embrace positivity and release negativity. I feel the life-giving pulse of nature flow through me, drenching me with compassion, love, and gratitude for my fruitful force. I let myself be. The Divine Great Mother's heavenly tones deepen my breath. In my true colours, I, her co-creator, step out, belonging here and everywhere, ready to bloom.

Our duty, as men and women, is to process as if limits to our ability did not exist.
We are collaborators in creation.
(Pierre Teilhard de Chardin)

4 THE EMPEROR'S NEW CLOTHES

The Emperor's New Clothes (HANS CHRISTIAN ANDERSEN)—*The following is a personal retelling of the tale:*

SYNOPSIS OF FAIRY TALE

Once in a kingdom far away lived a regal emperor who proudly wore the most opulent finery in the land. Even though his ornate robes were outlandishly garish on occasion, the townsfolk conceded that the emperor's wardrobe was fit for any king.

Ahead of his forthcoming appearance in a royal procession before the nation, he called for the best tailors from a neighbouring province to visit the castle and create an elegant suit for him. Finally, after toiling away for days, the tailors announced to the court that the new royal garments were ready.

In actuality, the tailors were seasoned tricksters making their living by fooling the rich and powerful. The emperor, none the wiser, paid their steep fees in gold sovereigns, without so much as a second thought. Still, his alarmed cries came only an instant later. The royal robes were nowhere in sight. Hastily the con-men cautioned that only those with the finest faculties could ever see such divine garments, tailored from a secret, exotic and invisible fabric only available to the elite. It made sense that if the fine apparel was not visible to someone, they must be ignorant and unfit for the ministry. Rushing to set things right, the emperor's acolytes smugly agreed that the new royal attire was exquisite and more so for only materialising before those with the highest intellect. The swindlers delighted in their folly and how easily the emperor and his underlings, fearing being seen as unfit for public office, fell for the ruse.

At last, the make-believe suit was complete. The garment-makers play-acted their way through the dressing of the duped leader. Within hours the emperor paraded himself before all his people. At first, wary of reprisals from the petty tyrant, the townsfolk played along with the pretence. Yet, they wondered what madness had befallen their monarch.

It was only when a guileless child, unable to contain his wonder, cried out that the emperor wore no clothes, reality struck. Waking to the truth, the crowd echoed his cry in a mocking chorus.

He might have embarrassed himself before his people, but the arrogant and pretentious emperor did not embrace his humiliation. With his head held high, the selfish sovereign continued to go about his business as though nothing had ever happened. **THE END.**

PSYCHOLOGICAL PROMPTS

4: Key soul learning: To develop skills for leading with humility (Self-Regulation)

The kitsch emperor fell prey to his vanity and pride, ego's feckless bedfellows hiding in shadow, turning a blind eye to both his instincts and moral reasoning and so, fell for the ruse. He does the forbidden, believing in his infallibility and putting faith in pretence. The cons played to the emperor's weaknesses he denied owning—being proud, pretentious, rigid, profligate, self-centred, callous and vain. His exposure was both literal and figurative.

Nobody likes feeling silly or wrong, and when finding themselves on the back foot become very defensive in efforts to self-protect. We justify our position or angrily blame someone else rather than own our shortcomings. With an unchecked ego in the driving seat, we mean to win at all costs, having the last word as though our survival depends on it.

Our prediluvian ancestors channelled the same primary drive into wildly aggressive acts necessary to bring home the kill and forestall adversaries. Without their machismo, we would not be here today to share our collective stories. Jung acknowledged such ancestry with his concept of the collective unconscious, where primitive and aggressive urges (depicted in fairy tales, myths and more) reside and are accessible through our dreams and deep reflections.

While it is natural to assert our truth (however we perceive it) to protect our position, an over-reaction, an ego-defence, attracts conflict. Our ego puts up its persona to shield itself against wounding, disbelieving empirical facts that counter assumptions held dear. Even if what we believe and what we observe contradict, we will likely favour the information confirming our biases, to feel we have the upper hand and are in control— a recipe for feuds.

Our shadow-self protects our ego (and vice versa) by attempting to stay hidden from conscious view. But we all know the guilty protest the loudest. The shadow holds our unclaimed guilt (among myriad negative emotions) and, when triggered, hollers like hell to break through the ego's fortifications. No wonder our distress: an unintegrated psyche is a mishmash of conflicting emotions.

The foolish emperor brimming with braggadocio falls for the illusion that he is in control. With his naked self-interest exposed, his reputation is irreparably damaged. Not a responsible protector, he was an impotent ruler unworthy of the respect of his people, who likely suspected he concealed malfeasance. Like mythical Narcissus, he gazed too long at his reflection and drowned in self-absorption. How could he have their best interests at heart?

Even when the jig was up, he acted (from blind ego) like the proverbial ostrich, refusing to see reality. Fancy a naïve but honest child exposing a mighty emperor who undressed to impress?

Are our behaviours analogous to his? If so, we hide our fears of being an imposter, or poseur, in our dark sides, play-acting an ideal image that could get found out, as happens in the universal dream of 'exposure'— that nightmare that puts our true colours on show for all to see.

But a full-frontal imbroglio for a high-ranking politician is a rude awakening, a harder fall. Envisaging the future: if the cavalier gets off his high horse, accepts his fall from grace and meets the fool inside, he will rise above his shame.

Like him, we must look fear in the face, forgive our folly and renew ourselves, co-creating with the Divine for a better world. If pusillanimous (a potential indicator of a contaminated anima), we must strip ourselves bare of fabrications and discriminate between substance and appearance. Secondly, we must embrace our positive masculine energy, welcoming back our animus. After our internal processing, self-respect and humility supersede pride, vanity and ignobility, re-instating our leadership strength. Epicurus predicted that if a leader's sense of virtue and responsibility ever grew stronger, they would overcome blame and hurt, thus enabling their people to live with faith, not fear.

How often have we hung on to a doomed plan rather than lose face, sweeping the dust under the carpet, repeating the same mistake? When we blindly follow worn-out life scripts—a schema of life patterns failing to serve us, we are like the grandiloquent emperor, becoming dissatisfied, stuck and easily duped.

The emperor with a fragile ego and predilection for role-power is not a victim but blessed with voice and choice. He can shift and lift his vibrations, stepping away from his superficial, superior and entitled stance. Self-aggrandisement never ranks above sincerity, humility and integrity, bringing only a disheartened air to an unfolding life.

To grow in contentment, the emperor should see leadership as a process with ongoing challenges to face with composure. He can find effective solutions by asking the right questions and collaborating with others.

It is the figuring-out process that empowers us. We adopt a trial-and-error approach to novel situations, not fearing failure but welcoming the opportunity to learn. A universal reciprocity is at work, seeing that we get back what we put in.

By getting back up, dusting ourselves off and starting all over again, we emerge stronger for the second round on our hero's path. How else will we hone our adaptability, flexibility, versatility, tolerance and resilience? We need these powerful attributes for our growth, especially in times of significant change and uncertainty. In environments of plenty, often with discriminatory policy, fortune, power, and privilege can come too easily for the few. Being indulged in celebrity treatment went to the emperor's head. When we are too spoiled to strive, we fail to thrive. But each fall ushers us into a process of redemption with fuel to light up our consciousness. If our inner wounds are made right, our lives on the outside follow, and real transformation and satisfaction begin.

Believing we are either powerless or possess absolute control is an illusion of the ego.

Our self-reflection and constructive feedback from others enlighten us, distilling an accurate picture of how we interact within the social construct. According to Johnson (1989), men are driven to act idiotically when suffering from a desperate sense of incompleteness within.

Had the selfish skite put his errant parts under the illuminating strobe of his Higher Self, he would have logically assessed what was best for all, and not been caught with his pants down—sans-culottes. But no, he surrounded himself with sycophantic pretenders with agendas. Have you noticed how males might stick together to defend a lie even when they know better? So, deep down, he was untrusting of himself and his social systems, failing to reach the benchmarks of the natural world, despite his efforts to mimic the great works of the Creator. After all, the ephemeral is no match for the eternal—understanding our limits is necessary before realising our supra-natural potential.

When we embody and regulate our authentic power and authority, we reclaim our sovereignty and innate ability to transform our creative longings into material form. We become genuine heroes on our personal mission. But before we reach our rewards, we must take sustenance from a slice of humble pie.

The pretentious emperor's opportunity is to journey from **Poseur** to **Leader**, emerging with heightened self-regulatory powers to act from humility and fidelity. No longer pseudo, supercilious, secretive and silly, untrusting of the inner voice guiding him to reign, he stands on the dais, wearing a new persona, reflecting his true power found only in that bona fide place within.

SELF-REFLECTIONS

You experience a reality check, as the emperor did. When you are central to your tribe, seen as a guiding light, there always come life tests where the teacher must be tested. Fortunately, you understand the spiritual journey in physical form is not straightforward but a circuitous and challenging path replete with pleasure and pain.

In response to revelations of truth, you take charge, enforce your intentions, and tell others that you plan to bring about fundamental change, promising a brighter future. However, there will be pitfalls on the road ahead with the long-awaited dividends hard-won.

As you know from past lessons, no good comes from pushing your agenda and then blaming others when things go awry. Face-to-face confrontation with others is inevitable, but you discover whom you are by recognising who you are not. Someone arrogant, materialistic and selfish serves as your teacher, forcing you to see, through their misguided actions, that only a humble approach brings lasting health and happiness.

To step up to the task, you must treat people as ends in themselves, not objects catering to your ends. No longer should any of us indulge in the 'I-It' paradigm, where we look at someone else in the context of how well they can (or cannot) instrumentalise our agenda and serve our needs. The lesson is clear: Focus on respect, humility and co-creation over a win-at-all-costs ethos. Otherwise, there is still much inner work to do. Contacting the emperor archetype opens the door to recalibrating your animus/anima and resetting your unconscious psyche.

Start the process by removing the ego's blindfold and recognising the negative traits projected onto someone of the opposite sex—This will help decode the inferior functions of your anima/animus within.

Once you establish your centre of gravity and walk your talk, good things will happen. A child or creative-offspring or the inner child is fathered. Embody the Great Father and stand erect in your yang energy, confident in authenticity, humbly conceding your humanness by accepting your flaws, the natural laws and social limits in the earthly arena. Admit and forgive your mistakes by growing beyond them, and the child within will feel loved.

Then, the 'I' can come to equal terms with the other, the 'thou'.

For those alone, the cosmos says: Thinking you are all-knowing repels others, for, after all, you provide no place for them (and their opinions) to be.

As someone wise once said, "It is a mature father that knows his own inner child and is ready to provide." You want it all: security, power, love and happiness. But remember, as you travel this narrow and high path, only a few manage to get through. Every 'emperor' in the end learns that one harvests what they cultivate. Journal what confuses you and spend time in contemplation.

Peel your eyes for the random rubble you encounter on the road to love. If you continue to put up the walls of your heart, you will prevent a soulful attraction from ploughing through. Your past paradigm meant always needing another to feel complete, and with broken promises, words without deeds, your unions overgrew with weeds. Take responsibility for your part in relationships, listen more, and temper your moods and appetites. Mean what you say and say what you mean. Merge your fiery masculine spirit with feminine grace, fuelling your Hero's Journey, kindling a spark between two hearts, weaving together physical and emotional threads, harmonising your strengths and fortifying your co-creations: This could be 'the one'.

If later, you face headwinds in your partnerships, stay in your Wholeness and respect and protect the trinity of I, thou, and the relationship. Kin will look to you for shining leadership and guidance, so rise again with true mastery, integrity, and confidence to lead from your Higher Self no matter how steep or rugged the road or how faraway the grail in the distance.

LIGHT QUALITIES (LEADER)	**SHADOW ATTRIBUTES (POSEUR)**
Masculine	Arrogant
Integrous	Rigid
Humble	Self-aggrandising
Protective	Play-acting
Co-creative	Selfish
Respectful	Callous
Responsible	Untrusting
Logical	Cavalier

PROVERB: Humble yourself, or life will do it for you.

AFFIRMATION: I fearlessly embrace my masculine creative powers.

GAME OF LIFE: Pretending to be superior, knowing-it-all and accepting only perfection (Consequence: Living a life devoid of soulful connections).

REFLECTION QUESTION: Am I leading with personal power or acting from fear?

ANIMAL SYMBOLISM: Magpie; Kookaburra

Magpie

The magpie represents lasting love, happiness, and material security. When we have much at stake, its black plumage signifies the shadow elements of trickery and deception.

Kookaburra

Kookaburras symbolise peace and prosperity, promising a time of plenitude, self-pampering and carefree happiness. The chortling kookaburra cautions, if one takes themselves too seriously, they risk making a jackass of themselves.

ONE SMALL STEP TO TAKE TODAY: I will practise regulating my egoic desires, so I lead with humility.

MEDITATION PREPARATION (to practice upon waking)

Inhaling golden light, I embrace positivity and release negativity. I envision a joyful day, connecting with nature and my masculine creative energy. In my centre, I feel my Whole truth: a leader ready to lead and inspire.

There is an inmost centre in us all, where truth abides in fullness.
(Robert Browning)

5 PUSS IN BOOTS

Puss in Boots (or The Booted Cat) – (PERRAULT/GRIMM)—*The following is a personal retelling of the tale:*

SYNOPSIS OF FAIRY TALE

When the poor miller of the village died, his youngest son, receiving his inheritance, was deeply disappointed. The bequest ranked according to birth order, with the two older siblings receiving the mill and mules, while the youngest was left only the barn cat. Even more surprisingly, the cat soon revealed his extraordinary nature, promising to make the young man's fortune. But first, the cat curiously demanded a bag, hat and a set of fine boots.

Before long, the booted and suited cat bagged a rabbit in the woods and presented it to the king on his master's behalf. The king appeared pleased with the clever cat's offerings and grew accustomed to receiving his regular gifts of fresh game, compliments of the so-called Marquis of Carabas.

Not long later, as it so happens, the king took his lovely but indulged daughter for a leisurely carriage ride to enjoy the warm sunshine and view of the wide, rolling countryside. Her gentle, lilting laughter swept like a summer breeze across the land to be heard by all. Catching on, the crafty cat, hastily hatched a plot to ensure the royals crossed paths with the miller's son.

First, he persuaded his master to remove his shabby clothing, take himself into the river for a cleansing swim, and wait until the carriage approached for further instructions. In the meantime, the duplicitous cat carefully hid the fellow's ragged attire under a rock.

Next, as the coach approached, the canny cat caused a fracas, feigning distress, he wailed, crying out the most frightful of cries. Abruptly, the regal coach came to a standstill, and the caring king descended to investigate. The cat coolly explained while the marquis was bathing, a band of vagabonds stole his fine apparel.

The king was quick to respond, ordering his servants to provide the young lord with fresh robes from his lavish trousseau before assisting him into the royal coach. Noting that his lovely little princess had instantly fallen in love at first sight with the handsome nobleman, the considerate king instructed his coachman to head directly to the marquis's nearby castle.

Unbeknownst to the confused miller's son, the dependable cat had already gone ahead days before, threatening the dutiful folk they must inform everyone who came to pass that these vast lands and fortress were now in possession of the Marquis of Carabas. If they did not obey, they would be severely penalised. Still, the calculating cat left nothing to chance.

Prior, he had gone to the chateau, majestically overlooking the glorious green fields of plane trees, wildflowers and the ribbon-like river flowing through the vast lands to confront the supernatural ogre in residence. He hotly demanded that the ogre, who bragged to all and sundry of his incredible talent to transform himself, show proof of his magical powers. First, he challenged the monster to become a lion, which he promptly accomplished. But then, when next tricked into becoming a mouse, was finished off by the sharp-witted cat.

Puss's ruse went as far as to convince the arriving king that the entire estate that spread for miles and miles before him was the grand property of the esteemed Marquis of Carabas. Finally, the impressed royal granted his approval for the so-called dignitary to take his daughter's hand in marriage. The cat's work was done.

Much rejoicing and salubrious ceremony followed, particularly in the case of the poor miller's son who, with a large new fortune, had climbed to the top of the social ladder, finding his happy place among the landed gentry. Who would have ever thought such a miracle possible?

His success was due solely to the supreme wisdom and shrewd schemes of the loyal cat he had inherited: an extraordinary cat that lives very comfortably nowadays as a peer of the realm, lording it over the estate's mice, enforcing their compliance with the house rules purely for his princely pleasure. **THE END.**

PSYCHOLOGICAL PROMPTS

5: Key soul learning: To develop social skills by heeding the voice of Higher wisdom (Social Skills)

Have we made a plan as the archetype Puss in Boots did, or are we aimless like the miller's youngest son? His forebears left him with only the legacy of a barn cat. Ironically, the cat made him aware of social rules and how to bend them, using them to his advantage. Had the son rejected the gift, he would have missed the dutiful cat's roadmap to success. With nothing left to lose, he committed to the cat's schemes. It was difficult to resist the cat with attitude, assuming command dressed in thigh-high boots and a feathered hat. Such masks denote and display one's station in a social hierarchy that the cat mysteriously understood. The fey feline had an innate intuition, allowing him to see around corners and mastermind a favourable fate.

He is an unlikely mentor, but the cat's anthropomorphic behaviours infer that balancing one's animal survival instincts with ego's logic is the key to a better life for masters and apprentices alike. The man (consciousness) and animal (id) must join forces to better both. Left with no other options, the son subordinates his limited reasoning powers to rely on the innate shrewdness and cunning of his human-like cat. Mentors who lead by shining example, practising what they preach, make the finest teachers, turning up when the student needs them most.

Like the miller's son, letting go of control, placing ourselves in the hands of a Higher Power or supernatural mentor (such as the cat), and trusting our best interests are being served is an exhilarating experience.

The fairy tale portrays the forbidden when the young man heeds a cat (symbolic of the natural order of things) over human artifice and plays the establishment at its own game—but despite the reversal, matters turn out right in the end. The manufactured institutions, status, wealth and power might control the masses but are mere illusions to him because they result from luck at birth—the fickle hand of fate rolling the dice. Society refused the poor fellow opportunities, so he wants to take his own chance on the wheel of fortune. Social order seems a mere fabrication if all it takes are acts of hypocrisy, rule-breaking, fancy masks, games and lies to achieve rank. Our desperate quest to survive will have us saying and doing just about anything to win.

The cat's visit to the king raises the ambiguity between the status quo and our authentic selves—the nobles might believe in their Divine right, but even a cat may look at a king. Instead of accepting our leaders have all the answers, suppose we listen reverently to Higher Wisdom instead. Does Puss see our human laws, which confer unfair advantages on the chosen, as fallible compared to nature, God's word and plan for us, and our faith?

Socrates received no advantage. According to Socrates' pupil Plato, the intolerant Deep State was responsible for his teacher's death (399 B.C.E.), imprisoning him for having his students question the accepted assumptions and conventions of the time. While waiting in misery on death row, Socrates poisoned himself with hemlock. Later, Plato's student, Aristotle, branded the State dangerously coercive for labelling opposing views as subversive. Religion might be the opium of the masses, but the State's stoking of fear in the people works just as well.

With an astute sense of timing, the faithful cat educates his master to obey nature's dominant but invisible rhythmic systems silently present in our lives. Similarly, the miller's son's story urges us to examine our priorities and motives. Do we value material worth over ethical values and a secure place within the establishment over our natural and spiritual selves? He demonstrates that despite our intellectual pursuits, humans still don't have all the answers to life's miracles and mysteries.

Suppose we subscribe to the hidden law of attraction, as the story suggests, and show our 'fine feathers to attract fine birds'. Had the cat not put on his glad rags before taking a look at the king, he would have copped the stink-eye from the self-righteous and patronising royal, and the theme recurs when the miller's son, an aspiring Marquis, a parvenu, dresses up accordingly.

However, there is a delicate balance between the racketeering rebel sticking it to the establishment and being opportunistic with what is available. The cat is a dependable model of his 'catness', and we humans have something to learn from him about how to be human. Puss teaches us that our duplicitous and disloyal behaviour and holier-than-thou attitude prevent us from grasping what really matters in the world.

It is time for us to balance our uniqueness within the social collective, think critically, act with integrity and humility and respect the power of truth. Whatever happened to Benjamin Franklin's (1706-1790) idea that honesty is the best policy? Are our self-idealisations of who, what and where we should be at odds with the truth of who we are, our true nature, our essence? If so, we must find the wisdom to reconcile the impossible with the possible. Puss implies if we have an ideal outcome in mind, only through taking a committed practical and steady approach can we hope to achieve it.

Puss shows us the folly of our guise as we struggle to make sense of ourselves as part of the social matrix. We fear missing out, stemming from believing that when someone else wins, we must be losers (i.e., the zero-sum mindset). Promoters would have us believe this spin because when we toe the line, pay our dues and redouble our efforts to win, putting our backs to the wheel, our participation, production, and consumerism favour them the most. Where is our sense of duty to those who benefit the least from the system, requiring a leg up, as was top of mind for the cat?

The archetype of Puss in Boots urges us to receive his message rather than follow his actions blindly. Clearly seeing the illusory nature of our earthly realm, he advises us, in times of confusion and uncertainty, to heed our Higher Wisdom. If life mysteries still confound, we must seek wise counsel possessing profound insights that transcend our understanding.

To live successful and authentic lives, we must balance being true to ourselves with our practical obligations to others and society. This requires transitioning from a **Hypocritical** mindset to a **Stalwart** one, in which we remain steadfast to our life philosophy and values while also fulfilling our responsibilities.

SELF-REFLECTIONS

Above all else, we must honour our true nature, like Puss in Boots. Our unique perspectives bring both rewards and challenges, attracting everything we are not and delivering conflict. However, in the end, those disputing our passage reveal who we truly are at heart. Life's natural rhythms persist, taking us up, down, and around again, whether we actively engage or choose to remain stuck. The miller's son chose the former path by following the congruent cat and found the right trajectory. He showcases the importance of aligning our thoughts, feelings, and actions with our beliefs and values.

Through his practical actions, Puss questions why humans often contradict their words with their deeds. He must wonder why we condemn others for things we ourselves are guilty of and then shy away from the truth. Nobody readily admits to being arrogant, preachy, or hypocritical, which reveals our collective need for improvement. Puss implies that God helps those who help themselves. In this vein, you are encouraged to take the initiative and rely on your own efforts. Remember that everyone fights to survive in the face of opposition.

If you find yourself in a highly competitive environment, much like the miller's son, struggling to fit in or progress within the social fabric, embrace your personal power and purpose. As Nietzsche (1844-1900) said, "He who has a why to live for can bear almost any how." Observe to sharpen your insight into the spiritual mysteries surrounding your interactions. Seize opportunities to make new connections when they arise. If you encounter fear and superficiality within your dark inner corners, redirect them with a keen perspective. Recognise your need for improved interpersonal skills to fulfil your secret longing for warmth and intimacy. Synchronising your spiritual intention with impactful actions strengthens your resolve and amplifies your capacity to authentically express yourself, positively impact others, and make meaningful connections.

Just as an unlikely mentor pointed the way for the penniless orphan, seeking wise guidance is worthwhile when navigating matters beyond your comprehension. Great mentors inspire confidence, balance, and steadfastness in action. They encourage respect and harmony between individual authenticity and the conventions and values of your community and tribe. The old self, who felt dissatisfied with themselves and others, must mature and progress through life's practical lessons with self-efficacy, without needing validation.

New partners may be cautious in sharing intimacy, expressing attraction through written words or lovemaking. Patience is necessary when others have yet to reclaim their shadows, as they may display contradictory behaviour. Forgiveness acknowledges the inherent paradox of our shared human experience. Nonetheless, an equal partnership requires adherence to the same rule book regardless of Puss's ability to bend and break it.

Look for a sincere willingness to grow. Reconciling our dark polarities is humanity's great test. If 'a cat may look at a king', our intolerance, dogma, and discrimination are unnatural and depressive to our collective spirit. Can we only expect to fit comfortably into hierarchical socio-economic structures and systems with fortunate circumstances of birth, upbringing, and education neatly tucked inside the knapsack of privilege upon our backs?

Puss in Boots (with a bag) challenges this notion. Amid negativities, feeling like an outlier for failing to keep up with tribal trends, learn from your experiences and heed Higher Wisdom.

Can you hear the cat whispering in your ear, "The past is history; tomorrow is a mystery, and today is a gift?" Don't look your gift horse in the mouth—record your story.

Our connection with the Puss in Boots archetype indicates our biological need to belong. How do we, as units of nature dressed up in society's garb, navigate the built bastion of materialism and social mores? When we engage in the systems of government, medicine, law, religion, education, finance, corporations and technology, we test our souls (and theirs).

There's a stark contrast between the human actions that align with the Divine and those driven by ego, impulse, or misadventure.

Standing atop the mountain, you share a hard-won but clear message: Progress is assured on the royal road by staying true to yourself, acting at the right time, balancing the needs of nature and society, and heeding Divine intent.

LIGHT QUALITIES (STALWART)	**SHADOW ATTRIBUTES (HYPOCRITE)**
Faithful	Hypocritical
Committed	Intolerant
Conventional	Patronising
Reverent	Self-righteous
Heedful	Disloyal
Loyal	Duplicitous
Dependable	Faithless
Dutiful	Rebellious

PROVERB: Above all else, be true to your own nature.

AFFIRMATION: I am true to my Higher Self.

GAME OF LIFE: Acting holier than thou while gaming the system (Consequence: Being lonely at the top).

REFLECTION QUESTION: Am I prepared to toe the line and pay my dues as I expect others to do?

ANIMAL SYMBOLISM: Domestic Cat; Australian Superb Fairy Wren

Domestic Cat

Cats move in sync with nature's rhythm and hold universal secrets beyond human understanding. They communicate telepathically and offer warnings (e.g., about self-deception) with signals and in our dreams. Their loyalty deserves reciprocity from humans who often fear their independence and superpowers.

Australian Fairy Wren

These birds symbolise social adaptability and survival through procreation, emphasising the importance of finding the right partner and environment.

ONE SMALL STEP TO TAKE TODAY: I will practise heeding the voice of Higher wisdom, guiding the development of my social skills.

MEDITATION PREPARATION (to practise each day at the same time)

Inhaling golden light, I embrace positivity and release negativity. I discover the hidden, supernatural laws in our world and adapt to them. Old angular patterns shift, making me feel stronger and more at peace. When I step out into society, I do so boldly, following my inner vision and Higher Wisdom as I go.

When patterns are broken, new worlds emerge. (Tuli Kupferberg)

6 CINDERELLA

Cinderella (PERRAULT/GRIMM)—*The following is a personal retelling of the tale:*

SYNOPSIS OF FAIRY TALE

When the beautiful wife of a rich man lay dying, she summonsed her lovely young daughter, Ella, reassuring her she would soon be lovingly watching over her from heaven. God would keep her safe, and if she remained faithful and kind, her life would be good. The father soon remarried. Ella's new stepmother was fair of face yet dark of heart, as were her two daughters.

The step-siblings insisted that Ella alone tend to all the chores, especially the fireplace. Their cruel taunts and tricks were a constant source of torment. One morning, when Ella emerged covered from top to toe in soot, the moniker 'Cinderella' stuck.

She made friends with the birds and animals to soothe her lonely, aching heart and spent nights huddled by the hearth to keep warm. Still, while humble Cinderella endured much suffering, her father, often absent due to his work, never knew.

Then came a royal proclamation: All kingdom subjects must attend the Royal Ball so Prince Charming can choose his future bride. Over the coming weeks, the stepmother and sisters prepared enthusiastically for the ceremony but ostracised poor Cinderella, emphatically opposing her when she pleaded for her invitation.

Finally, the long-awaited day arrived. After the three mean girls had dressed in their most glamorous attire, they left excitedly for the ball, leaving a crestfallen Ella behind.

But at just the right moment in time, in an ethereal haze from another realm, her supernatural godmother sensationally appeared out of the blue, granting Cinderella her wish to attend the ball. Could she be her loving mother in spirit form?

While the gracious Ella overflowed with love and gratitude, the kindness received came with a caution: she must be home before midnight when the spell's binding powers would dissolve.

In just a wave of the Godmother's magic wand, the mundane miraculously transformed into an array of enchanting apparel and animations. Radiant in her natural beauty, Cinderella donned an elegant gold silk gown and the most delicately cut crystal glass slippers before being whisked away in a gilded coach shaped just like the pumpkin from which it was remarkably formed.

No other young maiden at the ball came near the radiance of Ella. Dancing with the enraptured prince for most of the evening, she shimmered gracefully upon the palace floor.

Ella had never been more swept up in pure ecstasy than when in his arms. So, in rapture, she barely heard the clock when it began to strike twelve, stealing away with just seconds to spare.

One of Ella's glittering glass slippers fell loose on the long marble stairway as the prince gave chase, searching in vain for the vanishing goddess. Frantic, he darted here and there, all the while holding the mysterious slipper close to his wildly beating heart. Later, when he realised she had gone, he made it his mission never to give up until he found her.

Back at the palace, the royals were united in their decree that whomever the slipper fit was the true bride of the heir to the throne.

Meantime, the three jealous step-kin, unfaithful to royal orders, were doing everything within their power to restrict Cinderella's movements, preventing her from encountering the prince. Nevertheless, good fortune smiled on her that fateful day when a member of the visiting royal entourage spotted the shy maiden, demanding she come forward for her shoe fitting.

After much time-wasting with many fittings of the hopefuls across the kingdom, inevitably, it could only be Cinderella's foot that would be the right fit.

Her enraged step-family reeled in shock and dismay, trying their utmost to divide Cinderella and the prince. Resentfully, they even viciously slandered the innocent damsel. Yet, despite their vindictive slurs, the two soul mates could never be kept apart.

The sun shone brighter and longer on that special day as they rode off together on the prince's shiny steed. In a mutual state of rapturous romance and passionate bliss, the lovers anticipated joyously their future wedding and Ella's coronation.

Later, during the wedding breakfast, two white doves, ever-loyal to Ella, in one fell swoop, pecked out the eyes of the two back-stabbing, spiteful stepsisters. Their mother groaned, knowing her days would be consumed forevermore, ministering to her ungrateful daughters' needs. She would have too little time or energy left for royal balls and her giggly gossiping group.

How easy it was for Cinderella to forgive, and having pressed on to a better life, she soon forgot. And so it was, Ella and her handsome prince, living salubriously on high, were never to receive any news of the terrible trio ever again, going on to live the happiest of lives together, forever after. **THE END.**

PSYCHOLOGICAL PROMPTS

6: Key soul learning: To practise fostering forgiveness and gratitude through empathy (Empathy)

The tale of Cinderella explores matters of the heart and home. We contemplate the happy ending and how it relates to real-life romance. Archetype Cinderella representing love, contrasts with the divisive antagonists who withhold love. The story teaches us that human love is fleeting until we find eternal love, like mortal life transforming into an everlasting soul. While many of us struggle to understand, give and receive love, we are adept at knowing what it is not.

The mean-spirited step-kin in the fairy tale highlight the absence of love and the engagement of others only if they are useful to their gains. Eventually, we all face a painful reality check about love's authenticity and reciprocity.

Are our desires and expectations out of touch with reality? Are we more infatuated with the illusion of love than truly engaging from the heart? Do we desire someone solely because they fit our unrealistic fantasies until falling off the pedestal of our high expectations? Why do we refuse to settle for anything less than the ideal in a partner?

Often, our own imperfections drive us to seek perfection in others. We want to be completed by someone else, but Cinderella proves she is not inadequate nor helpless. By courageously assuming her right to attend the ball, she takes the first step towards transforming her life. We, too, have the power to turn our psychic wounds into glorious gifts.

Cinderella's forbidden act of attending the ball triggers a favourable destiny. Her self-actualisation is symbolised by her climbing out of the basement crying 'What about me' and slipping her foot neatly into the bespoke slipper. Similarly, we experience the same sense of completeness by unifying our unconscious and conscious selves. When we choose to do the noble thing, putting someone else in greater need before us, or we know it is time we took our shot at success, a charming kismet can occur, and our divinely ordained fate begins to unfold.

But, we often find it easier and safer to retreat into the shadows, when faced with constant tests. However, like maintaining physical fitness, we must use and support our personal growth or risk regression. Cinderella's self-empowerment meant more to her than captivating Prince Charming. Even though she felt a delicious visceral response on every level of her being, dancing in his arms, she tore herself away, prioritising her goals, trying to beat the clock.

Before her fairy-tale transformation, Cinderella's agency was dulled by ambivalence, just like us. She despaired about the lack of love in her life but feared making necessary changes. Intimidation leads to a mindset of 'damned if I do, damned if I don't'. Over time, we become stuck, feeling unable to create a more fulfilling reality.

Supernatural motherly magic (her superego) and the bird and animal motifs (representing her id) ignited Cinderella's soul-fire and self-love, affirming her worthiness to follow her dreams. We, too, can create fulfilling fusions within our psyches. The only hindrance is our resistance to admitting our shadows and change. But what we resist persists. Suppose we improve ourselves, becoming more loveable and loving; we will increase our chances of finding lasting intimate connections.

Through reflection, meditation, reframing our problem-story and saying positive self-affirmations, our consciousness guides us toward personal growth in giving and receiving love. We must question our motives and choose our path with care. Our potential partners, like us, are also navigating their shadow selves and relationships on the winding road of a hard-knock world. Few avoid contests, separation, and the harsh tests of their essence, values and skills.

What if we reframe our perspective and embrace gratitude for the lessons learned through our troubles? Can we accept that nobody is perfect and find contentment in someone who is 'good enough' and willing to share their life journey with us, as Wayne Dwyer (1940-2015) suggested? Will we choose a life in concert or conflict?

As we learn to love, no blame or shame can shield us from the realisation that we are all works in progress with much to learn about life, other people and how we relate. Suppose we reframe being right all the time with a stronger motive for shared happiness.

Cinderella's story teaches us that a harmonious relationship requires personal integration. We must know and accept ourselves before projecting our ungrateful, unfaithful, vindictive and resentful traits onto others. If the shoe fits, we must wear it.

Some suitors we have idealised adopt the mirage, convincing us they are 'the one', and only, in the end, reveal their true colours, too late. Still, Cinderella finds her ideal partner after facing opposition and stepping up to take her shot at the stars. Blending with another person is complex and requires behavioural adjustments. Achieving Wholeness is a significant personal undertaking, and we cannot dump our 'dirty work' onto someone else, making a 'Cinderella' of them.

Father time plays a role in our fate, as in Cinderella's, and our timing must be just right for us to achieve our Holy Grail. Still, our trial-and-error along the way helps us grow.

Cinderella, faithful to her promise of becoming, never lost sight of her Higher Self, being empathetic, passionate, authentic, and embracing her timely opportunities. Similarly, in the real world, our coherence of male and female energies within attracts spiritual synchrony (compliments of a fairy godmother, if you will), bringing us together with compatible partners.

Are we currently centred and aware, with open hearts, minds, and instincts on call? By integrating all aspects of ourselves, we gain the ability to identify our yearnings and make decisive choices on our Hero's Journey, enabling us to cope and resist impulsive urges with negative consequences for which we are solely responsible.

In the fairy tale, the pernicious stepsisters, overshadowed by their jealousy and cruelty, are blind to their own darkness, unable to reclaim and heal themselves. In contrast, forgiving and grateful Cinderella embraces change and transforms her existence from the dank depths of a doomed existence to an exquisite life of mutual love and light with her prince.

Despite her **Opponents'** threat to dim her loving light, Cinderella chose to stay grounded emotionally, synchronising with the timely intervention of the matriarchal spirit and realising her highest aspirations for **Partnership.**

Joy is the infallible sign of the presence of God. (Pierre Teilhard de Chardin)

SELF-REFLECTIONS

Life, like Cinderella's, tests your mettle. When you have an ego defence, you avoid confronting your issues. Nearly all of us go this route. We must consider two things: the quality of our relationship with ourselves and how we interact with others. If we remain in avoidance or denial, as our ego promotes, we reach a tipping point, and our suppressed issues spill over.

One issue is having feelings of emptiness— common for those who walk the path alone as *Cinderella* did in her early life. Every hero hearing the call of the heart's longing is urged to create change to achieve a deep connection with someone special. Somehow, Cinderella knew this to be so. She acted with certainty from her loving centre, stepping into the discomfort zone of the royal ball to transform her life from rags to riches, loneliness to love.

What does your past reveal about you and the choices you make? Our lived experiences provide the best information to guide our next move. While guidance comes in many forms, only you alone can find the right solution. Feeling exposed and vulnerable, you find yourself in a bind. Moments like these emphasise the importance of truth and immersing yourself fully in the situation to find it. Like Cinderella's cellar ponderings, you reflect, catching a glimpse of a brighter future. However, vacillating between self-affirmation and doubt, how can you gain the confidence Cinderella demonstrated in the pursuit of one's dreams. Your uncertainty is more about you than your circumstances. Author your preferred story, visualising who you truly are and what you want, and choose your path.

The hero's quest is to find love within and outside themselves. First, they must confront their inner conflicts reflected in their partners' (past and present) behaviours. You fight because the other person is ungrateful, jealous, or unfaithful, but have you not behaved similarly at some point? Is the stand-off between you merely an angry and vindictive payback or an attempt to establish healthy boundaries? Distinguishing between ego fantasies and reality is essential—a happy love life depends on it.

The chemistry of two produces a third entity: the relationship. Neglecting its need for forgiveness and nourishment will starve it. Every union requires mutual sacrifice and the ability to see things from the other person's perspective. When the behaviours of criticism, contempt, defensiveness and stone-walling (like those of the ugly step-sisters) creep in, our emotional intelligence is required more than ever for effective relationship repair and recovery (Gottman, 1999). We see our dualities in Cinderella's step-relationships: love versus hate, forgiveness versus resentment, and reality versus unreality. However, balancing positive and negative energies is crucial for healthier unions. Love is always a bumpy ride and accepting both the good and some bad is necessary to endure it.

Too often, we focus on what is wrong with the other person without knowing ourselves and our own flaws. We may resent that other people get to express those sides of themselves, while we don't: but if we express our anger through yelling, it will not heal a relationship. If love is blind, fault-finding soon cures its blindness. We all have two sides, dark and light. It is time to confront our shadow selves and process our past pain with the light of truth by acknowledging and forgiving our shortcomings before attempting to forgive and bond with others. Through dedicated practice, we become open, vulnerable, and authentic, inspiring authenticity from the ones we love. Empathy, forgiveness, and understanding are essential qualities that elevate our behavioural vibrations. As was the case for Cinderella: what was once hidden can now manifest. Two paths converge, adding value to each other's lives.

Maintaining gratitude and seeing our 'good enough' partner as a blessing—someone willing to share life's journey—is valuable. It's not about settling for crumbs.

Reconciling the desire for passionate love with the steady rhythm of partnership takes effort. Love heroes believe love finds a way, focusing on what works and daring to build a future together.

Yet something feels off when love is reduced to physical desire. A partner led by lust may struggle with self-love and deeper connection, relating more a 'I-It' than 'I-Thou' (Buber, 1923).

Unlike Cinderella's miracle prince, many lovers may have our bodies at their fingertips but keep their emotions at arm's length. Chemical attractions often fuel fleeting encounters that burn out before the lovers realise their incompatibility. How many times must one sacrifice their self-worth by leaping into bed with a stranger while dreaming of a never-ending fairy tale? Still, Cinderella's shining augury speaks the truth that an impossible love affair for one may be possible for someone else. However, tempering temptations and making conscious choices can prevent the dissonance between our words and actions, thereby enhancing our chances of success.

Sometimes, we must sacrifice the 'known' before gaining access to our potentially better 'unknown'. Although it may be painful to confront life's reality, you must set your ego aside, face self-defeating patterns, and address your issues with focused awareness. Otherwise, negative low-vibrational energy grows, leading to self-loathing unremedied by external rewards (as happened with the ugly step-kin). In the end, we all come to realise that love is all there is— it begins with the Self.

To discover one's Achilles' heel, one must look inward. The archetype demonstrates that we cannot fully understand someone else's journey or fit their shoes. However, we can acknowledge that we do not know everything, are not always right, and choose empathy over enmity, progress over perfection. These steps lead us to become more conscious partners—heroes embarking on the quest for loving intimacy. Jung spoke of how *the meeting of two personalities is like the contact of two chemical substances: if there is any reaction, both are transformed*— a sobering thought to ponder when selecting a partner.

The reward lies in truly knowing who you are and what you want and having the certainty that you can achieve it.

By daring to love with tenderness and grace and caring about the suffering of others, you walk the well-lit path, making a luminous and loving contribution to the universal field.

LIGHT QUALITIES (PARTNER)	SHADOW ATTRIBUTES (OPPONENT)
Forgiving	Vindictive
Thankful	Ungrateful
Unifying	Oppositional
Passionate	Jealous
Mutual	Unfaithful
Loving	Ambivalent
Decisive	Resentful
Self-affirming	Divisive

PROVERB: To err is human, to forgive Divine (Alexander Pope, 1711).

AFFIRMATION: I unify myself to unify with another.

GAME OF LIFE: I am right so you must be wrong (Consequence: Creating a lack of harmony and happiness in relationships).

REFLECTION QUESTION: Is it more important for me to be right than for us to be happy?

ANIMAL SYMBOLISM:

Blue Tiger Butterfly

The butterfly's magical motif inspires us to embrace vulnerability and openness to awaken. We also require courage to venture from the dark void into the unknown future, undergoing transformation from 'ordinary' to 'extraordinary'. Her short life is a metaphor for human existence: lasting only long enough to find a mate and create offspring until the cycle of life and death revolves again.

ONE SMALL STEP TO TAKE TODAY: I will practise being more empathic, forgiving, and grateful for how we complement each other rather than resent how different we are.

MEDITATION PREPARATION (to practise before going to sleep)

Inhaling golden light, I embrace positivity and release negativity. I leave betrayals behind, grateful for a fresh and vibrant start, feeling Whole and soulful. As I walk along, I see you in a shimmering haze on the distant skyline. Your warm aura of light beckons me closer, and I fall into your sweet embrace.

7 THREE BILLY GOATS GRUFF

Three Billy Goats' Gruff (Norwegians: PETER C. ASBJØRNSEN & JØRGEN MOE)—*The following is a personal retelling of the tale:*

SYNOPSIS OF FAIRY TALE

There once were three boy goats, the brothers Gruff, who realised there was little grass left for them to eat on their piece of turf by the river, but if they crossed to the other side, they would reach greener pastures. In a sunlit haze stood an overarching bridge leading to a lush meadow visible in the distance where they could fatten themselves up in readiness for another dry winter. The trouble was the bridge housed a horrible troll taking his toll with the blood of those attempting to cross.

Stories of the hideous creature's killing sprees were legend across the land, but the three brothers felt forced to make a choice. They would have to venture forth, testing their luck and survival skills against the might of the obnoxious obstructionist. The alternative was to stay put and perish from a lack of food, so, with nothing to lose, the three set off for the troll's bridge.

The Gruff brothers devised a canny plan. The youngest would make the crossing first, followed by the middle brother, and finally, it would rest on the largest and oldest goat to battle it out and overcome the heinous troll blocking their path.

Sure enough, as the smallest brother began to cross the bridge, the hungry troll threatened to gobble him up. True to plan, the goat persuaded the terrible troll to save his energy for when the bigger brother passed and eat him instead: he would make a much more gratifying feast. As the youngest billy-goat trotted on his way across to the other side, the next brother in line presented for permission to pass. The greedy troll salivated with anticipation as he eyed the bigger goat. Still, when the middle brother with self-preservation on his mind repeated the same argument, the bridge-blocker backed down: save your energy and wait for the most satisfying of suppers: the bulkiest billy-goat of the Gruff clan.

Much to his relief, the second goat was waved on. It was now the tallest and heaviest goats' turn to step up onto the bridge. The ravenous troll eyed off the brawny goat standing courageously calm before him, envisaging his sumptuous supper.

Then suddenly, with all his might, Billy-goat Gruff lowered his sharp horns and charged aggressively at the screeching creature, taking him totally by surprise. The troll was flung so high that he toppled into the raging dark waters below, never, ever to be seen again.

Brothers Gruff were ever so relieved and pleased with themselves. Their plan worked; the bridge was now troll and toll free, and all three brothers had rich green grass to eat on either side of the river through all the passing seasons of time. **THE END.**

PSYCHOLOGICAL PROMPTS

7: Key soul learning: To practise testing yourself in new settings (Intrinsic Motivation)

The tale of the three brothers serves as a powerful reminder of the significance of motivation and collaboration when facing challenges that may overwhelm any individual. While the younger brothers acknowledge the leadership of the oldest sibling, they willingly join forces to pursue their shared goals. Together, they devise a strategic plan to outsmart the bridge troll and manage to survive, thus living to recount their heroic adventure.

In assuming the role of the leader, the oldest billy-goat becomes the 'fall-guy' or 'scapegoat', immunising the team from blame (and death) should their plan go awry. However, in the event of a successful mission, they all reap the benefits. This approach mirrors a modern business ethos, wherein a team celebrates collective success while the leader shoulders the burden of failures.

It is heartening to witness the Gruff brothers' collaboration rather than succumbing to typical sibling rivalry, as children often do. Siblings learn valuable lessons from resolving conflicts and supporting one another through various stages of development. Unresolved disputes among siblings and the accompanying pain and hurt tend to resurface later in adult settings. These experiences can offer clues to help us resolve lingering issues when we encounter conflicts with colleagues, friends, family members, neighbours or partners.

For instance, if we find ourselves working alongside a colleague who is recalcitrant and unwilling to shoulder their fair share of work, we might recall the frustration and resentment we felt when a younger sibling did the same. Our parents blamed us for the incomplete tasks. Consequently, remnants of that resentment may surface from our shadow in new contexts, signalling it is time to address our underlying issues.

Much of our learning about interacting occurs within the family unit. Birth order and our sense of belonging shape our experiences. Often, overbearing and highly competitive siblings challenge us the most. In the absence of siblings, we derive these lessons through our other interactions, mainly when competition, fear and self-preservation are triggered.

Toxic sibling rivalry may be more prevalent in households where single or blended parents raise multiple children. In the case of the orphaned Gruff brothers, we can assume jealousy and competition existed among them regarding recognition, fairness, access, and equity. Nevertheless, in the face of a common enemy, a harmonious collective emerged to face it.

The eldest billy-goat is a courageous and positive role model, displaying a personal code characterised by decisiveness, proactivity, and democracy. With an engaging leadership style, he expects his younger brothers to take responsibility for overcoming their own challenges and contributing to the collective goals. He does not shield them from life's threats but instead encourages them to develop skills that will serve them long after he is gone, just as his parents had expected of him.

Throughout their journey, the goats encounter considerable resistance from the obstructive and petulant troll, as is typical for heroes on their quest. Despite the risk, they do the one forbidden thing—crossing the bridge—and it pays off. This experience strengthens their confidence, resilience and tolerance in dealing with the differences encountered in the world. Through rational thinking (ego-based), they negotiate and outwit the trolls' primal powers (his id). But, their destruction was inevitable, if they relied solely on unregulated brute force.

Three Billy-Goats Gruff addresses the duality of good and dark forces in reality and illustrates positive strategies for mastering our deep-seated fear and denial of them. However, the tale offers more than just this lesson.

The goat motif conveys that we can succeed if we possess the willpower to endure the craggy course, taking life in our stride and persisting until we reach the other side. By moving in harmony with nature, we establish a mysterious connection with the wild and tap into a force so potent that no earthly troll can resist our power.

The big billy-goat exemplifies an internalised parent figure (superego), coming to the fore with moral certitude when he assumes the driving seat, guiding his siblings to greener pastures—as is customary for many an oldest child. Resolute, he offered himself as the sacrificial lamb should the plan fail.

Despite their challenges, the goat family's practical optimism transformed them from potential victims to triumphant survivors. None was afraid: disallowing circumstances, competitiveness (such as blaming each other) or complacency to impede their progress. However, as victims, they would assume wrongly that the grass was just as brown on the other side, wasting energy contradicting each other's ideas and faltering diffusively by pulling in different directions. Contrastingly, the goats' unwavering belief was that they were undefeatable. Indeed, fortune favours the brave.

Suppose we confront the unconscious id-shadow parts of our ego, representing our unhealthy emotions and memories and deepest fears, with the power of mindful self-regulation, bringing them back into psychic harmony. As a balanced Self, we can pay attention to the way ahead, walking through the fire to the other side of our problems— to freedom. Then, we embrace change and look forward to growing ourselves in new settings. Nevertheless, as the fairy-tale archetype suggests, it takes maturity to overcome the trolls that dispute our passage and emerge victorious.

No more the **Resisters** of change due to fear. We are the **Motivators** who get things moving in life, like the team of goats who ultimately find their sweet spot.

SELF-REFLECTIONS

After experiencing an existential crisis, you confront the pain, stress, and lack of progress, seeking ways to overcome them. By perceiving challenges as opportunities for personal growth and increased drive, you follow in the footsteps of the Brothers Gruff. It is time to gather resources, tap into your desires, and forge ahead, embracing the cyclical nature of life.

The goats understood the importance of supporting each other rather than battling their difficulties alone. However, our defensive egos often keep us stuck, preventing us from accepting wise advice from each other. Nonetheless, mentors urge us to persist with unwavering determination.

Our aim is to mobilise and progress through a never-say-die attitude, adaptability, and agility. As we venture into new settings, our true selves are put to the test. Here, you will sharpen your problem-solving abilities, acquire new skills, and commit to completing what you start. By taking one step at a time, you inch closer to greener pastures. However, this path comes with a side note: Acknowledge and channel latent aggressive (i.e., assertive and passionate) tendencies to propel your achievements onwards. After all, reaching a place of fulfilment requires embracing both conscious and unconscious aspects, preparedness, understanding the challenges ahead, and discerning the next steps to advance.

In unfamiliar terrain, all heroes encounter rivals (from within and without) who place pressure on their emotional wellbeing. It proves best to go with the flow, for what we resist only persists and manifests as pain. Despite the ego's denial, the body cannot deceive. Anxiety intensifies when the shadow breaches its defences, triggering thoughts of inadequacy, scarcity, and vulnerability. Still, these trials are necessary for us to truly know ourselves at the core.

While some partners may be gruff and overbearing, they can catalyse our personal growth. Remaining with them becomes a spiritual test, teaching us the importance of balancing the bad with the good and reconciling differences.

If we anchor ourselves in a wounded ego, we go in circles, blaming others and distorting stories to fit misconceptions. The shadow expresses what the ego suppresses, shielding us from the truth. Instead of constructing walls through denial, justification, or projection of anger and hurt, suppose we develop a resilient Self and trust in our ability to overcome.

To illuminate your shadow side, summon the courage to confront the trolls of your psyche hindering your Hero's Journey. As you reflect upon the effects of harmful pressures stemming from sibling or peer rivalry you may discover you are too afraid to deal with conflicting emotions, making it difficult to maintain fulfilling relationships. Ask yourself which direction you lean. Are you ready to confront the obstacles standing in your way and 'challenge to evolve' or stay in avoidance mode? Can you act with empathy and altruism, or will you succumb to self-centricity, where avoidance, duality, and separation hold sway?

The territorial troll compromised his own survival by denying others their right to self-preservation. In stark contrast, the big billy-goat serves as a metaphor for the Higher Self, highlighting the efficacy of accepting one's role in shared problems and choosing the path of integrity.

Gracefully enduring challenges with a philosophical mindset will fuel the motivation to keep moving forward. Expand your perspective and horizons by staying focused on practical priorities and reflecting positively on how far you have come and crystallising this healthy perspective in a new personal story.

As you skilfully steer your destiny, renewed hope allows past troubles to fade in the rear-view mirror. Enriched by experience and blessed with an indomitable spirit, you confidently embark on new adventures. You tackle your tasks with gusto and take charge of matters concerning relationships; family; travel; legalities; education and spirituality. As an experienced tactician and caretaker charting a new course for yourself, community and tribe, you seize the reins, cross the gleaming bridge, and take the ride home, holding the golden cup of victory.

LIGHT QUALITIES (MOTIVATOR)	**SHADOW ATTRIBUTES (RESISTER)**
Motivational	Resistant
Resolute	Contradictory
Courageous	Afraid
Progressive	Obstructive
Strategic	Diffusive
Undefeatable	Over-bearing
Positive	Petulant
Collaborative	Rivalrous

PROVERB: Build a bridge and get over it.

AFFIRMATION: I take life in my stride when faced with new obstacles.

GAME OF LIFE: The grass is always greener on the other side (Consequence: Feeling discontented with where you are).

REFLECTION QUESTION: Can we ever play on the same team, or must we pull in different directions?

ANIMAL SYMBOLISM: Goat; Yowie

Goat

Symbolising male virility and feminine maternity, the goat indicates a need to balance yin and yang energies. Goats, both practical and mythical, embody faith and sure-footed independence, signalling readiness to ascend with full power and climb the summit.

Yowie

In First Nations stories, the **Yowie**, also called the Yahoo, is a huge, hairy, ape-like creature said to roam the remote outback, inspiring awe and caution. In our story, he takes the place of the troll, a creature of contrasts symbolising both timidity and aggression, reflecting our primal instincts when threatened.

ONE SMALL STEP TO TAKE TODAY: I will practise testing my assumptions and abilities in new settings with a positive and indomitable spirit.

MEDITATION PREPARATION (to practise at times of change)

Inhaling golden light, I embrace positivity and release negativity. Feeling inspired, I approach a bridge, my heart filled with the promise of a new beginning. With the universe's support at my back, I move forward to face challenges and claim my rewards. Once across, I marvel at the miracle of how much ground I have traversed. An invisible supportive presence whispers in my ear— All's well from here on.

Alone we can do so little; together we can do so much.
(Helen Keller)

8 BEAUTY AND THE BEAST

Beauty and the Beast (DE VILLENEUVE, PERRAULT/GRIMM))—*The following is a personal retelling of the tale:*

SYNOPSIS OF FAIRYTALE

Once upon a time, in a faraway land, there lived a wealthy merchant blessed with three sons and three daughters. Among them, the youngest and fairest was 'Beauty', christened Belle. Her beauty radiated not only from her physical charm but also from her kind and pure heart. She was thoughtful and well-read, her mind enriched with knowledge and wisdom.

As the father embarked on another trade venture, he gathered his daughters and offered them a special gift upon his return. The two older daughters, driven by their selfish nature, demanded exquisite dresses and magnificent jewels. However, with adoring eyes fixed upon her father, Belle humbly requested a sweet white rose.

Fate turned for the worse when the angry sea swallowed the father's ship in a fierce storm. Miraculously, he survived, but all his cargo was lost. The thought of returning home empty-handed and disappointing his daughters weighed heavily on his heart. With his head hung low, he trudged back, his spirit dampened. He stumbled upon an elegant palace on his way, seemingly appearing out of thin air. Inside, he found respite—a comfortable bed to rest his weary bones and a table laden with fine fare to satisfy his hunger. In this mysterious sanctum, he indulged in sleep and sustenance, unaware of the enchantment surrounding him.

As he prepared to leave, he came upon an enchanted garden, a hedge adorned with glorious white roses. One bloom shone radiantly among them, reminding him of his beloved Belle. Without a second thought, he swiftly cut the stem, only to be ambushed by an enormous man-beast.

The beast, filled with outrage at the merchant's ignorant actions—taking advantage of his hospitality and stealing his prized rose—pronounced that he would only pardon the beleaguered fellow if he agreed to send one of his daughters to the palace. Reluctantly, the hapless father, under duress, offered Belle, but his suspicions of the beast's intentions lingered in his heart.

On his return, the father was greeted with fanfare and celebration. However, intuitive Belle didn't take long to sense that something was amiss. She coaxed the truth out of her father—revealing the bargain he had struck with the Beast. Her father confessed that he chose her because he knew her love for him was unconditional and that she would go to the ends of the earth to save her family.

Beauty prepared herself for her handover to the beast. But when the time came, Belle was surprised to find that he possessed social grace, generosity, and attentive service, despite his repulsive appearance. She adapted to her life as the castle's mistress, finding solace in the beast's loyalty and provision.

Yet, despite Belle's repeated refusals, the ardent 'Beast' persistently sought her hand in marriage. As Beauty slept, she immersed herself in the same dream every night— a handsome prince became her confidante, with whom she shared her deepest love and truths. The beautiful maiden even wondered if 'Beast' had jealously hidden the prince of her dreams within the magical palace.

Although Belle found contentment living with 'Beast', her longing for her father grew stronger with each passing day. The beast, recognising her sorrow, granted her a short visit to her family on the condition that she returned to the palace precisely one week later.

With delight in her heart, Belle bid farewell, her arms filled with beautiful and curious gifts from the beast—an enchanted ring, a magic mirror, and oodles of opulent finery. The mirror possessed the power to reflect the palace scenes in real-time, and the ring, with three turns, could transport Belle back to the castle.

However, when Belle was greeted by her sisters, as anticipated, they self-indulgently snatched the elegant gowns she offered. With their covetous grasp, they reduced the precious gifts into mere rags. Yet, the enchanted garments restored their former splendours once donned by Belle. When the seventh day of Belle's visit arrived, the spiteful sisters rubbed onions into their eyes, pretending to weep and to delay Belle's return to the castle. Unaware of the dark schemes they had hatched, Belle, always trusting and tolerant, stayed behind to comfort them.

Yet, deep in her heart, Belle contemplated her broken promise to 'Beast'. Seeking solace, she turned to the magic mirror. To her shock, the reflection showed him lying by his enchanted white rose hedge, dying from heartbreak. In that instant, with three turns of the ring, Belle stood beside him, uttering words of love as her tears fell upon his heart. Miraculously, the beast transformed into the prince of her dreams. Bedazzled by this revelation, Belle learned the truth—the prince had been cursed by a vengeful witch, transformed into a beast for refusing her shelter in his palace bed. The only antidote for the dreadful curse was the true love of a beautiful and caring maiden. In the end, through the power of true love, she found lasting happiness alongside her handsome prince. **THE END.**

PSYCHOLOGICAL PROMPTS

8: Key soul learning: To develop managing your wild emotions (Self-Regulation)

At the behest of her father, a virginal girl (symbolised by a white rose) moves in with a beast to mediate the males' dispute and embark on her transformative journey to selfhood. The patriarch seeks absolution for his debt and guilt, having stolen the rose of purity, transferring his responsibility onto his most accommodating and forgiving daughter, thereby avoiding consequences.

In a state of fear, suspicion, and humiliation, the father's superego urges him to protect his daughter before himself. Yet, he submits to his shadow instincts, succumbing to the drives of his ignorant indwelling beast, reflecting the struggle between his duty and his primal desire (id) to avoid pain. Thus begins the young maiden's rite of passage, her Hero's Journey.

Stepping into this unknown territory, she quickly adapts, embracing her role as the mediator, appeasing the beast and saving her family from ruin. The tale subtly weaves historical themes of martyrdom and the plight of women as mere chattels in a man's world. Further, the father must save face as the primary provider within the social and cultural construct.

However, shadow elements surface, stoking the father's sense of loss and shame to bring out the worst in him. He steals from the hand that feeds him. Similarly, the beast resists owning his dark behaviours, projecting them onto the father. The hypocritical brute forces the father to hand over his daughter to settle a petty infraction—he is in no position to judge another's ethics. We all tend to see faults in others before recognising them within ourselves. Curiously, the father develops trust in the beast upon receiving parting gifts.

Behind the beast's frightful veneer hides a beautiful heart, a tolerant and strong character, and a handsome prince, reminding us that beauty is but skin deep and subjective. He defies the expectations of a wild and lustful creature, revealing a remarkable ability to self-regulate and resist his instinctual desires. He respects the woman, never seeking to violate her or exercise coercive control, a grace that Belle deeply appreciates. He holds but does not wield the lion's share of power. As we mature, we realise that inner beauty far surpasses external appearances. Through deep love for another, the perception of beauty becomes malleable. Our love interests may not be judged conventionally beautiful by others, but through our love-struck eyes, they transform into the most beautiful person on earth. But, when anger, fear, and loathing diminish our empathy, so does our ability to see the beauty within others.

Belle's agency evolves as she stands up for her dreams and refuses the beast's marriage proposals. Taking steps towards autonomy, she listens to her own counsel, trusts in it, and prepares for the consequences of speaking her heart's truth. However, her naive nature prevents her from seeing through the guise and guile of others. False tears usually arouse suspicion but fool her. Real tears from her trusting heart awaken the dying beast, proving the true power of love as an alchemical agent for healing.

The magic mirror serves as a metaphor for one who sees across space and time, reminding us of the importance of maintaining a mindful perspective free from false assumptions, bias, and maladaptive thinking. Pensive Belle awakens to her broken promise, like waking from a dream and faces reality with the courage of her convictions.

The enchanted ring and its three rotations symbolise our love connections' eternal and evocative quality, demonstrating their power to transform division and darkness. Promises, hope, and faith resonate in the tale, yet it also serves as a reminder that things are not always as they seem and will surely test our characters. Engaging in self-indulgence or taking loved ones for granted, as forbidden acts, carry repercussions.

With her delicate appearance but inner strength, the maiden unknowingly becomes the centre of a crisis caused by unconscious acts done in self-interest.

Sometimes, like Belle, those we expect to be allies become foes, and vice versa. Even our own family with ambitions for success may commit acts of betrayal. Forgiveness and understanding are necessary instead of placing blame. The Beauty and the Beast archetype underscores the need to tame the savage beast if we are to cope and take charge.

We must hone our insight, distinguishing between life's real and illusory aspects. Belle steps into the vast unknown, rife with real and imagined threats, but she emerges triumphant by achieving her heart's desires. Her visions, loyalty, empathy, forbearance, and inner strength propel her from an unsettling beginning to a victorious and glorious end. She proclaims, "Where there is a will, there is a way."

Unlike her father, Belle shows restraint, battling and balancing the contaminated masculine energies that are ignorant and beastly. Through the unique integration and self-regulation of wild and rational masculine (animus) and caring and intuitive feminine traits (anima), she finds the courage and strength to overcome the challenges she must face alone. The word 'courage' has its roots in the Latin word 'cor', meaning 'heart'. Without the spirit of a brave heart, love cannot endure.

Belle's journey exemplifies the transformative power of love, the importance of maintaining a balanced perspective, and the realisation that true beauty and power reside within.

Belle, possessing goodness, was a beautiful rose with self-preserving thorns. Her personal code, centred on compassion for others, underpinned her every action. Still, her ability to **Mediate** impulses with reasoning power, and to regulate ignorant **Force** with loving tenderness made her indomitable.

SELF-REFLECTIONS

Beauty and her Beast represent our instinctive nature concealed within the shadow. Our higher ego must navigate and conquer our fears, granting us the confidence to pursue our dreams. Failure to address these inner struggles allows anxieties to fester in the darkness, mirroring the predicament of the fairy-tale archetype. Before making life-altering decisions, we must confront our noble superego and primal id, quietening the din of neurotic thoughts and aggressive reactions, clamouring for our attention.

Crises provide opportunities for self-reflection and profound revelations, offering glimpses into our true character. In these moments of intense stress, our ego becomes the guiding force that restores rationality and equilibrium. Yet, our journey as heroes necessitates the summoning of inner strength—a meditative state of awareness that enables us to tame the wild 'tiger' dwelling within. It is through this act of self-discipline that we rise above self-centred concerns, embracing change and the challenges that await us in the outer world.

In contrast, when we deny, avoid, or suppress our primal and passionate urges, the dormant 'tiger' reacts with an antagonistic animus, threatening to unleash hostility and chaos.

At times, we are shattered by the realisation that we are not only vessels for love, beauty, and compassion but also anger, blame, resentment, and inappropriate lust. While anger, when channelled appropriately, can catalyse growth and transformation, uncontrolled anger becomes a dangerous adversary that holds us captive, held ransom to its destructive control.

To cultivate self-control and harmonise our inner landscape, we must embark on a journey of self-discovery, exploring the depths of our being and embracing both our shadow and light, our beastliness and beauty.

The beast's dominance over Beauty's family is a projection of his imprisoned identity. Only when the Beast lets down his guard, revealing his vulnerability, does Beauty return, showering him with a tender love that mends his wildness and unveils the hidden beauty he possesses. This tale aligns with the wisdom of Antoine de Saint-Exupery's *Le Petit Prince* (1943), reminding us that we only truly know (and are responsible for) what we have tamed.

Can you recall when you acted impulsively, driven by untamed passions, and turned a blind eye to the signs of potential failure? Our obstinate attachment to immature desires, fuelled by our wounded egos, ultimately diminishes us, not our vulnerability. Instead of succumbing to negative self-talk or surrendering to despair, let us reflect on the shadowy corners of our being and acknowledge and reclaim those unevolved traits we have previously disregarded and disowned. Admittedly, this task can be confronting, especially when, in the past, we have endured a succession of unfortunate events that have dampened our spirits. In this case, recording both our problem-story and its strengths-based reframe can deepen our understanding and support our emotional processing.

As we strive to transcend our trials, we may find that our untamed fragments (voiced by our monkey mind) jeer at our endeavours, reminding us of past failures and asserting that our fondest dreams are out of reach. However, once we embrace and integrate these fragments from the shadows, hence, allowing them to contribute to our vitality and creative potential, we unlock a newfound power to shape our reality and manifest our deepest desires.

The rewards of such pensive introspection and the reclamation of our personal power is invaluable. Moments spent in solitude, reflecting upon and reconciling our separated aspects, grant us a profound understanding of truth, light, and the transformative power of unconditional love in the realm of human existence. As we uncover our inherent goodness, doubts and fears dissipate, as happened for Beauty and the Beast. This process requires we self-regulate, enabling us to redirect our life-force energy to areas in need of change, restoring balance and re-igniting our motivation and zest for life.

Evolved Belle exemplifies a high-vibratory Self who transcends superficial attractions, status, power, money, and the pressure of meeting others' expectations. Instead, the focus is on fostering deep, loving, loyal, and lasting connections. Accessing your creative wellspring, once imprisoned by fear, unleashes a burgeoning artist, writer, healer, entrepreneur, or leader within you, ready to be expressed. Her archetype shows that when we establish a connection with the Divine, our loving tenderness surpasses any unhealthy emotional condition. Sending love to unsettling situations, whether through visualisation or by physically laying hands on sensitive areas of the reactive shadow-body, brings peace and healing to ourselves (and others). We move forward with trust in our innate abilities, encountering serendipitously and engaging with like-minded individuals fortuitously in new realms. In the end, love triumphs all.

LIGHT QUALITIES (MEDIATOR)	**SHADOW ATTRIBUTES (FORCER)**
Mediating	Forceful
Mindful	Wild
Strong	Beastly
Rational	Self-indulgent
Forbearing	Lustful
Tolerant	Blaming
Pensive	Ignorant
Trusting	Suspicious

PROVERB: Tame the tiger before letting it out of the cage.

AFFIRMATION: I am in charge of my emotions, adapting well to life's changing conditions.

GAME OF LIFE: Behaving in forceful ways to control others (Consequence: Finding that others avoid you).

REFLECTION QUESTION: Am I willing to take charge by controlling the negativity in my mind?

ANIMAL SYMBOLISM:

Tasmanian tiger

The extinct wild thylacine symbolises hidden spiritual insights available to us all. To tap into these, we must tame our turbulent emotions and connect with our intuitive higher self. The thylacine's enigmatic presence delivers cryptic messages from beyond, reflecting our dual nature. It exemplifies our bravery and resilience against peril, urging us to embrace adaptability.

ONE SMALL STEP TO TAKE AWAY: I will practise regulating my wild emotional impulses aroused during testing times.

MEDITATION PREPARATION (to practise when feeling emotional pain)

Inhaling golden light, I embrace positivity and release negativity. I envision a new day and ease into a feeling of tranquillity. With deep, even breaths, energy flows to my heart chakra, centring me. My faith and forbearance strengthen me for the grail trek ahead.

Beauty is not in the face; it is a light in the heart.
(Kahlil Gibran)

9 THE UGLY DUCKLING

The Ugly Duckling (HANS CHRISTIAN ANDERSEN)—
The following is a personal retelling of the tale:

SYNOPSIS OF FAIRY TALE

His story begins in a barnyard where a mother duck's eggs have hatched. All the little birds' features resembled their mother except one ungainly, taller bird that did not seem to fit. The mother duck had no idea that an egg of a different bird had accidentally rolled into her nest some weeks before. Sadly, the unusual baby bird stood out, enduring ridicule and physical torment for his individuality. He was very different from the small group of fuzzy ducklings.

While the little orphan was too confused and frightened and not yet strong enough to leave his surrogate family, he often gazed longingly skywards and across the local ponds, searching for a place where he might one day belong.

As soon as he was able, he wandered away from the barn without so much as a backward glance. Still, a tear glistened in his wee eyes as he quietly slipped into the lush lake habitat of the wild geese and friendly wood ducks. But, his peace was short-lived, as brutal game hunters arrived within hours, savagely slaughtering the friendly flocks while the poor duckling fled into the reeds, watching in terror.

Eventually tiring of his scary, solitary life, the battle-worn bird swam downstream to a rustic farm shed where, by chance, a kindly old lady took him in. She already housed an old snarly cat and a plucky hen who liked to rule the roost. The cat and hen taunted the strange duckling because of his different, non-ducky ways.

Then, one day, resigned to his sad reality, the young bird set out alone again to find peace. Each day, he made do with tiny morsels of food and just enough water, taking his comfort from the warming autumn weather. But out of the blue, as he gazed at the heavenly skies as he always did, he spotted a flock of migrating birds with rare natural beauty illuminated by sunlight, moving across the white feathery clouds. He closed his eyes, dreaming in his heart to join them one day.

Several weeks passed, and as deep winter set in and food sources waned, the poor starving bird faced another threat of freezing to death. Fortunately, a thoughtful farmer rescued him from the frozen lake and took him into his care. However, the farmer's boisterous children so terrorised him that he fled. He returned to the only place he knew: the icy lake. This time, he discovered a nearby cave where he could stay out of harm's way feeling unloved and alone.

A new day dawned, and the little hermit sensed a change in the air as the unusual and exciting cacophony of bird calls filled the surroundings. Feeling curious, he slowly emerged from the cave and waddled down to the lake to investigate. To his delight, as he looked around and took in the verdant scene, he saw that the sun was higher in the sky, and the day felt much warmer. Spring must have come at last, for he saw a familiar mother duck leading her parade of baby ducklings down to the water's edge. And on the thawing lake, he spotted a family of swans: a sight so majestic, so beautiful, it took his breath away, making him swoon. The young bird's instincts told him that his reclusive cave life no longer brought comfort. Without hesitation, he swam straight up to the beautiful swans gliding upon the lake. However, he secretly feared that he might be attacked again for being a bit odd, but he made his approach anyway. To his utter amazement and joy, the serene swans welcomed and accepted him as their own, swimming in circles around him and making gleeful sounds. In one serendipitous moment, he found his bliss.

The young bird felt a sense of peace as the sun crowned the blue sky and the gentle wind rustled through the long green grass. When he saw his reflection in the glassy water, he could hardly believe his eyes. He had transformed into an elegant specimen of superior beauty and strength: a swan no less, just like his newfound friends. With awe, gratitude, and a profound sense of inner knowing, he marvelled at his transformation as his brethren took to the skies. Suddenly, feeling a deep stirring to join them, he took flight at once, whooping with joy as he spread his magnificent wings and naturally fell into the formation of the wedge alongside his graceful kin. **THE END.**

PSYCHOLOGICAL PROMPTS

9: Key soul learning: To develop knowing the world within to understand the world without (Self-Awareness)

The Ugly Duckling is a teaching tale urging us to stay true to ourselves, regardless of the opposition we face. Its entwined themes of nature and nurture explore the profound and enduring effects adverse circumstances in our family life can have on our development. Growing up in an environment where we hear we are not okay and do not belong makes it harder to accept and love ourselves. Criticism and abuse from a mother create an insecure attachment, affecting us until we confront these old wounds. Many factors are at play.

For instance, mothers living in fear might desperately try to fit into the norms of the social tribe, fearing rejection if their child looks or acts differently. Some have an ambivalent, depressed, detached, or disorganised attachment style. Their maladaptive care behaviours manifest defensively and avoidantly. According to Clarissa Pinkola Estes (1992), children raised by deeply wounded mothers often feel alone and give in too readily, fearing taking a stand or demanding respect. They become afraid of expressing themselves creatively, scared of rejection, abandonment, and the unknown.

The would-be duck demonstrates that being the authentic self we were born to be requires courage. Raising a slightly different child requires a loving and heroic mother. He had the former but not the latter. The cygnet had all maternal protection withdrawn. Mothers facing hardships while caring for their children demonstrate grit and gumption. However, their struggle can be intensified by poor mental health issues like social anxiety and depression (and more). Narcissistic or self-absorbed 'me-first' mothers strive to remain children for as long as possible, failing to address childhood wounds and projecting and inflicting them on their children. An unwell psyche perpetuates family distress intergenerationally.

Overcoming childhood feelings of unlovability and non-belonging is challenging. In therapy, clients recount how their internalised maternal voice constantly reminds them of their inadequacy, unattractiveness, and uselessness. They might even hear the inner parent's (superego) disapproval during moments of intimacy and generally when they suspect they 'should' be doing better. But, like the swan, if we persevere, acknowledge our shadow fears, and process our pain, to enlighten and heal our emotional issues, we'll eventually restore our self-love. Through introspection, we gain clarity about ourselves, others, and the world around us. Moreover, we can choose to love and nurture ourselves in healthier ways than our original caretakers did, replacing the disempowering inner critic with a self-affirming one.

The outcast cygnet did not wallow or dwell on his mistreatment but chose to understand that others' cruelty was not his problem. He withdrew from hostile environments, accepting and adapting to necessary changes to feel comfortable in his own skin. But, only when he saw his reflection, did he become self-aware of his true identity—highlighting the value of self-reflection for all of us. He chose to move on when people and places were ill-suited, appreciating others' right to live their lives as he was determined to live his. His inner voice urged him never to give up. However, his sense of non-belonging saddened him, analogously illustrating the primary fear and pain of being human.

Negative self-talk keeps us mind-blind and stuck, draining the energy needed to survive and thrive. Against all odds, the cygnet did not succumb but entered the 'cave of despair' (Spenser, 1897), seeking solace and shielding himself, reassuring us that our soul-searching is the way to finding answers, renewed hope, and a fresh start. We must strive for higher ideals than the mainstream's groupthink deems good and worthy. When the 'mean' group goes low, we must go down into our deep core to go high, maintaining our empathic ethos. We learn from the intrepid swan (aka Hans Christian Andersen) that our sense of self-belief, self-worth, self-love, self-respect and agency—combined with emotional regulation—lead to a fulfilling life.

Humans have much to learn from the stoic maturity demonstrated by animals. The Ugly Duckling archetype shows how we must anchor to our authentic core to resist tribal and societal pressures. We are all born to be different; in that sense, we are all the same. Feeling threatened and driven by their animal instincts, humans behave harmfully towards others perceived as separate from themselves. Most of us have skewed perceptions, making assumptions based on unfounded fears and biases. Love is the antidote. But, we cannot force others to accept and love us, to fulfil our need for belonging, but we can choose to love ourselves.

As the tale's symbolism shows, when nature is ready to change seasons, everything else changes in concert. But before we soar, we must free ourselves from toxic shadow energy and establish meaningful connections with those who are there for us and us for them through the many challenges found along the hero's way. Our kind of people, the like-spirited, will naturally attract us to them when the time is ripe. The swan teaches us to spend quality 'alone' time in our inner world, enjoying our own company, to catalyse change in the outer world.

Psychologist Mihaly Csikszentmihalyi (1934 -) contends, "People who learn to control inner experience will be able to determine the quality of their lives, which is as close as any of us can come to being happy." Nothing is stopping us from seizing this life-transforming opportunity. Choosing not to dwell as a **Recluse**, hiding from the social noise, The Ugly Duckling was the **Seeker,** his lantern aglow, guiding his spiritual ascent to rediscover his kindred.

SELF-REFLECTIONS

In this intricate and chaotic web, we call life, it's easy to feel insignificant, lost, and pushed to the outer edges like an ugly duckling. But it's crucial to regain control of false egoic pride and hurt and stand confidently in who you are. Embrace the challenges that come your way because they offer opportunities to perspective take, uncover the truth, and re-establish real power.

You don't have to conform to groupthink that goes against your own beliefs. You might have tried to fit in and belong, but deep down, you still feel like a round peg in a square hole. The pain of exclusion (or missing out) is undeniable, but it's time to pause and reflect. There's a bigger picture beyond your current scope of vision.

Recognise that alternative worldviews often face opposition and criticism, leading one to retreat into a self-imposed cave. Reflect on the feelings of rejection and your beliefs about yourself and reality. Consider new paths for moving forward and growing.

While others may perceive you as self-absorbed with your struggles, you understand the power of choice within you. Remaining in environments that don't align with your true Self only adds unnecessary pressure, and these aren't where your soul can find nourishment.

Do you stay in adversarial contexts due to responsibilities or for security? This creates inner conflict, leaving you torn between fighting, freezing, hiding, or fleeing. It dilutes your power and prevents you from fully thriving. Instead, cultivate a positive outlook and engage in affirming self-talk. Nurture your self-esteem, rise above negative vibrations, and look for new paths. Still, accepting reality as it is, without resorting to magical thinking or trying to change it, is part of the challenge on your hero's path. Ask yourself, "Is this 100% true?" This helps identify incorrect assumptions causing unnecessary pain. Life's lessons are there to help you understand yourself better and to recognise your strengths and limitations. There's power in writing your stuck-story and reframing it.

Remember, you can't change others to fit your way of thinking. The only behaviour you can control is your own. Instead of being consumed by the actions of those who betray you, try to find the lessons in their poor treatment. But also consider whether you may have unknowingly rejected them first. Reflect on the self-rejection that may have led you to reject others. These factors often hide from our awareness. Reclaiming your true self requires solitude, patience, and significant inner work. It's a challenging journey (with no room for avoidance) but every effort you invest in expanding your self-awareness is worthwhile.

The story of *The Ugly Duckling* is a powerful metaphor. Confronted with persecution in unfamiliar surroundings, he chose not to let it define him. Tired of feeling lost and with nothing to lose, he leapt fearlessly into the unknown. By rejecting distorted perceptions foist upon him, he reclaimed his place and emotional freedom on the Hero's Journey. You, too, can follow his path, finding solace in the Danish saying, "What is lost without must be re-won within."

At the crossroads, distinguish between friends and foes, truth and falsehood, demonstrating your readiness to back yourself. Keep your emotions in check and trust that wisdom will blossom with time.

False egoism misguides those who segregate others. Forgive their hurtful actions, for they know not what they do. Focus on unpicking the behavioural patterns reinforcing your inner child's emotional response. If you work to your strengths, your heroic Self will emerge. Stand tall in your innate goodness, radiating the truth that you are more than just okay. By valuing the differences between you—such as contrasting levels of understanding—your mind begins to let go, fills with empathy, and allows what's beyond your control to simply be. Reclaiming your authentic Self may not be easy, but it's worth every step. Trust yourself, question assumptions, and know that your rebirth requires self-reflection and psychological work. You're not alone. With persistence and trust, you will emerge from the darkness, ready to make meaningful connection. Believe in yourself and let your higher frequencies shine and soar.

LIGHT QUALITIES (SEEKER)	**SHADOW ATTRIBUTES (RECLUSE)**
Alone	Lonely
Knowing	Mind-blind
Understanding	Assumptive
Self-reflecting	Self-absorbed
Soul-searching	Wallowing
Belonging	Withdrawn
Questioning	Rejected
Maturing	Avoidant

PROVERB: Self-worth cannot depend on the approval of others.

AFFIRMATION: I am aware of my Self and lovingly accept who I am in the world.

GAME OF LIFE: Fear of the unknown (Consequence: Rejecting new opportunities, becoming stuck).

REFLECTION QUESTION: Do I feel confident in my own skin?

ANIMAL SYMBOLISM: Duck; (Black) Swan; Emu

Duck

The use of duck imagery alludes to our watery emotions and the need for self-awareness when dealing with them. When we delve into our still waters, in quiet times of reflection, we get to the bottom of what we are seeking to know.

Black Swan

Sightings of swans (heavenly messengers), bring to mind the higher beauty and goodness of our natural world and our longing to atone with the Great Spirit. A black bird urges us to espy the hidden unknown, prepare for the unexpected and stay open. All swans signal a time to commence our deeper soul work.

Emu

Emus symbolise Divine protection. As large, swift birds, they demonstrate our untapped personal power and the need to regain self-confidence. Their flightlessness reflects our earthly competition and the challenges we face to overcome our limitations to rise.

ONE SMALL STEP TO TAKE AWAY: I will regularly practise self-reflection to become aware of my underlying patterns and motives for doing what I do.

MEDITATION PREPARATION (to practise at dawn)

Inhaling golden light, I embrace positivity and release negativity. I envision a spring day, feeling joyful anticipation for my next step. In the natural vista before me, sunbeams glisten on reflective pools where my knowing gaze invites me to embrace my full truth. I rise to higher spheres, my heart pulsating with loving light, knowing I am never truly alone.

Explore within to understand beyond.
(Socrates)

10 THE FISHERMAN AND HIS WIFE

The Fisherman and his Wife (GRIMM)—*The following is a personal retelling of the tale:*

SYNOPSIS OF FAIRY TALE

In a quaint hovel on the water's edge of the village, where the azure seas lapped rhythmically upon its doorstep, a poor fisherman lived with his wife. His days, simple yet pleasurable, were filled with the daily ritual of fishing for his trade and their daily repast.

One day, as he dropped his line to catch their dinner, a giant golden flounder miraculously appeared before him. To his astonishment, the flounder spoke, making an incredulous claim that inside, he was an enchanted prince trapped by a witch's spell. In an urgent plea, the flounder begged to be set free from the line, and without hesitation, the sympathetic fisherman released him back into the caress of the calm sea.

Upon returning home, he shared the baffling tale with his wife. She immediately flew into a rage, insisting he returns to the sea, catches the magical flounder for a second time, and demand that he grants them their fondest wish: a well-appointed home to replace their shambolic sea-shanty.

Obligingly, the fisherman returned to the sea to find the fascinating flounder but quickly became uneasy as the sea suddenly turned turbid. He beckoned the fish with a captivating rhyme, an old sea shanty sung from the heart. When the fish reappeared, he granted the fisherman his wish and, before vanishing, instructed him to go back and behold their new pretty cottage beside the sea.

At first, the fisherman was ecstatic with the magical gift bestowed upon them by the unfathomable flounder, but alas, his wife could never be satisfied. She demanded that the fisherman return to the sea, dictating that the flounder afford them a life of kingship with a home fit for royal office.

His wish, duly granted, the fisherman counted his bountiful blessings. Not so for his wife. She was never content, making one excessive demand after another. Fond of the simple and carefree life, the fisherman dared not refuse her orders, though they contradicted his moral compass.

He implored her to accept their newly acquired station and riches with grace and to desist from further testing the goodwill of the fish. Still, the articulate flounder stated with every magical manifestation: "Just return home again. It has already happened." Yet, every time, the sea mysteriously grew darker, more turbulent, and more menacing than before.

The fisherman begged his spouse to stop craving more than they needed and to start enjoying what they already had. Indeed, she must now be satisfied, wanting for nothing, he thought. But alas, she stridently proclaimed her greatest wish was to command, like God, the sun, moon, and heavens.

Despite the ominous conditions of the ocean, with a trembling heart, her harried husband approached the golden flounder once more with her grandiose wish. The now frustrated fish gave his usual reply, "Just go back home. It has already happened."

To the fisherman's amazement, the tumultuous waters subsided at that very moment, returning to their calm, crystalline, aqua beauty. They shimmered as if the hand of God had showered them with stars. However, spoiling the majesty of the scene was the sight of the fisherman's ungracious wife hanging limply from the window of their old humble abode. She stared blankly out to sea, realizing too late the poverty of her soul. **THE END.**

PSYCHOLOGICAL PROMPTS

10: Key soul learning: To develop learning life lessons with grace (Intrinsic Motivation)

The humble fisherman's ordinary life in the hovel by the sea lacks material comforts, yet he wants for nothing. At one with the natural world and its rhythms, the fisherman relishes his rich sense of belonging and met needs. The rise and fall of the ocean's swell evoke memories of the protective fluid of the maternal womb and his primal connection to life.

But when the fisherman hooks the magical flounder blessed with the gift of speech, life takes a mysterious turn for the better, giving him great abundance and upward mobility. Even miracles can manifest 'out of the blue' and when prayed for. However, fortune is fickle, as we will always experience alternating periods of challenges and unexpected blessings. Our lowest points precede a turn of the tide, symbolising the cyclical and dynamic nature of existence. Nothing stays the same, and all living things would stagnate otherwise. Cycles of the sea, nature, and celestial forms have long been symbiotically connected: as above, so below.

Optimistic and self-disciplined, the fisherman initially aspires to do the right thing. His actions attract kind and generous acts in return. What goes around comes around. However, strife ensues when his mismatched wife contradicts his principles. We attract opposites to fill the gaps we perceive within. The fisherman, undemanding and gracious, compensates with a rapacious partner who views his simple life as stuck and empty. She, his shadow archetype, assumes control, leading to insatiable desires that descend into addiction. He, with a poor self-image, surrenders to her, believing that he is inadequate on his own. Marriage, originating from the Latin root word meaning 'to gamble', hints at its uncertainty. Whilst the fisherman regrets his choice of such a driven and pessimistic partner on an unconscious level, he feels trapped between their opposing realities.

The straightforward fisherman values his free life, but excesses, at odds with the laws of nature, threaten his equilibrium. The more the fishers jealously covet, the more the sea responds with wild fury, turning a ghastly yellow-green, reflecting emotional turmoil. Denying the unsettling signs, he relegates unpleasant aspects to his shadow but cannot ignore the tremors in his heart when acting against his authentic values. Violet and cloudy waters serve as unmistakable warnings, yet the fishers, submitting again to unbridled ambitions, ignore them, driven by conflicting schemas that shape their destiny.

These adverse conditions represent spiritual poverty, lacking faith and being consumed by materialistic desires. The servile fisherman tries to absolve himself of guilt by blaming his wife's influence, but the messenger, a complicit toadie, is not let off the hook. Passive, he succumbs to a dangerous game, committing the forbidden act of 'selling his soul to the devil', similar to Eve in the Garden of Eden. He must learn to be accountable.

Tested at their lowest ebb, the fishers commit cardinal sins rooted in greed and desire, craving and taking more than they can handle. This contrasts starkly with Christ's spiritual teachings of humility, symbolised by the supersensible fish. Newfound increases in wealth and power often distort one's perspective, leading to a false sense of superiority. Finally, humbled, the fisherman hears the Divine whisper, "Selfish demands will not make you gods; only purification of the soul."

The Divine dimension transcends the base elements of our physical reality. It offers a means for growth and becoming better people. We learn from the fishers' choices about how easily we succumb to Spenser's (1897) seven deadly sins of envy, greed, gluttony, lust, wrath (anger), pride, and sloth. These traits, when reaching biblical proportions, impact nearly everyone at some point on their Hero's Journey.

We likely fall into the trap when we are successful but selfish, desiring more and more when we have much more than we will ever need. Those on this path soon become spoiled and entitled, ultimately facing a tipping point to test their character. The cycles depicted in *The Fisherman and His Wife* illustrate the primal survival needs at birth and infancy, while our ego and competitive nature are played out in our aspirational adulthood. Despite our drive to achieve, grace must guide our actions. Filling our lives with excess, clutter, and chaotic busyness only imprisons us, intensifying existential pressures.

Many stray far from their spiritual roots, only returning to simplicity and the motto of 'less is more' in the wiser, calmer stages of life. Through karmic lessons, we learn that love is what truly matters—self-love, love for others, and universal love, embracing care and respect for all forms of life. No manner of material abundance can control the uncertainty and constant external changes we must navigate. Still, staying alive, like everything else, has its price.

As the fisherman and his opportunistic wife spiral out of control, they become lost in a world of extravagance and power plays, driven by ego and societal aspirations. Humility and hubris emerge as two sides of the same coin. The fishers' pursuit of progressing from hovel to heaven lands them back at the starting blocks. God does not reside in billion-dollar basilicas but in the temple within.

The golden fish, symbolising Christ, offers a moment of truth, drawing us to return to our spiritual centre, where inner peace with ourselves and the world illuminates the illusory nature of the material world.

The consequences of greed, hatred, and ignorance lead to spiritual descent, while love and light fuel our soul-fire and spiritual ascent.

We cannot help but wonder, had the wife taken her tidings at their flood (as espoused by Shakespeare), she might have settled with a fortune. As a **Taker,** she opened the door to opportunities but responded without discernment and grace, alienating the divine **Giver**. Nature shows that everything ascending descends through the round of time before ascending again. There is a periodicity to events, a perfect storm or sunrise, beyond mere chance or coincidence.

The more we discover what matters in the world by experimenting with what doesn't, the better prepared we are for the hero's return and the sharing of our boon with those we meet along the way.

There is only one way to happiness and that is to cease worrying about things which are beyond the power of our will. (Epictetus)

SELF-REFLECTIONS

Having caught the wave to success, must we incessantly strive for more? Once we taste the good life, fear of slowing down, hitting a plateau or regressing creeps in. Some pause, counting blessings, grateful for having their needs met. A few pay it forward, recognising that owning less can lead to becoming more and making a positive impact on others' lives.

The lesson missed by The Fisherman and his Wife archetype lies in looking beyond wealth, power, and insatiable quests for success. Real abundance resides in the depths of the soul. To ascertain a life well-lived, we must project ourselves into the future, envisioning our last moments on Earth. What truly matters when our date with destiny arrives? Is it family, love, health, and kindness or the material illusions of the ego?

Our egos, masters of disguise, assign significance to superficial matters, generating grist for our regret. These are the life lessons that we have yet to fully grasp or accept with grace. Rather than regretting, we can prioritise our power of choice in navigating our ongoing tests. Having choices is like a spoonful of sugar that helps the 'medicine' go down. But we must choose wisely.

The tale of the fishers offers insights into the mysterious momentum constantly pushing us onwards. Our unique interactions with the external world yield inevitable outcomes. Every waking moment places us on the precipice of unexpected internal and external changes, shaping our existence. Our response to unforeseen challenges stirs emotion akin to calm waters or tumultuous seas (with the former sometimes masking the latter).

Anxiety often arises from knowing our choices carry consequences, leading us to postpone decisions and avoid discomfort before pursuing happiness or reaching our potential. Nevertheless, an invisible universal intelligence seems to observe the impact we cause, returning the natural effects of our choices to us and demanding that we take responsibility.

As the hero on your path, seeking resonance with natural cycles, you must be attuned to the swift shifting of situations and adapt with ease. Yet, any gamble or thrill that holds more potential for decreases than increases can carry far-reaching implications. Gambling with our freedoms—often taken for granted—leads to later lamentation, making it even more crucial to find a balance between it and unity with another.

At this juncture, you choose to persist until your dreams materialise, wrestling between the pursuit of perfection and the acceptance of 'good enough'. It is better to focus on making progress than making things perfect. Can you find a compromise? Some perspective-taking is necessary.

Entering the 'belly of the whale,' you reflect, weighing opportunities and limitations, guiding your strategy for Higher Living. Ongoing efforts sustain psychic progress and prevent regression into old, self-indulgent patterns.

If we slip backwards and feed our false ego, the more insatiable it becomes, fuelling desires that stem from feelings of worthlessness—catalysing a vicious circle. But our gracious acts of gratitude remedy low self-esteem.

By thanking our Higher Power for life's blessings, we signal our appreciation for our good fortune and draw more positive experiences towards us. We can write down our preferred story, embedding these elements, and make ready for a golden cycle.

Luck materialises when opportunity aligns with preparedness or, in other words, when our positive thoughts manifest through practical actions. Aligning yourself with the cosmic rhythm, you intuit guidance for timely changes. As the '60s anthem goes, 'to everything, there is a season'. Similarly, 'to catch a fish, one must go fishing'.

LIGHT QUALITIES (GIVER)	**SHADOW ATTRIBUTES (TAKER)**
Giving	Taking
Gracious	Rapacious
Accountable	Gambling
Valuing	Regretful
Optimistic	Pessimistic
Self-disciplined	Stuck
Driven	Materialistic
Aspirational	Demanding

PROVERB: What goes around comes around.

AFFIRMATION: I learn with grace the lessons evolving my soul.

GAME OF LIFE: Not taking responsibility for behaviours and choices (Consequence: Perpetuating negative patterns).

REFLECTION QUESTION: When new opportunities knock, am I prepared to open the door?

ANIMAL SYMBOLISM: Fish; Flounder; Whale Shark

Fish

Fish, motifs for our intuition and spiritual connection with the Higher Power, surface when our unconscious emotions are triggered, signalling our need to go within and commune with Divine goodness.

Flounder

The golden flounder signifies creativity, fertility, resilience, and fortune, although it urges us to adhere to our moral values to find true happiness.

Whale Shark

The sea's gentle giants remind us to see beyond the surface, diving deep into the truth and confronting reality— there is a grander perspective not seen yet. We must let go and trust in higher guidance.

ONE SMALL STEP TO TAKE TODAY: I will practise taking ownership of my choices and behaviours and accepting my lessons with grace.

MEDITATION PREPARATION (to practise at times of uncertainty)

I breathe in golden light vibrations, and as I exhale, I let go of my negative thoughts and feelings. I envision myself going about my day with a smile on my face and bliss in my heart. I sense an energy shift, aware that what has been lost is re-emerging in new form. I place my trust in the guiding hand of the benevolent Divine. Mother Nature's voice assures me that the fruits of my efforts are maturing in their own perfect time. In the serenity of stillness, I breathe in forgiveness and let go of excessive expectations as I slowly breathe out. With grace, I go with the flow, taking care of today, so tomorrow takes care of itself.

If we are to be happy, we must first react against our tendency to follow the line of least resistance, a tendency that causes us either to remain as we are, or to look primarily to activities external to ourselves for what will provide new impetus to our lives.
(Pierre Teilhard de Chardin)

11 RUMPELSTILTSKIN

Rumpelstiltskin (GRIMM)–*The following is a personal retelling of the tale:*

SYNOPSIS OF FAIRY TALE

A miller boasted to the king, promising that his daughter could spin straw into gold. If she could prove her skill, the king pledged to marry the young maiden, but he would condemn her to death if she could not fulfil the promise.

So, the king instructed the girl that she had the whole night until morning to spin the straw into gold and reminded her she would die if she failed. The young maiden sobbed all night long, knowing that she was incapable of such an extraordinary feat. At the eleventh hour, a little gnome-like fellow appeared in a puff of smoke out of nowhere. He hastily informed her that he would spin the straw into gold on her behalf in exchange for her gold ring. Without a second thought, she agreed.

When the king conducted his inspection the following day, he saw the spools of expertly spun golden thread. But the surprised king was not completely satisfied, sensing that some trickery must be involved. So, for good measure, he set the girl to the task twice more to ensure her magical skills were real.

The curious imp arrived again in the dead of night, took her glass beads in exchange for his superpowers, and proceeded to spin the bales of straw into gleaming golden thread. All stayed to plan, and the maiden began to feel that the king may spare her. But on the third night, she had nothing left of value to barter with the strange elf. Taking care to ensure that she would repay him eventually for his efforts, the imp looked ahead to when she would become queen. Her firstborn would be a fair trade for his services rendered in saving her life.

The young maiden was bewildered, having no inkling of ever becoming queen, let alone bearing children in the future. She believed the king would enforce his threat and take her life tomorrow after finding out that the silken strands of gold had reached their end. She quickly agreed to the deal, and the diligent imp spun the golden yarn all through the night.

When the king married the young maiden, she was so relieved she soon forgot her promise to the eerie elf.

As queen, she entered into a life of abundance and contentment and soon bore a lovely baby daughter. One day, as the loving mother nursed her child, the imp arrived, demanding that she honour their contract and hand over her child on the spot. The distraught queen sobbed hysterically. She never believed the funny little fellow with the Midas-touch would follow through on his threats. Couldn't he take her rich array of royal jewels instead, after all, adornments were enough for him in the past? But, he dug in his heels, refusing to sway; any deal was a done deal.

Then, in a moment of mercy or social justice (as curious as it may seem), he had a change of heart and became more reasonable, granting the young queen another way to settle their arrangement. Perhaps he perversely enjoyed prolonging her submission and worry, confident the queen would fail in her quest. Still, he told her, "If you guess my name within three days, I will go away and never return."

Predictably, over the next two nights, the uncanny elf showed up to challenge the desperate queen. She guessed every name she could ever remember and never gave up trying, but the peculiar little man-imp only smiled wryly, shaking his crooked little head.

Then on the third day, out of nowhere, there came a stroke of good fortune. A soldier passed through the realm and paid the queen an impromptu visit to tell her how he had witnessed a strange creature dancing around a fire in the moonlit forest. He overheard it singing a silly little song and repeated it to the queen, "The queen will never win my game for Rumpelstiltskin is my name." The queen listened attentively, thanked the soldier and knew what she must do.

That night, the self-satisfied looking little imp arrived in a jolly state, demanding she guess his name correctly, once and for all. The queen sat quietly and playfully said, "Is your name Trip Trap or Humpelby Bumpelby?"

""No!" came the imp's cocky reply.

Her Majesty waited a moment more before asking quietly and sweetly, "Then, is it Rumpelstiltskin?"

A look of utter disbelief flooded the little elf's face, and in a state of rage and fiery frustration, he stomped his feet so hard that he self-combusted, burning his way through the floor. Rumpelstiltskin was never seen or heard of again, much to the queen's solace and joy. **THE END.**

All that glitters is not gold. (William Shakespeare)

PSYCHOLOGICAL PROMPTS

11: Key soul learning: To develop trust that right prevails (Self-Awareness)

This shadow archetype shows us the consequences of lying, breaking promises, and making unfair deals. The miller-father, plagued by deep-seated insecurity and engulfed by envy, succumbs to the allure of lying, a consequence of Tall Poppy Syndrome that arises when he is confronted by the majestic presence of the king. An inflated ego drives all of us to exaggerate and do anything to feel better about ourselves.

While the miller desires a brighter future for his daughter, he fails to consider the repercussions of his deception. Societies that value social justice hold us accountable for our words, but in some cultures, such as Papua New Guinea, skilful lying is seen as a trait of strong leadership within a tribe. Still, all mammals and primates possess an innate sense of justice and closure. Studies show that our brains complete the picture or story when we see or hear something incomplete. Likewise, when something is untrue, amiss, taken, or owed to us, we feel uneasy until the matter is rectified.

The unfolding story reveals how the characters feel guilty because they act in ways that are wrong: being selfish, cowardly or forceful and reminding us that true justice requires unwavering fairness and righteousness.

Epictetus said, "Truth and justice are the sovereigns of humanity." The diligent, reasonable and just king values moral correctness (his superego), holding the millers to account. He shows that betraying authority has serious consequences, and when in its sphere, we need to be mindful of ourselves and our choice of words.

An imp aids the maiden unbidden, turning straw into gold akin to an alchemist or wordsmith, transforming the ordinary into the extraordinary. These instances illustrate the subjectivity of truth and its susceptibility to the observer's bias. In today's age of relativism and social media, laypersons' opinions seem to hold equal weight as those of expert researchers, shaping an arbitrary perception of truth. Lies can be seen as truth and truth as lies. However, universal truths ultimately emerge in the light of day, as Arthur Schopenhauer (1788-1860) explained, progressing through three stages of ridicule, violent opposition, and eventual acceptance.

Truth prevails when lies remain secret and hidden, allowing the truth to belong to everyone. It is no wonder that we find comfort in it.

A father is expected to protect his daughter's purity, health, and happiness. However, the miller becomes a self-serving bully, entangling his daughter in a mess and then passively sitting on the fence; a bystander disengaged from her struggles. Denying responsibility, fairness, and justice leads us to chaos. The daughter must navigate her journey to selfhood alone, symbolised by the relinquishment of her possessions—a gold ring and beaded necklace—representative of giving up her familial bonds to enter an arranged marriage.

Kings, whether in nations or industry, often exploit their subjects. Hence, the subversive message of the tale portrays the unjust penalties, and the sacrifices imposed upon their subjects through toil, blood, sweat, and tears. The decree for the maiden to labour for three nights holds symbolic meaning: her pending spiritual resurrection, overseen by the Trinity. Dante, in his *Inferno*, suggests that trines infer repentance for sinfulness such as wrath, envy and pride. The number three carries portent, invoking destiny's hand. It also represents the triangular interplay between the king and daughter-queen and the miller-father or imp, who form changeable coalitions to overcome a singular power at the apex. When the daughter fails to provide a third trinket, she faces a harrowing decision, a 'Sophie's Choice', to determine her fate.

Later, the family of three, consisting of the king, queen, and baby princess, owes its existence to the initiative of a fourth party, whether it is the miller-father, evil imp or good solder. Aristotle asserted that number four signifies that justice will be served through the squaring of debt (moral or material). The king consummates his promise and marries the maiden, exemplifying justice and fulfilment.

The imp, a creature from the deep primordial swamp, dancing around a fire in a moonlit forest indicates his presumption, the summoning of the Great Mother, and truth coming to light. Later, when he comes to collect the baby, enforcing his contract with the queen, she commits the one forbidden thing and breaks her word. A moral dilemma is sparked. The imp, compensating for his size with an oversized ego, takes perverse pleasure in the queen's torment over the sacrifice of the innocent. However, when she is granted another chance by the peculiar lawmaker, she outsmarts him, defying the sexist presumption of female guilt and burden. Ultimately, the imp's schadenfreude only leads to his fiery destruction. Desperate for recognition, the outcast and ignorant Rumpelstiltskin proposes a Faustian bargain, trading knowledge for the innocent child. Fancy the synchrony: the queen discovering the imp's distinctive name exactly when she needed it most. He embodies the dark intention to win at all costs, arising when we act without awareness, exposing the poor bargains we unwittingly make and urging us to recognise and reclaim our shadow elements. He is like a referee caught between two warring tribes, blind to his own bias. We must consider both sides of a story before jumping to conclusions and acting on them.

In the grip of men consumed by intense, instinctual desires and devoid of ethics, women, trembling with the dread of additional torment, are compelled into passivity. They place their hopes on the essential function of Divine justice to lift the veil of society's ignorance that can set them free.

But, like the young queen, their agonising wait can be transformed by the impact of just one soldier, a bystander who chooses to act for good. His active enlightenment dissolved the darkness of the Wesen.

Acting from the shadow, Rumpelstiltskin projects his soul's torment onto others. His grim behaviours serve as a poignant reminder, showcasing the profound significance of regulating our primal instincts and fears with the guiding light of our conscience, logic and rationality.

Though life sometimes **Enforces** a rough justice (as represented by the id archetype), seemingly beyond our control, influencing us to feel like disempowered victims or **Bystanders**, our words and actions possess a significant and lingering power, sparking reactions. Therefore, it is crucial to say and do the right thing, ensuring that our actions serve the wellbeing of others and ourselves, unwavering in our belief in the ultimate triumph of righteousness.

There are moments when encountering the truth that the mantle of responsibility befalls us, and only us, to climb down off the fence, ring the bell and see that justice is served.

By integrating both our dark and light elements and establishing unity in our being, we embrace the good soldier within whose clarity of judgment creates the potential for harmony in our relationships and paves the way for profound positive change.

Be careful what you wish for, you might just get it. (Aesop)

SELF-REFLECTIONS

Rumpelstiltskin revisits the principle of cause and effect, prompting us to learn and understand its significance. When others choose to fool, exploit, or condemn us, we have a choice in how we respond. Reacting with negativity only perpetuates the cycle, but by acting firmly with calmness and respect, we can subtly shift the dynamic and bring about the changes we wish to see in the world.

Transformation begins with us, as even one individual's changes can alter the chemistry between two people over time. Ultimately, in healthy environments, what we give is what we receive.

In the midst of a conflict, faced with an important decision, it is critical to weigh the pros and cons. Unlike the frantic fairy-tale maiden entangled in unfair deals, you must reason things through before reaching any agreement. Timing plays a crucial role, and it is imperative that you resist being coerced or rushed by someone else's agenda. A lesson unlearned is a lesson returned.

Seeking guidance from a wise mentor, actively listening and engaging in thoughtful deliberation unveils previously unseen solutions to the challenges we encounter on our journey. Stepping back from the situation and observing from the balcony of life also allows for a broader perspective.

It is essential to align our thoughts, choose our words and actions carefully, and make promises that we can square. Whether our deeds are recorded in the material world or in the Akashic archive of the ethereal realm, justice demands that debts be settled.

On the path of the hero, how we treat others reflects upon ourselves. The cruel tease inflicted by Rumpelstiltskin eventually turned back upon him. We must not be gullible in the face of trials, relying solely on others' loyalty and protection. Striking a balance between self-assurance and fairness is key.

Natural justice is always at work, superseding our human-made constructs, serving those who say what they mean and mean what they say (and those who do not). Both sides of the story deserve a fair debate. But, in unions where contention, control, one-upmanship, and indecisiveness overshadow empathy, an inevitable decline looms on the horizon.

While opposites may attract, understanding the essence of a vastly different partner requires openness and perception. If one remains closed off, there is ample space for assumptions, misinterpretations and deceptions to arise. In such relationships, significant effort is required as secretive partners, grappling with communication barriers and a failure to listen to others' needs, tend to prioritise their own interests in an attempt to compensate for the void.

When conflicts arise, it is essential to take perspective before jumping to conclusions. Are the individuals in your life intermittently employing passivity and aggression to confuse and exert control over you? If so, take opportunities for trustworthy third-party support in reclaiming your power, just as the queen did in the tale.

At the core of the imp's unfair bargains lies the maiden's first struggle to secure a better deal. Yet the moment she reclaimed her insight, agency, and the right words, she found power to advocate for herself.

Your choices today—in thought, word, and action—lay the foundation for your future.

Though justice may seem flawed, righteousness, slow but steady, prevails across relationships, work, law, and disputes.

When your story feels shaped by injustice, search for the exceptions where fairness was shown and reframe your narrative and live your path forward from there.

The tricky imp reminds us that the devil is in the details, underscoring the need for clarity and care when making agreements and contracts, for deceit returned in kind serves no one.

For every action, there is a reaction. Recognise the gravitas of promises made to one another and ensure that our expressions of love are genuine. While you may secretly wish that people did as you do, you cannot change others' beliefs and behaviours—so make conscious adjustments for your wellbeing.

As you embark on the hero's path, remember to anchor yourself in truthfulness and fairness, exercise prudence in judgment, and harness your instinctual drives. Your journey holds a profound lesson: to attract goodness into your life, you must first emanate it from within. Watch as the intricate workings of natural justice conspire to restore balance and harmony to your existence when you do. When one door closes, be ready for the next door to open wide, offering you a precious second chance to pursue your dreams and aspirations. Release the need to control every circumstance and instead surrender to the greater forces at play, recognising the valuable work you do every day. Most of all, embrace this 'golden' opportunity, for you have the power to become a guiding light, illuminating the way for others.

LIGHT QUALITIES (ENFORCER)	SHADOW ATTRIBUTES (BYSTANDER)
Just	Fence-sitting
Fair	Unjust
Observant	Unfair
Innocent	Self-serving
Diligent	Cowardly
Righteous	Guilty
Reasonable	Deceptive
Consummate	Tormented

PROVERB: Say what you mean and mean what you say.

AFFIRMATION: I do what is fair and just because it is the right thing to do.

GAME OF LIFE: Being a law unto yourself (Consequence: Closing oneself off to the good that surrounds you).

REFLECTION QUESTION: Am I open to seeing both sides of the story to resolve my relationship issues fairly?

ANIMAL SYMBOLISM: Koala; Imp-creature

Koala

The koala's name means 'no water', representing our fear of not having enough to sustain us. They are passionate and jealous during mating, but they adapt well to survive and conserve resources by sleeping. Koalas show us how to reclaim inner resolve through meditation and dreams.

Imp-creature

The imp creature symbol suggests that someone may have a hidden agenda, making it difficult to resolve conflicts. We need to consider both sides of the story to find a balanced perspective.

ONE SMALL STEP TO TAKE TODAY: I will practise aligning my thoughts and actions with the Higher Good, trusting that righteousness will prevail and lead to just outcomes.

MEDITATION PREPARATION (to practise when important decisions are to be made)

I breathe in golden light vibrations, and as I exhale, I let go of my negative thoughts and feelings. I envision myself going about my day with a smile on my face and bliss in my heart. Soaking in the warm glow of my faith in a just universe, I meet my Higher Self. I feel fully alive with my personal power, saying what I mean and meaning what I say.

A good name is better than great riches: and good favour is above silver and gold.
(Proverbs 22:1)

12 THE FROG PRINCE

The Frog Prince (GRIMM)—*The following is a personal retelling of the tale:*

SYNOPSIS OF FAIRY TALE

Life was idyllic in a faraway land in a picturesque kingdom of rolling green hills set under sweeping blue skies, ruled by a fair and just king with seven beautiful daughters. Spoiled by her doting father, the youngest princess always found life just as she pleased. Every day she wandered into the woods to play in a magical sanctuary beside the vine-covered wishing well beneath a canopy of tall whispering trees. She spent happy hours casting her gleaming golden ball into the air, catching it and delighting in the pure pleasure of how the globe glistened in the warm sunlight and reflected her pretty face.

One day, immersed in the sweet song of the larks, she threw the golden ball so high that it landed deep into the well. Her mood changed like a winter wind. As she wailed loudly and stomped her delicate foot, a mysterious male voice came from the dark depths of the well. "Hush now, let me help," he croaked before adding "for a fair exchange."

As she peered through the sun-dappled light on the rippled water's surface into the deep well, to her astonishment, an enchanted green frog appeared, offering to dive in and bring back her beloved ball. His only condition was that the princess must become his friend. "Very well", agreed the puzzled princess. But she recanted her promise the moment the frog retrieved it. She promptly turned on her heel, heading straight back to the comfort of the castle without so much as a nod of thanks.

Over dinner, the princess immersed herself in exciting banter with her sisters and quickly forgot about her pledge to the lowly pond frog. But the frog came to the king's castle later that night to collect on her promise. The polite royal family listened, and the princess grew sullen, but after hearing the frog's side of the story, the king spoke sternly to his youngest child: "You made a vow. Now, offer our guest some food and make him feel comfortable."

The young princess obeyed the king but shared her plate begrudgingly. Later, when bedtime arrived, the slimy frog hopped onto her pretty pink pillow. In a fury, she threw him against the wall. But he persisted until she relented. It was strange to feel the pond creature's presence beside her on her soft bed and know he watched her while she slept. The more she obliged, the more he wanted, even demanding the unpleasant ritual become a habit over the coming nights. The unwilling maiden had little choice but to resign herself to his recurring visits. For three nights, the clammy frog took pride of place on her dainty satin cushions, much to the disgust and disdain of the refined yet selfish daughter of the fair and just king.

But, late on the third night, to the wonderment of the worn-down princess, the cold and clingy frog demanded a kiss, miraculously transforming before her into a charming and handsome prince. She could not believe her eyes, but smitten, she soon knew it to be true when she felt his tender embrace and the warmth of his breath against her skin.

The prince whispered in her ear, sharing how an evil witch had cast a spell on him many years ago, which could only be broken if a beautiful princess let him eat from her plate and sleep on her pillow.

At once, the princess saw the error of her entitled ways, feeling relieved and glad she had honoured her vow and shown kindness to the frog. Realising the spell was broken, happiness lit up their faces as the sun lit up the day.

Together, they rejoiced at their good fortune of ever finding each other in that magical place under the canopy of tall whispering trees and were soon married with the kind king's blessing. **THE END.**

PSYCHOLOGICAL PROMPTS

12: Key soul learning: To develop handing things over in love and light to a Higher Power (Empathy)

The youngest princess has a golden ball, so ostensibly, the world is in her hands. Venturing into the woods alone, representing her rite of passage and coming of age, she seeks refuge in her private, happy place to escape the castle constraints. Her scrying of the unfathomable reflective waters of the well indicates her eagerness for change. The deep water mirrors her unconscious dreams and gestating future; its ripples signify impending unrest. Throwing the ball into the well (or her hat into the ring) signals her readiness to submit to the unknown, relinquishing her childhood and embracing her destiny. As she peers into the bottom of the mysterious well, she steps from her ordinary world towards becoming her own woman. Her journey encompasses transitioning from self-centredness to readiness for sexual fecundity (id) and motherhood. On such a threshold comes that moment of diving into the deep end, pursuing expansion without considering consequences. The ball landing in a dark well brimming with life spells excitement and danger. Hence, right on cue comes that croaky, unfamiliar male voice from the wild, offering help to the woman who struggles. However, the reality is that such assistance often comes at a price, to which the shallow princess impulsively agrees.

While it is a binding agreement to the green frog (he, a shadow symbol of the worlds of watery emotions and earthly, primitive desires) for the supercilious, sulky royal, it is an opportunity to fulfil her desires without any sense of obligation. Her charitable and popular king-father reminds her of her honour, appealing to her Higher Self. He emphasises the need to protect their good name, reputation, family, and kingdom (the superego). After all— heaviest is the head that wears the crown. As a responsible parent, he must impart his wisdom for higher living, guiding and shaping his young daughter's character, instilling the belief that one must always act prudently and do what is right.

The clash arises from the contrast between the primordial frog (who metamorphosises into a prince ultimately), and the civilised girl's sense of superiority. However, an allegory of complementary nature emerges between the frog in the well and the emerging woman, whose watery womb holds promise for future offspring. Nonetheless, a woman senses the danger when a man presumes that she is his for the asking (or taking). Many fear the stigma of being alone or childless, clinging to such patriarchal social norms and enduring their oppressive power.

Yet, this tale carries a stronger subversive message: the royals achieved personal evolution by 'lowering' themselves, becoming better versions of themselves. This paradox applies equally to all of us. There comes a time when we must voluntarily sacrifice personal status and dearly held assumptions (in shadow) for the higher moral good, surrendering to the wisdom and will of a Higher Power.

The reckless act of throwing the golden ball sets the princess's destiny in motion. Its reflective golden light is temporarily extinguished in the depths of the dark, stagnant well, transforming everything conscious into the unconscious. Within this mystical realm of universal life, the princess's primal nature converges with her untapped potential, heralding her age of consent and culminating in her profound union with the transformed animal-groom. Although the princess and society consider mingling with lower classes forbidden, she engages with the frog at her amicable king-father's behest. Is she merely subject to chance circumstances, or is she being guided along her rightful path by her budding intuition? The modest king's instincts, sense of reality, and moral code converge, signalling that this lesson is necessary for the spoiled young princess's ongoing development. He senses the time has come for the young woman to relinquish her childish vanity, self-righteousness, unforgiving prejudice, and pursuit of perfection. The more aware and empathetic she becomes, the less she will cling to her static and outmoded beliefs.

Always, there is the waiting in darkness, suspension, and endurance of a great unknowingness before the moment of revelation. Many spend sleepless hours ruminating, consumed in mental turmoil, contemplating what might be and procrastinating before taking the next step. At this juncture, we have entered the 'belly of the whale' on our heroic journey, reflecting on our hidden aspects where awakening the unconscious archetypal forces propels us into a new stage of life. Mythologist Campbell (1949) would urge us to let go of the life we have planned to live and welcome change. The frog metaphor urges us to plumb our depths, reclaiming, reframing and integrating our disowned dark side, catalysing our transformation from the denied animus archetype to princely Self.

The princess's Hero's Journey begins when she heeds the universe's call, restoring her sense of charity from the shadow and honouring her word. However, must we always expect tangible rewards when we give or fulfil our vows? Historically, an empty promise or a broken word from royalty led to anarchistic rebellion. If we prevaricate or postpone decisions and actions, events may eventually take charge, potentially resulting in disorderly consequences.

But there is a knack for controlling only those things within our control and releasing our need to control those things we cannot. When thrown out of balance, our tipping point prompts a turning point. Getting the timing right is crucial. We must navigate the landscape, recognising when to patiently let things be, let go, hand things over in love and light or dive into the vast unknown. It occurred to the frustrated princess to accept that her someday would come, trusting that the plan would unfold as it should. Her kissing the frog, initiates her process of integration and transformation. This transition requires emotional regulation but leads one to a newfound sense of emotional freedom and unity, transcending the feelings of relentlessness, constraint and separation. Similarly, the prince transforming from frog to ascended man, provides assurance that we are all capable of becoming our Higher Self.

We are encouraged by the tale of *The Frog Prince* to **Surrender** our stronghold on societal and personal ideals and resist **Clinging** to paradigms of the past that no longer serve our greater good. When matters are enigmatic and beyond our own powers, we must leave the details of our future outcomes to the Great Divine.

SELF-REFLECTIONS

The fairy-tale princess's surrender to her father's authority is a poignant reminder that, as mortals, we do not possess all the answers. It's better to relinquish control in futile situations and entrust our problems to a Higher Power. This act kindles a soulful knowingness that guides us in moments of uncertainty and helplessness. Sometimes we face situations with no simple solution, resulting in an internal conflict of polarities. The ego aggressively demands its way, attempting to overshadow the wisdom of the soul.

In your life, unsettling circumstances brew. You compare the external world with its alluring trappings to your simple philosophy of being. Others value status, power, and money while you honour love, truth, and light. Your ego and shadow deride you, while your authentic voice asks for acceptance, belonging, and love. One feels hamstrung when torn between these illogical comparisons within themselves. Putting these ambiguities into your recorded story helps bring cognitive understanding. Words can lead to a deeper awareness, an 'aha'.

When we feel frustrated and powerless, relinquishing the need to control conditions or other people can restore inner peace. The fairy tale illustrates the difficulty of changing others' beliefs and behaviours. Take the bewitched frog (id) who persisted after the princess made her promise but later said no. Fortunately, he had good intentions. Graciously accepting the things, we cannot change and courageously changing what we can is every Hero's ticket to a better ride. When living with emotional uncertainty, those unaware of their identity, place, and purpose might resort to escape through avoidance, mind-altering drugs, alcohol, or prescription medicines. Hence the need for developing emotional intelligence.

During conflict, reactive emotions often drown out our soul's quiet knowing. In such moments, we crave connection and comfort. If you've encountered others unwilling to repair relationships, leaving you disoriented and alone, there comes a time when you must face reality, accept the truth, and make necessary changes. Letting go of outdated beliefs, incompatible relationships, or impossible dreams lightens your load and serves your Higher Good.

Why cling to what no longer serves you? Obsessing over the past only sacrifices your present and future. You may feel disenchanted as you enter new terrain, but your desire for a better life is valid. Releasing the past is essential. It's time to reclaim and heal the wounded child within and reframe your story.

Eventually, insight will come—a dream, revelation, or wise words will catalyse action. You'll begin shedding stagnant parts of self and embrace a more grounded, authentic life. Letting go of pretence opens the door to self-acceptance and empathy. You stop clinging to idealised images of who you should be. Like the princess, you shift from perfection to love and experience a profound change of heart.

Committing to a way of life aligned with your higher vibrations does not happen overnight but is worth the waiting and effort. Hold this space for yourself as you stand on the precipice of discovering your true passion and purpose. Perhaps you are not meant to pursue more money and control but are being guided to perform charitable acts for loved ones or strangers in need or engage more in self-compassion. One thing is certain: Inside the cave, the Hero will experience a 'dark night of the soul' before seeing the light. They emerge with greater clarity, creativity, vision, empathy and energy to embrace their unknown future. Remember to let go and hang in there— by accepting 'what is' (as opposed to you resisting and it persisting) creates the head space that allows for better opportunities to enter your reality.

LIGHT QUALITIES (SURRENDERER)	**SHADOW ATTRIBUTES (CLINGER)**
Surrendering	Clingy
Releasing	Struggling
Accepting	Sacrificial
Promising	Procrastinative
Charitable	Ruminative
Modest	Stagnant
Metamorphic	Sulky
Amicable	Frustrated

PROVERB: My someday will come.

AFFIRMATION: I let go and let God.

GAME OF LIFE: Refusing to give up what no longer serves you (Consequence: Allowing life to become stagnant and cluttered).

REFLECTION QUESTION: Can I accept that all things happen in good time?

ANIMAL SYMBOLISM:

Green Frog

Frogs embody the cleansing power of water. During rain, their melodic chants connect us to memories of our early beginnings in the womb and our spiritual communion with nature. When we encounter frogs, it's a sign to let go of negative energy, mental burden, and painful memories—We must leap into self-healing for our transformative regeneration awaits.

ONE SMALL STEP TO TAKE TODAY: I practise surrendering myself to the Higher Good.

MEDITATION PREPARATION (to practise at times of solitude)

I breathe in golden light vibrations, and as I exhale, I let go of my negative thoughts and feelings. I envision myself going about my day with a smile on my face and bliss in my heart.

Gentle waves of relief wash over me, freeing me from my ties, one by one, as I enter a pool of tranquillity and bathe in the golden glory of the Higher Good. Emerging, with refreshed eyes, I see the rainbow colours of the world resonating with more vibrancy than ever before. Uplifted and renewed, I hand myself over to the waiting promise of my beautiful tomorrow.

The real voyage of discovery consists not in seeking new landscapes but in having new eyes.
(Marcel Proust)

13 SLEEPING BEAUTY

Sleeping Beauty (PERRAULT/GRIMM) —*The following is a personal retelling of the tale:*

SYNOPSIS OF FAIRY TALE

A beautiful baby daughter, Briar Rose, was born to a king and queen long ago. When the time came for her christening, twelve invitations were dispatched far and wide to the fairies of the kingdom, hoping to receive their blessings. However, they overlooked the thirteenth fairy, a mistake that infuriated her. The fairy, having been denied the opportunity to become one of the child's fairy-godmothers, stormed into the monarchs' celebrations. As she swept past the royal cradle, she unleashed a dark spell upon the innocent baby before vanishing into thin air. The curse dictated that on Briar Rose's sixteenth birthday, she would prick her finger on a spindle and die.

Luckily, the twelfth fairy to be invited was a good fairy who intervened to reverse the spell, but her white magic only reduced its dark potency. While death would not claim the princess, she would instead be plunged into a deep sleep lasting one hundred years that only a pure-hearted prince's kiss could break.

The king acted swiftly, ensuring all spinning wheels were banished from the castle. Despite these precautions, on the princess's sixteenth birthday, her curiosity led her to explore the unknown nooks and crannies of the grand palace. In the attic, she discovered a solitary maid (a spinster) diligently weaving. Excitedly, she succumbed to temptation, rushing to take her turn at the loom. In an instant, her finger pricked, and she fell into an enchanted sleep on the spot.

When the servants and royals finally discovered her, they were inconsolable, for they could not awaken the princess from the clutches of the curse. Desperate for a solution, they summoned the same good fairy who had white-washed the original dark spell and mitigated its sinister aura. Though she possessed great power, there were limits to what she could do.

Heartbroken, the grieving king made a decree: everyone in the castle would share the princess's fate, falling into the same trance so that she would never wake up alone and frightened.

A chilling frost encroached the day, indicating time had suspended its flight. The kingdom froze in time. The palace became enshrouded by a dense forest as time stopped within its walls but rolled by outside.

One day, a handsome prince, burdened by loneliness, ventured into the dark and tangled parts of the wood. He carried a quiver of arrows on his back and a large hunting blade at his side, his heart heavy with longing. As he pushed through the thicket, uncertain of his path, a nearby brook whispered life's deepest secrets. Then he hit an impasse where trailing bramble obscured the course, making him feel directionless, caught betwixt and between in a liminal space. Determined, he pressed forward until he stumbled upon a clearing. He could not believe his eyes. To his astonishment, a magnificent medieval castle stood before him, its inhabitants trapped in time. He tried to awaken them, but his efforts were in vain.

Finally, he reached the room where the beautiful princess lay, her face serene in sleep. Trembling with anticipation, he marvelled at her enchanting beauty, pondering how such a fate had befallen her. He felt the faintness of her breath and sensed her near-death state. Taking her delicate hand in his, he tenderly pressed a kiss upon it before leaning closer and gently brushing his lips against hers.

In awe, he watched as the princess gradually began to stir, her eyes fluttering open. She softly whispered, "My prince, I have walked with you in my dreams. You have come at last!"

Simultaneously, the castle's incapacitated inhabitants awoke, their unrestrained joy reverberating throughout the kingdom. News spread like wildfire that a prince of pure heart had come and, with a single kiss, had broken the curse of Briar Rose's eternal sleep. It was a time of great jubilation and celebration when the young lovers announced that they would soon be married.

And so, the tale of *Sleeping Beauty* came to a close, reminding everyone that even amidst darkness and despair, true love and the power of a pure heart can overcome the most formidable of life's curses. **THE END.**

PSYCHOLOGICAL PROMPTS

13: Key soul learning: To develop tuning into what really matters (Self-Awareness)

We learn from the thirteenth fairy that exclusion can be hurtful and potentially dangerous. The number thirteen holds various meanings: lucky for some, unlucky for others, and its lesser-known association with the pagan calendar of thirteen lunar months, assigned moon fairies, and the balance and harmony they promise. Thus, a snub of the dark fairy threatens the equilibrium of our earthly experiences.

Scorned, she gate-crashes the party, casting her dark magic, reminding us to respect others' sense of belonging. Otherwise, we may face their anger and revenge driven by irrational impulses (id). Rage can mete catastrophic consequences. The vexed fairy targets the innocent baby. However, the power of the twelfth fairy dilutes her wickedness: goodness can mitigate evil but not extinguish it completely. Still, positive influences turn things around. Grief and loss eventually give way to gratitude and renewal, allowing us to be reborn and fully appreciate life. We need to acknowledge the blessings in our lives.

The princess, overwhelmed with curiosity, does the one forbidden thing, pricking her finger on the spinning wheel. The spindle represents life cycles and the unique stories and patterns woven into the tapestry of our human condition. As she touches it for the first time, her sexuality is set in motion. However, the curse quickly arrests her blossoming, forcing her into a long sleep. The concept of death as a terminal slumber may dilute the fear of our inevitable final end in physical form.

As youths, we feel invincible, balancing the primal fear of death repressed in our unconscious. Our awareness of our life's expiry date is a fiery motivation for us to create, mate, and procreate.

The dark fairy's adversarial actions are indicators of the repressed fear, anger, and grief buried in our shadows and projected onto others. In contrast, the friendly fairy signifies the Sacred power of the number twelve. Aside from representing Divine order and authority, Wholeness and completeness, there are twelve apostles, angels, gates (doors), jury members, major Gods of Olympus, Herculean labours, paths on the Tree of Life, months of the year, and twelve steps on our Hero's Journey.

The fairy-tale royals, consumed by grief, suspend their kingdom in sleep—reflecting our tendency to escape reality through emotional withdrawal. Time's passage brings both nostalgia and relief, but it moves only one way, toward eternity's quiet triumph. The royals' sorrow invites us to surrender to time's mystery, letting go of the illusion of control.

The prince's unexpected discovery of the sleeping princess reminds us how seemingly separate paths can align by unseen design. Sometimes, to meet another, we must be still. In a dream, the princess releases her yearning into the ethers, and the prince responds, drawn by a shared resonance. Polar opposites merge—his outer journey meets her inner call, and a beautiful union is born.

When he takes her hand, she is no longer alone. Modern retellings soften the original tale's troubling themes of non-consent, replacing them with a symbolic, harmless kiss. Still, they caution against using physical power to exploit vulnerability. Respect and consent remain essential, guided by our moral compass.

Love and sex are not always intertwined. One arises from primal instinct; the other, from the deep human need to belong. The young royals embody both: raw desire and a tender bond that transcends it. Their story reflects how, in the pursuit of union and purpose, passion can coexist with compassion. When we honour each other with dignity, we tune into what truly matters—love not just as instinct, but as conscious, soulful connection.

The princess's unconscious belief in the goodness of her prince supported her endurance. Waiting and preserving one's virginity until finding a loving partner serves every person well. A woman's encounter with Mr Right can feel like a dream, making her question if she's truly awake and if his presence is real. This notion echoes Zhuangzi's famous quote: "I dreamed I was a butterfly, flitting around in the sky; then I awoke. Now I wonder: Am I a man who dreamt of being a butterfly, or am I a butterfly dreaming that I am a man?"

Sleeping Beauty holds the promise of our collective awakening, signalling that ignorance can only persist until humanity chooses to embrace the light and relinquish the darkness. Love's arrow pierces the ache of loneliness, peace supersedes suffering, good triumphs over evil, and the prince's kiss brings a resurrection of her animus. All's well that ends well. Sleep, that 'little slice of death' from which one can rise to see the world through refreshed eyes, suggests that our soul has eternal life. If we reframe our perspective, accepting endings as portals to new beginnings and counting how much we have learned rather than how much we have lost, we can find catharsis. Consider the relationship between the words 'exist and exits' to see the symbiosis.

After every fall, spending 'time-out' in the stillness of our indwelling place connects us with our unconscious. Then, we, ever-richer for our experience, begin to regenerate and dream of new possibilities. Endings are not our **Adversary** but our **Friend** who rings in the change that life demands. The door closes to the stultifying, now fading to black, allowing space for a new soul vibrancy to enter and fill our existence with light.

SELF-REFLECTIONS

Like an unconscious princess, our choices today can bury our dreams alive tomorrow, stifling their potential. Conforming to the herd leads to a monotonous existence, filled with fear of change and loss. By allowing our spark to fade to avoid pain, we unintentionally deprive ourselves of the subsequent pleasure that awaits. Paradoxically, the greater our preparedness to push through the pain, the higher our life satisfaction. Thus, the adage 'no gain without pain' holds truth.

Time brings both joy and profound grief, sometimes without relief. For some, there is no escape except through death. In these hardships, seeking respite in sleep is natural until the pain subsides. Many rely on drugs to cope with a life designed for survival, not thriving. The dark fairy would encourage us to consume poisonous potions, while the good fairy would purge our toxins.

In your own life, you stand at a crossroads, facing a choice between a lifeless existence that no longer serves you and an unknown path that evokes anxiety (i.e., undirected excitement). Despite hitting a dead-end, your ordinary life isn't finished but temporarily compromised. However, this impasse prevents progress, trapping you in a cycle of negative returns. It is time to stare down the abyss, and when it seems to be staring back at you, walk into its yawning void bravely. Take the risk, like archetype Sleeping Beauty, and believe you can handle uncertainty.

Any step away from the 'unaware' past is a step in the right direction for someone this immobilised. Looking back at the past through a rose-tinted rear window is deceptive. Glorifying our personal history goes hand in hand with the fear of change. The mere thought of a shift stirs up repressed emotions, paralysing us. However, when we look back as elders, we may regret our waste.

Unhealthy competition in relationships creates deadlock—where one must lose for the other to win. Such dynamics trigger behaviours rooted in repressed emotional pain, grief and trauma. Love and light cannot thrive in spaces dominated by anger and confrontation. Empathy walks when anger talks; our aggression and desire must be tempered with respect and reason. We must accept life's dualities: love and fear, light and shadow, life and death. Death is the ultimate circuit breaker—a dense, dreamful sleep from which we don't awaken.

Endings mark the point of no return and make change inevitable. Yet even painful endings offer grist for the mill, holding life lessons essential to growth. To deny the darkness in ourselves or others is to diminish the wholeness of the Self.

. When integrated, our shadow fuels transformation. Endings contain seeds of renewal. Let go and make the decision you've been postponing. Shifting gears opens new doors and allows your original Self to rise again. Journal your small steps, paying attention to your new-found strengths and progress.

Give your soul space to heal by acknowledging painful feelings like isolation and loneliness, rather than suppressing them. Catharsis takes time—but not a 'century'. Intense emotions accompany endings, but awareness, empathy, and forgiveness can transmute our suffering. Accepting impermanence brings deep relief. In time, you'll look back on dark days with quiet pride, knowing you transcended them. Awakened and grounded, you rise from the ashes to greet the green shoots of new life. This journey from womb to tomb is winding, shaped by allies and adversaries. Someone or something is soon to make a profound, positive impact on your path. Stay open.

LIGHT QUALITIES (FRIEND)	SHADOW ATTRIBUTES (ADVERSARY)
Friendly	Adversarial
Reborn	Implacable
Peaceful	Complicated
Relieved	Repressed
Transformed	Immobilised
United	Escapist
Dreamful	Excluded
Cathartic	Terminal

PROVERB: When one door closes, another opens.

AFFIRMATION: When I awaken from sleep, my eyes are refreshed.

GAME OF LIFE: Revenge (Consequence: Perpetuating 'bad-blood' retaliations).

REFLECTION QUESTION: Am I just projecting my shadow attributes onto others?

ANIMAL SYMBOLISM: Dragon fly; Brolga

Dragon Fly

The **dragonfly,** a creature of the wind, symbolises change and teaches us to distinguish between reality and falsehood, guiding us away from wrong choices.

With iridescent wings, it serves as a protective symbol against darkness and illuminates our path towards new beginnings.

Brolga

Brolgas are symbolic of our spiritual journey on earth. In Indigenous cultures, they represent the dance between the sacred feminine and masculine. A beautiful woman, sent to the Milky Way by an evil spirit, shines as a star—symbolising the essence of Divinity to which we are called to turn our gaze.

ONE SMALL STEP TO TAKE TODAY: I practise taking time out to dream, heal and begin anew.

MEDITATION PREPARATION (to practise before going to sleep)

I breathe in golden light vibrations, and as I exhale, I let go of my negative thoughts and feelings. I envision myself going about my day with a smile on my face and bliss in my heart. With faith, I lift my eyes skyward to the omnipotent One, envisioning a second chance to design my life. I see myself bravely making peace with my darkest fears, laying down calmly with them to rest beside a tranquil river. My soul essence harmonises with the water tumbling gently over the stones to dissolve my worries and strengthen my resolve. When I open my eyes, I feel accepted and regenerated, ready for fresh experiences.

Arise, my love, my beautiful companion, and run with me to the higher place.
(Song of Songs 2:10-15)

14 HANSEL AND GRETEL

Hansel and Gretel (GRIMM)—*The following is a personal retelling of the tale:*

SYNOPSIS OF FAIRY TALE

Deep in the dense forest of the fatherland lived a poor woodcutter with his wife and children, Hansel and Gretel. When a famine had taken its toll on the family, the wife devised a plan for the father to leave the starving children in the woods, where they would struggle to survive. The woodcutter reluctantly agreed to their removal, as it would give him and his wife a higher chance of survival. Unbeknownst to the couple, their children overheard their cold-hearted plot. Hansel and Gretel were afraid, but Hansel reassured his sister that they would always have each other and were in God's care no matter what.

When morning came, the children were taken into the deepest parts of the woods. But clever Hansel had kept his bread ration to make a trail for finding their way back home. Soon the father abandoned them, and when it grew dark, they turned around to follow the breadcrumb path left behind. Alas, the birds had eaten the trail, and as the panicked children looked around, they realised they were hopelessly lost. They wandered aimlessly through the woods, starving, tired, and frightened.

Come morning, a dazzling snow-white bird beckoned them to follow its flight path. So, they did. Before long, not believing their eyes or good fortune, they spied a cute gingerbread cottage in the clearing ahead. Without a second thought, they ran to it and began devouring its delicious rock-candy roof tiles and toffee-sugar-shard windows, piece by piece. Soon, their joy was interrupted by a strange and spooky voice from within the house. But overcome with hunger, they continued eating the crunchy sweet candy.

Next, a craggy crone with a crooked smile appeared and bade them inside. Lured by the promise that they would be fed, bathed, and put to bed in a warm and comfortable cot, the pair put up no resistance. Alas, the siblings had fallen into the trap of an evil witch. She was well-known in these parts for preying on and devouring abandoned children. In a quick act of force, she threw Hansel into a cage and enslaved Gretel.

Each day she checked Hansel's finger to see if he had grown fatter from his regular meals so that he would be worth the feast. Instead, clever Hansel showed the witch an old chicken bone he'd kept, tricking her into thinking he was still far too lean to bother lifting into a pot. Eventually, she grew tired and hungry from all the waiting and prepared the oven to roast him anyway.

She coaxed Gretel over to the large oven door to check on the fire, but sensing the dangers, Gretel gestured to the witch to first show her how to test its heat. The witch, growing impatient and angrier by the minute, leaned ever-nearer to the fire. A quick-thinking Gretel pounced on her, forcing the hag's bulky body into the flaming inferno. The oven door slammed shut on the screaming witch as she incinerated to ashes.

Gretel released Hansel from the cage, and together they looked over the cottage for what was salvageable. Much to their amazement, they discovered a treasure trove and quickly secured it into the folds of their clothes before setting off for home.

Spotting a shimmering lake in the distance, situated just ahead of their part of the woods, they soon found their way. Once there, a kindly white duck ferried them across to safety.

The woodcutter was shocked and overcome with joy when he saw that his children were still alive. He reassured them and explained that their mother had recently died and how regretful his life had been since he left them for dead in the woods that awful day.

Now reconciled with their father, the children excitedly shared their newfound treasure with him. They continued to do everything together, never bringing up the painful past, going hungry, or wanting for anything whatsoever ever again. **THE END.**

PSYCHOLOGICAL PROMPTS

14: Key soul learning: To develop doing all things in moderation (Social Skills)

Throughout history, there have been cases of abandoned or lost children found in wilderness areas, wandering naked, scarred from the harsh elements and unable to speak their native tongue after years of isolation. Some examples include the cases of John Ssebunya and Marina Chapman, who were allegedly abandoned in the wild and later discovered. You may recall the true story of Victor of Aveyron, who went from living as a wolf in the French woods in the late 18th century to living a human life in Paris. Unfortunately, extreme circumstances, such as war, famine, or lack of external support, have led some parents to desert, trade, abuse, kill or cannibalise their young. These unthinkable actions cut across different eras and cultures.

As fanciful as our tale of *Hansel and Gretel* seems, it reflects our forebears' brutal hardships. Their dynamic genetic traces survive, actively swishing in our DNA and collective unconscious today. We are more robust in our survival quest due to their capacity to overcome threats, privations and suffering.

Hansel and Gretel, like most children, are quiet observers and attentive listeners. Parents may be none the wiser, only sometimes mindful of how their offspring tightly hang onto their every action and word. Boys hear their mother's words but follow the father's behaviours, while girls mimic the mother's actions but hang onto their father's words.

This tale portrays the mother as cold and the father as emotionally unintelligent, but one who reconnects with empathy. The critical parental perspective (superego) is in high gear for the children's stoic mission of self-preservation.

There is no room for sibling rivalry as they bond to face a common enemy, harmonising to find the middle ground and reassuring each other as they quest for goals.

Life is not lived in a straight line, but our human experience moves us towards each milestone, maturity, old age, and death. Like Hansel and Gretel's vanishing trails, we can never find our way back to an earlier time. For our future's sake, we must accept and adapt to changes with resilience.

Hansel and Gretel's female and masculine energies unite symbiotically for a mutually beneficial outcome—the yin and the yang reconciled within oneself for full personal power.

Both protagonists confront the wicked witch, representing the dark forces and life's ordeals on their Hero's Journey. Despite feeling afraid and insecure in light of the power imbalance, they respond moderately. To them, theirs is a temporary setback from ordinary life, implying their conviction of faith in finding freedom in the future. They collaborate, utilising resources, animal cunning, and rational thinking to outwit the dark queen of chaos. Being darkly supernatural, the witch embodies the dark side of above and below. She emulates how humans house themselves in a sugar-coated persona to camouflage their inner negativity. Her hunger represents the excess appetite of human life that upsets the balance and harmony of nature. Under pressure, the ravenous children lose control and commit the one forbidden thing, devouring the candy house (akin to an infantile 'Oedipal' sucking and biting).

The witch, an outlier, symbolises the darkest aspects of human nature, acting out her feelings of alienation, revenge, and rage by consuming the village's innocents and in a vain attempt to assimilate their life-force. Her anti-social, confrontational and aggressive behaviours drove her to society's fringe. Hansel and Gretel, fearing 'death-by-witch' and acting in confluence, turn the tables, reducing her to ashes. The ruthless parents bred ruthless children, appreciating the necessity of desperate measures in desperate times.

Hansel's smart planning came from egoic-logic, while Gretel acted from her impulsive and instinctual id to garner the brute strength necessary for heaving the hag into the furnace. Gretel's newfound empowerment set Hansel free. The siblings become a blended pair: a balancing act of different psychic and gender chemistries and anima and animus.

Both are forged in the crucible of a life-threatening challenge, emerging stronger for the brave new world ahead. They dip their toes into the sacred stream of life, feeling blessed with riches far beyond the material level. A negative experience gets flipped by synchronistic and highly fortuitous acts of chance.

Victors often forgive their parents, knowing toxic emotions hold them hostage. Hansel and Gretel behave patiently and purposefully, finding the diamond in the rough, the light in the dark. Endowed with the treasure trove of absolution, they generously share wealth and wisdom with their flawed father. So often, children rectify their parents' mistakes and heal relationship rifts.

These heroes rise high like the phoenix. Neither the male nor female assume **Control** over the situation. They **Moderate** a mutual outcome, surviving a peak experience as self-actualised individuals, ready to take on the next challenge with calm confidence.

SELF-REFLECTIONS

In times of chaos, you may feel as shaken as the anxious children held hostage by the witch. Rest, self-healing, and positive change are long overdue for you.

As energetic beings, we naturally experience periods of balance and imbalance. However, when thrown off-centre, we yearn to regain control. Embracing the reality of continual outer change can help us return more smoothly to our inner resting place, our homeostasis.

Encountering overpowering individuals, and resisting their toxic control, can be exhausting. Their oppressive influence, however, presents an opportunity for self-discovery. By reflecting on the issues within us, we uncover the fears and shadow aspects that trigger our anxiety and unhappiness.

The Hero's quest is to remain calm in life's storms. Failing to regulate our chaotic emotions results in mounting imbalances that bring only more distress, disharmony, and dis-ease into our existence. Peace and emotional freedom follow the Hero, who remains steady, like Hansel and Gretel, navigating through challenging and uncertain times.

By emulating the dynamic duo and facing our ordeals, fears, and forgotten psychic fragments, we stand tall in our authenticity. As we illuminate our shadows and recognise unhelpful emotional patterns, we gain insight into our insecurities. Criticising others reveals more about our own sense of self. However, identifying dysfunctional behaviours in others doesn't necessarily mean we harbour the exact same traits in our shadows. We must thoroughly examine our light and dark characteristics to discern the nuances.

Like the emotionally intelligent protagonists in fairy tales, we can reframe and transform our shortcomings and the stories we tell ourselves about them. Achieving harmony in our inner and outer lives requires reunifying all aspects of ourselves. By bringing our personality traits into the full light, we can claim, balance, and regenerate our failings into strengths, thereby increasing our personal power.

While society often emphasises gender polarities, balance comes more from the harmonisation of yin and yang energies. Moderating aggression with passive tendencies allows us to assert ourselves without resorting to hostility or docility. It endows us enhanced communication skills and social competency and consolidates our authenticity, enabling us to co-create with others and feel deeply satisfied with our lives.

Turning our intemperate outbursts into calm but firm statements requires dedicated practice. However, we gain fresh and broader perspectives by exercising temperance and overcoming the self-inflicted consequences of overreacting, overthinking, and overdoing. We make a vow to stay on track, learning to take better care of ourselves and establish a healthy work-life balance.

Each trial from the past and present brings us closer to the summit of our soul's quest for us to regulate our wild impulses and appetites with common sense. Tests arrive when a third party enters our sphere, catalysing change. Can we moderate how we relate and interact with them, embodying temperance when they lose their heads? If so, we observe and actively listen in silence, resisting the urge to interject. When they go low, we choose to go high.

We tread carefully in the face of threats, negotiating our way wisely. Maintaining composure amidst imbalances and different stances is a joint responsibility. We must not allow ourselves to go out of whack because someone else's viewpoint differs from ours. By staying true to our Personal Code and appreciating the value of diverse realities, we unlock new levels of social connectivity.

Conflict and anger may arise, but we must strive to resolve issues in mutually respectful ways. When anger talks, empathy walks. Taking a pause, breathing, and consulting our Higher Self guides us towards balanced actions. Going with the flow, we wait for the right time and place to act, knowing that calmness follows every storm.

This newfound social adeptness brings positive feedback, causing us to vibrate at happier, higher frequencies. At this juncture, we reconnect with the creative cosmos, manifest our deepest longings and attract equal partnerships that enrich our lives.

Aligning our needs with our desires brings deep soul satisfaction. As old, debilitating patterns dissolve, we find contentment in peace, quiet, and life's simplest pleasures.

In your current situation, reasoned analysis and strategic planning are necessary to determine the best way forward. Follow the breadcrumb trail back to your roots, authoring your personal story, retracing your hidden strengths to rediscover your true identity. Temper impulsive urges, considering things rationally and intuitively before making important decisions.

Your reaching a higher octave fosters kindness, joy and empathy, allowing you to see life and love from both sides. When the Hero finds a happy medium, the treasure is found.

The curious paradox is that when I accept myself just as I am, then I can change.
(Carl Rogers)

LIGHT QUALITIES (MODERATOR)	**SHADOW ATTRIBUTES (CONTROLLER)**
Moderate	Controlling
Balanced	Imbalanced
Harmonious	Excessive
Purposeful	Confrontational
Reassuring	Insecure
Calm	Impatient
Patient	Abandoned
Confluent	Critical

PROVERB: With unity, there is greater strength.

AFFIRMATION: In shared purpose, I balance your needs with mine.

GAME OF LIFE: Refusing to share any excess (Consequence: Resources go out of balance).

REFLECTION QUESTION: Do I honour and balance my masculine and feminine sides?

ANIMAL SYMBOLISM: Fox; Rabbit; Dove; Goldfish; Duck; Chicken

Fox

As a symbol of unity and adaptability, the fox epitomises camouflage, quick-thinking, agility and cunning. Forever aware, he is an expert at leading enemies on a wild chase. No matter how far the fox must travel to evade the hunter, he always strives to get back to protect and reunite with his family.

Rabbit

As a totem of gentleness and faith, the rabbit's nervous demeanour shows how sharp reflexes keep one safe. Unpredictable, the rabbit says we must jump on opportunities despite our fears. Being one of the most social animals, wild rabbits live in multitudes in complex warrens, reminding us we must go along to get along.

Dove

Doves are the gentle spiritual messengers, bringing news from the Holy Spirit and Great Mother to say we are supported in our quest for finding joy and peace. Sightings of her signify how important it is that we calm our troubled minds with faith in kindness and goodness prevailing to restore inner balance and harmony to our lives.

Goldfish

The **goldfish** is an auspicious motif, conveying there are good tidings to come and abundance and good health to enjoy, no matter how dire things seem.

Duck

The imagery of the duck alludes to our deepest emotions and the need for self-awareness when dealing with matters hidden below the surface. When we delve into the still waters of the self, in quiet times of reflection, the duck symbol asserts that we will get to the bottom of what we seek (e.g., both our failings and virtues) and the other side of our problems.

Chicken

A coincidental sighting of a chicken, real or symbolic, foretells of good fortune, health, and abundance. This powerful and fertile motif also signifies protection against opposing forces.

ONE SMALL STEP TO TAKE TODAY: I will practise moderating my physical and spiritual sides, putting them into balance before interacting socially.

MEDITATION PREPARATION (to practise before making an important decision)

I breathe in golden light vibrations, and as I exhale, I let go of my negative thoughts and feelings. I envision myself going about my day with a smile on my face and bliss in my heart.

Calmly, I reflect on my strengths and weaknesses, calling into focus my masculine and feminine characteristics. My yin and yang, anima and animus energies entwine, strengthening my power for making choices with balanced judgment. When entering the path of challenges, I respond moderately, regulating my emotions, and see myself emerging boldly victorious.

But the fruit of the Spirit is love, joy, peace, patience, kindness, goodness, faithfulness—gentleness, self-control; against such things there is no law.
(Galatians 5:22-23)

15 BLUEBEARD

Bluebeard (PERRAULT/GRIMM)—*The following is a personal retelling of the tale:*

SYNOPSIS OF FAIRY TALE

Bluebeard was a blueblood aristocrat and widower: wealthy, powerful, and sought after as a prospective marriage partner. He married many times, always to innocent maidens whose families arranged their nuptials with great enthusiasm, if not imprudence. But mysteriously, all his young and beautiful wives seemed to disappear soon after going to live with him and join his privileged caste.

In the village, suspicions brewed. Were Bluebeard's status and palatial abode masking a much darker side, concealing a sinister secret? Soon the rumour mill churned out stories portraying Bluebeard as a dangerous man.

Still, after losing his latest wife, Bluebeard approached his neighbour for his daughter's hand in marriage. The unwitting neighbour threw a salubrious banquet so Bluebeard could survey his family of daughters and take his pick. The young women felt helpless and frightened about what the future may hold for them. Bluebeard chose the youngest daughter, whisking her away to his castle deep in the woods where they could be alone to consummate their vows.

Not long later, when the distinguished Frenchman announced he had to leave for a short while, he handed his wife the keys to the chateau, providing strict instructions for their use. She could open any door to rooms in the house where his riches were on display, but she must not enter the tower.

While he was gone, the young wife invited her sister, friends and cousins to visit for a small party. Later, once everyone else had retired to bed, she, overwhelmed by curiosity, ventured to the forbidden tower.

She could not believe her eyes. Shocked and horrified, she noticed a flood of blood dripping from decomposing cadavers hanging from meat hooks on the walls. Fleeing the stench of the gruesome scene, she stumbled, dropping the key. Alas, blood tarnished its surface, and despite her efforts to wash it clean, its dark crimson stain would not budge.

Shaking, she quickly gathered her loyal kin to share the grisly secret about what hung only metres above their heads in the tower chamber. All made a solemn vow to leave the castle of evil at daybreak. But it was not to be. Foiling their escape, Bluebeard unexpectedly returned before some of them had an opportunity to exit.

Bluebeard flared into a blind rage when he became aware of what had happened. He saw the blood-stained key and knew at once that his wife had betrayed her promise. The cruel and psychopathic patriarch, indifferent to the soulful existence of other beings, threatened to destroy his terrified wife and anyone who stood in his way. As he raised his sharp sword to deliver a fatal blow, the trembling wife begged passionately for a chance to share a parting prayer with her beloved sister.

Meanwhile, that morning's escapees had reached her family in the province, to muster aid. In the nick of time, her brothers burst into the middle of the melee, ran a sword through the startled tyrant, killed him in cold blood, and liberated their traumatised sister.

Later, the village-folk accepted the widow's account of events, and although she remained in the chateau, she arranged for the former wives' bodies to be respectfully interred. For many years to come, she used her inherited fortune to help other women in need.

Eventually, the young woman found true love and married a fine, upstanding gentleman the second time around. **THE END.**

PSYCHOLOGICAL PROMPTS

15: Key soul learning: To develop facing fears and reclaiming power (Self-Regulation)

Typically, in patriarchal societies, rich and powerful men are prized by parents practising the tradition of arranged marriages for their female offspring who have no source of income of their own. Marrying their daughter off to a man providing well for her material and social needs legitimises her womanly worth and instructs she must honour and obey.

But in the case of Bluebeard, there is a succession of obedient and naïve daughters who marry the devil incarnate himself, only to perish. Research confirms that a man known to a woman is likely the culprit of crimes committed against her, whether she has had her light slowly dimmed by emotional abuse or punched out by murder.

At first, the devilishly desirable Bluebeard hides behind his status, convincing everyone he is the poor victim of widowhood. But by the time he seeks his recent wife, the villagers have read his pathological pattern and spread the memo.

Despite the gossip and his niggling intuition, the father goes ahead with his daughter's wedding because the pairing potentially enhances his regional powers. Knowing what we know, his instincts, ego and superego are at loggerheads: the paternal inner voice drowned out by his egoic aspirations. In fairness to the father, he is in the thrall of the higher caste as any other in society, then and now.

Bluebeard is disingenuous, having two sides: the sanitised public persona brimming with boundless wealth and good standing and the underhanded, maladaptive, destructive other. Impious, he disrespects the Sacred and everything else— a monstrous devil using coercive control to overpower women and commit blue murder.

Bluebeard, the provocateur, tests the obedience of the fearful maiden, just as the serpent tempts Eve with the apple, and she falls for the near-fatal decision. She does the one forbidden thing. But when she turns the chamber key, she recognises the polarities of good and evil in the world, awakening her deepest sovereignty, and knows at once what she must do alone to survive.

Blood stains the key, symbolising both the blot on her innocence and body-readiness for motherhood—a calling yet to be initiated on her Hero's Journey. As a symbol of selfhood, it bears the imprint of the steep price she has paid to birth a new reality.

Inscrutable Bluebeard threatened his wives, "Do not unlock the door to my dark side, and learn the truth, or you will pay with your lives." Where someone romantic and in love with their partner offers the key to their heart, he is a cold conquistador, discarding those falling for his ruse.

Bluebeard is an extreme example of how a misogynist will gaslight, objectify (the I-It paradigm), having no integrity will go reduce and generalise women by saying, "You women are all alike". And on to say and do much worse. He has honed his aversive strategies by utilising fear, shame and other hurtful psychological pressure. Found in his rotten repertoire are skills to dismiss, discount, withdraw, blame, belittle, guilt-trip, de-rail and withhold. And as for the unheard, unbelieved, deluded or depressed women who come and then realise they must go, theirs is a 'damned if you do, damned if you don't' kind of existence until someday, they escape or sadly reach that vile dead end.

At first, the women will find him ardent, but then the derision, bad-mouthing and baffling double-standards will start. Next, in his forceful displays of overbearing masculine might, the women gradually realise they have been entrapped by a thin-skinned narcissist preferring to bring them down than share in an equal partnership. The seduction, communication without eye contact or any form of tenderness, is fuelled by fantasy and not to be mistaken as love and intimacy, no matter his odd, passionate proclamations (words are cheap). When love is absent, he is the 'I', and you are the 'It', leaving no room for 'Us'. Terrified women, subjected to Bluebeard's cold indifference, rage, and hostility, feel his denigration, possession, and ruthless control in every sense bitterly.

Life presents a double-edged sword for the worn-down wives who know the Bluebeard archetype's offensive capabilities but harbour mixed emotions about trying to escape his hell on earth. Filled with fears of hopelessness and failure, as they struggle to bring light into the dark man's home and avoid scandalising their father's name, women hit an impasse on their Hero's Journey.

The bloodied corpses of Bluebeard's wives suspended on hooks in the tower represent the oppressive and predatory patriarchal power on high that has striven to extinguish the threat of feminine strength since time immemorial. Suppose his misuse of power hasn't cut off a woman's head. In that case, he will tear at her life force using emotional and other forms of abuse, making her dead in different ways (at the time of writing, there have been at least 25 beheadings of wives in Western Europe alone in 2020). Others on the receiving end of relentless abuse claim their drained energy keeps them stuck.

When the ascribed potentially negative masculine powers (yang) of aggression, competition and brute force overwhelm the corresponding feminine energies (yin) of compassion, cooperation and caring (potentially in both genders), then a gross imbalance results: an inflated or possessed animus. To restore balance, there must be an inner marriage of each individual's male and female energies, the animus and anima archetype. Without this internal self-correction, one's external reality will likely bring more struggles.

Despite her planning and pleading, the young woman could not escape her spouse's dark grip when facing imminent death. Still, she did not act cowardly. Her maintaining connections and sharing of shameful secrets with loved ones helped bring about her timely rescue. As the moment of truth arrived, she, a victim-survivor, intended to cut ties with 'Diablo', but it took a concerted effort of male and female strength (her brothers and sisters) to overcome him—he who lived and died by the sword.

In Faust's thrall, the former wives could not leave his den of inequity. Receiving no sympathy or support, did they cut themselves off, put up no resistance to his violations, keep his secrets, and obey his every selfish command? Sometimes he is a Svengali, mesmerising all and sundry with his manipulative and charming accounts of his 'castle' life.

So, the wives' urgent cries for help from the villain's cruel trap go unheard, denied by fathers (and mothers and others) who told them they had made their bed and must lie in it? Blood draining from their bodies indicates how exhausting it is for these traumatised, fear-filled women, ridden roughshod over by hostile men possessed by the dark forces of their nature (e.g., bedevilled by some form of addiction).

If the woman is pregnant (unknown in the *Bluebeard* tale) and awash with hormones, she will be more restricted, dispirited, vulnerable and anxious about her escape and resettlement. She fears leaving because she knows he will hunt her down and even kill her (and her offspring) for daring to betray him and leave him alone to fend for himself. And this is how he, in his dysfunctional and compulsive-obsessive mind-storm, craves an excessive supply of attention, power and control to compensate for his hidden insecurities and feebleness. But his out-of-control behaviour reflects how he is a victim of the animal appetites he cannot control, and he knows it, compensating by exerting coercive control on another human being to project his victimisation.

His life is like a revolving door, with one woman passing as another arrives to enter his deadlock.

In the interest of fairness, women who marry only for convenience, security and status, feeling no love or compassion for the man, living a lie, might expect to receive some *harmless* short shrift in return. We might imagine their empty existence in the absence of love if not for their enmity. There always comes some bad with the good in relationships, so we must be prepared for both. But Bluebeard's morally bankrupt behaviour? Not that, never that. In the name of decency and humanity (not to mention law, morals and ethics), one would expect and hope for there to be some respect for the other party's right to exist. Indeed, there is no case for someone (male, female or non-binary) brutally extinguishing another being: physically, mentally, emotionally or spiritually.

Some advanced souls consider the other's dark traits as mirrors of the shadow parts of self that are not yet self-evident: A valuable perspective though not always applied or evinced absolutely in reality—a helpful starting point for self-reflection.

The tale's stone tower motif reminds us of the fortified façade we wear to hide our dark secrets from ourselves and the world. We can imagine Bluebeard stone-walling his wives, refusing and avoiding the conversations which might uncover truths that potentially heal (or end) their relationship.

While the husband is a remorseless dictator, we can assume wives who stick around are intimidated and controllable, afraid of his authority or desperately homeless without him. But they are not weak or deserving of our withering looks and what the Bluebeard archetype dishes out.

Despite Bluebeard's retrograde impact, preventing anyone from moving forward, can we dare to hope for his redemption? Can they transform from the benighted to enlightened? Sometimes even they are afraid of the dis-grace they create themselves. Given their disconnection and fall from the benign and benevolent stance to ingrained moral squalor, it will take devoted practice to light the spark of the Higher Self again. Their low and dark behaviours cast a long, deep shadow when the time comes for them to embark on the Hero's Road to Damascus.

Far from being a bitter dominatrix (i.e., the female's mirror image of him), the female protagonist is cautious concerning Bluebeard's abuse of power. But wouldn't the self-aware woman in this predicament accept she must unchain herself swiftly and worry about the details later? If only the outcome were as simple. Exits are more easily spoken about than done.

A woman in this position has had her identity and means to survive independently ruthlessly reduced over time by a cunning predator who has tortured her into submission. There is no easy climb out of the mire from rock-bottom back into a healthful existence for the subordinated or victimised. Bluebeard is a frightening beast of brawn, devoid of consciousness and moral fortitude. Nearly always, he is built physically stronger and more violently aggressive, making him potentially dangerous to the welfare of the woman and her children. Paradoxically, he, the fragile alpha male, is emotionally weak, fearing abandonment, isolation, separation and loneliness to the extreme. He is hung up on his past pain gone unprocessed, projecting it onto his victim so he may avoid it. He wants her to feel the pain, the inner turmoil he feels inside, mistakenly thinking it will save him, but the path he beats does not lead to enlightenment. He is split in half: an ego torn asunder from every psychic part. There is a schism of the soul: his deformed perspective and behaviours tell us so. He rails against any woman who says no to his demands or shows signs of her independence. Sadly, it seems that unless a woman has been lured and trapped into a relationship with a monstrous man, she will not fully understand or empathise with a woman brutalised and in desperate need of support to free herself from him. Until freedom arrives, she, with her life-force burned out, lives every day on the cusp of death, symbolic and egoic or mortal: hardly an empowering existence.

He, with a toxic anima, a wounded, pathological psyche, must be overcome and contained, but no one, even the law enforcers, seems to have the might to manage the task. Justice must be done wherever there is an abuse of power inflicted on any sentient being. Although it cannot compare to rehabilitation, atonement, forgiveness and healing, it is a step in the right direction.

Society must step up, providing a range of steadfast services and accessible options for those in need. So far, the system, needing significant reforms, continues to let victims down. As individuals, we must reclaim our awareness, agency, autonomy, and power of choice to restore the Self while waiting for the world to catch up.

We must not be duped into believing his kind of power makes him more of a man. The more blind and inflated his ego, the more air he needs to suck out of us to stay afloat.

Those of us fortunate to avoid the dangerous type but are intimate with someone disingenuous start by admitting the wounds that attract the wrong people to us in the first place (i.e., people who wish to use us as a means to their ends). It also helps to accept that we have gone off-course (as a spiritual-being) for a reason. Next, we have inner work to do on how easily we have been captivated and excessively obedient up until now. Through self-reflection, some realise they have been captivated by hedonistic love partners who prioritise their self-indulgence and personal gain at the detriment of others. Some women unveil their obsession with the notion of romantic love. Others find they compete in vain for attention and care from an indifferent partner whose priority is their addiction (e.g., power, control, gambling, sex, alcohol, other drugs, medications, acquisitions etc.). What's going on there? Are they attracted to partners who evoke the dysfunctional dynamics of their childhood so that they may try again to make things right? At the far end of the continuum resides the Bluebeard archetype—a serial killer of wives (uxoricide).

Thanks to his likes, we have learned that where there is a forceful control freak who incites fear to gain power, there will always be a biddable other enslaved by their unrecognised fears.

The 'one that got away' must identify her undealt with shadow that led her into the devil's lair. In the case of some arranged marriages (*the toxic ones*), we can appreciate a daughter's profound sense of duty and loyalty to her parents. These women around the world die an unpublicised death every day. If they rebel against and run away from an oppressive arranged marriage; or go along with it, potentially, they are tortured in either case. When they manage to escape the trap, some will be murdered when caught: Some choice?

Our liberated protagonist no longer dances to the tune of the devil. Surviving her downfall brings empowerment. The young woman is energised for a second chance at sovereignty. Now awakened, she has formulated a new personal code for Higher Living to share her inherited good fortune and genuine love for others. Having once been blighted by the possessive Bluebeard, she is now ever-grateful to be free to move on to an equal partnership. Yes, she will be wary, but experience need not embitter her. When she forms strong bonds with a good man willing to reciprocate lovingly the respect and tenderness she brings to the union, she will finally live a fulfilling life beyond her initial expectations.

N.B. *Bluebeard portrays the antagonist as male and the protagonist as female, but these roles can be reversed in the real world. In fact, one in three reported cases of domestic violence victims is male. Therefore, it is crucial to reject sexist generalisations about who is capable of committing acts of violence.*

According to current reports, both homeless females and males (of all ages) often escape from family violence and abuse without having a secure place to go. Unlike the young wife in our fairy tale, they lack functioning family members who can serve as liberators, offering a sympathetic ear and a helping hand to escape the traps that undermine their lives and souls.

Research shows that one in five people believe that abused individuals exaggerate their claims. This belief discourages victim-survivors from sharing their stories, not just with those close to them but also from speaking out publicly.

Sadly, for women victims, they are often disbelieved and blamed by men and women alike, allowing male perpetrators in court rooms to accuse them of abuse or mutual abuse or deny culpability. Consequently, perpetrators often get away with intimidation, coercive control, and domestic violence—tactics intended to erode women's sovereignty and self-worth. We must therefore approach with open minds, free of assumptions and bias, and truly listen to each person's story from the heart.

Bluebeard's wife may have embarked on her life journey as a naive Red Cap, lacking experience in the outside world and underestimating her own worth. However, the adulterated Bluebeard archetype has no right to degrade her. In the end, she shows how it is far better if women seek support to find the strength within to **Liberate** themselves from the emotional patterns that tie them to male **Captors** who possess a distorted perspective on life and love.

Bluebeard serves as a cautionary tale, reminding us to be cautious of the shadow side of individuals, regardless of gender, who have misguided goals and act as captors. They psychologically possess others by presenting a false sense of love, security, and stability, all while hiding shameful secrets. Beware of those who always assert their rightness, insist on having their way, and must have the final say. These individuals often have hidden agendas and view people merely as a means to their own ends.

SELF-REFLECTIONS

Do you fear the unknown, finding yourself in situations where you easily surrender your power? Acting sycophantic, as Bluebeard expected of his wives, means submitting to someone other than your empowered Self, creating a power imbalance. Pause and ask yourself if your actions are truly self-compassionate rather than striving to please others deemed more important or worthy. Remember, this is your one shot at life.

Societal groupthink dictates that we conform and dedicate ourselves to endeavours that enslave us, chasing after status and material possessions. We end up serving the very things we intended to serve us, only to realise that we've lost our time and the innocent joy found in life's simple pleasures. How did we replace carefree abandon with attachment to the illusions of the earthly arena?

By denying the truth, we inadvertently strengthen our negatives and subject ourselves to their influence. We must confront reality, which inevitably surfaces regardless, to reclaim our power. However, our personal history and repetitive toxic narratives can tempt us into the painful vortex of anxiety, depression, and self-punishment, taunting us with thoughts of what we should have done to be deemed worthy. We might ruminate on our perceived failures in finding lasting love or material success. No wonder we seek escape and feel unfulfilled on all levels of our being.

The ego remains indifferent, veiling the essence of our soul and obscuring our unconscious and spiritual aspects, fearing their overwhelming influence and perpetuating its falsehoods. *It actively seeks to entangle us in illusions that undermine the power of our soul.* The ego is extremely competitive.

Our blind ego denies the fault-lines within our shadow, afraid that acknowledging them will enlarge our weaknesses and failures, but the opposite is true. Additionally, the ego hinders our psychic integration, fearing demotion and preventing us from becoming Whole. An ego-driven life has us strutting through our days as if in a continuous job interview, oscillating between fear and bravado until we encounter emotional triggers that shatter the façade.

The ego, one-third of the psyche and seat of the mind, plays the game of life in pursuit of its own outcomes, propping up its sense of superiority by reacting defensively to perceived threats—like a wounded animal hiding its weakness to survive. Bluebeard serves as an example of someone anchored in the ego. Attempting to reconcile the ambiguity of the ego's coping mechanisms with reality and soul truth can lead to mistaken thinking, confusion, stress, and even addiction. Smokers claim that smoking helps them destress. Not hooked on substances, we may be addicted to emotional drama. An imbalanced ego leads us to excessively desire the wrong things or people, conditioning us to submit to pretence before honouring our Higher Selves.

Bluebeard's wives serve as a warning about the perils of acting without awareness, as it may lead to relationships with individuals who are indifferent, possessive, violent and worse. By reflecting on our own weaknesses while questioning self-imposed limits, we overcome manipulative forces and catalyse changes we must make. Exploring your psyche and understanding your internal patterns will shed light on the cause of your inability to act, unveiling deep-seated beliefs and fears that drive you to relinquish your power. When we fail to value ourselves, we often seek approval and affirmation from others, sacrificing our own agency, needs and desires in the process, perpetuating a self-defeating cycle. Fear plays a significant role in surrendering our power, as we may submit to others out of fear of rejection, conflict, and loneliness, believing that conforming to their expectations will grant us security. Our past experiences and conditioning contribute to this dynamic. When our power has been stripped or abused, we unconsciously develop a pattern of allowing others to exert dominance over us. Addicts, stopping at nothing to get satisfaction (and fearing, deep down their demise), become addicted to the power and control trip. These experiences shape our self-perception and perpetuate a cycle of disempowerment.

To liberate ourselves from this pattern, it is crucial to cultivate a sense of inner security through self-awareness and self-love. This entails acknowledging our strengths and inherent worth, regardless of others' opinions. It requires establishing boundaries and attending to our own needs and desires, even if it occasionally disappoints or upsets others. To be taken seriously and respected, we must say what we mean and mean what we say.

Nurturing unwavering self-confidence becomes paramount and involves advocating for ourselves, expressing our opinions and preferences (respectfully) and not relying on validation from others. Initially, it may feel uncomfortable, but with practice, such as journalling our story and reclaiming our power, asserting our autonomy becomes second nature.

Addressing our fears is vital to our emotional freedom. By confronting and challenging our fears, we gradually weaken their hold on us. This may involve seeking therapy, embracing meditation, mindfulness and self-reflection, or engaging in activities that push us beyond our comfort zone, gradually desensitising us to specific fears.

Reclaiming your personal power is an individual journey requiring self-discovery, honesty and emotional regulation. If ignored, our undigested shadow aspects manifest externally in our failure to attract the right people and circumstances into our lives. By recognising and addressing the underlying causes of your patterns, you can break free from the cycle of relinquishing your power to those who would misuse it (like Bluebeard) and step into your authentic Self, where living the dream becomes possible.

LIGHT QUALITIES (LIBERATOR)	**SHADOW ATTRIBUTES (CAPTOR)**
Liberated	Possessive
Captivating	Addicted
Boundless	Enthralled
Sympathetic	Destructive
Competitive	Hostile
Awakened	Indifferent
Wary	Coercive
Instinctual	Disingenuous

PROVERB: You never know someone until you live with them.

AFFIRMATION: I shine a light on my shadow to recognise my fears.

GAME OF LIFE: Stopping at nothing to get satisfaction (Consequence: Being difficult to love).

REFLECTION QUESTION: Am I putting others down to feel better about myself?

ANIMAL SYMBOLISM:

Tasmanian Devil

Tasmanian Devils symbolise our survival instinct and urgency to act decisively. Like these fiery marsupials, we might startle others with sudden outbursts. The Tassie devil shows that assertiveness is sometimes necessary over politeness. To achieve lasting love, joy, and satisfaction, we must confront our self-sabotaging defences and fears with unwavering honesty.

ONE SMALL STEP TO TAKE TODAY: I practise living with an air of love and light, so I may see and free my dark-side fears that separate me from the Divine.

MEDITATION PREPARATION (to practise when waking up in the middle of the night)

I breathe in golden light vibrations, and as I exhale, I let go of my negative thoughts and feelings. I envision myself going about my day with a smile on my face and bliss in my heart. As I shine a light on my blind-spots, I sigh with relief as I hand over my fear and error of ways to the forgiving Divine. Feeling safe in the warm breast of the Sacred, I draw the silhouette of my shadow close to me so we may walk together and become friends. At once, we are reconciled and my full power returns.

Some people are moulded by their aspirations, others by their hostilities.
(Elizabeth Bowen)

Bluebeard is a haunting, often adapted fairy tale about a wealthy man who forbids his wife from entering a particular room. Her defiance reveals his past murders. This punishment reflects historical patriarchal and misogynistic norms and female obedience. Bluebeard embodies toxic masculinity, coercively controlling wives through fear and violence. The women suffer not just for disobedience, but for daring to challenge his privilege and authority. *Bluebeard* is a cautionary tale about the dangers of male dominance and its grave outcomes.

Women, Men and Children experience violence. Reach out to these organisations for support in Australia or dial 000 now. 1800 RESPECT (1800 737 732); Men's Referral Service (1300 766 491); Kids Helpline (1800 551 800); LIFELINE (131114). Call 112 globally.

16 RAPUNZEL

Rapunzel (GRIMM)—*The following is a personal retelling of the tale:*

SYNOPSIS OF FAIRY TALE

Long ago and oh so far away lived a married couple expecting their first child. They lived next to a witch's well-tendered garden comprising several rows of luscious edible greens. When the young wife saw the rampion (also known as Rapunzel), she felt intense cravings, prompting her husband to steal some from the witch. The more his spouse ate, the more she craved. As he climbed back over the garden wall for the nth time with his green haul one moonless night, the angry witch snatched him 'red-handed'. Surprisingly, she granted his plea for clemency, but it did come with conditions. He could take even more of the lettuce for his pregnant wife on the proviso he agreed to hand over the child at the time of birth. Out of desperation, he accepted the witch's disturbing bargain.

Soon after, to their delight, a sweet baby girl was born. True to form, the crafty witch came to claim the innocent befittingly naming her Rapunzel. The child was well cared for and grew into a beautiful young maiden with long, lush golden braids.

But when she reached puberty, the possessive witch chose to protect her by isolating her in a tall tower set in the deepest part of the woods. The tower had no stairs or door; however, Rapunzel counted her blessings for a small window let in the light from the sun, moon and stars.

To tend to Rapunzel's needs, the witch visited every day at the same time. She stood beneath the tower wall, reciting the captivating refrain, "Rapunzel, Rapunzel, let down your hair so that I may climb thy golden stair."

Then one day, out of the blue, as Rapunzel merrily sang out from the tower, a passing prince heard her sweet melody floating lightly through the sun-kissed air. Entranced, the noble traced her lilting sounds skywards to the tower keep. He returned often to the secret spot to listen to the gentle angelic tones of her enchanting voice.

However, on one such occasion, while watching from the shadows, the prince was shocked to see an old witch climbing the stone rampart. He took note of how he might ascend it himself one day. So, he watched the wiry old witch descend and depart and took his chance, calling out to the lonely songstress in the same way as the crone had done.

When Rapunzel let down her golden stairway of hair, the bold prince nimbly scaled the tower wall and immediately embraced the beautiful maiden. Making his return often, he had fallen in love with the reclusive Rapunzel and soon asked for her hand in marriage. The plan to elope was complicated, but they wove silk into long golden braids, mimicking her own so that she could escape the witch's clutches.

Trouble struck. Before the lovers could carry out their plan, nervous Rapunzel let something dangerous slip to the witch. She merrily bantered away at her next visit, sharing how much lighter the prince was to draw up on her braids and how tighter her gown had become around her middle. Alas, the witch put two and two together. In a fit of blind fury, she cut off Rapunzel's crowning glory and, without warning or delay, took her deep into the woods to fend for herself alone.

Returning to the tower chamber that night, the vengeful witch waited for the love-struck prince to reappear. Rapunzel's severed braids in hand, she drew the duped lord straight into her trap, screaming obscenities and threatening that he would never see her beautiful daughter again. Taken aback, he struggled to be free of the woesome witch, leaping from the tower and landing hard on a thorny thicket that pricked out his sight.

The smitten prince wandered blindly through the deep woods, month in, month out, hoping that one day he would stumble across his beloved Rapunzel.

As soon as he heard that familiar ethereal voice trailing on the summer breeze from an eternity ago, he followed where its sweet scent led. Soon the voice rang louder and crisper, stopping the blind noble in his tracks directly outside the pretty cottage where Rapunzel and her infant twins now lived. Hearing footsteps approaching, anxious Rapunzel ventured outside. At first blush, she fell into her beloved prince's arms. They comforted each other, basking in the warm glow of a blazing sunset.

Rapunzel's joyful tears fell like the healing summer rain into the eyes of her blinded prince. Slowly he raised his handsome head and, with the miracle of his sight restored, beheld in full light his golden goddess— paradise lost was now regained.

Bonded together forever and joined by their young son and daughter, they made haste to his princely kingdom to live the free, richly loving and contented life always meant for them. **THE END**

PSYCHOLOGICAL PROMPTS

16. Key soul learning: To develop planning for the unexpected (Social Skills)

In various fairy-tale tropes, the poor with repressed desires, strike a forbidden bargain with a supernatural force, reminiscent of Eve's temptation in the garden, leading to their willing sacrifice of their child. Unfortunately, this reality was all too common in the European regions, including the origins of Rapunzel's tale, where starvation, malnutrition, war, natural disasters, disease, epidemics, famine, and poverty were everyday hardships.

During Rapunzel's gestation, the witch supplemented her daily diet with the mineral-rich rampion, akin to spinach or lettuce, known for its medicinal properties. In their wisdom, wise old women understood the importance of good nutrition for our health, even though their 'little bit of knowledge was a dangerous thing' in their time. Today, allopathic doctors acknowledge that lettuce, rich in folic acid, can protect a foetus's developing brain and spine. The tale also suggests another healing effect on mind and body through singing and music, which benefitted Rapunzel and later her twins. They survived the ever-prevailing mortality risks of childhood when the death rate was fifty per cent for children under five.

Despite her confinement, Rapunzel blossomed into a beautiful young woman, her glorious golden hair serving as a sign of her innate strength, glowing health and enlightenment.

However, we cannot overlook the consequences of her lockdown on her mental wellbeing. While the witch had always clutched at straws to keep her, her severed braids later symbolise her banishment and the arduous tests she must overcome alone. Vivid metaphors of clutching at and cutting ties are central in this trope, reminding us that despite hanging on too tightly to something, we will ultimately lose it.

The witch's bastide, symbolising our ego's defensive façade, hides Rapunzel's psychic wounding from childhood. Raised by a dark witch, she had ample time to think and brew, leading to feelings of fear and vulnerability when confronted with the aftermath of parental mistakes beyond her control. Nevertheless, Rapunzel's story teaches us that we can be reborn if we dismantle the walls around our hearts and live fully in the present.

The thorny witch, consumed by rage, jealousy, possessiveness, and covetousness, is emotionally triggered when the young lovers plot to overthrow her control. The stealing of Rapunzel's heart elicits an unforeseen violent response from the witch, highlighting the volatile force of nature and the capacity for unexpected and dramatic upheaval in our lives caused when our denied shadow aspects impact the reactions of others.

Had the couple hoped for the best but planned for the worst, they might have avoided the witch's ambush. The prince's blindness resulting from the fall, is a metaphor for falling in love, love being blind and uncertainty about the unseen future.

In the eyes of the world, a sovereign prince falling in love with a pretty commoner held captive by supernatural forces challenges societal norms. The prince must confront his unconscious shadow aspects and relinquish his sense of white male privilege that once defined him. As he falls in love with a plebeian, he realises the need for compassion and humility. The prince's descent from the tower alludes to the grounding of lofty ideals and past judgments that divided people into social castes. Pride comes before his fall, allegorically representing the disruption and collapse of a bygone era's unstable, and discriminatory belief system.

The severed braids symbolise Rapunzel's shocking but necessary Oedipal detachment from the archaic witch. The crone, stuck in her past, a Dickensian 'Miss Havisham', has lived vicariously through Rapunzel, assuming credit for how beautiful the girl has become.

Rapunzel's life undergoes a dramatic shift as she leaves her 'ivory tower' confines, embracing the realities and responsibilities of selfhood in modern life. Holding onto painful memories will only compound her problems in the future, urging her to let go, do the inner psychological work and embrace her authentic Self. She shows us that life begins when one steps out of their comfort zone.

Banished to the gloomy woods by the vengeful witch, the girl enters the cave of introspection. She emerges, having decided to bloom where she's planted, realising the necessity of survival-related tension for personal growth. She embarks on her Hero's Journey, establishing a home and single-handedly raising her twin babies—a boy and a girl. She renounces the witch's 'me-first' and over-protective mothering style, wanting what is best for her children. Conception symbolises our co-creative powers, hope, transformation and new beginnings. The twins embody the balance and stability that come from integrating feminine and masculine, anima and animus energies.

Rapunzel breaks free from the shadow-witch's influence by effectively processing her latent traits of anger, resentment, and frustration, resulting from her past entrapment. Recovered and emotionally liberated, she sings sweetly from her soul to her children in the cottage, displaying resilience and self-acceptance despite ongoing isolation, unplanned pregnancy, and separation from the father of her children. While she knows she can endure life's unpredictable disruptions and disappointments (symbolised by the witch) and forgives her damaged past, the possibility of reconciling with her man seems futile.

Meanwhile, the blind prince's unwavering search demonstrates the power of love as a magnetic, guiding force even in times of conflict, disillusionment and confusion when the horizon is beyond sight. The young lovers forge their paths with stoic resolve by taking risks and maturing independently. Ultimately, their paths converge, reuniting them rapturously, realising their love is here to stay even when edifices crumble.

Rapunzel's tears (constrained no more) cleanse the cloudy glaze from her hero's eyes, enabling him to face the truth—reality as it is. A revelation! For the first time, he saw the product of his love, their offspring. According to Aristotelian number symbolism, when two becomes four, a unit is complete, founded on security and a deep sense of belonging. The debt to each other was squared.

After enduring the ordeal, we draw upon Divine strength to rejuvenate ourselves, ready to face the new **Disruptors** with unwavering resilience. These storms bring refreshing rains to cleanse us of our past remnants, which no longer serve us, and prompt us to salvage what's valuable. As **Restorers**, we dismantle barriers to build stronger foundations and a brighter future. Through careful planning, we lighten the impact of life's tumultuous events, comforted by the ever-present beacon of hope at the end of the tunnel.

SELF-REFLECTIONS

When a storm surges and opposing forces clash, shattering your sense of security, your world is temporarily upended. Ignoring warning signs, akin to the inexperienced Rapunzel, will only delay your resettling. Amidst the chaos, anxiety, and stress in the 'season of the witch', a flicker of enlightenment emerges. Heed the signs.

This awakening, a cosmic call, reveals a new way on your Hero's Journey. Timely and profound, your spiritual lesson catalyses necessary changes. With unwavering determination, press forward, striding the fighter's path fearlessly, knowing your assertions will surpass uncertainty and fears.

In the teachings of life, like those provided by fairy-tale witches, mentors may not always align with our hopeful expectations. Nevertheless, a 'guiding influence' arrives at your doorstep to help restore stability to your daily affairs encompassing health, love, home, and work.

Similar to Rapunzel's narrative, upheavals force a paradigm shift to prepare you for the uncharted frontier ahead. Embracing newfound purpose and unshakable passion, you defy the odds, developing efficacy and confidence that lead to greater challenges and rewards. Although life happens while we are busy making other plans, as John Lennon's lyrics go, we still possess the power to choose our response and avert further pain.

In your case, reframe your story positively, and embody gratitude for the remaining comforts, irrespective of recent loss and pain. Remember, where you focus your energy, you will attract and expand.

Within every crisis lies opportunity, a double-edged sword that exposes dysfunctional aspects of life, liberating ego-driven parts that hinder progress. These self-saboteurs trigger exaggerated reactions to others' behaviours. Your dreams offer glimpses into the unconscious elements of your ego, revealing shadow wounds. By taking this philosophical perspective, you can avoid more negative consequences. As Jung elucidates, unaddressed contradictions and conflicts within our inner selves enlarge and manifest in our outer lives until we take action. Nature and our soul transmit signals to forewarn and fortify us, reducing the risk of being caught off guard, shocked and traumatised.

Now is the time to tend to our fragmented psyche when our words misalign with our actions. Are we truly listening, observing, and preparing to act? Rapunzel might have first overlooked the cues of her intuition, compounding her challenges, yet she stayed focused on the present moment. Reflecting on the 'whys' and 'should-haves' only prolongs pain and disillusionment, anchoring us in a regretful past. Once the shadow memory fragments are resolved, your eyes refreshed, you oversee the constructive reformation of life's pieces. Calmness returns, replenishing your capacity to live a satisfying existence. There is no retreat to the old, false haven—it is forever gone.

The tale of *Rapunzel* illuminates the fragility of relationship ties, cautioning us against clinging to what is not meant for us. Many associations fail the tests of truth, fidelity, friendship, or enduring partnership, at the end of the day. Some lovers lack empathy, offering little satisfaction to all involved.

Rapunzel's biography explores a social divide between peasants, witches, commoners, royalty, the supernatural, and the natural. Ultimately, the monarch outwits the cunning witch of the wild, possessing the ordinary yet beautiful

Rapunzel. Historically, witches were terminated (some of them mere herbalists offering folkloric remedies), no match for the so-called God-given king.

In your equation, clashing backgrounds and ideologies demand earnest efforts to repair relationships. Change shakes loose old patterns, propelling us into new lives. Let Rapunzel's hopeful song guide you, encouraging you to find your footing, start anew, and move in harmony with the rhythm of the universe.

Those grappling with separation and loss resist change but expecting eternity from the mundane is futile. Instead, we must prepare for such transitions. Death is an empty cup which promises a refill. Embracing our place in the continuum of existence, we must vault our inevitable encounter with eternal, and meantime, savour each precious moment.

When one loses everything, they may feel at the mercy of a Higher Power. However, Divinity recognises the unique strengths of every hero and guides them back onto their right path. Heroes understand that their soul worth exceeds what they have lost. With hearts expanded by brokenness, they have more room in it for others.

Standing between the ego's illusions and the real world, your perception sharper than ever, your inner healing equips you to better navigate the social interface—the threshold where your 'version 2' faces new tests and the making of new connections.

Rapunzel's tale encapsulates the transformative power of love, resilience, and self-discovery, teaching you to heal the past wounds that imprison you, dismantle emotional barriers, and embrace the present moment with refreshed eyes and a songful heart. Despite the trauma, fear and pain experienced in this phase of the Hero's Journey, each knock-down serves as catalyst for enhanced personal power. These peak challenges hold the potential for a transformative rebirth, akin to a phoenix arising from the ashes. By relinquishing the past, which no longer serves you, you create space for a future brimming with serenity, stability, and enduring love.

LIGHT QUALITIES (RESTORER)	**SHADOW ATTRIBUTES (DISRUPTER)**
Restorative	Disruptive
Reconciled	Stormy
Recovering	Unstable
Stable	Thorny
Revelatory	Constrained
Stoic	Damaged
Averting	Disillusioned
Refreshing	Shocked

PROVERB: There is always calm after every storm.

AFFIRMATION: I pick up the pieces and restore my foundations.

GAME OF LIFE: Clutching at straws (Consequence: Having nothing solid to fall back on).

REFLECTION QUESTION: Can I accept my past is dead so that my future may live?

ANIMAL SYMBOLISM: Owl; Goanna

Owl

The (Masked) Owl symbolises our instinct to guard our territory when threatened and represents unexpected enduring partnerships that start unexpectedly but bring a lifetime of love and companionship. With its mystical and spiritual qualities, the owl serves as a messenger from the wise Great Mother to remind us that we are not alone and to be mindful of upcoming life lessons. The owl encourages us to live authentically by removing our masks, lest we miss opportunities for transformative change.

Goanna

The lizard signs a return to primordial times, reminding us of the illusion of the built world. The goanna is our cautionary guide, symbolising the fusion of masculine bravery and stoicism and feminine intuition, ethics, and wisdom. It warns against neglecting common sense when falling in love, emphasising that true love is sacred, while material possessions are not.

ONE SMALL STEP TO TAKE TODAY: I practise being in my loving light, seeing and subsuming my dark fears that threaten to tear me down.

MEDITATION PREPARATION (to practise when waking up in the wee hours)

I open my eyes to a brand-new day. I breathe in golden light vibrations, and as I exhale, I let go of my negative thoughts and feelings. I envision myself going about my day with a smile on my face and bliss in my heart.

The Great Power urges me on, telling me I have the courage to overcome my obstacles bravely. My heart beats in rhythm with the natural world, strengthening my sense of Sacred connection as I make a straight and steady approach to a new horizon. Life is good.

Find a seed at the bottom of your heart and bring forth a flower.
(Shigenori Kameoka)

17 SNOW WHITE

Snow White (GRIMM)—*The following is a personal retelling of the tale:*

SYNOPSIS OF FAIRY TALE

A kind king and gentle queen once longed for a baby daughter.

One day, as the queen sat sewing at the castle window, she daydreamed wistfully, gazing out at winter's first snow and the soft flakes falling rhythmically upon the black ledge. Distracted, she pricked her finger. Three large droplets of blood fell onto the white-capped windowsill. Still deep in thought, the queen envisaged that one day she would hold a beautiful baby daughter in her arms with skin as white as snow, lips as red as blood and hair as black as ebony.

The queen gave birth to her baby girl but died not long later. As the mother slowly slipped away to heaven, she lovingly whispered her baby's name, Snow White.

When the grieving king grew lonely, he married again. His new wife was beautiful but vain, proud and envious. She had a magic mirror, all-seeing and truthful that she routinely consulted to find out who was the loveliest in the land. For many years, the faithful mirror assured the queen that she was by far the fairest of face.

Then one day, when Snow White had grown, her beloved father died, leaving Snow White alone with her stepmother.

The queen soon forgot the king, relying on her charming mirror for company. But her most dreaded moment arrived when it revealed her beauty was eclipsed by the sweet princess's. Suddenly, the jealous queen's heart turned dark and as cold as stone against Snow White, who only continued to blossom with each passing day. Unable to cope, the angry and hateful queen ordered the king's huntsman to take the girl away, murder her in the woods and bring back her heart on a plate. But try as he might to heed the queen's decree, the loyal servant could not bring himself to take Snow White's life. So, he let her go, leading her to the forest's impenetrable parts and taking a deer's heart back instead as proof of the done deed.

Snow White wandered for hours on end until she fell asleep from exhaustion. When she awoke to the high sweet mew of the birds, the forest animals had gathered near, and she knew at once to follow them. They led her deeper into the woods until the parched princess saw a strange little cottage ahead. The tiny cabin was warm and cosy, and after taking a small portion of food and drink from the table, she fell into a deep sleep in one of the seven beds.

Soon later, seven dwarfs who had worked hard in the nearby gold mine returned to the cottage. It surprised them to find disorder in their home, realising at once someone had snuck in and helped themselves to their belongings. They became so noisy and agitated, that Snow White showed herself and began to share the story of her ordeal. The kindly dwarfs agreed to let her stay but warned her to remain cautious with the infamously wicked queen.

Speaking of which, the evil stepmother consulting her magic mirror again learned, to her shock and horror, that Snow White was still alive and more beautiful than ever, living deep in the woods. Immediately, the rage-fuelled queen hatched a deadly plot to kill Snow White with her own hands.

In disguise, the sly queen went down into the thickest part of the forest to find the pure of heart, Snow White, alone in the dwarfs' cottage.

First, she tried to kill the maiden with a gift of white bodice laces which she tied so tightly across her torso that they took her breath away. But, in a timely stroke of good fortune, the dwarfs arrived home, cut her free and saved her. Secondly, the cruel crone tricked Snow White again with a poisoned comb for her hair. Once again, the dwarfs revived Snow White. On the third attempt, the queen pretending to be a harmless peddler lured the ill-starred Snow White with a luscious, red apple. Snow White was tempted but warier this time around. Ever-determined, the evil queen cut off the one untainted section of apple and swallowed it without consequence, encouraging Snow White to take a piece. The young maiden, faithful to the goodness of human nature, fell for the ruse. She ate the poisoned slice, falling instantly into a coma. Triumphant, the malevolent queen, made haste for the castle.

The dwarfs returned home, mortified to discover Snow White immobilised in an unconscious state. Despite their prolonged efforts, they could not revive her. Stricken with grief but resigned to fate, they placed her in a pretty glass casket in a quiet resting place in a glade of trees where they could share in their loss, mourning for the beautiful maiden they had grown to love.

One sunny day a passing prince caught a glimpse of the reflective coffin, quickly becoming entranced by the serene and radiant beauty of the languid Snow White lying inside. The royal asked the downcast dwarfs if he may open the glass case. As he stood mesmerised, admiring the young princess's beauty, he softly touched her cheek and kissed her gently on her cherry-red lips. Slowly, Snow White began to open her eyes.

As for the tenacious and spiteful queen, she came looking to annihilate Snow White once and for all. But her misadventure led her to the forest's edge, where she fell into a deep, craggy mine. The hard, deep earth, as dark and dangerous as her corrupted soul, swallowed her whole. Back at the palace, the prince and princess, planning their wedding, gave ne'er a thought to such demons of the past. You see, the young royals' life together was brimming with love, joy and hope. And so, it always would be. **THE END.**

PSYCHOLOGICAL PROMPTS

17: Key soul learning: To develop a sincere belief in the power of hope (Empathy)

The dearly departed mother-queen has left behind her picture-perfect infant daughter. The child possesses a star quality, with porcelain white skin symbolising awareness, crimson lips representing love-fire, and flowing ebony hair embodying shadow. Destined for a place among the ruling class, Snow

White is born into privilege. However, she is no more immortal than we are, and she must brace herself for the treacherous machinations of those envious of her birthright.

The tides of Snow White's fortune take an ominous turn when her father fails to protect her, and she falls into the merciless hands of her stepmother. Research by Takala (2008) reveals a chilling truth: step-children are more likely to endure physical, sexual, and emotional abuse, or even fall victim to murder compared to children residing inside their intact biological family unit. While their environments may not be as perilous as Snow White's, step-children are no strangers to pain. However, any amount of anyone's suffering is too much suffering.

Snow White's tale unfolds, exposing her cruel and irrational stepmother's envy for the glowing girl's God-given gifts. The huntsman, a rational and moral figure, stands as a wise man archetype in direct contrast with the shadow archetype of the witch. Did the bitter queen, (acting from her id), harbour sinister intentions of cannibalising and incorporating her young adversary's beauty and strengths when demanding he serve her Snow White's heart on a plate?

Stripped of her inner light and sense of rapture, the dark queen becomes possessed and psychically ruptured by the long-suppressed dysfunctional aspects concealed in her shadow. Bereft of her once youthful glow, she copes by projecting her seething rage and embittered resentment onto Snow White, determined to undermine her. It would have been far kinder to herself if she had drawn inspiration from her, envisioning a future as a dynamic and attractive elder, embracing her age and experience with confidence.

Tragically, the cynical queen finds herself ensnared by the pervasive allure of the beauty myth, mistakenly believing that a woman's power resides solely in her physical appearance. This fallacy, rooted in Greco-Roman culture, where beauty was considered a Divine blessing for both genders, has been etched into the collective consciousness throughout the ages. However, according to the magic mirror, one's outward appearance will betray the bitter truth if their inner self festers with spite. The queen's reliance on the mirror for validation indicates an over-reliance on her persona-mask and an imbalance in her psyche.

There is no growing old graciously for the narcissistic among us.

Immersed in her own toxic thoughts, the maladaptive matriarch succumbs all too easily to the three egoic poisons: delusion, desire, and aversion (or hate). Unbeknownst to her, her psyche becomes estranged from its innate goodness, distorting her perception of the unsuspecting Snow White, whom she falsely perceives as a threat to her survival, power, and control. The path to redemption lies in the denialist's reclamation of her dormant qualities, including her inner child's freshness, by reintegrating them into a regenerated psyche. Alas, her lack of self-awareness and empathy proves to be her greatest hindrance, leading her to shift blame onto Snow White as a twisted justification for her punitive actions. Throughout history, the pure and innocent have too often fallen victim to vengeful, dark oppressors.

But the resilience of the human spirit shines through, even in the face of unimaginable hardships. The dwarfs, emblems of childhood, industry, and perseverance, become beacons of hope for Snow White. With hearts made of pure gold (gold miners), they signify the maiden's rebirth if only she can reclaim her frightened and needy inner child. Named Bashful, Dopey, Sleepy, Happy, and so on, they point to traits she must reclaim from her shadow. Symbolically, the number seven is linked to our seven yearly stages of human development, to the heavenly realms, the Jungian concept of Wholeness, and to the Divine's 'cycle of completion', engendering hope that good will always outshine evil.

However, this tale also reveals the disparity between children born into the security of aristocratic families and the hard-labour-lives of less fortunate children. Youngsters, akin to the dwarfs, laboured in terrible conditions in the mines and chimneys across Europe during the time this fairy tale was penned.

The malevolent monarch makes three attempts on Snow White's life. The power of the number three, evoking destiny's hand, is a common notion in Western culture. We acknowledge the Trinity, the threefold path of good thoughts, words, and deeds, or the three virtues of faith, hope, and charity to live a good life. In her darkest hour, the people-pleasing Snow White teeters between temptation (id) and restraint (superego), similar to Eve's forbidden bite of the apple. She falls into a death-like sleep and has wishful dreams, where her idyllic fantasies interact with shadowy figures until she evolves into a voluptuous woman, ready to embrace her passions.

In this unconscious state, in the deep forest and in a crystal casket, Snow White receives the revelation, hearing the clarion call from the wild. Despite appearing weak, lying in a death-like trance, a shiny chrysalis, her smiling heart beats with magnetic and shining hope as she looks upward to the starlit sky of the night.

Directed by the morning star, a passing prince arrives to awaken her with a kiss. Sensing familiarity, she opens her eyes and falls in love with him at first sight. He is captivated by her radiant vision. But we must question the rescuing prince's motives. Does his attraction stem solely from her external beauty, or does he see beyond the surface to the depth of her soul? The metaphor of the glass casement reminds us that while we are often unconscious of our true selves, others can see straight through us to our hearts.

Snow White emerges from the depths of despair, resurrected with hope and optimism for a second chance. Her transformation serves as a poignant reminder that even the most fragile among us possess a reservoir of strength—we are blessed by a lucky star, after all. Through her actions, we catch a glimpse of her inner conflicts and her tendency to appease others at the expense of her own desires and wellbeing. She has faith in the milk of human kindness but must protect herself from victimisation by setting firm personal boundaries. The kiss from the passionate animus archetype will sort that out.

The multifaceted archetype unfolds against a backdrop of contrasting and polarising elements: light and dark, good and evil, love and hate, hope and fear, rich and poor, male and female, youth and old age. Her story stands as a testament to the transformative power of unity and communion, attracting love, balance and peace, while our separations from the Source repel love, sowing only emotional chaos.

The wicked queen's scheme backfires, plunging her deeper into the abyss of her shadow side. Yet, all is not lost for her; redemption remains within reach. It begins with embracing her buried beauty and reframing the hateful self-talk that poisons her soul. Denying our suffering causes our authentic selves to recede, but by acknowledging our pain, we take the first step toward reclaiming our true essence.

Snow White, aware of her beauty inciting the queen's wrath and the peril of her **People-pleasing**, chose not to dim her light. Instead, she shone her **Star**, radiating hope and optimism. She gifted herself forgiveness, gracefully letting go of her pain, and embraced a brighter future of new possibilities.

SELF-REFLECTIONS

Drawing from your lessons of naivety and trust, you've evolved into an insightful soul, more aware of who you are and others. Despite enduring setbacks, you hold a steadfast belief in the inherent goodness of most people. Embracing the virtue of seeing the good in everyone is at the core of your code for Higher Living. You don't let the darkness in. Each day, fuelled by unwavering faith and hope, love lights your way.

Similar to our beloved fairy-tale heroine, with change and growth underfoot, it is time to establish new personal boundaries for the present. As you stand at the threshold of a brighter future, a newfound eagerness arises to form new, meaningful connections. Your creative energy flows effortlessly through every facet of your life. Taking things slow, upholding your values, honouring yourself, and resisting risky temptations brings forth rewarding experiences.

The fusion of your inner goodness and outer beauty becomes a magnet, drawing others towards you. Some offer positive influences, while others, envious of your radiance, attempt to dim your light. Instead of persisting with those who undermine you, it is essential to stay clear and address vulnerabilities, following the example of the dwarfs.

In contrast, the witch's failure to acknowledge and heal her own dark fragments projected toxic energy onto Snow White. The dwarfs, on the other hand, reframed their story of sleepiness, grumpiness, dim-wittedness (Dopey) and bashfulness into a positive psychic framework to get the job done. Would the young princess have seen through the witch's facade had she known herself better? Would the witch have wielded as much power over someone less vulnerable?

As you traverse the path of life, tensions emerge to test your faith and resilience. Can you remain hopeful despite the guilty inner voice that questions your worthiness of manifesting your cherished wishes?

In the end, like all optimists, you perceive trials as catalysts for personal growth, forging ahead with unwavering faith and confidence.

Snow White's journey, from trials to triumph, serves as a blueprint for achieving love and truth—a journey that entails spending serene moments in the glory of nature alongside birds, animals, and true friends who offer comfort, joy, and spiritual upliftment. Engaging in self-reflection and dream journalling within the sanctuary of your deepest thoughts renews your energy and allows you to channel your innate gifts. Similar to Snow White, who discovered her destiny through dreams, you possess the intuition to sense when a potential partner enters your sphere, awakening to their presence.

Once your inner child is fully restored, a transformation occurs, and you emerge as a matured and dynamic soul, ready to employ and showcase your unique talents. Through the routine practice of reframing your story, meditation and affirmations, you carve new neural pathways, replacing outworn patterns of fear and doubt. Your emergence as an inspirational visionary serves as a radiant beacon of aspiration, positivity and passion, naturally attracting the same energy in return.

Should someone's words and actions ignite suffering, remember that they mirror elements of your own inner fragments. Acknowledging this shadow side becomes a catalyst for spiritual growth. You see that the futile denial exemplified by the toxic stepmother, whose spite tarnished her youth and beauty, underscores the importance of confronting and transcending one's remaining remnants of negativity or buried trauma.

Despite life's hardships, always remember that the darkest moments precede the dawn. Snow White imparts the wisdom that our unique stardust not only attracts light and love but also invites envy and attention. To embrace and nurture the flame of your inner light is to take the first step toward releasing the burden of others' judgments and the quiet oppression of their opinions. With a luminescent soul, you perceive the luminescence within others and they in you.

Frankl (1905-1997) taught us that optimism triumphs over pessimism, providing the necessary momentum for life's breakthrough moments. Kindred spirits gravitate towards your orbit during these transformative moments, indicating destined connections. But will your souls merge in lasting intimacy or fleeting chemistry? Others come for a reason, season or forever after. Discern, learning from Snow White's impulsive engagement with everyone she encountered by mapping the human heart before expecting commitment. Initially driven by the need for acceptance, the princess fell, but eventually reclaimed her true Self, becoming a shining example of confidence, love, and hope, and met her match.

This fairy-tale archetype, our original star-child within, offers an eternal and shining augury: Where there is hope, there is life; and in life, there is always room for hope to grow into new purpose. No matter that sometimes the sky darkens. We must open our hearts and eyes to its glory. Now, the same star of hope shines vibrantly for you, bringing a boon to your health and happiness. A ray of love-light shimmers in the near distance as continuously as the stars above, compelling you to follow where it leads. Like Snow White, someone special inspires you, positively shaping your future. **Stay radiant.**

LIGHT QUALITIES (STAR)	**SHADOW ATTRIBUTES (PEOPLE-PLEASER)**
Hopeful	People-pleasing
Visionary	Weak
Radiant	Superficial
Blessed	Needy
Wishful	Undermined
Dynamic	Envious
Inspirational	Cynical
Light	Denialist

PROVERB: Things are looking up.

AFFIRMATION: The universe conspires with me to attract light and love into my life.

GAME OF LIFE: Feeling guilty for being 'you' (Consequence: Attracting put-downs).

REFLECTION QUESTION: Can I renew my contract with my original Self, becoming a shining example of love and hope?

ANIMAL SYMBOLISM: Magpies; Possums; Rabbits; Horse; Cockatoos

Magpies

Symbolising love, joy and success, the magpie arrives after we emerge from hibernation to see the light of day. It signifies our universe's duality (black and white), urging us to look beneath surface appearances to find the truth. The chorister call of the magpie is an emblem of freedom, joy and our willingness to try again.

Possums

The nocturnal possum embodies caution amidst unknown mysteries, urging us to navigate with care. They teach us to embrace life while remaining vigilant. With their protective, caring nature and agility, possums combine sweetness with secrecy, intuition, and strategy, guiding us to outwit predators or bullies, taking them by surprise.

Rabbits

As a totem of gentleness and faith, the **rabbit's** image tells us that despite our jangled nerves, our sharp reflexes will keep us safe. Unpredictable by nature, the rabbit says we must adapt and leap on any opportunities despite our fears. Being one of the most social animals, often living in the wild in complex warrens of one hundred rabbits or more, she reminds us we must get along to go along.

Horse

The horse signifies our libido and desire for freedom. A red horse symbolises our unbridled passion; a dark horse represents our id appetites and dark side, whereas the sighting of a white or pale ahorse signifies our capacity for love and enlightenment.

Cockatoos

Her white and yellow crest feathers resemble the sun's rays, symbolising sunny times ahead. However, the bird's harsh calls warn against overexposure to the sun's fiery rays (or our unrealistic expectations) and the damage caused by flying too close.

ONE SMALL STEP TO TAKE TODAY: I practise being optimistic, loving and kind, believing I have a bright future ahead.

MEDITATION PREPARATION (to practise shortly after nightfall or when waking up in the middle of the night)

I breathe in light golden vibrations, and as I exhale, I let go of my negative thoughts and feelings. I envision myself going about my day with a smile on my face and bliss in my heart.

Dancing across starlit skies, I embrace the engulfing light, serenaded by an angelic voice reciting, * "*Starlight, star bright, first star I see tonight; I wish I may, I wish I might have the wish I wish tonight.*" Upon awakening, I watch in rapturous awe as the sparks of my dreams begin to twinkle like protostars.

(* Original composer is unknown—passed down through oral tradition over time.)

Arise, shine, for your light has come, and the glory of the Lord rises upon you.
(Isaiah 60:1)

18 EAST OF THE SUN AND WEST OF THE MOON

East of the Sun and West of the Moon (NORWEGIAN: COLLECTED BY PETER CHRISTIAN ASBJORNSEN AND JORGEN MOE)—*The following is a personal retelling of the tale:*

SYNOPSIS OF FAIRY TALE

In a land far back in the annals of time, a magnificent white bear approached a poor peasant, promising him great riches if he would hand over his youngest daughter. Reluctantly, the peasant's daughter agreed with her father's decision and was taken away to the bear's enchanted castle.

At night in the cold bastide, an unusual event unfolded. As the young maiden climbed into bed with the white bear, it seemed to transform, but the darkness obscured her view. After a time, she grew homesick and was granted permission to visit her family, with the condition that she would not speak to her mother alone.

But when she returned home, she confided in her mother about her peculiar life with the bear. Her mother suspected the bear was a troll and gave her some candles to assess his measure when he next came to her bed.

In the presence of the slumbering bear and the flickering candlelight, the daughter beheld a miraculous sight. The bear had another side and had transformed into a handsome prince. Startled by the revelation, she accidentally spilled three drops of melted tallow onto his white shirt, causing him to awaken. The prince bared his soul, revealing his captive existence at the hands of the trolls. He yearned for freedom to live his authentic life and shared that a spell cast by his future stepmother, the troll-queen, confined him. With only one year left to break the curse, he urgently prepared to depart and fulfil the trolls' demand of marrying the troll-princess in the kingdom east of the sun, west of the moon. Under the faint glow of the waning moon, the prince disappeared into the night.

When the enamoured girl awoke, she vowed to search for him high and low. Wondering how far she could go on her own steam, she embarked on her arduous quest, determined to find the mysterious castle. Through the dark, moonless night, she went until she encountered an older woman playing with a golden apple on a high mountain. But she did not know the castle's location. The woman gave her the apple and a horse and directed her to a neighbour who might have answers. The neighbour was also unaware but gifted her a golden carding-comb for her travels. Continuing her journey patiently, she met a third neighbour who offered a golden spinning wheel and a fresh horse to reach the place of the east wind, the wisest of all.

The east wind directed her to the west wind, which guided her to the south wind, and finally, leaving none the wiser, she headed to the home of the north wind. The north wind, recalling how he blew an aspen leaf that way long ago, escorted her to the cryptic castle east of the sun and west of the moon. Throughout the journey, she glanced at the waxing moon, cherishing the imagined presence of her prince's kind and gentle face, feeling his loving presence at her back. With hope in her heart, she pressed on.

Finally arriving at the castle, the troll-princess, captivated by the golden apple, sought to acquire it. The maiden negotiated a deal, asking for one night alone with the prince in exchange. Cunningly, the troll-princess slipped the prince a potent sleeping potion. Disappointed she could not awaken him, yet undeterred, the daughter made another pact with the troll-princess, trading her golden carding-comb for another night with the prince. However, the dormant prince could not be roused despite her anguished cries that echoed through the castle's hollow chambers. Within the tower, the imprisoned townsfolk overheard the girl's sorrowful sobs and secretly informed the prince when he awoke. Meanwhile, the maiden struck another deal with the trolls, securing a third night with the prince in exchange for her golden spinning wheel. Now aware of the situation, the prince resisted the drugged drink, and feigning sleep, awaited the girl's arrival. Their embrace overflowed with relief and joy as they conspired to break free from the trolls' clutches.

The following day, the trolls began to prepare for the wedding ceremony. True to plan, the prince used his royal authority, demanding that someone prepare his regal garments. The person worthy of marrying a monarch could remove the tallow stains from the prince's white shirt. Since the enchanted trolls could not perform such a mundane task, he called the young maiden into his chamber to prove her ability. Succeeding where others had failed, the prince boldly professed his love for her in front of the royal court, dispelling the troll's sorcery, and declared his intent to wed her. Their plan bore fruit as they liberated the imprisoned townsfolk, causing the enraged trolls to vanish into thin air. Before they departed, the young lovers discovered a secret cache of gold and silver that the prisoners had previously divulged, concealed within the castle's vaults. Full of love and hope, they gathered the treasure and loaded it onto her trusty steed, embarking on a journey south of the castle walls, east of the sun and west of the moon, toward his homelands bathed in warmth and light. And so, they followed the moonlit trail toward a brighter future. **THE END.**

PSYCHOLOGICAL PROMPTS

18: Key soul learning: To develop biding your time, until everything is revealed in the light (Self-Regulation)

A peasant father sells his youngest daughter in her prime, sacrificing something of irreplaceable value for a fleeting benefit. It's perplexing how humans often view sentient life as a mere commodity, a stock, readily exchanging it for financial gain.

The truth is not always visible, and things are not always as they seem. Like the daughter archetype, we often go to great lengths and suffer trials to uncover the hidden truths necessary for sustaining the essential stability and momentum of our lives.

When approached by a man in an animal suit (a white bear), the peasant-father's primal instincts are evoked. All rationality is lost, and he trades his daughter for money.

Beneath the bear's outward appearance lies his hidden humanness, which emerges only under the cloak of darkness, driven by his fear of vulnerability and exposure.

Does his desire for the young maiden emanate from his lustful cravings (id-animal) and need for domestic help (ego-man)? Courtesy of the troll-witch, his enchantment keeps him, by day, under the control of his fantastical persona. But if he faces his internalised traits (positive and negative) and integrates them, his false personality will lose its potency, threatening to extinguish his potential for true love, creativity and fulfilment.

The bear motif, symbolising an awakening from hibernation, points to the potential resurrection of the original Self—his pure white fur representing ascension above the arcane. The candle-lit scenario reveals that the outline of the authentic Self can be traced by others, despite the masks we wear.

The inquisitive maiden implies that we must risk shining a light on the hidden, turning towards the truth and accepting its consequences. Though we might not always approve of what we uncover in the shadows, we have a fleeting chance to illuminate the unconscious. Only by the grace of a moonbeam on a dark forest path can we find our way.

Our heroine's bewitched prince is not free to be hers. Moreover, the troll holding him hostage resides in a hard-to-reach place, symbolising life's intricate complexities and our struggles when we choose the path of most resistance.

Bound by the dysfunctional patterns of our past, endlessly repeating and exerting control over our present existence, we bear a striking resemblance to the entrapped prince. As we give away our power to self-deceptions, our authentic qualities diminish. When overwhelmed by the unproductive emotions of guilt, blame, shame, and pain, we hide behind our persona while yearning for our escape, as the prince did. But when he vents, revealing his pain and suffering, his circumstances start to shift.

He shows we cannot hope to synchronise with our deepest passions and discover our true path if we hide behind a false and misunderstood self. Life promises a fulfilling journey, not a constant struggle against instability, worry, depression, anxiety, and uncertainty. Reflecting on their final moments, individuals often lament the time squandered on unfounded fears that never materialised or dwelling in gloomy sentimentalities. They express a longing to have prioritised true love, embracing life with more enthusiasm and vitality.

Shall we strive as the maiden did to avoid the same regrets?

Embarking on a moonshot quest, she sets out to fulfil her destined purpose in an elusive destination, requiring her patience and perseverance. The benevolent cosmos is her unseen companion, guiding her closely as she seeks wisdom from the matriarchs who have traversed this path before her. These formidable warrior women, wielding fiery wands, ventured into the darkness in search of their battle-weary men, successfully bringing them back home for healing. If she survives her Hero's Journey, she will recount to her loved ones the tale of her unconditional love for her partner, who left to go into the untamed wilderness to rediscover himself. And through the authenticity of their love, they found their way back to each other.

However, the anxious maiden does not rely solely on blind faith. She approaches her challenges pragmatically, employing a practical mindset to solve her problems.

She travels from one neighbour's region to the next, seeking her prince by asking direct questions, actively listening, and giving something away to regain her love. Her allies provide her with the horsepower of their inspiring wisdom to meet her quest. By exchanging three gifts, including the golden apple, representing Eve's temptation, she begins to undo the deal with the devil (trolls). Having willingly relinquished her worldly wealth, including the metaphorical golden carding-comb and spinning wheel that portray the teasing out of truth from the threads of hers and the prince's lives and interweaving their destinies, she finalises the deal—three times lucky.

Inverting her father's trade, she exchanges material possessions for love, defying the patriarch's sacrifice of his daughter for fleeting personal gain.

Initially, the lovers' clandestine castle rendezvous was fruitless. Yet every hero must accept that everything unfolds in its own time and learn to bide patiently. The waiting space resembles an empty cup, ready to be filled with our special dreams. For the maiden, that dream was love. There is a natural gestation period between the darkness and dawn, occurring before each revelation or outcome. During the longest hour, we listen with psychic wonderment for our destined call, as the cycle of time gradually reveals its mysteries. Yet, unregulated, our imaginations venture into the cavern of fear, unleashing mental inventions that take us on white-knuckle rides in every direction.

The princess's act of washing the prince's shirt cleansed the unconscious fears lingering from the troll's duplicitous deeds. And when the released prisoners reveal the secrets of the vault, his profound awakening dawns, illuminating the transformative power of true love and setting free his heart of gold. Like the prince, we, too, must learn to free ourselves from the ego's illusions to get to our true feelings. How can we effectively navigate through life with minds burdened by doubt, fears and the weight of procrastination?

Love, light, truth and goodness can overcome secrets, darkness and chaos. If we accept this reality, we will have the energy to keep going despite the challenges and confusion we experience.

Our fairy-tale heroes embody pragmatism, proactivity, and persistence. As they travel east of the sun and west of the moon, they assure us that good things come to truth-seekers and tellers awaiting deliverance. Together, in love and light, the maiden and prince work to outmanoeuvre the opposing forces of darkness.

The lovers escape the castle prison with a treasure trove, a material manifestation of their golden bond, and follow their purpose, principles and passion to overcome their problems together. Their formula applies to our lives whenever we become lost on our journey somewhere east of the sun and west of the moon.

Liberated, the **Pragmatists** return home from their peak experience, all the wiser for their epic journey holding a brimming chalice. An **Illusionist** might see the gold and silver as the real boon, but these heroes are more concerned with their love, light and truth and sharing how they found it.

By your patient endurance, you will gain your souls. (Luke 21:19)

SELF-REFLECTIONS

As you lay awake at night, memories of the past mingle with worries about the future. Breaking free from endless rumination proves daunting. Do those who claim to care truly have your best interests at heart, or are they driven by self-interest? Seeking clarity so intently only makes it elude you further, circling back into the darkness. Finding your way to your mythical dream place, nestled somewhere east or west in the realm of time, seems impossible.

In this tale, the symbol of 'horses' represents a passionate desire that propels one on their quest to freedom, and the ability to control unbridled animus, while the three golden gifts signify a spiritual awakening, a journey through the gates of consciousness. They evoke the imagery of the three wise men following a star to behold the Messiah, urging you to strive for a soulful life to experience fulfilment.

To access the gateway to your soul's truth, take time to reflect and ask yourself profound questions: What do you truly and deeply desire? Is there a purpose beyond your immediate needs? Can you trust the relationships you have? Are you and your loved ones creating something loving together to share with the world? Let intuition, dreams, story-telling, and instinct guide your choices and actions, surrendering to the course mapped out by your soul. But how will you discern the right path?

Prepare to explore your inner depths, confronting your doubts head-on. Determine whether something you hold dear is mere fantasy or genuine truth. Probe, paying attention to the responses, focusing on what may be missing or concealed. Show courage in the face of uncertainty, recognising obstacles are surmountable, one step at a time.

It's essential to speak your truth and align your thoughts, words, and actions with who you are, as others can only understand you when you maintain congruency. If you find the prospect daunting, return to the cave and continue the inner work.

With the passage of time, the mysteries of existence, such as feminine fertility cycles, menstruation, gestation, childbirth, mothering, nurturing, or giving effective counsel, will gradually reveal themselves. Consider the slumber we surrender to beneath the moon's shadow, awakening only as the sun begins to rise, to understand the way we are enlightened by revelations. Delve into your dark recesses, searching for the glimmers of gold hidden amidst the dross. By mining these treasures from your psyche, you can tap into your intuitive and creative energies, elevating your vibrations and vitality. This newfound inspiration will infuse your artistic pursuits, whether in writing, art, music, dance, drama or any other expressive endeavour, bringing you new levels of satisfaction and joy.

Draw upon these spiritually nourishing emotions during moments of doubt and fear, as their positive energy, combined with consistent practice, will align your dreams with the workings of the universe. However, if you waver between your ego and soul, anxiety, instability, depression, and misunderstandings may cloud your life. Internal conflict leads to further suffering.

Quality sleep becomes vital for personal rejuvenation. Your dreams hold subconscious elements, and reflecting on them can unveil hidden intrigues. When analysing dream meanings, it's crucial to perceive the feelings they evoke as they are, rather than how we desire them to be. Two archetypal figures, the pragmatic moon-inspired maiden and the impressionable and enigmatic Little Mermaid, embody different perspectives on reality. Both seek to unlock their beloved's heart, but while the latter anticipates a miracle without ever confessing her feelings, the former's pursuit is validated when the bear-prince openly reciprocates their desire to be together. The truth never comes to light for the unrealistic Little Mermaid, but it does for the moon-maiden. By comparing these tales' outcomes, we learn the importance of clarity, honesty, confidence and patience in love. But before risking everything, it is essential to openly communicate our feelings, have the hard discussions, and ensure that our dreams are realistic, and love is mutual.

The animal-groom cycle serves as a reminder that love transcends external appearances, embracing the inner essence and true nature of individuals.

The mythic tale's golden augury promises the integration of our being. The apple symbolises wellbeing and success, while the carding-comb and spinning wheel represent the intricate weaving of our delicate strands, binding us together.

Ours is a journey of experiential learning (Kolb, 1984), forever evolving. It challenges our well-oiled perspective with diverse assumptions, beliefs, and opinions from others, urging us to review and expand our understanding.

Fears oppose love and demand our attention. If we succumb to them by resisting truth and healing, we risk entering co-dependent and unfulfilling partnerships in love, work, friendship, and other aspects of life. The subsequent brooding can lead to a sense of imprisonment, loneliness, and attracting others who also fear intimacy. Beware the calm before the storm, warns Jung. When it arrives, stay grounded and seek wise counsel to help regulate your thoughts and emotions.

Like the pragmatic heroes in the tale, patience and common sense are valuable resources for making necessary choices and practical changes in your relationships. If both parties openly love and share, without hidden agendas, your paths may converge once again. However, if one party leads a dishonest or double life, or if you persist in self-defeating behaviours, the divide will persist. You have the choice to embark on a fact-finding mission for the truth or ignore the tell-tale signs.

Romanticising the past, idealising it beyond reality, can erode the present's positive potential. Similarly, the other archetype, the mermaid, warns that fixating on a fantasised future distracts from the present moment, leading to missteps. It's better to take care of today, allowing tomorrow to take care of itself.

In our journey, we possess two selves: the present self and the one we are becoming. Like the fairy-tale's heroine, guided by moonlit hope through uncharted terrain, we must persevere. The Holy Grail awaits at our True North, where the Sun and the Moon merge, uniting the ego and soul. As a famous fairy-tale king once said, "Begin at the beginning and go on till you come to an end: then stop."

What we ardently seek will only reveal itself when we are ready to see it. Embracing this paradox helps us endure the wait with acceptance.

When the moment of truth arrives, you will find illumination, retrieve the treasure, and feel content with all you have experienced and accomplished. When the universe beckons, reach for the moon.

LIGHT QUALITIES (PRAGMATIST)	SHADOW ATTRIBUTES (ILLUSIONIST)
Pragmatic	Illusionary
Illuminative	Misunderstood
Persevering	Depressed
Inquisitive	Anxious
Listening	Confused
Imaginative	Self-deceiving
Venting	Worried
Biding	Doubtful

PROVERB: We all have two sides like the moon: our dark side hides our secrets.

AFFIRMATION: I will believe it when I see it.

GAME OF LIFE: Seeing only what you wish to see (Consequence: Losing faith in the vast unseen ahead).

REFLECTION QUESTION: What do my dreams and visions tell me, and how can I integrate their meaning into my daily existence?

ANIMAL SYMBOLISM:

Diprotodon

The **Diprotodon**, an extinct Australian megafauna from around 50,000 years ago, was the largest marsupial ever to walk the earth. It shares similarities with smaller cousins like the wombat and koala bear 'Diprotodon' means 'two front teeth', representing our determination to get stuck into solving life's mysteries. Our heroine in *East of the Sun, West of the Moon* rides a giant Diprotodon with long, sharp claws (like polar bears) for digging deep to get to the bottom of concerns. His eyes are small, but his keen senses, patience and resilience ensure accomplishment.

ONE SMALL STEP TO TAKE TODAY: I practise waiting calmly in the gestating stillness until the universe decides to reveal the full story.

MEDITATION PREPARATION (to practise in the moonlight)

I breathe in golden light vibrations, and as I exhale, I let go of my negative thoughts and feelings. I envision myself going about my day with a smile on my face and bliss in my heart. No longer spellbound by faulty beliefs, I sigh deeply, letting go, trusting the Great Unknown's secret plans for me. In tune with the slow beat of my patient heart, my intuitive powers glow, casting shiny auguries under the moon's silvery beams. Doubt's grey clouds disappear as the blessing of crystal clarity reveals my gifts.

As far as the east is from the west, so far has he removed
our transgressions from us.
(Psalm 103:12)

19 GOLDILOCKS AND THE THREE BEARS

Goldilocks and the three bears (ROBERT SOUTHEY, 1837)—*The following is a personal retelling of the tale:*

SYNOPSIS OF FAIRY TALE

Once upon a time, there lived a young girl with flowing, golden hair, aptly named Goldilocks—a name that matched her radiant appearance. Always curious and with a heart yearning for adventure, Goldilocks set out one day to go into the deep enchanted woods.

Before long, she stumbled upon a rustic cottage amidst the towering trees and marched straight inside, finding nobody at home. She saw a table set with three bowls of fresh porridge with an enticing aroma. Hungrily she took a mouthful out of the first bowl, but realising it was far too salty, she put it down with a jolt. She tasted the second bowl but, complaining it was too sweet, put it quickly aside. Finally, the last bowl of porridge was just right, so she ate every spoonful.

Feeling full and sleepy, she went to the cozy living room and reclined in a massive chair. It was much too hard for her delicate frame, so she tried the second chair, which was far too soft to support her. Finally, she sat on a small wooden chair, shattering it to pieces.

Unfazed, she wearily climbed the stairs to find a place to rest. She spotted three beds to try out. The first was much too hard; the second was too soft, but the miniature bed cradled Goldilocks' body perfectly, so she fell straight into a deep slumber.

While she was sleeping dreamily, the homeowners, a family of bears, returned. They saw at once that someone had snuck into their home and messed things up. Papa Bear growled, "Who has been eating my porridge?"

Then Mama Bear spoke next, demanding, "Who has been eating MY porridge?"

Finally, all eyes turned to Baby Bear, who was so upset he could barely get the words out: "And someone has been eating my porridge, and they ate it all up!"

Next, the family shuffled into the living room, where Papa Bear discovered someone had been sitting in his favourite chair; then, Mama Bear found the same. When they all looked at Baby Bear's chair, the alarmed little creature cried out, "And someone's been sitting on my chair, and they have broken it all up."

The grumbling bears ascended the stairs in haste. Papa Bear and Mama Bear were dismayed to see their rumpled bedding, but as for Baby Bear, he could not believe his eyes. He pointed and squealed excitedly, "Someone has been sleeping in my bed, and THERE she is!"

Goldilocks, overhearing the frightful fracas, shot straight up to see the three bears towering over her. They did not look happy. She hollered, taking off as fast as a fleeting fox, jumping out the window and heading back into the wild woods whence she came. The golden-haired girl was never seen again in local parts, much to the relief of the bears, but her mystery lingered on. **THE END.**

PSYCHOLOGICAL PROMPTS

19: Key soul learning: To develop faith in everything working out for the best in the end (Social Skills)

The prepubescent Goldilocks embarks on a journey to explore the vast wonders and dangers of the world, alluding to the marvellous but fleeting nature of conscious existence. The young only grow a set of wary eyes through their experience. Goldilocks seeks opportunities independently, defying adult authority and displaying a detachment reminiscent of the Oedipal complex. Unaware of the internalised voice of conscience, she disregards the consequences of her morally reprehensible behaviour, driven solely by her childlike wonder and the intense desire to find a new place to belong and nest.

The recurring motif of the 'rule of threes' in fairy tales is significant. Philosophers such as Pythagoras, Hegel and Jung attach importance to the number three, linking it to the three critical stages of life: childhood, puberty, and adulthood. Myths and fairy tales feature three-headed monsters, trios like the Gorgons, Fates and Graces, and three wishes, pigs, goats, horses and bears. Many believe that events occur in groups of three. The three bears symbolise the modern nuclear family, living within their means and adopting an eco-friendly approach to planetary life. Their timeless message evokes the trine of past, present, and future existing all at once in the ethereal.

Goldilocks embodies the ungrateful perfectionist who sees the world as an endless source of abundance, thinking everything should cater to her preferences. She epitomises the daring pursuit of personal desires, disregarding the impact on others. This self-centredness may be seen as narcissistic or even sociopathic, especially when patterns of disordered behaviour emerge. Goldilocks views the world as her oyster. However, even if she acquires what she desires, it falls short of her lofty standards. With such pernickety tastes, she is a 'glass half empty' archetype, yet to mature.

Despite her unintentional harm, Goldilocks trespasses and covets her neighbours' property, causing distress. Like feudal lords demanding the best produce from serfs, she takes without consequence, potentially depleting resources that sustain others. Even young children perceive the ethical violation in her actions, realising that the rules they are learning do not apply to her. Yet, the bears, in a remarkable display of 'human' understanding, acknowledge Goldilocks's youthful mistakes, recognising that everything Baby Bear possesses is 'just-right' for her. Through his overly emotional reaction, they are reminded that Goldilocks is still a vulnerable child herself. The bears, integral components of nature's matrix, refrain from retaliating, knowing better than to engage in a battle with humans (they might carry firearms).

The tale divides its audience regarding the consequences Goldilocks should face. Some children wish for moral justice, others feel relieved she escapes unscathed, and some remain ambivalent. Juvenile offenders often evade punishment and continue their lives as if nothing happened. While we desire legal retribution, we hesitate to impose severe penalties or label them criminals. Such stigmas may lead them to associate with seasoned lawbreakers, promoting repeated offences and hindering their potential for a better future which reflects on our whole society.

What prompts a well-groomed and seemingly well-cared-for young lady to behave brazenly, selfishly, and dangerously? Her intrusive actions do not seek attention or overt power over the bears but imply a sense of superiority and privilege. Some children misbehave because they feel inadequate, leading to negative and disrespectful behaviours that control their environments with chaos. They believe no one cares, which causes them to give up on themselves. These children require social support.

Goldilocks' character flaws, typical of adolescence, remind us to exercise rational control over our animal appetites as conscious beings. We have biological needs like food, shelter, and sleep, but our sense of belonging and being loved is equally essential. Ironically, fussy Goldilocks suggests we can delay gratification if something does not meet our approval or beliefs. Our pursuit of what we desire may require patience and experimentation. Serendipity, aligned timing with the universe, may also be necessary for our achievements to reach their zenith. True satisfaction and happiness lie not in material success but in honouring our integral part of the natural world.

Goldilocks exemplifies how humans run rough-shod over nature's kingdom. She jeopardises their survival by taking the youngest animal's food and resting places. Her over-indulgence in the porridge, representing to nourish and nurture, points to her lack of empathy. She acts as if she has complete control, answerable to no one. While humans often perceive themselves as caring custodians of the blue planet, our increasing population, overconsumption, and misuse of resources are unsustainable. The 'Goldilocks Zone' represents the ideal conditions for human life in our galaxy, but our greed and waste threaten its existence.

When author Southey revived the *Goldilocks* tale, only 1.6 billion people were on Earth. Today, our population has multiplied five-fold in the same space. As we spin under the sun and stars, as old as Genesis, at 1,000 miles per hour, we must consider the challenge of providing sufficient homes and sustenance. With its insatiable appetite and wilful power (like the Goldilocks archetype), will human life disappear one day as mysteriously as it came into being?

Tricky Goldilocks committed the forbidden by venturing alone into the wilderness to steal food and shelter. We must explore, take risks, and experiment to grow. However, Goldilocks failed to abide by the Golden Rule and neglected the wellbeing of others. The dark trilogy of narcissistic, psychopathic, and Machiavellian behaviours manifests in this seemingly golden and innocent child archetype, representing a spiritually unevolved humanity operating from the shadows. We cannot hide behind the excuse of youth's ignorance forever; we must consider the impact of our values, words, and actions on all living beings in our earthly arena. Goldilocks serves as a metaphor for individuation, the process of integrating conscious and unconscious aspects of our psyche to become Whole and fulfilled.

Her perfect 'blonde' appearance signifies a falsely assumed white superiority *irrelevant* to the struggle for survival occurring every moment on Earth. Can we not follow the example of other species and take only what we need? Instead of destroying it, can we nurture nature and live more sustainably, as advocated by Swedish teenager Greta Thunberg and millions sharing her sentiment worldwide? We unconsciously believe that Mother Nature is unaware of our human actions, good or bad—however, the image of the three bears cornering an intruder in their humanised habitat challenges this concept. Goldilocks flees in terror, getting a second chance to integrate her repressed shadow elements and become her Higher Self. Her encounter with the wild awakens her to a new reality beyond her self-centeredness. To truly belong, she must balance her ego with the laws of nature, society, and the perspectives of other beings. Her archetype teaches us that while we observe the natural world, it indeed observes us back.

Goldilocks is an idealistic, enthusiastic and free-spirited young girl who can be forgiven this once for her bold, entitled, and self-indulgent ways. Without these traits, she may never have the drive to venture beyond the familiar hearth and learn from her mistakes. This is how we grow and mature. Around puberty, the call to adventure beckons all of us, and we embark on our Hero's Journey, facing tests of survival.

Goldilocks, despite her precocious nature and foolish vanities, exhibits an inherent brightness that radiates through her playful demeanour and holds the promise of a joyful and successful life. Still unready to cross the pubertal divide, she is led by her instincts (id), risking life and limb without conscience (superego). The bears, a timeless and universal symbol of physical strength, wisdom, and power, observe her, hoping she will find where she belongs. When Goldilocks left them alone, the bears sighed with relief, for paradise lost was now regained. She is a metaphor for that pivotal and transformative moment when the child must become an adult, embracing responsibility, empathy, and the understanding that we are all interconnected in the great tapestry of life.

Post-travails, we envision Goldilocks realising that even with God-granted dominion, there are limits humans must observe. Grateful for her survival, she learns to value and **Nurture** all life, taking only her fair share. Embracing her true Self and the responsibility of a global citizen, she uncovers her soul essence and discovers her promised land. No longer seeking perfection, she understands that with faith and balanced progress, everything works out in the end. Having relinquished her **Narcissistic** tendencies, she becomes well-adjusted in social settings, illuminating rooms with her smile, vitality, love, and happiness.

SELF-REFLECTIONS

You recently stumbled, displaying poor judgment akin to the impetuous Goldilocks. However, your newfound enlightenment allows you to apply the lessons learned to your latest venture, instilling a sense of agency and optimism for the future. As a conscious being, you have expanded your awareness, tested the limits of your capabilities, and reflected, understanding better your place in the world.

You must conquer the fear of missing out (FOMO), the alluring materialistic illusion that plagues contemporary life. To avoid enduring psychic pain, you must reestablish your equilibrium, balancing your inner spiritual life with material aspirations. You are enough and have enough. With the guidance of a Higher Power, you possess the ability to navigate any challenge, transforming it into a catalyst for personal growth, creating harmonious and happy environments, and manifesting your dreams. You use your creativity to shine as someone special.

But can one be self-interested, starring in competitive environments, but humble, caring deeply for others and doing one's best to make the world a better place? The answer lies in harmonising your instincts, ego, and moral code to attain a state of Higher Living. It is through this alignment that you discover inner calm, transcending the attraction to superficial appearances and materialistic pursuits. The family of three bears set an example of living the good life with just the bare necessities, love, health and contentment.

Your raison d'être, more recently, revolves around both receiving and giving love in equal measure, unlocking new doors of opportunity and connection. Despite the dark days, you have forged ahead with unwavering faith, optimism and resolute determination. Your actions consistently emanate gratitude, as you share your blessings and empathise with others.

Reflecting on your progress, you recognise the importance of self-reward and self-care, diligently avoiding the pitfalls of over-indulgence. Your inspirational nature draws the admiration of those around you, serving as a shining example of what can be achieved through self-belief, hard work and perseverance.

Serendipity strikes, bringing a higher-frequency lover, resonating with your newfound energy and purpose. While golden times may not last indefinitely, the potential for enduring love remains within reach. As you navigate relationships, it becomes crucial to evaluate values and practical considerations, while respecting personal boundaries and avoiding undue intrusion into your personal space. Goldilocks entered a den of opposites and left knowing what her belonging place was not. Mindfully managing expectations, aligning with those who share the same relationship values, keeping lines of communication open and trusting, and nurturing intimacy dynamics are paramount, as is focusing on what truly matters in the external reality.

In your ongoing journey, obstacles will always arise, triggering occasional disappointment and testing stability. However, you possess the power to condition your thoughts with faith, effectively shifting your perspective to a positive outlook and seeing the dawn arise from the darkness. With passion, resilience and a can-do approach, things have a way of working out in the end.

Cultivating tolerance and curbing 'me-first' tendencies are essential aspects of personal growth. By fostering a loving and compassionate vibration within your relationship and reinforcing this philosophy for living in your story-telling, you create a space where both you and your partner can thrive and develop a golden bond.

With sincere efforts and intentions aligned, your spirit acts as a guiding force, keeping your ego in check and allowing you to navigate life's twists and turns with grace and wisdom. The path to fulfilment lies not in the relentless pursuit of external perfection (which leads to depression) but in embracing the Divinely orchestrated plan for your life. Its grace is revealed in the seeds of your dreams, progressive steps and unshakeable belief that your cherished goals will actualise. The best can and will happen in the end. By remaining positive, you open yourself up to remarkable opportunities and experiences, setting you on the hero's course for a stunning home run.

LIGHT QUALITIES (NURTURER)	**SHADOW ATTRIBUTES (NARCISSIST)**
Nurturing	Narcissistic
Idealistic	Insatiable
Enthusiastic	Intense
Happy	Brazen
Just-right	Self-entitled
Vital	Disrespectful
Successful	Vain
Bright	Intrusive

PROVERB: It is always darkest before the dawn.

AFFIRMATION: I light up a room with my love and happiness.

GAME OF LIFE: Thinking you are the centre of the universe (Consequence: Deflecting the loving admiration that would have otherwise come your way).

REFLECTION QUESTION: Can I see the glass half full rather than half empty?

ANIMAL SYMBOLISM: Golden orb spider; Bears; Sparrow

Golden orb spider

The sighting of a Golden Orb spider alerts us to our being conscious of the impression we make on others. We put a lot of energy into our self-image, ensuring we appear attractive on the social stage. This powerful symbol cautions us not to take ourselves as seriously as we do lest our vanity ensnares us.

Bears

The **bear** symbolises power, protection, strength, and freedom. If a bear is aggressive, it may indicate a downturn in one's fortunes, but if it is friendly, it suggests that better opportunities are on their way.

Sparrow

The sparrow is a symbol of the simple joys in life and working well with loved ones to achieve great things. Its presence encourages faith in the Divine, self-worth, high ideals, and nurturing dreams until they manifest.

ONE SMALL STEP TO TAKE TODAY: I will practise seeing the positives in new opportunities, going after my goals with Whole-hearted passion.

MEDITATION PREPARATION (to practise at noon)

I breathe in golden light vibrations, and as I exhale, I let go of my negative thoughts and feelings. I envision myself going about my day with a smile on my face and bliss in my heart.

I feel solace from worldly concerns in the warm presence of the sun and its shining promise of new experiences, assuring me things will work out for the best in the end. A cellular shift stirs deep within as I slowly open my eyes to all the blessings bestowed upon me. The vibrant rays of Universal Power fill me with gratitude, love, and light. The whole picture of my existence unfolds, leaving me wonderstruck by its triumphant splendour.

Find your sweet spot and cherish it.
(Daniel Coyle)

20 THE THREE LITTLE PIGS

The Three Little Pigs (JOSEPH JACOBS/ JAMES ORCHARD HALLIWELL-PHILLIPPS, 1890)—*The following is a personal retelling of the tale.*

SYNOPSIS OF FAIRY TALE

A wise mother pig sent her three adolescent children out into the world to fend for themselves and make their fortunes.

All three brothers decided to build their homes in the same section of the woods, but each used the different materials available nearest to their plot of land. The youngest brother wanted to be the first to finish, so he chose straw. The middle brother selected sticks in high supply in the nearby forest. But the biggest boy built his house from mud bricks for better protection from the harsh winter elements that came around soon enough, year after year.

Just as each little pig had finally settled in, a scary neighbour came looking for them.

A hungry wolf was on the prowl. Before long, he knocked on the door of the house of straw and shouted: "Little pig, little pig, let me in!"

But the terrified little pig called back, "Not by the hair on my chinny chin chin."

"Then I'll huff and puff and blow your house in," came the big bad wolf's retort.

Somehow, the youngest brother managed to make his escape to the middle brother's house of sticks. No sooner had he blurted out his frightening ordeal than the hungry wolf came knocking and shouting, "Little pig, little pig, let me in!"

But the petrified middle pig called back, "Not by the hair on my chinny-chin-chin."

"Then I'll huff and puff and blow your house in," the wolf replied menacingly.

The two brothers dashed out the back door, heading as fast as their little trotters could take them to their big brother. But lo and behold, within minutes of telling their terrifying tale, the big, bad wolf came knocking and shouting again: "Little pig, little pig, let me in!"

But the big brother pig called back, "Not by the hair on my chinny-chin-chin."

"Then I'll huff and puff and blow your house in," warned the ravenous wolf fiercely.

The third little pig calmed his younger brothers, reassuring them the wolf could blow as hard as he liked, but he would never blow down his house because it was made of solid brick. And he was right. Brawn did not work, so the wolf used a different strategy to outwit the pigs and make a meal of them.

The brothers tried to stay calm, sitting by the blazing fire to keep warm the whole time. Suddenly, they heard a shocking scratching and howling sound inside the chimney. In one piercing screech, it was the rangy wolf who came tearing down into the pigs' huge cooking pot below. Thinking quickly, the biggest pig slammed the lid on the pot tight and cooked the wolf for their supper.

All three little pigs were safe and sound at last (at least until the next hungry wolf was on the prowl in the neighbourhood). **THE END.**

PSYCHOLOGICAL PROMPTS

20: Key soul learning: To develop honing judgment skills to make the right decisions (Self-Awareness)

Most of us with siblings can see our birth order reflected in the behaviours of the three pig siblings. If we have older siblings who take on most of the responsibilities, we may identify more with the carefree younger brothers. They seem too eager for leisure and instant gratification of their animal appetites (id)—life is purely for pleasure, not pain. On the other hand, the elder brother is a self-aware pragmatist, subscribing to the 'reality principle'. He takes his responsibilities seriously, controlling his indulgent egoic and animal appetites and adapts effectively to the demands of the external world. However, we must strike a balance between these two archetypes of hedonistic pleasure and personal responsibility to live a fulfilling, satisfying life. Put succinctly, our journey entails reclaiming and integrating the irresponsible child archetype within our shadow, harmonising it with the wise and caregiving hero self.

Some of us never grow up choosing the easy way out (and making trouble), regardless of the consequences. Nietzsche (1844-1900) promoted living dangerously and pursuing our goals irrespective of repercussions. But won't our inattention prevent us from reaching the higher levels of success achieved through focus, hard work, patience, and perseverance? Nietzsche might advocate for taking risks, but he also emphasises the importance of fulfilling our responsibilities to develop into our authentic 'uber' selves. How can we balance taking charge and putting in sincere effort with our tasks and objectives while finding satisfaction, if not enjoyment?

The life test comes when we delegate the necessary onerous tasks to someone else. As Einstein observed, many people miss opportunities because they come dressed as hard work. Fearing the hard times, we procrastinate and fail to get started or maintain momentum. Integrating into an efficacious self requires utilising our hard-won experience to solve problems. However, the irresponsible younger pigs, unready to settle down, cannot be bothered. Their minimal effort for maximum gain approach only creates more trouble for them and unintended implications for others. The wise pig puts in the maximal effort today for the promise of minimal pain tomorrow, securing his present to take care of the future.

The contrasting archetypes reflect the inequitable situations in social structures, where some exploit the hard work of others. However, the striving for the collective's welfare proves more potent. Family values are tested when young slackers fail to secure themselves once they leave the nest. They swiftly discover that decisions made in haste breed repentance at leisure, compelling them to develop the capacity to discern wise judgments that establish solid foundations.

Regardless of age, some remain impulsive or are pig-headed with their opinions, while others choose a more measured and deliberative approach. Sometimes, speed pays off, other times, slow and steady wins the race. The younger pigs appear self-centric and rash, while the elder brother (with a conscience for doing the right thing) controls his id urges, working things through to arrive at the right solutions. Achieving the best outcomes requires putting all our operant psychic parts to work. Big-Pig, astute and unwavering in integrity, epitomises a tribe-centric ethos, distributing the rewards that stem from his diligent efforts and selfless sacrifices. By expecting the best but meticulously preparing for the worst, he has kept wild wolves at bay in the past. His modus operandi (M.O.) has a predictive quality that forearms him. He acts dutifully, upholding the right to shelter, survival and care. Having mastered his internal Self, he can defeat an external predator. As a reward for his altruistic contributions, he is his own man, living a purposeful and fulfilling life. This fellow does not wait under the oak expecting acorns to drop; he forages and feasts on truffles instead.

The primal, undomesticated wolf, a shadow and trickster archetype, symbolises our survival threats and fears. Confronting our fears and putting them into perspective with an aware and calm mind is achievable with a balanced psyche. There is a greater sense of emotional freedom and joy when we moderate ou id urges and observe our limits. Our superego guides us to do the right thing. Harmonising the ego, id, and superego is essential to mastering ourselves and our destiny. Big-Pig maintains composure in challenging situations, carefully assessing and managing risks with practicality, devoid of histrionics or hyper-vigilance.

Big-Pig's self-contained actions embody diplomacy and forgiveness. He leads by example, avoiding rebuke, blame, or deeming his brothers unworthy. He refrains from making them feel ashamed or lecturing them, knowing it would be like casting pearls before swine. In contrast, the wolf symbolises the dire consequences that arise from relentlessly seeking the destruction of others and their habitats. The wolf's pursuit of the pigs stems from survival and hunger, but his cruel taunts reveal a human-like predator with a bloodlust, reflecting the darkest facets of human nature that derive sporting pleasure from the hunt and kill.

The little pigs metaphorically represent our inner child, acting in curious, carefree and emotionally open ways that can lead us to do the stupid or forbidden, and our premature decline. But Big-Pig, the wise, caregiving hero, is more aware, thinks cautiously and plans to prevent susceptibility to harm. Life tests urge us to face reality and make difficult choices for our ongoing survival, security and belonging place. Once bitten is twice shy.

Justice prevails in the tale, with the ignorant achieving protection under the wise.

Prey can sometimes outmanoeuvre their predator, indicating that our creative solutions can overcome what initially seems impossible. By being well-prepared and seeing the world as it exists without falling prey to its darkest realities, our life will dominate death for a time longer—but this stance may take multiple attempts to overcome. Wisdom is a process that requires honing our judgment skills.

To mature from the unsettled, pleasure-principled days of youth into a reality-based existence, we must build our house brick by brick through experiences and lessons. We evolve through our Hero's Journeys entailing quests such as graduating, moving out of home, establishing new relationships, and coping with illness, troubles, disputes and hardships. Sharpening our self-awareness and reflecting on our experiences help us develop better strategies for the future. Life, ever our guiding teacher, enriches our soul through its tests.

Big-Pig, akin to Hercules, exemplifies the rewards of foresight, arduous labour, and endurance. His actions bring satisfaction while inspiring altruism on the Hero's Journey. With an understanding of his younger brothers' vulnerability and their inadvertent capacity for trouble-making, the Third pig reinstates stability, driven by his duty towards the common good. Swami Vivekananda (1863-1902) reminds us it is only by doing good to others that life's golden rewards are attainable for oneself. Similarly, Orwell's (1945) *Animal Farm* warns against prioritising a glut of power and pleasure over wisdom, ethics, and charity.

Finally, in the fairy-tale trope, we see again the charm of the magical number three. In Jungian terms, it symbolises the three stages of our human lifespan and the resolution of opposites and integration of conflicting elements into the harmonious Whole Self. Yet, the symbol also signals a promissory note from the universe, obligating us to be fair (i.e., *non-biased* and judgmental) when **Problem-solving** to settle the unresolved or redeem the unsalvageable in the chaos wrought by life's **Trouble-Makers.**

As The Three Little Pigs came to understand, everyone benefits when the one with the privilege of power does good for the less fortunate and those in need allow their help.

SELF-REFLECTIONS

Have you experienced a life-altering event recently? How well did you handle it? When faced with significant decisions, do you adopt a precautionary approach like the Third pig? Are your achievements a result of your ingenuity, luck, hard work, or a combination of these factors? Conversely, do you blame your broken dreams on unfair circumstances, the ineptitude of others, or the consequences of careless choices?

Reflect on the jigsaw pieces of your past and present life. Do you see patterns that your brain strives to complete? Through perspective-taking, you make sense of your reality and put the pieces into place. Begin to recognise how the challenging tests you faced have shaped you, reconstituting your core values and reinforcing your foundations. Reflect these understandings in your story-telling and the story reframes you write to propel your momentum. You become an individual of substance, akin to a house built with bricks.

As in the age-old tale of *The Three Little Pigs*, our ancestors used straw, sticks, and clay to construct different types of houses. Can you recognise the parts of yourself forged through the fires of life's threats and adversities? Have you transformed your emotional scars into strengths to positively impact the world? It is essential to acknowledge your weaknesses of character as well. Each schema influencing your life holds opportunities for redemption and growth. Rather than dwelling on your mistakes, own them, learn from them, and awaken your full potential on your Hero's Journey. But, before reaching this state of acceptance, it is natural to encounter frustration while managing new struggles. The hard-won lessons have taught you (and the younger pigs) that avoiding life's complexities merely bypasses the hidden opportunities they hold.

Accept the things you cannot change while rejecting the negative and embracing the positive elements within your control. Just like the Third pig, understand that the most satisfaction comes from the genuine connections forged with the people you care about deeply. Navigate the ups and downs of relationships, embracing both the bad and the good.

Family life is an integral part of this discussion. You are born into families and form bonds with others who may not always share your values, opinions, or personal codes for a higher way of living. As time passes, differences become apparent, often leading to divergent recollections and interpretations of shared events. Learn to coexist with opposing perspectives, discerning whether differences are tolerable, forgivable, or irreconcilable. The choice to stay or leave is paramount.

These differences can generate sceptical and disapproving energy between loved ones, sometimes escalating to mud-slinging and acrimonious break-ups—even arbitration and court judgments. When you believe you are perpetually hard-done-by, 'trying to keep the wolf from the door', you may view any differing viewpoint as a threat to your identity, sparking more conflict. If you have a low tolerance for opposing ideas, you often become defensive, huffing and puffing to protect your beliefs. Paradoxically, this overreaction stems from a sense of unworthiness, demanding validation through battle.

It is not surprising that communication falters when the unconscious holds fixed beliefs about being an 'underdog'. The feeling of shame, closely entwined with inferiority, further underscores the necessity for self-forgiveness, psychic healing, and integration. In this context, the younger pigs symbolise distinct elements—straw and sticks—which, when combined with clay and diligent effort, harmoniously integrate to manifest the triadic power embodied by the Third pig.

The pursuit of holistic integration in our inner life is further challenged by the wrenching burden of financial debt as we strive to achieve our dreams in the outer reality. Getting stuck in a rut, chained to the wheel of forging fortunes for our families, is a common trap. Often, we take today's small pleasures and our inner experiences for granted. It is crucial for you to assess the potential long-term consequences of excessive working hours, social isolation, poor health, relationship problems, persistent worry, or depression. These factors can have compounded effects that even imbibing in magnums of Foch champagne cannot cure.

On the other hand, if you only live for present happiness and indulge in the wrong things, your future may lack quality. But sacrificing too much pleasure now can lead to burnout and bitterness later, preventing you from fully appreciating the fruits of your hard labour. Reflective analysis may lead you to adopt the Third pig's code: to balance present wellbeing with future considerations. Self-awareness is key in answering important questions about your journey. Who are you, where and how are you going, and where are you heading next?

The Three Little Pigs highlights the diversity that can exist within the same family. These differing mindsets can create resentments and frustrations. However, attempting to force someone to change or adopt your way of thinking is futile. Encouraging respect and creativity in each other is essential for sustaining a partnership. When criticism and defensiveness overshadow affection and admiration, contempt seeps into the relationship. The elder pig in the tale did not judge his younger siblings' choices but worked together with them to solve their shared problem.

None of us can claim to know everything. Our dreams require collaboration and support from others. Recognising that we are all in this together, doing our best with what we have, allows us to judge less and appreciate different positions. Instead of separating from loved ones, consider rekindling mutual appreciation. By openly sharing your perspectives and attempting to understand each other, you can find common ground.

Put the past behind you, focus on one's redeeming qualities, and determine how to achieve mutually satisfying outcomes in the future. This is key to healing rifts, your reconciliations, and living a happier and healthier life.

Abandon delusions of easy rewards and embrace your reality-checker. Take responsibility for your choices and behaviours, both positive and negative. Rebuild yourself, brick by brick, adapting to whatever life throws your way. Good luck aside, it takes time for your efforts to bear fruit.

When you acknowledge life as a tough taskmaster, you will resign yourself to the job ahead and never give up. This is the route to becoming one's better version. Such heroes brim with optimism and see beyond the outmoded deceptions of the past, making a fantastic future finish possible.

You have made up your mind, once and for all.

Approach the path ahead with discernment, carefully weighing your choices, and treasure the ongoing journey as it unfolds before you.

LIGHT QUALITIES (PROBLEM-SOLVER)	SHADOW ATTRIBUTES (TROUBLE-MAKER)
Solution-focused	Trouble-making
Discerning	Judgmental
Deliberative	Hyper-vigilant
Diplomatic	Unforgiving
Self-contained	Unsettled
Settled	Unworthy
Meticulous	Irresponsible
Redeemed	Ashamed

PROVERB: Do not cast your pearls before swine (Matthew 7:6).

AFFIRMATION: If I take care of today, tomorrow will take care of itself.

GAME OF LIFE: Taking the easy way out (Consequence: Having to repeat lessons).

REFLECTION QUESTION: Can I settle this once and for all by forgiving past mistakes and making matters right?

ANIMAL SYMBOLISM: Pigs; Dingo; Bees; Ants

Pigs

The porcine promise is one of prosperity and plenitude if we are prepared to dig for rewards or retrieve the pearls of wisdom of our suffering. On the other hand, pigs negatively refer to our tendency for laziness, overindulgence, and the undervaluing of intelligence.

Dingo

The dingo is a wild dog native to Australia, originating from the Asian grey wolf (Canis lupus lupus). It symbolises teamwork and leadership. Dingoes are a reserved species, signalling that we should refrain from unsubstantiated opinions and employ well-tested strategies to solve problems.

Bees

The bee society is well-structured with bees symbolising teamwork, meticulous effort, and loyalty to a leader. They are self-reliant creatures and represent the importance of hard work before reaping a sweet harvest.

Ants

Ants, like bees, have structured societies, teaching us to organise resources, prioritise collective needs, and work diligently for prosperity. They inspire personal growth, strategic planning, and hard work for the future we desire.

ONE SMALL STEP TO TAKE TODAY: I practise being realistic when sizing up situations so that I discern my best choices.

MEDITATION PREPARATION (to practise when facing important decisions)

I breathe in golden light vibrations, and as I exhale, I let go of my negative thoughts and feelings. I envision myself going about my day with a smile on my face and bliss in my heart.

I see how indulgent I have been, prioritising my desires over the needs of the greater good and taking the easy way out. I ask the Great Spirit to help me to forgive myself, so I may finally settle past wrongs and make them right in my soul.

I release a deep sigh as my feelings of unworthiness dissolve, and a warmness in my consciousness opens to all things being made loving and brand new, light and right, stable and secure.

Once you make a decision the universe conspires to make it happen.
(Ralph Waldo Emerson)

21 VASILISA: THE BRAVE, BEAUTIFUL AND WISE

Vasilisa the Beautiful (collected by Russian folklorist Alexander Afanasyev)—*The following is a personal retelling of the tale:*

SYNOPSIS OF FAIRY TALE

Once, a long time ago in a Slavic place bordering the Baltics, so the storytellers say, there was, and then there was not, a travelling merchant who lived in exotic parts with his wife and only child they named Vasilisa. Sadly, the beautiful little girl's mother died eight years later. On her death-bed, she gave Vasilisa a small wooden doll with magical powers, sustainable with a bit of daily sustenance. If Vasilisa looked after the doll, it would take care of her. Vasilisa tucked the supernatural doll out of sight in the pocket of her skirt so that it could accompany her everywhere she went.

Later, when her father grew lonely, he took on a new wife who came with two daughters. Vasilisa tried to make friends with her new stepsisters, but they had other ideas. They demanded Vasilisa do the heaviest outdoor chores where her beauty was bound to fade in the harsh elements. Luckily for Vasilisa, her tiny doll performed magic to help her quickly complete the endless string of tiring tasks. Her doll was also her wise confidante and a kind and reassuring friend in times of despair.

Years later, when Vasilisa had bloomed into a wholesome and beautiful maiden, many bold and handsome suitors came to the house to woo her. Secretly, the cruel stepmother shooed them away but not before asking them to consider courting her mean girls instead. Unsurprisingly, no decent man seemed to want to take on her spiteful daughters as their wives.

Vasilisa's merchant-father was too often away, unaware of the skulduggery back home. One day, behind his back and without warning, his wife sold the family home. She took all three young girls with her to live in a dark and secret region of the woods dominated by the infamous and turpitudinous ogress, Baba Yaga. The blood-thirsty witch was renowned in these parts for killing and eating villagers: children mostly.

Clearly, the stepmother had evil on her mind. As soon as the sun rose each morning, she sent Vasilisa deeper into the more dangerous parts of the woods, but without missing a beat, the maiden returned every evening with her beloved pocketed doll close at hand.

Having grown so angry and frustrated, Vasilisa's stepmother hatched a new plan that no one, not even Vasilisa, could survive. Suddenly in the dark of night, she snuffed out the candles and doused the fire that lit and warmed the home. In the blackness, the unkind matriarch cried, "We cannot complete our work in this darkness —and because only Baba Yaga has the power of fire and light, one must go to her and bring it back to us, or we will all perish."

The two stepsisters were only faking and making excuses when they claimed they could not knit or see their needle-work, let alone find their way through the dark woods. Their recalcitrance much pleased their scheming mother, who was hellbent on Vasilisa undertaking the dangerous task.

Terrified, the beautiful maiden took her first steps into the dead of the cold black night, not knowing where she was placing her feet or what horrific fate awaited her. But as she fed her little magic doll, she heard its familiar calming voice whisper, "Vasilisa, go to the hut of Baba Yaga and ask her to give you the light. I will guide your steps along the way, so do not be afraid."

Vasilisa trembled as she trudged through the night, holding her doll close to her heart as she ventured into the unknown depths of the forbidden forest.

Then, just as dawn broke across the sky, a horseman upon a white horse appeared from nowhere, riding all in white. Bewildered by the powerful image, she pressed on, nevertheless. As the golden sun rose above the mountains, another mysterious rider came into view. He approached on a red horse donned in red garments from top to toe. Silently, and for some time deeper into the wild, he rode beside her as she wended her way cautiously down the unbeaten path toward the witch's hut.

Finally, arriving at a clearing, she stood stunned, staring at a strange, unearthly-looking place emitting a sickening odour. A fence made of flaming skulls encircled a shambolic shack, resting atop a curious concoction of old scaly bones and giant chicken legs. It could only belong to the fabled Baba Yaga. Even the gates bore a set of gaping jaws with razor-sharp teeth to scare away would-be intruders. Vasilisa felt paralysed with fear. As the darkness began to creep in, she despaired over how she would ever retrieve a light source from such a dark place.

Then, in a flash, a horseman, all in black upon a black horse, galloped towards her but abruptly turned, riding rapidly to disappear through the gates. As nightfall descended, the fence skulls burned brightly with an eerie glow, and Vasilisa, frozen to the spot, feeling all alone, clutched desperately at her small doll.

She looked nervously about her, worried about the strange skulls that lit up the forest and wondered about making a quick escape. Suddenly, she heard a horrid creaking sound: the crowning sky billowed and heaved while the earth below began to shake and shudder. A tower of birch trees watched on, some bellowing, others moaning as she made her approach. Vasilisa stood stiff, her small doll hugged close to her chest. She could not believe her eyes and ears: before her, she saw what could only have been the grotesque ogress Baba Yaga. Incredibly, the horrible hag rode high upon a cavernous cauldron, a most mysterious looking mortar-cum-sledge.

The warty old witch began to sniff at the air as a dog might lift its snout on the hunt. "I smell a human; who is there?" she demanded to know.

As her feet stepped slowly forward, her voice followed, and Vasilisa, quivering in terror, obediently replied, "I am Vasilisa. I come on behalf of my stepmother requesting the light and flame; our house has become cold and black." She froze as the hot stale wind of the witch's breath encircled where she stood.

Baba Yaga knew of the stepmother. She demanded that Vasilisa stay to do some tasks. If she completed the work, the light would be hers. If not, she would kill and eat Vasilisa.

Baba Yaga commanded her iron gates to open and rode in with a riotous rush. Before the grinding gates clashed behind their master, Vasilisa made haste to enter, shuddering at the thought of their wolf-like jaws snapping shut on her neck.

Baba Yoga wasted no time giving orders, instructing Vasilisa to bring her the enormous pot of food bubbling on the stove along with the rye, mead, beer and wine from the cupboard. Ten men would have been satisfied by the meal, devoured alone by the greedy witch. Before bed, she left only a crust of bread on her plate for Vasilisa while providing her with a long list of tasks for the next day.

As Vasilisa drew her magic doll closer, she wondered whether her completed yard-work, sweeping, cooking, and washing tasks would ever satisfy the witch. After all, separating mildewed corn kernels from the good ones was a cause for anyone's concern. She must also remove all of the black spots left on the corn. It was a fiddly and arduous job, but Vasilisa resigned herself to it, knowing that she would be cooked and eaten should she resist.

Before long, Vasilisa heard guttural snorts raging like a thunderstorm. She peered and caught a glimpse of the witch's long, pointy nose scraping and rattling along the hut's roof, tapping a beat in rhythm with Baba Yaga's gurgling breath: an ungodly scene, indeed.

As Vasilisa fed her tiny doll the bread crust, she counselled Vasilisa to leave her thinking until the day lit up the night. Finally, the girl fell asleep. When the maiden awoke at dawn, Baba Yoga was already up and about. Vasilisa stole to the barn to find her tiny doll studiously picking the last remnants of the black spot from the corn kernels. It relieved her to know the magic doll had completed the complex work, leaving only the hag's supper for her to prepare. The daylight passed quickly in these realms, and night's dark cloak began to fall again.

Vasilisa could see the light glowing like crimson-red cinders from the skull posts on the chalk-white fence: an unsettling sight to behold. She felt the earth move and heard the ancient trees creak before laying her eyes upon the hulking Baba Yaga. "Have you done as I have asked?" demanded the ever-doubting witch.

"Yes," came the confident reply of young Vasilisa, "Look, and see for yourself."

Stunned by her miraculous performance, Baba Yaga appeared strangely angry and upset that Vasilisa had done the tasks. The hungry witch had had a preference to consume the girl yet said without complaint, "Very good." But then, in a mysterious-sounding voice, she summoned to the spirit world and commanded solemnly, "My faithful servants, grind wheat!" In an instant, three pairs of ghastly disembodied hands seized and crushed the corn prepared by the tiny doll before vanishing into thin air. Next, the ogress gobbled down her supper and, before retiring, ordered Vasilisa to perform the tedious tasks all over again the next day. This time she was tasked with sorting poppy seeds from grains of dirt.

Tomorrow came, and as Baba Yaga departed in her mortar, Vasilisa and the doll finalised the job, again visited upon by the ghostly grain-crushers. On her return, Baba Yaga inspected the completed work, bade the three pairs of disembodied hands their leave and watched as they disappeared into the underworldly shadows with the bin full of poppy seeds.

The witch turned and sternly asked if Vasilisa had any questions, scolding her for her timidity and telling her that not every question comes with the right answer. Vasilisa decided to speak up, asking about the three mysterious riders.

Baba Yaga told her they were her faithful servants: the white horseman, representing day; the red rider, symbolising the rising sun; and the black, signifying night. Too frightened to enquire about the disembodied hands, Vasilisa went dead quiet. She held the small doll ever- closer to her wildly beating heart when Baba Yaga shrieked, "Now, I have a question I would like YOU to answer: How on earth have you completed all of these chores so quickly?"

Vasilisa promptly replied, "With my mother's blessing."

Baba Yaga screeched, "Silence! Speak no more of blessings. I will have no such talk in my house. Begone, Vasilisa!"

With that, she shoved the maiden out the door and through the gnashing gates. But before she sent her back into the gloomy woods, the witch gave her a parting gift. She handed her a lit skull that hung from a long, crooked stick, declaring, "Here is the light source for your stepmother and her daughters. Take it to them and be forever gone!"

The return through the primaeval woods was long and arduous, but after walking into the daylight hours, Vasilisa spotted the family home, a faint speck in the long distance as the fog lifted. She carried the staff topped by the ghostly skull ablaze with glowing hot coals and watched how the shadows grew deeper and darker the closer she got. Each time she felt a shiver go down her spine (like someone had walked on her grave), needed a rest or decided she must give up, a muffled warning would come from the spooky skull about her step-kin needing its light and for her to stay the course. So, she pressed on towards her destination until day became night again.

Finally, with the helpful doll's navigation, she, exhausted and in pain, made it back, nearing the cabin's threshold with the eerie, illumined skull held high. In the distance, she saw the horizon's haunting deep crimson hue, and knew at once, all the birds had up and flown. Suddenly, the skull took on a blazing life-form of its own: like a bolt of lightning from out of the blue, casting a gimlet eye from its scorching hollows onto the spellbound step-kin. Its laser beam turned their sight to soot. Blinded and mortified, they scuttled about, but the relentless skull never let them from its fiery, coal-charged stare. By morning, all three were ash.

Vasilisa and her tiny doll, the radiant mother within, miraculously survived the ordeal. Unharmed, the beautiful and brave maiden remained in the creepy cottage, trying in vain to restore her inner peace. But after a while, she decided to bury the supernatural skull with its all-consuming and destructive powers, longing to start her life anew away from these horrible parts. The skull, its darkness now dispatched, required but a ray of sunlight to break into bud. So, soon after, when Vasilisa took leave, searching for some company in the neighbouring town, a beautiful rose bush bloomed in its place.

She found lodgings with a kindly older woman who gave her some flax to weave. From the flax, industrious Vasilisa wove an exquisite white fabric fit for only the upper echelons of society. She offered it to her gracious host, who presented it to the Tsar.

The Tsar was so impressed with the magnificent beauty of the cloth he rewarded the kindly woman with exotic wares before sending her back home. However, the tailors in his court refused to make shirts from such a sublime material lest they spoil it, so the Tsar turned to the old lady again.

She confided that it was Vasilisa's handiwork, not hers, leading to the maiden receiving a commission to create ceremonial apparel for the oligarch. Entranced by the beauty of her craft, the Tsar demanded that he finally meet this fine needle-woman. Vasilisa made her way to his royal palace, and the moment the Russian emperor laid his eyes upon her, he was so captivated by her beauty, bravery and wisdom he wanted her as his bride.

Eventually, Vasilisa's merchant-father returned from his trading in faraway places. After receiving an invitation to live with Vasilisa at the palace, he accepted and took the friendly older woman with him. Once reunited, they all lived a satisfying family life of contentment and love.

One can still hear the whisperings of the helpful doll once blessed by Vasilisa's mother, coming from the pocket of the beautiful tsarina's robes whenever the tsardom's people need a wise and kindly act or two. **THE END.**

PSYCHOLOGICAL PROMPTS

21. Key soul learning: To develop illuminating and embracing the divinity in all life (Empathy)

There are different versions of the Slavic folktale Vasilisa. The retelling above is from my childhood and is closely relatable to the cyclic trope of the Hero's Journey.

Vasilisa is every woman's initiation story, where she must sally forth into the unknown world and bravely face the odds to emerge stronger, wiser and more soul-beautiful.

Vasilisa is an only child who develops independence in middle childhood when the seeds of empathy start to sprout. When her mother dies too early, she becomes the orphan archetype, looking to build bonds beyond her family hearth. However, she lacks the confidence to handle her newly blended family's toxic jealousies and thorny competition. Blessed with her mother's mitochondrial strengths, Vasilisa is entrusted with a supernatural doll as a proxy for her mother's moral code (superego), aiding her in navigating the world in her absence. The doll, a metaphor for the anima and the earth mother archetypes, takes care of all practical and domestic matters while the mother's blessing represents the much higher calling of women: To co-create with the Divine, the miracle and gift of bringing new life into the world.

As the doll carries out the burdensome chores, the never-ending 'dirty work', we are reminded of the long list of thankless domestic duties demanded of women throughout the ages. No one seems to acknowledge the conscientious women with babies on their backs and untamed toddlers alongside them as they gather, sort, cook, and clean to feed and care for the tribe. Every woman's secret wish for a visit from an enchanted fairy to lighten the burden is fulfilled through the doll. The doll, connecting the girl to her inner mother, not only helps with tasks but serves as a sage confidante, surrogate mother, and mentor.

An echo of Little Red Cap surfaces in Vasilisa's journey with both girls penetrating the primaeval woods, overarched by matriarchal expectations that they will survive and emerge confident, worldly and wise.

Vasilisa's father is absent (familiar to many fairy tales), leaving her at risk. Clarissa Pinkola Estes (1992) suggests that adolescents with absent or careless fathers may struggle to adapt effectively to the wiles of the world. On top of her shaky start, Vasilisa must confront an embittered ogress (the loss of light and love), haunted by past persecution, and bring light and warmth back to her mean-spirited stepmother's house. These metaphors point to a girl's journey into womanhood, where her triumph over trials, jealousy, oppression and bullying is the making of her.

Vasilisa encounters three male horse riders along her unfolding path, alluding to the continuous cycle of the dawning day and the black night. She learns to be patient and calm, waiting for the right time to act. A well-ridden horse symbolises our will to power, controlling unbridled animus with noble intentions. The magical number three carries portent, invoking destiny's hand: change is afoot. Vasilisa's psychic maturation is assured.

Vasilisa's instinctual fears stir as she approaches Baba Yaga's grisly and absurd domain, hearing the chilling low howls escape from the bones of the long-departed. Skull embers burning bright, red hot allude to the illumination of all that has been dark and hidden in the subconscious. Like Vasilisa's, our spiritual fire sparks if we are prepared to go into the shadow and face our darkest traits and fears. Our reflective gaze leaves no stone unturned, enlightening our consciousness. Lighting up the darkness is our switched-on ego's inner seeking, reflecting in sharp relief the secret corners of one's mind where a rationale for reality is grasped and understood.

Baba Yaga's mortar and pestle sledge speaks to the churn of her under-worldly power in the natural world. Although she claims to be the keeper of day and night, life and death, the foreboding grandmother of grandmothers brings forth nothing but chaos.

While Vasilisa's savvy is rooted in maternal nurturing and guidance, Baba Yaga's poisonous paranormal power makes her an ominous and manipulative dominatrix. She embodies a stark schism from the good Source, evoking images of skulduggery, Voodoo rituals, and human sacrifice. Her light originates from the external, never emanating from within. In contrast, Vasilisa is a blazing beacon of eternal love and light in a transient world, threatening to put it out. However, she is afraid to assert herself and feels inadequate when set challenges by the dark mother, shadow archetype, such as sorting good corn from cankered kernels and poppy seeds from the dirt (like wheat from the chaff). Corn and poppy seeds, metaphors for healthy goodness, fertility, and rebirth, take a twisted turn in her rotten realm. Their mildewed, dirty, hallucinogenic elements in the cauldron signify a brew of blighted spawn, a manifestation of Baba Yaga's murderous curse on life itself. The unearthly imagery of disembodied hands grinding grain in our human dimension evokes the transcendental maternal role of seeding our continuance long after we have ceased to exist. They caution, though, that we reap from what we sow.

Vasilisa's extended exposure to the intense negativity of her step-kin, who belittled her, made her unsure of herself but tolerant of the likes of the harping wood-witch. Just as mildew threatens the corn and dirt the poppy seeds, we risk stagnation if we don't confront our self-doubts in shadow and embrace the good life fully. Vasilisa recognises that completing her tasks and conquering her fears is essential for her personal growth, emotional freedom and self-actualisation. As the Jedi would say hundreds of years later, "Fear is the path to the dark side."

Like Vasilisa, we of the earthly arena may feel very alone in times like these, but spiritual succour will guide us in our quest if only we remember to ask for help. Vasilisa does, and she receives the gift of fire. To achieve it, she dared to do the forbidden twice. Firstly, she sought light from Baba Yaga, a figure seen as an unbeliever and a devil incarnate. Secondly, she invoked the 'goodness' of her mother to counteract evil. In her defiance, the witch rejected all that was wholesome and virtuous, banishing them from her fallen realm. This defensive stance mirrors the marginalised Russian crones who, under the shadow of fear cast by the Orthodox Church and the harsh Tsarist laws threatening their lives, began to be seen as wielding their wisdom and healing powers in harmful ways.

An emboldened Vasilisa lights a match to her fears to find her way out of conflict. But to finish what she starts, she makes a consecrated contact with the archetypal earth mother (via the doll), which ignites her brave spirit to round each dangerous corner and carry on. She waves her magic lantern to return with the rewards of her labour. Facing infernal difficulties on the path is one thing; exorcising demons is another.

Mother Nature, majestic, unbidden, revives the day and night, trees, water, wind and earth, promising an inescapable cycle of life, death and rebirth. Vasilisa felt it in her bones as she went by the light of the fiery skull, radiating a vibrancy so vivid it blinded and toasted her callous kin. Curiously, the blowtorch knew to leave her be, seeing good for goodness's sake and evil for evil. It stubbornly pursued only the unillumined until its natural justice was done.

A parallel and paradox exist with the superstar Joan of Arc, the immortalised icon of female power. She symbolises liberation, unity, bravery, and victory but, in reality, was persecuted and tortured by enemies accusing her of heresy and witchcraft. Joan bypassed church authority by drawing direct inspiration from the Divine. Dressed as a man to confuse her assailants, Joan confronted past traumas of rape and violence but was captured and burned alive by rival forces at just 19 years of age, unlike the mythic Vasilisa, who incinerated her foes, reversing history.

The persistent *Hammer of Witches* propagated the belief that women were inferior to men and required male oversight. To them, witches received it from the devil. Different outcomes emerged in different times for similar women driven on by the power of their faith in the Great Mother. Joan (in battle) and Vasilisa appeared as fire-breathing chimeras, not to intentionally destroy but to enlighten and restore. Vasilisa's strobe might have opened their eyes and turned them away from darkness and towards forgiveness and love—but alas, it did not.

Though seemingly insignificant compared to Joan and Vasilisa, the neophyte Little Red Cap personifies the universal rite of passage of confronting perilous trials and emerging fortified by life's lessons. She embodies the folly of fairy-tale archetypes' beginnings. At the same time, Vasilisa epitomises their wisdom, authenticity and holistic integration by journey's end—these spirited models of leadership contrast with incomplete women reduced by resentment and rage when disputed and violated. Take the mythical Medusa. Her natural beauty, ravaged by inner hate (from Athena's curse), transformed her into a cold and bitter ugliness with a headful of snakes and a gimlet eye for turning men to stone. Toxic emotions fail to serve us well, and victim-survivors must keep faith's flickering flame alive for their sakes.

Archetypes, historical and mythical, teach us that those who are magnanimous, enlightened and directly connected to the Divine provoke those who are not. Threatened helmspersons in any disconnected social construct still hold power to cast out the soulful, as the shadow-ridden step-kin and irrational Baba Yaga did to Vasilisa. Yet, embracing the principle of 'doing unto others as she desired in return', the empathetic archetype left an everlasting imprint, surpassing human evanescence.

Vasilisa teaches that one must endure the trials of darkness to reach the light of day. By harnessing the impetus of our troubles, embodied in the metaphorical Baba Yaga threatening our peace, stability and happiness, we ignite our inner fire of creativity and passion, compelling us to act assertively and progress, seizing opportunities. Overcoming these challenges allows us to return home as triumphant heroes.

In how Vasilisa cared for her inner doll (and vice versa), we must mature to mother and nurture our inner child, sustaining her with daily doses of respect, wisdom, and dignity.

When Vasilisa felt the earth quiver beneath her feet in the tundra forest (her unconscious), she did not run or think it was the end of the world, for she knew it spelt a new order of things to come.

Each time we venture deep into the woods, exploring new paths diverging in different directions, we continue our courageous quest to conquer the novel experiences that expand our reality. Reaching the horizon, we can finally stand tall, accepting ourselves as we are, calling a spade a spade.

Vasilisa urges us to develop our powers of observation and reflection, enabling our keen insight for planning and anticipating what lies ahead without fear. Hers is another rags-to-riches story, symbolised by her artistry (with her inner doll) in crafting resplendent robes for Russian royalty, mirroring her remarkable ascent. Aristotle would say that the cosmos squared the debt to Vasilisa between the four examples—the maiden, the magic doll, the kind older lady, and the Tsar.

A better reality becomes accessible when we uncover the root cause beneath the symptoms of our grief and regret. Like antennae scanning for truth flying on a random wind, we see smoke and find the fire. But we only see when we focus our eyes to a squint.

To live with a modus vivendi, we must reclaim and tame the shrew within, igniting a bonfire of her psychic deadwood. May the vexatious drive us to our vertex as they did Vasilisa, who got her meteoric rise despite stiff opposition. Then, like fresh undergrowth, we emerge empowered, worldly-wise, brimming with new vitality.

Amidst the tension of life and death, heaven and earth, exaltation and despair, Vasilisa transformed from the naïve **Fool** to the self-reliant **Sage**, a radiant beacon of hope in the darkness, ever-ready to brave the next summit.

As day follows night, she will sight a host of unbidden wildflowers on the other side of the peak: those splendid, fragrant roses of success, pressing their glorious faces into the gentle rays of a sunlit morning sky crowning a clearing where ghastly old bones and ash once took root.

SELF-REFLECTIONS

Your life, mirroring Vasilisa's journey, has come full circle, bringing personal growth and conscious awareness to once-hidden realms of your inner being. Embracing your authenticity demands bravery, yet it harmonises and liberates your mind, body, and soul, culminating in triumphant accomplishments in the outer world.

Before this awakening, you faced unfinished business and struggled with emotional chaos and pain. Through your soul-searching and the wise counsel of spiritual mentors, you discerned the dualities defeating your purpose and draining your passion. The quest is always challenging, but perseverance pays off.

You remain poised, acknowledging further trials that await in the round of time. However, these days you see them as vehicles ushering in fresh opportunities for developing even higher levels of self-efficacy, just as Vasilisa overcame her Herculean tasks. The intrepid leader in you stands tall.

Gratefully embrace this new phase of effort and reward with a sense of creative freedom, and your actions will align with the forces of good. By wholeheartedly tackling your responsibilities with a spirit of acceptance, you will reap the gratifying fruits of your labour like Vasilisa did. She was a sharer, retrieving the light for darkened souls, unexpectedly receiving the gift she gave away—the eternal flame of the Holy Spirit. And darkness, existing only in the absence of light, ceased to be.

Your quest is to embody the warrior-woman archetype (with fulsome feminine firepower), labouring through tests that push you to your limits. Learning from challenging circumstances puts you in the right place at the right time for welcome windfalls. Like Vasilisa, refuse to be beaten by your troubles. Trouble your troubles and never take anything for granted again.

As part of the social tribe, much of our learning comes from earth-bound experiences: survival, reproduction, relationships, creation, aging, loss, birth and death. To transcend the material constraints, we must let go of ego-driven desires and empty ourselves, allowing the Divine essence to fill us with its goodness. The Sufi prophet Rumi says, "Life is a balance between holding on and letting go." Discerning what, how and when to surrender is key.

When you find your breath out of alignment with nature's circadian heartbeat, take a step back to nourish your soul and hear your inner child's gentle voice again. Restful sleep, harmonious breathing, and a joyful heart contribute to a balanced waking state.

With newfound assertiveness, you allow life to take you in new directions. Motivated by bold visions for the future, you become an explorer, venturing into exotic places or spiritual realms. All this is to live a soul-inspired life and share your light with the world. Refusing to be controlled by irrational fears, you patiently observe the Sacred mysteries at play and motivate to speculate in your brave new field of unlimited possibilities.

When the going gets tough, the tough get going, fostering unification over separation, and creating loving partnerships founded on mutual admiration. As you deepen your connections with others, you realise the transformative power of one's authenticity. Reflecting on what you see, you recognise how narrow views, and negative behaviours hinder one's growth. Still, you embrace the differences in others and appreciate their unique perspectives while subtly influencing them with your shining example.

Rather than becoming frustrated and overwhelmed by relationship (personal and professional) problems, you seek practical solutions. Your old thinking, swinging between acceptance and rejection, has been replaced by a deeper sense of empathy and stability. To you, the world is akin to a golden egg, its protective shell concealing a fertile yolk imbued with an abundant richness and goodness, ready to be cracked open and savoured. In this reframed story, your refreshed reality, new or renewed partnerships emerge, taking one to rewarding environments in far-flung climes.

Even the most profound and authentic connections require ongoing care and attention. Vasilisa's relationship with the Tsar began superficially but grew into a meaningful and loving partnership. To reach your own Holy Grail of love, cultivate both the anima—your inner feminine qualities of empathy, intuition, and receptivity—and the animus—your inner masculine qualities of creativity, determination, and assertiveness. Resonating with feelings of deep gratitude and reverence for the blessings in your life is the catalyst for progressive change.

Like Vasilisa's hidden doll, tap into your inner child's innate curiosity and potency to accompany you on your quest for personal growth. Recognising and harnessing the immeasurable support of others sharing your journey, envision the heights you can ascend with their caring presence. There are already too many *unsung* allies, steadfastly contributing to another's success.

We are never truly alone. Drawing upon the backing of the invisible Eternal Presence, we must prove our efficacy to ourselves and the world by overcoming seemingly insurmountable obstacles. Even in the darkest moments, the realm of spirit awaits our cries for help. Remember, when we ask, we shall receive.

All of us must face the litmus test to conquer the mother of fears—our subterranean fear of death. While some see a burning skull on a stick and think annihilation (the Templar crusaders carried silver skull heads to invade and eradicate), Vasilisa saw it as a tool for fire and light. But as the adage goes, "What must die, dies." Unless we embrace this profound reality, akin to how our mythic hero did (and the witch did not), our existence shall be etched upon cold and unyielding stone. Like Vasilisa, keep the flame of faith burning, keep moving, knowing that the hand of spirit has your best interests at heart.

Alone, the shimmering torch-bearer for a new age embarked on a quest for light, prioritising enduring spiritual growth over fleeting material success, and faced her perils without succumbing to victimhood or self-pity. Her life was far from perfect, but her future, growing from the skull of conflagration, promised to blossom like glorious pink roses. From the ashes of destruction, she discovered her budding self-worth, agency, and transformative power for bringing good from even the worst circumstances. Her story takes her from trauma to triumph.

Like the indomitable archetype, trusting in the daylight of new beginnings, you have the whole world in your hands, entwining with the very fabric of the universe, as you round the bend of your soul's homecoming.

Beneath the façade of everyday life, something brave beautiful, and wise comes into being. You have become a light of the world, contributing to cosmic consciousness and elucidating the Divine way for fellow seekers of truth, love and light.

The Eternal Feminine draws us onward. (Goethe)

LIGHT QUALITIES (SAGE)	SHADOW ATTRIBUTES (FOOL)
Assertive	Foolish
Worldly-wise	Unassertive
Authentic	Under-worldly
Enlightened	Irrational
Magnanimous	Stubborn
Wholesome	Incomplete
Integrated	Mean-spirited
Emboldened	Chaotic

PROVERB: She doth teach the torches to burn bright (Romeo: Shakespeare).

AFFIRMATION: I strive to be authentic to live a life well-lived.

GAME OF LIFE: Getting others to do your dirty work to avoid getting your fingers burnt (Consequence: Disempowering yourself).

REFLECTION QUESTION: Am I doing unto others, as I would like them to do unto me?

ANIMAL SYMBOLISM: Wedgetail eagle; Eastern Brown Snake

Wedge-tail eagle

Eagles' sharp vision symbolizes the all-seeing Self, capable of a broader perspective, objectivity, forgiveness, and rising above blame and shame. They embody strength, bravery, power, and confidence in the return of that which once took flight.

Snake (Eastern Brown)

When brown snakes reveal themselves, life changes are afoot. These potent totems utilised in ancient rituals and belief systems, signify the duality of existence. For example, where wisdom and light exist, there is darkness and ignorance. While snakes shed skin, we need to soul-search before basking in the sunlight of our renewal.

ONE SMALL STEP TO TAKE AWAY: I will practise serving my authentic Self and all sentient Life in the earthly realm.

MEDITATION PREPARATION (to practise when at the crossroads)

I breathe in golden light vibrations, and as I exhale, I let go of my negative thoughts and feelings. I envision myself going about my day with a smile on my face and bliss in my heart. I ask the Great One to direct my soul, illuminating all that is true and wise, extinguishing stale energy contesting my passage to success. Feeling uplifted, every fibre of my being dances in concert with the world around me. I embrace the simple joys of living with trust in the spiritual goodness of humanity.

Fairy-tale archetypes serve as lanterns guiding us into the depths of our psyche, where our shadow aspects reside. They beckon us to embrace the darkness within, for only by facing our fears and acknowledging our hidden desires can we truly know ourselves and experience profound growth.

19 OUR EARLIEST MYTHIC LITERATURE

Questing for enlightenment to become more knowledgeable about the great mysteries of our existence and to evolve into better versions of ourselves is nothing new. Even the ancient archetype, the great hero of Sumerian mythology, Gilgamesh, from four thousand years ago, eventually made this his raison d'etre. Like us, the proud semi-mythic king understood that seeking wisdom will not grant it—but find it, we must.

His deeds were recorded on a cache of clay tablets, taking him from the ancient city of Uruk (or Erech: modern-day Iraq) to the vast wilderness and back again. Three centuries later, the Babylonian priest Sin-liqe-unninni (and other contributors over time) revised the clay tablets, containing episodic poems including *Gilgamesh and the Netherworld*, into its Akkadian literal form, the cuneiform script. The newly inscribed narrative heralded the birth of the *Epic of Gilgamesh.*

In this preserved state, archaeologist A.H. Layard rediscovered the recorded epic on clay tablets at Nineveh (Iraq) in 1849 C.E., with scholars recognising the written composition as one predating the collective text of the Bible.

Gilgamesh's narrative came to life again from the rubble of Assyrian King Ashurbanipal's palace library. Much of the story is corroborated by historical accounts, with its elements—such as the battle with Agga, King of Kish, and a great flood—that echo entries from the Sumerian King List and appear in Mesopotamian and Biblical traditions. The Akkadian *Epic of Gilgamesh*, often seen as the first chronicled Hero's Journey, predates Homer's *Iliad* and *Odyssey* by over a thousand years and is widely regarded as the world's oldest surviving epic. As fictionalised history and the world's oldest recorded scribal story, many contend that components reflect the oral traditions of the earlier civilisations of the 10,000 B.C.E. Neolithic revolution but this idea remains speculative.

From as far back as the archaic philosophies of ancient China, India, Egypt and Mesopotamia (within the Fertile Crescent), we have received guidance on navigating the complexities of the human condition. In the Sumerian culture, the sun god advised a desolate Gilgamesh to embrace mortality, urging him to find joy in each passing day: "Day and night be thou merry; make every day a day of rejoicing."

Each time-honoured school of thought presents various ways of living, encompassing myriad mundane, moral, and spiritual codes to assist us in overcoming our limitations and finding relief from the struggles and suffering we face as everyday journeymen or women. Recognising myths as narratives that blend natural history with primitive spirituality and social morality, Campbell (1993) acknowledged the links between myths and history and the difficulty of distinguishing between the two.

Enduring wisdom of the great teachings of Lao-Tzu's Taoism (600-501 B.C.E.) and Confucius (551-479 B.C.E.) crystallised in written form much later than the Gilgamesh era. Millions worldwide have also found comfort in *Song of the Spirit* (i.e., the conversation, better known as the *Bhagavad Gita,* between

Arjuna and Lord Krishna on the battlefield of Kurukshetra) *written down* much later by the Hindu Rishi, Veda Vyasa, around 2,500 years ago. And millions again find direction and purpose today by listening to what the man (Jesus of Nazareth) said two millennia back. In contrast, the rest find solace in diverse spiritual sources that feel right to them. No matter the Source, there is a shared belief that all journeys for inner transformation begin with surrendering our egoic control.

The Maxims of Good Discourse, composed in the hieratic script by the Egyptian Ptah Hotep, around the same time as Gilgamesh's reign (and story-recordings), recommended (in the form of proverbs), telling and hearing the truth, advancing justice and becoming morally conscious for our lives to be happy. Yet, according to humanity's first recorded literary work (about Gilgamesh and his triumphs and travails), nothing could have been further from his mind. The demi-god king (one-third human and two-thirds divine) is an ambiguous hero, prioritising actions to oppress his people and defy the gods. He embarks on a self-serving journey in the hope of great fame and immortality, only to discover something unexpected, more precious.

All these years later, the Hero's Journey of the part-real king of Uruk is as relevant to us and our quest to master our internal demons and achieve transformation as it was to his tormented people, yearning for relief from his gall, gore and gloom.

Come now to explore the story of Gilgamesh, whose mythic-historical feats, inscribed upon clay, live on, writ in stone, adorned with metamorphic gems in the darkest annals of unverified history.

Write your name upon the face of life in big letters.
(Kahlil Gibran)

ANCIENT MYTHOLOGY: THE EPIC OF GILGAMESH

SYNOPSIS OF MYTH

A long-ago story takes us back to a faraway and vibrant place in ancient Mesopotamia, where the semi-mythic King Gilgamesh reigned. Known as a mighty warrior with superhuman strength, Gilgamesh ruled Uruk with an iron fist, driven by his instincts and desires. He built opulent stone temples, towering mud-brick ziggurats, and long sandstone walls to fortify their city, all while oppressing his people. Yet, beneath his majestic facade, his heart carried the burden of arrogance.

Prosperous Uruk, with its green fields, abundant orchards and festive civil celebrations, should have been a utopia, but Gilgamesh's abuse of power, malice and violations of the flesh brought suffering to the people. Constant warfare, forced labour, and the humiliation of virgin brides consumed their lives. Angry men sought solace in Ishtar's temple, finding comfort with sacred prostitutes. However, their cries went unheard as their selfish sovereign cared little for their welfare.

One day, the populace reached their breaking point, pleading with the gods for mercy and an end to Gilgamesh's malignant rule. The goddess-mother of creation, Aruru, answered their call. She crafted a companion for Gilgamesh from clay and water, a wild-man named Enkidu. Enkidu, embodying two-thirds animal to Gilgamesh's two-thirds divine and mirroring his stature and might, would counterbalance the king's dark side, restoring the harmony once enjoyed in her husband's reign.

Trappers witnessed Enkidu's primal nature as he suckled from a deer's breast and drank from its waterhole. Worried by his untamed ways, they believed that Enkidu must embrace his humanity to become Gilgamesh's trusted friend and equal. It was a temple prostitute who domesticated Enkidu through sacred sexual rites and life teachings, causing his animal kin to shun him for entering the realm of humans.

The giants finally met when Enkidu confronted the headstrong king, outraged by his attempt to defile a virgin bride. They clashed, wrestled, and fought, but their struggle forged a bond deeper than blood. Pleased with her son's triumph, Gilgamesh's goddess-mother, Ninsun, adopted Enkidu as her second son.

Time passed unremarkably in Uruk until Gilgamesh urged Enkidu to join him on a quest to the Forbidden Forest of the gods. Their aim was to remove the tree sentinel and cut down the twelve sacred cedars. Gilgamesh longed for fame as the warrior who bravely challenged the gods, immortalising his name in stone. Initially resistant, Enkidu eventually relented and accompanied him on the fateful mission.

Meanwhile, Ninsun sought the assistance of Shamash, the sun god, to protect her son in battle. Just in time, Shamash stirred up a wind that momentarily paralysed the forest demon Humbaba the Terrible. However, Gilgamesh, egged on by Enkidu, failed to seize the moment and spare the forest guardian—with one blow, he fell hard like a giant cedar. The gods, enraged by Gilgamesh's gall, planned harsh consequences.

Gilgamesh and Enkidu boasted of their victories, unaware that their lack of piety and prudence could destroy them. The goddess Ishtar, impressed by Gilgamesh's magnificence, threw herself at him. Aware of Ishtar's history with lovers as the ruthless Black Widow, Gilgamesh rejected her advances, sparking her vengeance. Ishtar implored her father, Anu, the sky god, to unleash the divine Bull of Heaven to destroy Gilgamesh and his palace. As a result, famine struck the kingdom for seven years, and the Bull of Heaven wreaked havoc upon Uruk's leader.

In revenge, Gilgamesh and Enkidu slew the gods' mighty beast, unleashing a dark storm of celestial fury. The angry gods assembled and decreed that Enkidu must die for their insolence, condemning him to a slow and agonising death. Enkidu, meant to be a moral influence on Gilgamesh, had only encouraged the king's dastardly deeds, embodying only impiety and rebellion.

During his untimely demise, dying Enkidu entered the netherworld, where he dreamed disturbing death visions that he retold to his beloved brother. Gilgamesh grieved deeply, feeling betrayed and forced to confront his mortality. Seeking to escape his human destiny, Gilgamesh resolved to find Utnapishtim, the only man granted eternal life.

Thus, robed in wild animal skins, and with twelve loaves of bread to sustain him, Gilgamesh embarked on a long journey fraught with peril and hardship. He traversed vast fields and wildlands and ventured to where the twin peaks of Mashu stood. Onwards he pressed, through a deep dark tunnel, guarded by two scorpion monsters, and only after he had traversed twelve leagues of darkness, did the glorious sun rise in the sky again. After surviving the Waters of Death, he encountered Siduri, the veiled tavern keeper, and Urshanabi, the boatman, who would ferry him to the ends of the earth to meet Utnapishtim. Before parting, Siduri cautioned Gilgamesh to be content with mortal pleasures, as he would never find the Holy Grail he sought.

Enduring more trials, Gilgamesh finally arrived at the far eastern edge of the world where all the rivers ran, and the trees were laden with jewels. He met Utnapishtim, 'he who saw life, though he saw death'. Utnapishtim revealed the mystery of how the ocean god Ea instructed him to build an ark to save all living creatures from the Great Flood brought by the angry god Enlil, and that Ea rewarded him (and his wife) with eternal life. Despite Utnapishtim's urging to accept the inevitability of human mortality, proud Gilgamesh refused to listen.

To test Gilgamesh's worthiness, Utnapishtim challenged him to stay awake for seven days and nights. Exhaustion eventually overcame the king, and he fell asleep. Before parting, Utnapishtim's wife, touched by Gilgamesh's desperation, gave him a gift to uplift his spirit: a magical plant, a box-thorn rose, the elixir of youth to restore his former glory. Filled with hope, Gilgamesh headed homewards. However, while bathing along the road, a cunning serpent snatched the magical plant, ate it, shedding his skin before vanishing into the green undergrowth. In deep anguish, Gilgamesh cried out loudly to the gods, "What shall I do now? All my hardships have been for nothing!"

Empty handed and weary, the hero continued to Uruk. Nevertheless, in the end, he had learned valuable lessons, whispering to himself in the dead of the black night, "Where is the man who can clamber to heaven? Only the gods live forever …but for us men, our days are numbered, our occupations are a breath of wind."

He had been transformed by his remarkable odyssey, shedding his despotic ways. He sought to heal the wounds inflicted on his people, abolished unjust laws, and listened to their concerns. Uruk prospered in a new age, and Gilgamesh became a just leader, admired for using his strengths for good. Though he had lost his beloved Enkidu, through loving him, Gilgamesh had found what it meant to be human.

The name of the Sumerian king engraved in carnelian and lapis lazuli at the base of Uruk's high stone ramparts immortalised the legend of Gilgamesh's heroic exploits. His journey had not been in vain. **THE END.**

PSYCHOLOGICAL PROMPTS

The epic journey of Gilgamesh holds deep psychological significance in its narrative, symbols, metaphors, themes, and tropes. Through these literary devices, the epic delves into the complexities of human experiences, inner conflicts, and existential questions concerning mortality, power, the struggle between humanity and divinity, the duality of human nature, and the transformative journey of self-discovery.

Gilgamesh, a half-god with super-human powers, embarks on a quest not to become a better man but, according to Sandars (1998), to prove his divinity and immortality to the gods. However, fate has a twist in store for him.

Initially a proud and brutal tyrant, he gradually comes to accept his mortality and integrates the conflicting aspects of his psyche. Themes such as hubris, humility, wisdom, and compassion reflect his duality and journey to himself. The wild-man (id), demi-god (ego) and assembly of gods (superego/conscience) allude to the disparate components of our psychic makeup.

Gilgamesh's personality parts clash, leading him to suffer and project his pain. To achieve Wholeness, he must harmonise the human-god dyad within him, embracing the reality of his human condition and taming his animalistic drives. While he fails to prove his place in the pantheon, conquer mortality or attain eternal life, Gilgamesh undergoes a glorious transformation by accepting his limitations. Paradoxically, his quest for immortality ends when he succumbs to the power of sleep, as death is likened to an eternal slumber, and yet, humans need sleep to stay alive.

The epic draws upon archetypal frameworks such as the tropes of the Hero's Journey and the battle between good and evil. It explores the relationships between humans and gods, tapping into the collective unconscious and resonating with our universal human experiences. Gilgamesh's mission mirrors our modern motivations, desires, struggles, and search for meaning and purpose.

Metaphors, such as the serpent devouring the box-thorn rose and shedding its skin for a new roomier one, and the rose-thorn as a symbol of rebirth, encapsulate the psychological processes of personal growth, self-realisation, and coming to terms with life's impermanent beauty. Gilgamesh must let go of the old to embrace the new and expand himself. The emergent hero evolves from hubris to humility, from cruelty to compassion. His divine heritage may not guarantee immortality, yet his legacy, etched in stone, symbolises the enduring impact we all have on subsequent generations.

Lapis lazuli, the stone of the midnight sky, becomes an emblem of truth, friendship, and the essence of Gilgamesh's trials. Its radiant deep blue hue and glow illuminates the depths of our unconscious, beckoning us to reflect, dream, and delve into hidden mysteries.

Gilgamesh and Enkidu defy societal norms and engage in forbidden acts.

The epic hints at a clandestine same-sex love affair. Their rebellion against the gods suggests repressed emotions and concealed non-conformity with sexual conduct laws. While there is no direct evidence, speculation arises about Gilgamesh's dramatic show of unbridled animus compensating for and disguising his latent leanings.

The 19th century philosopher Schopenhauer said, "No one can escape from their individuality"—something the flawed hero found to be true. He denies his mother's warnings and invites the wrath of the gods. Only when the rose was lost to the serpent did his nascent awareness spark. The rose-thorn is a sacred symbol of God's protection (thorns) and miraculous work on earth (rose). Its heavenly perfume transports us into the realms of rapture, transcendence, revelation and truth.

Through Gilgamesh's journey, we learn that truth goes through stages of ridicule and opposition before being accepted as self-evident (as Schopenhauer contended). Even over 3,000 years later, Galileo's (1564-1642) support of Copernicus' heliocentric theory serves as a historical example of violently opposed truth due to groupthink. Charged with heresy and tortured, Galileo was imprisoned during the Inquisition. Some truth! Some opposition!

As a model of redemption, Gilgamesh emphasises that all people, regardless of social status and norms, must bravely confront the truth in their lives—the sooner, the better. The quest for truth and acceptance requires us to remain optimistic despite the cold hard facts and the popular perception of truth being negative, awaiting us in our real-world settings.

The epic's nature motifs, such as sacred forests, wilderness, mountain peaks, tunnels, and deep waters, represent facets of our duality, aspirational climb, fears of abandonment and death, and emotional complexities on our journey to reality. The blurred lines between spirituality, animalistic desires, and profanity exemplify our struggle and the need for restraint to belong as civilised and valued members of society.

The recurring number twelve in the Gilgamesh text, symbolised by references to twelve cedars, loaves, and leagues of darkness, holds significance in ancient Mesopotamian culture. It influenced their concepts of time, astronomy, measurement, and mathematics. The twelve major gods known as the Anunnaki further reinforce the symbolic importance of the number twelve, representing cosmic governance, order, and completeness, mirroring Gilgamesh's failed pursuit of Godhood and his healing journey toward Wholeness.

Gilgamesh, the ancient archetype, embodies the dual nature of light and darkness within us all. He symbolises our potential for growth and change. We must let go of pride, arrogance, rebellion, and controlling behaviours, recognising them as shadow aspects and hindrances to our personal development.

Four thousand years later, Gilgamesh's trials continue to resonate, revealing our negative tendencies and highlighting the importance of acknowledging weaknesses and striving for our Higher Self. Pascal's (1623–1662) insight that humans are the 'glory and scum' of the universe captures both our greatness and fallibility. The latter rings true to those tortured, enslaved, wrongly accused, exploited, neglected, violated, ostracised, oppressed, and abused the world over. Greek philosopher Sophocles (496–406 B.C.E.) asserted that many things in life are both wonderful and terrible, but none more so than humankind. Our souls are wonderfully divine; our personalities, terribly flawed. By confronting our inner demons, we embrace our better angels and contribute love, light, and truth to the world (and beyond). The epic underscores how accepting truth reduces ignorance and increases compassion towards all sentient beings. Schopenhauer (1840) argued compassion for animals is synonymous with goodness, and if someone is cruel to an animal, they cannot be good. The proud and foolish king learned this bitter truth—though not before delivering immense suffering. Pascal wrote two centuries earlier that we know the truth not just by reason but by the heart. When ignorant Gilgamesh's heart broke, he had a change of heart—and was better for it.

According to the Bhagavad-Gita, humans can develop divine qualities with devoted practice, leading to ethical behaviour, virtue, liberation, and spiritual transformation. Transcendentalist poet Ralph Waldo Emerson (1803–1882) wrote: "Every man is a divinity in disguise, a god playing the fool."

In the grand tapestry of human experience, the *Epic of Gilgamesh* weaves a timeless tale, promising renewal when we remain open, adapt to new ideas, and embrace the flow of life. Reflecting on our behaviours (the noblest way to learn) and calling a spade a spade prepares us for the next chapter of our journey, a more challenging peak experience. As we grow, our perspectives expand, reshaping our minds and equipping us to venture into the vast unknown. When Gilgamesh emerged from the dark tunnel, the glorious sun rose on the horizon, casting its radiant glow upon the world—symbolising his impending rebirth and promising a profound ascent for all humanity.

20 REFLECTIONS IN THE MYTHIC MIRROR

We have unpacked mythic and fairy-tale archetypes, correlating them with contemporary human behaviour patterns. Yet such typologies are indicators, not absolutes, and the author's insights are by no means the last word.

Each of us exists in shades of grey, with intricate layers defying simplistic categorisations of pure good or absolute evil. Still, we can categorise the primary actions of the semi-mythic king Gilgamesh as belonging to a dark cultural archetype of hierarchical and patriarchal power.

Like us, there are two sides to the Gilgamesh mould. His behaviours embody traits such as wilful aggression, oppression, narcissism, and uncontained animal lust—abhorred today just as in the past.

We also distance ourselves from those exhibiting neuroticism like Gilgamesh: erratic, moody, fearful, anxious, worried, frustrated, jealous, riddled with shame or guilt. However, we all sit somewhere on this spectrum.

Stress causes dysregulated and maladjusted behaviour. But we can choose to do the inner work, reflecting and undergoing the psychological process of reassembling our fragmented mind into a cohesive narrative and getting back on track as quickly as possible.

The most favoured human traits are openness, conscientiousness, extraversion, and agreeableness. Mythic and many fairy-tale heroes regenerated these positive characteristics only once their Hero's Journey, replete with tailored trials and tribulations, was complete.

We are not our traits, but our traits count when others sum us up, playing a role in how they choose to include or exclude us. Moreover, our attributes contribute significantly to our decision-making processes, choices and outcomes. It pays to become aware of our behaviour, regulate what lets us down, and practice more of what serves us well.

It is no mystery to us, knowing the difference between our respectful, functional behaviours and those that are toxic and dysfunctional. If we are blind to them, we can certainly pick them out in others.

Seeing the truth humbled the once-ignorant Gilgamesh. Never mind that the gods and his subjects pointed it out for years—it took him seeing it with his own eyes and owning it with his heart before remedying his self-deception. With a human heart now broken and opened, his innate divinity stepped into the breach, guiding his choices and future direction.

When doing things against our better nature, we may reflect, confess and atone, relieving ourselves of the burden of guilt. Otherwise, we may justify, deny or excuse what we have done, blaming others for making us act harmfully. People claim they can't help it since it's in their nature: their traits make them who they are and what they do. This implies the person lacks self-control. What is natural about being vicious and violent like the archetypes Bluebeard or Baba Yaga? If our animal behaviours from the id part of the psyche tell us to attack a threat or force ourselves sexually on the object of our desire, and we allow it free rein over our more evolved rational thinking, we are in the grip of our over-reactive dark side. There is no scientific evidence that human brains are hard-wired for violence and cruelty. We are capable of atrocities when under fire, but it is not inborn in us to behave perversely any more than we expect other animals to deviate from their inborn compass.

Depending on our environmental conditions, we learn dysfunctional ways to cope and self-preserve. We behave counter-intuitively. Did our significant caregivers in early life nurture our intrinsic nature and survival needs or not? What genes, behaviours, and narratives-for-living did they pass on, model or cultivate?

Gilgamesh may have grown into an overbearing leader in response to the hedonistic, patriarchal pleasure paradise of his existence. Does it spoil one living in an oasis where abundance prevails and women, flushed with sexual eagerness (or not), serve every erotic fantasy?

We understand the warrior harboured a fear of death, the mother of all fears. From his authoritarian rule we can estimate he feared losing control and the ramifications should he take his heavy hand off the reins. The few townsfolk, known for their raucous revelry and excessive indulgence, mirroring Gilgamesh, held the potential to turn their society into a dystopian state.

Like him, before we uproot the dark parts of self dwelling in the netherworld of our psyche, we must come to that place where we see the light. That moment of truth arrives when we reflect on our behaviours in the context of the role-models we aspire to become or undergo a hard-won reality check.

When introducing progressive social reforms, the Prussian conservative statesman Bismarck (1815–1898) quipped, "Only a fool learns from his own mistakes. The wise man learns from the mistakes of others." Was he also saying that we are fools to ignore history, for when we do, we must repeat the lesson?

Those going before us, like these examples, travelled the same human road experiencing similar psychological struggles that eventually befall us. The main takeaway from cruel despots is that vanity, pride, and arrogance do not serve us, others, or our quest to evolve spiritually during our brief time on earth. In his sonnet *When I Have Fears*, the romantic poet John Keats (1795–1821) alludes to us being 'merely fair creatures of an hour', our fame sinking ultimately to nothingness. In this transient vale of soul-making, where our days are numbered, if we face our true nature—dark side and all—accentuating and spreading our light, we will emerge more powerful than ever, just as the heroes before us did.

Unlike the dry and hardened clay tablets upon which Gilgamesh's history was indelibly writ, he proved adaptable to change when his typical ways of being wrought horrible consequences. Prior, as almighty king, he was undergirded by the three pillars of the so-called 'dark triad' (narcissism, Machiavellianism and psychopathy). After his fall from grace, the demi-god's more profound nature as a man came to light. But not before he saw his human frailties of fear, rage, lust, greed, and destruction manifest in manifold ways, returning in spades at fate's hand to cut him down to size.

When Gilgamesh's love and joy fell to grief and loss, he found his mentor Utnapishtim, showing it was time to reset his depths and follow the light of his original and better design. We can follow suit, for as Confucius says, this is the penultimate way to learn our lessons.

According to Albert Bandura's (1977) Social Learning theory, we learn by observing and mimicking others' actions, values, and attitudes. When mentors inspire us, we follow their lead and pick up new perspectives, knowledge and skills. Jung (1959) also argued persuasively that knowledge and learning were deeply rooted in direct observation.

Our brain plasticity allows for bending its circuitry and blending inborn personality traits with new conditioning. Our environment feeds into our innateness in different ways, nurturing us positively, bringing out our best, or hindering us and activating our worst. Once we become aware of our personality parts not compassionately serving us (or others) or conflicting with our purpose, there are compensatory actions we can take to address our underlying arrears.

Humans can amend the quirks of their underlying dispositions and behaviours with different forms of retraining or spiritual education and devotion. The *Mythimo* method provides an accessible, practical, and eclectic way: self-administered or with supervision. Still, one must be committed to self-improvement for any personal transformation to take place. As we all find out, deep-rooted inclinations seem immutable when we try to improve others' behaviours to suit our preferences.

Familiar traits and patterns, when bunched together, are associated with specific typologies, such as the 'dark triad' of a disordered personality.

Taxonomies for classifying and understanding human behaviour are myriad and hail from scientific and mainstream sources or alternative schools of thought, ranging from Jung's archetypes to the astrological signs of Eastern and Western astrology. When Jung (1959) classified us into two basic types (introverts and extraverts), depending on how we approach and feel about the world, many were keen to identify as outgoing extraverts because popular culture promoted them. However, as Jung contended, we have an instinctive predisposition to either pull back or lean into a world that approaches us. While the introvert likes a quiet home, the extravert wants to host a party.

Another straightforward way is classifying us into four human types of Optimistic, Pessimistic, Trusting and Envious (the latter is the more populated, incidentally). When someone becomes aware they are envious and resentful about another's success, they can decide to work through their envy, building their capacity to admire and respect the high achiever. Acting when jealousy has turned into hatred and cruelty becomes more urgent. Otherwise, one can redouble their efforts and go after the same dreams they see social expanders making possible for themselves.

Evolutionary psychology sheds light on why we continue to behave in ways non-conducive to our Common Good, such as why some leaders choose to dictate and oppress their people. Such negative leadership styles tend to make large populations afraid for their survival, making them compliant with the policies of the oppressor to avoid punishment. Some see in the end that they went along to get along, ever-fearful of making difficult decisions on their own.

We already know that the dark king Gilgamesh used the control method of violence to restrain his people. Consequently, Uruk's upstanding citizens possessed no inclination to imitate or follow him.

Returning to Social Learning and imitating how our mentor (or spiritual leader) operates, we, as the master's apprentice, can adopt their ways if inspired without losing our authentic essence. And we do it not because we are afraid we (and our offspring) will fail to survive or reproduce and continue the legacy of our tribe. We do it because being in the shade of our mentor's light makes us want to become a better person.

But if we choose the bitterest path, like most fairy-tale and mythic archetypes, learning from trial and error and our mistakes the hard way schools the mind and grows the soul. Our living cells carry within them our ancestral forebears' life experimentations and education. Chances are that we are coping with our survival stresses in the same way (different contexts, same pain) our great-great-great-grandparents and beyond did. Whether we have good instincts for fighting things out, freezing, fawning, or fleeing the threat, choosing dependable partners for reproducing offspring or managing our resources through collaboration or competition with others has much to do with how our ancestors answered these same existential questions. Sometimes these inherited ways of being serve us, while other times they do not, and we of the 21st century need the wisdom to know (and act on) the difference.

No one said it is easy to do the inner work, transforming our negative aspects into positive ways that value us and others and mobilise our highest aspirations. Deep-rooted inherited but flawed coping mechanisms will compete rigorously with a mind full of logic. But it is a fallacy to say we have no choice in how we behave as we are in the hands of destiny, or we are powerless trying to control our nature. Like Gilgamesh, once messed-up, wandering lost, but now self-realised, we, dwellers on the threshold of self-improvement, can prime our brains to the positive by leaning into the light.

When a specific range of circumstances and conditions occur on any given day, a role 'type' carried around within us (imbued with the nuances of our individual genetic, cultural, social, historical, familial, environmental, and idiosyncratic characteristics) will rise to meet the occasion. Human beings are more than the three dimensions of a type. An archetype's dimensions refer to the different aspects of its universal patterns or images. They include a. Unique physical presence (name, appearance/unique features: body); b. Unique disposition (personality, traits, behaviours: mind); c. Individual story (its contextualised trope of recognisable patterns commonly found in storytelling).

Ken Wilber (1949–) suggests that humans have four fundamental dimensions: the mental and emotional (mind), physical (body), and spirit (soul). These dimensions encompass various aspects of human experience and consciousness put to work in search for meaning and connection with something larger than oneself. A neat way to differentiate between the archetype and the human being is to say the former is mind and body, but the latter is body, mind and soul. In other words, to be human, take an archetype and add soul. Our fourth ethereal, spiritual dimension is sometimes called the subtle body. Within our physical embodiment, the interplay of DNA and our original soul essence weaves the fabric of our uniqueness.

The capacity for reflection or introspection, mental time-travel, decision-making, and dynamic creative self-expression adds layers of individual uniqueness that archetypes do not possess outside of their story-byte.

Archetypes are universal patterns shared across cultures and time, offering a symbolic framework that individuals uniquely interpret through the intricate nuances of their own lives.

In a nutshell, what sets us apart from universal archetypes is the unique interplay of our genetic makeup, personal experiences, and individual conscious selfhood.

Still, our actions can exemplify archetypal patterns in our various roles, such as teacher, parent, counsellor, doctor, mentor, or leader. However, if what we do lacks the depth of our innate soul essence, we may fail to birth knowledge in our learners. A teacher's universal aspiration is to impart wisdom and empower learners to improve their lives. Yet, without a soulful connection, a teacher may fulfil duties without engaging or transforming the students.

When we allow archetypes to overshadow our authentic Soul Self, we risk becoming trapped in the mythic. Our engagement in the illusory, rather than reality, engenders our duality, fragmenting our integral being into conflicting dark and light traits. For example, when teachers are 'dismissive', they fail to connect with students and meet their individual needs with empathy. Teachers must actively reflect on bridging the gap and cultivating heartfelt connections with learners. *Learners only care what a teacher knows once they know their teacher cares.*

By addressing the sources of resistance hidden in our shadows, we reclaim our authenticity and overcome archetypal reactions that hinder student-centred praxis. We can effectively transmit our light and prevent negative traits from overshadowing our efforts by embracing our integrated Wholeness.

Rather than rush in, attempting (in vain) to cast out our shadow selves, we must instead use the patterns of behaviour and lessons of the archetype as a path to self-discovery and an opportunity to accentuate its positive characteristics. First, we must understand our strengths and weaknesses.

Dark traits which cause negative energy to manifest in our real-world can be reincorporated into light. We must name, reclaim, and reframe them to regain our inborn authenticity, embodied by our inner child. As Matthew (18:3), the apostle, said, "Truly I tell you, unless you change and become like little children, you will never enter the kingdom of heaven."

So, we have a double blessing: returning to our innate goodness and light, symbolised by our original inner child, and reconnecting with the Sacred and Divine.

Returning to the subject of our dark traits for a moment: there is a time and place for 'anger', typically categorised as a negative behaviour. It has another side. Well-channelled anger fuels our drive, propelling us away from harm's reach and surmounting mountains of grief. It beckons us to embark on the initial steps of our thousand-mile journeys, akin to the legendary Gilgamesh or moon-maiden from *East of the Sun and West of the Moon*.

To establish a framework mirroring our human duality, attributes of *Mythimo's* twenty-two fairy-tale archetypes embrace both the positive and the negative inherent within us. Any traits considered negative have proven harmful in the context of the specific fairy-tale trope (and real life) and as played out by its lead antagonists. Anger is not always a negative expression (toxic or impotent), but it is when it harms the giver, the receivers, or the perceivers. Strategically steered anger can lead to incredible feats, such as compelling Gilgamesh's return journey to humanity. It helps us to overcome, along with grief, our denial, passivity, depression, procrastination, and immobilisation. But any anger (passively or aggressively expressed) turned 'toxic' is potentially harmful behaviour. Turning anger inward on ourselves causes depression. When we deny our anger or justify and excuse it without owning it and making amends to the harmed, our anger finds a welcome home in our shadow.

If we were indeed at peace with our angry outbursts, there would be no need to deny or justify them. We would own our out-of-control behaviour, and there would be no need for vowing to get a grip next time. But here is the rub. The denied anger intermingles unrestrained with all sorts of other negative emotions in the shadowed recess, becoming more contaminated, enlarged and trigger ready.

We already know that in our psyche, our ego (and conscientious superego) is doing everything possible to have us looking good and feeling accepted with glowing colours in social settings. Then, we have the unappealing remnants of self that the ego has disowned and banished to our mental dungeons. Yet, being out of sight does not mean that these elements of the self are out of mind. The shadow springs into action, triggered when the enlightened aspect of the self (conscious ego) becomes emotionally overwhelmed. Our body absorbs, swallows, and syncretises the shadow's off-colour emotional contents, assuming the shadow's form and conditions. If our shadow is angry or resentful, our body is eaten alive; the same happens when we harbour hateful emotions; if our dark side is rife with unclaimed fears, our mind-body reacts anxiously. The shadow, sometimes called our 'pain-body' (or shadow-body), is the psychical source or metaphysical cause of our dis-stress and dis-ease manifested as physical symptoms. It is tangible, accessible and mutable.

How can we ever be surprised when we contract an illness? Our body (and pain-body) provides many early indicators. Our pain only worsens when our shadow ambushes us.

Once we become integrated (an ongoing cycle), taking note of our organism's hints, the ego, now checked, no longer needs to deny or avoid a displeasing reality. We unhook its thinking triggers by reframing them with healthy coping thoughts and accepting and pushing through reality—the good and the bad—and keep going head-on like Vasilisa towards the grail.

In the season of Gilgamesh's discontent, his negative outputs attracted miserable returns. He suffered intense symptoms when grieving his beloved Enkidu. Grief unearths buried emotions such as guilt, anger, shame and hurt, leading to fatigue, nausea, headaches and other bodily aches and pains. Sorrow depresses the mind, and the body follows, sinking into immobilisation.

Are we similar to Gilgamesh's first incarnation, acting as our worst enemy, leading not because others choose to follow us but because they fear us? Gilgamesh symbolises the duality within us all, that dyad of good self, bad self.

Do we choose to be empathetic and kind like the latter-day Gilgamesh or his selfish, self-centred and judgmental version before his fall? None of us is black and white: there are always nuances of grey and an array of our true colours shining through. But we all know what taking the high or low road means and feels like in our interactions with others. The secret is acknowledging how we err and reframing how we perceive our behaviours in ways helping to harness and steer their positive power.

To emphasise again: when anger is harnessed and used effectively, rechannelled as a source of spirit fire or energy, it mobilises a depressed (or flooded soul) into action. Take the grieving Gilgamesh, who lost his way after Enkidu's death. His angry determination drove him into a dark tunnel, racing against the dawn, seeking to overcome his human limitations.

Within the ancient epic, the timeless dualities of darkness and light, and the eternal clash between the forces of good and evil, resound within our souls, akin to the sacred pages of the 'good book' that unfold across distant ages. In these profound reflections, we discover a mirror that unveils the trials we face on our Hero's Journey as we seek the power of purpose, depth of meaning, and sense of belonging that unite us with nature and all sentient beings, both great and small.

Like Gilgamesh, when our sense of safety is threatened, our organism's cells ignite, tirelessly safeguarding our existence even in the realm of sleep and dreams. Within each cell, we bear the indelible imprint of our ancestors' ancient struggle for survival, coursing through our neural networks and bodily systems. However, in our complicated modern times, relying solely on our instinctual cell programming for tailored responses is unlikely. Nevertheless, these refined resources, honed through millions of years of evolution and experimentation, remain vital. Sometimes, we must transcend the cellular imperative to merely survive and embrace the pursuit of thriving—a profound lesson the once warmongering King of Uruk was destined to grasp. To achieve it, we must evolve, and to evolve we must love.

The written story of *Gilgamesh* is the oldest in the world, even predating the West's *Iliad, The Odyssey* and the *Hebrew Bible*. His is the classic Hero's Journey not because he sets out with the noble cause to evolve or free others from their suffering but because he returns a better man through his suffering. Gilgamesh walks the highs, the lows, the divine, human and the animal sides of life and is described in the end as one who has 'seen everything, experienced all emotions, suffered all and accomplished all'. Implicit is the philosophy that one cannot achieve great heights in our human-spiritual existence without loving profoundly and having endured great suffering in kind.

Gilgamesh's epic is a universal tale, encompassing every journey the journeyman or woman must take before reaching the crossroads to ask for forgiveness of their flaws and failings and proceeding upwards to their Higher Selves. "Suffering is a swift steed to our redemption," said Nietzsche. Like Gilgamesh's, our first lessons are to know that foolhardiness runs counter to wisdom, and arrogance must not be mistaken for strength and courage. Our disregard for prudence and the natural laws and hierarchy brings harsh consequences. Gilgamesh shows no one can force others to follow their lead. Only by inspiring others can we hope they will look to us for leadership in conducting themselves.

Despite the valuable insights that the ancient Gilgamesh myth offers contemporary leaders (in professional and personal settings), the twenty-two fairy-tale archetypes curated and presented in *Mythimo* also allow us to deepen our understanding of ourselves, others, and the universal tests imposed by our reality. Our resultant sharpened clarity will prove helpful in those challenging moments we must face bravely through these uncertain times.

The emotional ups and downs of Gilgamesh from ancient Mesopotamia (part of the Fertile Crescent that coexisted with Egypt, the Far East, and parts of Eastern Europe) are traceable through worldwide myths, narratives, fairy tales but, most of all, mirror our human condition and the essence of stories of our contemporary existence. From time immemorial, our flawed natures, suffering and moral learning have held the power to transform our psychological reality. Life's learning, as perennial as the grass, reveals the use of the world and our place in it, providing the vital impetus to get us across the Rubicon.

What is the best thing of all for a man to ask of the gods in prayer?
That he may be always at peace with himself continually…
Of what effect are righteousness and courage?
To advance the common good by private pains…
(Homer)

MYTH'S WEALTH OF HEART

Across the mythic canon, East and West alike, myths whisper a timeless truth: gold, power, and fleeting desires always give way to the enduring labours of the heart and the rewards of love.

When overlaying Gilgamesh's heroic tale upon the fairy tales recorded and shared in the Baroque era thousands of years later, we see that despite vast societal changes, certain constants endure. Most strikingly, the human condition—our nature and behaviours—remains much the same as that of our ancient forebears. Though we benefit from greater knowledge and resources, the inner and outer challenges we face, though different in form, remain deeply connected to the past.

Our enduring quest to transcend ourselves, whether through conscious effort or unconscious drive, remains central to our experience. It is only by embracing these challenges and learning from hardship that we can evolve. Through the mythic journey, the archetypes show us the path—from chasing illusions and unreachable desires to confronting fears and accepting reality as it is.

Death, bordering every one of our lived days, becomes an intimate reality for all of us, sooner or later. A grieving Gilgamesh teaches us what he learned from his pain and troubles as he strayed like a beast through the dark wilderness, relying only on his instincts to survive: We must live our lives imbued with loving grace as if each day were our last because one day, it will be.

Turning our gaze to the East's great Siddhartha Gautama, who lost his sense of identity while living in a place of plenty, we learn that we may face similar trials as we take our Hero's Journey, searching for answers concerning our human condition, meaning and purpose. The curious Buddha, confronted by suffering, sickness, old age, birth, and death, wondered why a beautiful life seemed unattainable. After much wandering, he sat under the bodhi tree, refusing to move, and called out to the cosmos for a revelation before falling asleep. When the morning star appeared, he woke. The Awakened One's epiphany set him free: he learned the noble truths about suffering: suffering exists; it has a cause; it has an end, and it has a cause to bring about its end. He realised if we encounter unpleasantness, are separated from the pleasant or cannot gain what we desire, we suffer.

Had he been born much earlier and met the Mesopotamian, and sometime later, the Greco-Roman demi-gods, he would have warned that greed, ignorance and hatred only cause trouble and pain. Siddhartha Gautama lived around 563–483 BCE—long after the legendary Sumerian King Gilgamesh of 2100 BCE and the legends of the Pantheon circulating orally, 1200 BCE, and immortalised by Homer 8BCE.

By the time the Buddha was teaching the path to enlightenment in India, the foundational myths had already shaped a millennia of storytelling and spiritual thought in the globe's far-reaches. Gilgamesh had an elixir to share: Our attachment to getting what we want at all costs is the source of much of our suffering. Its only antidote is to let go, surrendering our grip on preconceived outcomes and being realistic about the world. After all, it is a 'place where the heart must feel and suffer in a thousand diverse ways' (Keats, 1819).

So, if we do not suffer, how will we learn? If we had a beautiful life in a utopian place like Uruk—that particular 'no place' where would we find the motivation to rise above our problems? Wherever there is darkness, the light will ultimately reveal itself. Buddha said, "There has to be evil so that good can prove its purity above it."

We can only recognise the light once we have seen the dark.

Gilgamesh was devastated by his failures. He lost true love and the fountain of youth, realising that the Tree of Life and immortality were beyond reach. Although we are not eternal, our stories are. The king's unrealistic desires let him down, but his struggles led him to the Eden within. After surrendering his vain desire to manipulate the cosmos, Gilgamesh's mortal destiny unfolded as it should. Is this the 'letting go' that is the key to personal transformation, emotional freedom and the next step towards our next quest?

Only now, we must step onto that spiral stairway of higher elevation with our awakened Self lighting the way for others to follow. At this juncture, Gilgamesh bestrode two worlds—the master of the beastly self he left behind and his new reality where he accepted becoming human. Gilgamesh's high stone ramparts have writ upon them: "He who saw all, who was the foundation of the land, who knew (everything), was wise in all matters." Finally, in peace, love and grace, the brave, beautiful, wise warrior came home to himself.

We can overlay this picture with an image of Jesus, the holistic healer, radiating golden light and hearing his tender voice whisper gently, "Your faith has made you well. Go in peace." In the spirit of his healing power, Jesus reminds us that diverse paths, guided by love, light, and compassion, converge at the nexus of our shared human experience.

Can we harken to our calling from the yon primaeval wild, urging us out from the woods where the shadows darken and deepen to courageously shine our blazing light on truth and love? As the unforgettable Jesuit, de Chardin suggests, when we do, we unify with all of creation, participating in the evolutionary expansion of consciousness and the great harmonic convergence of the universe. Our Wholeness and healthier, happier and loving ever-afters depend on it.

Among your kindred, you'll find a wealth of heart
It's worth more than a thousand precious rings
And love, not battle glory, life's great gift.
(Siduri)

AFTERWORD

As we conclude—only to prepare to begin again—our next *Mythimo* journey, we are reminded that we are, and always have been, mythopoeic beings. We make myths about ourselves, one another, our cultures, our societies, and the cosmos. While this book has primarily unpacked fairy tales to recognise, release, and temper their archetypal power within the psyche, the same correspondences can be found across myriad myths and stories from diverse cultural traditions, all meeting along a porous boundary. The permutations are as numerous as we are.

Gilgamesh revealed our animal nature, our hubris, and our fear of death. Yet, once he passed through the gates of sunrise, he began to see the light. Our personal narratives echo his journey, just as they mirror that of Odysseus, who endured physical and psychological trials, descended into darkness, received guidance from the dead, and returned home transformed—matured by suffering, and capable of restoring his kingdom.

When we hear the word *mythology*, many think first of the Greco-Roman pantheon. Yet these myths were preceded by Mesopotamian stories more than four thousand years old, and long before them, Australia's First Nations peoples carried oral narratives across tens of thousands of years. Central to their culture is Dreaming: a sacred framework guiding spirituality, law, and creation. An Indigenous Australian friend once explained that if non-Indigenous people wish to understand First Nations peoples, they must first understand this spirituality and reverence for the Creator, approached with balance and respect. Through oral transmission, cultural continuity—and survival itself—was ensured.

Evidence from the ancient Shanidar caves in northern Iraq suggests that Neanderthals engaged in ritual behaviour some sixty-five thousand years ago. These findings hint that symbolic meaning-making, and perhaps myth itself, reaches far deeper into prehistory than we once imagined. Many people of European and Asian ancestry still carry traces (1-2%) of Neanderthal lineage within them.

From this tangled unconscious web of collective human experience, we are invited to tease out our Self-stories and rediscover who we are.

Fairy tales emerged much later, carrying the same moral and ethical dilemmas as myth, yet rendered more accessible—softened for daily digestion. Regardless of genre, what matters is our capacity to recognise ourselves within them. As Ruebsaat (2013) suggests, the most compelling journey is our descent into the psyche's dark recesses—the realm the Greeks called the Underworld. When Odysseus entered it, he received guidance that enabled him to survive what lay ahead.

Allegory, archetype, symbol, motif, trope, and metaphor convey unconscious knowledge across myths and fairy tales alike. The unconscious is where we go in nightmares, but we also enter it through dreams, deep reflection, meditation, visualisation, and altered states. These experiences connect us with archetypal material—often powerfully, sometimes unbidden.

By now, you have read my memo. *Mythimo* refers to how mythical meanings are elucidated through personal reference points—*IMO*, 'in my opinion.' Archetypal inquiry is never singular. Meaning emerges collaboratively between counsellor and client, and each interpretation carries value. *IMO* may also be read as 'in memory' of myth and its enduring power, or as myths' dynamism— '*in motion*'. In *Mythimo* they carry us from novice to sage, from Little Red Cap to Vasilisa, retracing the spiritual arc from zero to hero. *Myths in motion* is unanimously more resonant.

Myths are embellished, irrational, subversive, or obedient to the norms of their time. Yet their creation stories, rites of passage, and symbolic expressions—whether through story-telling, song, ritual, cave painting or dance —remain deeply relevant. When John Keats (1817) born in the Romantic Era like the Brothers Grimm, wrote that 'imagination is the queen of truth' he may well have been speaking to the same truisms fairy tales hold.

Myths live in our cellular memory. Across time, archetypes—noble and ignoble alike—reflect the human condition in all its contradiction and splendour. Jung observed that the stories we tell ourselves shape our lives through archetypal patterns, exerting unconscious influence unless brought to light. As Roesler (2006) reminds us, reclaiming this material allows us to redirect its power.

We are myth-makers by nature. Yet if we are to reach any kind of spiritual apotheosis in the one short life we have, we must follow that internal flicker back to its source, capture the fire, and set it into motion on the hero's path.

First Nations peoples describe life as a journey of 'coming to know'—supported by learning spirits who guide individuals toward their heart, face, and foundation. Their stories evolved to transmit spiritual wisdom and practical knowledge intergenerationally, using symbolism to make learning memorable and enduring.

Perhaps, now, you have glimpsed your own multifaceted self among *Mythimo*'s twenty-two archetypes, recognising yourself as one of Campbell's thousand faces. If so, you have already begun the work of integration.

Samuels (1986) warns that unacknowledged shadows grow denser the more they are denied. Yet, like Vasilisa, when we enter the shadow realm consciously, we can discern what must be discarded and what must be kept, allowing roses to bloom from ashes.

Mythimo is not a prescription. It does not dictate what one ought to do. Rather, it invites us to reclaim who we are beneath ego and conditioning. If Aristotle feared myth as a tool of social control, this work seeks the opposite: liberation through recognition. Hercules reminds us that virtue, not denial, defeats vice.

Engaging imaginatively with other perspectives returns us to what matters—self-interest aligned with the common good. Emotional and moral intelligence are essential to becoming who we are capable of being. Transformation does not require perfection, blame, or cancellation of the past. Awakening, in its original sense, is a Buddhist beatitude: an enlightened state of consciousness. It resembles that liminal magic between twilight and the dawn.

Mythimo draws eclectically from mythological, philosophical, spiritual, and psychological traditions. A Jungian lens reveals the human longing for the Higher Self and the redemptive power of a spiritually informed path.

While embracing diversity and gender inclusivity, *Mythimo* speaks of masculine and feminine energies as forces to be balanced within us all. Myths have long acknowledged androgyny, and fairy tales such as *Hansel and Gretel* illustrate the fluid, symbiotic nature and balance of opposites. All twenty-two archetypes belong to everyone.

Fairy tales show us that the world is messy and ambiguous, populated by flawed yet fundamentally good humans. One poor choice can change a life; one inspired idea can redeem it. These stories restore hope—a second chance.

Myths arise from unconscious processes. Freud saw them as projections; Jung understood them as biologically perpetuated archetypes. Dreams access not only personal memory but ancestral knowledge. When we encounter archetypal material, we are often transfixed—on the threshold of transformation. Still, our self-regulation is essential. Without it, we remain governed by negative archetypal patterns.

The journey inward is not a checklist of strengths and weaknesses, but a lived process of awareness, regulation, and renewal as we follow the compass of the heart. Healing is not fixing. Nothing within us must be cast out. Everything must be owned and integrated.

Mythimo begins with our reflection, utilising the beautifully illustrated and emotion-evoking *Mythimo Cards*. When both visual and verbal information are presented to humans, the Dual-Coding theory (the 70s) argues that information is more engaging, quickly processed and retained, leading to improved learning outcomes.

But the journey does not end there. It is a syncretised self-growth therapy of proven and accessible approaches such as mindfulness, meditation, visualising, controlled breathing, journalling our stories and dreams, self-affirmations, and more. Some folks choose to undertake their fairy-tale archetypal work with a trained narrative counsellor to collaborate, customise and craft the best way forward to their psychic integration and a life well-lived.

Freud (1856-1939) argued that fairy tales, resembling dreams, use symbols and metaphors to express repressed conflicts, anxieties, and forbidden desires in the human psyche. For the sensitive souls addressed earlier: Remember that you are finely tuned intuitive instruments designed for sensing vibrations, dreaming dynamic dreams and feeling intense passion for living life creatively. If you are channelling your gift into acts of empathy and compassion, the world needs you more than ever. Hopefully, the fairy-tale archetypes help you see how your imaginative insight and sensitivity sharpen and heighten your feeling frequencies, sparking your flame of love and light and empowering you to stand tall in full voice.

Take heart from your kindred spirit, John Keats (1817), who spoke earlier in this Afterword about imagination's truth and affirms it again when he writes: "*I am certain of nothing but the holiness of the heart's affections and the truth of imagination. What the imagination seizes as beauty must be truth, whether it existed before or not.*"

We have gone into the woods to meet twenty-two fairy-tale protagonists, born from the imagination, each on an individual journey where they come to a fork in the road, see cause to change, and discover their future. In taking the first step out of their comfort zone into the wild unknown, helped along the path by their learning spirits (and their antagonists), they grow from their trials. When the time arrives, they emerge from the woods, knowing and appreciating their full measure and return ready to share their boon, their truths.

Can fairy tales help us move beyond the fears and boundaries of our egoic selves to face the next horizon offered on the hero's path? Yes. Yet, a simple flick of the magic wand falls short.

There is inner work to undertake. Undoubtedly, the darker archetypes spell what feels wrong to us, so we can see what we really want. Sometimes we must find out what we are not— to know who we are. But as for experiencing happiness, according to archetypes such as Jack, Cinderella, The Little Mermaid, and a cast of thousands more, *happiness is having what we want and wanting what we have.*

The Little Mermaid and *Le Petit Prince* explore themes of love, sacrifice, and personal growth. Both tropes emphasise the importance of looking beyond appearances, finding beauty in simplicity, and the transformative power of love. Both stories end with the characters dying and becoming spirits but continuing to impact the world positively. They share that our happiness is found by *cherishing the things and people we care about.*

You may recall my childhood reminiscence of living a mermaid's life, swimming in rapture beneath open skies. Years later, carrying that indelible imprint, I embarked on a solo journey into the vast blue in a single-engine aircraft. Gliding through the clouds, I confronted my fears and found solace for a love-torn heart. I continued on, following my bliss, singing jazz in small clubs, and—perhaps tellingly—even as adults, a sister and I returned to the sea to play mermaids, keeping childhood wonder alive. No longer was I the mute mermaid, the Orpheus muse, the doormat or machine for suffering. I had found my sea legs and my voice. In being myself—authentic and unadulterated—I discovered a quiet satisfaction, even contentment.

Through the arcane alchemy of fairy tales, I healed a thousand wounds, expanding my poetic soul with love, light, and learning. *Self-transcendentalists* will recognise this exhilarating psychic expansion: the moment one begins, at last, to live within their total reality.

Our path is lit by archetypal truths, igniting our spirit as we continue to navigate parts of life's unexplored woods. It is a journey, a story like no other, with a life all its own and explanations only falling short. The essence of the experience I describe resides inside the individual, tappable only once one is genuinely engaged on the hero's path of getting to know themselves—really know themselves just as they are.

We all have one story that calls from our soul, fired by the breath of the Sacred Divine. An opportunity for discovery awaits through the looking glass of fairy-tale archetypes.

Fairy tales, mythopoetically expressed, intertwine our innate symbolic, mythic and timeless patterns, enabling us to tap into the collective unconscious as our dreams do.

Artist Simo has infused his work with these magical elements to evoke aspects of the shared human condition, resonating with our inner world and sparking our beliefs, emotions, and memories.

As we delve into the reflective realm of the *Mythimo Cards*, we create an emotional connection that empowers us to illuminate the universal symbols and themes with profound insight, enhancing our understanding of the complexities within our ever-evolving personal reality.

Wish as we might, we can't just click our ruby-red heels together to reach our Holy Grail.

And that is why I must venture forth again, taking the long and winding road home, for only then will I fully grasp what I am trying to say.

Just as well because according to Frank (1995), when one person recovers their voice, many people begin to speak through that story. And so, this is my wish for you, dear friends.

Seek the wisdom that will untie your knot; seek the path that demands your whole being.
(Rumi)

RECOMMENDED READING

Aarne, A. (1961). *The types of the folktale: A classification and bibliography*. Helsinki: The Finnish Academy of Science and Letters.

Ainsworth, M., Blehar, M., Waters, E., & Wall, S. (1978). *Patterns of Attachment.* Hillsdale, NJ: Erlbaum.

Aronson, E., & Patnoe, S. (2012). *Cooperation in the classroom: The jigsaw method* (3rd ed.). London, England: Pinter & Martin.

Bettelheim, B. (1976). *The Uses of Enchantment: The Meaning and Importance of Fairy Tales.* London: Penguin Books.

Bloch, A. (1980). *Murphy's Law Book Two: More reasons why things go wrong!* Los Angeles: Price Stern Sloan Publishers, Inc.

Bray, W. J. (2012). *Quantum Physics, Near Death Experiences, Eternal Consciousness, Religion, and the Human Soul.* USA: CreateSpace Independent Pub.

Buber, M. (1970). *I and Thou* (W. Kaufmann, Trans.). New York, NY: Touchstone Books.

Burguez, J. (2025). *Mythimo Cards*. Brisbane, Australia: Synchronicity Press.

Cajete, G. (2000). *Native Science: Natural Laws of Interdependence.* Santa Fe, NM: Clear Light Publishers.

Campbell, J. (1949). *The Hero with a Thousand Faces*. USA: Bollingen Foundation and Pantheon Books.

Campbell, J. (1993). *The Hero with a Thousand Faces.* Fontana Press: London.

Davidson, B. (2020) *Find your Light.* Macmillan Australia: Sydney.

Dias, D. (2017). *The Ten Types of Human: A New Understanding of Who we are, and who we can be.* London: William Heinemann.

Dreikurs, R. (1968). *Psychology in the Classroom: A Manual for Teachers.* NYC: Harper & Row.

Durham & Lisbon Universities (2016). Comparative phylogenetic analyses uncover the ancient roots of Indo-European folktales. *Royal Society Publishing, 3*(1). Retrieved December 1, 2022, from https://royalsocietypublishing.org/doi/pdf/10.1098/rsos.150645

Esquith, R. (2007). *Teach like your Hair's on Fire: The Methods and Madness inside Room 56.* Manhattan: Penguin Random House.

Estés, C. P. (1992). *Women Who Run with the Wolves: Myths and Stories of the Wild Woman Archetype.* New York: Ballantine Books.

Ford, D. (2010). *The Dark Side of the Light Chasers: Reclaiming your Power, Creativity, Brilliance, and Dreams.* NYC: G P Putnam's Sons.

Forsyth, K. (2022). *Long-Lost Fairy-Tales.* https://kateforsyth.com.au/book/long-lost-fairy-tales

Frank, A.W. (1995). *The Wounded storyteller: Body, Illness, and Ethics.* London and Chicago: The University of Chicago Press.

Freud, S. (1913:1900). *The Interpretation of Dreams.* NYC: Macmillan.

Freud, S. (1930). *Civilization and Its Discontents.* London: Penguin Books.

Freud, S. (1966). *The Psychopathology of Everyday Life.* London: Earnest Ben Limited.

Glasser, W. (1998). *Choice Theory: A New Psychology of Personal Freedom.* New York: Harper Collins.

Goleman, D. (1995). *Emotional Intelligence.* New York: Bantam Books.

Grimm, J., & Grimm, W. (1812). *Grimm's Household Fairy Tales*: The Original 1812 Collection. Germany: Self-published.

Harris, T.A. (2004:1969). *I'm OK, You're OK.* Manhattan: Penguin Random House.

Hillman, J. (2015). *Archetypal psychology*. USA: Spring Publications.

Johnson, R. A. (1989). *He: Understanding Masculine Psychology* (Rev. ed.). New York, NY: Harper & Row.

Jorgensen, J. (2019). The Most Beautiful of All: A Quantitative Approach to Fairy-tale Femininity. *Journal of American Folklore*, 132, 36-60.

Jung, C.G. (1959). *Archetypes and the Collective Unconscious.* England: Routledge Kegan Paul.

Kolb, D.A. (1984). *Experiential Learning: Experience as the Source of Learning and Development.* Englewood Cliffs, New Jersey: Prentice-Hall.

Maslow, A. H. (1943). Hierarchy of Needs. A Theory of Human Motivation. *Psychological Review,* 50, 370-396.

Payne, M. (1993). *Reading Theory: An Introduction to Lacan, Derrida, and Kristeva.* Cambridge, USA: Blackwell Publishers.

Quinn, S. (2023). *Mythimo: Favourite Fairy Tales Reimagined Under the Sunlit Australian Skies* art series.

Robertson, R. (1987). *C.G. Jung and the Archetypes of the Collective Unconscious.* New York: Peter Lang.

Robertson, R. (1992). *Beginners Guide to Jungian Psychology.* York Beach, ME: Nicolas-Hays.

Robbins, R.A. (2006). Harry Potter, Ruby Slippers and Merlin: Telling the Client's Story using the Characters and Paradigm of the Archetypal Hero's Journey. *Seattle University Law Review, 29*(767). Retrieved December 1, 2022, from

https://digitalcommons.law.seattleu.edu/cgi/viewcontent.cgi?referer=&httpsredir=1&article=1871&context=sulr

Roesler, C. (2006). A Narratological Methodology for Identifying Archetypal Story Patterns in Autobiographical Narratives. *The Journal of Analytical Psychology*, 51*(4),* 574-586.

Rotter, J. B. (1954). *Social Learning and Clinical Psychology*. NY: Prentice-Hall.

Ruebsaat, S. (2013). What Does a Mythopoetic Inquiry Look Like? *SFU Educational Review*, 6: https://doi.org/10.21810/sfuer.v6i.372

Samuels, A. (1986). *Jung and the Post-Jungians.* UK: Routledge Kegan Paul.

Sandars, N.K. (1998). *The Epic of Gilgamesh.* United Kingdom: Penguin Publishing Group.

Spenser, E. (1897). *The Faerie Queene.* London: J M Dent.

Tarantino, Q. (Director & Writer). (2019). *Once Upon a Time in Hollywood* [Motion picture]. Sony Pictures.

Takala, J.-P. (2008). Evolution of Violence. In L. Kurtz (Ed.), *Encyclopedia of Violence, Peace, & Conflict* (2nd ed.). London: Academic Press.

Thompson, S. (1977). *The Folktale.* Berkeley, Los Angeles: University of California Press.

Teilhard de Chardin, P. (1959). *The Phenomenon of Man.* Harper & Row.

Triandis, H. C. (1995). *Individualism and collectivism.* Boulder, CO: Westview Press.

Vogler, C. (1996). *The Writer's Journey: Mythic Structure for Storytellers and Screenwriters.* London: Boxtree.

Wadsworth, B.J. (1989). *Piaget's Theory of Cognitive and Affective Development.* UK: Longman Publishing Group.

Walsch, N.D. (2009). *When Everything Changes, Change Everything: In a time of Turmoil, a Pathway to Peace.* USA: Spiritual Legacies.

Willans, J. (2012, November). *The Hero's Journey as a Metaphor for Personal Transformation.* 10th International Conference on Transformative Learning, San Francisco, United States. Retrieved December 1, 2022, from

https://www.researchgate.net/publication/302576163_The Hero's Journey as a Metaphor for Personal Transformation

Williamson, M. (2013). *A Year of Miracles: Daily Devotions and Reflections.* New York: Harper Collins Publishers.

Wolf, N. (1993). *Fire with Fire.* New York: Random House.

Zipes, J. (2012). *The Irresistible Fairy Tale: The Cultural and Social History of a Genre.* Princeton: Princeton University Press.

Half the harm that is done in this world is due to people who want to feel important. They don't mean to do harm, but the harm does not interest them. Or they do not see it, or they justify it because they are absorbed in the endless struggle to think well of themselves. (T.S. Elliot)

GLOSSARY

Term or Name	Description
AARNE-THOMPSON-UTHER INDEX [ATU] (1910, 1928, 1961)	The Aarne-Thompson-Uther Index (ATU) was first developed by Finnish folklorist Antti Aarne in 1910. American scholar Stith Thompson translated, revised, and expanded it in 1928 and 1961. German folklorist Hans-Jörg Uther further updated the index, which now bears all three names. This catalogue of folk and fairy tales remains a key tool for folklorists, helping them analyse human stories across 7cultures.
Active learning	A method, encouraging learners to become experientially involved in the learning process such as 'having a go' and learning through 'trial and error' and to control their own learning directions and outcomes.
Active listening	Active listening means fully holding space for another—leaning in, giving small encouragers, and paraphrasing or summarising their words to show you've truly heard their story.
Adaptive behaviour	Active coping within social norms shows we are well-adjusted and have adapted our behaviours effectively to challenging circumstances.
Aggressive	Aggressive individuals speak or act in ways that threaten, intimidate, or provoke fear and retaliation in others.
Allegory	A narrative where characters, events, and details represent abstract ideas, moral qualities, philosophical/spiritual concept—an extended metaphor, as in Orwell's *Animal Farm.*
Analytical psychology	Carl Jung's (1875–1961) analytical psychology links a person's inner drives and symbolic or spiritual experiences to the archetypal patterns of their socio-cultural positionality and the collective unconscious.
Anima Archetype	The anima (Latin for 'soul') is the feminine aspect of the unconscious in both men and women. Jung called it 'the

	woman in the man'. A balanced anima fosters sensitivity, nurturing care, creativity and intuition.
Animus	The animus (Latin for 'mind' or 'spirit') is the masculine aspect of the unconscious in both women and men. Jung called it 'the man in the woman'. A balanced animus fosters assertiveness, strategic thinking, creativity and healthy competitiveness.
Jungian psychologists hold that anima and animus dwell deeply in both the personal and collective unconscious. They are among the most challenging archetypes to integrate, and serve as gateways to the unconscious universal field. Their integration is visceral, marking the emergence of one's felt Wholeness (a non-static state).	
Anthropomorphism	Anthropomorphism is attributing human traits, emotions, or intentions to animals or non-human beings. Fairy-tale animals are often anthropomorphised, as in *The Little Red Engine That Could*, where the engine shows human grit and determination to reach the top of the hill.
Archetypes	**Archetype** derives from Greek *archein* ('to begin/rule') and *typos* (type), meaning the original pattern from which copies derive. Archetypes function as universal typologies—like the Hero—that shape human stories and behaviour. While each person expresses the Hero differently, core qualities (courage, sacrifice, transformation) remain constant. In Jungian psychology, archetypes arise from the collective unconscious and manifest through myths, dreams, art, and symbols. Archetypes have three dimensions: physical presence, disposition, and individual story. However, humans have a fourth dimension—the unique soul and spiritual layer.
Assertive	Assertive individuals put forward their perspectives and preferences in a confident but non-aggressive manner.
Case-Study	A case study is a written document, used in social sciences, which explains the who, what, when, where, why, and how of a person's (or entity's) situation to gain an in-depth, multifaceted understanding. It examines the individual's strengths and limitations,

	their environment, circumstances, challenges, opportunities, and past actions taken, as well as the goals to be achieved. This enables collaborative exploration of solutions addressing complexities that affect progress towards those goals.
Collective Unconscious	Jung introduced the concept of the collective unconscious to describe a deeper layer of the psyche beyond the personal unconscious. This realm holds all the inherited, universal material shared by humankind since the dawn of life. It contains archaic archetypes, myths, memories, metaphors, primordial ideas, images, and symbols—the collective reservoir of knowledge. truth and experience common to all humanity.
Confirmation bias	Confirmation bias (in our unconscious mind, leads us to dismiss information that challenges our existing beliefs while favouring data that support them.
(Critical) Reflection	This mental process involves pausing to engage in introspection—examining closely what has happened around us and the fundamental ways we think and behave. Since time immemorial, humans have been meta-thinkers, reflecting on their thoughts, actions, and behaviours. The drive to improve and become better versions of ourselves is hardwired into our nature, pushing us to continually move forward.
Duplicitous	A two-faced or incongruent way of behaving—where our actions betray our words. It is considered an untrustworthy or a double-dealing way to operate.
Gypsy	The term *gypsy* historically refers to the Romani people, an ethnic group originating from South Asia. However, many Romani consider the word derogatory because of its association with negative stereotypes. To show respect, it is better to use 'Romani' or 'Roma'. That said, when the author refers to her personal heritage, she embraces the term *gypsy* not as a slur but as an expression of pride in her Romani roots.

Hero's Journey	Joseph Campbell (1949) developed the Hero's Journey, building on Jung's work. This monomyth follows a hero who embarks on a brand new adventure, overcomes challenges, and returns transformed—ready to master both their old world and new reality. The journey unfolds in 12 steps grouped into four stages: the Call to Adventure, completing the mission, returning home, and applying the gained wisdom. Psychologist James Hillman expanded on this, showing how everyone's life and personal story can reflect the Hero's Journey in some way.
id	At the centre of the psyche lies the instinctive self, including sexual, survival and other organic impulses (hunger). Because these instincts can clash with the socially adapting ego, the ego often represses the 'savage' parts, sending them into the id—what Jung calls the shadow self. The author combines Freud's and Jung's ideas into the term 'id-shadow'.
Individuation	Individuation is a natural but uncommon unconscious process. According to Jung (1959), it occurs only in those who have undergone the challenging yet essential task of integrating their unconscious aspects. The result is the reward of Wholeness.
Instincts	Instincts are our hardwired behaviours driven by survival needs—such as hunger, sleep, procreation, and sex—reflecting our animal nature. For example, the innate fear of snakes found in many animals illustrates this deep-rooted survival instinct.
Journal Notes	Note-taking helps solidify memories of important dream details, recurring themes, or significant elements of internal dialogue. It provides a reference to revisit, reflect on, and prepare for future inner work like meditation or self-reflection.
Karma:	Karma is a belief found in Hinduism, Buddhism, Jainism, and Sikhism, and is also used in secular contexts as the law of cause and effect.

	While Christians may speak of 'reaping what you sow', they differ from Eastern traditions regarding reincarnation. Karma represents the cycle of life—what goes around comes around. It acts as a metaphysical ledger, recording positive and negative actions that influence our spiritual ascent, descent, or rebirth. Everything we think, say, and do is energy that does not vanish but affects realities beyond our ordinary senses.
Libido	Libido is psychic or emotional energy originating from primitive physical urges, often directed towards achieving a goal. Influenced by Freudian theory, it is commonly associated with sexual drive. More broadly, libido can be understood as the strength of our life force.
Locus of Control:	We view control over life's events in two ways: either as shaped by our own choices and actions (internal locus of control) or as governed by fate, with little influence from us (external locus of control). A balanced locus of control means taking responsibility for what we can change while accepting what lies beyond our control.
Maladaptive behaviour	Maladaptive behaviour is any response that fails to effectively cope with new or challenging stressors, preventing positive adaptation and hindering our best interests and goals. Examples include avoidance, denial, withdrawal, addiction, passive-aggression, self-harm, anger, aggression, violence and escapism.
Metaphor	A metaphor is a figure of speech that implies a comparison, such as saying, "She's a princess"—instantly conveys meaning beyond the literal words. Narratives might describe eyes as 'a pool of water' or call someone 'a wolf in sheep's clothing'. Metaphors offer vivid, visual shortcuts to express complex ideas. In mythology, they carry symbolic meaning; for example, water often represents the unconscious mind or

	emotional states, adding deeper layers beyond its physical presence.
Metaphysical	Metaphysical refers to realities beyond the physical—spiritual, transcendent, or unknown. It encompasses mysteries, intuition, and experiences beyond ordinary perception.
Myth	Myths are often misunderstood as fabricated or false stories, contrasting with historical fact. However, many myths have been passed down through oral tradition since prehistory, focusing on creation stories and helping to shape culture, religion, language, customs, and traditions. Mythology reflects the collective psyche. As Campbell (1993) put it, myths serve as a form of natural history—a practical guide to primitive faith and moral wisdom.
Mythopoeic	Mythopoeic means the specific act of creating myths—myth-making. Humans are naturally mythopoeic, crafting mythologies, rituals, ceremonial music, drama, dance, poetry, stories, and artworks throughout history to pass stories and wisdom across generations.
Mythopoetic	Mythopoetic refers to the poetic evocation of mythic themes and archetypes, often with emotional or cultural resonance that help explain the world, natural phenomena, human psychology/behaviour, and the mysteries of existence.
Persona	The persona is the 'mask' we wear to shape how the world sees us. It is our outward identity that protects the ego by hiding our less desirable traits. As a mask, it can feel inauthentic, concealing our true self—flaws and all. Yet, without this persona, we risk social rejection, tapping into a deep collective fear of being an outlier.
Personification	Personification is a figure of speech that attributes human qualities or personality to inanimate objects or non-human beings. For example, saying, "The artwork really spoke to the deepest parts of me," personifies the artwork, since it cannot literally speak.

Projection	Projection is an ego defence mechanism where we unconsciously transfer our pain and shadow aspects onto others, avoiding facing our own dark side. Also, we may project an idealised image of a partner onto a lover. When they fail to meet this ideal, disillusionment follows, often ending the relationship. This cycle of projecting and disappointment can become a recurring pattern—putting someone on a pedestal only for them to inevitably fall.
Psyche	The term *psyche* originates from the Greek heroine Psyche, the lover and wife of Eros (Cupid in Roman myth). Universally, *psyche* encompasses the totality of the human mind and spirit, including both conscious awareness and the deeper, often hidden layers of the unconscious. It represents the complex and dynamic inner life—an integration of thoughts, emotions, instincts, memories, and the various facets that make up our mental and emotional being.
Psyche–Tripartite	Freud (1923-1966) described the psyche as a tripartite structure of **id**, **ego**, and **superego**, shaping all human behaviour. The **id**—our instinctive, shadow side—drives raw desires and survival needs. The **superego**—our internal critic or moral voice—restrains and judges. The **ego**, aided by the outward **persona**, mediates between these forces and the demands of reality, creating a functional balance unique to each individual.
Role-play	Role-play is the act of performing the part of a person or character to simulate real-life situations. It is widely used in learning, therapy (e.g., Gestalt), and creative settings.
Schadenfreude	Schadenfreude is the pleasure or satisfaction we feel at another's misfortune, often fuelled by rivalry or a sense of justice.
Schema/Schemata	A schema is a mental pattern or framework that shapes how we perceive and interpret the world. Archetypal

	schemas arise from the unconscious or collective unconscious.
Self-actualisation	Self-actualisation, as described by Maslow, is the innate drive to realise one's potential and live with purpose, which can lead to the integration of the self and movement towards (Jungian) 'Wholeness'.
Shadow	Shadow is the archetypal repository of our repressed instincts, emotions, traumas, and disowned traits—what Freud called the id. It forms as we suppress behaviours and desires, from anger or shame to even unvalued positive qualities, to meet societal expectations. We encounter our shadow in dreams, projections, trauma triggers, or intense emotional reactions. It also carries inherited ancestral patterns. Though it cannot be erased, consciously integrating the shadow—acknowledging and balancing these hidden parts—supports healing from trauma, personal power, and the journey towards Wholeness.
Symbolism	Symbolism is the use of a concrete or abstract representation—human, animal, object, or idea—to convey deeper meaning. For example, a red light symbolises the command to stop. As Freud (1913) noted, "Symbol formation is the initial stage of concept formation."
Transpersonal	Transpersonal refers to experiences where the individual transcends personal identity to connect with broader aspects of humanity, life, psyche, universal field or the cosmos.
Vasilisa	Vasilisa—Traditionally, the Russian fairy-tale heroine is known as Vasilisa the Beautiful. However, multiple versions of her story exist. The author uses her title interchangeably as Vasilisa the Beautiful, Vasilisa the Wise, or Vasilisa the Brave, Beautiful, and Wise to reflect the varied story-tellings of her childhood.

N.B. Mythimo often refers to the shadow as the 'id-shadow' or 'shadow-id' to represent Jung's model of the shadow whilst incorporating Freud's original concept of the 'id'.

MYTHIMO ARCHETYPAL READING CARDS

0 Little Red Riding Hood

1 Jack & The Beanstalk

2 Little Mermaid

3 Our Lady's Child

4 Emperor's New Clothes

5 Puss in Boots

6 Cinderella

7 Three Billy Goats Gruff

8 Beauty & the Beast

9 The Ugly Duckling

10 Fisherman & his Wife

11 Rumpelstiltskin

Every man, when he gets quiet, when he becomes desperately honest with himself, is capable of uttering profound truths. We all derive from the same source. There is no mystery about the origin of things. We are all part of creation, all kings, all poets, all musicians; we have only to open up, to discover what is already there. (Henry Miller)

Thumbnails of Twenty-two Mythimo© Cards (Continued)

12 The Frog Prince

13 Sleeping Beauty

14 Hansel & Gretel

15 Bluebeard

16 Rapunzel

17 Snow White & the Seven Dwarfs

18 East of the Sun, West of the Moon

19 Goldilocks & the Three Bears

20 Three Little Pigs

21 Vasilisa

Reverse-side of Cards

Mythimo logo

Email: info@mythimo.com to enquire how to purchase *Mythimo* products.

ABOUT THE AUTHOR

I have known Janice since the early 1990s.

In my capacity as an announcer on 4BC Brisbane—and, later, as the station's Program Director—I came to know, like, and respect Jan enormously.

By the time we met, Jan had already built a reputation as a dream analyst and I was keen to introduce her to our wider audience, with whom she quickly built a strong rapport as the *Dream Diva.*

As a Talk station, 4BC encouraged listener interaction with our guests and Jan was always one of our most popular contributors.

All the announcers—including Peter Dick, Anthony Frangi (now Manager at ABC Brisbane) and John Scott–invited her on regularly. The response from our large audience was always enthusiastic and there was never a shortage of people wanting to chat with her.

As Program Director I would regularly conduct focus groups and the feedback on Jan was always positive and respectful. She was consistently one of our most popular 'regulars'.

The reasons for that are apparent when you hear her: a lovely voice, a gentle and pleasant nature, and a deep knowledge in her chosen field.

Her enthusiasm was matched only by the depth of her expertise and a willingness to share it.

Dreams are immensely fascinating, and, like all great communicators, Jan possessed the ability to make the complicated both accessible and interesting.

It's wonderful that she has pursued her studies (including taking a deep dive into fairy tales and archetypes) so that others might benefit, and I recommend her without reservation (and with great pleasure).

Greg Cary (Formerly Broadcaster and Program Director at Radio 4BC Brisbane). Author (*An Absence of Certainty, A Fascinating Investigation, and A Colour of Blue*): gncary@gmail.com

Someday, after we have mastered the winds, the waves, the tides and gravity, we shall harness for God the energies of love. Then, for the second time in the history of the world, we will have discovered fire.

(Pierre Teilhard de Chardin)

The
End

www.ingramcontent.com/pod-product-compliance
Lightning Source LLC
LaVergne TN
LVHW010556100826
845148LV00014B/2739
* 9 7 8 1 7 6 4 5 3 1 3 0 6 *